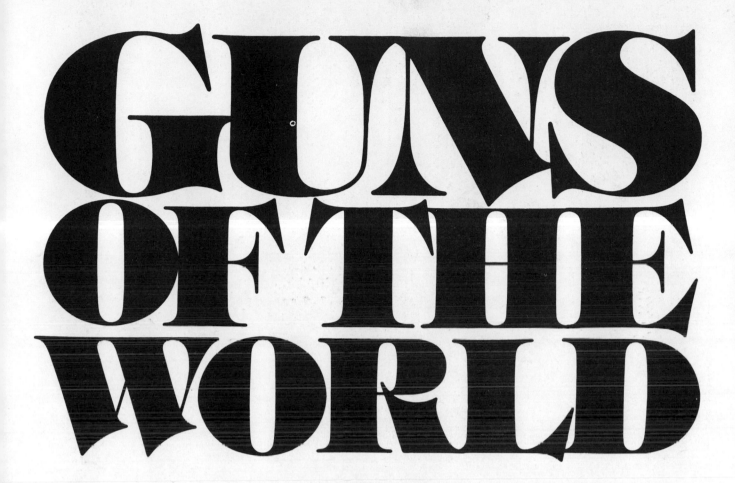

GUNS OF THE WORLD

HANS TANNER / EDITOR
ROBERT I. YOUNG / ART DIRECTOR
AL HALL / MANAGING EDITOR
HARRIS BIERMAN / TECHNICAL EDITOR
ALLEN BISHOP / ASSOCIATE EDITOR
TERRENCE S. PARSONS / ASSOCIATE EDITOR
STEVEN L. FULLER / TECHNICAL CONSULTANT

Bonanza Books
A Division of Crown Publishers, Inc.
One Park Avenue
New York, New York 10016

CONTENTS

INTRODUCTION

by Hans Tanner, Editor

How many times have you been to a gun show and seen something on a table and wondered what it was? It may have had a low price tag on it, but you passed it by only to discover later that the value was very much higher, and in fact you passed up a scarce item. If this is the case then "Guns of the World" is for you. In it you will find evaluation of the most common as well as the most obscure and rare, the cheapest and the most expensive firearm or edged weapon you are ever likely to find.

The hobby of arms collecting has always been strong in the U.S. and now it is beginning to catch on throughout the world, despite restrictive laws on ownership. Clubs have begun to blossom from Germany, Switzerland and Italy to Argentina and Uruguay. Cartridge collectors can be found from Finland, Norway, Belgium and France to Australia and New Zealand.

The collecting of ornate early arms and armor has become strictly a wealthy man's hobby; this type of material is still available but few and relatively minor examples are within the financial means of the average collector.

The same situation applies to the great American collectables, Colt and Winchester, in which fields a relative fortune has to be spent in order to even approach near completeness.

There is no doubt that gun collecting is a good investment.

Inquiries to several well known dealers reveal that the values in a large number of cases have tripled in the last few years. One such dealer informs us that material he has sold is often repurchased by him at a higher price than he sold it, but then he has no difficulty at all in selling it once again at another profit. Thus the values spiral ever upwards.

While the strongest movement has been in U.S. weapons, such items as Lugers and Mausers as well as other rare early European pistols have sky-

rocketed. Twelve years ago, a friend was offered a Luger Carbine for $150.00. Today, its value is around $1700. A rare Schlegelmilch semiautomatic pistol was sold for $200.00 12 years ago; the same pistol realized *over* $3000 when sold last year.

What then is left for the average collector? The activities at the hundreds of gun shows throughout the country is unabated. Every Saturday and Sunday, thousands of people trade and buy to add to their collections. The high prices of collecting in certain areas has caused people to turn to collecting accoutrements, knives and bayonets. Antique Bowie knives which were readily available a short time ago have now become higher priced than some firearms. Some bayonets are worth *more* than the long arms to which they belonged, and there is a strong movement in the collecting of other edged weapons—American and European swords, and above all, Japanese sword blades.

With the controls on the import of surplus military rifles from abroad, the free and easy attitude on these items has changed. Selling for as little as $9.95, these military surplus rifles were converted to sporters in huge quantities but the stocks have been slowly drying up. Because of the fact no more are being brought in, the military rifle collecting field is one with a tremendous potential for investment. Collectors are finding many varieties that they never knew existed which makes this field an extremely interesting one. As more and more research is done and results published, so the incentive to collect is stimulated.

Another factor is that the increased interest in Europe and other foreign countries has begun a movement to return some of the more collectable items to these parts of the world, where prices are often higher than in the U.S In this way a number of rare items have been whisked away from under the very noses of U.S. collectors. Military rifles in mint con-

dition were common a few years ago but most of them have disappeared into private collections and it has become harder and harder to find those in perfect or near-perfect condition. Low serial numbers meant very little in the past, but now when a low serial number is encountered, there is a healthy premium to be paid for it.

Research has also revealed that some items considered common because of the apparently large numbers on the dealers racks were in fact quite scarce. Perhaps 1000 examples were produced, but the buyer was deceived by seeing so many of them all in one place when in fact, what he saw was all that remained available!

A collector friend turned down an 8mm Japanese Murata for $25.00 because it was in poor condition, but in the last five years of attending shows we have seen only one other example.

The buyer would be well advised to do some research before he turns down something as "too common," or draws *any* snap conclusions.

Another field that could be rewarding is that of the European sporter. There is a healthy trade in American sporting rifles and the majority of the fine British sporting rifles have already reached prices beyond the means of the average collector. The European sporters have not had much of a following because of the weird and wonderful collection of calibers in which they come. The ammunition for many of these is not universally available in the U.S. and some of the cartridges themselves are collector's items. Nevertheless, for those who like to shoot their collector's item, some of the European calibers are available through specialized dealers and quite a number of the arms are available at very reasonable prices.

A question foremost in every collector's mind is how to safeguard his collection in these days of ever increasing crime. Obviously insurance is important, but at the most it can just be a financial solace to some way compensate a loss. It is usually very difficult to replace a comprehensive collection with any money received as the result of insurance. Nevertheless insurance must be considered. A word with your insurance agent can quickly give you an idea of what it will cost and what additional safety requirements such as the installation of a burglar alarm, will be required. The NRA has an insurance service for its membership. This consists of a shooter's insurance and a collector's insurance, the latter being cheaper as it does not include coverage for shooting.

It is most important to keep a catalog of your collection complete with description and serial numbers; this is the only way any stolen pieces can hopefully be retrieved.

The best way perhaps, is to keep your collection from being an obvious attraction to criminals. Keeping the collection out of sight preferably in a separate room that can be locked and at least burglar proofed to some degree are preventative methods. Use common sense, and do not make your collection public to just anyone who comes along!

Once again, we would like to stress that every collector should be aware of those legislators who would take our hobby away from us. Gun collecting is a hobby as is stamp, coin and antique collecting. A man's involvement in a hobby has a beneficial effect, and as such is of benefit to the nation—let us keep it that way.

The editors would like to take this opportunity to thank the many people who were of assistance in the compilation of this book:

Mr. Clemente Bosson of the Musee d'Art et d'Histoire, Geneva, Switzerland; Dr. Hugo Schneider of the Schweizerisches Landesmuseum, Zurich, Switzerland; Tom Hall of the Winchester Museum; Mr. E. V. B. Norman of the Wallace Collection, London, England; Mr. Hutchinson of the Western Australian Museum, Perth, Australia; Mr. Basil W. R. Jenkins of the Francis E. Fowler, Jr. Foundation Museum, Beverly Hills, California; General Cuenca Diaz, Secretary of Defense of the Republic of Mexico; General Somuano, Secretary of the Department of Archives, Correspondence and History, Mexico City; Mr. Manuel Gonzales Cosio, Advisor to the President of Mexico; Colonel T. Olavi Lechti of the Finnish Embassy, Washington D.C.; Mr. Charles Abegglen, Swiss Consul, Los Angeles, California; Fritz Hausler, Edmund Fasnacht and Fred Datig of Switzerland; Her Majesty's Tower of London, England; Metropolitan Museum of Art, New York; Mr. Martin B. Retting of Culver City, California and the staff of the Retting organization; John Malloy, Danbury, Connecticut; Chris Anderson and Dick Reyes of Fort Carson Arms & Antiques, Carson City, Nevada; Ray Howser and Bob Ellithorpe of Pony Express, Encino, California; Jim Thompson and Steve Tidwell of California Arms, Santa Monica, California; Carl Ring, commercial sales manager of Interarmco, Alexandria, Virginia; Robert N. Green, Mexico City; James B. Hughes, Jr., Houston, Texas; William H. Woodin, Tucson, Arizona; Frank Wheeler, Osborne, Kansas; John Pickering, Santa Monica, California; Bob Hill, Northridge, California; Jack Harker, Warren Odegard, Chick Evans, David M. Sachs, Mike Greene, Bill Evans, John Plimpton and Kearney Bothwell all of Los Angeles; Jerry Knight of Kerr's Sport Shop, Beverly Hills, California; Jacques P. Lott, George Hoyem; Jack Brickell; Will Hoffeld of the Eagle's Nest, Los Angeles; R. Q. Sutherland for permission to use photos from his fabulous collection.

In the Bowie knife section we would like to thank Lou Kosloff, Walter O'Connor, Robert Stephen, Gordon Frost, the Alamo Museum and the Mississippi State Historical Museum, Jackson, Miss., for their permission to illustrate knives from their collection. In the preparation of the color section we wish to thank the following persons for access and loan of pieces from their collections: Garry James, British weapons; Mario Pancino, Mausers; Robert J. Neal, Smith & Wesson; W. M. Hawley Japanese swords and accessories; Tom B. Buckley, Sharps; and Jim Helms.

1. Long arms require considerable space in order to display them properly. Rifles may be stacked in vertical fashion, which allows for more space, but precludes easy viewing and will eventually discourage frequent inspection for corrosion and dust.

2. Not many private collections have received the careful housing as found in the Winchester Gun Museum, but then such displays as this are very costly to organize and build. The cannon is an experimental model built in 1865 by Timothy Tufts in a Massachusetts blacksmith shop. In the display case in foreground are experimental Winchester revolvers.

1   2

THE KENTUCKY RIFLE

DEVELOPED AS A NECESSARY TOOL ON THE PENNSYLVANIA FRONTIER, THE LONG RIFLE HAS BECOME ONE OF THE MOST TREASURED EXAMPLES OF AMERICAN ART FORMS. **by James E. Serven**

The autumn foliage around Freeman's farm in upper New York afforded excellent cover for Timothy Murphy when on that October day of 1777 he crept to within 300 yards of the British camp. Carefully he lined his sights on the bright-hued uniform of General Simon Fraser. A puff of smoke, and a lead ball sped unerringly to its target.

That lethal ball from Murphy's Kentucky rifle brought to an end the brilliant career of one of Great Britain's ablest officers, and was a factor in General Burgoyne's decision to surrender his force to the Americans at Saratoga a short time later.

Timothy Murphy was a member of Col. Daniel Morgan's rifle company, one of eight such companies from Pennsylvania. Two rifle companies from Maryland and two from Virginia had also responded to General Washington's call for riflemen during the early days of the Revolution.

The rifle was used sparingly during the war, principally by skirmishers and snipers, but it served the colonists well, and in some instances tipped the scales in their favor. Such an occasion was recorded three years to the day after Murphy's rifle ball had fatally wounded General Fraser.

On October 7, 1780, 900 American riflemen under "Nolichucky Jack" Sevier and other backwoods leaders soundly defeated a larger British force commanded by Major Patrick Ferguson at King's Mountain in North Carolina. The British suffered 242 killed and wounded, and 664 were taken prisoner. Of the American riflemen there were 28 men

1. Daniel Boone leads a group of pioneers through the Cumberland Gap into the Kentucky region. From the painting by George C. Bingham in the Washington University art collection in St. Louis, Missouri.

2. Ancestors of the Kentucky. These short, heavy European rifles came to America with the early settlers. Note wooden trigger guards on the lower two rifles and sliding wooden patch boxes on the top and bottom pieces.

killed and about 90 wounded. This defeat broke the back of British power in the South.

It was ironic that Major Ferguson should be among those killed by a rifle ball at King's Mountain. He was one of the few British officers who long had been advocating the use of the rifle and had designed a breech-loading flintlock rifle, specimens of which are among the most treasured collector's items.

Apparently still another war was needed to convince the British that the American rifleman was not a man to take lightly. So it was that on January 8, 1815 in the final confrontation of the War of 1812 the British "lobster-backs" were almost annihilated in their attempt to take New Orleans. Losses for Great Britain's proud redcoated veterans were at the unbelievable ratio of 100 to 1 when confronted by the deadly fire of entrenched American riflemen.

A short time after the war a sentimental ballad was written about the Battle for New Orleans which gave special credit to the "Kentucky riflemen." This helped to popularize "Kentucky" as applied to long rifles.

There were earlier circumstances, too that tended to associate the name "Kentucky" with these deadly ac-

curate American-made rifles. In 1769 Daniel Boone and a few other hardy backwoodsmen had shouldered their long rifles, penetrated the Cumberland Gap and spent two years exploring the virgin wilderness beyond. This rich but uncharted territory, loosely comprising what are now the states of Kentucky and Tennessee, became popularly known as "Kentucky," a name derived from an Indian word meaning "dark and bloody ground." This forbidding name had special significance for the Indians as there was constant conflict between the tribes to control the rich hunting grounds there.

Boone's glowing reports of the Kentucky country soon led to establishment of "The Wilderness Trail," a rough road that was to be traveled by hundreds of settlers seeking the flat farm lands west of the Appalachians. Nearly all carried a long rifle. By popular usage, and by a series of circumstances the name "Kentucky" caught the imagination and thus the long rifles made in Pennsylvania, Maryland, Virginia and North Carolina became "Kentucky Rifles," and so they are known today.

The superiority of the American rifles over those of Europe and England in the late 18th and early 19th centuries led General George Hanger, one of England's leading marksmen, to declare: *I never in my life saw better rifles (or men that shot them better) than in America.*

In design the Kentucky rifle evolved from the bulky, relatively short barrel "Jaeger" hunting rifles of Central Europe. The long, light fowling pieces popular in England may have had some slight influence also in establishing the American rifles slender silhouette. Gunsmiths who emigrated to America from Germany, Switzerland, Austria and adjacent borders, including some French Hugenots, like Le Fevre and Ferree, brought with them gunmaking craftsmanship learned through long apprenticeship. There were a number of reasons why these talented craftsmen gave up their homeland for a new life in America, but principally it was to escape religious persecution, avoid onerous military service, or just in the hope of a better life.

Entering the colonies mostly through the port of Philadelphia, these emigrants spread out into the interior regions of Pennsylvania, the earliest and largest concentration being in the Lancaster region.

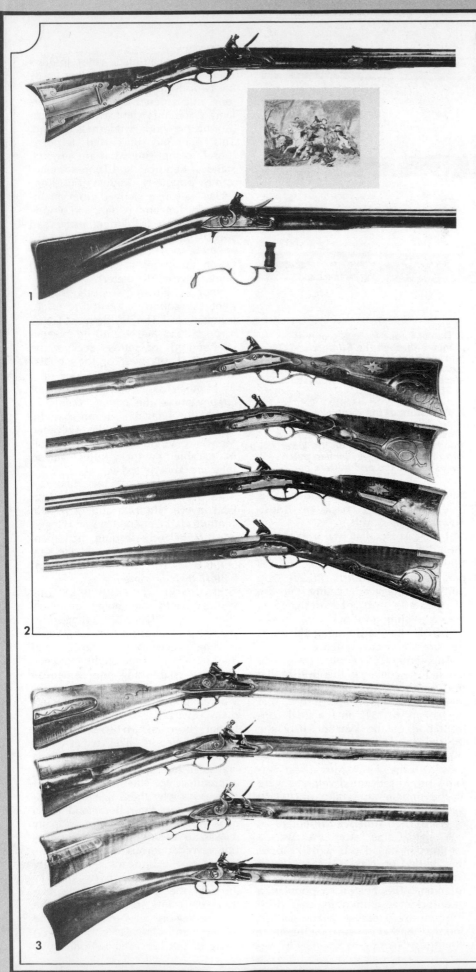

THE KENTUCKY RIFLE

This was all virgin or sparsely settled territory and here the rifle was even more important than the axe. It was the means of supplying food and buckskin (the cloth of the frontier) for clothing; it provided protection from dangerous animals and hostile Indians. The gunmaker became a very important and respected man in the pioneer settlements.

Along the coastal regions the traditional muskets or fowling pieces long retained their dominant position. They could be used for military service and for loading with either shot or ball when the situation demanded. Most could be fitted with a bayonet for military use. They were easy and quick to load. But smoothbore barrels lacked accuracy except at close range. If a ball was used it tended to tumble and follow an erratic flight, not having the spinning motion given by a grooved bore.

On the other hand, the Kentucky rifle, while it took longer to load, used less powder and a smaller ball, made less noise, could be held steadier than the musket, and was infinitely more accurate, having a deadly range at 100 yards and a dangerous range up to 400 yards.

In the interior regions, then, the rifle was the more effective weapon and its environmental development attracts our major interest.

The evolution that brought the bulky European-type rifles to the most highly developed stage of Kentucky rifle production was not accomplished quickly. Qualified students of Kentucky rifle history estimate that the earliest guns were made about 1720 but it was not until the 1790-1815 period that Kentucky rifles reached their zenith in standards of art and craftsmanship. This does not mean that there were not earlier or later rifles of fine quality, but pertains to the period when more top quality rifles were made than any other.

The period of Kentucky rifle manufacture extended from the flintlock period, about 1720, through the Revolution and well into the caplock period approaching the War between the States. In the greater part of this era the Kentucky rifle was the premier rifle of the world and one of the most beautiful.

The late Joe Kindig, Jr., a great student collector and author has stated that the Kentucky rifle was as symbolic of American freedom as the eagle itself. A religious man, he also declared that *"When God wishes to change the earth, he first develops men to do the job, and then the tools for them to work with."* In any case, these rifles were graceful in line, economical in consumption of powder and lead, fatally precise and most important, distinctly American products.

Production of the long rifles was conducted in a relatively limited geographical area centered on Pennsylvania. The gunsmiths fanned out in three major directions. Following the movement of the frontier westward they first favored Pennsylvania's Lancaster County, then into York County and north into Lebanon and Dauphin counties; eventually gunsmiths were established in what are now Adams, Cumberland, Franklin, Bedford and Somerset counties. Another route of migration led up the Schuykill and Delaware rivers north through what are now Reading, Allentown and up along the Susquehanna to New York state. The third route turned southward to Maryland, Virginia and into North Carolina.

New England's environmental needs favored muskets and smoothbore fowling pieces in the flintlock period, and as a result few Kentucky-type rifles were made there. Those that came from New England shops were quite plain guns, with almost as much relevance to English sporting guns as to the typical Pennsylvania pattern. Many had walnut stocks. Among the few prominent New England makers were Silas Allen of Shrewsbury, Massachusetts, Martin

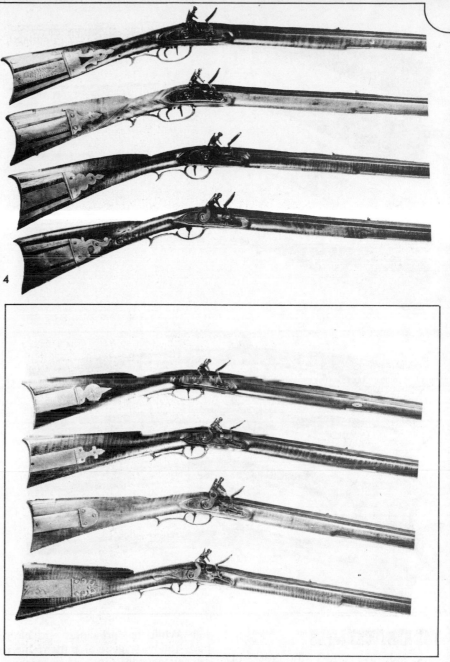

1. Major Patrick Ferguson, inventor of the famous breech-loading rifle shown was killed by American backwoodsmen with using Kentucky rifles. Lithograph depicts scene.

2. Relief carving on Kentucky rifle butts was of reasonably uniform style. Taking the form of a "C". Quality and amount of decoration varied greatly.

3. Early American long rifles showing the transition from the European to the American style. A graceful form is beginning to emerge.

4. A further development in the Kentucky rifle, and the most distinct to the layman, is the brass patchbox with side bars. The upper two rifles are of a later period than the lower.

5. Representative pieces with very plain patchboxes. From top: New England type rifle by Martin Smith; unsigned but well-made rifle with fleur-de-lis on patchbox hinge; rifle by J. Dickert with Dreppard lock; rifle by J. Shriver with fine carving.

Smith of Greenfield, Massachusetts and the Stillman brothers of Farmington, Conneticut. Usually these New England guns have a very plain brass patchbox with no side bars. While a few Kentucky-type rifles were made in Ohio and New York, major production there was bordering on the caplock period and favored development of the half-stock rifles.

From the mid 1700s, the gun, the axe and the plough had been helping to transform parts of the American wilderness into prosperous farms and industrious villages. Each year saw this movement edge away from the coastal areas and toward the West. As has been said, Daniel Boone's favorable reports of the

unknown country beyond the Cumberlands served to inspire an accelerated movement westward.

As pioneers pushed into new wilderness areas the rifle was an indispensable and primary part of their equipment. This increased the trade in and reliance on Kentucky rifles. The Revolution had caused Americans to realize that they must no longer depend on importing their needs from England or Europe but must learn to produce vital necessities like rifles here in the Colonies.

The gunsmiths of Pennsylvania, Maryland, Virginia and North Carolina responded to the increased demand with dedication, ingenuity a combination of skills and dawn-to-

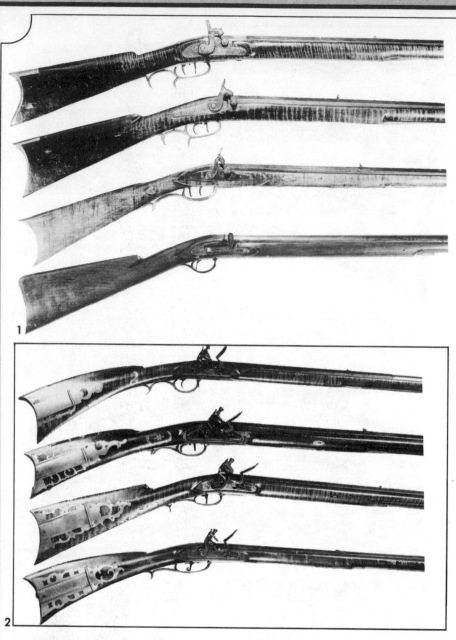

Lancaster buttstocks have a distinct nose but straight top and bottom lines. There is very little drop to the buttstock.

Bethlehem (Allentown) rifles, developed close to the same time as those around Lancaster, show a pronounced curve on the top and bottom lines of the buttstock and thus a sharper drop.

The Reading buttstock profile, said to be developed around 1765, is a compromise between the Lancaster and Bethlehem area guns in that it retains the curved comb, called a "Roman nose" of the Bethlehem profile but has a relatively straight underline like the Lancaster pattern.

Down in Maryland the buttstocks, many showing beautiful raised carving, are said to have reached prominence about 1800. They had a negligible nose, the straight line of the comb only slightly raised above the line at the wrist. The top and bottom lines of the Maryland stocks are about equal in length, whereas those made around Lancaster have a shorter to pline than that of the under part. The butt of Maryland-made guns is usually quite thick and broad from the heel to the toe.

Latest of the buttstock profiles was developed in western Pennsylvania in Bedford and Somerset counties and is generally called the Bedford school. This is a sort of Johnny-come-lately in Kentucky rifle making for Bedford-type rifles were primarily of the caplock era, coming into popularity about 1835 when the production of

1. Four different forms of lock illustrated in this group of late percussion rifles. None have patch boxes. From top: a commercial bar action lock with minor engraving; back action lock on a rifle by Sells; typical Bedford County rifle by William Defibaugh. Note the long, narrow hand-forged lock and the high, angled hammer; mule-ear lock on a rifle by W. Gardner of New York State.

2. Patch boxes with pierced head and side bars were considered the most decorative. The top two rifles are not identified; the bottom are by L. Crosby and S. Miller.

3. Believed to have originated north and west of Lancaster, a few over/ under rifles were made. They are among the most desirable.

4. Three Kentucky rifles from the Winchester Collection. From left: a New England rifle, circa 1780; a smoothbore circa 1800 by J. P. Beck; another smoothbore by Nicholas Beyer.

5. These three rifles illustrate the variety of finish and style that spans several periods and schools.

THE KENTUCKY RIFLE

dark industry. Under the spur of necessity they accomplished great things, and it must always remain a source of wonderment that fine rifles could have been produced with such limited equipment and under the conditions of their manufacture.

It has been said that only he who realizes the intimate relations between the tools of a nation and its institutions really understands its history. Thus the long rifle story embraces not only the product itself but the men who made and used it along with the communities where it was made and used.

For the moment we shall focus on the areas where the Kentucky rifle was produced, and here we find somewhat different schools of de-sign. While the principles and basic parts follow a general pattern there are variances in form and decoration which help to identify the areas of origin.

One of the latest publications on this subject is *The Kentucky Rifle - A True American Heritage in Picture* published by the Kentucky Rifle Association in 1967. Albert M. Sullivan, an officer of that association, has worked out a set of profiles which picture the varying identifiable major buttstock contours for rifles in the areas of Lancaster, Bethlehem (Allentown), Reading, and Bedford County in Pennsylvania as well as a general type produced in Maryland.

The Lancaster profile or silhouette, probably the first to evolve from the old German or Swiss heavy butt-stocks, was fully developed by 1750.

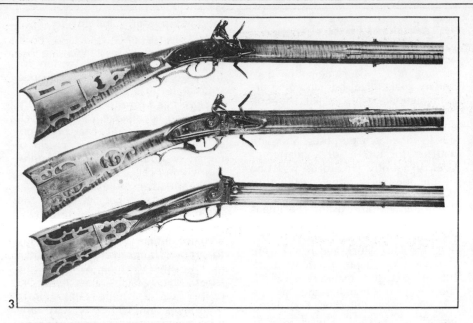

Kentucky rifles in areas farther east was falling off. The Bedford profile presented a rather narrow look with straight top and bottom lines and little or no nose. The stock has a sharper angle of break at the wrist than any of the others. A characteristic feature is a long, narrow, hand-forged lock plate and a high, angled percussion hammer.

While there are certain features of the Kentucky rifle forestock which may help to identify a maker's work, the forestock by itself really offers little to establish the maker of an unmarked gun. It is in the butt end where lock, trigger guard, patchbox, carving, engraving, inlays and other features tell the biggest story.

In Joe Kindig's tremendous 561-page volume, titled *Thoughts on the Kentucky Rifle in Its Golden Age*, he enlarges on the five major areas outlined by Mr. Sullivan and lists nine area schools of workmanship, namely: Lancaster, Bethlehem, Womelsdorf-Reading, Lebanon, Dauphin, York, Littlestown, Emmitsburg and Chambersburg. The term "schools"

is used in the sense that gunsmiths in given areas shared some similar pattern ideas.

These schools of workmanship and design are relative to the flintlock at its best in the 1790 to 1815 period. It should be noted that additional schools of design are indicated outside of Pennsylvania for Maryland, especially those of Cumberland, Emmitsburg and Frederick. It is assumed that the gunmakers of Virginia and North Carolina, many of whom emigrated from Pennsylvania, followed the designs prevalent in the areas whence they came.

Eventually gunsmiths appeared in Tennessee. A recent study of arms from that area by Robin C. Hale indicates that these were rather plain, inexpensive, full-stock guns, a distinctive characteristic in many being an oval recess for grease in the butt-stock or a simple patchbox with a long, narrow lid called a "banana patchbox."

The primary goal of all these individual gunsmiths, regardless of the community wherein they served, was

THE KENTUCKY RIFLE

to produce a conveniently portable, accurate, sturdy and dependable hunting rifle — a game-getter. Secondary goals might be handsome ornamentation or, as match shooting sport developed, heavier and specially sighted barrels might be produced for match purposes. Shooting matches for turkeys or a quarter of beef at country crossroads was one of the few recreational pastimes of the backwoodsman.

We know from existing specimens that even the plainest rifles have a graceful line and an appeal to the eye. The lock, stock and barrel were the basic or major assembly parts, but it was the manner in which these were put together and how the whole rifle was finished that determined the appeal to critical buyers.

Toward the accomplishment of American goals the old Jaeger (sometimes spelled Yaeger, Yager, Jager or Jaeger) rifles went through these transformations:

The thick, heavy buttstocks were thinned down, given a more comfortable contour and the flat musket-like butt plates were slimmed and changed to a modified crescent shape, better suited to holding securely in the armpit and having a sufficient point at the heel to keep the rifle from slipping when the butt rested on ground for loading.

Easily damaged sliding wood patchbox covers were replaced by spring-latched hinged brass covers. These patchboxes offered a great range of design and provided a major feature of decorative beauty for the rifle.

Some of the early Jaeger trigger guards were of wood and easily damaged. Those that were of brass were massive and frequently sculptured.

In America, sturdy but smaller brass trigger guards were adopted, having a plain oval bow protecting the trigger, a slightly curved extention for the finger grip and a crescent-shaped spur at its rear terminal.

Barrels and forestocks were lengthened and slenderized. The barrels were made of soft charcoal iron, slowly formed by welding a strip of metal around a rod or mandrel (sometimes called a "needle"). The barrel was then ground to octagonal shape, bored, straightened, rifled and fitted with a breechplug. The name rifle, incidentally, comes from an archaic German word *riffeln* meaning to groove. Bores were smaller than in the large yawning barrel of the Jaeger, the average being about .45 caliber. Barrel lengths ranged from 40 to 44 inches, with some very early guns even longer. About one-third of the barrelmakers used seven-groove rifling, one-quarter used eight grooves and a few used a straight form of rifling. Most rifling, however, has a slow twist. A relative few were smoothbore to be used with either ball or shot.

European walnut was replaced in America by the native maple. Some of the well-cured hard maple used for Kentucky rifle stocks showed beautiful striping or curl. Where this was not present occasionally a decorative striping was applied by fire or by applying acid or stain. A light stain might be applied to the wood before rubbing it to a fine patina with oil. It is said that maple trees which grew on thin rocky soil produced a tighter, curlier grain than trees which grew on open ground and heavy soil. After being cut into two-inch planks the wood required a drying period of about four years to be at its best.

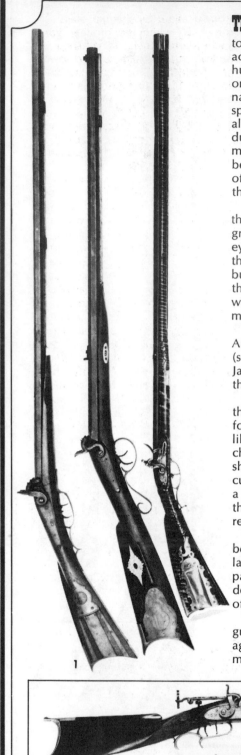

1

2

1. At left are two unusual variants of the Kentucky-type rifle with side-by-side barrels. Both are late examples. At right is a classic example of the long rifle which was made when the form had reached its highest point.

2. In the caplock period, gunsmiths turned to making heavy target rifles with half stocks. The bottom piece by Leman of Lancaster retains some of the earlier characteristics.

3. A pair of top quality Kentucky pistols with English locks.

4. A group of representative Kentucky pistols originally in the Herman Dean collection. Sometimes these handguns were made in pairs, as are the two at top left, but more often than not were single pieces.

One of the features which made the Kentucky rifle superior to its predecessors was the method of loading. In the Jaeger a large naked lead ball was forced into the grooves by hammering it down with an iron loading rod. This tended to deform the bullet and greatly reduce accuracy. The Kentucky muzzle loader, however, used a ball slightly smaller than the bore. This was wrapped in a thin greased muslin or leather "patch" and thus the ball could be easily and snugly pushed down the rifling with a light hickory rod. The patched ball gave a tight seal, retaining pressure behind the ball and giving it velocity, a good spinning motion, accuracy and range. Further,

the patch helped clean the barrel as it was expelled. This method of loading also reduced wear on the barrel.

There were important differences in those early Jaeger rifles used for the stag and boar hunting in Europe as compared to their American descendents that were designed to down the bear, panther, wolf, deer and even a hostile Indian. Slings used extensively in Europe might have been handy for carrying the shorter Jaeger rifles but they were not practical for the long slender Kentucky rifles. Bone, pearl, and ivory decorations found little use on Kentucky rifles, where the durability of iron, brass and silver were required.

These were the major changes

brought about by gradual steps from 1720 when the pioneer gunmaker Martin Meylin set up shop and the long rifle moved forward toward the perfection of its excellence. Photographic illustrations can better describe this slow design metamorphosis than the pen, but for a start, very plain American-made rifles with sliding wood patchboxes started the parade toward greater excellence from about 1720.

The brass patchbox, a wholly American innovation, was the next step forward and appeared on rifles about 1750. Thereafter it was used exclusively on long rifles except for those few very cheap "hog rifles" which have merely a round hole in the right face of the buttstock to hold grease. Pre-revolutionary patchboxes usually consisted of a plain, hinged lid. Very few had side bars. A slight amount of carving on the stocks began to appear.

Few of these early rifles bore a name or initials to identify them. Several theories have been projected to explain this. One is that the maker wished to conceal his identity from the British. Another is that some could not write. And again, the work of local gunsmiths was so well-known in their community that they felt no need to scratch up the barrel of their rifles with initials, names, addresses or dates.

This, of course, makes it hard to identify guns as to maker and sometimes as to the period and area of manufacture. But there are certain motifs and characteristics peculiar to each gunmaker that often help toward identification and dating.

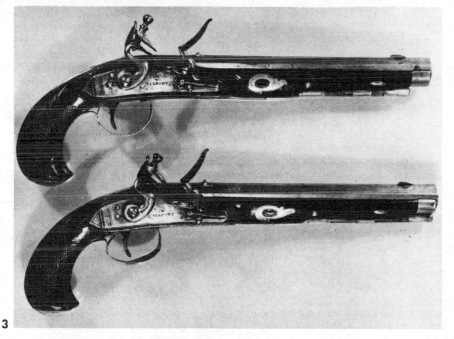

3

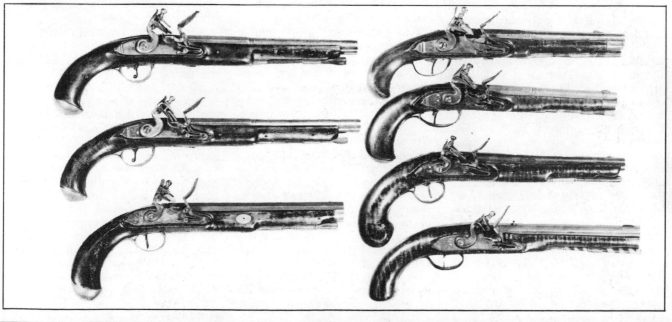

4

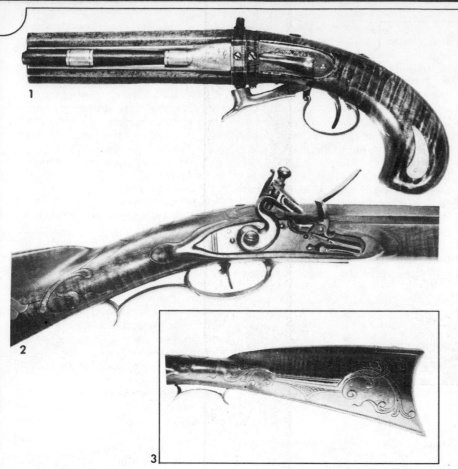

1

2

3

THE KENTUCKY RIFLE

Hand-forged locks are associated with the early periods as well as their plain frizzen springs without a roller and the gooseneck cock or hammer. Later flintlock locks have a reinforced hammer and an advanced form of pan, frizzen, and frizzen spring with roller. Thick sideplates with beveled edges opposite the lock are indications of early design.

One of the first popular designs found on Kentucky rifles was a flower resembling a daisy at the head of the brass patchboxes. Many rifles that carry a variation of this design are unidentified, but toward the end of the 1700's, Jacob Dickert, a well-known citizen of Lancaster, adopted a distinctive form of this pattern which serves to identify his work. Using variations of this motif were gunmakers Graeff, Resor, Henry, Albright, Haeffer, Brong, Fondersmith, Haga and quite a few others who produced rifles in the 1790 to 1815 period.

Patchbox designs took on many forms. A few featured a horse head (sometimes used by Henry Albright and Melchoir Fordney). A bird or elaborate rococo designs were frequently used. Hinges varied a bit for

the lid which covered the recess for patches, etc.; sideplates might be straight bars, fancy designs or pieced work. This became a focal point in the rifle's decoration best suited for artistic metal design and engraving.

While the metal furniture and inlays were very important, it is quite probable that the quality of the raised and incised carving in the "Golden Age" rifles determined the rifle's quality and value. The customary carving on the right side of the buttstock was a stylized "C" or double "C". Carvings are also noted around the barrel, lock, sideplate and trigger guard. Incised mouldings are found along the length of the forestock, along the lower edge of the buttstock, and under the cheekpiece. Sometimes a small tube or eyelet under the cheekpiece moulding held a pick to keep the touch hole clean. An occasional design feature under the cheekpiece, such as Leonard Reedy's triangle enclosing stylized crossed hatching, helps to give a clue to an unmarked rifle's identity.

The cheekpiece flat on the left side of the buttstock is the usual location for the most prominent inlay. A favorite here is the birth star with side points extended and the top and bottom points of equal,

shorter length. The work of John and Peter Moll could be recognized by a stylized and engraved birth star within a circular silver band.

Another favorite inlay on the cheekpiece after the Revolution was the eagle. There are some eagle designs which are sufficiently distinctive to identify the maker. Such a one was that used by John Armstrong of Emmitsburg, Maryland. Other standardized eagles were used by the Voglers of the Salem school in North Carolina; they used eagles for the head section of their patchboxes as well as for the cheekpiece inlay. Others occasionally used eagles but most lacked the uniformity of Armstrong and Vogler designs.

It should be remembered that many of the "deutch" (Pennsylvania Dutch) settlers of Pennsylvania had strong superstitions. Some insisted in having an X inscribed in their gun as a hex to keep away witches and evil spirits. X was the mark for Christ as in Xmas. XXX marks were also signs of quality such as on barrels of flour or whiskey. Another familiar religious symbol was the fish, and the religious derivation is sufficiently complex that we must omit it here; suffice it to say it had a strong talismanic significance.

The birth star, mentioned previously, was also a strong talismanic decoration along with the half or crescent moon. It will be found that usually the half moon (with recognizable face) will be positioned in the stock so that the inner curve faces down. Other and perhaps less potent but meaningful inlays were the heart, tulip, teardrops, shield, etc. Inlays were usually of silver, often hammered out of a silver coin.

Although not especially significant in number in the discussion of Kentucky rifles, perhaps it should be mentioned that a few double barrel guns were made. The majority were of over/under design with a swiveling breech so that the barrels could be rotated and fired by the one lock. These and side-by-side double barrel Kentuckys proved to be heavy and gained little favor. Kentucky pistols, however, were a more useful product. Some were carried by officers in the military service and others by travelers. A pair was said to be used by one of the men who helped to spirit away the Liberty Bell and hide it from the British during the Revolution. An interesting chapter on these pistols was added to Captain John Dillin's book, *The Kentucky Rifle*.

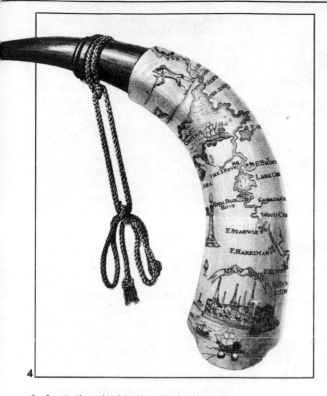

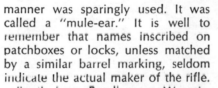

4

5

1. A rotating double barrel pistol with underhammer made for President William H. Harrison by Jonas Hess of Heidelberg Township, Pennsylvania.

2. A closeup of the lock area of a high-quality Kentucky rifle. Note the carving on the wrist of the stock.

3. An example of the graceful carving found on many high-quality long rifles. Each maker developed his own style. This particular piece, though unsigned can be identified as the work of Leonard Reedy.

4. Among the most historically important accessories are the powder horns with maps on them.

5. Typical accessories carried by the rifleman on the frontier.

Most of the gunmakers stuck to the manufacture of single-barrel rifles and as the years rolled around changes were made in gunmaking processes. The gunmaker could now buy locks made in Germany and England cheaper through Philadelphia importers than he could hand forge them. Some American makers of locks such as Drepperd appeared to flourish but foreign locks marked *Warranted, Ketland, Golcher* and other names began appearing on Kentucky rifles in increasing number. German-made locks usually bore die-stamped initials on the inside of the lockplate while English locks were usually engraved on the face. In the caplock period an odd lock with a striker that moved sidewise rather than up and down in the normal

manner was sparingly used. It was called a "mule-ear." It is well to remember that names inscribed on patchboxes or locks, unless matched by a similar barrel marking, seldom indicate the actual maker of the rifle.

South from Reading on Wyomissing Creek, sometimes known by residents as the *Schmutz Deich,* there is said to have been nine dams in a three-mile stretch — all these dams provided the waterwheel power to run barrel-making shops. Here welders, grinders and borers worked a 12 to 14-hour day, turning out Kentucky rifle barrels that sold from $2.00 to $3.00 apiece. A few barrels were finished in a half-round, half-octagon design but most were octagon. The name Pennypacker stands out prominently in the Pennsylvania barrel-making trade.

It was not, however, in the locks and barrels that the architectural and artistic personality of a rifle depended. The individual gunmaker often cut the rifling, shaped the stock, designed the hardware and assembled all in one package that would end up in a handsome, individualized, straight-shooting product.

After invention of the percussion cap, great changes occurred in arms manufacture. The trend toward large manufacturing plants in America had

gained impetus with the activation of the government armories at Springfield and Harper's Ferry. Private firms like that of Eli Whitney and other New England arms manufacturers began to prosper. Philadelphia attracted to it a number of qualified gunmakers and manufacturing plants.

By the late 1830s, the backwoods gunsmith was on the way out, but he did not meekly fade away. While the so-called "Golden Age" in the making of Kentucky rifles may have passed, some outstanding rifles were produced in following decades before the breech loader superseded the muzzle loader.

Makers of these percussion Kentuckys sometimes attempted to replace by an abundance of fancy inlay the artistry of the earlier flintlock guns with carved stocks. Bores became smaller as the big game disappeared. This led to frequent reference to the later arms as being "squirrel rifles."

Apparently the gunmakers in the western sections of Pennsylvania were the last to abandon substantial manufacture of Kentucky-type rifles. William Defibaugh, the Border family, John Enos, Elias Crissey and some others excelled in making Bedford-type rifles in this late period. One of the last of this breed was

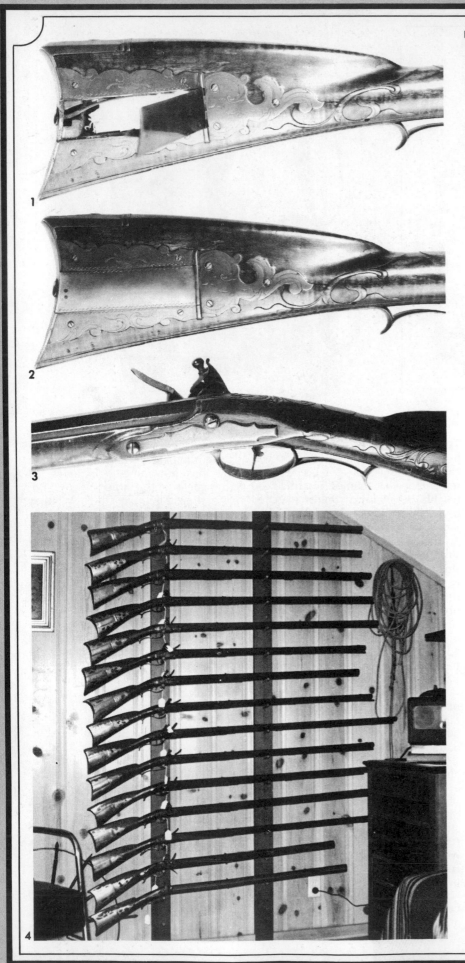

THE KENTUCKY RIFLE

John H. Johnston who later operated a gun store in Pittsburg. It is my good fortune to have a 1911 account of these late gunmaking days written by Johnston's son, who bore the same name as his father. Excerpts follow:

"My father learned his trade of Carlisle at Shippensburg and moved up to Cumberland County where he opened his shop. I was born there in 1836 and began working at the bench when I was 14 years old. I was so small at that time that they built a little platform for me to work on. We used to work harder 50 years ago than we do now — 12, 14 and 16 hours were nothing unusual as a day's work. The popular opinion is that in those days one man made and finished a rifle from one end to the other, but that is a mistake. Of course, the gunsmith who employed no help did so, and no man was considered capable who could not do so in a pinch. But whenever a riflemaker had enough business to warrant his employing two or three hands, as my father did, there was a specialization of the work, just as there is today. One man would devote his attention to rifling barrels and fitting breech plugs; another might be particularly handy about working patch-boxes and ornaments out of brass and silver, and some men were more skillful than others in laying out stocks and fitting in the actions.

"We had a few lock makers in this country, but most of the gunlocks used were imported, for at that time in England lockmaking was a distinct trade.

"Barrel making was also a trade of considerable importance, and rifle barrels in the rough were a part of all hardware men's stocks. We used to get our best barrels from a stretch of country that ran from Dauphin County down to Philadelphia. All through those hills, wherever there was sufficient water power to work a triphammer and a grindstone, you would find the shops of the barrel makers. Prominent among these workers were the Pennypackers. Of all men who understood this art when I was a boy only one is living. He came from a family of barrel makers and has a little shop up in the mountains, where he forges out barrels just as his father did

many years ago. Of course very good barrels are now drawn by machinery, but in the old way, under the hammer, the metal was worked over and over until all impurities and specks and grays were removed, and it became tough and smooth and rifled beautifully. Barrels were ground to an octagon on an ordinary grindstone, and a good workman would do this as accurately as a modern planing machine.

"Father had a great reputation as a riflemaker, employed four men beside myself, and used to send guns all over the country. We never kept rifles in stock, but our customers would come in from a hundred miles or more, and sometimes spent several days around the shop and consuming a great deal of tobacco, cheese, crackers, raisins and hard cider. After the size and length and weight of the new gun were decided upon, we would go to work upon it. Curly maple was the popular wood for stocks. The lumbermen up on South Mountain used to save us their choicest planks, and we would season them very carefully before laying them out. Patch boxes were cut to pattern from sheet brass and set into the woodwork. Some extravagant men would ask for silver, which necessitated rolling out a silver coin or two in a little hand roller that was part of the equipment of every shop, and then with cold chisel and file we would work out circles, stars, crescents and other ornaments.

"The boring and rifling of the barrels, the setting of the trigger and the adjustment of the sights were delicate matters that sometimes would have to be gone over repeatedly, until everything was as perfect as was possible to be made.

1. View inside the patch recess of a Kentucky rifle showing the spring activated fastening latch.

2. Same rifle with patch box lid shut.

3. Early, best quality rifles usually feature a heavy, beveled plate surrounded by raised carving opposite the lock.

4. These Kentucky rifles in the author's collection are among the many he has owned and studied.

5. The studies of Albert M. Sullivan reveal the major gunstock profiles of different gunmaking areas.

"When our customer called for his new rifle we would walk across the road from the shop, put up a mark and then test and show its accuracy. Riflemen were as peculiar in those days as they are now and some men would detect a harshness or drag in the trigger, or something irregular about the way the bullet set, and this would necessitate first one adjustment and then another, until everything was satisfactory. Of course, we were always experimenting with bores, twists and depths of rifling, but generally settled down to about one turn in every 36 inches."

Widespread appreciation of the Kentucky rifle is increasing and along with it greater collecting activity. Not only are the guns admired for their artistry and historical background, but they inspired modern craftsmen to match their skills with those of the 18th Century gunmakers and to produce replicas that not only are works of art but which also perform well at frequently-held muzzle-loading shooting matches.

In a long career of collecting and studying the Kentucky rifle the author has owned several hundred of these fascinating guns. Some were well preserved, some showed the honest wear of time, and some gave evidence of injudicious repair or deceptive restoration. But despite any defects each has represented a real and visible link with our dramatic national past. Few objects of any age can equal the Kentucky rifle as a symbol of pioneer America.

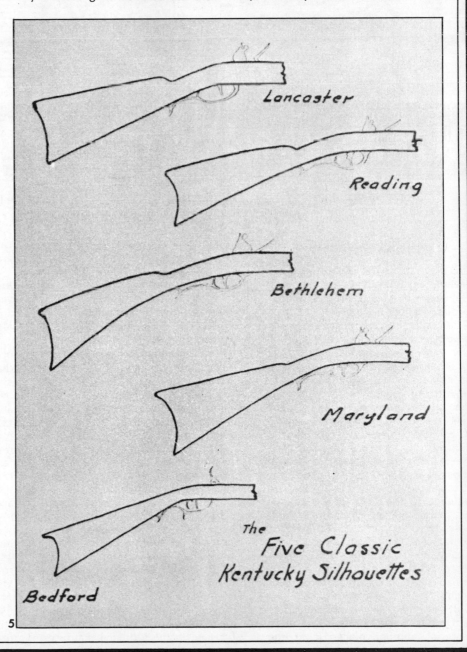

Lancaster

Reading

Bethlehem

Maryland

Bedford

The Five Classic Kentucky Silhouettes

5

THE STORY OF TWO GUNS

ONE WAS OWNED BY AN INDIAN BRAVE, THE OTHER BY A HORSE SOLDIER —THEY MET AT LITTLE BIG HORN

by Rick Saccone

In the annals of history certain events are subject to such bountiful publicity that even the poorest scholar, or most remotely situated citizen, signals recognition when the subject arises. Such an event is "Custer's Last Stand." In Western lore, no other historic occasion has been the subject of as many books, articles, paintings, and in fact, speculation. Controversy surrounds so many facts . . . as to, how and when did Custer die? In what sequence did the individual events transpire and among the eyewitness accounts, whose was supported by the truth?

However, some incontrovertible evidence in the form of artifacts of the battle have come forth and these concrete reminders of history are fallible only when they are not accompanied by sufficient provenance. What is sufficient provenance? Perhaps, just enough facts to be convincing. In fact, it becomes very difficult to discount completely *any* item whose type, model, condition or serial number places it in the area and period.

So begins the story of two long arms, a model 1873 Springfield carbine, serial #41743, and an H. E. Leman, percussion, trade model, saddle gun.

The accepted serial number range for "Custer" Springfield carbines is #39,000 to #44,000; #41743 is only 243 digits from dead center of the range. Starting in March of 1876, 14 changes were made in the model 1873 carbine. The first was a modification of the thumbpiece which cut away the underside of the firing pin guard rather than only notching it. The subsequent changes were ordered in January of 1877 and March, April, May, June and October of 1878. These involved changes in the configuration of the rear sight, breechblock, firing pin, barrel, extractor, hinge pin and receiver. Many 73s still in service or in storage during later years received these and additional alterations stemming from the model changes in 1879 and 1884. Serial #41,743 bears none of these changes. It remained unaltered! Unaltered, that is, except for the effects of a stay on the Montana prairie exposed to the elements as it lay con-

cealed from view in the tall buffalo grass.

It would be pure speculation as to how it arrived at its resting place. Was it discarded and lost in the grass and rocks by a trooper as he made a futile attempt to reach safety? Did a Sioux brave, laden down with trophies from the most convincing Indian victory in the annals of the cavalry decide that this gun, among his other prizes, was the least desirable and with no second thought let it fall to the blood-soaked turf? Or, did an Indian owner, sometime later, while revisiting the site of Yellow Hair's defeat, encounter a circumstance which caused him to lose his trophy on the site of its capture? All that is actually known about the post-issue period of the arm's history is that some circumstance left it waiting to be discovered late in the summer of 1904 by a young man looking for some relic of the event which filled his imagination with the war whoops of men revenging themselves against the Manifest Destiny.

The average Indian traded for his firearm. The trader saw to it that he paid top dollar. In some instances

more than $300 worth of skins were pushed across the counter for a $10 rifle. A number of makers supplied the fur companies and the government with "trade guns." One of the most aggressive companies engaged in this business was that owned by Henry E. Leman of Lancaster, Pennsylvania. Of the 160 muzzle-loading rifles surrendered in 1877 by bands of Sioux and Cheyenne, who chose to remain in the United States, rather than follow Sitting Bull into Canada, 94 were examples of the craft of Henry Leman. The example featured here is one of those pieces.

The best way to tell the story of the piece is to relate verbatim the contents of a note found inside the patch box.

"This Leman buffalo gun was made for sale to the Indians and was one of a lot sold by the U.S. Government to Francis Bannerman sometime after the Indians surrendered a lot of guns in the late 70's. It was one of a lot purchased by Western Costume Company sometime in 1920's. Bannerman's catalog mentions this government lot. I obtained it from Western in Mid 1930's. This gun could have been one of used in the Little Big Horn fight.
(Signed)
1957 D. Franklin"

Since virtually every able fighting man under Sitting Bull's command was engaged against Custer's forces and since this arm was surrendered by a member of a tribe in this confederacy, it is almost certain that this rifle was carried into battle against the doomed 7th. While atypical of a "type" of gun, this specimen is also unique. Unique, in the sense that the decoration applied by its Indian

owner is, although not the most extraordinary stylistically speaking, nevertheless, a design dictated by personal taste. Then, again, the hard usage associated with an Indian saddle gun did a lot to change its configuration, rendering each surviving specimen slightly different. One of the most common wear patterns was a stock break, either fore or aft of the breech. The Indian solved this problem by either lacing on, or wrapping wet rawhide on, the affected area. This served to pull the pieces together in a vise-like grip. However, in the instance of this specimen, careful usage and luck precluded the need for this treatment. Although the stock bears numerous small line cracks, chips and scratches, the arm is structurally sound, as well as mechanically sound enough to be fired today.

Through the deep patina on the 23½-inch, .52-caliber octagonal barrel, one can see the stamping, "H. E. Leman Lancaster, Pa, warranted." The decoratively engraved percussion

1. Low Dog, an Ogalla Sioux Chief, in much the same costume he must of worn on the Custer battlefield. Kicking Bear, a Sioux veteran of the massacre, was commissioned in 1898 by artist Frederic Remington to put into a pictographic painting his eyewitness account of the battle. Note Custer's body in center.

2. A fine example of the craft of Henry Leman. Of the 160 muzzle-loading arms surrendered in 1877 by Sioux and Cheyenne who chose not to follow Sitting Bull into Canada, 94 were Lemans of this type.

3. This Model of 1873 Springfield caliber .45/70 carbine is a veteran of the Custer campaign. Only a handful of these exist today that can qualify as true "Custer guns." The elements that must be considered are the serial number range, lack of alterations and the origin of the individual arm.

4. Page 7 of the Francis Bannerman Catalog issued in April of 1889. The 50 arms offered, as is the case of the subject arms, were part of the lot surrendered near the Canadian border.

lockplate bears the stamp, "H. E. Leman." The breech, although at first glance resembles a conversion from flint lock, was assembled new with a conversion drum-style nipple mounting, thereby avoiding the higher production cost of a bolster forged directly on the barrel itself.

In 1866, a law was passed making it illegal to sell or trade arms to Indians. This law, as well as the end of the percussion era, curtailed the manufacture and distribution of this type of weapon. However, for years to come, unscrupulous traders sought out remaining stocks of these and other Indian arms and helped set the stage for the battle which would cause the first meeting of a model 1873 Springfield carbine, serial #41743, and this example of the craft of Henry E. Leman.

sharps rifle cartridges

The legendary buffalo and target rifles used an extensive variety of ammunition, specimens of which are among the most desirable to the collector. **by George Hoyem**

Identifying the early American single-shot rifle cartridges can be a problem because so many were manufactured without headstamps. Even headstamps can be misleading as there was a tendency for ammunition makers to identify many of these loads by caliber and weight of powder charge alone. While this is complete enough identification for many repeating rifle cartridges, such as the old .44-40, it doesn't work as well for single-shot rifle loads because, over the years, many different powder charges and bullet weights were developed for use in a few basic cartridge cases.

The Sharps rifle cartridges have been organized into five groups to show all of the rimfire and centerfire case sizes used in these rifles. Two factors—the caliber and the cartridge case length—should be considered in identifying each cartridge case. The shape of the case must be added in the .40 caliber group to avoid confusing straight-case and bottlenecked loads with the same powder charge.

The first group contains an example of the linen combustible cartridge and the rimfire rounds. The others represent the four centerfire sporting rifle calibers in which the Sharps was made—.40, .44, .45 and .50. Several centerfire specimens shown are duplicates in case size and caliber to illustrate the differences in powder charge and bullet weight.

A comprehensive collection of Sharps centerfire cartridges including all the factory-loaded variations in bullet weights, bullet types and powder charges could easily number five times as many as shown here. In order to avoid misleading the reader, only those cartridges which have been positively authenticated as Sharps-originated, or developed specifically for the Sharps rifles are discussed. A few Sharps rifles were made to special order for the thick-walled everlasting cartridge cases developed by other manufacturers, but Sharps did not advertise nor approve of such cases, asserting that their own would last just as long through repeated loadings.

The production of the Sharps rifle extended over that period in arms development when the primitive paper cartridge containing only powder and bullet was replaced in turn by a combustible linen-case cartridge, then the copper-case rimfire and finally the drawn-brass case, reloadable centerfire cartridge. The short-lived Sharps breechloading percussion rifle of 1857, or "pistol-rifle" as it was frequently called, was also made to use a metallic percussion cartridge.

Christian Sharps' first patent, issued September 12, 1848 covered a single-shot rifle action with falling breech-block operated by a lever which formed the trigger guard. The upper edge of the breechblock was constructed so it would shear off the rear portion of a paper cartridge case when the block raised to close the action, thus exposing the powder

charge for certain ignition by the percussion cap.

Sharps rifles were made under several company names. The early arms were manufactured by Sharps Rifle Manufacturing Company at Hartford, Connecticut from approximately 1852 to 1859 when the company name was changed to C. Sharps & Co. and the plant moved to Philadelphia where it operated under that name until 1863.

The company name was again changed to Sharps & Hankins in 1863 and used that name until 1872. However, the firm moved back to Hartford in 1870 and only lasted two years before it failed. Re-organized at Hartford in 1874 as the Sharps Rifle Company, the firm continued operation there until 1876, moved again to Bridgeport, Conn. and finally closed down in October 1881.

EARLY PAPER, LINEN AND PERCUSSION AMMUNITION

The .52 caliber Sharps linen combustible-case cartridge was an advancement over the earlier paper case ammunition because it was less susceptible to damage in handling and there was no need for the rear portion of the cartridge to be clipped off to expose the powder charge. The cartridge was inserted fully into the chamber. The rear portion of the linen powder container was covered with thin paper which was easily penetrated by the hot flash of the exploding percussion cap.

The .52 caliber rifle and carbine

employing either the paper or linen cartridge was the principal Sharps military arm used during the Civil War. However, these early Sharps rifles were also made in calibers .44 and .36 for sporting purposes, and a .56 caliber Sharps was produced, reportedly for sale in Great Britian. All used paper and linen cartridges.

An early attempt to modernize Sharps ammunition was the percussion "mule ear" cartridge made in calibers .31 and .36. Christian Sharps and Dr. Edward Maynard came up with similar ideas of a metallic cartridge made with a flash hole in the rear to admit the igniting explosion of the percussion cap. Both employed a prominent metallic "ear" or extension projecting at right angle from the base of the case which stuck out the top of the gun and served as a handle for extraction purposes.

Used in the modified breechloading percussion rifle introduced about 1857, the brass-case Sharps "mule ear" cartridges were laboriously hand made and have been found loaded with roundnose and pointed lead bullets. The projecting ear of the cartridge case was made in two shapes—one tapering and the other key-shaped, or wider at the point than at the cartridge base. The mortise in the chamber of these rifles is shaped to accept one or the other.

Unfortunately, quite a few of these little cartridges have been handmade in recent times, some by collectors whose only motive was to shoot their rifles. It is sometimes difficult to tell the difference between an original specimen and one made later. This state of affairs is a plague to collectors of early percussion ammunition and a competent authority should be consulted and a guarantee

1. Combustible linen and rimfire cartridges, from left: .52 linen combustible, 1½-inch. Sharps called for 50 to 55 grains of powder; .52 Sharps & Hankins 1 5/32-inch rimfire rifle, 55-grains powder, 465-grain bullet; .52 Sharps & Hankins 1⅛-inch; .52-70 Sharps rimfire conversion.

2. Page from 1878 Sharps catalog.

of authenticity requested before purchasing such a cartridge. This comment is not meant to cast doubt on the originality of the many authentic specimens owned by serious and discriminating collectors, but is intended as a warning to save the new cartridge enthusiast from pain and expense.

RIMFIRE CARTRIDGES

Another rifle action was patented by Christian Sharps on July 9, 1861 which employed a different action. This single-shot arm, known as the Sharps & Hankins, was also opened by pulling down on the opening lever. A rod connected to the lever and the underside of the barrel

moved the barrel forward away from the breech along an extension of the frame which also served as a forearm. A .52 caliber rimfire cartridge was developed for this arm.

The first, known as the Sharps & Hankins rifle cartridge was loaded with 55 grains of black powder and a 465-grain bullet. The second is an earlier version referred to among collectors as the Sharps & Hankins carbine round. The carbine load is distinguishable from the rifle cartridge by its flat-pointed bullet and slightly shorter case. The .56-52 Spencer rimfire cartridge was also used in the Sharps & Hankins, though it is shorter than the original cartridges.

Some 1500 Sharps & Hankins car-

Cartridges.

CALIBRE.	LENGTH OF SHELL.	WEIGHT OF POWDER.	LENGTH OF BULLET.		WEIGHT OF BULLET.	PRICE PER 1000.
	INCHES.	GRAINS.	INCHES.		GRAINS.	
40/100	1 7/8	50	1 5/8	Patched.	265	$37 00
40/100	2 1/4	70	1 7/8	"	330	39 25
40/100	2 1/2	90	1 7/8	"	370	47 75
44/100	2 1/4	75	1 1/8	Naked.	297	39 25
44/100	2 1/4	75	1 1/8	Patched.	405	41 25
44/100	2 1/2	90	1 3/8	"	500	53 00
44/100	2 6/8	105	1 13/32	"	520	55 00
45/100	2 1/10	70	1 1/10	Naked.	400	40 25
45/100	2 1/10	70	1 1/10	Patched.	420	41 25
45/100	2 6/10	100	1 13/32	"	550	55 00
45/100	2 7/10	100	1 3/8	"	500	54 00
50/100	1 1/4	70	1	Naked.	425	39 75
50/100	2 1/8	100	1 1/8	Patched.	473	53 00

Bullets.

CAL.	LENGTH OF BULLET.	WEIGHT OF BULLET.	KIND OF BULLET.	PRICE PER 1,000.
	Inches.	Grains.		
40/100	3/4	238	Naked (2 cannelures).........	$8.75
40/100	1 5/8	265	Patched and Swaged.........	9.25
40/100	1 1/2	330	" "	10.25
40/100	1 1/2	370	" "	11.50
44/100	7/8	297	Naked (2 cannelures).........	10.25
44/100	1 1/4	405	Patched and Swaged.........	12.50
44/100	1 3/8	500	" "	13.00
44/100	1 13/32	520	" "	14.50
45/100	1 1/10	400	Naked (2 cannelures).........	11.75
45/100	1 1/10	420	Patched and Swaged.........	13.00
44/100	1 3/8	500	" "	13.25
45/100	1 13/32	550	" "	15.00
50/100	1	425	Naked (3 cannelures).........	12.25
50/100	1 1/8	473	Patched and Swaged.........	13.50
45/100	1 13/32	550	Special Long Range, patched.	18.00

The bullets comprised in the above list are made with the greatest care, the lead being alloyed to a proper degree to insure accuracy and prevent leading the rifle barrel. The patched bullets are swaged under powerful presses, which secures the greatest uniformity in density. The patches are cut of bank note paper of even thickness, manufactured for this Company expressly for the purpose, and are put on with the utmost exactness. The special long-range bullet composed of an alloy known only to and exclusively manufactured by this Company, is giving very fine results.

1   2

sharps rifle cartridges

bines are known to have been purchased by the United States War Department between 1862 and 1865. Some, intended for navy use, were made with a leather-covered barrel—a measure designed to protect them from the corrosive action of salt air.

The fourth specimen in this group is the .52-70 rimfire used in the early Sharps rifles and carbines converted to use metallic, self-contained ammunition. A .52-70 Sharps centerfire was also loaded. It was nearly identical in dimensions to the rimfire round. A limited number of the Sharps rifles and carbines were altered to take these rimfire and centerfire conversion cartridges before the better idea was conceived of reaming out the barrels full length and sleeving them with liners chambered and bored to take the .50-70 rifle or carbine cartridge, the then-standard military loads. Consequently, both the .52-70 rimfire and centerfire cartridges are rare.

CENTERFIRE CARTRIDGE COMPONENTS

Factory bullets in Sharps ammunition, whether loaded by Sharps, Union Metallic Cartridge Company, Winchester Repeating Arms Company, E. Remington & Sons or United States Cartridge Company, were either paper-patched or "naked" as Sharps referred to grooved lead bullets. Paper-patched bullets were predominate, as they offered the advantage of preventing leading in the rifle bore, as only the paper touched the bore directly.

The theory was that the paper, cut by the rifling would fly off the bullet as soon as it left the bore because of its spinning action. This was a good theory but experiments since have shown that, in actual practice, the paper didn't always leave the bullet. One technique used in obtaining a good, snug fit of the two wraps of paper patch was to dampen the paper before putting it on the bullet. Consequently, it shrunk tightly around the projectile. Some shooters made a practice of making a slit in the paper lengthwise to the bullet to help it fly off. The paper remaining evidently made little difference, though, as these rifles firing long, heavy bullets were famed for their accuracy. After American rifle teams using Sharps rifles soundly trounced British and Irish marksmen, the European shooters lost no time acquiring Sharps rifles

of their own. British ammunition nearly identical to Sharps is well-known to collectors and specimens exist head-stamped "J. Rigby & Co." and "Fraser, Sdinburgh," as loaded for these gunmakers by the British ammunition manufacturers, Eley.

The influence of British rifle and ammunition developments may be seen in some Sharps ammunition. The "Express" rifle originated by James Purdey firing relatively light bullets with very heavy powder charges evidently appealed to some American riflemen, so Sharps offered light "express" bullets for the .44, .45 and .50 caliber rifles. The 1879 catalog, discussing the Sharps Borchardt hammerless rifle reads, in part:

"EXPRESS RIFLE, Model 1878 . . . .45 caliber, 26-inch barrel, single trigger, 2⁷⁄₈" chamber, for straight shell, holding 100 to 120 grains powder . . . We warrant this arm to be quite as effective as the best English Express Rifle made. The price is about one-third the cost of an imported gun . . . The whole secret of the term "Express" consists in using large charges of powder with a light projectile, which is given so great an initial velocity that gravity is largely overcome, and the bullet will fly 150 to 175 yards without a perceptible fall toward the earth, thus making a very flat trajectory."

Describing the bullets used in the Express loads, the catalog further states:

"The Bullet is made with a hollow point, in order to give, with the same weight of lead, additional bearings

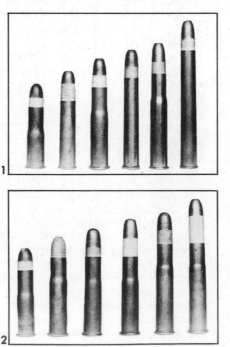

1

2

upon the grooves of the barrel, and to properly adjust its balance . . . The hole in the point of a .44, .45 or .50 caliber Express bullet is made to take a long .22 caliber rimfire cartridge blank . . . so that the hunters of grizzlies and other ugly game can use them as explosive bullets . . . We are prepared to furnish Express cartridges, Express bullets, and Express moulds . . . together with the .22 caliber blanks for explosive cartridges."

The ammunition and bullet lists included here as examples from the Sharps catalog show some of the bullet weights available. Also, independent ammunition makers developed a few of their own. The original catalogs are not infallible references since some (apparently typographic) errors appear in them here and there.

Sharps cartridges loaded early in the era were made with plain heads but U.M.C. and Winchester adopted headstamps later on, showing maker and caliber. E. Remington & Sons made ammunition at one time with the company name embossed on the head but these "raised" headstamps do not show the cartridge identification. U. S. Cartridge Company and Sharps Rifle Company itself never used headstamps on these cartridges to our knowledge.

Early catalogs frequently identify many of these Sharps cartridges as "Sharps and Remington," because Remington did adopt many of the well-established Sharps cartridges for their own single-shot rifles using their own style of bullets and a distinctive rounded or beveled-rim head on the cartridge case. Primers found in the early ammunition are the large Ber-

1. Centerfire .40 caliber, from left: .40-1 11/16-inch, necked, 50-grains powder, 265-grain bullet; .40-1⅞-inch straight, same loads as above; .40-2¼ necked, 70-grains powder, 330-grain bullet; .40-2½-inch straight, same loads as above; .40-2⅝-inch necked with 370-grain bullet; .40-3¼-inch straight, 90-grains powder, 370-grain bullet.

2. Centerfire .44 caliber, from left: .44 1⅞-inch necked, 60-grains powder, 395-grain bullet; .44 2¼-inch necked, 77-grains powder, 395-grain grooved bullet; .44 2¼-inch necked, 77-grains powder, 470-grain bullet; .44 2¼-inch necked, 90-grains powder, 470-grain bullet; .44 2⅝-inch necked, 90-grains powder, 500-grain bullet; .44-2⅝-inch necked, 105-grains powder, 520-grain bullet.

3. Sharps Model 1874, .45-2⅞-inch.

4. Page from 1879 Sharps catalog.

dan type while those loaded later contain the smaller Boxer primers.

CENTERFIRE .40 CALIBER

Because the .40 caliber Sharps group contains three necked cases and three straight cases, it is necessary to include the case shape of the cartridge in the name of each in order to avoid confusion. To say a rifle is

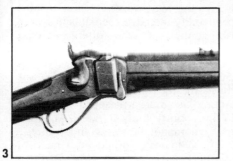

3

chambered for the .40-.50 Sharps cartridge (.40 caliber with 50 grains of powder) does not tell the whole story, as two cartridges in the line may be called this over-simplified name. The same situation goes for the .40-70 and the .40-90.

The .40-2½-inch straight case was also loaded with 65 grains of powder, but this is evident only if the cartridge is found in an original box so labeled. Some collectors have reported a .40-65 Sharps with a 2 7/16-inch straight case. This load does not appear in any of the Sharps catalogs or ammunition manufacturers' lists. Consequently, it is not included here. It seems inconceivable that the company, or anyone else, would produce a special case 1/16-inch shorter than the normal 40-2½-inch case which was so widely used. Both Ballard and Maynard .40 caliber cartridge cases

were made 2⅜ inches long and it is very easy to mistake one of these for a Sharps cartridge, especially if it is found with a typical Sharps paper-patched bullet loaded in it.

The .40-90-3¼-inch Sharps straight case was not a standard load developed by the company. Sharps would make rifles for this long case but it was a special order situation. The ammunition was made by U.M.C. and Winchester.

CENTERFIRE .44 CALIBER

The .44 caliber group contains three basic cartridge cases, around which a number of loads were developed with wide variations in bullet weight and powder charge. All Sharps .44 caliber centerfire cartridges are bottlenecked, which simplifies identification.

The .44-60, made for mid-range target and hunting rifles, may be found with either the paper-patched or "naked" grooved bullet. The 1891 United States Cartridge Company catalog illustrates the .44-60 loaded with both grooved and paper-patched bullets, but with a *straight case*. This is an example of the errors that crept into some of these early publications and which confuse the subject of arms research today. There was *never* any such thing as a straight-case .44-60 Sharps cartridge. No variations appear in the original company catalogs or other cartridge manufacturers from the 395-grain bullet with 60 grains of powder loaded in the necked 1⅞-inch case.

The following three specimens of the .44-2¼ inch cartridge show the variations in loading possible with one case. The first two are both .44-77's but with 405-grain plain lead and 470-grain paper-patched bullets respectively. The longest cartridge of the three is a Winchester-head-stamped .44-90 with the same 470-grain bullet. The bullet looks much heavier in this one because the powder charge takes up most of the room in the neck, leaving only a short space for the base of the bullet. Shooters undoubtedly had to exercise care in handling such ammunition as the bullets are easily removed with the fingers.

The .44-2¼-inch case was loaded in variations from .44-70 to .44-90 and with 293-grain to 550-grain bullets.

The third Sharps-originated .44 is represented by specimens five and six. Cartridges using this 2⅝-inch case were made up using 500-, 520- and 550-grain bullets and powder charges varying from 90 to 105 grains.

CARTRIDGES.

CALIBRE.	LENGTH OF SHELL.	WEIGHT OF POWDER.	LENGTH OF BULLET.		WEIGHT OF BULLET.	PRICE PER 1000.
	INCHES.	GRAINS.	INCHES.		GRAINS.	
40	1¼	50	1⅝	Patched.	265	$37 00
40	1⅞	45	1¹⁵⁄₁₆	"	265	39 00
40	2¼	70	1⅝	"	330	39 25
40	2½	65	1½	"	330	41 25
40	2⅝	90	1¼	"	370	47 75
40	2⅝	100	¾	Express Nk'd.	190	47 75
44	2¼	75	⅞	Naked.	297	39 25
44	2¼	75	1⅛	Patched.	405	41 25
44	2⅝	90	1⅜	"	500	53 00
44	2⅝	105	1¹¹⁄₃₂	"	520	55 00
44	5⅝	100	1¹⁵⁄₁₆	Express Nk'd.	277	50 00
45	2¹⁄₁₀	70	1¹⁄₁₀	Naked.	400	40 25
45	2¹⁄₁₀	70	1¹⁄₁₀	Patched.	420	41 25
45	2⁴⁄₁₀	100	1¹³⁄₁₆	Long Range.	550	55 00
45	2¹⁄₁₀	100	1½	Special L. R.	550	56 50
45	2⅝	100	1⅝	Patched.	500	54 00
45	2⅞	110	1¹⁵⁄₁₆	Express Nk'd.	293	54 00
50	1¾	70	1	Naked.	425	39 75
50	2½	100	1⅛	Patched.	473	50 00
50	2½	110		Express Nk'd.	335	52 50

BULLETS.

CALIBRE.	LENGTH OF BULLET.	WEIGHT OF BULLET.	KIND OF BULLET.	PRICE PER 1000.
	INCHES.	GRAINS.		
40	¾	190	Express, Naked (2 cannelures)...	$10 25
40	¾	238	Naked (2 cannelures)............	8 75
40	1⅝	265	Patched and Swaged...........	9 25
40	1⅛	330	" "	10 25
40	1¼	370	" "	11 50
44	1¹⁵⁄₁₆	277	Express Naked (2 cannelures)...	12 50
44	⅞	297	Naked (2 cannelures)	10 25
44	1⅛	405	Patched and Swaged	12 50
44	1⅜	500	" "	13 00
44	1¹¹⁄₁₆	520	" "	14 50
45	1¹⁵⁄₁₆	293	Express Naked (2 cannelures)...	13 25
54	1¹⁄₁₀	400	Naked (2 cannelures)	11 75
45	1¹⁄₁₀	420	Patched and Swaged	13 00
44	1⅝	500	" "	13 25
45	1¹³⁄₁₆	550	Long Range, patched	15 00
45	1½	550	Special Long Range, patched...	16 50
50	1	425	Naked (3 cannelures)	12 25
50	1⅞	473	Patched and Swaged	13 50
50	1¹⁵⁄₁₆	335	Express Naked.................	13 50

4

sharps rifle cartridges

Another cartridge in this group—the .44 2 7/16-inch Remington Special—is frequently included with the Sharps specimens, but it is actually a Remington development. However, some shooters must have preferred the Remington .44 case as some Sharps rifles have been found chambered for it. It is also necked but easily distinguishable from the Sharps cartridges by its length and different location of the shoulder on the case.

CENTERFIRE .45 CALIBER

The .45 caliber straight-case cartridge gradually superseded the .44 necked loads which Sharps originally developed for long-range target and big-game hunting rifles. One reason for this was the longer life of a straight case which was often fired and reloaded many times.

Five authenticated case lengths exist and, as in the other groups, each of the .45 case was used to make up loads varying in powder charge and bullet weight. The first three specimens show this. The .45-70 and .45-75 are both loaded with the 405-grain bullet. The .45-80, using the same 2 1/10-inch case, has the 500-grain bullet.

Sharps developed the 2.4-inch, 2.6-inch and 2⁷⁄₈-inch cases but declined to go beyond this last case length, insisting that the 2⁷⁄₈-inch cartridge case was long enough for any useful powder charge. Obviously, they were overruled by riflemen who wanted something even more powerful. U.M.C. and Winchester both produced the big 45-3¹⁄₄-inch cases and, consequently, Sharps made the rifles to order for the cartridge. Bullets as heavy as 550 grains were commonly loaded in the longer .45 caliber cases and Winchester experimented with an enormous 650-grain paper-patched slug for the .45-3¹⁄₄.

CALIBER .50 CENTERFIRE

Although the .50-70 cartridge was not a Sharps development, many of the sidehammer guns, both military conversions and later sporting models, were chambered for it. Since the .50-70 was the U.S. military cartridge only from 1869 to 1873 before it was superseded by the .45-70, probably more .50-70 cartridges have been loaded for sporting purposes than for military. The cartridge was also loaded with the paper-patched bullet.

The second cartridge shown is a

variation of the .50-70 and is somewhat of a mystery. Some collectors have referred to it as a .50-75. It is included here as a probable Sharps sporting variation because its bullet exactly matches that in the next cartridge shown, the .50-2-inch. This two-inch long cartridge case is listed in the 1875 and 1876 catalogs under "Brass, Centre Fire Re-loading Shells" with no other data given. The bullets in catridges two and three are probably the 500-grain listed in the same catalogs. The .50-2-inch cartridge case is one of the least-known in the Sharps line, and we have found it loaded only with this grooved bullet.

The .50-2¹⁄₂-inch Sharps, or "Big Fifty" as it was known, was a popular round for the buffalo rifle. It was also known as the .50-90 or .50-100 depending on the powder charge used.

1. Centerfire .45 caliber, from left: .45-2 1/10-inch, 70-grains powder, 405-grain bullet; .45-2 1/10-inch, 75-grains powder, 405-grain bullet; .45-2 1/10-inch, 80-grains powder, 500-grain bullet; .45-2.4-inch, 90-grains powder, 500-grain bullet; .45-2.6-inch, 100 grains powder, 500-grain bullet; .45-2⁷⁄₈-inch, 110-grains powder, 500-grain bullet; .45-3¹⁄₄-inch, 120 grains, 550-grain.

2. Centerfire .50 caliber, from left: .50-1¾-inch, 70-grains powder, .425-grain bullet; .50-1¾-inch, loading unknown, 500-grain bullet; 50-2-inch, load unknown, 500-grain bullet; .50-2¹⁄₂-inch, 90-grains powder, 473-grain bullet; .50-3¹⁄₄-inch, 140-grains powder, 473-grain bullet.

1

2

The last and most impressive of all Sharps centerfire loads was a late development. The .50-3¹⁄₄-inch case was never offered but Sharps made a few rifles for it on special order. Since the buffalo were gone by the time it arrived, it is difficult to figure out what anyone found to hunt with such artillery. Rifles handling this cartridge and the big .45-3¹⁄₄ are excessively heavy. The fact is, the cartridges were not in the least necessary, but in all probability the advertisements of British gunmakers who offered their single- and double-barreled rifles chambered for the .450-3¹⁄₄ and .500-3¹⁄₄ Express loads spurred enthusiasm for the longer cartridges among the more wild-eyed riflemen in this country. Only U.M.C. is known to have made the cases and bullets for it. Winchester produced a nearly identical cartridge case—the .50-140 Express—but loaded it with a flat-nosed copper-tubed hollow-point bullet. Any other bullet loaded in the .50-140 Express is not original.

Bullets found loaded in the big .50-3¹⁄₄ Sharps case range from 425-grain to 700-grain. Since so many of the existing .50-3¹⁄₄ cases have been found as primed empties, the .50-70 paper-patched bullets have been used to load them up. Both the .45- and .50-caliber 3¹⁄₄-inch cases are scarce items because the Sharps Rifle Company went out of business in 1881 shortly after the loads were introduced to the market.

Other interesting specimens in the Sharps cartridge line are sought after by collectors. Some of the target cartridges were produced with nickeled cases and the company offered solid steel shells with a reduced powder chamber for gallery use with round balls in .40-2¹⁄₂ and .45-2 1/10 sizes. A .45-2⁷⁄₈ case in the author's collection has an enigmatic "3" deeply cut on the head with no other marking. Another collector found three .52 Sharps shot cartridges in a packet of .52 Sharps Linen loads, an indication that some Civil War soldiers supplemented the army diet with a few birds now and then. Undoubtedly, many other interesting facts remain to be ferreted out by collectors.

For the man whose principal interest in cartridges is to shoot his Sharps rifles, James Grant's *Single-Shot Rifles* has a wealth of information and practical instructions for working up loads. Originally published in 1947, it has been reprinted since and is still available through book dealers.

COLT'S COMMEMORATIVE GUN COLLECTOR'S
ASSOCIATION OF AMERICA, INC.

1

COMMEMORATIVES

A NEW FIELD IN COLLECTING WITH GREAT INVESTMENT POTENTIAL

By Wallace Beinfeld

Since ancient times, people have built memorials to significant persons, places and events. These memorials range from small medals or pins to such works of art as the Taj Mahal in India. In America, we have the Liberty Bell, the Washington Monument and numerous other locations commemorating famous persons and events in our history.

In the past decade, we have seen a new idea in commemorative art take very solid and popular form— the commemorative firearm. Repeatedly, we have been told how indispensable the rifle, pistol and to a lesser degree, the shotgun were to our nation's birth and growth. And the fact is that they were, and still are, despite frequent misuse by criminals.

Colt and Winchester, two of the most important American gunmakers have been regularly issuing limited-production versions of their products, either individually, or in sets that re-

call important persons, places and events in our short, turbulent history. More recently, Marlin, Remington, Harrington & Richardson and Ruger have also entered this field.

Colt alone, since 1961, has issued more than 75 different commemorative handguns, based around the Single Action Army, its smaller brother the Scout and the government Model .45 Automatic. By far, they have been the most prolific producers of commemoratives. Winchester has based their commemoratives on their famed Model 1894, last of the traditional lever actions that made them so famous.

Around these diverse pieces has grown a whole new field of collecting; commemorative collecting. Most commemorative pieces are bought as investment items with no intent on the part of the purchaser to ever shoot them (we have, however, seen some very well-used commemoratives!). Since their numbers are few, they become collector's items as soon

as they pass out of production. Most all bear special serial numbers and are carefully cased or packaged by the factory along with historical information. Certain commemoratives have been issued in pairs, while others are single pieces.

The accompanying list has been prepared by Cherry's Sporting Goods of Geneso, Illinois 61254, and is as complete as possible. Especially interesting are the current prices—well above the original retail tab. New commemorative issues will continue to be offered by the arms makers in succeeding years, and this fascinating field, though growing, is really just beginning!

1. The Colt's Commemorative Gun Collector's Association contributes a trophy as an award at major gun shows around the U.S. The trophy is at center of this display.

2. The Savage 1895 Anniversary Model is indicative of the importance placed on this field by manufacturers.

2

COMMEMORATIVES

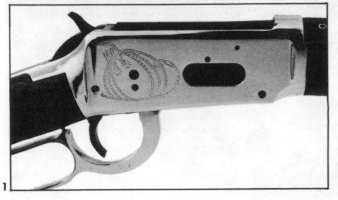

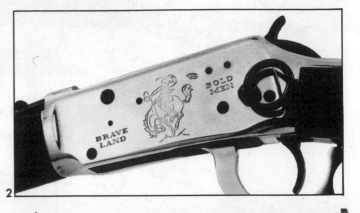

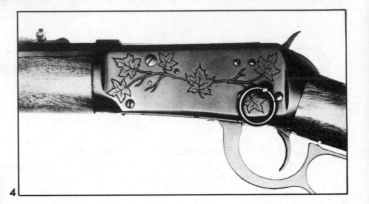

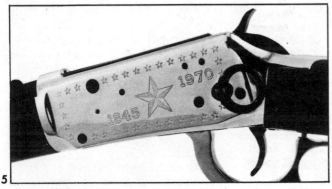

1. The Cowboy Commemorative done with a nickel-plated Model 94 Carbine. This limited edition lever action saddle gun was authorized by the Cowboy Hall of Fame and was made available only in 1970.

2. The inscription on the left side of the receiver shows a bronc-riding cowboy flanked by the words: "Brave Land—Bold Men."

3. Winchester's Canadian Centennial which was made available in 1967.

4. An engraved maple leaf motif decorates the highly-polished black chrome receiver. Five leaves on each side symbolize the 10 Canadian provinces; the larger maple leaf centered on the left side represents the two northern territories.

5. Winchester's Lone Star Commemorative was produced to celebrate the founding of the State of Texas.

6. Winchester's Golden Spike Commemorative, produced to honor the famous linking-up of the country by rail.

7. One of the more intriguing commemorative Colt revolvers was the Golden Spike Centennial of 1969.

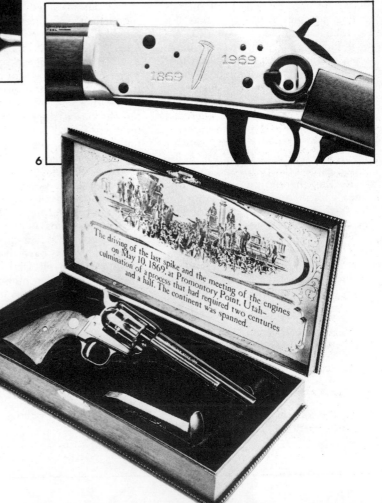

8. The Buffalo Bill Commemorative, a traditional Winchester .30/30 caliber lever action in both carbine and rifle styles.

9. Remington Montana Territorial Centennial 600 rifle. 1000 were made in 6mm Remington, however five more were made in .222 Remington.

COMMEMORATIVE ISSUE	MANUFACTURER AND MODEL	CALIBER	YEAR ISSUED	QUANTITY	CURRENT VALUE
Abercrombe & Fitch Trailblazer,					
New York	Colt NF SAA	45LC	1966	200	$850.00
Chicago	Colt NF SAA	45LC	1966	100	850.00
San Francisco	Colt NF SAA	45LC	1966	100	850.00
Abilene Anniversary	Harrington and Richardson	22LR	1967	300	95.00
Abilene, Kansas Cowtown	Colt Scout	22LR	1966	500	195.00
Alabama Sesquicentennial	Colt Scout	22LR	1969	3001	150.00
Alamo	Colt Scout	22LR	1967	4250	150.00
Alamo	Colt SAA	45LC	1967	750	325.00
Alamo, Combo	Colt Scout,	22LR	1967	250 }	495.00
	Colt SAA	45LC	1967	250	
Alaskan Purchase Centennial Carbine	Winchester 94	30-30WCF	1967	1501	450.00
Appomattox Centennial	Colt Scout	22LR	1965	1000	195.00
Appomattox Centennial	Colt SAA	45LC	1965	250	350.00
Appomattox Centennial, Combo	Colt Scout,	22LR	1965	250 }	550.00
	Colt SAA	45LC	1965	250	
Arizona Territorial Centennial	Colt Scout	22LR	1963	5355	175.00
Arizona Territorial Centennial	Colt SAA	45LC	1963	1280	350.00
Arizona Territorial Sesquicentennial	Colt Scout	22LR	1969	3500	110.00
Article II, Carbine	Marlin 39	22LR	1967	3000	125.00
Article II, Rifle	Marlin 39	22LR	1971		125.00
Bat Masterson, Lawman	Colt Scout	22LR	1971		195.00
Bat Masterson, Lawman	Colt SAA	45LC	1967	500	375.00
Battle of Gettysburg Centennial	Colt Scout	22LR	1963	1019	195.00
Browning 2000000 Commemorative	Browning Arms Automatic 5	12 Gauge	1970	2500	575.00
Buffalo Bill Carbine	Winchester 94	30-30WCF	1968	118,799	99.00
Buffalo Bill Rifle	Winchester 94	30-30WCF	1968 in Above		99.00
California Bicentennial	Colt Scout	22LR	1970	5000	135.00
California Gold Rush	Colt Scout	22LR	1964	500	225.00
California Gold Rush	Colt SAA	45LC	1966	130	495.00
Canadian Centennial Rifle	Remington 742	308 Win	1967	1000	199.95
Canadian Centennial Rifle	Ruger 10/22	22LR	1967	2000	99.95
Canadian Centennial Carbine	Winchester 94	30-30WCF	1967	90,301	99.00
Canadian Centennial Rifle	Winchester 94	30-30WCF	1967 in Above		99.00
Canadian Centennial Matched No. 1 Rifle	Ruger 10/22	22LR	1967	30 }	750.00
	Remington 742	308 Win			
Canadian Centennial Matched No. 2 Rifle	Ruger 10/22	22LR	1967	70 }	450.00
	Remington 742	308 Win			
Canadian Centennial Matched No. 3 Rifle	Ruger 10/22	22LR	1967	1900	219.00
	Remington 742	308 Win			
California Charter Tercentenary	Colt Scout	22LR	1963	300	250.00
California Charter Tercentenary, Combo	Colt Scout,	22LR	1963	250 }	475.00
	Colt SAA	45LC	1963	250	

COMMEMORATIVE ISSUE	MANUFACTURER AND MODEL	CALIBER	YEAR ISSUED	QUANTITY	CURRENT VALUE
Chamizal Treaty	Colt Scout	22LR	1964	250	175.00
Chamizal Treaty, Cased Pair	Colt Scout	22LR	1964	100	395.00
Chamizal Treaty	Colt SAA	45LC	1964	50	550.00
Chamizal Treaty, Combo	Colt Scout,	22LR	1964	50 }	750.00
	Colt SAA	45LC	1964	50	
Cherry's Sporting Goods 35th Anniversary	Colt Scout,	22LR	1964	100 }	475.00
Combo	Colt SAA	45LC	1964	100	
Chisholm Trail, Kansas Trail	Colt Scout	22LR	1967	500	150.00
Civil War Centennial	Colt M1860	22 Short	1961	24,141	60.00
Coffeyville, Kansas Cowtown	Colt Scout	22LR	1966	500	195.00
Col. Sam Colt Sesquicentennial					
Presentation	Colt SAA	45LC	1964	4750	395.00
Deluxe Presentation	Colt SAA	45LC	1964	200	850.00
Special Deluxe Presentation	Colt SAA	45LC	1964	50	1850.00
Colorado Gold Rush	Colt Scout	22LR	1966	1350	175.00
Columbus, Ohio Sesquicentennial	Colt Scout	22LR	1962	200	425.00
Cowboy Commemorative Carbine	Winchester 94	30-30WCF	1970	27,500	99.00
Dakota Territory	Colt Scout	22LR	1966	1000	175.00
Dodge City, Kansas Cowtown	Colt Scout	22LR	1965	500	195.00
Fort Hays, Kansas Fort	Colt Scout	22LR	1969	501	130.00
Fort Larned, Kansas Fort	Colt Scout	22LR	1969	501	150.00
Fort Riley, Kansas Fort	Colt Scout	22LR	1970	501	130.00
Fort Scott, Kansas Fort	Colt Scout	22LR	1971	501	130.00
Fort Findlay, Ohio Sesquicentennial	Colt Scout	22LR	1962	110	425.00
Fort Findlay, Ohio Sesquicentennial,	Colt Scout	22LR	1962	20 }	2000.00
Cased Pair	Colt Scout	22 Magnum	1962	20	
Fort McPherson, Nebraska Centennial	Colt #4 Derringer	22 Short	1963	300	150.00
Fort Stephenson, Ohio Sesquicentennial	Colt Scout	22LR	1963	200	450.00
Forty-Niner Miner	Colt Scout	22LR	1965	500	195.00
General Hood Centennial	Colt Scout	22LR	1964	1503	175.00
General John Hunt Morgan Indiana Raid	Colt Scout	22LR	1963	100	550.00
General Meade Pennsylvania Campaign	Colt Scout	22LR	1965	1197	175.00
General Meade Pennsylvania Campaign	Colt SAA	45LC	1966	200	425.00
General Nathan Bedford Forrest	Colt Scout	22LR	1969	3000	150.00
Geneseo, Illinois 125th Anniversary	Colt #4 Derringer	22 Short	1961	104	325.00
Golden Spike	Colt Scout	22LR	1969	11,000	150.00
Golden Spike Carbine	Winchester 94	30-30WCF	1969	70,015	99.00
H. Cook 1 to 100, Combo	Colt Scout,	22LR	1963	100 }	495.00
	Colt SAA	45LC	1963	100	
Idaho Territorial Centennial	Colt Scout	22LR	1963	902	250.00
Illinois Sesquicentennial Carbine	Winchester 94	30-30WCF	1968	30,073	99.00
Indiana Sesquicentennial	Colt Scout	22LR	1966	1500	150.00
Joaquin Murietta, Combo	Colt Scout,	22LR	1965	100 }	575.00
	Colt SAA	45LC	1965	100	
Kansas Statehood Centennial	Colt Scout	22LR	1961	6201	195.00
Lone Star Rifle	Winchester 94	30-30WCF	1970	38,400	99.00
Lone Star Carbine	Winchester 94	30-30WCF	1970 in Above		99.00
Maine Sesquicentennial	Colt Scout	22LR	1970	3000	120.00
Marlin Centennial Matched Pair--Engraved	Marlin 336	30-30WCF	1970	1000 }	850.00
	Marlin 39-A	22LR	1970 in Above		
Marlin 39 Century Limited	Marlin 39	22LR	1970		125.00
Marlin 90th Anniversary	Marlin 39-A	22LR	1960	500	295.00
Marlin 90th Anniversary	Marlin 39-A	22LR	1960	500	295.00
Missouri Sesquicentennial	Colt Scout	22LR	1971	3000	125.00
Missouri Sesquicentennial	Colt SAA	45LC	1964	851	275.00
Montana Territorial Centennial	Colt Scout	22LR	1964	2300	195.00
Montana Territorial Centennial	Colt SAA	45LC	1971	5000	375.00
Montana Territorial Centennial	Remington 600	6mm Rem.	1964	1005	200.00
Nebraska Centennial	Colt Scout	22LR	1968	7001	125.00
Nebraska Centennial Rifle	Winchester 94	30-30WCF	1966	2500	295.00
Nevada Battle Born	Colt Scout	22LR	1964	981	175.00
Nevada Battle Born	Colt SAA	45LC	1964	80 }	850.00
Nevada Battle Born, Combo	Colt Scout,	22LR	1964	20	
	Colt SAA	45LC	1964 in Above		550.00
Nevada Statehood Centennial	Colt Scout	22LR	1964	3984	150.00
Nevada Statehood Centennial	Colt SAA	45LC	1964	1688	295.00
Nevada Statehood Centennial, Combo	Colt Scout,	22LR	1964	189 }	395.00
	Colt SAA	45LC	1964 in Above		
Nevada Statehood Centennial, Combo	Colt Scout,	22LR	1964	577 }	475.00
with Extra Engraved Cylinders	Colt SAA	45LC	1964 in Above		
New Jersey Tercentennial	Colt Scout	22LR	1964	1001	175.00
New Jersey Tercentennial	Colt SAA	45LC	1964	250	425.00
New Mexico Golden Anniversary	Colt Scout	22LR	1962	1000	225.00
N.R.A. 100th Anniversary, 4¾" Barrel	Colt SAA	357 Mag.	1971		250.00
N.R.A. 100th Anniversary, 5½" Barrel	Colt SAA	357 Mag.	1971		250.00

COMMEMORATIVE ISSUE	MANUFACTURER AND MODEL	CALIBER	YEAR ISSUED	QUANTITY	CURRENT VALUE
N.R.A. 100th Anniversary, 7½" Barrel	Colt SAA	.357 Mag	1971		250.00
N.R.A. 100th Anniversary, 4¾" Barrel	Colt SAA	.45LC	1971		250.00
N.R.A. 100th Anniversary, 5½" Barrel	Colt SAA	.45LC	1971		250.00
N.R.A. 100th Anniversary, 7½" Barrel	Colt SAA	.45LC	1971		250.00
N.R.A. 100th Anniversary	Colt Gold Cup	.45 ACP	1971		250.00
N.R.A. 100th Anniversary	Harrington and Richardson M1873 Springfield Officers Model Rifle	.45-70	1971		250.00
N.R.A. 100th Anniversary	Winchester 94 Rifle M64	30-30WCF	1971		119.95
N.R.A. 100th Anniversary	Winchester 94 Musket M1895	30-30WCF	1971		119.95
Oklahoma Territory	Colt Scout	22LR	1966	1334	175.00
Old Fort Des Moines Reconstruction	Colt Scout	22LR	1965	600	195.00
Old Fort Des Moines Reconstruction	Colt Scout	45SAA			395.00
Old Fort Des Moines Reconstruction, Combo	Colt Scout,	22LR	1965	200	650.00
	Colt SAA	45LC	1965	200	
Oregon Trail	Colt Scout	22LR	1965	1995	150.00
Pat Garret, Lawman	Colt Scout	22LR	1968	3000	175.00
Pat Garret, Lawman	Colt SAA	45LC	1968	500	350.00
Pawnee Trail, Kansas Trail	Colt Scout	22LR	1968	501	150.00
Pony Express Centennial	Colt Scout	22LR	1961	1007	350.00
Pony Express Presentation	Colt SAA	45LC	1964	1000	450.00
Pony Express Centennial Presentation Combo	Colt Scout	22LR	1964		800.00
	Colt SAA	45LC	1964	in Above	
Robert E. Lee	Colt Navy	.36 Perc	1972	5000	250.00
Rock Island Arsenal Centennial	Colt M1860	22 Short	1962	550	125.00
St. Augustine Quadricentennial	Colt Scout	22LR	1965	500	195.00
St. Louis Bicentennial	Colt Scout	22LR	1964	502	175.00
St. Louis Bicentennial, Cased Pair	Colt Scout	22LR	1964	150	395.00
St. Louis Bicentennial	Colt SAA	45LC	1964	200	350.00
St. Louis Bicentennial, Combo	Colt Scout,	22LR	1964	250	550.00
	Colt SAA	45LC	1964	250	
St. Louis Bicentennial	Ithaca Mod. 49	22LR	1964	200	125.00
Santa Fe Trail, Kansas Trail	Colt Scout	22LR	1969	501	150.00
Savage 75th Anniversary Rifle	Savage M1895	308 Win	1970	9999	195.00
Shawnee Trail, Kansas Trail	Colt Scout	22LR	1969	501	150.00
Sheriff's Model, Blued & Case Hardened	Colt SAA	45LC	1961	478	450.00
Sheriff's Model, Nickel	Colt SAA	45LC	1961	25	2000.00
Single Action Army 125th Anniversary	Colt SAA	45LC	1961	7390	325.00
Stevens Favorite '71	Stevens Favorite	22LR	1971		75.00
Texas Ranger	Colt SAA	45LC	1970	800	650.00
Texas Ranger, Deluxe	Colt SAA	45LC	1970	200	1500.00
Theodore Roosevelt Carbine	Winchester 94	30-30WCF	1969	52,243	99.00
Theodore Roosevelt Rifle	Winchester 94	30-30WCF	1969	in Above	99.00
Ulysses S. Grant	Colt Navy	.36 Perc	1971	5000	250.00
West Virginia Statehood Centennial	Colt Scout	22LR	1962	3452	195.00
West Virginia Statehood Centennial	Colt SAA	45LC	1963	600	350.00
Wichita, Kansas Cowtown	Colt Scout	22LR	1965	500	195.00
Wild Bill Hickok, Lawman	Colt Scout	22LR	1969	3001	150.00
Wild Bill Hickok, Lawman	Colt SAA	45LC	1969	500	350.00
Winchester Centennial Rifle	Winchester 94	30-30WCF	1966	106,666	195.00
Winchester Centennial Carbine	Winchester 94	30-30WCF	1966	in Above	195.00
World War 1,					
Battle of 2nd Marne	Colt M1911	.45ACP	1969	7400	175.00
Battle of 2nd Marne, Deluxe	Colt M1911	.45ACP	1969	75	650.00
Battle of 2nd Marne, Special Deluxe	Colt M1911	.45ACP	1969	25	1250.00
Belleau Wood	Colt M1911	.45ACP	1968	7400	175.00
Belleau Wood, Deluxe	Colt M1911	.45ACP	1968	75	650.00
Belleau Wood, Special Deluxe	Colt M1911	.45ACP	1968	25	1250.00
Chateau Thierry	Colt M1911	.45ACP	1967	7400	250.00
Chateau Thierry, Deluxe	Colt M1911	.45ACP	1967	75	700.00
Chateau Thierry, Special Deluxe	Colt M1911	.45ACP	1967	25	1300.00
Meuse-Argonne	Colt M1911	.45ACP	1969	7400	175.00
Meuse-Argonne, Deluxe	Colt M1911	.45ACP	1969	75	650.00
Meuse-Argonne, Special Deluxe	Colt M1911	.45ACP	1969	25	1250.00
World War 2					
European Theater of Operations	Colt M1911	.45ACP	1970	11,500	250.00
Pacific Theater of Operations	Colt M1911	.45ACP	1970	11,500	250.00
Wyatt Earp Buntline	Colt SAA	.45LC	1964	150	795.00
Wyatt Earp, Lawman	Colt Scout	.22LR	1970	3001	175.00
Wyatt Earp, Lawman	Colt SAA	.45LC	1970	500	750.00
Wyoming Diamond Jubilee	Colt Scout	.22LR	1964	2357	175.00
Wyoming Diamond Jubilee	Winchester 94	30-30WCF	1964	1501	395.00

THE ARMS OF
SPRINGFIELD

FOR OVER 100 YEARS, MORE VARIATIONS THAN ONE CAN IMAGINE HAVE EMANATED FROM THE FORGES OF THIS NATIONAL ARMORY

by Bob Hill

To the American arms collector, particularly the individual who is especially interested in military arms, the products of our National Armories hold great fascination. These armories, such as the Springfield Arsenal, grew with the United States. From these forges emerged the requisite small arms to keep the new republic free and independent. To say that the production of small arms was prolific at Springfield Armory would be a misnomer. The rate of production depended on the national climate. In time of war, full effort was given to new innovations and mass production. In times of peace, however, there was quite a bit of backsliding due to lack of funds and the need to conserve at every production turn. In spite of the vagaries of time and lack of funds, the artisans at work for the Armory plodded on and produced arms that served in the War of 1812, the Mexican War, the Civil War, the Indian Wars, the Spanish-American War, the Philippine insurrection, both World

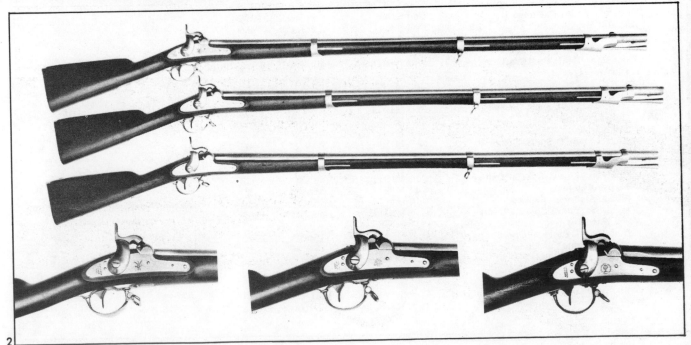

Wars and the Korean Conflict. The M14 must also be mentioned as it too has been used in the Viet Nam Conflict and had been produced at the Armory in small, developmental quantities.

Springfield Armory is now closed, serving presently as a museum, but the arms that have emanated from its shops over the years are still available to the collector. One such collector, Mr. Bob Hill, has made collecting arms manufactured by the National Armories (Springfield, Harper's Ferry and Palmetto) his life's work. The arms pictured here are from the Bob Hill Collection unless otherwise indicated. They represent not only the great and varied quantity of experimental and service arms, but America's tremendous production and technical potential during the Industrial Age. ♕

1. *New York National Guardsmen in this obviously posed shot in 1898 are armed with the Model 1896 Krag.*

2. *Model 1842 Muskets, caliber .69 as manufactured at Harper's Ferry, Springfield, and Palmetto (top to bottom, locks, left to right). Palmetto version uses brass guard plate and trigger bow.*

3. *First type Maynard alteration of 1835 flintlocks, marked "H. Maynard Patentee". At bottom, a Remington-Maynard alteration of a Model 1816 flintlock musket.*

4. *From top to bottom: First type Model 1855 Rifle-Musket, Springfield; Model 1858 Cadet, Springfield; Model 1855, Harper's Ferry. Springfield did not produce this model.*

5. *Lock detail of Model 1858 Cadet and Model 1855 Rifle. Both are fitted with Maynard tape primer feeds.*

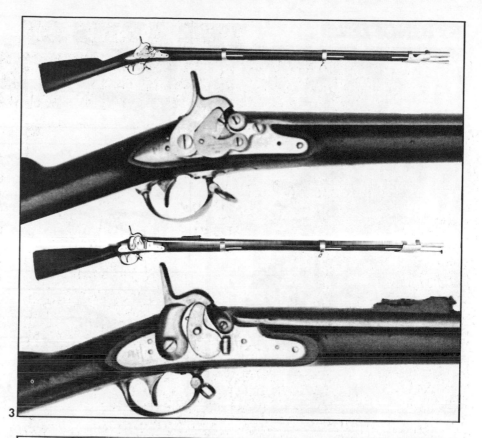

3

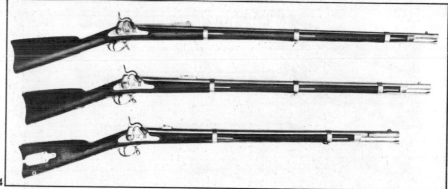

4

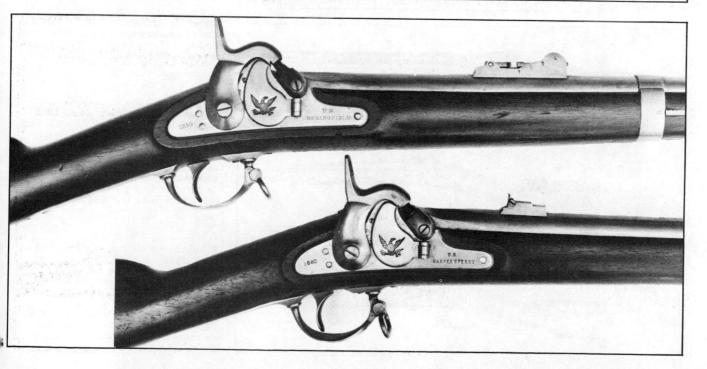

SPRINGFIELD

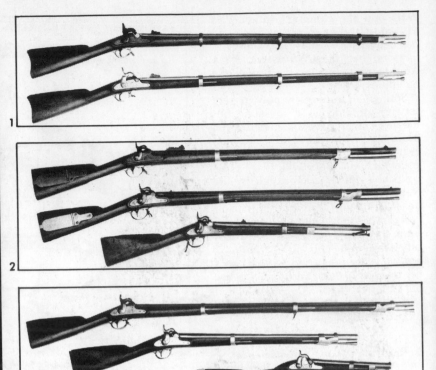

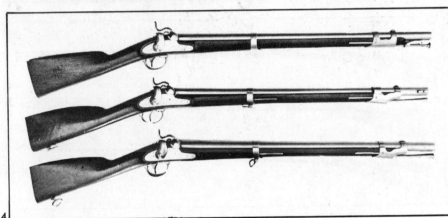

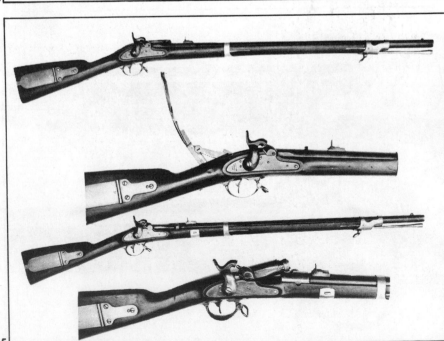

1. At top, a very early Model 1863 Musket with case hardened lock plate and hammer. Barrel bands are blued. Bottom, a Model 1861 Musket, dated 1861; both Springfield manufacture.

2. From top to bottom: Model 1841 Rifle, altered to .58 caliber with long-range sight and lug for saber bayonet; Model 1841 Rifle, caliber .54; Model 1855 Rifle Carbine, dated 1855. Only 1020 were made in 1855-1856.

3. From top to bottom: Model 1851 Cadet Musket; Model 1842 Musketoon, one of approximately 200 altered from Sapper's Musketoons for Naval issue; Model 1855 Pistol-Carbine, .58 caliber.

4. From top to bottom: Model 1842 Cavalry Musketoon; barrel bands, butt plate and trigger guard are brass; Model 1842 Miner's and Sapper's Musketoon. A total of 830 were made at Springfield between 1848 and 1856; Model 1842 Artillery Musketoon, manufactured at Springfield between 1848 and 1859. Total made, 3359.

5. Two conversions of the Model 1841 Rifle. At top, the Merrill, at bottom the Lindner, both shown with breech detail. The Merrill has been quoted as having 14,000 rifles so altered, however scarcity would indicate a misprint; 1400 is probably the correct figure. Only about 150 Lindner conversions were produced for General Buller's expedition to Ship Island.

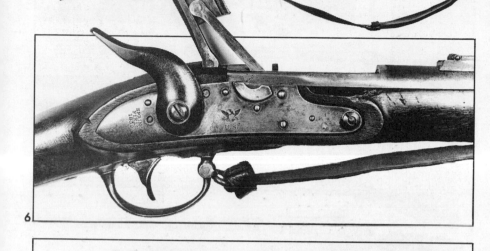

6. The Morse was the first breech-loader to be made at Springfield to take a metallic cartridge. A total of 2000 such conversions were authorized in 1858, with a payment of $10,000 patent rights to Morse. In November, 1859, the project was terminated, only 60 having been completed. From the collection of Mr. Bob Penny; Bob Steele photograph.

7. Two Joslyn conversions, both based on Model 1863 Muskets. The upper piece is caliber .50 rimfire, 1603 were so altered in 1871. In November of 1871, 1266 were subsequently changed to caliber .50 centerfire, lower rifle.

8. From top to bottom: Springfield-Remington conversion of Model 1863 Musket; Roberts conversion of Model 1855 Musket; Miller conversion of Model 1861 Musket. At right, details of the Roberts falling block and Miller rising block conversions.

9. Needham alteration of the Model 1863 Musket. Note side hinged block.

UNLESS OTHERWISE NOTED, ALL ARMS ARE FROM THE BOB HILL COLLECTION

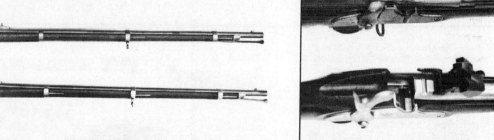

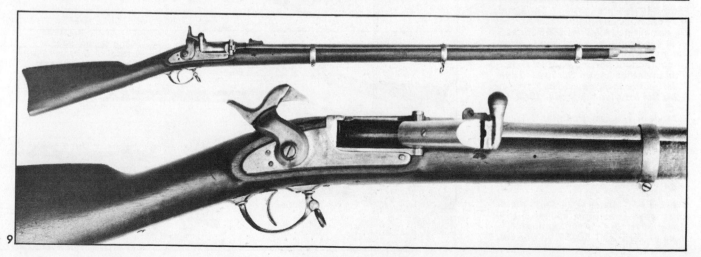

SPRINGFIELD

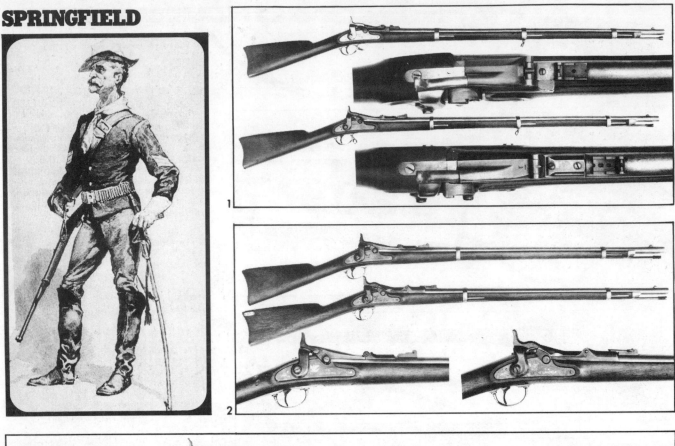

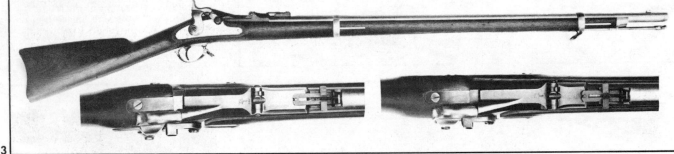

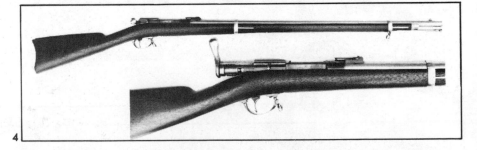

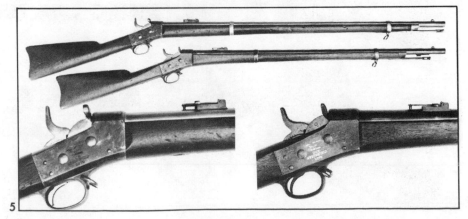

1. At top, the Model 1865 alteration of the Model 1861 Musket, commonly known as the "First Allin Alteration". Below, Model 1863 Musket with the Second Allin Alteration, the Model 1866. Caliber .58 centerfire.

2. Model 1866 Cadet Rifle, caliber .50/70 and the Model 1869 Cadet Rifle, also caliber .50/70. Only 320 Model 1866 Cadets were made at Springfield in 1867. Specially manufactured, they are not cut-down Model 1866 Rifles as is commonly believed. Every effort was made to lighten them, as a result 14 component parts do not interchange with any other known Springfield rifle. At left is the lock, dated 1867; at right, the lock for the Model 1869.

3. Model 1870 Experimental Rifle, caliber .50/70. Top views of Model 1868 Rifle, left, and Model 1870 shows the shortened breechblock of the '70.

4. Model 1871 Ward-Burton, caliber .50/70. Springfield made 1015 in 1871.

5. From top: Model 1871 Springfield-Remington Army Rifle, caliber .50/70; Model 1870 Springfield-Remington Navy pattern, cal. .50/70. At bottom, breeches of the Army, left, and Navy.

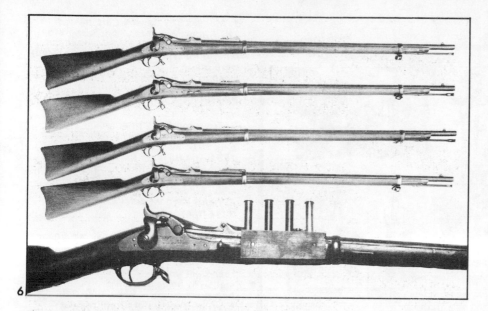

6. Four versions of the Model 1873 "Trapdoor" Rifle. From top to bottom: Early specimen, made in 1874, showing all features of the so-called "First Model"; Model 1873 with Metcalf attachment; 1008 were made at Springfield in 1876; Model 1873 with the improvements of 1879; Model 1884; detail of the Metcalf attachment from the Paul Parsons collection.

7. At top, the Model 1873 Cadet Rifle with 1879 improvements; bottom, the Model 1884 Cadet Rifle.

8. Model 1875 Officer's, first type. A scant 290 were made between 1875 and 1879. Bob Penny collection, Bob Steele photograph.

9. Model 1875 Officer's, second type. Differences from the first type are the improvements of 1879, style of vernier tang slght and the addition of pistol grip. Between 1879 and 1885, only 187 were built. Bob Penny collection, Bob Steele photograph.

10. At top, Chaffee-Reese, caliber .45/70. Springfield made 753 of these bolt-action repeaters in 1884. At bottom, the Springfield-Lee vertical-action rifle, caliber .45/70. Only 143 were made at the Armory in 1875.

UNLESS OTHERWISE NOTED, ALL ARMS ARE FROM THE BOB HILL COLLECTION

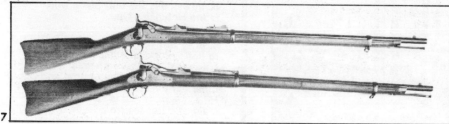

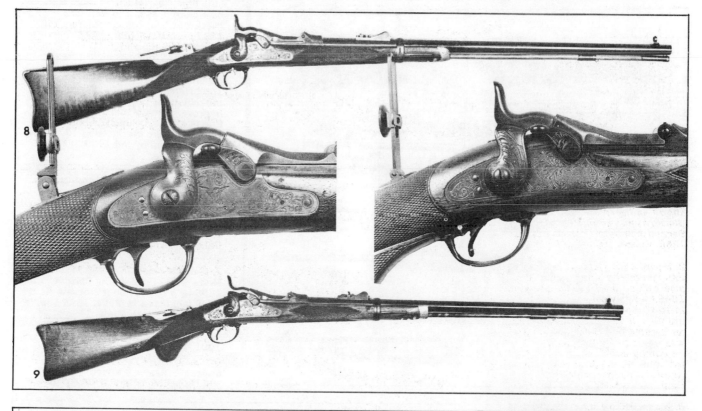

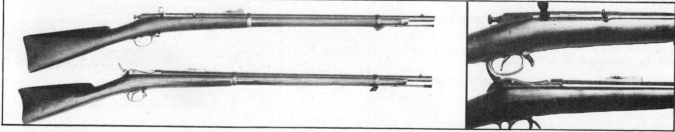

SPRINGFIELD

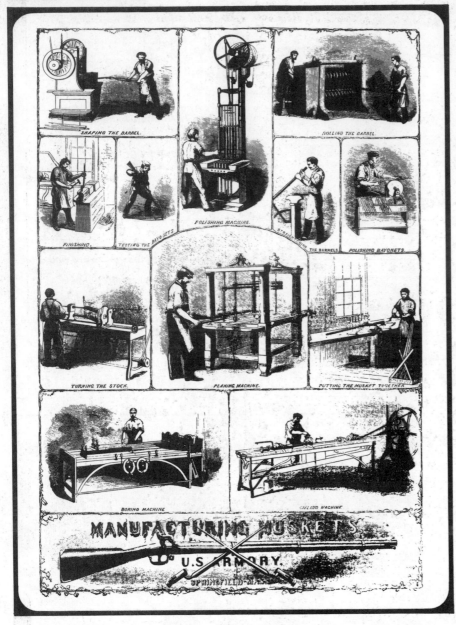

MANUFACTURING MUSKETS
U.S. ARMORY.
SPRINGFIELD MASS.

1. Model 1873 Cavalry Carbine with 1879 improvements. (Winchester Museum). Model 1882 experimental carbine, third type. Designated "XC", 1000 were made in 1886 as a possible weapon for both foot and mounted troops. Inset, the unusual sling swivel on the 1882.

2. From top to bottom: Model 1880 Triangular Rod Bayonet Rifle of which only 1014 were made in 1881; Model 1884 Rod Bayonet Rifle; 1003 made from 1885-1886. Rifle has first type Buffington rear sight with gear-driven slide; Model 1888 Rod Bayonet Rifle. At right, bayonet details of the three rifles.

3. Long Range Rifle, caliber .45/80 (80 grains powder). Springfield made 24 in 1881. They featured Sharps tang rear sight and spirit level front sight. No holes are drilled in the barrel for a conventional rear sight. Drop of stock differs from regular issue as does the butt plate, which is the Hotchkiss type.

4. Krag-Jorgensen rifles, from top to bottom: Model 1892 Rifle, early type made in 1894 with solid upper barrel band. First type ramrod and other early features; Model 1895 Cadet Rifle. Cleaning rod is second type. Major differences from issue rifle are absence of sling swivels, lightening cuts under barrel and in butt. The butt plate is solid (no trap for oiler), but has contour of later Model 1895 buttplate; Model 1892 altered to Model 1896. Cleaning rod groove filled, and Model 1896 rear sight fitted. Butt drilled to accept three-piece cleaning rod; Model 1896 Rifle; Model 1898 Rifle; rear sight changed to tangent curve pattern, other minor improvements; Model 1898 Gallery Practice Rifle, caliber .22 rimfire. After 200 were produced in 1906, they were replaced by the 1909 Gallery Practice Rifle.

5. Details of the Model 1892; Model 1895 Cadet and Model 1894 altered to 1896, from top to bottom.

6. Action detail of the Model 1898 Gallery Practice Rifle, caliber .22.

7. Krag carbines, from top to bottom: Model 1896 Saddle Ring Carbine; Model 1896 with replacement stock of Model 1899 length; early Model 1898 Saddle Ring Carbine with Model 1896 stock; Model 1899 Carbine, late issue with headless cocking piece and Model 1901 rear sight.

UNLESS OTHERWISE NOTED, ALL ARMS ARE FROM THE BOB HILL COLLECTION

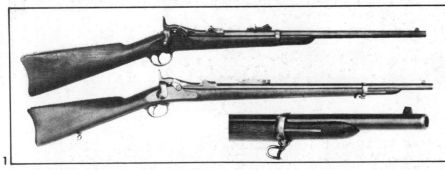

1

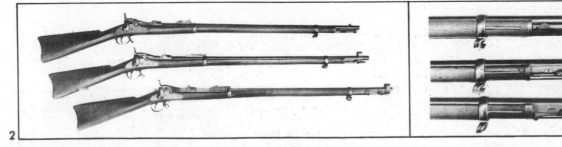

2

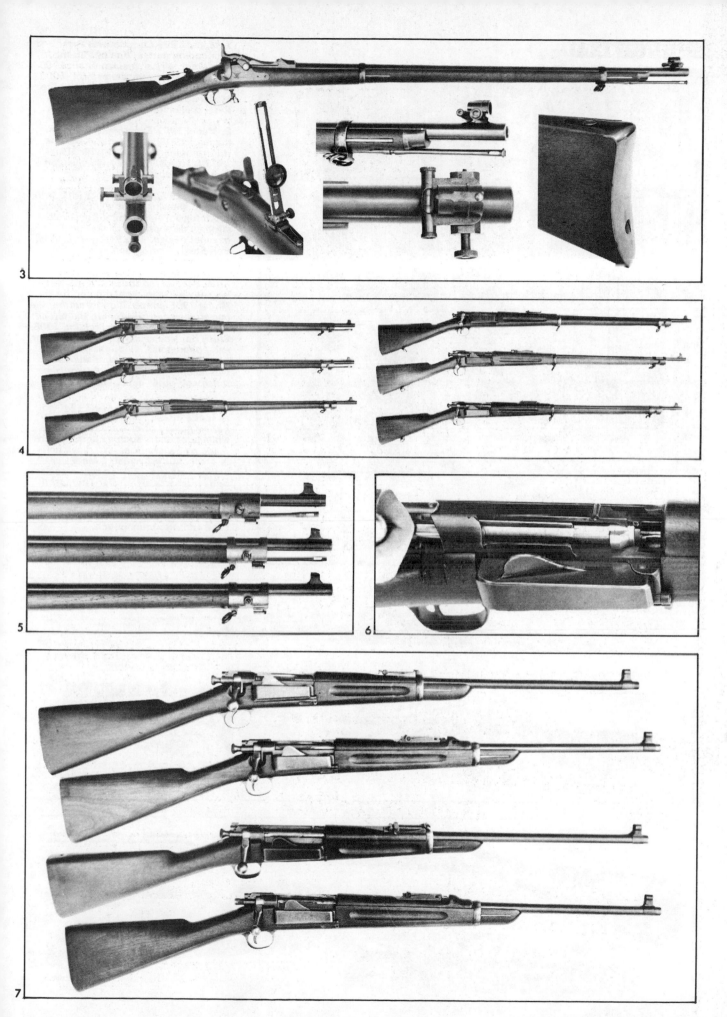

SPRINGFIELD

1. Model 1899 Carbine with Parkhurst clip loading device, one of 200 made experimentally at the Armory in 1900. Though successful, the project was dropped with the development of the Model 1901 Experimental Magazine Rifle, progenitor of the Model 1903.

2. Model 1901 Experimental Carbine, made in 1902, note serial #29. This rifle combines Krag and later Model 1903 features. Bob Penny collection, Bob Steele photograph.

3. Model 1903 Rod Bayonet Rifle with closeup showing front sight and lock catch for bayonet. Teddy Roosevelt strongly disapproved of the rod bayonet design. Bob Penny collection, Bob Steele photograph.

4. From top to bottom: Model 1905 Rifle, chambered for the .30-03 round. Virtually all were rechambered for the Model 1906 ammunition by setting the barrel back and shortening the forend; Model 1903 Rifle, manufactured 1908. Stock has one recoil bolt above trigger, early handguard, all metal parts are blued; Model 1903 rifle, made 1917; two recoil bolts in stock, Parkerized finish and other detail changes.

5. Model 1909 Gallery Practice Rifle as made in 1913, caliber .22 Short. Earlier gallery rifles were rebarreled, while later ones, such as shown, were made as gallery rifles. No recoil bolts in stock, but otherwise a Model 1910 stock. Note the "22" on rear receiver bridge. Inserts are Hoffer-Thompson.

6. Model 1903 Rifle with Pedersen Device complete with metal carrying case and magazine pouch.

UNLESS OTHERWISE NOTED, ALL ARMS ARE FROM THE BOB HILL COLLECTION

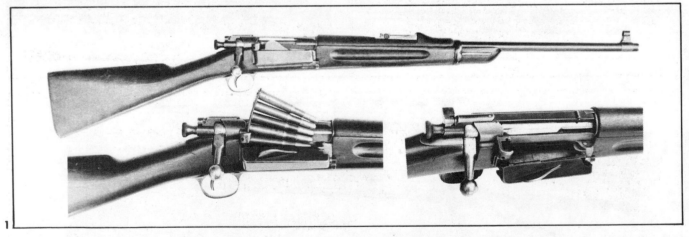

1

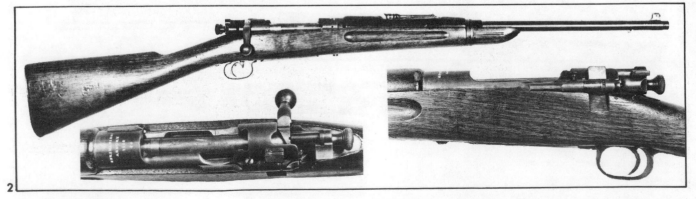

2

3

4

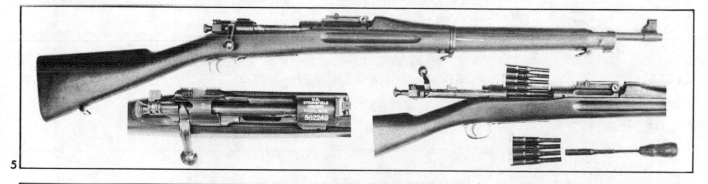

5

6

BOWIE KNIVES

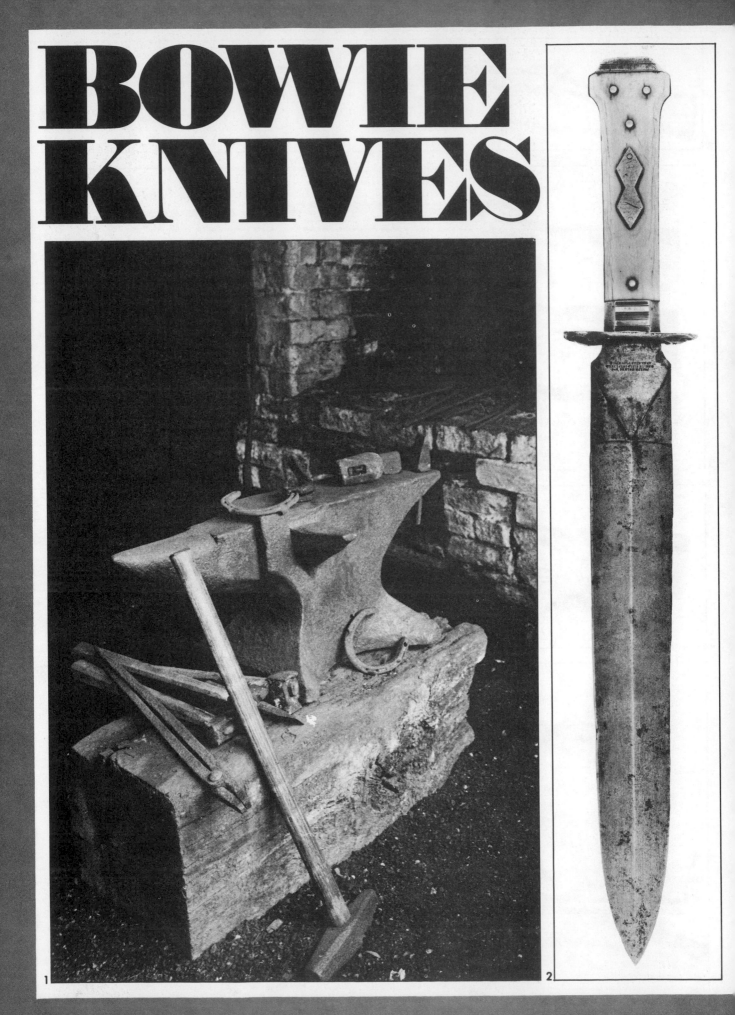

1

2

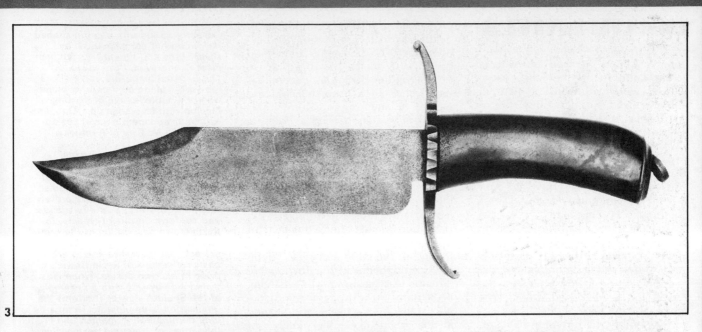

3

WHEN THE BOWIE WAS INTRODUCED, IT BECAME ". . . . MOST IN VOGUE" ACCORDING TO THE CONTEMPORARY PRESS. PRESENTLY, THE COLLECTING OF KNIVES IS "MOST IN VOGUE."

by William R. Williamson

"The Bowie knife is the weapon most in vogue," was the observation of F. C. Sheridan of the British Foreign Office, July 12, 1840, when he wrote an official report concerning the Republic of Texas. "It may not be uninteresting here to state that the greater number of these weapons are manufactured in Sheffield and Birmingham and brought over on British ships as a profitable speculation. I have seen one manufactured by "Bunting & Sons" of Sheffield, the blade of which was 18 inches long, and ornamented in beautiful tracery on the steel as a genuine "Arkansas Toothpick" and I have been offered anoth-

1. With these simple tools the 'smith forged the implements of peace and weapons of war. These included horseshoes and Bowie knife blades.

2. "Arkansas Toothpick" is stamped under the name of the maker, Joseph Holmes of 5 Cross Smithfield, Sheffield, on both sides of this large knife with an 11½" blade made circa 1837. Arkansas Toothpick was a term used interchangeably with Bowie Knife during the period and was applied to blades whether single edged with clip point or double edged with spear points.

3. Some clever fellow inserted a percussion cap box (removed from a pistol butt) into the hilt of this knife to serve double duty as a combination pommel and cap holder. Backwoods Bowies of this type were made by local smithies and individuals. This specimen is reasonably well done.

er for sale also of English make, the vendor of which hinted that I ought to pay him a dollar more than he demanded, as he assured me it had tasted blood."

In 1827, before he had carved his way into American history and legend, James Bowie became involved in the personal and political differences of one Samuel Levi Wells and Doctor Thomas Maddox. These disagreements ultimately culminated in the now famous Vidalia Sandbar Duel, and subsequent rough fight which served to catapult James Bowie and his knife to fame. Dr. Maddox issued a challenge which was accepted by Wells. The date arranged was September 19, 1827, the place a Mississippi river sandbar across from Natchez in Concordia parish of Louisiana. The principals arrived with the usual seconds and a small group of friends on each side, each group antagonistic to the other. Twice, shots were exchanged by the two duelists, apparently neither a sharpshooter, without effect. The aggrieved pair was satisfied. Differences between members of the attending parties however were at the boiling point and a wild fight ensued. Two men were killed and others badly wounded. Bowie, shot by his enemy Norris Wright, was down but managed to rise as Wright rushed in to finish him with a cane sword. Drawing a large hunting knife Bowie, using his last reserve of strength, was able to kill his attacker. The several wounds which James Bowie received were so severe that his recovery was in doubt. Walter W.

Bowie later wrote that James was saved by his unusually strong constitution.

The Bowie knife was launched! The newspapers wrote of the bloody affair with lurid descriptions. Bowie's reputation as a knife fighter was spread rapidly and enlarged all out of proportion to the actual facts. Soon men were asking for a knife like Jim Bowie's, and then simply for a Bowie knife. The "Red River Herald" in Natchitoches, Louisiana stated, "all the steel in the country, it seemed, was immediately converted into Bowie knives." All this steel was not enough to satisfy the demand for the knife, eastern dealers and English cutlery firms were called upon to meet the increasing need. Schools teaching the techniques of Bowie knife fighting were established. The knife became not only an instrument of the frontiersman, gambler and adventurer but it was held in high esteem by all strata including politicians, business and professional men. Mottos used on British made Bowie knife blades as, "I'm A Real Ripper" or "I Never Fail" held real meaning and appeal in the day of single shot pistols with frequent misses and misfires. At an even later time another Englishman Sir William Russell in, "My Diary North and South" refers to that area south of the Mason-Dixon Line as "the land of lynch-laws and Bowie knives." Friends "warned against the impolicy of trusting to small-bored pistols or to pocket six-shooters in case of a close fight, because suppose you hit your

BOWIE KNIVES

man mortally, he may still run in upon you and rip you up with a Bowie knife before he falls dead."

The severity with which an alarmed public viewed the increasing 'rule of the Bowie' is evidenced by support for restrictive legislation. Stringent laws with severe penalties were passed in several southern states. An example was one in Tennessee titled, "An Act To Surpress The Sale And Use of Bowie Knives and Arkansas Toothpicks In This State." This was in 1838 and the local newspaper in Nashville viewed the new law with great optimism. "The bill passed in January by the legislature against the sale and use of Bowie knives deserves to be reckoned among the most salutary Acts of the late General Assembly. Its provisions will effectually stay the use and sale of one

of the most bloody instruments of death known to the present age. Every friend of humanity and good order must rejoice that the practice of wearing this barbarous weapon has been rendered a misdemeanor, and its use in any way, a felony." This optimism was short lived as sales of the Bowie continued to accelerate and did not peak for another two decades. That the Bowie knife continued to be a favored weapon with members of the Southern aristocracy there is no question. Attorney Benjamin Hardin prosecuted Judge Wilkinson and friends after a rough fight at the Galt House Inn in Louisville, Kentucky. The good judge had "done in" one opponent with a Bowie knife described as having a white handle, eight to 10 inches long in the blade, two inches wide, heavy and shaped at the point like other knives of that name.

1. A fine American Bowie knife of the early 1830s with a coffin-shaped hardwood hilt complimented by silver studs and mounts. Escutcheon plate is engraved, "Bowie No. 1." The unusual blade/hilt angle aligns the 13⅜" blade on a parallel plane when the knife is held in fighting fashion with true edge up. "On a line with your opponent's navel" as advised by C. M. Clay of Kentucky.

2. The prototype of the original Bowie knife appears to be the "Spanish Dagger," a design long-favored by the Italians, French and Spanish. The top two knives are early presentations from Rezin Bowie to friends, and conform, in most respects, to Rezin's own description of the original Bowie knife. It seems safe to project that these two knives are basic reflections of Rezin Bowie's pride in his own design. When illustrated side-by-side with an example of the Spanish dagger (bottom) the implication is undeniable. In an area long dominated by Spanish and French influences of style and design, this trend is not surprising.

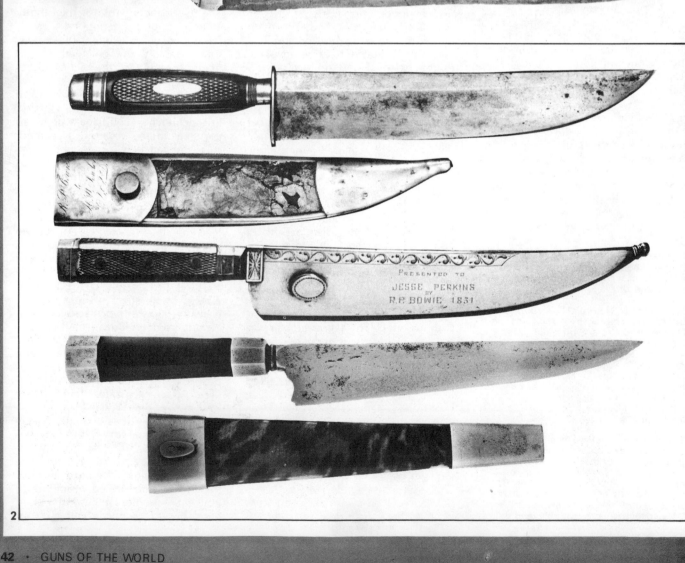

Before the jury, Hardin expressed this view in an attempt to discredit Judge Wilkinson because of his high position, "Go to Louisville when a portion of the city is enveloped in flames, and you will see a thousand mechanics rushing into the devouring element for the protection of property, while the lawyer and the judge, and the haughty aristocrat walk about as spectators with their hands in their pockets . . . Where, then, are your Bowie-knife and pistol-gentry, your duelists, and your despisers of the man who lives by the sweat of his brow? Gentlemen, one question is, are we to tolerate the Bowie knife system under the false pretense of self defense? I say, let your verdict act like an ax laid to the root of the tree, and many a prayer will bless you for your timely check of its growth. Many a woman is made a mourning widow, many a child made a pitiable orphan, and many a father childless by this accursed weapon." Hardin's impassioned plea fell on deaf ears for after 15 minutes of deliberation the jury acquitted the defendants.

In "Tait's Edinburgh Magazine" of June, 1846, an English traveller observed, "Above Dubuque, Iowa we refueled and I walked into a bar room to see the type of people. There were two cutthroat-looking men whom I should not like to meet on a dark night. One fellow was picking his teeth with a frightful looking Bowie knife; another with a similar weapon, was whittling on a piece of wood. Almost every man on this boat was armed with a Bowie knife, a detestable weapon with which the most frightful murders are constantly perpetrated. The owners made no attempt to conceal them, but appeared rather to take pride in their display."

The first of these frightful looking Bowie knives, as observed by our British friend, were forged from the best materials obtainable by the local blacksmith. Others were simply made from old files. The earliest example of a specialized industry was the craft of the 'smith. In almost every primitive American settlement of the period they were the fabricators of essential implements for the weapons of war and the tools of peace. Folklore credits a select few of these artificers with powers they did not possess, but are now accepted by many as fact. The tempering of steel blades has long been associated with

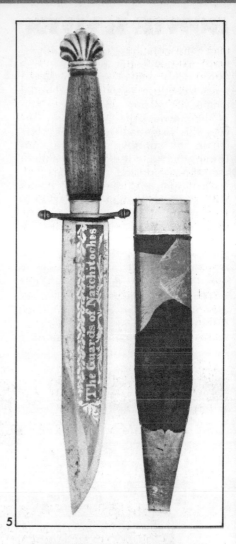

5

3. Excellent Bowie knives were made in India during the 19th Century. The 12⅛" blade of this large and unmarked specimen is inlaid with silver scroll work. Iron cross guard and mounts of one-piece stag hilt also display fancy silver inlays. Quality knives fabricated in old Madras province of India are often found signed by makers such as Arnachellum, Salem or Austin.

4. A seafaring man in search of California gold must have been the owner of this unusual American Bowie knife. The ivory hilt terminates in eagle head with scrimshaw designs and the leather sheath is reinforced with plaited twine. The 9½" clip point blade is inscribed, "Job Churchill, Maker" on one side and "Gold Hunter" on the other.

5. "The Guards of Nachitoches/They Yield to None" is acid-etched on the blade of this handsome American Bowie knife. There is no maker's name inscribed on it, but it was fabricated by a master cutler. Pommel and ferrule are of German silver and the one-piece hardwood hilt has an escutcheon plate on the other side of the hilt. The piece may be dated at about 1838. The local newspaper, "The Red River Herald," of Nachitoches, Louisiana, publicized the rise in popularity of the Bowie knife after the famous John Bowie sand bar duel.

3

4

BOWIE KNIVES

magic formulations, mystic methods and guarded secret processes. Possibly no weapon of relatively recent times has become so enmeshed in the tangle of folklore and pure fiction as the Bowie knife. When one surveys this legendary mix, three basic factors of controversy evolve concerning the knife itself; the invention, the fabrication, and the design.

The often-told legend of James Black, the Washington, Arkansas blacksmith, is a case in point, as all three elements are incorporated in the story. The opinion of most advanced collectors today was adequately expressed by Ben Palmer in, "The American Arms Collector", July 1957 issue. "Some American legends are of modern invention, although those persons who accept them as authentic folklore are not aware of it. So it is with the legend of James

Black, the 'smith who according to present and popular belief made the first Bowie knife by a secret process now lost. I believe the legend of James Black was born of the recollections of Daniel Webster Jones, of Arkansas, respected both as a member of the bar and governor of the state from 1897 to 1901. Certainly no record of it has been found which predates his account, which was written in 1903. I do not agree with the "Houston Chronicle," that it is true simply because Governor Jones wrote it. There is no evidence to support the legend. On the contrary there is fact to discredit it." Palmer further asks, "Where are the knives which, according to Governor Jones, poured in such volume from his (Black's) shop? Could these beautiful weapons, gleaming with the inlay of precious metals, have escaped us all these years? Would a silversmith-cutler, proud of his skills and jealous of his

fame, have failed to mark at least a few of his masterpieces?" The answers seem obvious. No such knife has made its appearance to lend credence to this tale. Knives claimed to be the unsigned work of James Black, when researched, can lead to such obscure places as the little village of Amozoc, Mexico where silversmiths inlaid blades and guns, or to the Indian subcontinent where Arnachellum and others made silver-inlaid Bowie knives in Salem town, located in the old Madras province of India.

A reference to Black written earlier than 1903 has been found. In 1895 William F. Pope, also an Arkansas

1. If one possessed the "gold coin" in 1871, both Bowie knives and baby carriages could be purchased from William Beck & Son.

2. These three knives display some distinctive and similar features. Note the almost straight back blades have worked designs and unusual notched or cut out choils. The top knife was made by Thomas Lamb in 1847 at Washington City (now D.C.) and has a blade length of 8⅞", brass mounts and hilt of ivory. Center knife was found in the French Quarter of New Orleans, the cutler's name is stamped as J. Cab (actually Jean Cabau, of Paris, France). This French Bowie was made in the 1840s and reflects superior quality with its fancy worked steel guard and carved hilt of ivory. Blade length is 9 3/16". Bottom knife with ivory handle and 10¾" hollow ground blade is by contemporary maker Gil Hibben of Springdale, Arkansas.

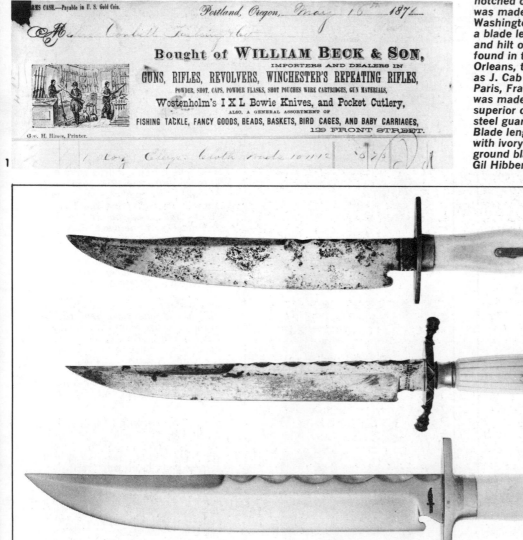

ARMS CASH.—Payable in U. S. Gold Coin.

Portland, Oregon, May 16ᵗʰ 1871

Bought of WILLIAM BECK & SON,
IMPORTERS AND DEALERS IN
GUNS, RIFLES, REVOLVERS, WINCHESTER'S REPEATING RIFLES,
POWDER, SHOT, CAPS, POWDER FLASKS, SHOT POUCHES WIRE CARTRIDGES, GUN MATERIALS,
Wostenholm's I X L Bowie Knives, and Pocket Cutlery,
ALSO, A GENERAL ASSORTMENT OF
FISHING TACKLE, FANCY GOODS, BEADS, BASKETS, BIRD CAGES, AND BABY CARRIAGES,
129 FRONT STREET.
Geo. H. Himes, Printer.

judge, refers to Black in his "Early Days In Arkansas". The revelations are not so detailed as Jones', and in Pope's version, Rezin Bowie (James' brother), went to Black with a carved wood model of the knife for Black to execute. Pope's expressed conclusion is, "I do not hesitate to make the statement that no 'genuine' Bowie knives have ever been made outside the state of Arkansas." This judicial decision, made without hesitation, is based on very flimsy, if any, evidence.

From Iberville, Louisiana, August 24, 1838 Rezin Bowie wrote the following to set the facts straight after reading a newspaper account with which he did not agree. These are his own words, "The first Bowie knife was made by myself in the parish of Avoyelles, in this state, as a hunting knife, for which purpose, exclusively, it was used for many years. The length of the knife was 9¼ inches, its width 1½ inches, single edged, and blade not curved." He continues, "Colonel James Bowie had been shot by an individual with whom he was at variance and as I presumed that a second attempt would be made by the same person to take his life, I gave him the knife to be used as occasion might require, as a defensive weapon. Some time afterwards, and the only time the knife was ever used for any purpose other than that for which it was intended, or originally designed, it was resorted to by Col. James Bowie in a chance medley, or rough fight, between himself and certain other individuals with whom he was then inimical, and the knife was then used

3. "How Gamblers Win or the Secrets of Advantage Playing," written in 1866 advises, "In these fast days every traveling gambler is armed with pistol and Bowie knife and is only too eager to use either." Professional gamblers and others of the sporting crowd favored the San Francisco-made daggers. The knife at upper left and the one at top are by M. Price. The other three by Will & Finck.

4. Confederate Bowie knives are usually rather crude affairs, yet this was executed by an accomplished cutler. In almost any and every form they were popular (especially in early Civil War years) with the men wearing gray. This knife, made from a file, has a 9 11/16" blade with a cross guard of iron and hardwood grips. The old label states, "Secesh Knife—Taken from a Rebel after a skirmish near Kirkpatrick's Mill in Johnson County, Mo., Dec. 18th, 1862." Grommets holding the old leather sheath together are flattened .31 caliber bullets.

BOWIE KNIVES

only as a defensive weapon, and not till he had been shot down; it was then the means of saving his life. The improvement in its fabrication, and the state of perfection which it has since acquired from experienced cutlers, was not brought about through my agency. I would here assert also, that neither Col. James Bowie nor myself, at any period of our lives ever had a duel with any person soever."

It has been further reported by members of the Bowie family that a white blacksmith, in the employ of Rezin P. Bowie, by the name of Jesse Cliff actually made the knife under Rezin's supervision.

Despite Rezin P. Bowie's apparent rejection of dueling and violence there is hard evidence that he did bask in the reflected glory surrounding his brother James and the knife. Rezin seems to have taken great pride in making presentations of Bowie knives to friends. Several of these are now in museums and private collections. One of the most important of these is a specimen with its sheath presentation engraved and dated, "Presented to Jesse Perkins by R. P. Bowie 1831." This significant knife was donated on May 28, 1918 to the Department of Archives and History, Jackson, Mississippi by the grandson of Jesse Perkins and is on display in the State Historical Mu-

seum. Another presentation Bowie in the Alamo Museum, San Antonio, Texas was made by Searles—Baton Rouge and bears the inscription on the sheath throat, "R. P. Bowie to H. W. Fowler, U.S.D. (United States Dragoons). These two knives are interesting reflections of "improved fabrication by experienced cutlers" which incorporated blades very similar in both size and shape to Rezin's original knife as described in his own words. The inference is as obvious as it is understandable. Rezin Bowie, a prideful man, desired the presentations knives made, accepting small modifications, based on his original pattern. When illustrated side by side with an example of the

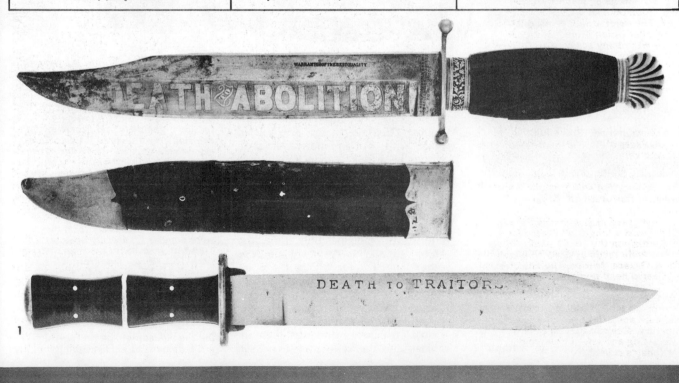

THE
SLAVE'S FRIEND.

VOL. III. No. II.   WHOLE No. 26.

DEC. INDEPEN.   BIBLE

PUBLISHED BY THE AMERICAN ANTI-SLAVERY SOCIETY, and for sale at their office, No. 143, Nassau street, New-York.

☞ Price—One cent single; 10 cts. a dozen; 80 cts. per hundred; $6 50 per thousand.

THE
SLAVE'S FRIEND.

VOL. III. No. II.   WHOLE No. 26.

DEATH ABOLITION

BOWIE KNIFE.

These horrid weapons are usually called *Bowie* knives. They were invented by a man who lived in the state of Louisiana. His name was Buie. It is a French name, and is pronounced *Bóo-e*. Afterwards he went to Texas, and was killed there in battle.

People in slave states often carry such knives about them. When they get angry they draw the knife, and sometimes *stab one another*!

A man who keeps a shop in Broadway, New York city, sells Bowie knives.

2   SLAVE'S FRIEND.   [18

Several people in New York sell them. I saw one at his window. It had two words on the blade, *etched in*, as they call it. Perhaps you have seen razors with mottoes on the blade, in the same style. Do you want to know what two words were on the blade? I will tell you— "DEATH TO ABOLITION." I asked the man a great many questions about these knives. He said they were imported from England by several merchants in this city. He told me the names of two of them. One keeps his store in Pearl Street, and the other in Maiden Lane.

The man said also that Bowie knives are made at Newark, New Jersey, and Springfield, Massachusetts, but he never saw any with the words, "death to abolition," on them, except those imported from England. But one seller said he could have the words put on here if purchasers wished it. How wicked to make such knives! How wicked to sell them!! How wicked to use them!!!

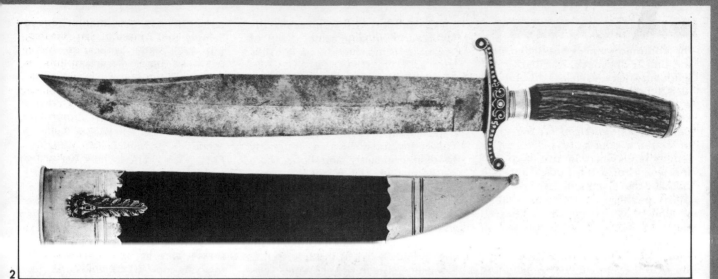

2

'Spanish dagger' these two presentation knives project an implication that is undeniable. The prototype of the original Bowie knives appears to to be a design favored by the Italians, French and Spanish long before R. P. Bowie was born. This development is not surprising considering the French and Spanish influence still existing in the area after years of dominance. It would indeed be difficult for Rezin Bowie or the cutlers involved to be far removed from design motifs of traditional acceptance. The clip point blade, as ap-

1. "The Slave's Friend," printed prior to the Civil War, was obviously not written by a scholar but reveals some interesting observations on the Bowie knife. Knives representing both northern and southern sentiments were marked accordingly. The Bowie knife bearing the words, "Death to Traitors" on its 9" blade was the inspiration of J. D. Chevalier, New York. The reverse side is inscribed, "Chevalier Union Knife." Hilt is of brass with ebony scales, cross guard is also brass. "Death to Abolition" knife is signed by the George Wostenholm firm of Sheffield. It is also stamped "Celebrated Cast Steel Bowie Knife." The one-piece ebony hilt has German silver mounts, 8 9/16" blade.

2. A German-made Bowie knife by Fernando Esser of Elberfeld. The Germans enjoyed very little success competing with the English in the American Bowie knife market. Esser also made very fine combination knife/pistols; blade length of this beauty is 12⅜".

3. "The brave man who attacks me I'll send on a long trip" is etched in Spanish on the 10½" blade of this Bowie knife made by Guillermo Maldonado, Oaxaca, Mexico. The cross guard and eagle head pommel are of brass and the hilt is carved bone. Mexican cutlers incorporated such engaging mottos on their blades as, "Death to whites," and others even less complimentary. Mexican Bowies offer an interesting and unexplored field for today's collectors.

3

plied to the Bowie knife, soon followed and, likely as not, was introduced by the English.

An interesting description of a clip-point Bowie knife written by Charles Hooten, observed while travelling in the U.S., was printed in his, "St. Louis Isle, or Texiana", London, 1847. "It is made of varied sizes; but the best, I must say, is about the size of a carving knife, cast perfectly straight in the first instance, but greatly rounded at the end on the edge side; the upper edge at the end for about two inches is ground into the small segment of a circle and rendered sharp; thus leaving an apparent curve of the knife, although in reality

BOWIE KNIVES

the upturned point is not higher than the line of the back. The back itself gradually increases in weight of metal as it approaches the hilt, upon which a small guard is placed. The Bowie knife, therefore, has a keen, curved point; is double edged for the space of about a couple of inches of its length; and when in use falls with the weight of a bill hook. Certain it is that I have, myself seen skulls of Mexicans brought from the battleground of San Jacinto that were cleft nearly through the thickest part of the bone behind, evidently at one blow, and with sufficient force to throw out extensive cracks, like those of starred glass.''

America's fascination with the Bowie knife and the demand created for fine knives did not go unnoticed by the British who had dominated the import cutlery market in the U.S. since colonial days. It would have been difficult not to observe the potential market with many English journalists awed and intrigued by the Bowie knife sending home vivid reports which appeared in newspapers and books. Great Britain as the world's greatest maritime nation, during this period, was constantly seeking new markets and enlarging established ones for the products of an industrial economy. Sheffield steel, developed to a stage of technical excellence, was combined with superior fabrication to produce Bowie knives of unexcelled quality. An examination of blade stampings on these knives reveals inscriptions as, ''Superior Bowie Knife'', ''Best English Cutlery'', ''Adamatine Edge'' and others which extoll the virtues of the product. In addition to the family or company name, pride of the maker is indicated by trade marks such as, I*XL, XCD, NON-XLL, SUPERLATIVE, XLALL, B4*ANY and other devices.

The numerical preponderance of British-produced Bowie knives compared to American makes existing in collections today is mute testimony to their popularity and lion's share of the market. This is not to suggest that surviving specimens are in abundance, as they are not. It must be recognized that American capacity for quantity knife production was extremely limited. It was not until the mid-1830s when the J. Russell & Company—Green River Works was organized in Massachusetts, that British cutlers were confronted with any serious competition. The fledgling U. S. cutlery industry was represented by firms as Russell, Meriden Cutlery Co., Empire Knife Co., Waterville Knife Co. and others concerned with products other than Bowie knives. At a much later date, the Russell company produced some hunting knives of Bowie-type design. The making of fine-quality American Bowie knives and daggers for discriminating members of 'the Bowie knife and pistol gentry' became the lot of a few accomplished individual cutlers, family firms and small businesses or partnerships. Cutlers as Reinhardt — Baltimore, Rose — New York, Chevalier—New York, Marks & Rees—Cincinnati, and R. Heinisch—Newark, were specialists in surgical and dental instruments. The superiority of their Bowie knives reflect this expertise. Other American cutlers whose knives collectors should search for include, Thomas Lamb—Washington City, Dufilho—New Orleans, Samuel Bell—Knoxville, W. M. Cotton—Leominster, Mass., Rees Fitzpatrick—Natchez, Hassam—Boston, A. G. Hicks—Cleveland, Lamonthe—New Orleans, C. Roby & Co.—W. Chelmsford, Mass., Buck Brothers—Worcester, Mass., Alfred Hunter—Newark, Will & Finck—San Francisco, Schmid—Providence, R.I., and M. Price—San Francisco, to list a few, and few there were. They are not to be counted in the several hundreds as is applicable to British makers who made Bowie knives and daggers for the American market. When one does locate a signed American made Bowie knife he has a real prize, and they are not all in collections.

Almost everyone, collector and non-collector alike, recognizes that antique firearms have value. The same awareness does not apply to knives. There are 'sleepers' to be found. When the same intensive search conducted for antique arms is applied to knives, who knows what

1. A 19th Century Sheffield ''hull'' where a colorful group of grinders plied their trade. The grinder in the foreground is seated on a wooden saddle or ''Horsing'' with the rough or course grinding wheel in front of him. Each grinder was assigned a separate trough or trow containing several wheels. A set of three, as shown, was described as ''three deep.''

2. ''Cast Steel Bowie Knife'' and ''Cast Steel'' are often found imprinted on Bowie knife blades. This high grade steel was made in clay pots or crucibles and melted at intense heat, below the foundry floor. Long metal tongs were used by a strong and agile ''teemer'' to extract the fiery crucible, with its molten mass, in a flash of blinding light and heat. This furnace is at Abbeydale Works, Sheffield, England.

treasures will be unearthed. With the increasing collector interest in this area new specimens will be located and makers, American, British and other, as yet unknown and unlisted will become recognized. This will be true even to a greater extent concerning Bowie types made in Mexico, France, India, Germany and other countries. These, to date, have been largely neglected and offer an interesting and fertile field. Of the thousands of Bowie knives produced, why so few seemingly exist today is often a question of speculation. Again, compared to a fine firearm which constituted a major investment and received an occasional coat of oil and reasonable care, the knife did not. When a favored arm was retired, it was carefully put away but seldom thrown away. A knife did not become obsolete because of changes in ignition systems, discontinued ammunition or unavailable parts. The knife received hard and continuous use on the frontiers, in wars and camps for chopping, digging, mending equipment, prying, dismembering game, as well as for fighting and picking the teeth. Blades were worn away by sharpening, broken, lost and discarded. In later years, large fighting-type blades were sometimes shortened and ground down to make them more utilitarian for general use around the home or hunt. Even now, antique Bowies are located, still being used, in a kitchen drawer, fisherman's kit and camper's gear! Recently a fine large specimen was found by a collector at a watermelon garden, the proprietor was using it to split melons rather than skulls.

The thread of contributions made by the British cutlers is interwoven throughout the period when the Bowie knife was, 'the weapon most in vogue'. Certainly they were the most imaginative in introducing different blade shapes, sizes, hilt and pommel designs, interesting blade etchings and mottos. As previously observed, the majority of fine and highly prized Bowie-type knives and daggers, in collections today, are of British origin. Most of these knives were made in Sheffield but some were fabricated in London. Birmingham does not stand out as an important contributor in this area. Occasionally, Bowie knives will be found marked Salisbury where, in earlier years, cutlers had gained a high reputation for excellence. Small quantities of cutlery were produced there during the 19th century, but it is believed that blades so marked on Bowies originated in Sheffield. The concentration of knife production during the reign of the Bowie knife in America was in Sheffield. Very little historical information has been made available to the American collector concerning Sheffield's cutlery trades and practices. An examination of background material which may answer some questions and help lay foundations for greater understanding and interest in this popular area of collecting is in order.

The earliest origins of Sheffield's cutlery history are shrouded in the mists of antiquity. There is documentary evidence dating as early as 1272, but the beginnings of cutlery making in the area date much earlier. In the 14th century, Chaucer wrote a

3. Only a door, but through it passed the cutlers who made the prized half horse, half alligator pommel Bowie knives and others. It leads into a workshop off a small central court at 36 Howard Street, Sheffield. Collectors will recognize this address as that of Woodhead & Hartley and then George Woodhead. Many of these historic old buildings were bombed out during World War 2, and others were torn down thereafter.

4. "For ev'ry man was half a horse and half an alligator" and "We'll show him that Kentucky boys are alligators, Horses," are two lines extracted from the lyrics of "The Hunters of Kentucky" written about 1815 to honor Kentuckians who fought the Battle of New Orleans. Illustrated with the original sheet music are knives made in the 1840s with pommels of German silver incorporating the frontiersman's brag. Left to right are Bowie knives made by Woodhead & Hartley, 36 Howard Street, Sheffield; R. Bunting & Son, Sheffield; and W & S Butcher, Sheffield.

description of the Miller of Trumpington in his tales of the Pilgrimage to Canterbury, "A Sheffield thwytel bare he in his hose, Bounde was his face and camois was his nose." The Sheffield 'thwytel' became known as a whittle and was an all-purpose sheath knife with a pointed tang. This tang design is still produced today and is known as a whittle-tang.

Several of these old whittles, dating the 16th and 17th centuries, were found during excavation of the old Sheffield Castle moat. They were forged of iron rod, case hardened in charcoal, and have a hardness near that of modern steel.

Sheffield during these times was an obscure little village bounded by a great moorland with surrounding

BOWIE KNIVES

forests of stately trees. Two important rivers, the Don and Sheaf, with their tributaries provided ample water and a power source for turning the many waterwheels soon to be built along the banks. All the elements necessary for the development of cutlery production were concentrated in the area, namely iron ore, wood for charcoal, natural sandstone for grinding wheels and water power. Before the pilgrims landed at Plymouth Rock, the water wheels of Sheffield were set in motion. Two centuries later they were still turning the grinding wheels that cut Bowie knife blades from Sheffield steel.

Steam power was introduced with the first engine put into operation in 1786. Acceptance was slow, but it was the beginning of the end for the old water wheels which had been so instrumental in building Sheffield's reputation for quality cutlery products. By 1865 steam driven grinding wheels outnumbered those relying on water power about five to one. At the end of the century only about a dozen of the old time water-driven grinding wheels were still in use, and today they are museum pieces. Shepard's Wheel and the water wheels, forges, furnaces, and so forth at historic Abbeydale Works have

been preserved and restored. A visit to both of these sites provides a fascinating experience for today's visitor to Sheffield.

Under the auspices of the Lord of the Manor of Sheffield, Earl of Shrewsbury, a court issued the first private mark for the marking of iron knives in October of 1554 to William Elles. This was the first of hundreds to follow of which many are familiar to collectors of knives today. The 'star and cross' mark of Joseph Rodgers & Sons originally issued in 1862, the 'heart-pistol' mark of Jonathan Crookes issued in 1780, or the I*XL mark granted in 1787 but reissued to George Wostenholm in 1826 are examples of those found on 19th Century Bowie knives and are, in fact, still in use today.

An important event in Sheffield's cutlery history occurred in 1624 when The Company of Cutlers In Hallamshire was founded as a self-governing body with jurisdiction embracing the Sheffield-Hallamshire area. The Cutlers Company assumed responsibility for trademarks in addition to administering the good order of government set forth in the bill of incorporation relating to cutlery. Each year a Master Cutler has been elected as the highest official. Knife collectors will recognize the names of many Bowie knife makers among those who served in this im-

portant capacity for among them were Thomas Ellin, William Butcher, William Webster, F. T. Mappin, George Wostenholm, Henry Harrison, Thomas Turner and many others. The Cutlers Company still functions after 350 years, and that is stability even by British standards.

"Cast Steel Bowie Knife" and "Cast Steel" are often found imprinted on the blades of Bowie knives and daggers made in Sheffield. This high-grade steel, of precise formula, was made in small clay pots or crucibles. The mixture was melted, at intense heat, in a furnace below the foundry floor. A "teemer" using long tongs, manually extracted the fiery crucible with its molten mass

1. The bust of General Zachary Taylor stands out in high relief on the German silver pommel of this Bowie knife made by S. C. Wragg, 25 Furnace Hill, Sheffield. The knife dates about 1847. Also incorporated are the words "Old Zack" and the motto, "I Ask No Favors And Shun No Responsibilities." Taylor, as a Mexican War hero, was a favored design motif used by Sheffield cutlers. The overall knife length, including the 8⅞" blade, is 13 11/16".

2. An illustration from an old George Butler catalog of a scene at Trinity Works. This picture has the following caption: "Showing a process in Hand-Forging "Cavendish" Hand-Forged Double Shear Steel Blades, the Finest in the World."

in a flash of blinding light and heat. His legs were swathed in wet sacks which still ignited, and the act of removal and pouring the molten steel into iron molds required great physical strength and dexterity. Bowie knife blades marked "Shear Steel" were made of a steel produced by heating steel faggots to welding heat and forging with a heavy hammer into bars, repeat and you have "Double Shear". Provided with quality steel some 'Little Masters' would make a complete Bowie knife by providing their own enterprise, capital and labor. Some others did out-work at home for larger firms by delivering the goods and drawing their money at the week's end. This practice was known as "liver and draw", and the names found on some Bowies are actually those of factors for whom they were made.

A completed Bowie knife would normally pass through the hands of three basic specialists; the hand forger, the grinder and the cutler. Forging of large Bowie knife blades was normally engaged in by the forger and a helper, or striker, wielding a double-handed hammer. This was known as double-handed forging. Today the hand forger has virtually disappeared from the Sheffield scene and the situation is best expressed in the words of an old gravestone epitaph:

"My sledge and hammer lie reclined
My bellows too, have lost their wind
My iron is spent, my steel is gone
My sycthes are set, my work is done
My fire's extinct, my forge decayed
And in the dust my bones are laid"

The second basic procedure in the fabrication of a Bowie knife was that of grinding the blade, finish grinding, glazing and buffing. The grinders were certainly the most colorful group engaged in the cutlery trades with their prodigious consumption of beer, their tinted skins, rough jokes, horseplay, suspicion of strangers, and air of recklessness enhanced by the fatal nature of their calling. The activities of the grinder took place in a room or "hull" which was not the most salubrious place. The building was normally of stone, later of brick, with unglazed windows, bitter cold in winter, poorly lit, damp and dusty. All was covered and permeated by "wheel swarth", an ochre combination of iron fragments, grindstone mud and dust produced by wet and dry grinding Wet swarth dyed the grinders skin and clothes a yellow hue from head to toe. A large natural grindstone about four feet in diameter and nine inches across the face was used for blades of Bowie knife size. Grinders sat mounted on a wood

saddle, or horseing as it was called, behind the grindstone and faced the light which fell on the stone. Among the numerous dangers confronting them was the breaking of a speeding grindstone due to hidden flaws or unequal grain, flying particles of red hot iron endangered the eyes, and "grinders asthma" or silicosis was the greatest hazard of all. The problem of silicosis became even more acute with the advent of steam powered hulls of smaller size, more grinding stones and poorer ventilation. A 'dry' grinder was fortunate to attain the age of 35 years. It was not

3. The Bowie knife and California's gold were popular items in the 1850s. The distinction of having its name inscribed on more antique Bowies than any state belongs to California. Blades were marked, "California Knife"; "California Bowie Knife"; California Toothpick"; "Chevalier's California Knife," and with gold rush references as "I Can Dig Gold From Quartz" and "For The Gold Searchers Protection." Illustrated with an old knife polisher in the background are the "California" Bowies.

4. An impressive Bowie knife, signed Marshes & Shepard, Pond Works, Sheffield, dwarfs a diminutive Derringer pistol. Made about 1838 the 11⅛" blade is stamped, "Superior Bowie Knife" and possesses the sharp false edge found on many fighting types. The shaped hilt is rosewood with German silver mounts.

BOWIE KNIVES

until very late in the 19th Century that artificial wheels even began to supersede natural sandstone in Sheffield. The words of an old song are self expressive:

"To be a Sheffield grinder, it is no easy trade
There's more than you'd imagine in the grinding of a blade.
The strongest man among us is old at thirty-two
For there's few who brave the hardships that we poor grinders do.
And every working day we are breathing dust and steel,
And a broken stone can give us a wound that will not heal,
There's many a honest grinder ground down by such a blow

For there's few that brave such hardships as we poor grinders do."

An artisan specifically known as the "cutler" completed the third and final stage in the construction of a Bowie knife. With his drills, files, glazers, buffs and other implements the cutler assembled and finished the guard and hilting materials on the completed blade. This constituted a relatively simple procedure on most Bowies as compared to cutling a picket knife. A separate industry supplied the demands of the cutler for hafting materials. Scale cutters furnished completed two-piece hilt coverings of pearl, ivory and the like. One firm alone in 1872 had in its inventory 122 tons of ivory and in 1887 it is estimated the horn industry supplied 72,000 stag handles and

scales per week to cutlers of various types of knives.

In the 1870s celluloid and other synthetic materials began to make inroads on natural products used for knife handles. Shortly before the beginning of the Bowie period a new alloy was introduced to the cutler in Sheffield. This combination of nickel, copper and zinc, containing no silver, was known as German silver and nickel silver. Cross-guards, plain-to-fancy mounts, and complete handles utilizing this metal were attached to Bowie knife blades. Embossed, chased, stamped, engraved, cast and filed into German silver were designs, mottos, and patriotic motifs designed for strong appeals to American tastes.

So it came to pass that Sheffield had emerged as a world cutlery center leaving London far behind. London cutlers has originally considered the Sheffielder as provincial country hicks but as early as 1592 the London

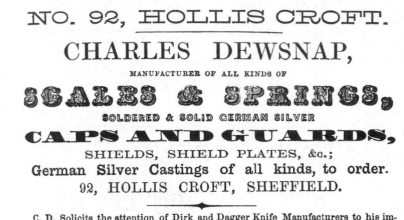

1

1. Charles Dewsnap was one of many supplying the Sheffield cutlers with knife parts and pieces in 1856 when this ad was published.

2. Contemporaries of the Bowie knife are these lock-back, pocket daggers. Most of the type were produced circa 1825 through the Civil War period by many of the same Sheffield people who made Bowies. The survival rate among these aristocrats of the folding knives is small and each may be regarded as a desirable collector's item. The smallest illustrated is 8¼" overall when open and the longest is 16⅛".

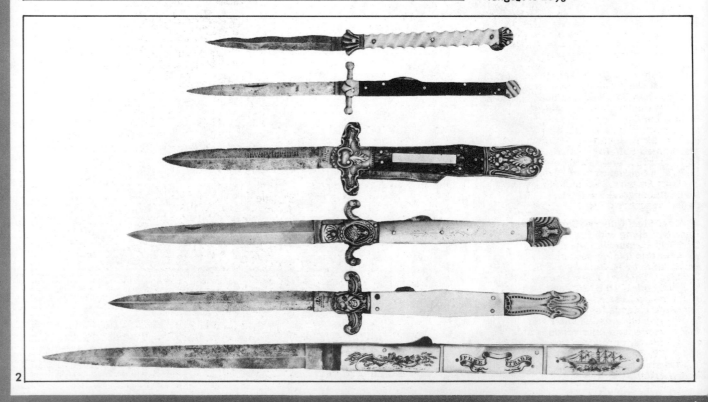

2

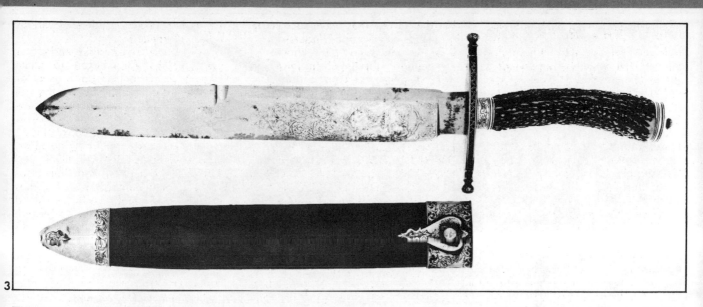

3

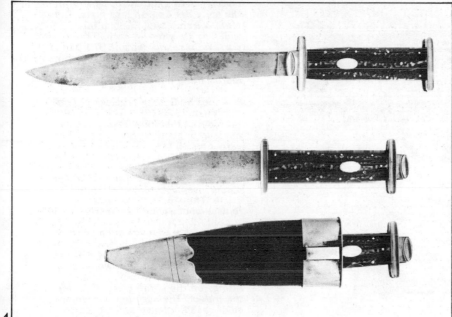

4

Cutlers' Company complained of "English foreigners" hawking in the London streets and highways with deceivable wares. During the 19th Century only a few cutlers were producing knives in London but the Bowie knives they made were most often beautifully executed and finished. Collectors should take note that the quality and scarcity of London-made Bowies will eventually be recognized with the inevitable rise in demand and price. Many Sheffield Bowie knives and daggers, minus the word Sheffield, are found bearing a London dealer's name and street address only, but the law forbade inclusion of the word London. Only those knives actually made there, other than complete misrepresentations, were stamped 'London'.

The Bowie knife was born of turmoil and violence in the 1820s. Its popularity and use were established in the 1830s, expanded in the 1840s and reached its peak in the 1850s as a fighting weapon. The knife diminished in favor as an instrument of death after the Civil War and by the mid-1870's, for the most part was relegated to its original role as a hunting knife. Man-made laws were not responsible for its demise. The times had changed, law and order prevailed to a greater degree but the killing efficiency, mechanical reliability and widespread distribution of the revolver was the nemesis which retired the Bowie knife as 'the real life defender'. The Bowie had reached a transitional period in its colorful history but its career did not end. Man's desire to possess a Bowie knife whether for sport, defense, exhibition or whatever continued and some exceptionally fine knives were made during the last quarter of the 19th Century and the years following. Military use initiated a revival of the Bowie knife as a fighting weapon during this century and today's contemporary cutlers are producing some exceptional specimens using modern steels and new hafting materials. The Bowie knife period instituted on that obscure Mississippi river sandbar 150 years ago offers today's knife collectors exciting opportunities be their tastes for antique, modern or in-between. A great and growing collector interest exists pertaining to knives in all categories, from all places and all times. This development will continue to expand. It is the Bowie knife, however, as an integral part of American heritage, in fact and fancy, which still stirs the imagination and collecting instinct. The Bowie knife is destined to remain, as in the past, "the weapon most in vogue." ♔

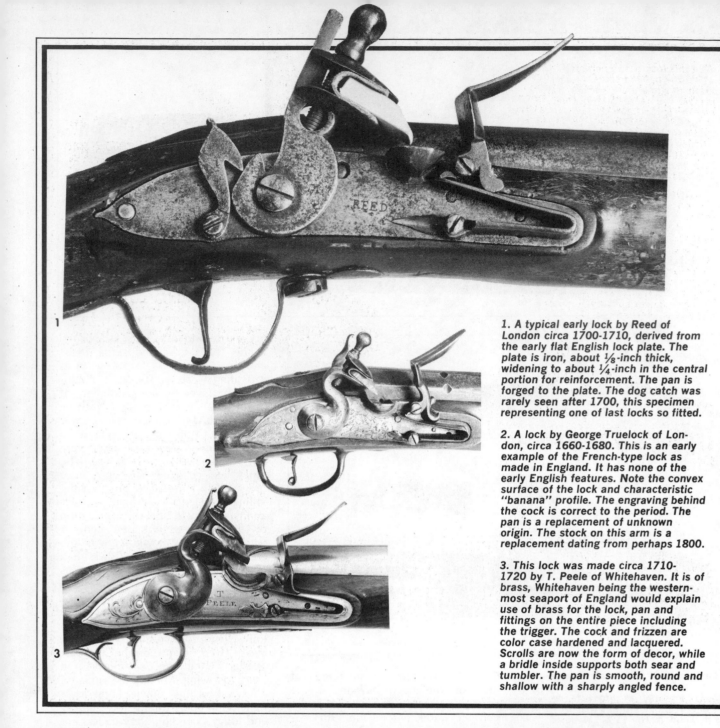

1. A typical early lock by Reed of London circa 1700-1710, derived from the early flat English lock plate. The plate is iron, about ⅛-inch thick, widening to about ¼-inch in the central portion for reinforcement. The pan is forged to the plate. The dog catch was rarely seen after 1700, this specimen representing one of last locks so fitted.

2. A lock by George Truelock of London, circa 1660-1680. This is an early example of the French-type lock as made in England. It has none of the early English features. Note the convex surface of the lock and characteristic "banana" profile. The engraving behind the cock is correct to the period. The pan is a replacement of unknown origin. The stock on this arm is a replacement dating from perhaps 1800.

3. This lock was made circa 1710-1720 by T. Peele of Whitehaven. It is of brass, Whitehaven being the western-most seaport of England would explain use of brass for the lock, pan and fittings on the entire piece including the trigger. The cock and frizzen are color case hardened and lacquered. Scrolls are now the form of decor, while a bridle inside supports both sear and tumbler. The pan is smooth, round and shallow with a sharply angled fence.

ENGLISH GUNSMITHS DEVELOPED THE STYLE OF FLINTLOCK THAT ORIGINATED IN FRANCE. THIS ARTICLE PICTORIALLY TRACES THIS DEVELOPMENT FROM THE 17TH TO THE 19TH CENTURIES.

the French Lock in England

by Charles R. Suydam

Antique arms collectors recognize several snapping locks which employ a piece of flint or similar stone to strike a sharp blow against steel, causing sparks to fall into and ignite powder in a small pan, the fire of which, in turn, passes through a small hole and ignites the charge in barrel of the piece. Among these are the snaphaunce, the miquelet, and the Baltic, Madrid, Roman, English, and French locks. The last named survived to become what is now known as "the" flintlock. It is about

4. *In this lock of the period 1725-1735, the banana shaped lock has given way to a more slender, narrow profile. The hammer face is flattened and the breast thinner. The pan is very round with a well-angled fence; there is still no bridge between pan and frizzen pivot. Note engraved toe of steel. The vase-shaped trigger guard finial helps to date this piece before 1750. The maker was J. Jones, London.*

5. *Both lock and the complete arm are difficult to date because the maker, Perry, worked circa 1780, but this lock dates from circa 1750. Probably there were two Perrys, the earlier unknown at the present. All the characteristics of this lock date it from 1750, including the round, shallow pan, lack of bridge between pan and frizzen pivot and fully rounded cock. Note the acorn pattern on the trigger guard finial, another feature of the 1750 period.*

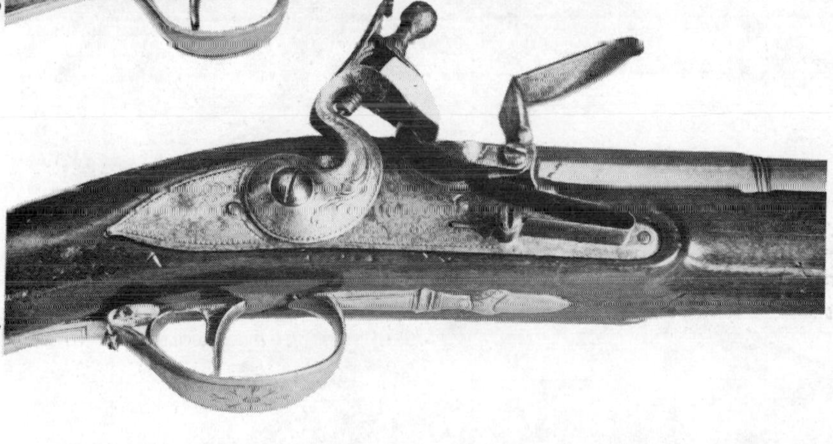

6. *This lock by J. Richardson of Manchester was made circa 1780-1790, and is shown here to prove that not all gunsmiths followed contemporary trends. Specifically, there is no bridge or bridle connecting the pan and frizzen, though this feature became common after 1770. All other features date it; flat lockplate and cock, deep pan with short fence, engraving style, straight trigger, and well-defined acorn finial. Data lists Richardson as 1790-1832.*

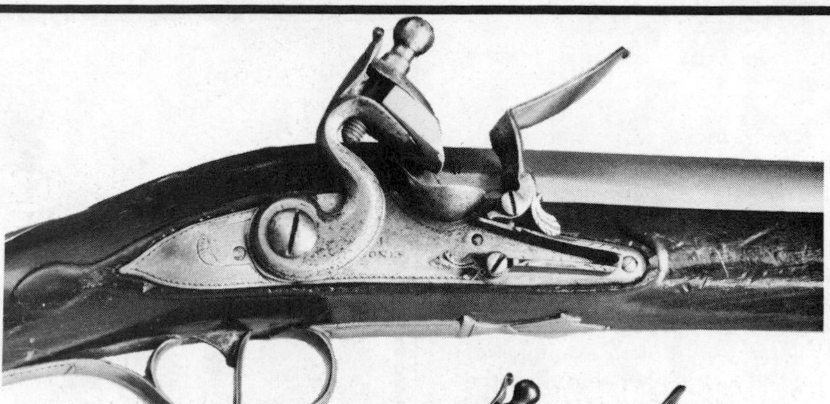

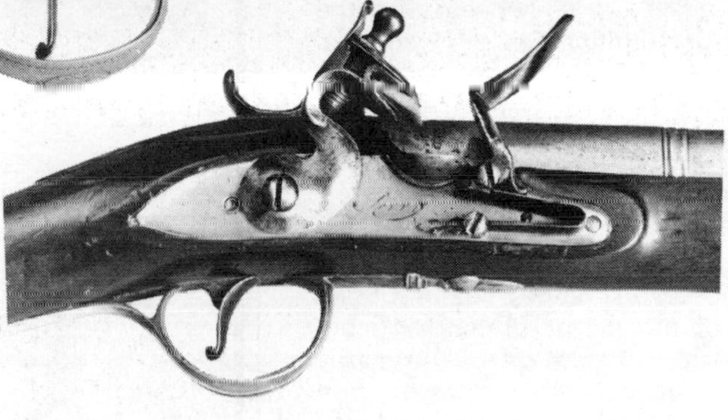

7. *Although dating from somewhat later, this lock is typical of the period 1750-1760. It was made by Griffin & Tow of London in the period 1770-1780. However, a bridge now appears between the pan and frizzen pivot. The bridge first appeared circa 1750, but did not come into general use until 1770.*

its development with which this article is concerned.

The earliest flintlocks used in England (circa 1575-80) were snaphaunces derived from Dutch patterns (or actually Dutch locks) which had a horizontally-acting sear extending through the lockplate to catch a projection on the heel of the cock, and a two-piece steel and pan cover.

The first English modification, adopted about 1630 and now called the English lock, was to combine pan cover and steel. The tumbler was still pinned to a shaft forged to the cóck ("hammer" today). The snaphaunce sear was used with a halfcock notch cut into the tumbler, along with a bridle connected steel ("frizzen") screw and steel spring

screw. A stop against the breast of the hammer kept it from falling too far, the lockplate was flat with an odd elongated shape, and a "dog ketch" safety was located behind the hammer.

The French lock varies greatly from all other snapping "flintlocks." Externally, the pan cover and steel are combined, pivoted before the pan, and controlled by a small external spring variously called the steel spring, feather spring, or frizzen spring. The cock is fitted to a square shank forged to the tumbler, and held in place by a screw. Additional external features appeared as the lock evolved: they include a bridle from pan to steel screw, a sliding lock or safety behind the cock, a

small wheel on the steel spring or bottom of the steel itself (rarely), a free-standing ("waterproof") pan, and a variety of hammer patterns. The face of the lockplate is rounded.

Internally, the French lock has a long V-shaped mainspring forward of the cock, which presses against the toe of the tumbler. There are two notches on the tumbler: shallow full cock and deep halfcock or safety. The sear is a simple L-shape, releasing the tumbler when pushed vertically upward by the trigger, and controlled by a sear spring. Evolutionary developments include a supporting bridle which covers the sear and tumbler, a swivel link from tumbler to main spring, and a detent on the tumbler to prevent set

the French Lock

trigger sears from catching in the half-cock notch.

The outside surface of the Dutch and English locks were necessarily flat to accept all of the devices fastened to them; the shape of both was long and awkward, with a decided lobate finial at the back end. Earlier English matchlocks had plates with curved outside surfaces which generally resemble the plates of the French lock. Early British examples of the French lock—henceforth "the lock" or "flintlock"—followed two patterns: one with a flat lockplate, the other rounded, depending on whether they derive from the English lock or more directly from the French pattern.

Determining the date of origin of an English flintlock may be aided by several factors: known dates of activity of the maker (if marked); actual dates on the plate (primarily military pieces); known association with specific persons or events; physical characteristics of the lock and/or its gun, and (rarely but most accurate when possible) interpretation of date stamp of silver or gold fittings. ♛

1. The period 1770-1780 was one of transition for the English lock, this specimen by Wm. Jover of London showing the changes which were appearing. Note the sliding safety behind the cock. The cock and pan are still rounded, but slight touches of engraving appear in a number of areas.

2. Two further improvements in locks which appeared in the 1770's can be seen on this left-hand lock of a fowling piece by Williams of London. The first is a small wheel added to the tip of the frizzen spring (it was fitted to the toe of the fizzen itself). The second, not visible, is a swiveling link between the tumbler and the mainspring which helped to shorten lock time. The lock plate is flat as is the face of the cock. The rounded front trigger guard post is unusual on English arms.

3. This lock by Thomas Twigg of London was made circa 1810 and shows the small sliding safety which was reintroduced after being dropped for a time. In comparison to the first ones of circa 1750, they were small and hard to manipulate. The acorn trigger guard finial has been replaced by a pineapple—possibly a memento to Capt. James Cook, killed by islanders in 1779 (?).

4. The last major improvement in the flintlock arrived about 1775, but did not come into general use until later. This was the waterproof or "teaspoon pan" which stands free of the fence and frizzen bridle. The ultimate development of this design—not shown—was a very tiny pan completely divorced from the fence and bridge. The frizzen was very tightly fitted to these, and they were indeed almost waterproof. This 1810 lock is by Thewlis of Huddersfield.

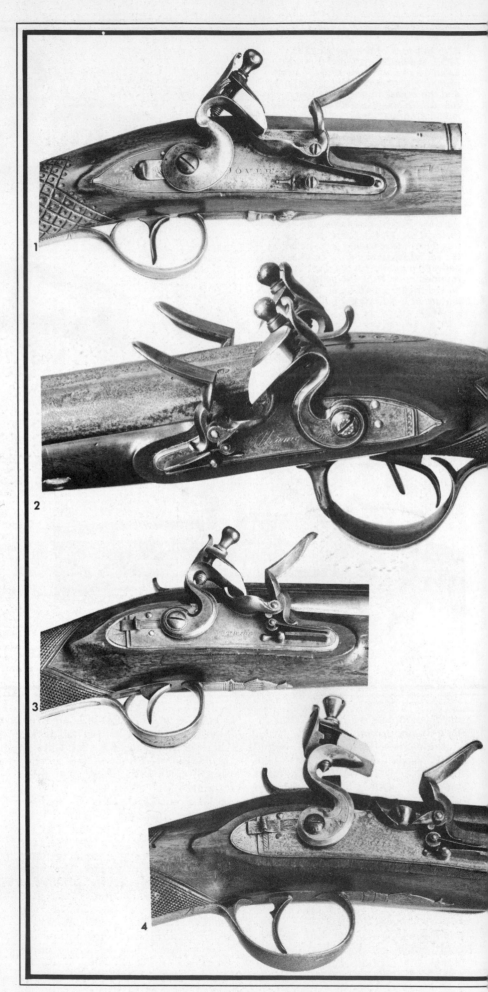

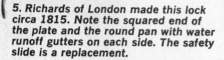

5. Richards of London made this lock circa 1815. Note the squared end of the plate and the round pan with water runoff gutters on each side. The safety slide is a replacement.

6. A London-made lock of the period 1815-1820 which has a very unusual feature for a high-quality English gun—no maker's name. The lock plate is now rounded, and the cock has a double throat. The engraving is both extensive and of high quality. The priming pan gutters are very pronounced.

7. This small pocket pistol and its lock represents the ultimate in the flintlock, both in quality and development. It was made circa 1830-1835 by William Jackson, a gunsmith who worked with the legendary John Manton for 18 years, the piece reflecting Manton's influence very strongly. Note the fancy spur beneath the jaws on the cock. It has been said that the test of a fine flintlock was to prime the pan, then turn the piece upside down and pull the trigger; a high-quality lock would fire the powder before it could fall out of the pan.

8. An India Pattern military lock, circa 1812. A lock by Manton could be a work of art; a military lock was at best utilitarian. Time has obliterated all marks from this lock, but it is typical of those used from 1740 to 1830. The double-throated cock replaced the "swan neck" in 1809. There were pattern variations throughout its life; this is generally the lock used on all India Pattern Brown Bess muskets.

SIGNIFICANT DATES IN THE DEVELOPMENT OF THE FRENCH STYLE LOCK IN ENGLAND*

1660 — The Restoration — beginning of the reign of Charles II

1662 — Mention of a French lock with "back ketch"

1685-1700 — Wide, straight and flat lockplate

1685 — Reign of James II begins

1687 — William III on the Throne

1700 — Bridle on tumbler, end of dog lock

1702 — Reign of Queen Anne begins

1710 — End of upward tang screw, end of three-screw lock plate

1710 — Beginning of foliated trigger guard finial

1714 — Reign of George I begins

1720 — Trigger guard finial becomes "vase with leaves"

1727 — Reign of George II begins

1740 — Outside bridle to steel screw (military)

1745 — First side lock safety

1750 — Acorn trigger guard finial

1760 — Reign of George III begins

1770 — Wheel on frizzen spring, swivel between tumbler and main spring

1775 — Second side lock safety, early waterproof pan, sear spring screw and sear screw visible behind hammer

1780 — "Pineapple" trigger guard finial

1800 — Late waterproof pan

*All dates are approximate, with possible variations as much as ten years.

COLLECTING
COLT
FIREARMS

SAMUEL COLT HIMSELF WAS THE FIRST COLT COLLECTOR
by R. L. Wilson

Samuel Colt was a compulsive achiever. He did things, and he made things happen. As a bright little boy in New England, he learned the basics of science. Within a matter of a few years he developed an underwater mine, worked with Samuel F. B. Morse in creating an early telegraph operation, evolved a road show based on the application of laughing gas on audience volunteers, and invented, patented, promoted and manufactured a product which made

him rich and famous—the revolver.

It is not generally known that Samuel Colt himself was the first Colt collector. Fully realizing the impact of himself and his firearms on the 19th Century, he began early in the 1850s to assemble an arms collection of selected pieces of his own manufacture, plus weapons related to the evolution of the revolver. Colt's own arms group is now displayed in the Wadsworth Atheneum and the Connecticut State Li-

brary, both museums in his home town of Hartford, Connecticut. One of the author's first Colt books, The Arms Collection of Colonel Colt, was based on the Colonel's pieces in the Atheneum.

Gun collectors like history, tradition, mechanical and artistic design, and quality. Colt—known as the specialty in gun collecting—offers all these characteristics in spades. It is no surprise that Colt collectors outnumber any other specialty group.

Their numbers go beyond the boundaries of the United States and Canada, to nearly every country in the world. Thousands of fine antique Colts leave the States every year, enroute to collectors in Europe, many of whom have specimens that would be the envy of most American specialists. The Colt man shares his interests with many names famous in other areas of American life—two members of the Ford family of Detroit are keen collectors, one of the Mellons (banking, finance, philanthropy), one of the Phillips (Phillips 66), entertainers Mel Torme, Johnny Cash, and Hank Williams, Jr. are all Colt aficionados, and so is Congressman Bob Sikes of Florida. One of the Russian Czars was so keenly interested in firearms that Sam Colt personally gave him three lavishly gold-inlaid revolvers. The Czar's pieces are still in Russia and are now part of The Hermitage Museum armory, in Leningrad. Obviously the man who collects Colts shares his enthusiasms with a lot of class!

How many persons are actively collecting Colt firearms at this writing? Nobody knows for certain, but a reasonable guess would be somewhere from 25,000 to 50,000! Annual sales figures are easily into the millions of dollars. And the current record price for a single antique firearm is held by a Colt. The Colt field is big by any standard. Over 400 distinct models have been produced,

totalling in excess of 25 million pieces, since the company's beginnings in Paterson, New Jersey, in 1836. Only a very limited number of well-heeled collectors can afford to put together a complete group of Colt's manufacture, having at least one specimen of each model represented. The vast majority of collectors decide to specialize in distinct areas and have fixed goals and standards to which they abide religiously. For most individuals the two factors determining their specialization are funds available for purchases and their own esthetic inclinations. The man with plenty of money to spend may lean toward engraved, historic, and mint-condition pieces. A person with a limited budget may collect only deringers or cartridge longarms, or memorabilia. However, there are many quite wealthy collectors who also go in for the less expensive models. And thus it is not unusual for the collector on a limited budget to be the proud possessor of some fine pieces that his wealthy counterpart would like greatly to own.

Before delving too deeply into buying up Colt guns by the gross, the collector would do well to spend about $100.00 on a good reference library. The two prime reference works are James E. Serven's Colt Firearms From 1836, and the Wilson-Sutherland tome, The Book of Colt Firearms. A detailed bibliography appears at the end of the present article; the more of these publications one owns, the better off he will be. In arms collecting, books are by far the best investment for the money. By studying the Serven and Wilson-Sutherland and Colt texts, one can

1. A cased pair of Texas Paterson pistols in mint condition—one of of the most magnificent collector prizes in the entire Colt field. These guns were purchased approximately 10 years ago from a country auction in New York State. It is possible that more sets like this one await discovery by the astute collector. From the collection of Richard P. Mellon.

2. Only a few hundred Paterson Colt rifles were made, yet they seldom are sold today at prices nearing the high values placed on the more numerous Paterson hand guns. A fine Paterson rifle or shotgun can still be bought from between $1000 to $2000.

3. This charger for Paterson longarms is of much greater scarcity than any model of arm for which it was made. Only three are known!

4. One of the classics in Colt's entire firearms line is the Walker Model of 1847. This fine specimen, marked "A Company Number 19," was stolen from the Connecticut State Library Museum, at Hartford, and has yet to be returned. A substantial reward has been offered.

select an approach to collecting, and plan a course of action that will satisfy his collector instincts.

No hard-and-fast classifications exist in Colts, because the field is so vast. However, the major categories are as follows: Percussion handguns, percussion longarms, conversions, Single Action Army revolvers, deringers and pocket pistols, double-action revolvers, automatic pistols, cartridge longarms, commemoratives, engraved firearms, historic firearms and memorabilia. There exists some overlap in virtually all of these specialties. Engraving, for example, can include specimens from all the other fields, and percussion handguns can even encompass the commemorative, and vice versa. Each collector employs an individual approach, and many thus alter a specialty to fit personal tastes. As we shall see, there are specialties within the major specialties, and even the sub-divisions

COLLECTING COLT

thereof can be further divided. From over 26 million pieces it is logical that the choice is broad.

PERCUSSION HANDGUNS AND LONGARMS

Piece for piece, the percussion Colt handgun category ranks as one of the most expensive and difficult areas in which to assemble a complete collection in fine condition. Only slightly more than one million percussion Colt arms were produced, in a period of about 37 years (circa 1836 to 1873). Sales were made worldwide, and the vast majority of these weapons saw hard use. Perhaps as many as a third of this million-plus production was lost on battlefields, in fires and floods, and to town dumps when more modern guns came along. Scrap drives for World Wars 1 and 2 also ate up some of the surviving percussion Colt relics. Known survival figures indicate two factors of significance in the percussion Colt field: A high percentage of loss from reasons noted above; a surprising percentage of specimens still to be brought to light from attics, cellars, and bureau drawers.

Only about 150 original Walker Colts are known, out of the production run totalling 1100. About 300 of them were lost when the model was produced, due to burst cylinders on the battlefield. An estimated 300 or 400 more were lost by natural and manmade disasters. This means that perhaps 250 Walkers are yet to be discovered! So far the author has seen several times that number of aspirants—all fakes. An even rarer model of early Colt, the Whitney-ville-Walker Dragoon (successor to the Walker) was made in a total of only about 240 specimens. Of these about a dozen are known to the collecting fraternity. Again most pieces are lost forever, but probably at least another dozen or more are awaiting discovery by the knowledgeable Colt student.

One of the most exclusive areas of specialization is the Paterson Colt. One aficionado had 32 specimens at his peak in that area, and now has trimmed these down to a total of 19. His intent has been to put together a group of all variations in the Paterson field. Many years were required to assemble this select group, along with many thousands of dollars spent in time and acquisitions. The Paterson collection was formed by a man of means who is the expert in that period of Colt manufacture—the fact that it took over 30 years of patient

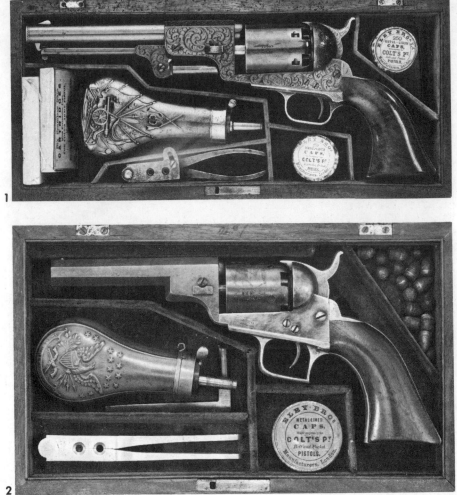

effort to put together the 19 pieces proves a point: It takes more than just money to assemble a fine Colt collection.

Another collector chose as his special field the Dragoon Models. Only 21,000 were made, including the Walker, and the survival rate is low due to the wide use of these big handguns in the Indian Wars. As with the Paterson approach, the Dragoon collector has to have a good supply of cash on hand, and an expert eye to detect the fakery that high-value arms inspire.

The Colt collector can find other areas of percussion specialization every bit as exciting and challenging as Patersons and Dragoons—but with notably less expenditure—by going into the Model 1848 or Model 1849 Pocket revolvers, or the Model 1851 Navies, the Sidehammer Pocket pistols, the Model 1860 Army, the Model 1862 Police and Pocket Navies, or the variety of Colt longarms. Over 330,000 Model 1849 Pocket pistols were made, and they are by far the most common of percussion Colts. P L. Shumaker of the Ohio Gun Collectors Association wrote a 150-page book only on these arms; itself quite an indication of the popularity of

that model. Nathan Swayze's '51 Colt Navies, a 243-page book, covers in exhaustive detail the Model 1851 Navy. For collectors of the Sidehammer Pocket pistol two excellent monographs have been published, each detailing the minute variations in the short production run of that model. A monograph was done some years ago on the Model 1860 Army, and still another publication is planned on that subject.

The collector specializing in percussion Colts has the advantage of an ever expanding interest and an ever growing selection of specialized publications. Despite the large body of information already in print, there is more to come, and new sources of information continue to come to light. One of the great thrills in collecting is discovery. In percussion Colts particularly, there is much information remaining to be discovered and published just as there are many fine arms "in the brush" waiting to be found by the diligent and the lucky.

Colt percussion long guns were recently given a considerable boost in popularity by the extensive detail published in The Book of Colt Firearms. Only about 19,000 revolving

Colt longarms were produced, and these offer infinite variants and a background of frontier and combat use nearly as colorful as Colt's percussion handguns.

Accessories for percussion Colts have themselves become a collector specialty. Such items as bullet molds, flasks, screwdrivers, nipple wrenches, cappers, cleaning rods, cases, keys, extra barrels or cylinders, cap tins and paper cartridges are often of greater rarity than the firearms they were made for. Each percussion revolver was sold with a bullet mold and L-shaped screwdriver/nipple wrench as standard equipment. The buyer who intended to carry his pistol on his person would often need a flask as well, while cased sets offered the most complete equipage. Due in part to their small size, the accessories were easily lost. No doubt many a rare Paterson capper was pitched into the trash by housewives unaware of the piece's high value. Such items as special holsters for extra cylinders, telescopic rifle sights, tin-foil car-

tridges, and replacement cylinders (without serial numbers) rank in rarity with some of the hard-to-find models such as Walkers and Patersons. Despite their rarity, prices for these items—when you can find them for sale—are reasonable; usually in a range of from $100.00 to $500.00, and only rarely going for about $1000. The record price for a Colt bullet mold was about $1700, paid by Herb Glass at auction in 1970 for a Walker two-cavity mold.

CONVERSIONS

The Ohio Gun Collectors Association booth at the 1972 NRA meetings in Portland offered the rare opportunity to observe a complete col-

lection of Colt factory conversions. Beginning in the late 1860s, with the Thuer design, Colt altered some of their percussion models to fire the new metallic cartridges. The NRA showing, based on the extensive collection of Willis Neuwirth, covered the Thuer Colts, and factory alterations to Dragoon, Pocket, Navy, Police and Army Models.

Conversions are a challenging field within Colts. The original factory shipping ledgers are nearly complete on these guns, but they are quite limited in providing details specific to the configuration of each model. Locating specimens of each model presents a problem, in that a large majority of the production was shipped abroad, or to Mexico and

1. An exquisitely engraved Dragoon model revolver, presented to gunmaker Eli Whitney Jr. by Colonel Samuel Colt. The serial number, 12405, dates the piece at about the year 1852. Accessories are complete: Two packets of combustible paper cartridges, bullet mold, powder flask (stand of flags embossed design), percussion caps, and L-shaped screwdriver nipple wrench. The standard factory casing, of mahogany, is lined in velvet.

2. The Model 1848 Pocket revolver; also known as the Baby Dragoon. A smaller group of accessories accompanies this diminutive handgun. Again, the factory case is mahogany, lined in velvet. A characteristic feature of the Colt revolvers made during the 1847 through 1851 period was the so-called squareback trigger guard. Clare Short Collection.

3. A specimen of the most common of all Colt percussion revolvers— the Model 1849 Pocket revolver. Over one hundred major and minor variations have been tabulated for this highly popular model.

4. The Model 1851 Navy was brought out as an intermediate handgun between the pocket pistols of .31 caliber and the large Dragoons of .44 caliber. Chambered for .36 caliber, the Navy proved to be one of Colt's best selling percussion firearms. Over 215,000 were made in Hartford; over 40,000 were produced at Colt's London factory. R. Q. Sutherland Collection.

5. Colt's London factory, in operation from 1852 through 1857, manufactured versions of the Model 1849 Pocket, the Model 1851 Navy (shown here), and the Third Model Dragoon. Most of the Navy model production was bought by British Ordnance. The specimen illustrated is a civilian model. R. Q. Sutherland Collection.

3

4

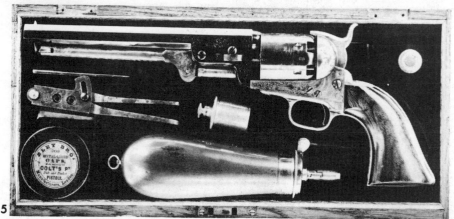

5

COLLECTING COLT

South America. These pieces were widely used and abused. Except for the Thuer models, most conversions of Colt guns are in bad condition today. The Thuers had a relatively high survival rate because they were so impractical that only a few were given much use at all.

The collector has an extra dimension to confront his knowledge and judgment in the field of conversions. Not a few percussion Colts were altered outside of the factory, often quite expertly. The factory-made piece is, as a rule, more valuable and important than any non-factory alteration. Many non-factory pieces are so skillfully altered that their true origin can be determined only by careful, part by part, examination. Fortunately many excellent experimental and production conversions are in the Colt Factory Museum, now in the Connecticut State Library, Hartford. Comparison with those speci-

mens provide vital clues in unraveling an otherwise perplexing situation.

The evolutionary sequence from the percussion Colt into the true cartridge Colt only spans about four years. Since less than 50,000 conversions were made by the company in that period, these arms have never been common, and are a fruitful area for specialization. Only in recent years have they received any special degree of attention, and thus prices for most specimens are still beneath

what they should be. A collector should expect to buy most Colt conversions at prices from $200 to $1200, for average condition pieces of the standard models. Note that Thuers usually go for $2000 to $4000 and are seldom seen offered for sale.

DERINGERS AND POCKET PISTOLS

With the purchase of the National Arms Company in the late 1860s,

1. Cased sets are highly prized collector's items. This mint Sidehammer pocket revolver has complete factory accessories, including the rare combustible paper cartridges. The Sidehammer was a flop in both handgun and longarm configurations. Most are found in good condition because they saw only limited use. H. A. Redfield Collection.

2. Sidehammer rifles (top and bottom), a musket (second from top), and a shotgun (second from bottom). The cylinder pins have been removed for comparison purposes. The Sidehammers were the only percussion Colts having solid frames; all other models were in a basic three-piece takedown construction of frame, cylinder, and barrel. From R. Q. Sutherland Collection.

3. A rare prototype Model 1860 Army revolver, serial number 6. Prototypes and experimentals from the percussion period are all advanced collector rarities. Thieves made off with this specimen from an inviting exhibit arrangement which left the sides of the display case wide open. The piece is still missing; it had been in the Colonel Colt collection of the Wadsworth Atheneum, Hartford.

4. A historic matched pair of Model 1860 Army revolvers, cased, inscribed, and deluxe finished for presentation by Colonel Colt to Union General Irvin McDowell. Double casings and Sam Colt presentations are high on the list of Colt rarities. Jerry D. Berger Collection.

5. The recipient of this exciting, cased, engraved, and inscribed Colt Police revolver was college professor and author J. D. Butler. Butler helped write a eulogistic biography of Samuel Colt, published by the inventor's grieving widow. George R. Repaire Collection.

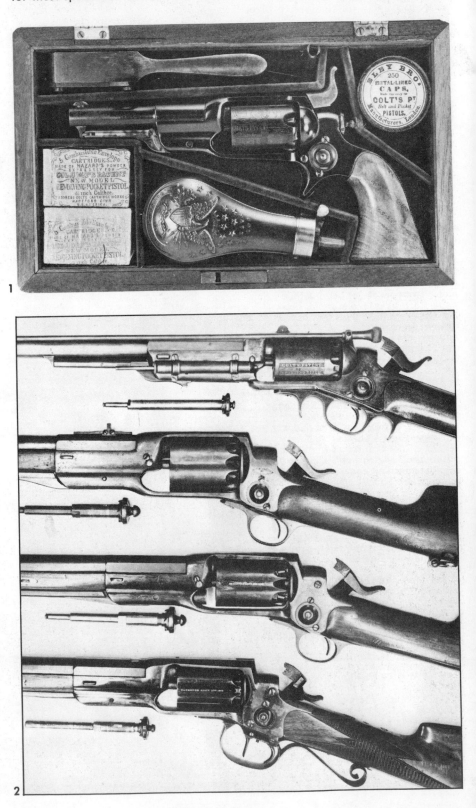

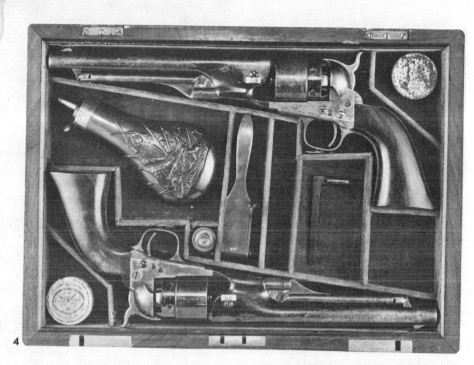

3

Colt moved with considerable gusto into the field of concealable cartridge handguns. The period circa 1870 to circa 1910 saw the company manufacture and sell a total of several hundred thousand .41 caliber single-shot derringers and Old Line and New Line pocket revolvers. Most specimens of these pistols today sell for less than $500.00, and it is possible to put together quite complete and intriguing collections which have the advantage of taking up limited amounts of space. Since nearly all types predate 1898, they are usually exempted from the Federal Firearms Act of 1968.

These diminutive handguns played quite a role in the colorful times in which they were produced. The Colt Cloverleaf revolver (so named because its four-shot cylinder had a cross-section like a four-leaf clover) was used by Edward Stokes when he shot playboy financier Jim Fisk,

4

in an encounter over a prostitute. Dance hall girls, gamblers, and even some lawmen and gunfighters (Wild Bill Hickok included) took a liking to the deringers and to the pocket-size Old and New Line revolvers. A most desirable selection of the New Lines was presented by Colt's to their major dealers in 1874. These were engraved, inscribed, and cased up in pairs.

The most extensive assemblage of New Lines is in the Holbrook collection in Florida. In this selection of several hundred pieces is an infinite variety of features. The great many calibers, weights, markings, finishes, casings, engravings, and other variations presents quite a challenge to the collector. New Lines and deringers offer the potential of a big collection, with considerable histor-

5

COLLECTING COLT

ical and mechanical interest, but at a price within the reach of most active collectors.

SINGLE ACTION ARMY REVOLVERS

Four excellent books have been written on this engrossing subject, and a fifth is now in preparation. The Single Action Army offers an almost endless number of variations, the major categories of which are: Calibers, martially (U.S. Government) marked pieces, target models, the Bisley and Bisley target, the rimfire series (a specially serial-numbered group totalling less than 2000), the Sheriff's Model, Buntline Special and odd barrel length types, the Battle of Britain series, engraved guns, experimentals and commemoratives. There are even collectors who pursue only specimens made since 1955, the year in which Colts renewed SAA manufacture after production had been discontinued due to World War 2.

Single Action Army Colts have been studied in the most minute detail. The pioneer book on the subject, The Peacemaker and Its Rivals, by John E. Parsons, has been printed and reprinted for over 20 years, and is one of the all time best sellers in the field of arms collectors' publications. Author Parsons meticulously went through all the original Colt shipping ledgers on the SAA. His tabulations produced the first production chart giving serial number sequence by year, and totals of manufacture broken down into each caliber for the SAA target, the Bisley, the Bisley target, and (in a fourth group) all other Single Action Army types.

The Colt Single Action Army has a unique attraction to gun collectors. It is hailed by many as the "handgun that won the West." In history and tradition its position is unique. Factory ledgers document Single Actions which were used by Buffalo Bill Cody, Pawnee Bill Lilly, Bat Masterson, and Marshal Bill Tilghman. Other known shooters who swore by their Single Actions were Theodore Roosevelt, Wild Bill Hickok, John Wesley Hardin, the Earp brothers, Pat Garrett, Texas Ranger Frank Hamer, General George S. Patton, and many others. In history, tradition, mechanics, and design, the Colt SAA is a true classic.

It is safe to say that considering collectors who specialize in one model of Colt, the Single Action Army ranks as the most popular of all Colt

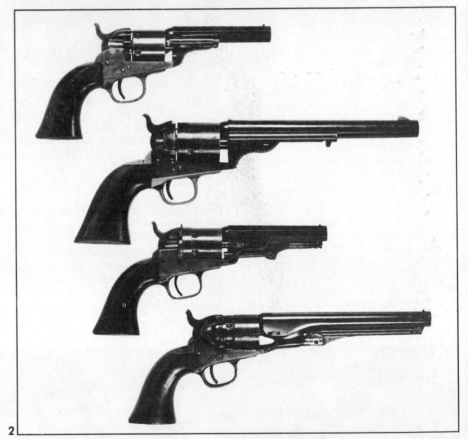

firearms. Because of this demand, and the relatively limited supply, prices for fine specimens are often over $1000. Most standard-frame models, however, sell for from $350.00 to $1000, depending on condition and such features as markings, caliber, barrel length, and details of the documenting letter from the Colt factory.

DOUBLE ACTION REVOLVERS

Samuel Colt himself had no enthusiasm for the double-action mechanism. As a result no Colt revolvers were made in quantity with that operative system until the Lightning Model of 1877. The Lightning and its big-framed companion, the Model 1878 Frontier, were distinct departures from Colt's tried and true single-action revolver line. Pulling the trigger automatically cocked the hammer and turned the cylinder. On both the Lightning and the Frontier models, the mechanisms were none too reliable; they are often found today with broken actions. Many a torrent of unprintable expletives have emitted from irate gunsmiths trying to repair one of these abominations, of which the Lightning is by far the most exasperating.

Despite their practical weaknesses, both models have a growing collector following. They are early enough guns to have seen use in the Wild West. Furthermore they share some basic design similarities with the Single Action Army, and on the exterior at least are well designed and handsome weapons. Billy the Kid is credited with preferring the Lightning model, Rowdy Joe Lowe is known to have owned a Frontier model (serial #2655), and photographs of Westerners taken during the last quarter of the 19th Century indicate some degree of popularity for these guns.

Similar to the Single Action Army, the Lightning and Frontier double-action revolvers offer the collector quite a number of variations, mainly in calibers, barrel lengths, finishes, and markings. One Lightning as yet undiscovered bears the intriguing backstrap inscription: *To Will Cravens from Heck Thomas.* Thomas was a well-known lawman in the Old West. Artist Frederic Remington purchased a .41 caliber Lightning (serial #98951), also as yet unknown in any Colt collection. A deluxe engraved and inscribed Model 1878 Frontier revolver was made for His Excellency Senhor Felippe Lopez Netto. That gun too awaits discovery by a lucky collector.

Although some collectors specialize in the Lightning and/or the Frontier DA revolvers, most try to take in all the double actions, stopping early in the 20th century, or choosing some later date as a termination point. All other DA Colts had swing out cylinders, and thus did not have the Single Action Army look as found on the Lightning and Frontier models.

The swing out cylinder double-action Colt revolvers look like modern revolvers—even the first model brought out in 1889. Partly for this reason, these pieces do not have the same appeal as do the Single Action Army or the Model 1877 Lightning and the Model 1878 Frontier. The

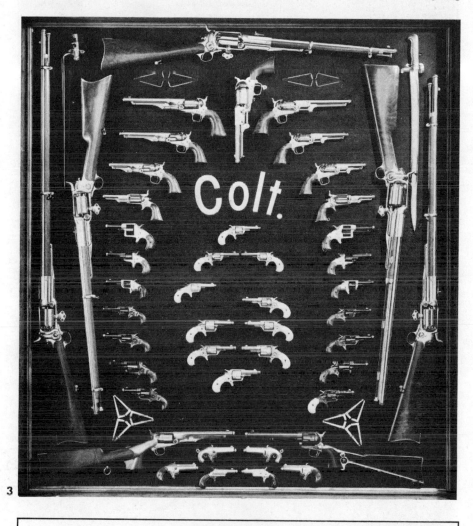

3

4

1. The ultimate in Thuer conversions. Colt's pulled out all the stops when they made this truly fabulous outfit. This elaborate, engraved Model 1860 Army is plated in gold and silver, and fitted with relief-carved ivory grips. An exchange cylinder permits firing the gun with the percussion system. The extra large deluxe rosewood case is complete with specially finished accessories.

2. Four conversions dating from 1870 to 1874. The Colt factory was never one to throw out obsolete parts. When the percussion system was giving way to the metallic cartridge, Colt's found it judicious to alter many weapons in the process of manufacture from the old system to the new. The top and second from bottom guns are experimentals; the bottom and second from top are a Thuer Model 1862 Police conversion and an Open Top .44 CF. Connecticut State Library Collection.

3. A unique collection of Colt percussion and early cartridge firearms, assembled in 1877 by the firm of Hartley and Graham, New York City. This is the only original display board of Colt guns to survive intact from the 19th Century. Interestingly, the percussion models are finished in the white—none are blued. Every piece is in mint, unfired condition. R. Q. Sutherland Collection.

4. One of the earliest Colt revolvers made to fire the metallic cartridge; the Old Line "Open Top" in .22 rimfire. This piece was produced from 1871 to 1875. Sam Colt failed to recognize the great potential of the metallic cartridge. Despite the historic interest of the Old Lines, they are quite inexpensive on today's market. Sutherland Collection.

COLLECTING COLT

fact that most DA Colts postdate 1898 also tended to limit their interest to collectors. 1898 is the arbitrary cutoff date established by the government (1968 G.C.A.) as a rule of thumb in separating "modern" guns from collector guns.

However, in recent years collectors have been drawn increasingly to the double-action swing out cylinder revolvers. The relatively high prices of percussion and many pre-1900 cartridge Colts have limited the possibilities for success in those areas for the collector on a limited budget. But success for the same collector comes with less financial effort when he turns to the swing out cylinder DA revolvers. In the process, collectors have found that they too are rich in tradition and history. Among the original users of the Model 1889 DA revolver (the first Colt swing out cylinder model) were Sam Colt's son Caldwell, a coterie of Turkish Sultans, a Siamese Prince, and lawman Heck Thomas. Theodore Roosevelt carried a New Army and Navy DA revolver during his Spanish-American War service, and the Wells Fargo express company was a quantity buyer of this model. Many other colorful figures from American history are known to have owned swing out cylinder DA Colt revolvers. In modern times, Presidents Truman and Eisenhower were recipients of presentation DA's, and a specimen was made for presentation to Richard M. Nixon while he was Vice President, but the gift was never made.

Some models of DA Colt revolvers are extreme rarities. Among these are the Model 1905 Marine Corps (total production only 926 pieces), the Border Patrol Model of 1952 (only 400 made), and the unique single-shot Camp Perry target pistol (2525 made). One area of increasing collector interest is in DA Colts having special service markings. For example, among the various butt stamps used on the Army Special Model (1908-1927) were N.J.S.P. (New Jersey State Prison), N.O.P.D. (New Orleans Police Department), P.P.D. (Pontiac, Michigan, Police Department), and F.W. P.D. (Fort Worth, Texas, Police Department).

The DA Colts, with a manufacturing total to date in excess of four million pieces, in over 35 basic models, offer the collector a wide range of choice, and at quite reasonable expenditures. It is the unusual piece in this area of specialization which costs more than $500.00. Furthermore, since most specimens post-

date circa 1900, it is possible in some instances to have personal knowledge of the weapon's original user. Sometimes purchase can be made directly from that individual.

AUTOMATIC PISTOLS

The same opportunity to have a direct knowledge of a weapon's history is offered by the Colt Automatic pistol category, the total production of which has been in the 20th Century. From the first Colt automatic, the Model 1900, over five million pistols have been made, in a total of 25 major models One excellent book has been published on this field, Donald B. Bady's Colt Automatic Pistols. From historical and mechanical standpoints, the automatics are captivating.

Variations of caliber within each model are quite limited, and do not compare with most types of Single and Double Action revolvers; the automatic Colts are basically cham-

bered for .22 rimfire, and .25, .32, .38, .380, and .45 ACP's. Some models were made in tremendous quantities, and these by themselves are collector specialties. Most prominent of the high-production autos are the Model 1911-M1911A1 series, of which over three million have been made to date. In the Woodsman .22 over 500,000 have been produced, and the Model 1903 and 1908 Pocket Automatics totalled well over 700,000 when discontinued in 1945. Some commemoratives have even been issued as automatics; so far the model used has been limited to the .45 ACP caliber (World War 1 M1911 and World War 2 M1911A1).

Some collectors who are interested in the automatic Colt pistols avoid them because of restrictive local, state, or federal laws. As a result, the number of specialists in this area is less than it would be if conditions were more favorable.

Other than pistols made for military use, one expects to find most

Colt automatics in very good condition, with plenty of original finish and crisp markings. Quite a bit of the market for Colt autos is more as a used piece, rather than as a collector's item. Prices are quite reasonable, seldom exceeding about $400.00 per pistol. And some of the most intriguing historic specimens have yet to be discovered. Among these are Buffalo Bill's gold-inlaid Model 1902 Military pistol, serial # 14940, and C. L. F. Robinson's (Colt's President), gold-inlaid Model 1903 Hammerless Pocket pistol, serial #89776. The Robinson pistol was gold inlaid with portraits of George Washington, Abraham Lincoln, and U. S. Grant, and had the Colt coat of arms and a monogram in gold. A few models of service-type automatics were shipped with such romantic markings as W.F. &Co. (Wells Fargo & Co.), Shanghai Police (China), Ejercito Mexicano (Mexican Army), and T.H.D. (Texas Highway Department).

Some of the production mechan-

1. *Advertising the National No. 1 and the Colt No. 3 (Thuer) Model deringers. Colt's bought out the National Arms Co. and took over the production and sale of this firm's 1st and 2nd Model pistols. The 3rd Model was a Colt design, and remained in their product line from 1875 through 1912. It was reintroduced in 1959 as a .22 calibered arm. John Hintlian Collection.*

2. *A deluxe Single Action Army with ivory grips. The beauty and romance of this early specimen (circa 1876) helps explain the Single Action Army's unique hold upon those of the Wild West. The renowned craftsman L. D. Nimschke engraved this piece. Dr. R. L. Moore Jr. Collection.*

3. *A Bisley Single Action in the scarce flat top target version. All Bisleys were designed as target revolvers and shared the serial number markings with the S.A. Army series. Only 976 Bisleys in the flat top configuration were made. From the R. Q. Sutherland Collection.*

4. *This D.A. Official Police revolver, serial number 718128, once belonged to Ian Fleming, author of the James Bond novels. It was purchased in London in 1967 at a used gun price. Careful buying can still lead to bargains in Colt collecting. R. Q. Sutherland Collection.*

5. *A Colt Courier, representing one of the scarcest variations in the company's D.A. revolver production. Rarities exist in the later models of Colt arms just as they do in the 19th Century types. Sutherland Collection.*

6. *The Model 1902 in caliber .38 Automatic with its military livery. Note the evolutionary details of the checkering on the front of the slide which provides a gripping surface. Original holsters from the period are scarce. R. Q. Sutherland Collection.*

COLLECTING COLT

ical variations that strike a collector's fancy are unusual sights, unusual finishes (e.g., special-order sandblast or Parkerizing, cutaway specimens (extreme rarities), combination holster/ shoulder stocks (Model 1905 .45 Auto), and foreign-language markings. Of the latter an interesting group of 14,500 Model 1911 pistols was made for the Russians in 1915 and 1916, marked ANGLO ZAKAZIVAT.

CARTRIDGE LONGARMS

The reputation of Colt firearms was built on handguns. When most persons think of a Colt, they consider only revolvers and automatic pistols. Many collectors are unaware of

1. A medium frame Lightning slide action rifle in cutaway form. This piece was probably used as a salesman's sample or for reference use in the assembly shop. Lightnings were the most successful Colt longarms series produced for the civilian market. Sutherland Collection.

2. The Colt automatic shotgun; one of the scarcest of modern-day Colt longarms to locate. Only a few of these are now in collections as most are used by shooters who have no idea that their now obsolete Colt is a collector's item. Production ran from 1962 to 1966. They were made in Italy. Sutherland Collection.

3. One of the finest double barrel shotguns made in America was the Colt Model 1883 Hammerless. One of the devotees of this model was President Grover Cleveland. His 8 gauge custom-made double weighed 12 3/16 pounds; his name was neatly gold inlaid on the trigger guard. The piece illustrated is an experimental with engraved action, Circassian walnut stock, forend and no serial number! R. Q. Sutherland Collection.

4. The carbine version of Colt's only production lever action firearm. The Burgess Model Colt had only one production run, and sold for approximately two years in the mid-1880s. Though a sound looking arm it had some mechanical weaknesses. It appears that this design was forced off the market by a threat from Winchester to enter the revolving handgun business. R. Q. Sutherland Collection.

5. Cutaway firearms were introduced by Samuel Colt as early as 1850. Though never made in anything but limited numbers, over 25 distinct models (from 2nd Model Dragoon to M16 Assault Rifle) have been "cutaway" by Colt machinists over the years. The M1911A1 illustrated was made for use by Colt's armorers' training school during World War 2. R. Q. Sutherland Collection.

6. Some commemorative collectors go all the way. Charles Kidwell's collection of serial number 8 Colt Commemorative issues took up four tables at the Tulsa Gun Report Show of 1969. Two more tables would take the rest.

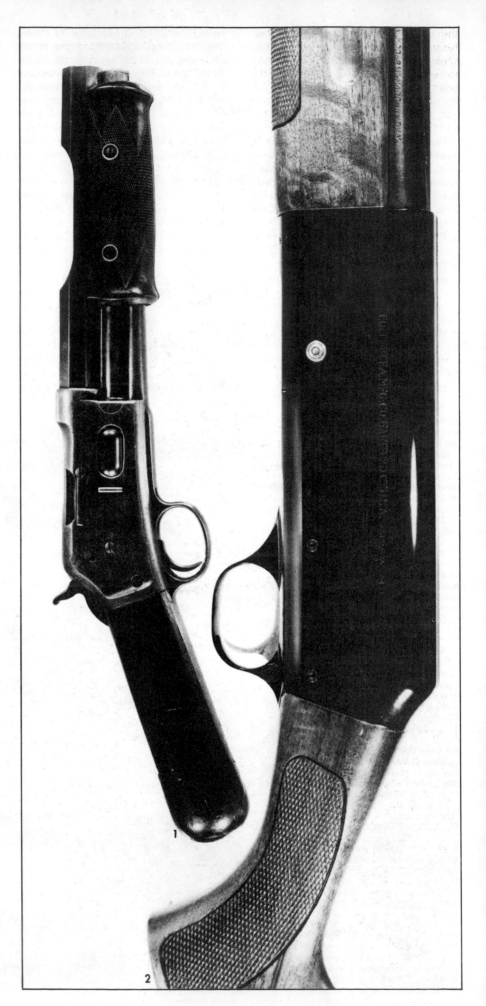

the Colt firm's substantial manufacturing total of cartridge longarms. Over 20 distinct models numbering in excess of 500,000 pieces have been produced by Colt since 1866 in rifle, shotgun, carbine, and musket configurations (not counting over 3,000,000 current M16 rifles). The first cartridge weapon made in quantity by Colt was not a handgun, but the Berdan single-shot breechloading rifle. Colt's Franklin Military rifle of 1887-88 was one of the earliest U.S.-made bolt-action repeaters. Connoisseurs of quality gunmaking consider the Colt Model 1878 Hammer and Model 1883 Hammerless Shotguns as among the finest shotguns produced in America. One of the great rarities in gun collecting is the Double Barrel Rifle brought out by Colt in about 1879. Colonel Colt's son Caldwell is credited with the basic design, the only double-barrel cartridge rifle made in any quantity by a major American gunmaker.

Colt gave Winchester a scare by bringing out the Burgess Lever Action rifle, in 1883. According to tradition, Winchester threatened to bring out a series of handguns if Colt persisted in marketing the rifle. In 1885 the Colt-Burgess was dropped from the product line, after only 6403 were produced. One of the owners of this short-lived but handsome weapon was Buffalo Bill Cody. His was inscribed, engraved, and silver inlaid.

Three basic frame sizes of Lightning slide action rifles were produced, in calibers ranging from .22 rimfire to the .50-95 Express. Over 180,000 of the Lightnings were sold from the early 1880s to the early 1900s. Collectors who specialize only in these longarms have a fertile area which has yet to be restricted by high prices. Among the more popular and desirable variations are the 401 rifles in .44-40 caliber made for the San Francisco Police Department. Each is especially numbered on the lower tang S.F.P. 1 through S.F.P. 401. A few medium-and large-frame rifles were made in military types with slings and bayonet lugs. Sam Colt's son Caldwell ordered a .22 rifle, #1669, with a special short magazine, adjustable trigger, buttplate of iron, and a cover of canvas. One of the large-frame "Express" rifles was custom made for "Texas Charley" and was so inscribed.

Colt's export sales in the Lightning rifle era were substantial. Several thousand were shipped for sale through Colt dealers in Australia and Europe. Lightnings are so well made that they are popular to this day as shooters. The .44-40 carbines sell quite well in parts of Europe for use in hunting rabbits and other small game.

Quite difficult for a collector to obtain are Colt bolt action rifles and

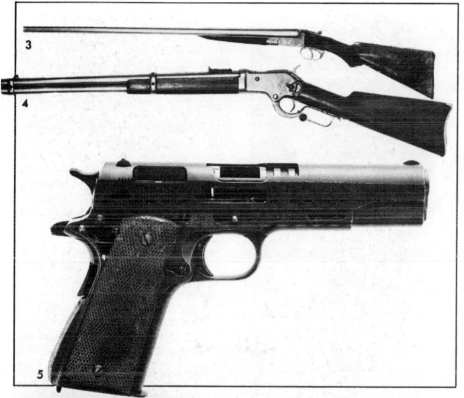

COLLECTING COLT

pump and semi-automatic shotguns. These items are all discontinued models and were only available in limited numbers and for limited periods. Unfortunately, most owners are current shooters unaware of the scarcity of these Colt weapons. As a consequence, the place for a collector to locate a specimen is by chance in the hands of a hunter.

There is a lesson to a handgun maker like Colt in the sales failure of nearly all the longarms they have produced. Four times in the last 136 years the company has attempted to carry a line of sporting longarms, in addition to their handguns. In every instance the attempt has ultimately failed. Of all its rifle production only the AR-15 (M16) has been a solid success, but that is not yet in the realm of a collector's item.

COMMEMORATIVES

Colt's was the first gunmaker to enter the commemorative field; in fact, they were creators of this concept with the Sheriff's Model .45 and the 125th Anniversary .45 Single Action revolvers of 1961. The company has carefully and wisely nursed the commemorative concept along, avoiding glutting the market (by limiting the numbers of each issue), and, in general, carefully selecting every theme. The basic models have been the Frontier Scout .22 and the Single Action Army .45, the .45 Government Model Automatic, and the newly introduced Model 1851 Navy.

Nearly every Colt commemorative has proven a sound investment for the collector, some even selling among collectors at prices above retail before the model is fully on the market. Only a few collectors can afford to purchase one each of every Colt commemorative made—since 1961 there have been over 75 models—so most buyers concentrate on specific areas. Among these are: State and territorial themes, historical personages, historical events, cities, towns, trails, forts, and company and corporation models The next major model promises to be one of the best of the lot—the Centennial of the Single Action Army, some of which will be chambered for the popular .44-40 cartridge.

Commemorative enthusiasts have joined together in the only collecting organization devoted exclusively to Colts—the Colt's Commemorative Gun Collectors' Association of America. Founded in 1968 and already over 3000 members strong, the CCGCAA publishes a quarterly journal with news of events in the commemorative field, holds annual meetings, and in general keeps collectors in tune on their field of interest.

The standard reference in the field is the author's, Colt Commemorative Firearms, published by Charles Kidwell in 1969.

ENGRAVED FIREARMS

Engraving on Colt firearms dates back to the very earliest pieces, and has remained popular to the present

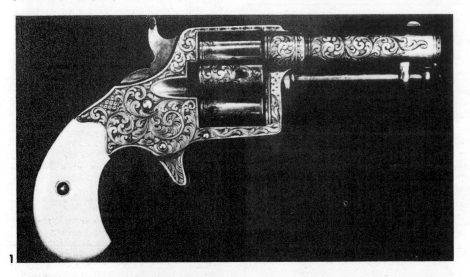

1

2

World War I Commemorative Colt .45 Automatic Pistol

THE BATTLE OF CHÂTEAU-THIERRY

3

4

5

day. The collector of engraved Colt pieces is in the very big leagues! Consistently the highest prices in the Colt field go for deluxe engraved specimens, primarily percussion revolvers. Cases and presentation inscriptions are usually present and add to the value of the weapon. Condition is a factor of considerable significance in evaluating the collector importance of engraved arms. It is not unusual for the exceptional engraved, cased, and inscribed Army, Navy, or Dragoon revolver (in excellent condition) to have a value in excess of $15,000.

The first reference to deal in some detail with elaborate Colt guns was this author's book, *Samuel Colt Presents*, published in 1961 by the Wadsworth Atheneum. Some of the finest percussion Colt guns known are pictured and described therein. Winchester Press, will publish in 1973 a detailed study of Colt and Winchester firearms engraving, which will be the pioneer work in this very exclusive and popular field.

The basic factor to bear in mind in studying Colt engraving is that each craftsman worked in his own style. Thus, the decoration on Colt arms is one style from 1852 to circa 1869 (G. Young), and another style from circa 1871 to 1921 (C. Helfricht). From about 1920 through around 1950, the decoration shows the hand of Wilbur A. Glahn, and in the post-1950 period, most engraving was by the late Alvin F. Herbert or by the renowned Alvin A. White.

Because engraved Colts are usually high-value items—except for deringers and pocket revolvers, they rarely sell for less than $1000; this area of collecting has attracted a few shady individuals who create *excellent* fakes. The collector is well advised to be certain of the honesty of the person from whom he is making a purchase. It is strongly recommended that a documenting Colt factory letter or opinion from a recognized expert be solicited before pulling out one's checkbook.

Samuel Colt himself was a keen fancier of finely embellished firearms. He was lavish in presenting such weapons to potential clients. It is surprising to learn that the finest single group of Colt presentation percussion arms is now in The Hermitage Museum, Leningrad. These were gifts from Colonel Colt to the

1. Just a Cloverleaf pocket revolver, but the rich engraved coverage by L. D. Nimschke made an otherwise rather ordinary gun into a highly desirable specimen for the collector of engraved Colts. From the Dr. Robert G. Fox Collection.

2. An exquisite example of the gun engraver's art, cut on an Officer's Model target revolver made in the year 1909. The superbly executed scrolls and the relief-carved pearl grips are identifiable by style as the work of master engraver Cuno Helfricht. David S. Woloch Collection.

3. In commemorating the 50th anniversary of the First World War, Colt's revived the .45 ACP calibered Model of 1911 Automatic Pistol in four versions. Pictured here is the first of these, the Chateau Thierry. In addition to the regular models of this type, a total of 100 engraved and gold inlaid pistols were made selling for $1000 each, and 300 engraved pistols sold for $500 each. Most Colt commemoratives have been in calibers .45 Long Colt and .22 Long Rifle, the hand engraved variations are limited issues.

4. A masterpiece of the engraver's art, and one of the finest Colt revolvers ever made. Samuel Colt presented this gold inlaid and engraved Dragoon to the Sultan of Turkey. The mate went as a gift to Czar Alexander II of Russia. That's a portrait of George Washington on the cylinder, in gold. Locke Collection.

5. A gun collection in a single piece. This engraved, silver inlaid, and ivory gripped Texas Paterson is the finest gun known from the early period of Colt manufacture. From the inventor's personal arms collection, now in the Wadsworth Atheneum, Hartford.

6. A deluxe, gold inlaid Government Model Automatic pistol, serial number WW II S-2. One of the finest collector's guns made in Colt's post war production. Former Colt's President W. H. Goldbach (Weapons Div.) ordered this pistol and five other handguns in building a unique group of engraved and gold inlaid Colts. Alvin White engraved all but one.

7. This deluxe Sheriff's Model Single Action was made for western gunfighter Marcelino Baca. Baca is shown in the book, "Law and Order Ltd." From the N. Brigham Pemberton Collection.

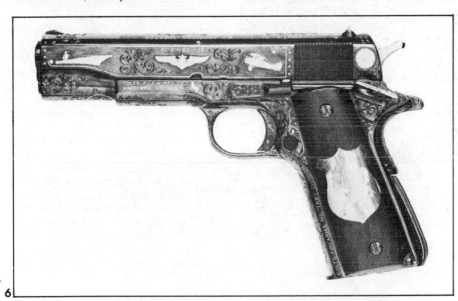

6

7

COLLECTING COLT

Czars Nicholas I and Alexander II, and to the Grand Dukes Michael and Constantine. Three of these revolvers were exquisitely gold relief inlaid, one of them featuring the Capitol of the United States wrapped half way around the cylinder in gold! In our opinion, the collecting of engraved pieces is the highest plain of collecting in the Colt field. However, all other areas of Coltiana have their own special fascination, and what counts in the final analysis is each collector's own individual taste and interest.

HISTORIC FIREARMS

Usually, the historic firearm is also an engraved piece. It is unusual to be able to prove that a specific piece was owned by a famed individual or used in a special event unless the firearm was in some way engraved or inscribed. Thus, when the Colt factory presented a cased pair of revolvers to General George B. McClellan, an inscription was neatly lettered on each backstrap. When Lt. William Morris, U.S.A., ordered a deluxe cased and engraved Navy revolver, Colonel Colt added the inscription: *W. H. Morris U.S.A.*, on the backstrap. To document this latter piece (serial #6354), an original letter was recently discovered in a Connecticut museum from ordnance inspector W. A. Thornton to Colt, ordering the complete set, with inscription.

The author has had the good fortune to document over 100 historic weapons through time consuming re-

1. One of the most valuable Colt revolvers, steeped in history as the personal Single Action Army of Theodore Roosevelt. L. D. Nimschke engraved the elaborate designs, one motif of which is a TR monogram on the recoil shield and on the right side of the ivory grips. Documentation of this revolver was provided in part by an early photograph of the revolver in the TR Collection at Harvard. From the Richard P. Mellon Collection.

2. Colt's letterhead of 1855 to 1870 showed off the company's premises. The Mr. Brown on the billing was none other than John Brown, the Abolitionist. Kansas State Hist. Soc. Collection.

3. Some publications of interest regarding Colt firearms.

4. Finding an original cardboard box for a pre-World War I Colt is a feat by itself. Paper and leather items were easily lost, and until recently most collectors had no interest or appreciation of these relics. The Lightning revolver in this box dated from about 1900. From the R. Q. Sutherland Collection.

search in original Colt factory records and in museum documentary sources. Nearly always the subject historic arm bears special engraving and an inscription.

Generally speaking, the weakest documentation is a letter from a usually somewhat distant descendant or second-hand acquaintance stating that he or she remembers (vaguely) the old timer having said he carried such and such revolver in the Wild West. Letters of that nature are easy to prepare, and the notarizing of them only guarantees that the signature of the signer is genuine. One of

Theodore Roosevelt's sons has been quoted as saying he has seen at least 50 different revolvers which his father carried up San Juan Hill! It is well to remember this anecdote when assessing documentary letters accompanying so-called historic weapons.

Credibility should not be given to any stories connected with a weapon unless there is solid supporting evidence. By far the best documentation is the Colt factory letter. Colt ledgers are nearly complete from 1860 through today. A description of your piece, plus $15.00, addressed to M. S. Huber, Historian, Colt's,

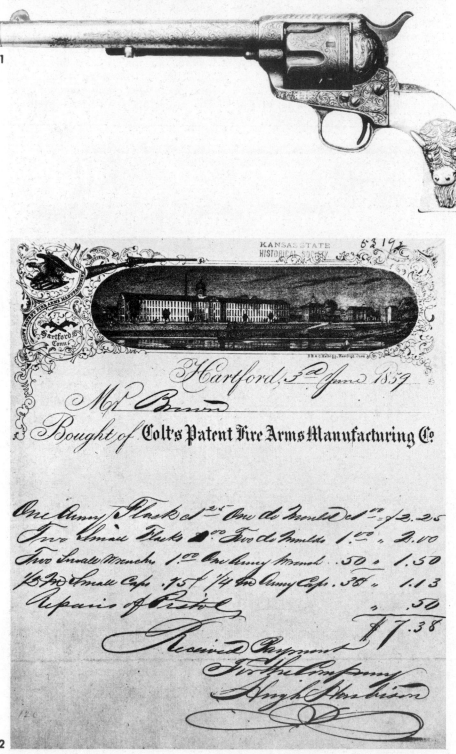

SELECTED COLT BIBLIOGRAPHY

BARNARD, HENRY
ARMSMEAR.
Hartford: Mrs. Samuel Colt, 1868.

EDWARDS, W. B.
THE STORY OF COLT'S REVOLVER.
Harrisburg: The Stackpole Company, 1953.

HAVEN, C. T. and FRANK A. BELDEN
A HISTORY OF THE COLT REVOLVER.
New York: W. Morrow and Company, 1940.

KEOGH, G.
SAMUEL COLT'S NEW MODEL POCKET PISTOLS.
Ogden: Published by the author, 1964.

MITCHELL, J. L.
COLT THE MAN THE ARMS THE COMPANY.
Harrisburg: The Stackpole Company, 1953.

PARSONS, J. E.
THE PEACEMAKER AND ITS RIVALS.
New York: W. Morrow and Company, 1950.

PARSONS, J. E.
PERCUSSION COLT REVOLVERS.
New York: The Metropolitan Museum of Art, 1942.

SAMUEL COLT'S OWN RECORD.
Hartford: The Connecticut Historical Society, 1949.

ROHAN, JACK
YANKEE ARMS MAKER.
New York: Harper and Brothers, 1935.

SERVEN, J. E.
COLT FIREARMS FROM 1836.
Santa Ana: The Foundation Press, various editions since 1954.

SHUMAKER, P. L.
COLT'S VARIATIONS OF THE OLD MODEL POCKET PISTOL.
Beverly Hills: Fadco Publishing Company, 1957.

SWAYZE, N. L.
'51 COLT NAVIES.
Yazoo City: Published by the author, 1967.

ULRICH, A. L.
A CENTURY OF ACHIEVEMENT.
Hartford: Colt's Patent Fire Arms Mfg. Co., 1936.

VIRGINES, G. E.
THE SAGA OF THE COLT SIXSHOOTER.
New York: Frederick Fell, Inc., 1969.

WILSON, R. L.
COLT COMMEMORATIVE FIREARMS.
Wichita: C. Kidwell, 1969.

WILSON, R. L.
THE ARMS COLLECTION OF COLONEL COLT.
Bullville, N.Y.: Herb Glass, 1964.

WILSON, R. L.
THE RAMPANT COLT.
Spencer, Indiana: T. Haas, 1969.

WILSON, R. L.
THE EVOLUTION OF THE COLT.
Kansas City: R. Q. Sutherland, 1967.

WILSON, R. L.
SAMUEL COLT PRESENTS.
Hartford: Wadsworth Atheneum, 1961.

WILSON, R. L. and R. Q. SUTHERLAND
THE BOOK OF COLT FIREARMS.
Kansas City: R. Q. Sutherland, 1971.

3

4

Inc., 150 Huyshope Avenue, Hartford, Connecticut 06102, will result either in a documenting letter or the return of the $15.00. This documentation, based on the original factory ledgers, lists model, serial number, caliber, date and destination of shipment, and various other facts such as engraving (if present), finish, type grips, number of similar type guns in shipment, and so forth. The research letter is one of the best investments a collector can make in assembling a collection. The classic episode about such letters is that of a collector from Illinois. By paying the modest research fee, he learned that his old nickel-plated Single Action Colt .45, #112737 had been shipped on July 30, 1885 to W. B. "Bat" Masterson, one of the West's greatest gunfighter/adventurers. The collector had just purchased the gun for a total of $90.00!

MEMORABILIA

It is possible to be an advanced Colt collector without owning a single firearm—specialize in memorabilia. The number of items in this relatively new approach to Colts is phenomenal. Many such objects are more rare than most firearms, yet this rarity is seldom indicated by price. Whether a document, catalogue, price list, medal, antique photograph, print, gauge, tool, shoulder patch, workman's pass, tie bar, or tobacco humidor, it is the marking "Colt" which says: "I am a collector's item." There are more genuine Walker Colt revolvers known than there are Samuel Colt calling cards, or rampant Colt coachman's coat buttons. A broadside advertising the Colt cylinder roll die scenes (circa 1850) is so rare that only about three specimens have survived the ravages of time. Letters from the factory on the elaborate Colt letterhead are seldom seen outside of museum collections. Catalogues from pre-World War 1 years are so scarce that the first edition (February, 1888) easily brings $250.00. In catalogues alone, a complete set from 1888 through today is nearly impossible to assemble; approximately three such sets are known—and none of these belongs to the Colt factory. Original advertising prints such as the George Catlin lithographs of the 1850s are better known to art collectors than to arms fanciers.

The magic identifying markings in seeking these specimens of memorabilia are not only the word Colt (or Colt's), but the famed rampant Colt trademark. That classic symbol, one of America's oldest (in use since

COLLECTING COLT

the 1830s) has been so widely employed that it served as the central theme for this writer's book, The Rampant Colt, published in 1969. This 108-page illustrated volume became the standard text of memorabilia collectors and is already nearing a second printing.

COLLECTING COLTS AS AN INVESTMENT

The boom in arms collecting in the years since World War 2 has proven Colt collecting to be the major blue-chip field in antique firearms. Every specimen has held its value in the inflationary spiral, and nearly all have increased substantially in cash worth during those years. Originality of condition has been a major factor in assessing value; the best performances have been by the percussion handguns, particularly the engraved, inscribed, or cased specimens.

The publication of new books on all aspects of Colt arms and memorabilia has added to the desirability of the field for the collector. The commemorative Colts have created many new aficionados, and the active interest of the Colt company in arms collecting is still another important growth factor. The ever increasing number of wealthy buyers has tended to push prices to top levels. And interestingly enough, today a professional dealer may have as many monied clients in Europe as he does in America. One dealer states his European customers use The Book of Colt Firearms as a combination source book and catalogue. They see pictured a type weapon they would like to own, and he sets out to buy it for them.

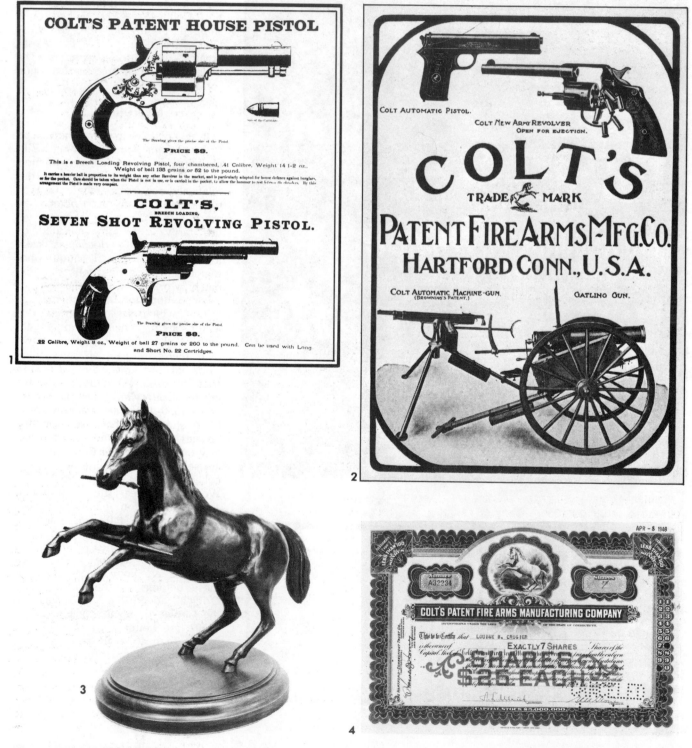

CATLIN THE CELEBRATED INDIAN TRAVELLER AND ARTIST, FIRING HIS COLT'S REPEATING RIFLE BEFORE A TRIBE OF CARIB INDIANS IN SOUTH AMERICA.

5

6

1. On this page from a scarce Colt broadside of 1872, the early models of Cloverleaf House (top) and Old Line revolvers are advertised. The skillfully executed drawings even depict the fine scroll engraving and the wood grain in the grips. John Hintilian Collection.

2. Hartford city directories yield some extremely collectible advertisements of Colt products. The company ceased to use illustrated ads in this medium prior to World War 2. The promotional piece illustrated was featured in Geer's Directory, 1909.

3. The rampant colt, Colt's trademark since the 1830s. This bronze by sculptor-engraver Alvin A. White is part of a limited edition authorized by Colt's. Samuel Colt himself had commissioned all types of luxury items on which the rampant colt appeared, even the family silver.

4. An original stock certificate, signed by A. L. Ulrich, Secretary, and S. M. Stone, President. Colt's went public in the early 20th Century, and is now a relatively small part of the giant Colt Industries Corp. The corporate headquarters is in New York City, but the firearms division remains in Hartford, its continuous home since 1847.

5. One of six prints made as a set for Colonel Colt by the artist, George Catlin. Each subject showed Catlin proving the effectiveness of a Colt firearm, usually before a tribe of Indians. An original print may sell for as high as $750 if one is fortunate to find one.

6. A collector's dream. This was the original Colt museum as displayed at the factory in the 1940s and 1950s. In 1957 the collection was given to the State of Connecticut by the Colt Company.

waiting to be discovered. The thrill of discovering new pieces is one of the many rewards of gun collecting. Because of the high value of many Colt pieces, that fresh discovery may be like striking a gold vein or drilling a gushing oil well.

If Samuel Colt were alive today, one can be certain that the inventor, showman, entrepreneur would still be collecting products bearing the great Colt name. He always liked adventure, mechanics, design, and quality—and he was always a genius at making investments. But then, if he were actively collecting in this modern era, it would make matters difficult for the remaining Colt collectors. With his enthusiasm and inclination to possess, Samuel Colt would want to own every fine piece that hit the market. At present we collectors are lucky. The field is shared only with somewhere between 25,000 to 50,000 proteges of that pioneer in Colt collecting—Colonel Samuel Colt.

With an estimated 25,000 to 50,000 active Colt collectors, and ever increasing values and prices, one would think the time to collect is now many years past. The fact is that most areas within Colts still offer fine condition specimens at reasonable prices. Several of these fields are noted in the text. A prospective collector would do well to consult C. E. Chapel's Gun Collector's Handbook of Values for a general idea of what can still be purchased at prices in the hundreds of dollars, and in the thousands. By buying quality and originality, and by buying from a reputable professional dealer, a fine collection of good investments

can be built, and the results are much more tangible and intriguing than a stack of bank savings account books or a portfolio of stocks and bonds.

The collector should also bear in mind that diligence and good luck may turn up some fine buys from attics or cellars. There remain many thousands of virgin Colt guns yet to be discovered. A survey of presentation arms in Colt ledgers indicates over 75 gifts of fine cased weapons were made in the 1860s. To date only about a dozen of these have been located by collectors. Some of the balance were lost or destroyed, but it is likely that most of these sets are in private homes,

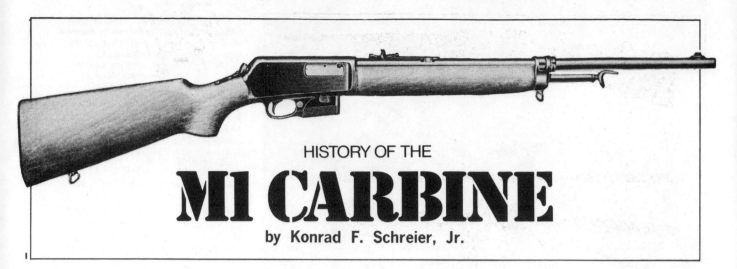

HISTORY OF THE
M1 CARBINE
by Konrad F. Schreier, Jr.

Volumes have been written about the U.S. Carbine Cal. .30 M1 since it was adopted on September 30, 1941, however all these histories have missed some interesting portions of the story. In order to begin the story of the M1 carbine you have to go back to the days when the Army adopted the M1903 Springfield.

Until the adoption of the '03 Springfield rifle there had always been a regulation carbine for the U.S. Cavalry, but the carbine died when the '03 was introduced. A carbine was a shortened, handier version of the regulation infantry rifle specifically designed for use by mounted troops. In order to eliminate the carbine, the new '03 rifle was made in what was then a radically short length by making its barrel 24 inches long instead of the 28 to 30 inches as was customary in military rifles. Carbines usually had 20- or 22-inch barrels. The '03 rifle was just 43½ inches long overall, and and an equally handy arm for either infantry and cavalry. Both Infantry and Cavalry were delighted with the new rifle.

The next element which contributed to the development of the M1 carbine was the introduction of the U.S. Pistol Caliber .45 Model of 1911. This .45 service automatic was adopted after some 20 years of extreme difficulty with the Army's service pistols. The first problem came about when the Army tried to adopt the fragile double-action .45 Colt "Alaskan Model" revolver to replace the old .45 Colt Single Action Army Model of 1873. Then some idiots tried to replace the .45 revolver with a .38 revolver which was mechanically acceptable but of too small a caliber to instantly stop a determined hostile. The result of these inadequate revolvers led to troops in the field continuing to use the old .45 Colt Army Model revolver, which,

despite its age and tendency to shake apart, did the job when it was asked to. So did the new .45 automatic pistol, and the Army was more than happy to be able to finally take the antique Colt Army Model revolvers out of service. The .45 automatic pistol could do its job so well that it soon became the pet of everyone who carried it.

The men who used the new .45 automatic pistol and '03 rifle during their early years were truly a special breed. The Regular Army was composed of soldiers who were trained from the soles of their boots to the peaks of their campaign hats, and they were taught to shoot expertly. The Army's reserve component was the National Guard, a volunteer force which made a point of learning military skills because they felt it was their duty to their country, and the National Guardsmen also learned to handle small arms very well. In fact, many National Guard units prided themselves on being better small arms shots than similar units of the Regular Army. This was the state of affairs when the United States was drawn into World War I, and then new problems relating to the use of small arms began to cause difficulty.

Although the drafted men who were the majority of the troops in the vastly expanded Army could be taught to use the rifle reasonably well in the time allotted for training, it proved almost impossible to teach these men how to use the pistol effectively. The situation was such that, in the hands of the drafted men with no prior service or weapons experience, the pistol became more of a badge of office than a useful tool.

In order to give men who couldn't handle the pistol a weapon they could use for short-range combat, the Army issued a large number of the regular guard and riot 12 Gauge Winchester Shotgun Model 1897 to front line troops. The riot gun had a 20-inch barrel, and it made a very handy (and deadly) weapon, but it lacked the range capability for use over 50 yards.

Another Winchester weapon went into the trenches and caused a lot of thinking, the .351 Winchester Self-loading Rifle Model 1907. This 20-inch barrel self-loader was originally used in World War I by the French as a secondary weapon on multi-seat combat aircraft. Limited numbers of these rifles were acquired completely outside the scope of regulations for use in the trenches.

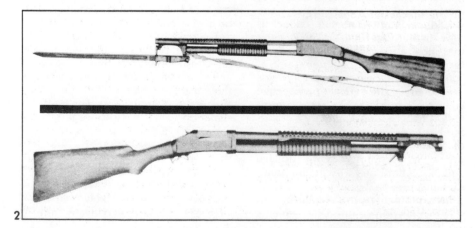

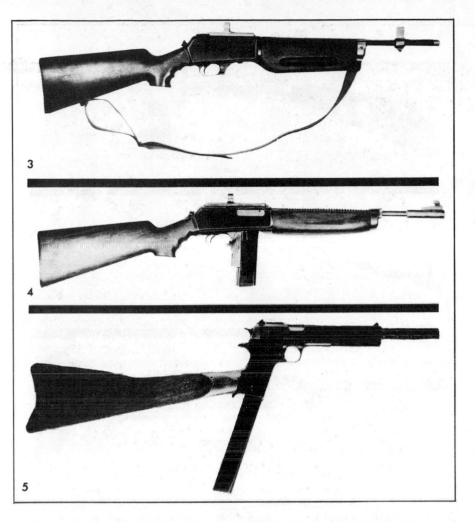

3

4

5

Although the .351 Winchester Self-Loader wasn't a particularly good military weapon because it was somewhat complicated and fragile, it was very effective because of the stopping power of its ammunition up to several hundred yards range. Its short length and 7½-pound weight made it very handy to use. Many of the .351's that found their way into the trenches were in the hands of men who would normaly have been armed with pistols, and the success

1. Winchester 1907 self-loader in caliber .351. In many respects, this weapon may be called the grandfather of the carbine.

2. The Winchester Model 97 12-gauge shotgun in "riot" form. Some were still in use in Viet Nam. A deadly weapon at close ranges.

3. The Woodhull experimental .30 caliber light rifle was actually built from a Model 1907 Winchester.

4. Woodhull submachine gun built from a .401 Winchester Model 1910.

5. The .45 M 1911A1 as modified by Colt into a carbine with stock, extended magazine and lengthened slide/barrel group. A European concept which did not find favor here. Photo courtesy the late Col. B. R. Lewis, USA, ret'd.

of the Winchester Self-Loader started a number of men considering a new weapon for the Army.

After the end of World War I, a specification and requirement was developed for a light rifle, similar to the .351 Self-Loader and with a 300-yard effective range, and intended to replace the pistol among front-line troops. Since there was no money available for the development of the new light rifle, the pistol remained standard as it still is. There are many combat situations in which there is still no reasonable replacement for the handgun. However the idea for a light rifle was imbedded in the Army, and then the Thompson submachine gun came into the fore.

The Tommy Gun, or .45 Thompson Submachine Gun Model 1928, was developed to give extended range and firepower in a weapon firing standard pistol ammunition. The development of the Thompson followed the German development of submachine gun firing their 9mm pistol ammunition. Although it had many characteristics of the light rifle, the Thompson proved to be an entirely new breed of weapon, however it did serve to keep the idea of a light rifle alive. Then World War 2 began to evolve, and money be-

came readily available for the development of new weapons for the first time since the end of the first World War.

In June 1940 the U.S. Army Chief of Infantry revived the light rifle project to eliminate the pistol, and the Secretary of War approved the expenditure of funds on the project. On October 1, 1940 the Army published an invitation to all arms manufacturers and designers to submit weapons for the light rifle tests. The weapon was to be a five-pound rifle with a 300-yard effective range, capable of selective full- or semi-automatic fire, and be chambered for a .30-caliber cartridge similar to the .32 Winchester Self-Loader Rifle Model 1905 cartridge. The reasons for the choice of caliber are a complete mystery.

The .30 Carbine cartridge was suggested by Mr. Edwin Pugsley of Winchester, but why he suggested it or why the Army adopted it is very puzzling in the light of previous U.S. Army knowledge and experience. One of the inspirations for the light rifle, or "carbine" as it soon began to be called, was the .351 Winchester Self-Loading Rifle Model 1907 which had seen limited but effective, and illegal, service in World War I. Just eight years before, the Army had scrapped the .30 Pedersen devices for the '03 rifle because of the basic ineffectiveness of its ammunition. The Army was still familiar with the utter failure of the .38 revolver because of its inadequate caliber. There were still men around who remembered the basic inadequacy of the .38 revolver, and that the cal. .45 automatic pistol had been developed to overcome the .38's weaknesses.

The idea of adopting the basic cartridge design of the Winchester Self-Loading Rifle was excellent because the ammunition for this rifle had been in use since 1910 and was highly perfected. The Self-Loader cartridges were also an intermediate design between regular pistol and rifle ammunition, and that was exactly what was indicated for the new carbine. The Winchester Self-Loader was made in four calibers: .32 SLR, .35 SLR, .351 SLR and .401 SLR. The .351 had replaced the .35 in 1907 because the .35 wasn't quite enough of a cartridge, and the .401 had been brought out in 1910 in answer for requests for a more powerful model of the Self-Loader. One of the primary uses of the Self-Loader was among law enforcement agencies who needed a weapon more powerful and easier to handle than a pistol but still not as powerful as a military

M1 CARBINE

caliber rifle, and that is the requirement the new carbine would fill.

The cartridge the carbine was developed from was a modification of the .32 SLR round which fired a 110-grain bullet with the same profile as the .45 pistol cartridge bullet. The .30 Carbine cartridge was adopted without any developmental testing to speak of, and this is very unusual in the U.S. Army. If an ammunition development program had been conducted, it's a sure bet that modifications of the .351 and .401 Self-Loader cartridges with new lighter bullets would have been tried along with the .30 caliber cartridge. Then, perhaps, a .35- or .40-caliber carbine might have been adopted instead of the .30, and the biggest single deficiency in the carbine—its ammunition's ineffectiveness—would have been avoided.

The difficulty with .30 Carbine ammunition is that the bullet is too light, and frequently doesn't transfer enough energy to a target. The .30 Carbine bullet is also very stable in flight, and it tends to make a very clean hole in a target without doing much damage to it. As a military weapon on which men's lives can depend it should have all the shocking and damaging power possible, but it hasn't. Although the carbine was a popular weapon in World War 2, many men issued carbines replaced them with .45 pistols, .45 submachine guns and .30 M1 Garand rifles after using the carbine in combat. They did this simply because they wanted weapons with more stopping power.

One unusual weapon presented during the carbine tests did have enough stopping power and showed some men were thinking along those lines. It was a modification of the .45 automatic pistol with a special long barrel, a shoulder stock, and an extended magazine. This impractical weapon was dreamed up by Mr. Val Browning and submitted by Colt in late 1941, but it was withdrawn before it was tested.

The series of weapons submitted for the first tests under the original light rifle specifications included samples from Harrington and Richardson, Savage, Springfield Armory, Woodhull, Bendix Aviation and Auto-Ordinance (the makers of the Thompson), but none of these arms met the requirement. The Woodhull carbine was actually rebuilt from a Winchester Self-Loader! When the tests were completed in July 1941, the Springfield Armory and Bendix

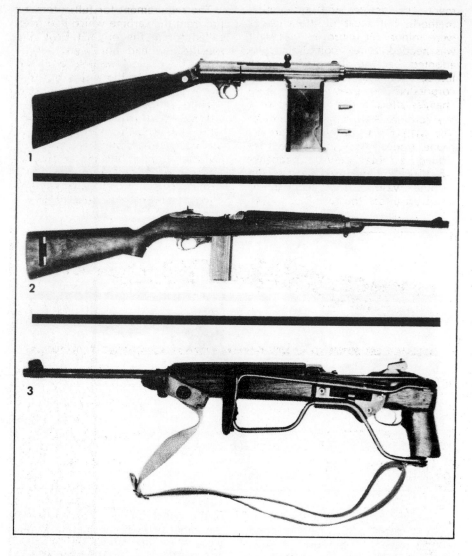

samples were selected for further development, while the other designs were dropped as unsatisfactory. However, the next trial sessions were left open for anyone who wanted to submit a new weapon for test if it met the specifications.

Several more carbines were submitted in the next several months including the Turner, the Hyde (the improved Bendix), the improved Springfield Armory, the Reising (an improved Harrington and Richardson), and the Winchester. The Winchester was a very simple weapon combining the Williams tappet gas operating system with the Garand rifle bolt system. In the experimental model, which was welded and brazed together in a manner totally unacceptable in a military weapon, the Winchester showed more merit than any other design. The Winchester was also easier to manufacture on the scale the Army wanted.

In carbine tests held in September 1941, the Winchester won hands down, and it was adopted by the Army with requirements for six minor changes, the most serious of which

was better and more rugged sights. In the light of production capability and reliability the Winchester designed U.S. Carbine Caliber .30 M1 was undoubtedly the best of the designs submitted. All told 6,117,827 .30 carbines were manufactured during World War 2, more than 30 percent more than the next most manufactured weapon: the .30 M1 Garand rifle!

During World War 2 the carbine went through a series of improve-

1. Smith & Wesson's 9mm light rifle built in 1940. It was foredoomed due to its caliber.

2. Second prototype Winchester carbine in .30 caliber. The design inherited many features from the old self-loader rifles, Models 1907 and 1910.

3. A production M1A1 carbine. This weapon was designed for paratroops.

4. Standard production configuration of the Caliber .30 M1 carbine. The M2 selective fire version had a heavier forend construction.

5. Drawing of the .30 carbine round. Tolerances were established February 21, 1941. Courtesy Winchester-Western Division, Olin Mathieson Chemical Corp.

ments in design and production methods, but most of the changes were minor. An improved rear sight was needed, a new bolt design was adopted because the original type lacked endurance, a bayonet was incorporated; however none of these changes affected the basic design of the carbine. A folding stock model (the M1A1) was developed for airborne troops. Accessories even included a rifle grenade launcher which was seldom used because the carbine wasn't strong enough to stand up under the recoil.

The requirement for full-automatic fire from the carbine which had been called for in the original light rifle specification had not been met by any of the original models, but it was not forgotten. In the spring of 1944, the Army adopted the selective-fire version as the U.S. Carbine Caliber .30 M2, and many earlier models were altered to this configuration. In any version the carbine was a handy, reliable weapon, but it wasn't an effective one. Although the U.S. Armed Forces kept using it until after the end of the Korean War and

many armies still use it, the carbine still lacks the stopping power it should have to be a really good military weapon, forever damning it in the eyes of modern armies.

Had the carbine been adopted in a larger caliber, it would have been a different story. Either a .35 or a .40 carbine would have had all the power the .30 caliber lacks, and there is no sound reason why the excellent Winchester carbine design couldn't have been built in either .35 or .40. The carbine would have been somewhat heavier in a larger caliber: about 5³⁄₄ pounds for the 35 caliber and 6¹⁄₂ pounds in 40 caliber as opposed to five pounds which the .30 caliber weighs. The additional weight would have tended to balance the somewhat heavier recoil of the larger calibers overcoming any complaints on that score, and the weight would still have been well within the light rifle category. The length of the carbine wouldn't have changed, but its ammunition would have been somewhat heavier. The effective range would have been reduced somewhat because of the ballistics of the heavier bullet in a larger caliber, but this would have had not real effect on the combat utility of the weapon.

Unfortunately the action of the .30 Carbine is too small to rework to a .35 or a .40 caliber, so building a carbine in either of these calibers would have been difficult, though many parts of the existing model could interchange. But the question of why the carbine is a .30 caliber weapon remains a puzzle. Why didn't the Army do any ammunition development and testing before the carbine was adopted? An ammunition development program would have added very little time or cost to the program, and it could have made the carbine a much more effective military weapon.

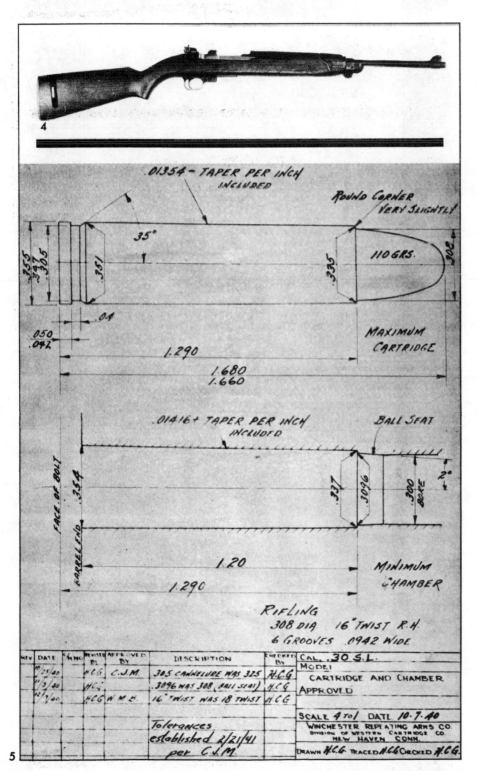

BALLISTIC TABLE

Carbine Cal.	Bullet Wt.	Muzzle Vel.	Stopping Power Factor*
.30	110 grs.	1950 fps	1
.35	130 grs.	1850 fps	1.5
.40	150 grs.	1750 fps	2

*Note: The stopping power factor is an old idea of the late Gen. Julian S. Hatcher. It rates the stopping power of a weapon by combining bullet weight, muzzle velocity, bullet diameter, and several other things of a very minor nature. It is a figure of merit for the shocking power of a given weapon, and Gen. Hatcher demonstrated that it works, and that caliber—the largest possible for the requirements—counts.

THE NEWTON STORY

ADVANCED THINKING BACKED BY MARGINAL FINANCES CUT SHORT THE CAREER OF CHARLES NEWTON'S PRODUCTS.

by Allen Bishop

It was an opressively warm, silent summer day in upstate New York. No wind shuffled the brilliantly green trees or the neat meadows, but flocks of birds intervened at broken intervals with their singing. Few sources of real noise had ever disturbed this quiet — the man-made types — and it would be some years before any would. A buggy maybe, now and then. There had been in recent years the deep-throated chug of a well-to-do motorist's Panhard-Levassor or Winton passing on a nearby dirt road now and then, however.

Most of the thinly distributed farming population in this region was quite used to the sounds of firearms being discharged occasionally; shotguns mostly, big 10-gauge doubles and smaller 12's and 20's especially in the early morning during the fall season. And rifles? Sure, who hadn't heard the somber crack of a .32-40 on the 200-yard offhand range? Real enthusiasts had even gathered one recent 4th of July to see the New Springfield rifle demonstrated by the State militia. What an event; especially when the troopers disconnected the cutoffs and discharged a rapid-fire staccato. Chances were good though, that if you were sharp enough to pinpoint the location of an isolated shooter, a cloud of white smoke would drift away in the wind that carried the sound with it.

Any listeners on this particular summer day were in for a surprise, however, because a gentleman from Buffalo had set up a 100-yard range of his own to do some unusual shooting. His Winchester High Wall single shot certainly didn't appear unusual as he settled it down into a pile of

blankets used for a rest. The 10X Malcolm scope was unusual, though. Those devices were expensive.

Suddenly, the air was penetrated by the snap of a small bullet travelling at an unheard-of velocity, followed instantaneously by the piercing muzzle blast of the rifle, sort of like the New Springfield rifle, but more like a firecracker.

With a quick, almost cadenced step, the shooter made his way out to his target. Light passed through a tiny hole, dead in the center of the bull. Of the bullet, nothing; blown to atoms on a rock outcropping which served as a backstop. Satisfied with the results, the shooter sat down in the grass and took off his hat, revealing a balding head, partly offset by a thick moustache. Most distinctive, though, were his sharp, penetrating eyes, which seemed to be

fixed on a point somewhere in the countryside. But Charles Newton, the lawyer from Buffalo, wasn't really studying the countryside — he was thinking.

The shooter of today should remember this man for what he really was: a successful wildcatter, one of that innovative breed here in America which includes names like Howe, Niedner, Roberts, Kilbourn, Donaldson, Dubiel, Gebby, Hutton, Ackley and others who were not content to blast away with loads from the ammunition factories. Many people parallel him with Roy Weatherby, which leaves Newton a seeming failure. Though he tried, he was never able to really produce a successful line of rifles for his advanced cartridge designs. Unlike Weatherby, Newton despite his training as a lawyer, was never able to handle business or

financial problems. Furthermore, a study of the literature published by Newton showed that he could be incredibly naive, and certain of his statements are downright humorous to the modern reader. Humorous, at times, naive, yes, but Charles Newton, the first commercial proponent of high velocity was not just a pipe dreamer or stupid.

Long before he began any commercial venture, Charles Newton did a lot of private experimentation with existing cartridges of his time, and no doubt with some of the very early "wildcat" loadings. Some of these loads were of his own concoction, while others were the developments of other experimenters. Most wildcats of that era were existing cases necked down to .22 or .25 caliber, since the arrival of stable smokeless powders had resulted in high-velocity enthusiasm. Following suit then, his initial success was a .22 centerfire, based on a rimmed case (the .25-35 Winchester) and adaptable to any strong single-shot at the time. A number evidently were built on a custom basis for interested parties, and in the single shots it was undoubtedly a good cartridge, even with the powders available at that time. All this began in 1905. In 1910 or 1911, Savage Arms Co. took notice of this cartridge, especially the relative ease with which it would adapt to the rotary magazine of their Model 99 lever-action rifles. It was adopted by them and became the

famous .22 Savage Hi-Power. Unlike today's .22 centerfires, its 70-grain bullet mikes out at .228-inch, instead of .223 or .224. For the reloader, it did not fill the bill in the lever action due to its rear-locking bolt which permitted too much case expansion when fired. Subsequent reloadings overworked the brass, and it was not safe to load the round to its ballistic potentials. Often referred to as the "Imp," many shooters agreed fully with that term, and not from a favorable standpoint. But in those halcyon days, the "new velocity" was as exciting as the "new morality." Early gun and hunting publications tell of its fantastic effects on big game, i.e. animals larger than deer. The game it *failed* to take probably runs two to one to that which was downed by it. Today, C.I.L., Canada's main cartridge producer, DWM and RWS in Germany still offer the .22 Savage. In Europe, where it gained some use, it is called the 5.6 x 52R (rimmed). The current Canadian load has a listed muzzle velocity of 2800 fps and a muzzle energy of 1220 ft.-lbs.; not too hot when compared with a modern .22 centerfire, but well within the safe limits of the Savage action.

Newton's second commercial effort came in 1912, again for Savage, and was one of his best designs. Certainly it has been the longest-lived, for what shooter hasn't heard of the .250-3000? This time, Newton started with the Mauser rimless case profile, shortened and necked down to hold

.257-inch bullets. The original factory loading had an 87-grain bullet, and wtih about 30 grains of the old Du Pont #21 powder, 3000 fps muzzle velocity was attained. Though this was a milestone, Newton evidently experimented with 100-grain bullets at .30-06 velocities, but Savage wanted the more spectacular figure. Again, this cartridge made its bow in the Model 99 where it gained tremendous popularity. One of the earliest specimens was tested by Townsend Whelen and his average of 10 groups, 10 shots each from rest at 100 yards averaged just under three inches — with peep sights. Along with this inherent accuracy was a low recoil, but a good, sharp muzzle blast; good psychology for

1. Cover of one of the numerous Catalogs issued by Newton. This is "A" from his second, or "Buffalo" Newton company. This catalog dates from the early 1920's.

2. An example of Newton's first design. This rifle has a very fine stock, both in design and figure. It has the optional striker-mounted peep sight.

3. A first model Newton rifle with optional engraving and additional stock checkering. All Newton rifles had set triggers.

4. A second model, or "Buffalo" Newton rifle. Note unusual set trigger design and bolt handle profile. The front sight is not original. These later Newton rifles generally are not of the same quality as the earlier versions.

THE NEWTON STORY

the shooter. Unfortunately, the little 87-grain pellets were effective on larger game only under the best of conditions. It was not until 1932 that Peters Cartridge Company introduced the 100-grain load.

At the tail end of World War 1, Savage introduced their Model 20 bolt-action sporter, the first quantity-produced sporting arm of that type of action in the U.S. It was in this and subsequent bolt-action rifles, commercial and custom that the .250-3000 further sustained its reputation for being versatile especially on different game. Recently, in the current wave of nostalgia Savage reintroduced the .250-300 in the Model 99.

Newton's two successes with Sav-

age no doubt gave him confidence in his ability because it was not long after — shortly before World War 1 — that he began to develop his own line of cartridges which would bear his own name, and eventually his own rifles for them. Naturally, we have condensed a considerable span of time and work down to a few words, the results of which were nonetheless far-sighted and in many ways practical.

When his company became a reality, at least on paper, Newton contracted with the ammunition companies of the day to produce given quantities of his designs. Both the U.S. Cartridge Company and the Union Metallic Cartridge Company did so, these early loads being head-stamped "Newton Arms Co." along

with the caliber. Later, Remington (ex-UMC) and Western continued to market the .256, .30 and .35 Newton rounds until World War 2 offered the opportunity to rid themselves of these and some other limited-demand calibers. Newton ammo of the 1920-1940 period is relatively scarce, which indicates that smaller lots were produced. There weren't enough Newtons floating around to shoot up large amounts, especially in the .30 and .35 calibers, though the .256 had limited popularity. These examples of inventiveness and advanced thinking bear some detailed examination.

One of the best-known American gunsmiths of the early 1900's was Fred Adolph, who based himself in Genoa, New York for many years.

1. Closeup of a first model Newton. The styling was very advanced for the time—circa World War 1. Both front and rear sights were mounted by bands.

2. First type Newton stripped. The floorplate was released and rotated, unscrewing the barrel/receiver from the stock. An interesting design, but production tolerances could not keep bedding tight enough.

3. Newton and Springfield sporters compared. The Newton is more slender and lighter by a pound.

4. Barrel markings on the first model Newton. All Newton rifles have very low serial numbers: roughly 6000 of the first model were produced. The last lot was assembled by the person who assumed control of the first company after its failure and are reputedly of poor quality.

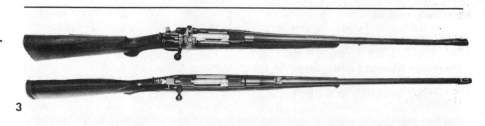

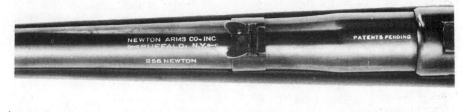

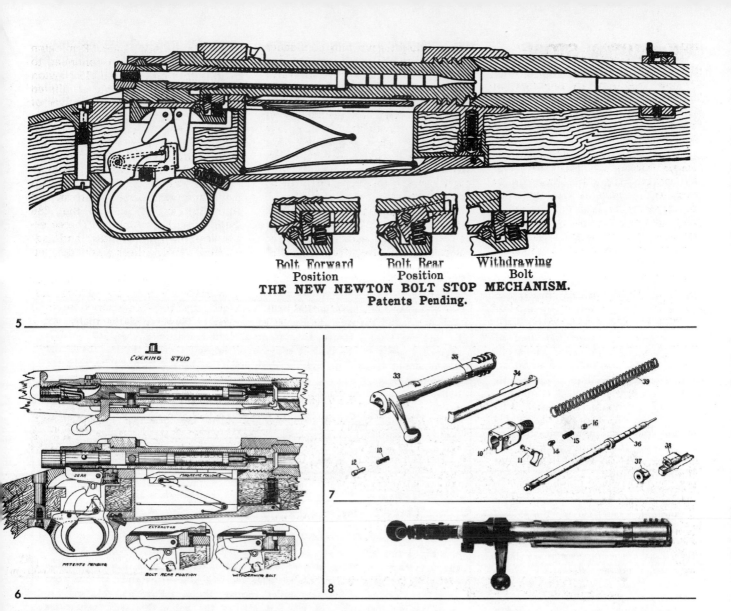

THE NEW NEWTON BOLT STOP MECHANISM.
Patents Pending.

Bolt Forward Position   Bolt Rear Position   Withdrawing Bolt

5

COCKING STUD

6

7

8

5. *Original sectional drawing of the first model Newton. Note the multiple lugs on the bolt and unique set trigger design. Below the chamber is the single-screw bedding layout.*

6. *Cutaway of the second Newton rifle. The setting trigger faced rearward. The same system of bedding was used. The bolt stop (inset) evidently gave trouble on these rifles, the stop piece was not properly hardened and would wear from the bolt body striking it during operation.*

7. *First type bolt fully dismantled. The extractor is similar to a Mauser.*

8. *First type Newton bolt showing its seven forward, and two rear lugs. The safety wing is on the right side of the striker head.*

He possessed tremendous talent, and built combination and double rifles which followed the best European style of the time. Around 1912-13, he had Newton develop a powerful .30-caliber load for custom rifles. A true "proprietary" round, empty brass was constructed in Europe for it, most likely by DWM, but ultimately loaded here by Adolph according

to demand. These cases, naturally, had Berdan primers, and the complete round was named the "Adolph Express." How many rifles were made for it is not known, but the count would be very low if tallied. Shortly thereafter, when Newton established his first commercial venture, he retained the design, simply calling it the .30 Newton. The .30 Newton did not survive the demise of his rifles for very long, but in retrospect, it stands as the first all-American .30-caliber "magnum" load to be produced in quantity. Had this cartridge been available in a non-takedown bolt-action rifle weighing a minimum of say, eight pounds with scope, the .30 Newton just might still be with us. The lightweight, takedown Newton rifles however, whacked the average person just a bit too hard for comfortable shooting. Again, Townsend Whelen enters the picture with 100-yard test results on this cartridge: two groups measuring 5½ and 9 inches with iron sights. These not especially encouraging spreads were produced

sometime during the World War 1 era with what the Dean of American Rifleman states was "Newton factory ammunition". This would place them as being from a very early commercial load put up by U.M.C. or the U.S. Cartridge Co. The bullet used in this case was the Newton-designed 172-grain flat-base spitzer with a muzzle velocity of 3000 fps and a muzzle energy of 3440 ft.-lbs. So here we have a .30 with ballistics comparable to the current .300 H&H loads, and only slightly below the .300 Winchester Magnum. The one big difference is the generally fine rifles the last two had for them from their very inception.

Carrying this theme one step further, Newton also offered the .35 Newton. On paper, this round — the .30 Newton necked up — would surpass the .375 H&H in velocity and energy, but with lighter bullets. Again, the proper rifle was lacking. Though we have never fired either a .30 or .35 Newton, contemporary reports are sufficiently vivid in their descriptions of the recoil these two

THE NEWTON STORY

generated. The slender combs on the Newton rifles must have given the shooter's cheek a working over, not to mention his shoulder.

The .35 Newton is listed in his company's catalogs as having a 250-grain bullet with a muzzle velocity of 2975 fps and an initial energy of 4925 ft.-lbs. Newton gives the load as 67 grains of DuPont #10 or #15; both were early slow-burning nitro powders. Later, 270- and 300-grain bullets were used in it.

In relation to these two loads, Newton really comes through in his ability for making understatements. The 14th edition of his first company's catalog says this about the .30 Newton: *"The recoil of this rifle is not noticeably heavier than that of the Springfield rifle using the same weight of bullet"* and goes on to quote Colonel (then Lieutenant) Whelen's more favorable comments on the rifle. Whelen, however, stated, that the .30 Newton had heavy recoil for the unaccustomed shooter, in his book *The American Rifle*, but that it would not be noticed under hunting conditions.

Newton's comments about his .35 are more candid yet: *"The .35 Newton, when used in a 7½-pound Mauser, shoots fairly pleasantly, the recoil not being noticeably above that of a 12-gauge shotgun with a trap load, fired at a stationary target, and good target work at 200 yard offhand can be done with it. Here we have a rifle equal to the elephant gun in energy, far superior in killing power, due to its higher velocity,*

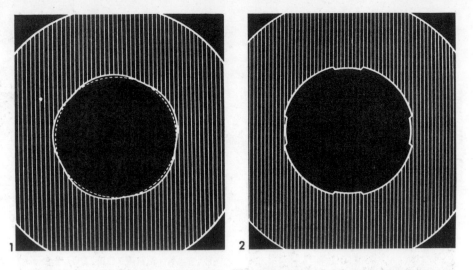

1

2

None of the above devices will work properly here, since there is not enough friction between the copper of the jacket, however weakened it may be, and the tissues struck, to prevent a clean puncture. When soft lead is exposed directly to the flesh it clings upon impact, tearing the lead back and mushrooming the bullet, and the flesh itself is thrown forward, tearing the adjoining tissues, resulting in a wound such as the .22 Savage high power bullet has made familiar to all.

To meet this condition Mr. Newton has designed and patented the Newton Patent Protected Point Spitzer bullet the principle of which is readily seen from the cuts.

FIG. 1   FIG. 2

PATENTED MAY 12, 1914

Fig. 1 consists of a jacket brought well toward the bullet point, by which the upsettage on firing is prevented, with a copper wire inserted in the center of the point. This copper wire receives and withstands all the accidental batterings which the bullet receives in handling, and stiffens the point against bending, yet when it strikes the game this wire penetrates like a needle, thus letting the flesh strip back the lead point and mushroom the bullet without difficulty. The wire itself, as soon as the bullet is

3

1. Newton's segmental rifling, similar to Metford type. Newton praised the ease with which it was cleaned and said it deformed the bullet less.

2. Standard rifling which Newton considered inferior. He also employed a ratchet type of rifling in later designs because of longer life.

3. Drawings of two Newton bullet designs. The soft noses were protected by sunken wire.

4. From left: .256 Newton; .30 Newton; .35 Newton. At far right is the .276 Enfield which Newton at one time planned to commercialize. Both the .256 and .30 rounds are Western loads with hollow point bullets. The .35 is an example of the post-war Speer load made in limited quantities.

5. Newton cartridge designs, from left: .40; .35; .33; .30; .280; .256 256; .250 Savage; .22; .22 Hi-Power. Only the .250 Savage survives, recently being revived by Savage Arms. The .22 Savage Hi-Power is still loaded in Canada by CIL.

6. At left is the 20-round box into which Speer packaged his .35 loads. At right is a pre-war box of .256.

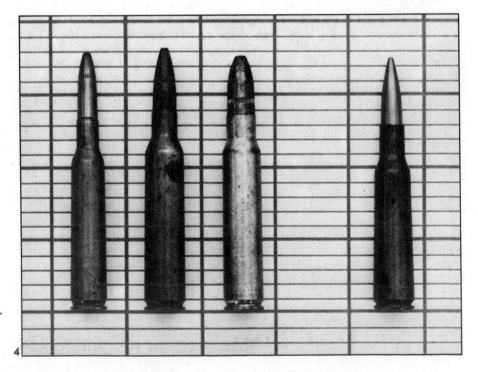

4

light enough to be carried by the sportsman himself, and free from disagreeable recoil. Its accuracy is of the best and for those who wish the most powerful rifle they can get it is just what they want." So be it. Note that Newton's wording says "7½-pound Mauser". The rifle he was comparing directly his .35 to was the .450-3¼" Nitro Express, the "rifle (singular) for which weighs 12 pounds, must be carried by a gunbearer, and almost kicks the shoulder off."

First of all, few .450 doubles weighed more than 10 pounds, and we tend to think a fine English double might just be a little better balanced than the average Newton rifle. Now without even going into the ancient "high-velocity" versus "big-caliber" argument, let it be simply stated that anyone who tried to take on an elephant with one of Newton's patent bullet designs hopefully had someone

with a .450 backing him up! We have, on occasion, fired the .450-3¼" Nitro, and though it has a tremendous muzzle blast, the recoil did not almost kick our shoulders off! Despite these somewhat acid criticisms of Newton's promotional writings, the same statement we made about the .30 Newton applies in regards to the .35: Had a proper rifle been built for it, it very likely would be with us today. Its ballistics are in no way obsolete, and with modern powders and bullets, would be even better.

Again, referring to catalog "A" of Newton's second company, we find that he planned to offer target, midrange and short range loadings of the .30 and .35 cartridges. The target loads were attempts, evidently, to duplicate .30-06 ballistics, the .30 round using a 180-grain full-jacket bullet, the .35 a 200-grain full-jacket. The midrange loads were to du-

plicate the .30-30 and .35 Remington in the .30 and .35 Newton cases respectively. Short-range loadings of the two duplicated, according to Newton, revolver ballistics. The .30 and .35 used a 115-grain and 170-grain bullets respectively at about 1000 fps. If any of these reduced loads were produced, the numbers were precious few.

Evidenlty, the .35 Newton received at least one instance of baptisim under fire, Newton quoting the famed African hunter, Charles Cottar as using one to take a rhino "striking it in the stern, the bullets raking its body the entire length and coming out the chest."

Two of Newton's cartridges which were developed bu only saw very limited distribution were the .22 Newton and .33 Newton. The .22 Newton is listed as having a muzzle velocity of 3100 fps with an energy

THE NEWTON STORY

of 1921 ft. lbs. with a 90-grain bullet. Not bad, by anybody's standards, even today. Charles Newton thought it was especially nice. *"Think of a .22 caliber rifle of power equal to the .405 Winchester at 300 yards and more powerful beyond that range."* Think of it. However, the .22 Newton was developed almost simultaneously with the famous .256 Newton, and the latter cartridge was given preference over it commercially.

The second aborted Newton round was the .33. Of it, Newton says the following in his 14th edition catalog: *"The .33 Newton we have decided to abandon as there was very little demand for it, most sportsmen who wanted anything more powerful than our .30 caliber taking the .35 caliber. While the expense of placing this cartridge on the market was comparatively (?) trivial, yet in the absence of a considerable demand, dealers would not carry the cartridges and the sportsmen would be obliged to send to the factory for them. In fact we think the sportsmen are logical in that anyone requiring anything more powerful than the .30 might as well go to the .35, as the weight of the rifle is no more and the recoil*

not at all serious." Damn those dealers! Probably the differences in recoil between the .33 and .35 were negligible — take your choice, both were heavy.

Very little information remains on the .33 Newton. The late Phil Sharpe stated in his book, *The Rifle in America* that he had some notes in his files on this round which said the round had a 200-grain bullet, 3000 fps. muzzle velocity and 4000 ft.-lbs. energy. The same ballistic figures are given in the Newton catalog, 14th edition, so he may have found the information there originally. He had evidently discussed the load with Newton, but Sharpe at that time (1937), had ever seen the round. No doubt a few were made and possibly were just the .30 Newton necked up. However, it looks like our .338 Winchester existed, at least in prototype form, around 1914!

Three cartridges mentioned in various pieces of Newton literature are the .276, .280 and .40. It is highly doubtful if they ever went beyond the "pipe dream" stage, though there is a steel engraving by Western of the .280 Newton, so they could have made a few. The .276 is described in a small 12-page supplement to the

14th edition of the Newton Arms Company's catalog. All in the world it amounted to, was the .276 British, developed experimentally for the Pattern 13 Enfield rifle just prior to World War 1. Newton evidently planned to load the British-developed case with American primers, powder and bullets. No doubt it would have been an outstanding 7mm round. Newton stated that *"Not until our own cartridge factory is running, which will be in February, 1917, can we manufacture these cartridges and develop the charges."* He hoped to better the British ballistics somewhat, as their loadings used cordite, a wholly unsuitable propellent for such a case. The .276 was dropped due to World War 1, but the P-13 became the P-14 in .303 British and later, the design in .30-06 became the U.S. M1917. The Newton never was.

But at the time he envisioned all this, he stated flatly that the .276 would become the British military round after the war. A simple, clever plan unfolds in his words, *"In view of the tendency of the Briton, both at home and abroad to use the army cartridge for sporting purposes, coupled with the fine design of the cartridge itself, we have decided to bore and chamber our rifles for it,*

ORIGINAL BALLISTIC FIGURES OF NEWTON CARTRIDGES

Cartridge	Bullet Weight (grs.)	muzzle	Velocity (fps.) 100 yds.	200 yds.	300 yds.	muzzle	Energy (ft.-lbs.) 100 yds.	200 yds.	300 yds.
.22 Savage	70	2800	2453	2131	1833	1190	911	687	510
.22 Newton	90	3103	2891	2689	2496	1921	1660	1445	1247
.250-3000 Savage	87	3000	2657	2340	2042	1740	1375	1061	783
.256 Newton	123	3103	2891	2689	2495	2632	2288	1980	1709
.256 Newton	129	2964	2758	2562	2375	2528	2193	1883	1625
.256 Newton	140	2920	2729	2552	2387	2660	2310	2030	1778
.276 Newton	165	3000	2817	2642	2474	3300	2920	2557	2244
.280 Newton	160	3000	2809	2625	2450	3200	2816	2464	2144
.30 Newton	150	3208	2950	2707	2477	3445	2910	2445	2040
.30 Newton	172	3000	2804	2631	2439	3440	3010	2618	2287
.30 Newton	180	3000	2812	2632	2460	3600	3168	2772	2430
.30 Newton	225	2610	2470	2333	2202	3470	3060	2723	2430
.33 Newton	200	3000	2758	2530	2312	4000	3400	2852	2382
.35 Newton	250	2975	2737	2512	2297	4925	4175	3500	2950
.40 Newton	350 ?	3042	2784	2541	2310	6180	5220	4320	3570

The accompanying ballistic chart of the Newton-designed loads, real and pipe dream, was compiled from several editions and supplements of his catalogs. He claimed that all figures were obtained with his standard 24-inch barrels, but the oft-repeated "magic" 3000 fps muzzle velocity makes the reader a bit suspicious. His .250 Savage being the first commercial cartridge to achieve this initial velocity was quite an accomplishment at the time, and Newton evidently didn't want anyone to forget it! The .276 figures were copied from available British figures by Newton, and "adjusted" by him to what he felt would be the performance with nitro powders.

Ballistics for the .40 Newton are quite interesting — and maybe just a little fantastic. No doubt such figures could be achieved today, but not with a cartridge of a necked-up .35 Newton's capacity, without having some exotic pressure figures. They are given in the 14th edition of his catalog, but the bullet is listed as a "H.P." only. Later editions do not list this caliber.

The remaining figures seem realistic, and it can be seen that the .256 and .30 Newton cartridges used a variety of bullets at different times. The Western loadings of these are almost invariably found with hollow-point bullets.

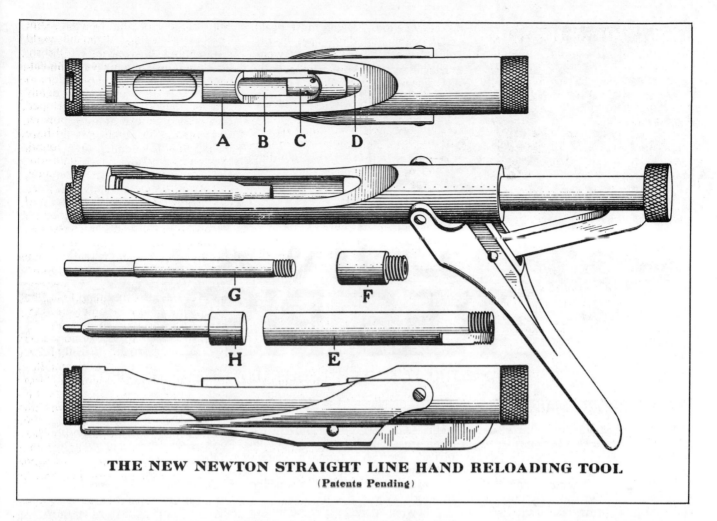

THE NEW NEWTON STRAIGHT LINE HAND RELOADING TOOL
(Patents Pending)

principally for the benefit of our customers in Great Britain and the Colonies."

The .280 Newton is described in "Catalog A" of the Buffalo Newton Rifle Company (Newton's second organization) circa 1920. Here Newton states that the fine .256 *"fell a little below requirements for an ideal game cartridge,"* and thus the reason for the .280. Never having actually seen a .280 Newton we can only surmise, but the following statement, again Newton sums up his intentions! *"Although the shell is of different form the caliber and powder space of this shell are the same as the .280 Ross."* Earlier to this Newton had decried the Ross round as being too large in capacity.

From all appearances the .280 was created by necking the .30 Newton down to 7mm.

"We offer the .280 Newton rifle in full confidence that it will speedily become the standard big game and target rifle of the sporting world." Ballistics with a 160-grain bullet were stated as being 3000 fps, and 3200

ft.-lbs. energy. Around 42 years later, Remington announced a new round, the 7mm Remington Magnum. Ballistics? With 175-grain bullet, 3070 fps at the muzzle, 3660 ft.-lbs. energy! And the 7mm Remington Magnum certainly hasn't left the makers "in the red."

Least known of the Newton cartridges is the .40. The "Supplement to Catalogue B" of the Buffalo Newton Company says that they have been too busy setting up for manufacture to bother with it, but that it would use a 350-grain spitzer bullet in a necked-up .35 Newton case at 2800 fps muzzle velocity, with 6125 ft.-lbs. energy. Nice — but not in a Newton product. It's very doubtful if any were ever made, except in experimental form. By this time, the last Newton company was going rapidly and the end was near.

Of all the cartridges which Charles Newton developed for his *own* rifles, the .256 was undoubtedly the best, this round coming to light about 1915. Originally, bullets no heavier than about 130 grains could be used in the .256 rifles, due to their 1-in-10 rifling twist. The earliest loadings had a 123-grain bullet but the final load used a 129-grain. The later "Buffalo Newton" rifles had a 1-in-8 twist,

permitting a 140-grain bullet to be utilized. The .256 is based on the Springfield '06 case, necked to 6.5mm. However, it is shorter in length than the current 6.5/06 variety of wildcats. The Newton rifles adapted perfectly to the recoil, etc. of the .256, and its popularity alone no doubt was a major factor, at times, in tiding Newton over for his mistakes, financial and otherwise. Like other early high-velocity loadings, the Newton was pushed well beyond its sensible game-stopping limits, but somehow managed to come out smelling more like a rose than the others. Though decidedly superior to the .250-3000, it was unfortunately never adopted by one of the major rifle companies, and the .270 Winchester (introduced 1925) and the .257 Remington-Roberts (introduced 1934) pretty well finished off this pioneer development. At the risk of being really repetitious, we can say that the .256 Newton might, too, still be on the available list today had not circumstances been against it from the start.

Today, the surviving Newton products represent an important and interesting segment in the development of the modern sporting cartridge and rifle.

EUROPEAN FREE PISTOLS

AN UNUSUAL AND THUSFAR MUCH NEGLECTED FIELD FOR THE COLLECTOR

BY THEODORE MAINO

Collecting is a passion. The collecting of guns goes a step further to become an all-encompassing passion. The author was first exposed before World War 2, and during that time and after the war, he collected anything that struck his fancy.

He gradually settled down to collecting the European free pistols when he purchased a Flobert pistol in mint condition. After this find, he purchased a German .22 caliber free pistol and the hunt was on.

Presently, 68 free pistols make up the collection. The most important items are the free pistols made in Germany between 1890 and 1942. The author now has 46 German-made .22 caliber single-shot pistols of every type, from a copy of the Stevens through Floberts to superb Tells, Lunas and Records. These were the pistols that dominated Olympic competitions before World War 2. In addition, the author has six pistols from additional European countries other than Germany.

Ernest Frederick Buchel originated the famous William Tell pistol which won the World's Championships at Rome in 1911 and Biarritz in 1912, and again at Camp Perry in 1913. This pistol held its position as the premier free pistol through the years, culminating with the World's Championships at Reims in 1924 and in Rome in 1926.

Buchel then brought out a new pistol, the Luna, similar to the Tell, but with a different cocking lever to continue his domination of world free pistol competition. The Buchel firm was taken over by Udo Anschutz of Zella-Mellis, whose record match pistol smashed all records in Berlin in 1936. The U.A.Z. Company continued to make the Luna along with the Record until all such work was halted by World War 2.

Following World War 2, the firm of Hammerli in Lenzburg, Switzerland, took over the leading position held by Udo Anschutz with their excellent match pistols.

World records were made at the 1947 Championships in Caracas, in the 1948 Olympics in London, the 1949 World Championships in Buenos Aires, the 1950 World Championships in Guatemala, the 1951 World Championships in Cairo, the 1952 World Championships in Oslo, the 1952 Olympic Games in Helsinki, the 1956 Olympics at Melbourne, the 1957 International Match Week in Lucerne, the 1958 World Championships in Moscow, again in 1959 at Caracas, the 1959 World Championships at Milan, the 1960 World Championships at Emmen and the 1962 World Championships at Kingston, Jamaica.

The presently available Hammerli 106 is still one of the finest competition pistols made; having continued its domination of World and Olympic Championships through 1964 at the Tokyo Olympic Games.

The Russian Vostok TOZ-35 is included in this section because it is the leading free pistol in use today. It made its first appearance outside the USSR in 1962 at the World Championships at Cairo, where Vladimir Stolypin used it to win the Gold Medal in the 50-meter event. Since Cairo, this pistol has won gold medals in nearly every International and Olympic meet.

This piece has a most unusual trigger. It can be adjusted to fire from pressure in any direction, by rotating a tilting table which, when moved by the trigger action releases the sear. The entire trigger mechanism can be removed intact by undoing a screw situated in the fore-end and removing one pin. Once removed, the tilting table can be set so that the pistol can be fired by moving the trigger forward, backward or sideways—in fact, in any direction through the complete circle of 360 degrees.

Many free pistols were made by recognized manufacturers, and are so marked, but a greater number were apparently made by individual gunsmiths to personal specifications of the buyer; some being copies of the designs of recognized gun manufacturers, others were personal designs of private 'smiths. Some of these items are found without any markings as to who made them or where they were made. Others are recognizable by their fine workmanship and German proof marks. Many free pistols were made for the dedicated sportsman—at his special request—and these pistols will remain one-of-a-kind specimens.

1. The Hammerli match pistol Model 106; basically the Hammerli that started winning world championships in 1947. This model has an improved trigger pull, adjustable between 5 and 100 grams. McLain Photography.

2. Rare ball-handled pistol in .22 caliber with shotgun-type action and outside hammer similar to a cap and ball pistol. Made by Max G. Fisher of Berlin, this custom-made piece sports an 11⅛" tapered, fluted octagon barrel and a single set adjustable trigger.

3. A one-of-a-kind free pistol made by U.A.Z., the famous German pistol maker, successors to Buchel of Tell fame. Basically a Tell pistol with a 15¾" octagon barrel and a full-length walnut stock. This fine pistol is marked H. Scherping, Hanover. The original owner's name is engraved on a plate inletted on the front of the grip. The single set trigger is set by the large side lever, the smaller top lever is for removing the action.

4. Kommer original Meister-D.R.G.M., a falling block pistol with 14½" octagon barrel. This pistol has fully-carved rosewood grips and the finest engraving of any free pistol the author has seen, save the one below. Single set trigger is set with lever shown just above trigger.

5. This pistol by George Knaak has the same beautiful engraving, but more conventional wood work. Barrel is octagon, 14½" long. Falling block is dropped by pulling on trigger guard. Action is removed by turning lever.

EUROPEAN FREE PISTOLS

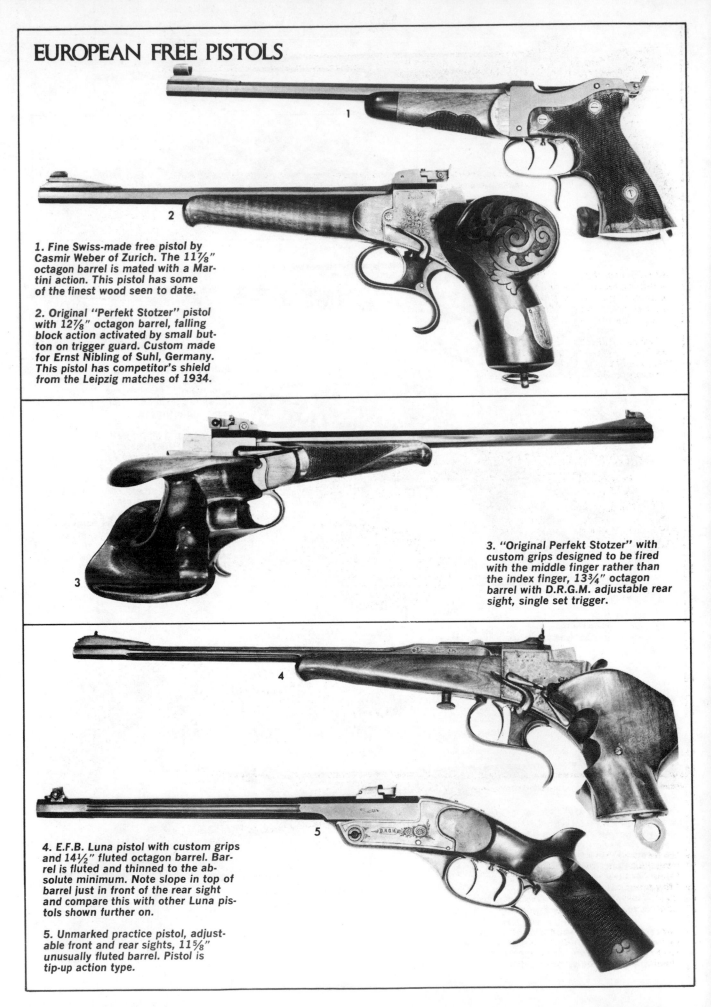

1. Fine Swiss-made free pistol by Casmir Weber of Zurich. The 11⅞" octagon barrel is mated with a Martini action. This pistol has some of the finest wood seen to date.

2. Original "Perfekt Stotzer" pistol with 12⅞" octagon barrel, falling block action activated by small button on trigger guard. Custom made for Ernst Nibling of Suhl, Germany. This pistol has competitor's shield from the Leipzig matches of 1934.

3. "Original Perfekt Stotzer" with custom grips designed to be fired with the middle finger rather than the index finger, 13¾" octagon barrel with D.R.G.M. adjustable rear sight, single set trigger.

4. E.F.B. Luna pistol with custom grips and 14½" fluted octagon barrel. Barrel is fluted and thinned to the absolute minimum. Note slope in top of barrel just in front of the rear sight and compare this with other Luna pistols shown further on.

5. Unmarked practice pistol, adjustable front and rear sights, 11⅝" unusually fluted barrel. Pistol is tip-up action type.

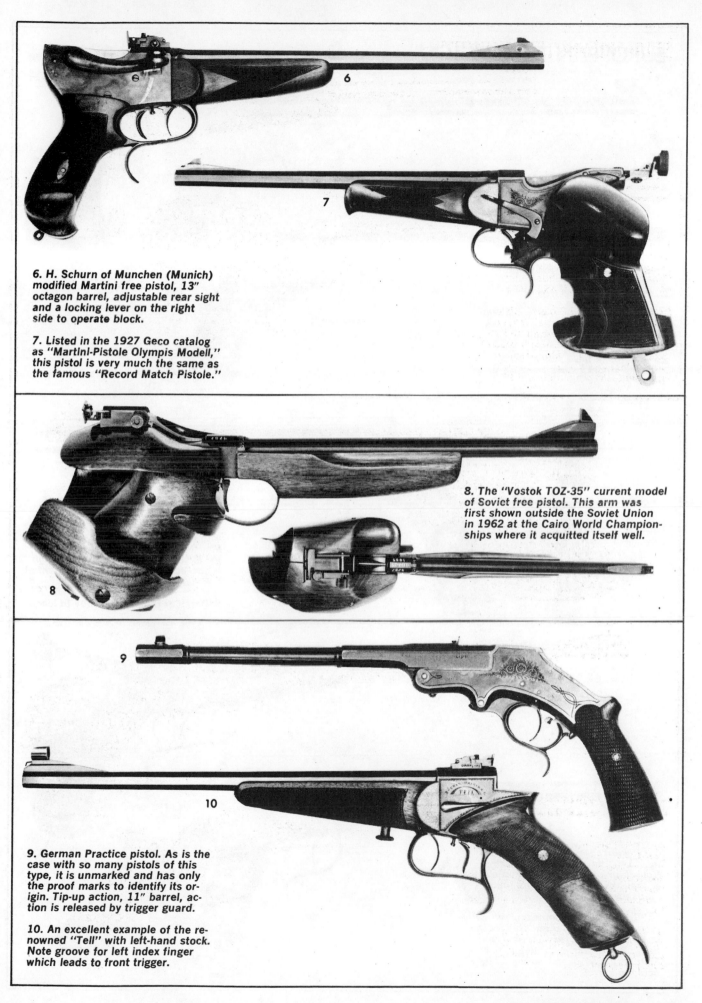

6. H. Schurn of Munchen (Munich) modified Martini free pistol, 13" octagon barrel, adjustable rear sight and a locking lever on the right side to operate block.

7. Listed in the 1927 Geco catalog as "Martini-Pistole Olympis Modell," this pistol is very much the same as the famous "Record Match Pistole."

8. The "Vostok TOZ-35" current model of Soviet free pistol. This arm was first shown outside the Soviet Union in 1962 at the Cairo World Championships where it acquitted itself well.

9. German Practice pistol. As is the case with so many pistols of this type, it is unmarked and has only the proof marks to identify its origin. Tip-up action, 11" barrel, action is released by trigger guard.

10. An excellent example of the renowned "Tell" with left-hand stock. Note groove for left index finger which leads to front trigger.

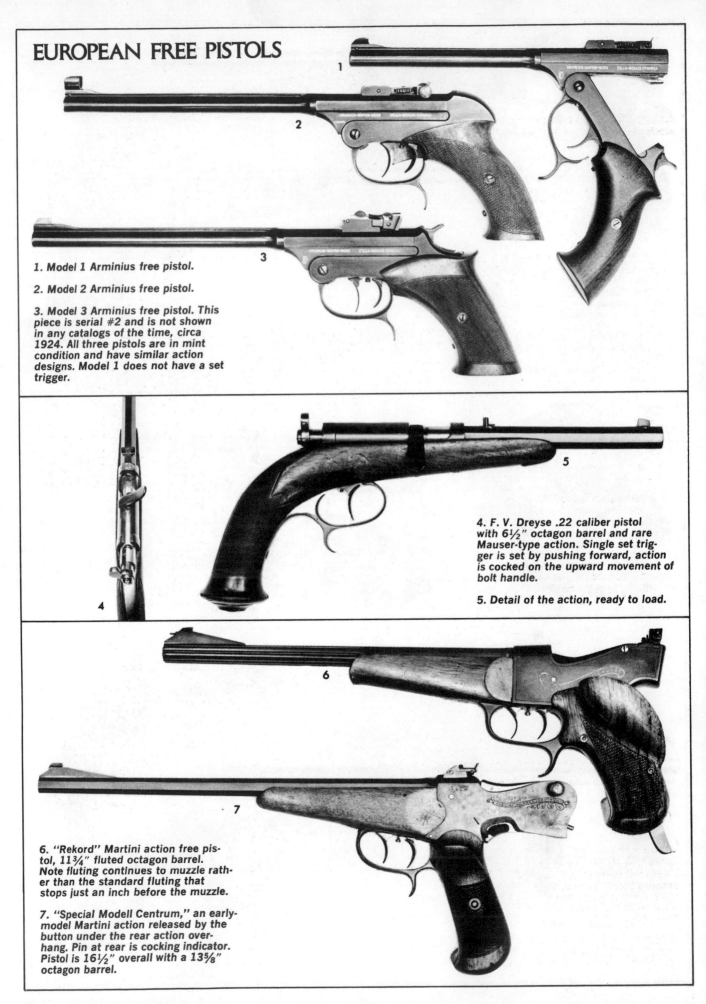

EUROPEAN FREE PISTOLS

1. Model 1 Arminius free pistol.

2. Model 2 Arminius free pistol.

3. Model 3 Arminius free pistol. This piece is serial #2 and is not shown in any catalogs of the time, circa 1924. All three pistols are in mint condition and have similar action designs. Model 1 does not have a set trigger.

4. F. V. Dreyse .22 caliber pistol with 6½" octagon barrel and rare Mauser-type action. Single set trigger is set by pushing forward, action is cocked on the upward movement of bolt handle.

5. Detail of the action, ready to load.

6. "Rekord" Martini action free pistol, 11¾" fluted octagon barrel. Note fluting continues to muzzle rather than the standard fluting that stops just an inch before the muzzle.

7. "Special Modell Centrum," an early-model Martini action released by the button under the rear action overhang. Pin at rear is cocking indicator. Pistol is 16½" overall with a 13⅝" octagon barrel.

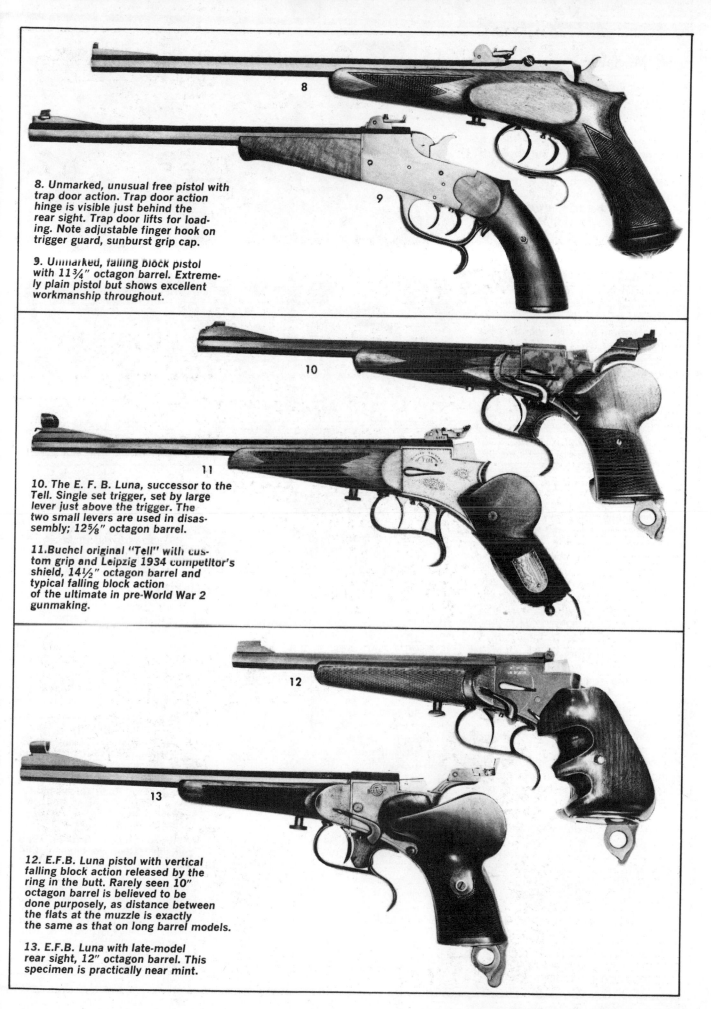

8. Unmarked, unusual free pistol with trap door action. Trap door action hinge is visible just behind the rear sight. Trap door lifts for loading. Note adjustable finger hook on trigger guard, sunburst grip cap.

9. Unmarked, falling block pistol with 11¾" octagon barrel. Extremely plain pistol but shows excellent workmanship throughout.

10. The E. F. B. Luna, successor to the Tell. Single set trigger, set by large lever just above the trigger. The two small levers are used in disassembly; 12⅝" octagon barrel.

11. Buchel original "Tell" with custom grip and Leipzig 1934 competitor's shield, 14½" octagon barrel and typical falling block action of the ultimate in pre-World War 2 gunmaking.

12. E.F.B. Luna pistol with vertical falling block action released by the ring in the butt. Rarely seen 10" octagon barrel is believed to be done purposely, as distance between the flats at the muzzle is exactly the same as that on long barrel models.

13. E.F.B. Luna with late-model rear sight, 12" octagon barrel. This specimen is practically near mint.

by W. M. Hawley

In 1543 a Portuguese trader put into Tanegashima, an island off the west coast of Japan, after being driven off course by a storm.

He wanted food and water which were supplied to him by the governor of the island.

He carried with him a matchlock gun, and as no guns had ever been seen in Japan, he demonstrated it for the governor who instantly recognized its value as a weapon and tried to buy it. The trader refused to sell claiming that he had to have it to supply his crew with food, but the governor persisted, making all sorts of offers which the trader continued to refuse. Finally, the governor, perhaps to soften him up, put on a big going-away feast complete with music, drinks and geisha.

At this feast the trader got a glimpse of the governor's daughter who was an outstanding beauty. That did it! He offered to trade the gun for the daughter! To make a long story short, the governor finally gave in and the trader gave instructions in how to make the barrels and gunpowder and took the girl to Portugal, where he married her.

Immediately, the governor set up a factory for the manufacture of guns which became known as Tanegashima from the location of the factory.

With one or two exceptions, the copying of the lock presented no difficulty to the Japanese, who were superb craftsmen. The steel coiled spring baffled them so they substituted the folded brass spring that is characteristic of these weapons for most of the time they were made. Plugging the barrel also gave trouble as they had no way of cutting threads at first.

When flintlocks were introduced later, some were made and some of the matchlocks were converted, but somehow they never replaced the older matchlock mechanism which continued to be made right up to the Restoration in 1868. The same can be said of the wheellock and percussion.

Actually, guns, though accepted as necessary weapons, were never considered sporting and never replaced the sword as the main fighting weapon. Also, they were almost useless in the rain.

Many types were developed, all individually handcrafted, ranging from a whole assortment of pistols of from one to four barrels; pistols concealed

TANEGASHIMA
JAPANESE MATCHLOCKS

in various ways as fans, writing kits, etc.; a pistol attached to the side of a sword; and even a tiny 2-inch working model used as a toggle (netsuke) to hold a pouch or *inro* suspended from the sash.

Hand cannon that weighed from 15 pounds up to 40 pounds also were produced to batter down gates, etc.

Nearly all models were decorated with brass inlay on the stocks reminiscent of the Near-East Arab guns, and with sometimes very elaborate inlay of gold, silver, copper and brass on the barrels.

Bore varies considerably, as do lengths, weight, styles of muzzle, and all other features. Nothing seems to have been standardized. In fact it is hard to find two identical guns. The hand cannon had bores that ranged from about 5/8-inch to 2 inches or more.

The Japanese described the size of the gun by the weight of the ball in momme (.1325 oz.). A 1 momme ball

would be 8.517mm in diameter.

Most gun barrels were signed. Signatures were concealed by the stock. Many signatures have been faked—the "Honcho Buki Meikan" lists 112 names that have been faked on guns. There are probably more. 🏵

BIBLIOGRAPHY

Ko Ju (Old Guns) by Yoshioka Shinichi 1965. English introduction and index. 112 pages 7½" x 10". Out of print. Illustrated

Hinawa-ju (Fire Rope Guns) by Tokoro 1965. Well illustrated. No English. 240 pages 6" x 8½" Available about $12.00

Hojutsu (Gunnery) by Yasunari 1965 Well illustrated. No English. 264 pages 6" x 8½" Available about $12.00

Koju Jiten (Dict. of Old Guns) Quite the most thorough book on old Japanese guns and foreign prototypes. 270 pages & 4 color plates. Mostly illustrations with many detailed photos and drawings of locks. No English. 6" x 9" Available about $16.00

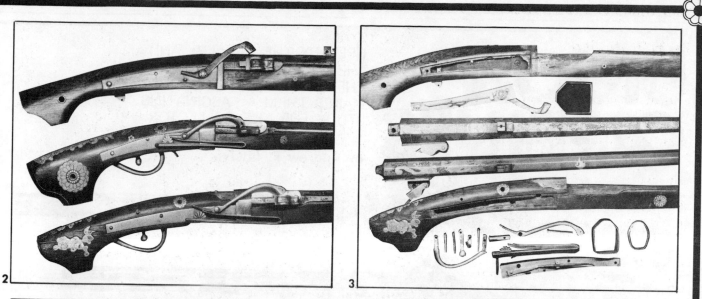

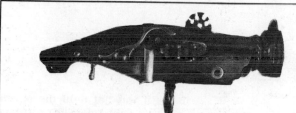

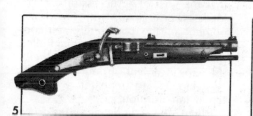

(Actual Size)

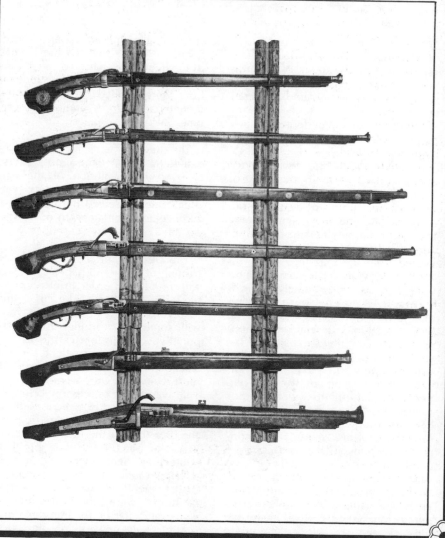

1. A print by Kuniyoshi from his series of "50 Famous Generals of the Taiheki Period c. 1600. Ina Uye Dai-kuro Masatada using a hand cannon.

2. Tanegashima locks and typical decorations.

3. Disassembled locks. From the early days and not quite up to the early 19th Century the Japanese were unable to make steel springs, properly tempered. Consequently all springs were made of brass. The matchlock was manufactured up to the Meiji Restoration (1860). Although flintlocks and percussion arms were known these too were conversions of matchlocks. Guns generally were considered unsportsmanlike and inimical to the Samurai code of battle therefore firearms were not very popular.

4. Netsuke, a miniature matchlock handgun (shown full size) was used as a toggle to hold a bullet pouch in the sash.

5. Matchlock pistol of approximately .40 caliber. Fowler Collection.

6. Seven matchlock muskets of various calibers ranging from .40 to .75 caliber. Varying degrees of decoration were used from none at all to very elaborate silver, gold and copper inlays on barrels and stocks. Damascene work was not uncommon.

UNION CARBINES

USED BY THE CAVALRY AND
THE NAVY DURING THE CIVIL WAR,
THE DIVERSITY OF THEIR DESIGN
MAKES THEM A FASCINATING
STUDY FOR THE COLLECTOR.

by Andrew F. Lustyik

A
B
1 C

The decade preceding the Civil War marked the dawn of a new era in the evolution of firearms in the United States. The four-year conflict further accelerated their development and at no time before or since have arms undergone such rapid changes in design and principle over such a short period.

In the early 1850s, the flintlock ignition system, a military favorite of most nations for 200 years, had uttered its final throes of death, before demission to the percussion system. Even with the new percussion action, almost all firearms still had to be loaded from the muzzle. A fairly intricate operation under normal conditions, it was an extremely difficult feat for even an experienced cavalryman to perform while mounted on his horse. One can imagine that it was practically impossible during the confusion of a battle. This fact, coupled with the gradual amelioration in the tactics of warfare, rendered the smoothbore muzzleloading carbine inadequate under most combat conditions. The same was true for the pistol and sabre, both short-range weapons at best, and common arms of the mounted soldier. It became imperative to equip cavalry with a more effective weapon for use at longer ranges. As surely as the percussion system had displaced the flintlock, the breechloader began to

supplant the muzzleloader. Consequently, this era became the heyday of the light, short-barreled, rifled carbine, as many breechloading innovations were applied to arms for the mounted soldier. A number of carbines also were placed in service aboard naval vessels.

The development of the breechloader was dependent almost entirely upon the evolution of the cartridge. In their earliest forms, cartridges merely served the purpose of a convenient container. In many cases, the container was used as wadding, if of a suitable material.

The next important step was the treating of linen and paper cartridges with nitrates, in order to effect complete disintegration of the entire unit following ignition. The main fault with some early carbines using these primitive combustible cartridges was that they were not gas-tight and the chambers or breech-joints leaked almost every time they were fired. Not only was this most discomforting to the shooter, but on occasions these eruptions proved more injurious to the user than to the intended victim.

As the war drew closer, internally ignited, gas-tight metallic cartridges, as known today, were still in the embryo stage. New types of metallic cartridges were appearing on the scene and began forcing the combustible types towards obsolescence.

Actually, it was not until the advent of the gas-tight metallic cartridge that the goal of a successful breechloader was attained. With the development of the completely self-contained metallic cartridge (i.e.: Bullet, powder and primer within the shell), the advancement from single-shot breechloader to repeater was hastened into fruition.

When the conflict erupted, few really good arms existed in the hands of our troops. Arms on hand in arsenals, often antiquated or obsolete, were rushed into service. Foreign arms also were purchased, but most proved to be of inferior quality. A profusion of serviceable arms was needed and as a result, "necessity became the mother of invention." It was logical that perplexing times such as these would appeal to inventors, and many directed their efforts to designing a weapon which they hoped would prove suitable for rigorous military use. This resulted in numerous patents covering breechloading arms and there appeared a rapid succession of new arms, or improved versions of existing carbines as the imaginations of inventors ran rampant. However, some of the gimcrack contraptions that were offered to the government seemed to have been hatched by their makers during a night of insane revelry. Consequently, it became necessary to exercise extreme caution before purchasing a quantity of any particular type. As might be expected, this fascinating multiplication of intriguing breechloading mechanisms, combined with their historical significance, make the carbines of our Civil War a fertile field for students and collectors.

The breeches of most carbines are opened for the loading operation by a motion, sometimes quite intricate, of the breech-block, barrel, or chamber. Included are: Falling, sliding, tilting and hinged breechblocks; rotating, sliding and tilting barrels; and revolving, rotating, hinged and tilting chambers. Regardless of the mode of operation, serious collectors agree that the most convenient method of classification for study purposes is to group the carbines on a basis of their ammunition. Either they use unprimed units, ignited by a separate percussion cap, or they utilize self-contained rimfire cartridges. The separately primed carbines are further divisible into two sub-groups; using either a metallic or other non-com-

1. Muzzle loading cavalry arms made at Springfield Armory and utilized during the Civil War. A) The U.S. Cavalry Musketoon, Model 1847, .69 caliber (smoothbore) with 26" barrel, and an overall length of 41". Lockplate marked "U.S." under a spread wing eagle, also marked "Springfield 1851". Brass furniture. From 1847 to 1859, 6703 of these arms were made. Many were later altered from original form by removal of sling ring bar and addition of a bayonet stud, or modification of the swivel ramrod attachment to a sleeve chain fixture. B) The U.S. Rifled Carbine, Model 1855, .54 caliber with 22" barrel and overall length of 36¾". Markings are similar to (A) above but for the year, 1855. Brass forend cap, iron furniture. About 1020 made during 1855-56. C) U.S. Pistol/Carbine Model 1855, .58 caliber, 12" barrel, overall length with stock, 28¼". Marked and dated similar to rifled carbine. Maynard tape primer magazine. A total of 4021 were made.

2. Hall-North Breechloading Percussion Carbine, Model 1843, .52 caliber (smoothbore). Barrel length 21", overall length 40". Breechblock marked "U.S.-S. North-MIDLtn-Conn-1846". Specimens made after 1848 are marked "steel" on barrel. About 11,000 of these were produced.

bustible cartridge with a perforated base to admit the flame from the exploding percussion cap, or combustible envelope cartridges of linen, paper or skin. At no other time in history and in no other type of weapon, did our forces have such diversity of mechanical principle and ammunition on the battlefield at one time.

Needless to say, one of the biggest headaches of the unit supply detachments was created by the confusing array of weapons in the field, most of which required their own special cartridge. Each carbine manufacturer usually chambered his weapon for a cartridge of his own design. Hence, some of the "designs" appeared to be sinister and monetary, as well as technical in nature, as the inventors figured that the government would have to give them the order for future ammunition replacements. Keeping the highly mobile cavalry units supplied with the proper type of ammunition for the particular carbine they were issued must have required extraordinary planning. This was another of the major objections to introducing a great variety of breechloading carbines into service.

A question frequently asked is: "Which carbines actually are Civil War carbines?" The point is debatable, but the facts are that many carbines made before or during the war were used in combat, whereas others manufactured during the war weren't delivered until after the cessation of hostilities. Dozens of breechloading carbines were invented or produced in hopes of securing a government contract, but many never passed the trial or experimental stage.

To John H. Hall belongs the distinction of having the first breechloading percussion carbine introduced into the United States service. After initial experiments in 1833, Hall carbines were issued to the First Regiment of U.S. Dragoons for an expedition among the Indians liv-

ing between the Rocky Mountains and the Mississippi. During the next 10 years, several models of Hall carbine were adopted by the government, each being identified by the style of lever used to raise the breechblock for loading. Most Halls had been withdrawn from the field and sold as "unserviceable" by the time the Civil War began. However, a well-documented case on record reflects that in mid-1861, 5000 unused Model 1843 Hall carbines stored at New York Arsenal were sold to Arthur M. Eastman, Manchester, New Hampshire, at $3.50 each. Within a month, these smoothbore carbines had been sold to Simon Stevens of New York City, rechambered, rifled and resold, for $22.00 each, to Maj. Gen. J. C. Fremont, Commanding the Army Dept. of the West. There was a public outcry when it was learned that the government had bought back its own weapons at more than six times the selling price. However, investigation by a Congressional Committee revealed no collusion on the part of those involved. In fact, it was revealed that several months prior to buying the carbines, Eastman had proposed to alter and rifle them for the government at less than $1.00 each. When the offer was rejected, Eastman decided to buy up the arms.

The seven-shot Spencer repeater was undoubtedly the most famous and favored of all Civil War carbines. It was the first truly successful magazine repeater firing self-contained metallic cartridges.

The U.S. Ordnance Department was slow to accept the arm, but its value became evident midway through the war. Armed with this seven-forked lightning, Union regiments often defeated a much larger force armed with other contemporary arms.

Christopher M. Spencer, the inventor, devised his carbine while a mill superintendent at the Cheney Silk Mills, Manchester, Connecticut. Strangely enough, the leaders in Washington, D.C. did not leap at the opportunity to examine the new Spencer gun. Contrary to popular belief, it was not the Army or Cavalry that first tested the arm, but the Navy! Fortunately for Mr. Spencer, Charles & Frank Cheney knew Gideon Welles, Secretary of the Navy, and they suggested he examine the repeater. Welles was quite impressed and penned the following brief, but historic, note to Capt. John A. Dahlgren, Commander of Washington Navy Yard:

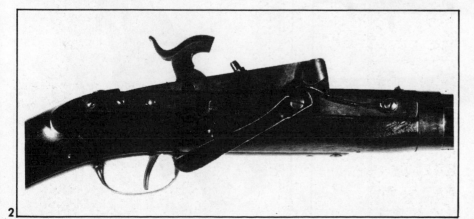

2

UNION CARBINES

"I take pleasure in introducing to you Messrs. Cheney of Hartford, Gentlemen whom I am happy to number among my special friends, and whom I commend to your very favorable regard.

"They have a newly invented breechloading arm, which they and others think superior to anything invented; and I, with them, desire to have your opinion respecting it, or at all events wish you to give it such experimentation as your time will permit.

"I need not say to you, that my friends the Messrs. Cheney are among our best citizens and that any attention to them I shall deem a special favor."

Spencer was off to a good start, but Dahlgren granted no special favors and gave the design a severe test. The Navy was quite impressed and ordered 700 repeaters and 70,-000 cartridges. The Navy tested the piece further, obtaining permission to have Army Capt. Alexander B. Dyer, later Brig. General and Chief of U.S. Ordnance, conduct the tests. After firing for rapidity, covering the action with sand, immersing the gun in salt water and leaving exposed to rusting for 24 hours, the repeater was loaded and fired without difficulty. Captain Dyer regarded it as one of the very best breechloading arms he had ever seen.

The future began to look bright and the Spencer Rifle Manufacturing Company was organized. The company leased one-half of the large Chickering piano factory in Boston, Mass., in which to commence manufacturing. However, General James W. Ripley, Chief of Ordnance, was not known for his receptiveness to innovative changes in weaponry and would have nothing to do with the newfangled Spencer.

In November, 1861, Maj. Gen. George B. McClellan directed an Army Board to test the Spencer at Washington Arsenal. The board commented:

"In firing it is accurate, the range good; the (powder) charge used smaller than is generally used in small calibre; the cartridges, being in copper tubes (shells) are less liable to damage. The rifle is simple and compact in construction, and less liable to get out of order than any other breechloading arm now in use."

Shortly afterwards, Charles Cheney again went to see Mr. Welles, who in turn contacted James G. Blaine of Maine, Speaker of the House. After a meeting between Cheney, Spencer, Welles, and Blaine, the Secretary of the Navy, in what may have been an unprecedented act, ordered 10,000 rifles for the Army. Thomas A. Scott, Assistant Secretary of War, agreed to countersign the contract in the presence of the jubilant Mr. Spencer.

In June, 1863, Col. John T. Wilder became the first commander in history to fight a battle with the basic repeating rifle when his force cut to ribbons a far larger Confederate force at Hoover's Gap, Tennessee. Many of Wilder's men, upon learning that they could not obtain Spencers through regular Army channels, had purchased them with their own money. Other units did likewise, as Spencer bypassed the disinterested Army Ordnance in Washington and set out with samples of his repeater on an extensive and successful tour of battle fronts, selling the design to appreciative regimental commanders. As Spencer repeaters appeared more frequently in the hands of Union infantry and cavalrymen, the battle story was usually the same, even when Union soldiers were heavily outnumbered. Confederate formations, charging what they believed to be troops armed with muzzleloaders, were cut down by the repeaters long before the Federal lines were within range of the Confederate arms. In battles such as Hoover's Gap, Yellow Tavern, Winchester, Franklin, Five Forks, and Gettysburg, the grey-clad forces found themselves victims of the infernal widow-maker in the hands of the men in blue.

In August, 1863, President Abraham Lincoln personally fired the Spencer and had its mechanical features explained by the inventor. Highly impressed, Lincoln insured that the troops received the arms more rapidly. In short order, General Ripley was replaced with a new Chief of Ordnance, Gen. George D. Ramsey, who reported:

"Repeating arms are the greatest favorite with the Army and could they be supplied in quantities to meet all requirements, I am sure no other arms would be used. Colt's and Henry rifles and Spencer carbines and rifles are the only arms of this class in the service. Colt's is both expensive and a dangerous weapon to the user. Henry's is expensive and too delicate for service in its present form, while Spencer's is at the same time the cheapest, most durable and most efficient of any of these arms."

The Spencer action is simple and sturdy. A tubular magazine in the buttstock holds seven stubby rimfire cartridges, which are fed forward by the action of a compressed spring

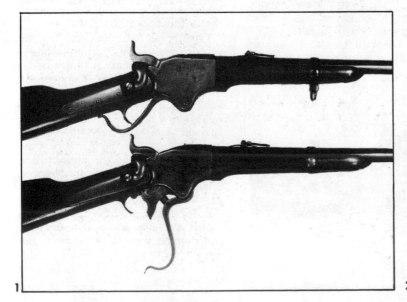

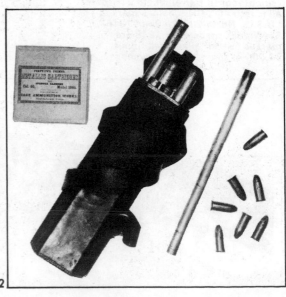

inside the tube. Lowering the trigger guard lever drops the breechblock, extracting the fired case, if any, and the closing stroke of the lever carries a cartridge from the magazine to the chamber. Some later Spencer carbines were equipped with a magazine cut-off device, invented by Edward Stabler of Sandy Springs, Maryland. It limited the lowering of the breechblock and prevented the cartridges from feeding from the magazine. In this way, the arm was used as a single-loader, retaining the contents of the magazine for an emergency.

Before the end of the war, the loading procedure was expedited even further by the development of the Blakeslee Cartridge Box. Invented by Col. Erastus Blakeslee, whose 1st Connecticut Cavalry was armed with Spencer carbines, these contrivances contained from six to 13 tubes, each of which held seven cartridges ready to empty into the magazine well.

As the demand for Spencer repeaters increased, the Burnside Rifle

Co., of Providence, Rhode Island, was subcontracted to complete orders. Many of the arms made near the end of the conflict bear the marking of this company.

The Sharps carbine was the leading single shot and the second most popular breechloader of the war. First tested by the Army in 1850, early boxlock and slanting breech specimens used wrapped paper cartridges. The carbines first became famous due to their part in the anti-slavery fight in Kansas territory. It was here they picked up the nicknames: "John Brown Sharps" and "Beecher's Bibles," as they were shipped to abolitionist John Brown in Kansas from the east in cases marked "Bibles" and delivered partly through the efforts of Henry Ward Beecher, a Brooklyn clergyman.

Although small numbers of the early model Sharps carbines evidently were carried in the Civil War, two nearly identical later models made up the bulk of those used. These were

the "New Model 1859" and "New Model 1863" carbines, which fired a combustible linen cartridge with nitrated paper base. A Sharps pellet priming device was incorporated in the lockplate. A thin brass tube of waterproofed primer discs was in-

1. Spencer's Repeating Breechloading Cartridge Carbines. Top piece is the .56-52 caliber, 7-shot with a 22" barrel, overall length of 39". Marked "Spencer Repeating Rifle Co., Boston, Mass.-Pat'd March 6, 1860" and "M-1865" with serial number. A cartouche bearing the government inspector's mark is stamped on left side of butt. Earlier models lack the "M-1865" marking. Second piece is the .56-50 caliber model with 20" barrel, overall length of 37". Either marked as above, or "Model 1865" and "Spencer Repeating Rifle-Patented March 6,1860-Manufd at Prov. R.I. - by Burnside Rifle Co." and serial number. This specimen has Stabler cutoff.

2. This 10-tube Blakeslee quickloader for the Spencer holds 70 cartridges.

3. An assortment of Sharps and Sharps & Hankins breechloading carbines. From top to bottom: Model 1853 or "John Brown" model, .52 caliber, barrel 21⅝", overall 37¾". Markings on barrel, "Sharp's Rifle Manufg Co.-Hartford, Conn"; on lockplate, "Sharps-Patent-1852"; on tang, "Sharps-Patent-1848" along with serial number. Brass furniture. Sharps pellet primer magazine in lockplate. The Massachusetts-Kansas Aid Committee purchased 200 of these carbines to send John Brown in Kansas. Model 1855 features same basic specifications and markings as the Model 1853 except lockplate is unmarked. Gate of tape primer is marked "Edward Maynard-Patentee 1845". Rear of barrel is marked "U.S.-JH-P". Ordnance Department purchased 400 in April, 1855. New Model 1859, in .52 caliber, barrel 22", overall 39". This vertical breech carbine is marked, on barrel, "Sharps Rifle Manufg. Co.-Hartford Conn."; on lockplate "C. Sharps' Pat. Oct. 5th, 1852" and "R.S. Lawrence' Pat.-April 12th, 1859" (covering pellet cutoff feature); on left side of frame, "C. Sharps, Pat.-Sept. 12th, 1848", and the serial number on tang. Brass furniture, early production, iron later. New Model 1863 carbines are identical to the New Model 1859s except for markings on barrel as to model. After March, 1864, a "C" prefix was used for serial numbers "over 100,000," i.e. number "C,24688" would mean 124,688. Patch boxes were deleted at the same time. Sharps & Hankins Army Model 1862, caliber .52 (No. 56 S&H) 23⅝" barrel, overall, 38⅝". Serial number on tang. Right of frame marked "Sharps & Hankins-Philada", left side "Sharps-Patent-1859", brass butt plate. In 1863 Army ordered 1217. Navy Model 1862. Similar to Army model but Navy inspector's mark is "P/H.K.H.", barrel is covered by a 1/16" thick leather tube met at muzzle by an iron ring/sight base. Navy ordered 6320. Note sling ring.

3

UNION CARBINES

serted into the magazine. The discs were moved forward one at a time by spring tension and an arm actuated by the descending hammer. The carbines also had a feature patented by Richard S. Lawrence which enabled the pellet magazine to be cut off and held in reserve to permit the use of regular percussion caps.

The Sharps action consists of a vertical sliding breechblock which operates in a mortise cut through the receiver. The face of the breechblock had a gas-escape check designed by R. S. Lawrence and Hezekiah Conant, consisting of a sliding steel plate with expanding flange. It proved to be the most successful gas check used in any of the Sharps percussion models. After the war, thousands of the Sharps carbines were altered for rimfire and centerfire metal cartridges.

Around 1853, Christian Sharps, the inventor, had left his manufacturing concern in Hartford, Connecticut, shortly after Samuel E. Robbins and R. S. Lawrence of Windsor, Vermont, took over much of the manufacturing responsibility. Sharps set up a small shop in Philadelphia, Pennsylvania, and was ready with a larger shop when war came. In conjunction with William Hankin, he produced a sturdy sliding-barrel carbine in two basic models. The early type (1861) had a firing pin integral with the hammer face and the later type (1862) had a separate, floating firing pin. A safety device on the frame slides under the face of the hammer, at the shooter's discretion. The 9th and 11th N.Y. Volunteer Cavalry Regiments were armed with these Sharps & Hankins carbines.

Third in popularity was the Burnside carbine, invented by Ambrose E. Burnside, later a Civil War general. The carbine was first patented on March 25, 1856 (Pat. No. 14,491) and developed through four basic models from 1856 to 1864. Most unique was its cartridge, a conical type with rearward tapering brass case. The loaded round resembled an ice cream cone and had a small hole in the base to admit flame from the conventional percussion cap.

To digress slightly, we will note that of the three principal Civil War carbines, each one falls into one of the previously mentioned categories of ammunition classification, that is: Spencer (completely self-contained metallic cartridge); Sharps (separately primed combustible envelope cartridge); and Burnside (separately primed metallic cartridge).

Around 1855, General Burnside organized the Bristol Firearms Company, Bristol, Rhode Island, with hopes of far reaching sales of his breechloader. In August, 1857, Burnside's carbine received a complete and careful examination by a trial board of military officers at West Point, New York, along with guns submitted by a dozen and a half other inventors. Although the board was of the unanimous opinion that of those tested the Burnside was the best suited for military service, only several hundred carbines were ordered for additional trials. A combination of a lack of orders, under-capitalization, and the depression of 1857, eventually caused the financial collapse of the concern. With the company in bankruptcy, Burnside signed everything of value over to his creditors.

On July 16, 1861, General Ripley wrote to Charles Jackson, President of the old Bristol Firearms Company, stating:

"There are required immediately by this department 800 of Burnside's carbines, for which the same price last paid will be allowed. Please inform me of the shortest time possible you are prepared to furnish them."

Ripley was actually writing in behalf of Gov. William Sprague of Rhode Island, who wanted the carbines to arm a mounted brigade of Rhode Island troops. The price Ripley referred to was "$35.00 per arm," as this was the price agreed upon for each of 709 carbines sold to the

government by the concern on an earlier contract of Sept. 21, 1858.

On July 18th, Mr. Jackson acknowledged and accepted the order for 800 carbines, stating: " . . . having perfected the arm during the past two years, I have recently reorganized under the name of the 'Burnside Rifle Company', Isaac Hartshorn, agent . . . your order can be delivered in December next, in whole or in part, probably the whole. This is the earliest moment that we can safely promise them. If you desire it, we can furnish loaded cartridges with electro silver-plated cases at $3.00 per hundred. The cases now used are tinned . . . "*

These arms, which were "Second Model" Burnsides were finally delivered by March, 1862. The carbines had several improvements over the "First Model" Burnsides, lacking a concealed Maynard tape primer and side locking lever found on the earlier model. The two most noteworthy improvements were a redesigned locking latch contained inside the bow of the lever and the use of a tapered metallic cartridge case having a recess or grease-chamber within the projecting bead carried around the front end or ball mouth of the case. Early Burnside cartridges were of wrapped foil, without the bead. The main purpose of the bead or case collar was to lubricate the bullet with grease or tallow and seal the joint of the breech. Both of these improvements were the invention of George P. Foster, plant foreman at Bristol and Providence.

A "Third Model" Burnside was soon developed. It had a wooden forestock and a modified hammer. By 1864, this evolved into the "Fourth Model" which was by far the most common type produced. It carried as major improvements a hinged, double-pivoting breechblock and easily removed breechblock hinge pin patented by Isaac Hartshorn.

Gilbert Smith, a physician of Buttermilk Falls (near West Point), invented and patented a break-action carbine which ranked fourth among carbines purchased by the Ordnance Department. The carbine was tested at Washington Arsenal in the spring of 1860. The trial board commented:

"This arm uses an India Rubber cartridge case and has no escape of gas. It is the simplest form of breechloader presented to the board for trial. The gun is divided, the barrel from the breech, by a hinge, and the parts when closed are held together by a spring projecting from the barrel and fastening over a stud . . . It was fired 1000 times without weakening the spring. This gun, from its simplicity of construction, apparent strength of parts, the ease with which it is loaded, and the general accuracy of firing, recommends itself strongly; and is particularly adapted to the mounted service."

The board recommended adoption of the arm for further tests in active service on a campaign. At first, only 300 carbines were ordered. When war came, Thomas Poultney and David B. Trimble, Baltimore, Maryland, agents and proprietors of the Smith carbine, contracted with the government and arranged to commence manufacture

of the Smith carbine at the Massachusetts Arms Company, Chicopee Falls, Massachusetts. In August, 1863, the company was desirous of dropping production of the Smith in favor of the Maynard carbine. To complete existing contracts, the Massachusetts Arms Co. made arrangements with American Machine Works in Springfield to assist with part of the manufacturing, that of making the breech piece for the Smith. In September, 1863, Mr. Poultney, perturbed by the attitude of the Chicopee concern toward the Smith, made his own arrangements with Philos B. Tyler of American Machine Works to take over the manufacture of the entire Smith carbine on another government contract that he had signed.

The "Poultney's Patent Metallic Cartridges" used in the Smith carbine during the war were actually patented by Thomas J. Rodman and Silas Crispin on Dec. 15, 1863 (Patent #40,988). The patent, which was assigned to Poultney, covered cartridges having a *"metallic case formed of thin wrapped sheet metal . . . combined with an internal or external strengthening disk or cup . . . said disk being made of paper, metal, or elastic material."*

The fifth ranking breechloader in terms of purchases was another in the long line of arms contributions supplied to the government by the famous Starr family. The Starr name had become well known during the years 1798 to 1845 for the family had numerous contracts for swords, sabres, cutlasses, artillery swords, pikes, flintlock rifles, and muskets.

Patented on Sept. 14, 1858, by Ebenezer Townsend Starr of N.Y.C., it was one of the very few Civil War carbines that started as a percussion arm and ended as a cartridge arm. Other examples were the Joslyn and Gallager carbines.

In January, 1858, Maj. William H. Bell tested the Starr carbine, stating: *"The carbine performed remarkably well, the accuracy of fire not being*

1. From top to bottom. 2nd Model Burnside .54 caliber, barrel 21", overall 39½". Markings on lockplate, "Burnside Rifle Co.-Providence R.I.", on barrel, "Cast Steel 1861"; on frame, "Burnside's Patent-March 25th, 1856" over the serial number; on lever "G.P. Foster Pat-April 10th 1860". Second models were also made earlier by "Bristol Firearms Co." and are so marked. Neither type had forestock. 4th Model Burnside. Similar in markings and specs to 2nd model. Frame marked "Burnside's Patent-Model of 1864. Double pivoting block, lever unmarked. Maynard, early model, calibers .35 or .50, 20" barrel, overall 36½". Markings, right side of frame, "Maynard Arms Co.-Washington" left side, "Manufactured by-Mass. Arms Co.-Chicopee Falls". Exterior of patchbox marked "Maynard Patentee"-Sept. 22, 1845-May 27, 1851- June 17, 1856", first date is usually absent. Equipped with tape primer magazine. Serial number stamped inside primer door. Many have tang sight. No sling bar and ring, some have ring on lower tang. Patchbox cover hinges on buttplate. Some were used by the Confederates since many were stored in U.S. arsenals "down south." Late Model .50 caliber, 20" barrel, 36⅞" overall. Marked on right of frame, "Manufactured by Mass. Arms Co.-Chicopee Falls", left side, "Edward Maynard-Patented-May 27, 1851-Dec. 6, 1859". Serial number found on bottom of barrel and/or lower tang. Date "1865" also on lower tang of late production. Late carbines have sling bar, no Maynard primer, tang sight or patch box.

2. Smith Carbine, .50 caliber, barrel 21⅝", overall 39½". Markings, right side of frame "Address-Poultney & Trimble-Baltimore, U.S.A." over "Smith's Patent-June 23, 1857". Other typical frame markings include, "Manufactured by-Mass. Arms Co.-Chicopee Falls"; "Manufactured by Am'n M'ch 'n Wks-Springfield-Mass." or; "American Arms Co.-Chicopee Falls". Serial number is usually found on the bottom of the frame near the hinge. Smith carbines occasionally have sling swivels on the butt stock and barrel band. Starr Carbine, .54 caliber, barrel 21"; overall 37⅝". Marked on lockplate and barrel, "STarr Arms Co Yonkers, N.Y.", and on breech tang, "Starr's Patent-Sept 14th, 1858". Serial number appears on breech block follower. Brass furniture. Starr Carbine for the .56-52 Spencer. Specifications and markings identical to above. Serial number is on right rear of barrel. Brass or iron furniture.

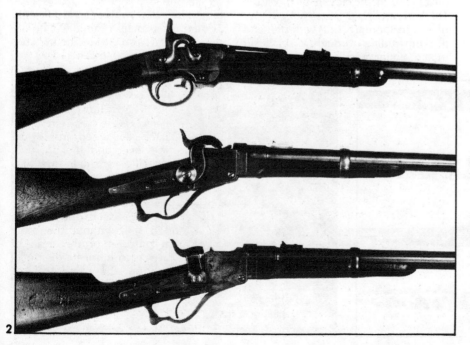

UNION CARBINES

exceeded previously at the (Washington) arsenal." Although the piece never misfired and was remarkably accurate, there was a small amount of gas leakage at the breech. Major Bell felt that if the leakage could be entirely stopped, the arm would be superior to the Sharps, since it did not cut open the rear of the cartridge and spill powder around the breech mechanism. Most of the Sharps carbines used in the 1850s depended upon the sharpened front end of the rising breechblock to cut through the rear of the chambered cartridge, exposing the powder for quicker ignition. While similar in appearance to the Sharps, the Starr lever-action breech mechanism differs in that the split breechblock is pivoted and swings down backwards. A deep annular groove in the breechblock face encloses the breech end of the barrel. The breechblock is forced against the barrel by action of a locking wedge.

Starr linen cartridges closely resemble those of the Sharps, but instead of a grooved lead bullet, have a characteristic ridge or raised band around the bullet base. The cartridges cost $24.75 per thousand, according to a contemporary Ordnance list.

After purchasing over 20,000 percussion carbines during the war, the

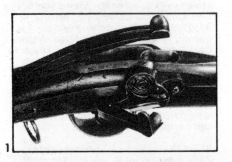

1

Ordnance Dept. contracted with the Starr Arms Company on February 21, 1865 for 3000 carbines at $20.00 each, chambered for the .56-52 Spencer metallic cartridge. An additional 2000 cartridge carbines were ordered shortly thereafter. The major physical change in the guns was the vertical-shank hammer, breechblock design, and added ejection feature of the cartridge model. The company also furnished close to 48,000 Starr revolvers during the Civil War.

One of the best performing carbines of the war was invented by the widely celebrated dental surgeon, Dr. Edward Maynard, of Washington, D.C. In spite of his many contributions and the international honors bestowed upon him in the field of dentistry, Dr. Maynard is best known for his improvements in firearms and cartridges.

Early in his career, Dr. Maynard invented the "Maynard Tape Primer," the best known and most widely used automatic priming mechanism in the Service. Its purpose, like the Sharps pellet primer, was to eliminate the step of manually placing a percussion cap on the nipple each time a weapon was readied for firing. A number of pre-Civil War percussion breechloading carbines have Maynard primer magazines affixed to, or built into, the lockplate or frame.

Maynard's Patent No. 4,208 (Sept. 22, 1845) specified that little lozenges of percussion fulminate, spaced about ¼-inch apart would be placed between two narrow slips of paper which were cemented together and varnished in order to secure the mixture from the action of moisture. The primer strip was coiled and placed in the magazine with one end just protruding through a small slit in the upper part of the magazine.

Magazines had two basic types of feeding mechanism; a "sprocket-wheel" or a "finger feed" type. When the hammer was cocked, it moved the next primer over the nipple. Squeezing the trigger caused the hammer to fall, its sharpened under edge cutting off a lozenge and carrying it down instantaneously to the top of the cone where it was exploded.

The government standardized the Maynard primer lock in 1855 and continued its use until about 1860. The system functioned well under favorable conditions, but did not possess the reliability of the percussion cap during inclement weather. Nevertheless, some tape-primed arms did see service in the conflict.

Maynard's cartridge patents of June 17, 1856 (No. 15,141) and January 11, 1859 (No. 22,565) rank high, not only among his own inventions, but among the entire avalanche of other pre-Civil War metallic cartridges. The former covered a tubular metallic shell with the rear aperture closed by waxed paper. It had a lubricated bullet. The latter patent covered a perforated steel disk soldered to the perforated base of a brass shell. This wide, flat base of steel facilitated manual extraction, but soon gave way to a brass base. The springy walls of the cartridge expanded when fired to form a perfect seal, preventing gas and flame leakage at the breech joint. This invention solved what for years had been a major problem in breechloaders and hastened the end of the percussion ignition period.

Like the cartridge, Maynard's carbine also was simple and efficient. Testimonials to its superiority, based upon actual use, were many. Extracts from several follow:

2

STATEMENT OF CARBINES AND AMMUNITION PURCHASED BY THE ORDNANCE DEPARTMENT FROM JANUARY 1, 1861 TO JUNE 30, 1866				
Type	Number	Cost	Cartridges	Cost
Spencer	94,196	$2,393,633.82	58,238,924	$1,419,277.16
Sharps	80,512	$2,213,192.00	16,306,508	$347,410.57
Burnside	55,567	$1,412,620.41	21,819,200	$547,490.05
Smith	30,062	$745,645.24	13,861,500	$377,569.78
Starr (*)	25,603	$586,773.79	6,860,000	$140,768.30
Gallager (*)	22,728	$508,492.94	8,294,023	$211,893.92
Maynard	20,002	$489,399.78	2,157,000	$72,207.50
Remington	20,000	$436,752.00	4,257,000	$68,600.00
Merrill	14,495	$374,804.63	5,502,750	$105,779.32
Joslyn	11,261	$282,586.00	515,416	$12,935.37
Gwyn & Campbell	9342	$199,838.29	6,300,000	$132,007.27
Warner	4001	$79,310.54	1,028,000	$27,472.00
Hall	3520	$64,763.50	Unknown	
Ballard	1509	$35,140.00	3,527,450	$57,945.05
Gibbs	1052	$27,995.25	Unknown	
Ball	1002	$25,387.00	Used Spencer Ammunition	
Palmer	1001	$20,918.50	Used Spencer Ammunition	
Lindner	892	$19,895.00	100,000	$2,262.00
Wesson	151	$3,491.75	254,000	$3,666.60

NOTE: This table is not a complete record of all the carbines used by the U.S. Government during the Civil War. Carbines purchased privately by various regiments and States, as well as small quantities of carbines produced by other manufacturers and earlier models of several types listed above which were purchased prior to 1861, are not included. (*) Figures for Starr and Gallager carbines include percussion and cartridge models.

On July 14, 1859, Lt. Col. B. S. Roberts, U.S. Regt. of Mounted Riflemen, wrote: " . . . its peculiar advantages are the motion of the barrel, raising the breech for loading, its metallic cartridge, and the primer . . . at 700 yards the penetration was two and a half inches in oak . . . discharges ten times per minute easily and with certainty of aim . . . for cavalry service, and for light troops or skirmishes, the Maynard is the most destructive war weapon that has ever been invented."

In October, 1859, a trial of the Maynard carbine was conducted under the supervision of Cmndr. John A. Dahlgren, Washington Navy Yard. Mr. William P. MacFarland, agent for the arm, and Dr. Maynard personally demonstrated a .50-caliber carbine, equipped with tape primer device. Accuracy was quite good, on one occasion 237 rounds being fired at 200 yards on a 3x6-foot target, without a miss. At 1300 yards, the bullets penetrated to their length in seasoned oak planks. After firing over 600 times, only a slight foulness had accumulated. As a part of the test, two metallic cartridge cases were reloaded alternately and fired over 200 times, remaining as serviceable as at first.

The Hon. Howell Cobb, Secretary of the U.S. Treasury, wrote to the Maynard Arms Company on December 15, 1859: "Ample testimony from sources every way entitled to confidence, having been furnished this Department, of the superior merits of the Maynard Breechloading Carbine, it was, after due consideration, determined to introduce it on board the Revenue Cutters, to take the place of different kinds of small-arms in use on board these vessels . . . Since the introduction of this arm

into the Cutter Service, it has met with unqualified approbation, and the Department now takes much pleasure in hearing testimony to its great superiority over all other small arms heretofore furnished it."

On January 16, 1860, A. M. Ball, Master Armorer at the U.S. Armory, Harper's Ferry, Va., stated: " . . . I am fully convinced that no arm of the same calibre and weight of metal can compare with Maynard's as to force and accuracy . . . I feel no hesitation in saying, that I believe it to be the very best breechloading arm in the world . . . "

Surprisingly, the Maynard was not purchased in greater numbers or used to a greater extent. It weighed only about six pounds and was only 36 inches in overall length, making it one of the lightest and shortest carbines in military service. The recoil was considerable, but not greater than could be expected from a piece so light. As a tribute to its quality, Maynard continued to produce single-shot arms which were improvements on this basic system into the 1890's, some 25 years after most other Civil War breechloaders had been discontinued and long forgotten.

On May 25, 1838, William Jenks of Columbia, South Carolina, patented a carbine which first appeared with flintlock ignition. The system was modified and refined several times as a percussion arm, ultimately attaining the distinction of being the only "mule ear" sidehammer breechloader ever adopted in the U.S. Service. It was also the first U.S. military arm to incorporate the Maynard primer and one of the first firearms to use the drilled cast-steel barrels developed by Samual Remington of E. Remington & Son, Herkimer, N. Y.

The Jenks had a novel arrangement of a plunger sliding into the rear of the chamber. The plunger was drawn back by a top lever for loading. When the lever was depressed, the plunger and associated parts were forced to a closed position where the parts constituted a species of toggle joint, in almost a straight line from the breech to the extreme point of action. No fastening of any kind was required and the piston could not be forced back by the discharge of the piece.

From 1841 to 1845, the U.S Navy ordered 6200 Jenks carbines. Of these, 5200 were made by the Ames Manufacturing Co., Chicopee Falls, Massachusetts, and 1000 (with tape

1. Jenks (Remington) is similar to "Ames" manufactured carbines, but lockplate marked, "Remington's-Herkimer-N.Y." Breech marked "Wm Jenks"-USN-RC-P-Cast Steel-1847". Carbine has double-eared lever, straight-shank hammer, and Maynard tape primer device. Serial number stamped inside primer door, which is open to view.

2. Jenks (Ames) .54 caliber, rifled barrel 24¼", overall 41". Marked "N.P. Ames-Springfield-Mass." on lock and "Wm Jenks" on lockplate and barrel. Serial number on all major parts. A number have smoothbore barrels. Either a round or oval loading aperture in top of breech. An unusual arm with a mule-ear (Side-swinging) hammer, full length stock, brass furnishings, and browned and lacquered barrel. The Merrill alteration featured the same fittings of the Ames but has a patented breech-lever marked, "J.H. Merrill-Balto-Pat. July 1858". Lever locks on rear sight base. Mule-ear hammer replaced by a conventional side hammer as was nipple and cone. Merrill (Early Model) .54 caliber, 22⅛" barrel, overall, 37⅜". Lockplate marked, "J.H. Merrill, Balto.-Pat. July 1858-Apl 9, May 21-28-61" and serial number. Top lever marked "J.H. Merrill, Balto.-Pat. July 1858", and serial number. Lever has flat knurled, release-latch. Stock has tapered forearm tip, brass furniture, and patchbox. Merrill (Late Model) similar to above, but with rounded button-like lever release-knobs. Lockplate has stamped eagle and date, such as "1863", but lacks serial number. Tips of stock eventually became more rounded and patchbox was eliminated.

3. Remington-Rider (Split-Breech) using the .50 caliber cartridge barrel 20", overall 34⅛". Breech tang marked, "Remington's Ilion, N.Y.-Pat. Dec. 23, 1863, May 3 & Nov. 16, 1864". "U.S." stamped on butt plate. Serial number under barrel and on front of frame, hidden by forearm. Late production models have sling swivels. The .46 caliber model with exact specifications and markings as above, except "U.S." deleted. However, most parts are smaller and lighter.

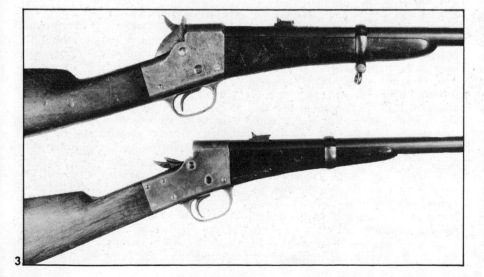

3

UNION CARBINES

primer) by E. Remington & Son. Cost ran from $15.00 to $19.00 per arm. The Army tested the carbine extensively in 1842, firing one of the pieces submitted a grand total of 14,813 times with the only sign of wear being a split nipple which was easily replaced. However, the Army only ordered 44 carbines (Ames) for field trials. Tests in the hands of the First Dragoons did not go well and the weapons were considered *"impossible to load on horseback . . . generally inferior to Hall carbines . . . and not worth the storeroom they occupy."* Unfortunately, the Dragoons had never received instructions for loading the arms and had mistakenly tried to load with an improper paper cartridge. Actually, Jenks carbines were meant to be loaded with a round ball followed by loose powder from a special charging flask. In some cases, where the soldiers did charge the carbine with loose powder and ball, they used the 100-grain charge for the Hall carbine instead of the 65 grains for which the Jenks was designed. Ignorance of correct loading technique caused clogging, fouling, and rendered the arms useless.

Although the Navy never had any major problems with the Jenks carbines, they were lying unused in government arsenals in the late 1850's. At this time, James H. Merrill, of Baltimore, Maryland, saw a chance to update the obsolete carbines by altering them to fire combustible cartridges. Initial tests in February, 1858, proved that the Merrill alteration of the Jenks was not only costly and cumbersome, but required a great deal of work to convert the arm. Undaunted, Merrill improved his invention and presented another model for trial in June, 1858. The alteration, which used a conventional side hammer and nipple, worked well and was favorably recommended after tests conducted by Lieut. F. K. Murray at Washington Navy Yard. Merrill was authorized to deliver only 300 altered Jenks carbines and 5000 suitable cartridges. The converted guns were accepted on January 26, 1861, in time for Navy use during the war. It was impractical to alter "Remington" made Jenks carbines to Merrill's system due to the tape device in the lockplate.

Mr. Merrill was not a stranger in the gunmaking business. Around 1855, with partners Ferdinand C. Latrobe and Philip E. Thomas, Jr., he

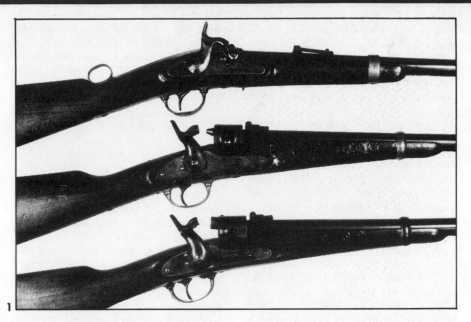

formed "Merrill, Latrobe & Thomas" of Baltimore. Although purchased by the government, Merrill's early faucet-breech carbine (patented in 1856) was, like his first attempt to convert the Jenks, cumbersome and not a success. Around 1860, Latrobe dropped out and Lewin W. Thomas joined, creating "Merrill, Thomas & Co." The Merrill Patent Fire Arms Company was formed shortly before hostilities began and both of the latter firms seem to have been active during the war years.

Merrill's wartime carbine was available in two models, each identified by the type of lever latch employed. Advantages claimed by the inventor were *"Simplicity and strength of construction; the efficiency of the carbine not being dependent upon any patent metallic or india rubber cartridge case, but using the paper cartridge, or loose powder and ball, and the ordinary percussion cap."* This, he felt, secured one of the indispensible conditions of an arm of war. Merrill's disparaging remarks concerned the rubber cartridge of the Smith carbine and the patent metallic types, such as were used in the Burnside and Maynard.

In September, 1862, Col. Wm. A Barstow wrote to Mr. Merrill, advising that all 1200 men in his 3rd Wisconsin Cavalry were armed with the Merrill carbine and they *"considered it superior to any arm of any kind in the service."* In February, 1864, Col. S. T. Spear, 11th Pennsylvania Cavalry, wrote that his entire regiment was currently being furnished with Merrill's carbine and he had advised the 1st New York Mounted Rifles and 5th Pennsylvania Cavalry, then under his command, to

obtain the carbines. A number of other officers did not have such esteem for the carbine.

Mechanically, the Merrill is similar to the earlier Jenks system. To operate, the hammer is first cocked and top-lever drawn upward and backward, sliding a piston to the rear. This piston has a copper disc at its front end forming the rear face of the chamber. Firing the arm caused the disc to expand slightly, forming a gas seal. A small projection on the right side of the lever clears the fired musket cap from the nipple on the upstroke and also serves to lock the mechanism when the hammer is completely down.

The most familiar name among the wartime carbine makers would probably be Remington, the oldest active gunmaker in America. Founded in 1816, their long-livedness is due to a combination of factors: Simplicity in arms design, durability, practicality and reasonable cost, resulting in the production of quality arms in quantity.

The Jenks carbine contract helped Remington put a foot in the door and when the rebellion came, they supplied many types of efficient arms in defense of the Union. Among these was the "split-breech" carbine, the forerunner of the world-famous rolling-block action. The "split-breech" system was designed by Leonard Geiger, an armorer with the concern. Joseph Rider, of Newark, Ohio, a company engineer, improved Geiger's system and assigned the patent to himself and Remington. The frame of the carbine has very high walls, containing a breechblock which swings backward and downward. The hammer pivots within the split breechblock, its nose striking the rimfire cartridge through a slot in the top of the block.

On October 24, 1864, 15,000 "split-breech" carbines, caliber .56-50, were ordered at $23.00 each. Delivery was completed on May 24, 1866. Another 5000 carbines were contracted for on January 19, 1865, at $17.00 each. These carbines were similar, but had smaller frames and used a .46-caliber rimfire cartridge. They were furnished to the War Department by June 30, 1865. After the war, Remington bought back most of the .50-caliber "split-breech" carbines, at $15.00, and resold them to France.

Pre-Civil War Joslyn carbines used a combustible paper cartridge, fired by a separate percussion cap, whereas later versions utilized self-contained metallic rimfire ammunition.

The percussion Model 1855 Joslyn has a large oval ring on the top lever, located at the small of the stock just in front of the comb. Moving the ring forward unlatches the long hinged breechlever. This radial lever is then raised vertically, exposing the breech orifice for loading. The escape of gas was prevented by an arrangement of split metallic expanding rings in the face of the breech-strap.

Benjamin F. Joslyn foresaw a limited market for the Model 1855 breechloader and quickly effected the transition to metallic cartridge at the beginning of the war. In the spring of 1861, Joslyn brought his newly designed side-swinging breech-system to the attention of both the Army and Navy. The side-swinging breech series included two basic models (Model 1862 and Model 1864), with a total of five production variations. The movable breech cap had a cleverly designed extractor system, or "curved wedge-formed projection." In effect, one inclined surface inside the breech seats the cartridge upon the closing of the breechblock, while another inclined surface withdraws the cartridge suf-ficiently upon opening, so as to allow for its ready extraction by hand.

Various tests were made by the Service, but as the war neared the halfway mark, Joslyn still had not received any substantial contracts. The War Department authorized the purchase of 860 Joslyn carbines at $35.00 each, from Bruff Brothers & Seaver, New York City agents. Deliveries were made between November, 1861 and July, 1862, with 660 carbines being assigned to the State

1. Joslyn Carbines. The "percussion model" in .54 caliber, barrel 22½", overall, 38¼". Marked on lockplate, "A.H. Waters & Co.-Milbury, Mass." and on top lever, "Patd By-B.F. Joslyn-Aug. 23, 1855". Serial number stamped on breech bolt lever. Brass furniture. Model 1862, .52 caliber, (.56-52 Spencer), 22" barrel, overall 38⅞". Marked on lockplate, "Joslyn Fire Arms Co-Stonington-Conn." and on the top of the breechblock, "B.F. Joslyn's Patent-October 8th 1861-June 24th 1862" over the serial number. Among other characteristics are, brass furniture, long tang strap, hook-like breechblock operating projection, single breechblock hinge, and screw-on extractor plate. A few carbines were mechanically altered during the transition to Model 1864 by fitting a contoured and checkered finger-piece into the underside of the hook to lock the breech more effectively. Model 1864, similar to the Model 1862 but uses the .56-56 Spencer or special .54 Joslyn cartridge. The date "1864" is added to the lockplate. Breech-block markings, with exception of serial number, are on back instead of top of cap. Iron furniture. Butt plate stamped "U.S." Changes include circular firing pin shield, gas vent on top of breechcap, firing pin shield, shorter tang strap, double hinged breechblock after serial No. 11,000.

2. Breechloading percussion carbines from top to bottom. Gallager Percussion Carbine, .50 caliber, 22¼" barrel, overall 39-3/16". Lock marked, "Manufactd by-Richardson & Overman-Philada"-Gallager's Patent-July 17th 1860" and serial number. Made without wooden forearm. Gibbs Percussion Carbine, .52 caliber, 22" barrel, 39" overall. Lockplate marks, "Wm F. Brooks-Manfr New York-1863" and stamped with a spread eagle. Breech marked, "L.H. Gibbs-Pat'd-Jan'y 8, 1856". Cosmopolitan (Gross) Carbine, .52 caliber, 19" barrel, overall 39". Lockplate marked, "Cosmopolita Arms Co." in a curve over "Hamilton O.U.S.-Gross' Patent-1859". Frame marked, "Union-Rifle". Serial number usually appears on all parts. Assembly number is stamped too. Gwyn & Campbell, .52 caliber, barrel 20", overall 39". Lockplate marked "Gwyn & Campbell" in a semi-circle over "Patent-1862-Hamilton, O" and "Union Rifle". Serial number on all major parts. An outgrowth of the Cosmopolitan. Lindner, .58 caliber, 20" barrel, overall 38¾". Top of breechblock marked, "Edward Lindner's Patent-March 29, 1859".

UNION CARBINES

of Ohio. Larger contracts finally came and deliveries commenced on August 20, 1863. Prices ranged from $23.50 to $25.00 per carbine. When the end of the war came, about one-half of Joslyn's final contract was still undelivered. It appears that the government then "found" some deficiency in Joslyn's carbines and no longer considered itself bound to the contract. In April, 1866, Joslyn was still trying to induce the government to take the remainder of the arms. His efforts were unsuccessful and most of the carbines were unloaded on the civilian market.

The Gallager system was patented in 1860 by Mahlon J. Gallager of Savannah, Georgia. Depressing the operating lever caused the barrel to move forward about one inch where the breech end elevated for loading. One-half of the cartridge chamber was in the breech, the other half in the barrel. After the piece was fired and the breech opened, the cartridge case usually protruded from either the chamber of the barrel or of the breech piece. The cartridge used most frequently was Poultney's Patent of brass and paper, but cases of iron foil covered with paper (Jackson's Patent) and drawn brass also were available.

Cartridge extraction was a problem and a major objection to the Gallager. In July, 1862, Brig. Gen. J. T. Boyle, commanding the District of Louisville, Kentucky, wrote to the Secretary of War: " . . . *Gallager guns are unquestionably worthless, Officers do not want them . . . the cartridge hangs in after firing, often difficult to get out with screwdriver . . . men throw them away and take any other arm . . . Can we get Sharps or Wesson's or Ballard's or some other kind? Sharps best! We are much in need of carbines . . . "* The screw-

driver referred to by General Boyle was a combination tool, consisting of nipper, wrench, and screwdriver, which was furnished with each Gallager carbine. If the empty case became stuck after firing, the circular end of this special wrench was slipped over the projecting case to facilitate removal.

In March, 1865, the government ordered 5000 Gallager carbines, chambered for a Spencer metallic cartridge. They were delivered shortly after the war ended.

One carbine that found favor with some units from the midwest was the invention of Henry Gross, of Tiffin, Ohio. Although Gross was granted a number of breechloading patents between 1855 and 1864, carbines of early manufacture were based mainly on his Patent No. 25,259, issued August 30, 1859.

On December 23, 1861, the Ordnance Department offered Edward Gwyn and Abner C. Campbell, of the Cosmopolitan Arms Co., Hamilton, Ohio, a contract to produce 1140 Gross Patent carbines for units being formed by Governor Richard Yates of Illinois. These carbines were made without forends, as were later models. Pulling the curved lever down and forward pivots the face of the breechblock upwards as the entire block swings down and away from the breech. A separate breech aperture cover, with a loading groove on top, drops down at its front end to form a loading trough, allowing a combustible cartridge to be guided into the chamber.

A change in style becomes apparent on carbines produced under Patent No. 36,709, issued to Messrs. Gwyn & Campbell on October 21, 1862. The vast majority of the carbines produced after 1862 incorporate this patent, which features a simpler breech arrangement in which the action of the lever merely drops

the front end of the grooved breechblock for loading.

This carbine did not make any names for itself on the battlefield, but managed to acquire many an appellation in later years. In spite of the fact that practically all Civil War carbines were known by the inventor's name, this one has been known as the "Gross" for the inventor, "Cosmopolitan" for the manufacturer, "Union" due to a marking on the carbines, "Gwyn & Campbell" for the later patentees and operators of the Cosmopolitan Arms Co., "Ohio" for the State of manufacture, and "Grapevine" due to the snake-like curves of the trigger guard lever and long ungainly hammer.

The Warner carbine was a very handsome weapon, being the only brass frame carbine purchased for the Service. The initial patent was granted to James Warner on February 23, 1864 (No. 41,732) covering "*a semi-cylindrical recess within the breech*" long enough to receive the proper type of fixed ammunition and of a width sufficient to receive the rim of the cartridge. When the action is opened by swinging the breechblock upward and to the right, the cartridge is guided in an exact line with the barrel both in loading and withdrawing the case. A subsequent patent (No. 45,660—December 27, 1864) covered a device which facilitated movement of the breechblock.

A total of 4001 Warner carbines were purchased. Of these, 1501, using special caliber .50 Warner rimfire ammunition, were contracted for between January 13 and November 11, 1864, all being delivered by November 15, 1864. An additional .56-50 carbines, chambered for the .56-50 Spencer cartridge, were contracted for on December 26, 1864, with final delivery being made on March 15, 1865.

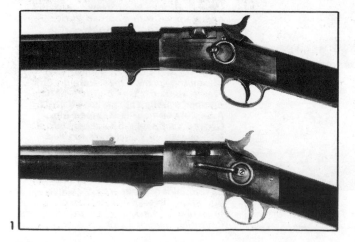

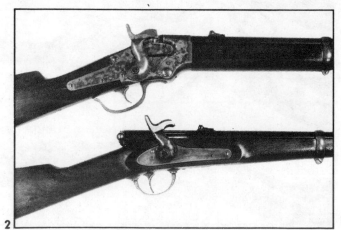

1

2

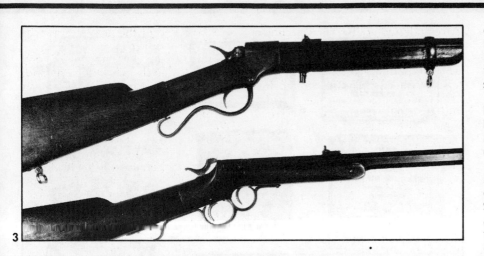

3

Warner carbines were manufactured in two basic styles, each easily identified by the markings which appear on the frame.

On "James Warner" marked specimens, the breechblock is released by upward pressure on a hook projection on the left side of the block. A thumb lever locking device, on the left side of the frame adjacent to the hammer, must first be depressed to allow the breechblock to be swung up and over for the loading operation. A sling ring on the left side of the frame is held by a heavy eye bolt inserted completely through the frame.

Warner carbines manufactured by "Greene Rifle Works" have a knurled sliding button release on the left side of the breechblock. This locking device eliminated the need for the thumb lever found on James Warner specimens. A sling bar and ring is affixed to the left side of the frame. The Greene Rifle Works, South Worcester, Massachusetts, was originally known as the "Lower Junction Shop" or "South Junction Shop". Prior to the Civil War, a number of early Joslyn firearms were manufactured at this location.

All things considered, the Warner was not a bad carbine, but others available were better. Some of the problems with the Warner centered around unreliable ammunition, poor extraction and a weakness in the design of the buttstock. The extractor was manually operated by the rearward movement of a stud-like handle located under the forend in front of the trigger guard. It proved unpopular because insufficient leverage was provided in case of a swollen shell. Furthermore, to eject the shell from the breech after extraction, an extra movement was required, either by using the fingers or by inverting the carbine.

The remaining government pur-

chases of carbines during the war were relatively insignificant, amounting to little more than 1000 or so, at most, of each type. Included in this group were the Ball, Ballard, Gibbs, Lindner, Palmer and Wesson carbines. All were metallic cartridge arms, excepting the Lindner and ill-fated Gibbs. The latter, patented by Lucius H. Gibbs of New York City, seemed destined for greater use, except for extenuating circumstances.

On December 13, 1861, the Ordnance Department contracted with William F. Brooks, 8 Spruce St., New York City, for 10,000 Gibbs carbines at $28.00 per carbine, including appendages. Brooks was a brass and flue manufacturer, who associated with William W. Marston, a practical armorer, to have the arms manufactured at the Phoenix Armory, 2nd Ave. & 22nd St., New York City. The barrels were to be made by Dinslow & Chase, Windsor Locks, Connecticut. Deliveries did not commence until May and June, 1863. With only 1052 carbines delivered, the Phoenix Armory burned to the ground on July 13, 1863 during the Draft Riots. All of the barrels, stocks, mountings, small parts, and gunmaking machinery was destroyed and that was the end of the Gibbs contract.

The operation of the Gibbs was similar to the Gallager carbine. The lever locking device is released, allowing the lever to be pushed down and forward. The barrel slides forward a short distance and the rear end tilts upward for loading. Affixed to the face of the breech is a circular collar (gas seal) surrounding a hollow cone (piercer), which enters and transmits ignition fire to the rear of the combustible cartridge.

At least three types of Lindner carbine were fabricated during the Civil War. The first type consisted of imported Austrian arms, cut down and altered to Lindner's system. The

other two types were produced almost in their entirety by Edward Lindner at the Amoskeag Manufacturing Co., Manchester, New Hampshire.

The breech cover is turned to the left by a flat knob and the breech-block tilts up in similar fashion to a Hall carbine. A paper cartridge was used.

On November 6, 1861, Lt. Col. William Maynardier, Ordnance Dept., requested that 400 Lindner carbines, at $20.00 each, and 40,000 cartridges, at $20.00 per thousand, be delivered to Washington Arsenal within eight days for use by Col. Thornton F. Brodhead's 1st Michigan Cavalry. While leading his Lindner-armed regiment at the 2nd Battle of Manassas, Colonel Brodhead was fatally injured in an encounter with the 12th Virginia Cavalry.

The Ballard carbine was a very simple and sturdy lever-action system. Like the Maynard, it lasted well into the post-war era. The original patent (No. 33,631) was issued to C. H. Ballard, Worcester, Massachusetts, on November 5, 1861. The dropping

1. Warner Breechloading Cartridge Carbines .50 caliber Warner or .56-50 Spencer, 20" barrel, 37½" overall. Marked on brass frame, "James Warner, Springfield, Mass.-Warner's Patent". Serial number is on inside of breechblock and/or butt plate. Sling ring on eyebolt. Bottom carbine is of similar specification but brass frame marked, "Greene Rifle Works, Worcester, Mass.-Pat. Feb. 1864". Serial number on inside of breechblock and frame.

2. Ball Repeating Cartridge Carbine, .50 caliber Ball or Spencer, 20¾", overall 37½". Left side of frame, "E.G. Lamson & Co.-Windsor, Vt.-U.S.-Ball's Patent-June 23, 1863-Mar. 15, 1864". Serial number inside frame and lockplate. Palmer Breechloading Cartridge Carbine, .50 caliber (.56-50 Spencer), 20", overall 37¼". Marked on lock, "U.S."-"E.G. Lamson & Co.-Windsor-Vt."-"1865". Receiver marked, "Wm Palmer-Patent-Dec. 22, 1863".

3. Ballard Breechloading Cartridge Carbine, .44 or .54 caliber, 20", 37¼" overall. Marked on left of frame, "Ball & Williams-Worcester, Mass." over "Merwin & Bray-New York"; on right, "Ballard's Patent-Nov. 5, 1861"; on top "No. 44 and serial number. Hammer marked, "Patented Jan. 5, 1864" to cover auxiliary percussion device in breechblock. Wesson Breechloading Cartridge Carbine, .44 caliber, 24" octagonal barrel, 39½" overall. Barrel marked "F. Wesson's Patent-Oct. 25, 1859 & Nov. 11, 1862"-"F. Wesson-Worcester, Mass." and "B. Kittredge & Co-Cincinnati, Ohio." Serial number stamped on trigger guard extension.

UNION CARBINES

breechblock was unique, containing both the trigger and hammer, bringing the latter to half cock when the breech was opened.

Although the Ballard originally was intended for use with rimfire ammunition, Joseph Merwin & Edward P. Bray, of New York City, patented an auxiliary percussion device (No. 41,-166) on January 5, 1864. In a sense, the novel device was a retrogression, but most handy in event the supply of fixed ammunition was exhausted. A nipple and vent were located midway in the breechblock, below the hammer nose slot. Either combustible or loose ammunition (powder and ball) could be used, but the breech would not be gas tight. A better method was to make use of the spent rimfire cartridge casing. The base of the case was pierced and the case loaded with powder and ball. A percussion cap was placed on the nipple and detonated by the

1. Full packages of Civil War carbines: A) Smith B) Merrill C) Sharps D) Starr E) Burnside F) Gwyn & Campbell G) Gallager H) Maynard (paper wrapped) I) Maynard (brass case).

2. Cartridges and related items for Civil War carbines. (Top row) Packet of 12 percussion caps and loose percussion caps; cylinder of Maynard tape primers; and brass tube of Sharps disc primers. (Second row) .69 Buck and Ball, cavalry musketoon; .50 Gallager (paper and brass); .50 Gallager (iron and paper-Jackson's Patent); .54 Joslyn paper; .50 Maynard (Poultney's paper wrapped); .56 Merrill paper; .52 Sharps paper; .52 Sharps linen; and .50 Smith India rubber. (Third row) .50 Smith (Poultney's Pat.); .54 Starr linen; .50 Ball rimfire; .44 Ballard; .54 Burnside (brass); .54 Burnside tinned case; .50 Gallager drawn brass; .54 Joslyn; and .58 Joslyn. (Bottom) .35 Maynard; .50 Maynard brass; .46 Remington (split-breech); .52 Sharps & Hankins; .56-56 Spencer; .56-52 Spencer; .56-50 Spencer; .56-50 Spencer blank; and .50 Warner.

3. Accessories for the carbines (from left to right top) Sharps .52 caliber, 6-cavity bullet mold; Jenks Navy flask; Wesson (Bennett's Pat.) cartridge box; leather socket buckled to saddle. An early form of scabbard, it held carbine; Joslyn mainspring vise; wide leather sling has brass buckle and was worn lanyard fashion with steel snap hook engaged on carbine sling ring to prevent dropping or loss in battle; Burnside single cavity bullet mold. (Bottom) Appendages: (From left) bullet screw for Springfield musketoon or Pistol-Carbine, and; combination tools for Ball, Burnside, Gallager, Maynard, Merrill, Palmer, Remington, Sharps, Sharps & Hankins, and Spencer carbines.

neck of the hammer during its normal fall. The flame from the cap entered the breech, which was now rendered gas tight in a fashion similar to the Burnside and Maynard designs with their separately primed metallic ammunition.

Although a limited number of Ballards were purchased by the U.S. government, notices in Harper's Weekly magazine in the spring of 1865 indicated that almost 20,000 Ballards were then in active field service with militia units of the State of Kentucky, who had high praise for the arm.

On June 20, 1864, Ebenezer G. Lamson & Co., of Windsor, Vermont, secured government contracts for 1000 Ball repeating carbines, at $25.00 each, and 1000 Palmer single-shot carbines at $20.50 each.

Albert Ball, the inventor of the Ball repeater, was superintendent and mechanical genius of the Lamson company. One of the greatest inventors and mechanics that New England ever produced, he spread his work over an extraordinarily wide field for over 70 years. In addition to his firearms patents, Ball held about 135 patents for major improvements in other fields.

The breechblock of the Ball repeater is formed by a trough-like "cartridge-carrier," which is employed not only for receiving a cartridge from the magazine and transporting it to, and inserting it in the barrel chamber, but is employed after discharge for extracting the empty shell. The "split" cartridge chamber in the barrel is unique, in that the upper and forward half of the chamber is partially constructed

in the frame at the rear end of the barrel. The lower and rearmost portion of the cartridge chamber is formed by the "cartridge-carrier" itself. The carbine fully loaded holds nine .56-50 Spencer cartridges or 12 of the shorter ".50 Ball Carbine" cartridges.

The Palmer was invented by William Palmer, of New York City, and is based upon his Patent No. 41,017, December 22, 1863. The primary claims of Mr. Palmer were "a collar applied around the breech-pin (bolt) and carrying a spring-latch (extractor) that draws out the cartridge case, in combination with a spring-ejector that delivers the empty case from the breech." The hammer on the Palmer functioned in similar fashion to that of the Ball carbine, a projection on the face of the hammer directly striking the rim of the shell. The Palmer had the distinction of being the first bolt action shoulder arm, using metallic cartridges, obtained for United States martial use.

The government originally desired both carbines to be in .44 caliber, and the question of caliber delayed Albert Ball in obtaining these carbines on a manufacturing basis. Late in 1864, the government authorized use of the newly designed .56-50 Spencer cartridge in arms then being manufactured. The Ball and Palmer carbines were delivered on May 14th and June 15th, 1865, respectively, too late for wartime use.

The smallest of the wartime carbine contracts was for 151 Wesson carbines. General Ripley purchased 150 carbines on July 7, 1863, at $23.00 each. The carbines were purchased from Benjamin Kittredge & Co., Cincinnati, Ohio, a dealer in guns and accessories. An additional carbine was purchased from Schuyler, Hartley & Graham, New York City, on August 1, 1863, at a cost of $24.25. Mr. Kittredge, an ardent supporter of the Wesson carbine, also furnished 1366 to the State of Kentucky, 760 to Indiana, and hundreds more to various regiments.

The Wesson features a double trigger guard with barrel releasing trigger in the smaller forward guard bow. The barrel pivots at the forward end of the metal frame, tipping up at the breech. Up to 15 shots per minute could be discharged with good aim. The empty shell was withdrawn by the fingers, no mechanical means being provided. Often a ramrod was necessary to drive out a stubborn shell.

As the Civil War neared its conclusion, the general superiority of certain carbines and types of ammunition over others became apparent. It also became obvious that the glowing testimonials of many officers in regard to certain carbines came as a result of their limited exposure to a single carbine. Having seen no others for comparison, they were impressed by the performance of any breechloading carbine as opposed to muzzleloading arms. Consequently, many of the breechloading carbines in the service were ineffective and tolerated only in the emergency of war.

Even the government was becoming aware of the need for a change. On December 5, 1864, Brig. Gen. A. B. Dyer, Chief of Ordnance, wrote to Edwin M. Stanton, Secretary of War:

"The experience of the War has shown that breechloading arms are greatly superior to muzzleloaders for infantry as well as for cavalry . . . It is important that the best arm which is now made shall be adopted and that all breechloaders thereafter made by or for this department shall conform strictly to it, and that no change shall be made until it shall have been clearly demonstrated that the change is a decided and important improvement. With a view, therefore, to carry out these measures, I have the honor to request that a board, to be composed of ordnance, cavalry, and infantry officers, be constituted to meet at Springfield Armory, and at such other place or places as the board may direct, to examine, test, and recommend for adoption a suitable breechloader for muskets and carbines, and a suitable repeater or magazine carbine, and that the arm recommended by the board may, if approved by the War Department, be exclusively adopted for the military service."

The trial board convened at Springfield Armory, on January 5, 1865 and began the arduous task of testing approximately 65 different breechloading systems submitted by inventors and manufacturers from across the country. Included were some systems previously issued for use during the War. The first day of the trial officially rang the death-knell of the percussion ignition system, as it was decided that only cartridge arms would be considered. On April 6, 1865, the board rendered an opinion that the Peabody single-shot and the Spencer magazine systems each combined more advantages than any of the arms of this description presented to the board.

However, further testing was deemed necessary and another board assembled at Washington, D.C. on March 10, 1866 to complete the tests. In June, 1866, the final report of the board indicated that the experience of the late war as well as all experiments by the board had proven the Spencer magazine carbine as the best service gun of the kind yet offered, but recommended a delay in adopting definitely a pattern "for future construction of carbines for cavalry service." The dreadful carnage of war had ended and additional experimenting with new or patent type arms seemed unnecessary as many improvements in arms were foreseen prior to the time further use would be actually required or anticipated.

Since there was a large number of arms on hand capable of economical alteration and the Ordnance Department was faced with the usual post war retrenchment in funds, this was a point in favor of the system of Erskine S. Allin, a Master Armorer at Springfield Armory. Allin's principle was a good one and could be applied to the muzzleloading arms available with little difficulty. The conversion was accomplished by milling open the breech section of the barrel and inserting in this opening a hinged bolt, which was affixed to the top of the barrel. This system eventually became the forerunner of the single-shot "trap-door" Springfield breechloader, issued for over 25 years. ⚔

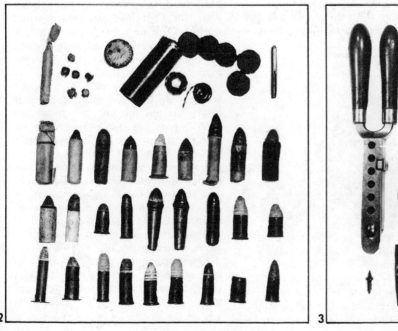

2

3

FORGOTTEN FOR A CENTURY

A DISINTERRED COLT NAVY WITH LOADED CHAMBERS COULD NO DOUBT TELL A FASCINATING STORY. OTHERS LIKE IT HAVE BEEN FOUND, AND MORE AWAIT THE CAREFUL SEARCHER.

by Walter L. Rickell

Finding an old firearm is always a rewarding experience, even though it might be far beyond repairs, usually due to severe rusting conditions. From the first time you pick it up your mind wanders, "Wonder how it ended up here?" Was it the reason for a gun fight? Who used it? If only these old arms talked!

These questions still run through Ken Carrell's mind about that old rusted 1851 Colt Navy of his, which was originally found by Gale Jones while skin diving in the Rogue River near Brushy Chute, Oregon. The old pistol having retained some of its silver plating, reflected the sunlight in the cool, clear waters, attracting Gale's attention. When found, most of the pistol was buried in the river bottom, but the exposed silver-plated grip frame marked its resting place.

Soon after the piece was found it became the possession of Ken Carrell of Grant's Pass, Oregon who, being somewhat of a student on guns, initially identified the piece as a Colt 1851 Navy model, .36 caliber, percussion revolver, serial number 15,-262. Later discussion with a local historian revealed that several sailors had jumped ship near what is now known as Crescent City, California about 150 miles to the southwest, and during their escape they passed through the Brushy Chute area. They had stolen several pistols of this type from the ship and possibly they could have dropped it while swimming the Rogue River.

Incidentally, when found the gun was fully loaded, capped with the hammer on a safety pin. These are small pins protruding from the rear of the cylinder, located between the nipples, allowing six rounds to be carried safely with the hammer in the fired position.

Although the metal was badly rusted, the brass grip frame was still intact and usable with much of the original silver plating evident. This indicates that it must have been a new or nearly new piece, since this plating was quickly worn off in use.

The historian's story seemed to jibe, with this being a low-serial number 1851 model, the sailors jumping ship in 1851, and this being a Navy sidearm. So the next step was to check with Colt Firearms to see what they had on their records for this particular model since he had the serial number. This proved to be a brick wall, for Colt lost all their records during a fire in 1864, set by Confederate agents. The most recently recorded number was 98,000 being manufactured in 1861.

This didn't settle with Ken for he still wanted to know more about that Navy, so he began to study the 1851 Navy Colt itself. The more he learned the more his interest grew. The first Colt 1851 Navy models began manufacture in 1851, hence the model number. The first 4200 pieces had square-backed trigger guards, of this there were two different variations with the first 1250 referred to as the first model and the remainder as the second model.

Ken's specimen is numbered 15,-262, so it fell into the third model class; these have small round or oval trigger guards. It was manufactured

2

3

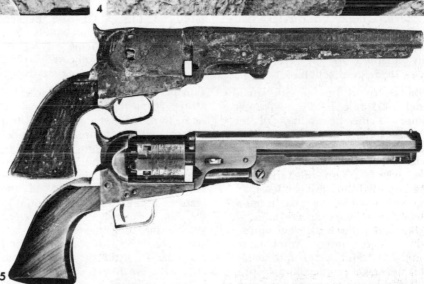

4

from serial numbers 4200 through 85,000. The fourth and last model, having a large round trigger guard, went from there to 215,000 when the production ceased in 1873.

Some recently discovered records found in an attic at Colt's Hartford plant indicated that 1851 Navy Models numbering in the 30,000 range were in production during 1854. So, using a little mathematics, it works out to about 8000 pistols per year, and would date the rusted relic about 1852. But still it could have been made in 1851; who knows? In any case, it's entirely possible that it could have been on the ship, sailing the Pacific in 1851.

But further checking revealed that the Navy never purchased any of these pistols until around 1858, and they were delivered with iron back-straps and trigger guards, plus the serial numbers began with 55,000. So the pistol in question was not a Navy gun, a fact or not a fact??? It could have been privately owned by some officer on the ship???

The reference to its name as Navy model has always been credited to the design being used and made for the United States Navy. The facts are when Sam Colt introduced the model in 1851, he called it the ''Ranger'' model. Now, wanting to enter the

military market, he had engraved on the unfluted cylinder the most recent military engagement of any significance. This happened to be a battle between the Texas Navy and the Mexican Navy in 1843. Soon after the gun was out, the name Ranger was dropped and it was from then on referred to as the Navy model, due strictly to its cylinder scene.

So the interest grows and grows, each time Ken has looked into the history of the old relic the picture grows bigger and bigger; if only that old pistol could talk.

5

1. Left side view of this unusual 1851 Colt Navy shown alongside the new Colt reproduction revolver.

2. Bottom view reveals the serial number 15262 on the trigger guard.

3. Top view shows that the pistol was carried on the safety notch. Note that the silver plating is still evident on the backstrap.

4. Front view shows pistol is still loaded. Note ball in chamber.

5. The Rogue River of Oregon has taken its toll of this relic-grade gun but it did look like the new Colt repro model in its better days.

WINCHESTER
MODEL 70

A 20TH-CENTURY CLASSIC

by Ted Komula

In 1866, Winchester Repeating Arms Co. made history with the introduction of their first lever-action rifle. The Model 1866 and its successors were the rifles by which all others were judged. Except for highly specialized target shooting, the various Winchester models adapted themselves to all forms of use to which a rifle can be put.

The emergence of the turn-bolt repeating rifle was looked on with suspicion by the American rifleman, both as a military and sporting arm. Though our armed forces adopted the Krag repeating turn-bolt system in 1892, the civilian shooter clung to the lever-action Winchester. Although the Krag rifle was not well suited to civilian use, its cartridge easily adapted to the Winchester Model 1895 lever action.

The adoption of the Springfield Model 1903 rifle mildly awoke the shooter to the possibilities of the turn-bolt system, and its completely revised cartridge, the .30 Government Model 1906. The high power, high velocity bolt action rifle and cartridge sounded taps for the lever action, which could not take modern ammunition's working pressures. A lot of men used the "New Springfield" rifle/cartridge combination during 1917 and 1918, and its effectiveness against the ultimate prey resulted in a strong demand for turn-bolt sporters in the decade following

World War 1. Savage and Remington responded to this demand by 1920 with high-powered bolt action sporters, but Winchester marketed only the Model 52, a bolt action .22.

It was not until 1925 that Winchester introduced their Model 54, a very sleek, beautifully made bolt action big bore with features which up to that time had been present only in custom-built Mauser- or Springfield-based sporters. On good looks alone, the Model 54 was a winner, and appearances were backed up in balance and performance. Introduced simultaneously with the Model 54 was Winchester's .270 cartridge. Based on the .30-06 case necked down to accept 6.8mm bullets. This cartridge remains on the market today, though always hotly argued over by writers in the shooting sports.

In 1937, Winchester introduced the Model 70 to replace the Model 54. Actually it was nothing more than a revised edition of the earlier Model 54 design, the improvements were so significant that the 54 was almost forgotten overnight. Here was a commercial rifle incorporating all the features heretofore available only in the super-expensive class sporters. Winchester took the initiative and commercialized two popular Holland & Holland cartridges, the .300 and .375 with the Model 70.

To a collector, the Model 70 is now classified into three main

groups: those built before World War 2; those built after World War 2; those built after 1964, when a number of major design revisions were put into production. From this point, we come to style variations such as the Sporter, Target, Carbine and National Match models, plus the Varmints and Featherweights. Following this are caliber variations. The Model 70 has been available in a variety of calibers over the years, and some rifles in odd calibers are extremely scarce. Taking this theme to the advanced level, we find that the Model 70 has undergone numerous inevitable production variations over the years. This ranges all the way from changes in bolt handles to safety wings and checkering patterns.

Today, 35 years later, the Model 70 is still with us. Indeed, it is a different Model 70 in many respects from the original model, but the past two years has seen it returning to the original format in stocking up— a welcome return. No matter what range the serial number falls into, a good 70 is a good rifle, be it a sporter, varminter or target style. However, the Model 70, in its numerous variations (there are many) is rapidly becoming an object for the collector. Several individuals have discovered this fact, and are building fascinating and extremely diverse collections based on this, the traditional, all-American turn-bolt production sporting rifle.

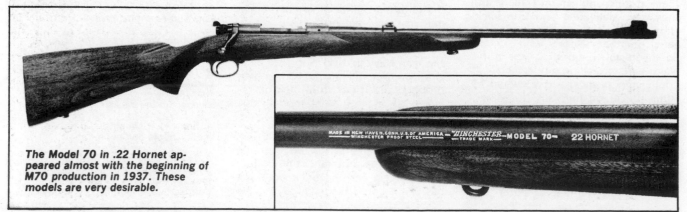

The Model 70 in .22 Hornet appeared almost with the beginning of M70 production in 1937. These models are very desirable.

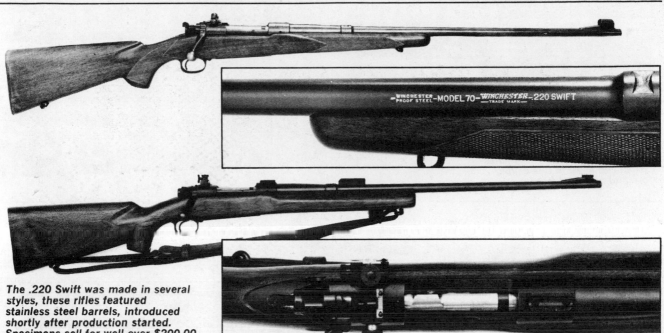

The .220 Swift was made in several styles, these rifles featured stainless steel barrels, introduced shortly after production started. Specimens sell for well over $200.00. The National Match version is quite rare.

M70s in .243 Winchester are common in standard weight barrels but the Varmint and Target barreled arms are scarce. Specimens are in the $200.00 to $300.00 category based on condition.

The .250-3000 M70 is quite a rare bird. Chambering was offered before and after WW 2. Few are found, specimens command high "tariffs."

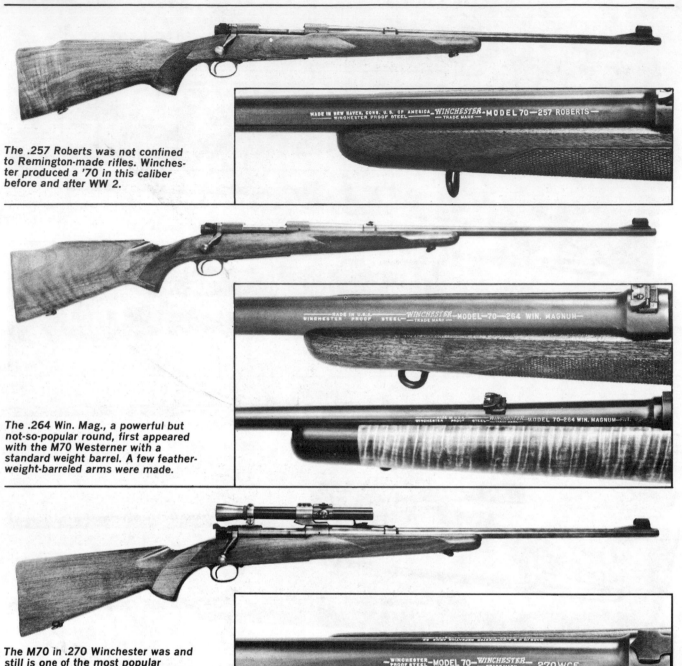

The .257 Roberts was not confined to Remington-made rifles. Winchester produced a '70 in this caliber before and after WW 2.

The .264 Win. Mag., a powerful but not-so-popular round, first appeared with the M70 Westerner with a standard weight barrel. A few featherweight-barreled arms were made.

The M70 in .270 Winchester was and still is one of the most popular chamberings going for the Olin firm. Pre-war rifles are quite desirable as collectors guns now when in mint condition, some can bring $175.00 to $225.00.

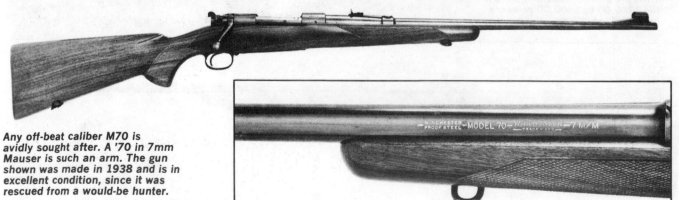

Any off-beat caliber M70 is avidly sought after. A '70 in 7mm Mauser is such an arm. The gun shown was made in 1938 and is in excellent condition, since it was rescued from a would-be hunter.

Almost unheard-of except to collectors, the M70 in .300 Savage is a rare bird. A high-buck item on the list of scarce '70s, it is eagerly sought after.

The 70 was America's first factory production sporter to chamber the long ranging, hard hitting .300 H&H Magnum cartridge. Winchester introduced the .300 H&H as well as the .375 H&H with the M70. Some time after introduction the .300 H&Hs were made with stainless steel barrels as this cartridge was highly erosive on the throat and lead of barrels.

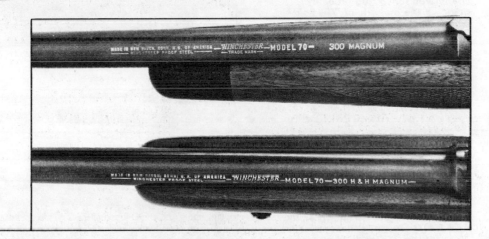

Winchester Bull-barreled target rifles are favorites of precision riflemen. The "Old Model" variation was chambered in .30/06, .300 H&H. .220 Swift, and .308 Win.

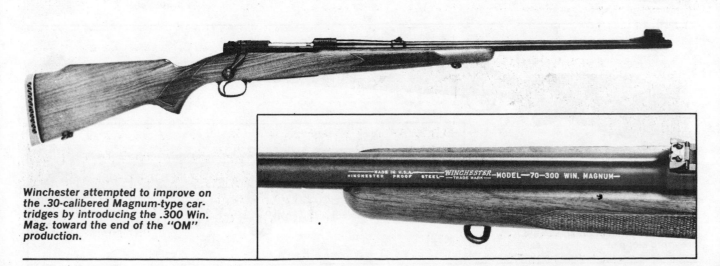

Winchester attempted to improve on the .30-calibered Magnum-type cartridges by introducing the .300 Win. Mag. toward the end of the "OM" production.

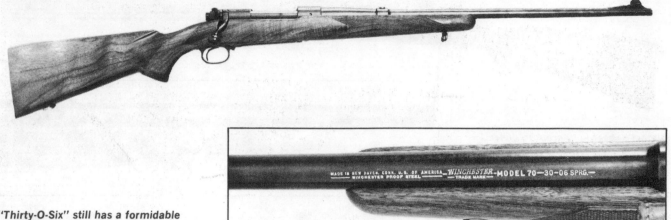

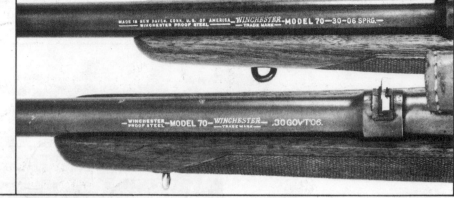

"Thirty-O-Six" still has a formidable ring to it just as it did in "the-good-old days". It was the most popular cartridge for long range hunting in the United States before introduction of the Magnums. M70s chambered for .30/06 probably made up the majority of '70s sold before discontinuance of the "OM". Shown are the late and early marking styles.

The introduction of the .308 Winchester cartridge, also known as the 7.62 NATO brought in heavy competition for the .30/06. First appearing about 1951, the .308 has risen to great popularity.

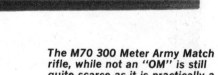

The M70 300 Meter Army Match rifle, while not an "OM" is still quite scarce as it is practically a custom gun. Specimen shown is a prototype.

The .338 Winchester Magnum appeared about the time the "Old Model" was on its way out. Early specimens show fine fitting and finish. Late production specimens are more sloppy.

This M70 in .35 Remington was made just after WW 2. Quite scarce it was not a popular chambering, now a premium collector's item.

The .308 had variations on its case the .243, as previously discussed, and the .358 Win. as shown. A scarce chambering now, it is very desirable.

The .375 H&H Magnum is still one of the most popular big game cartridges in use today. Winchester pioneered in chambering a factory rifle for it. The specimen pictured with scope is a very early model with a straight taper, heavy barrel chambered for .375. This piece is probably one of the first M70s in .375. It is also the "Super Grade" variation, making it extremely desirable. The other rifle is standard grade that had a butt-pad retrofitted. Also shown are the two marking styles for early and late production guns.

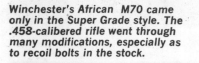

Winchester's African M70 came only in the Super Grade style. The .458-calibered rifle went through many modifications, especially as to recoil bolts in the stock.

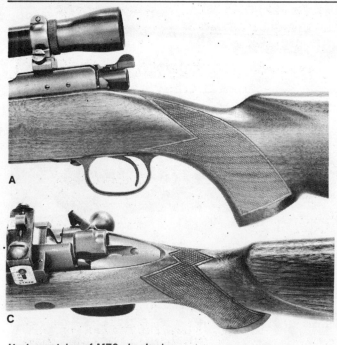

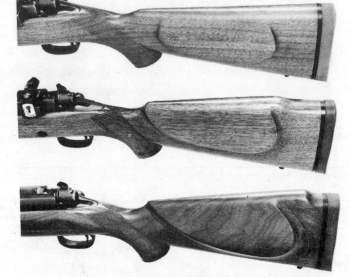

The M70 came with two basic stock styles; the low comb (standard) as seen on top left and the Monte Carlo comb left, bottom. Super Grades came in two basic varieties, low comb with cheek piece and Monte Carlo with cheek piece, right, bottom stock has an unusual cheekpiece design and is a "factory" gun.

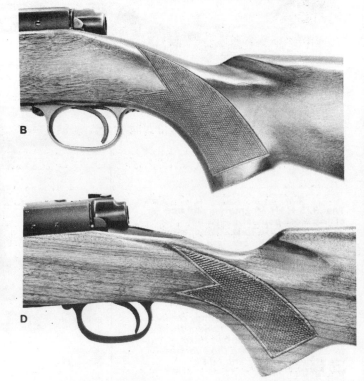

Various styles of M70 checkering are: (A) Pre-War 21 points per inch; (C) Super Grade post-War at 18 points; (B) Standard post-War, 18 points; (D) late production, 18.

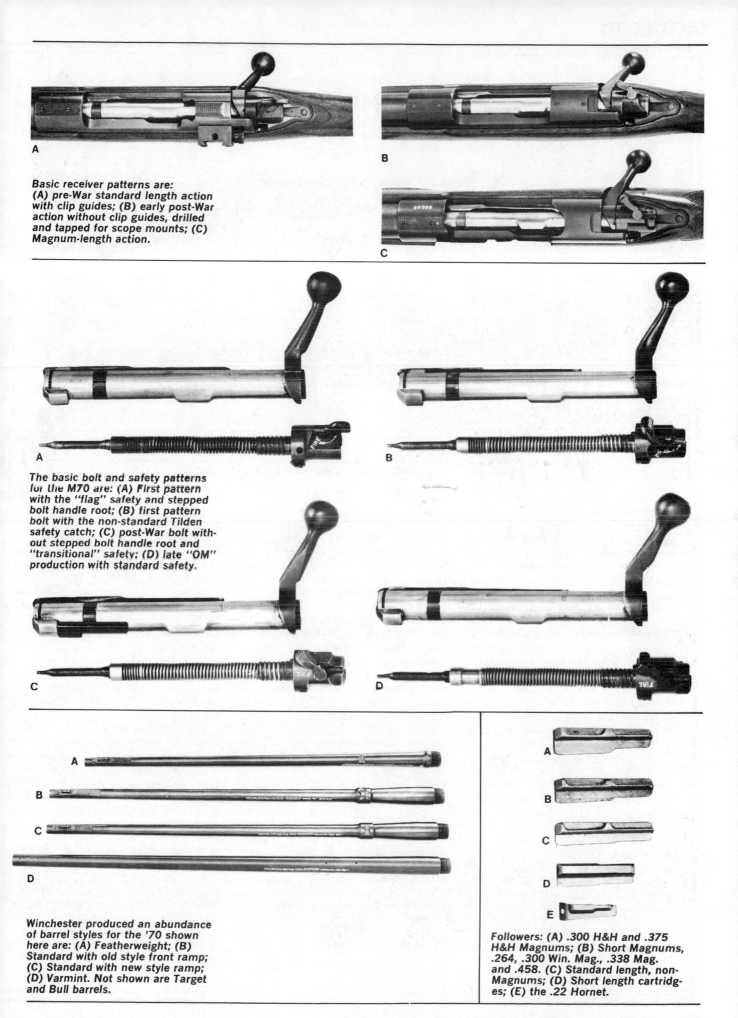

Basic receiver patterns are: (A) pre-War standard length action with clip guides; (B) early post-War action without clip guides, drilled and tapped for scope mounts; (C) Magnum-length action.

The basic bolt and safety patterns for the M70 are: (A) First pattern with the "flag" safety and stepped bolt handle root; (B) first pattern bolt with the non-standard Tilden safety catch; (C) post-War bolt without stepped bolt handle root and "transitional" safety; (D) late "OM" production with standard safety.

Winchester produced an abundance of barrel styles for the '70 shown here are: (A) Featherweight; (B) Standard with old style front ramp; (C) Standard with new style ramp; (D) Varmint. Not shown are Target and Bull barrels.

Followers: (A) .300 H&H and .375 H&H Magnums; (B) Short Magnums, .264, .300 Win. Mag., .338 Mag. and .458. (C) Standard length, non-Magnums; (D) Short length cartridges; (E) the .22 Hornet.

SMITH & WESSON

PIONEER IN SINGLE ACTION REVOLVERS
by Robert J. Neal

When Horace Smith and D. B. Wesson formed their first partnership in 1852 it marked the beginnings of two great firearms companies, Smith & Wesson and Winchester.

The original partnership was formed to develop a practical magazine-type firearm for later manufacture. This effort culminated in the issue of patent No. 10535 on February 14, 1854. On June 20, 1854, Horace D. Smith, D. B. Wesson and Courtlandt Palmer formed the Smith & Wesson company for the actual manufacture of these arms. The company held magazine arms patents of Walter Hunt, Lewis Jennings and Horace Smith issued between 1849 and 1851. These were all basic magazine arms patents and control of them was essential to avoid possible patent suits. It was the exterior and interior design shown in the February 14, 1854, patent which was closely followed.

Production was started in Norwich, Connecticut, in 1854 and continued into 1855 with a total output estimated at less than 2000 pistols. These were primarily in .30 caliber with 4-inch barrel and .38 caliber with 6- or 8-inch barrel. The arms were generally marked on the barrel flats "SMITH & WESSON NORWICH,

CT." "CAST-STEEL" "PATENTED FEBRUARY 14, 1854." The frame was of cast steel with the smaller model being round butt and the larger square. These arms are exceedingly rare and highly desirable collectors items. Even more desirable would be one of the very rare .50-caliber rimfire rifles they made on an experimental basis. One such rifle now resides in the Winchester Museum.

Smith & Wesson's interests turned from magazine arms to revolvers using a cylinder which was bored through from end to end so as to accept a rimfire cartridge inserted from the rear. A rimfire cartridge had been shown in their magazine arm patent, though not claimed. They had taken out a patent on a rimfire cartridge on August 8, 1854, however.

In June of 1855 the partners sold their interests in the magazine arms company, including machinery, parts, stock and patents to the Volcanic Repeating Arms Company of New Haven, Connecticut. This company produced magazine arms similar to the Smith & Wesson marked arms except that they had brass rather than steel frames. Markings were changed to "VOLCANIC REPEATING ARMS COMPANY NEW HAVEN, CONN. PATENT FEB. 14, 1854." This com-

pany went into receivership in February of 1857 and one of its stockholders, Oliver Winchester, bought out the remaining assets. Winchester then formed the New Haven Arms Company to continue production of the arms we now call the "Volcanic" type. These were marked "NEW HAVEN CONN. PATENT FEB. 14, 1854." The New Haven Arms Company continued until 1865 before it was reorganized into the Henry Repeating Arms Company and only one year later into the Winchester Repeating Arms Company.

The fact that the Smith & Wesson, Volcanic, and New Haven arms all used the same type of caseless ammunition, were of very similar design, and were all made under the same patent has led collectors to call them all "Volcanics," which is actually incorrect. Each had its own characteristics and name. The Smith & Wesson arm was the first to bear this great name and was also produced under a patent taken out by Horace Smith and D. B. Wesson which was to become the basis under which the Henry and Winchester rifles were later to be made. Thus it represents the beginnings of two of the greatest names in firearms in the world.

In connection with their new venture into revolvers, Smith & Wesson purchased the rights to patent No. 12648 of April 3, 1855, issued to Rollin White. This patent covered the use of a revolver cylinder bored through from end to end, thus allowing the use of metallic ammunition inserted from the rear. Assignment of these rights was not made until November 17, 1856, and by that time it is believed most of the design of the original revolver, later to be known as the No. 1, had been done. Rights to this patent gave the company a monopoly on the production of a practical cartridge revolver until its expiration on April 3, 1869.

The account books of the company were opened on November 18, 1856, and thus began the second Smith & Wesson partnership. This one was to build into the great revolver producing company we know today.

Work was started to set up production facilities and the first income from production was recorded on October 18, 1857. Thus began sales of the first revolver which was a small seven-shot .22 rimfire of very limited power. This pocket-size revolver was known as the No. 1. The decision had been made to name the models (by numbers) in order of size. After several years and several models this was found to be impractical and dropped in favor of descriptive names.

Since this numbering system is sometimes confusing, some detailed explanation seems to be in order. As stated, the first model, called the No. 1, was introduced in 1857. It continued in production, with several modifications, until 1881. 1861 saw the introduction of a belt-size pistol, the No. 2. This was a six-shot revolver chambering the .32 rimfire Long cartridge. In 1865 another .32 rimfire revolver was introduced. This

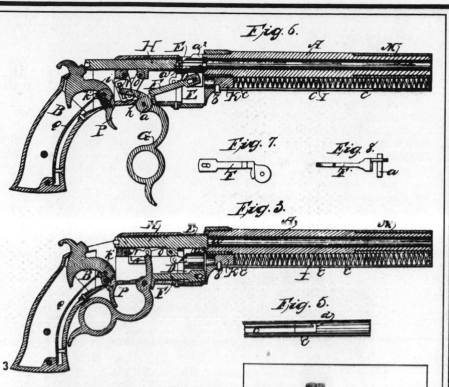

one was a five shot and somewhat smaller than the No. 2. It was named the No. 1½ as it fell between the No. 1 and the No. 2 in size. In 1870 a six-shot .44 caliber revolver in what was considered "army" size was put on the market. It was called the No. 3.

This type numbering system was continued in use until about 1885. By this time it had all become rather confusing since several actions in each size had been produced and double actions had come into the picture as well. All sizes had been included within the numbers 1, 1½, 2, and 3. By 1882 there was no more No. 1; there were three sizes of double actions and three sizes of single

1. Small frame "Smith & Wesson" pistol in .30 caliber.

2. Large frame "Smith & Wesson" pistol in .38 caliber.

3. Magazine pistol patent, U.S. No. 10,535 issued to D. B. Wesson, on February 14, 1854.

4. Model No. 1, First Issue in gutta percha case with ammunition.

5. Smith Wesson experimental magazine rifle in caliber .50 rimfire. Winchester Museum.

SMITH & WESSON

actions. It was about this time the company ceased to use the numbering system.

It was not until about 1960 that the company decided to again use numbers for model designation. This time they kept the descriptive names in addition to the numbers. To avoid possible confusion with numbers used with these early models, the 1960 numbering system started at 10 (thus the numbers 4 through 9 were never used) and the number had no relation to size.

The No. 1 First Issue was put on the market late in 1857 and was the first cartridge revolver commercially produced. The frame was brass and the barrel, cylinder, and lockwork was of steel. The cylinder held seven .22 Short rimfire cartridges of Smith & Wesson design and manufacture. This was a hinged-frame design which pivoted at the front of the top strap and latched at the front of the bottom strap. Pivoting the barrel upward allowed removal of the cylinder for loading and unloading. Empty cases were pushed out of the cylinder one by one with the rammer pin lo-

cated under the barrel. Though this system was certainly inferior to the modern ones of later years, it was far faster than reloading the cap-and-ball revolvers of their competitors. This basic design is known as the "tip-up" revolver.

Smith & Wesson manufactured cartridges for their revolvers until about 1868. They held two patents for rimfire cartridges and found the business profitable as well as necessary as no other firms had yet begun production in enough quality or quantity to supply the needs of S&W purchasers.

Problems with bulging of the early copper cases required several design changes in the No. 1 revolver to keep fired cartridges from jamming the cylinder. Within a little over a year, improvement in case material and design had alleviated the cause.

Barrel length was 3 3/16 inches

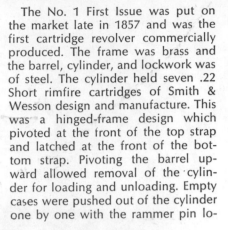

1. Box of Smith & Wesson-made .22 Short rimfire cartridges.

2. Gutta percha case for the Model No. 1, First Issue made by Littlefield & Parsons.

3. Variation of the above, having a more explicit explanation of the intended contents.

4. From top to bottom: Model No. 1, First Issue; Second Issue; Third Issue.

5. Factory engraved pieces, from top to bottom: Model No. 1, Third Issue; Model No. 1, Second Issue; Model No. 1½, Second Issue; Second Model .38 Single Action.

6. From top to bottom: Model No. 1½, First Issue; Model No. 1½, Transition, Model No. 1½, Second Issue; Second Model .38 Single Action.

throughout production. The first engraved revolvers were produced in 1858 and marked the beginning of S&W presentation grade guns. Cylinders of early pistols were marked "White PATENT Apr. 3, 1855" with the mark later changed to "PATENTED Apr. 3, 1855." In June of 1859 the patent date June 15, 1858 was added. The top of the barrel was marked "SMITH & WESSON Springfield, Mass."

This model was available in two types of gutta percha cases made by Littlefield and Parsons & Co. One type had a reproduction of the revolver molded on the lid and the other a design featuring six draped flags in the center. The cases are quite rare and desirable items.

Production of the model continued to 1860 and about serial No. 11,671. There is no exact ending serial as there was some overlap in serials with the following model. This holds true of all the models where a replacement model continued in the same serial series.

Operations had been carried on in a small shop at 5 Market Street in Springfield until 1860. At this time, work was completed on a new factory

on Stockbridge Street and production was moved there in time to start on the new Model No. 1 which collectors call the No. 1 Second Issue. The Stockbridge plant was continually expanded over the years and remained in use until 1952 when new facilities were completed at 1200 Roosevelt Avenue.

The oval-sided frame of the First Issue was changed to a flat-sided one and the small round side plate was replaced with a larger, irregularly shaped one. The frame was still of brass but access to the lockwork was greatly improved. The old type cylinder stop had been activated by a split hammer. The act of pulling the hammer back by the thumb piece pivoted the upper section of the hammer nose upward. It contacted the bottom of the cylinder stop and pushed it up and out of the stop notch. This system was changed to use a projection on top of the hammer nose to ride the stop upward on a spring ramp on rearward movement, a great improvement over the old system. This model continued in production until 1868 with serials remaining in the same series with the prior model.

Barrel length remained at 3 3/16 inches as in the prior model and patent markings continued to be carried on the cylinder. Beginning in December of 1861, some of this model with minor defects in finish of frame casting were marked "2D.-QUAL'TY" and sold at slight discount. The defects did not effect safety or function so the pieces were allowed to be sold in an effort to reduce huge back orders. A total of 4402 such revolvers were sold by the end of production in 1868. A large number of these were sold to dealer B. Kitteridge & Co. of Cincinnati, Ohio. Most of the pieces had the second quality stamp on the side of the barrel flat just forward of the cylinder. On many so marked, Kitteridge was very careful to stamp their house mark over the second quality mark so it could not be read. The author strongly suspects they retailed the revolvers at full prices!

By 1861 the problem of case bulging encountered with early ammunition had been overcome and calibers larger than .22 became practical. The company was anxious to put something of larger size on the market in order that they might have a re-

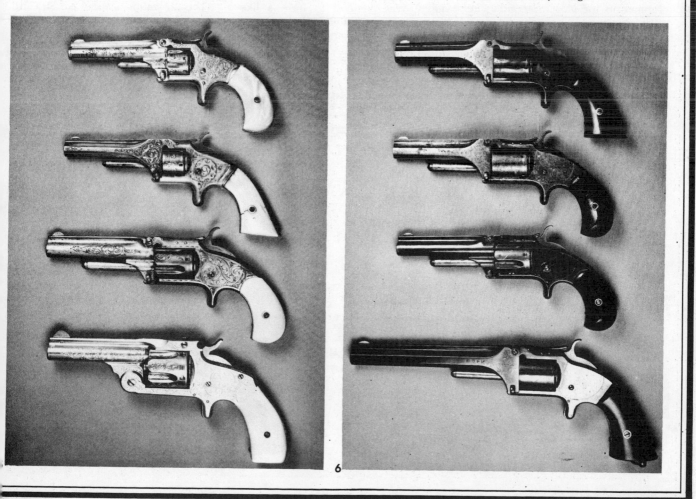

6

SMITH & WESSON

volver to sell in competition with the percussion revolvers. In this year they introduced the Model No. 2 Old Model, or Army as we now call it. Overall design was like the No. 1 Second Issue except that it was scaled up in size considerably to chamber six .32 rimfire Long cartridges. The model gained the name "Army" in later years because it was purchased in fairly large quantities by military personnel to be carried as backup or belt gun. It has even been classed by some writers over the years as a "secondary martial," inferring it was purchased by the government for issue to troops. This is not the case however, as there were never any military purchases of this model.

The model continued in production until 1874 and enjoyed wide popularity. Barrel lengths were 4, 5, and 6 inches with the four-inch length being introduced in April of 1866 and produced in very small quantities.

Between 1863 and 1871, 35 of this model were marked "2D.QUAL'TY" and sold at slight discount. These had minor defects as explained in reference to the No. 1 Second Issue.

The year of 1865 brought the introduction of a .32 rimfire revolver very similar to the No. 2 Army, but somewhat smaller and chambering five instead of six cartridges. This was called the No. 1½ by the factory and further distinguished by collectors as the "Old" or "First Model."

This model was the first to carry patent dates on the barrel rib along with the company name and address. It was also unique in that it was the only "tip-up" revolver to have its cylinder stop in the bottom strap. This new stop was activated with a spring-ramp by the hammer and proved to be rather delicate and often broke. As a result this was the only revolver to use this design. Standard barrel length was 3½ inches with four inches becoming available in April of 1866. Few were furnished in the longer length and are scarce.

Production continued until 1868 and into the 26,000 serial range. Six of this model were marked "2D. QUAL'TY" and sold in 1867, thus producing a *very* rare variation.

In December of 1868, while switching from production of the No. 1½ First Model to Second Model it was found that about 1500 First Model barrels were left on hand. As D. B. Wesson was never one to be wasteful, it was decided to have a like number of non-fluted cylinders made up and the combination assembled on Second Model frames. This created what collectors now call the "Transition" Model No. 1½. Although the 1500 barrels were to be made up into a like number of arms, sales records indicate only 650 completed pieces were actually sold. These were made in March of 1869 and fall into the serial range of No. 27,200 to 28,800. Sales to dealers were as follows:

March 27, 1869—50 to C. W. May for sale in Japan.

April 19, 1869—200 to J. W. Storrs.

May 17, 1869—400 to C. W. May for sale in France.

1868 brought the introduction of a new model in both .22 and .32 caliber. The primary improvements over the replaced models were in exterior design or styling. The No. 1½ First Model was replaced with the Second Model which had a new "bird's head" style grip and round rather than hexagon barrel. The non-fluted cylinder was replaced with one with long flutes. The previously described hammer-activated cylinder stop of the old model was replaced with the old type found in the No. 2 Army. The production run of some 100,000 guns went from 1868 to 1875.

The .22 caliber Model No. 1 Third Issue replaced the Second Issue also in 1868 and carried the same exte-

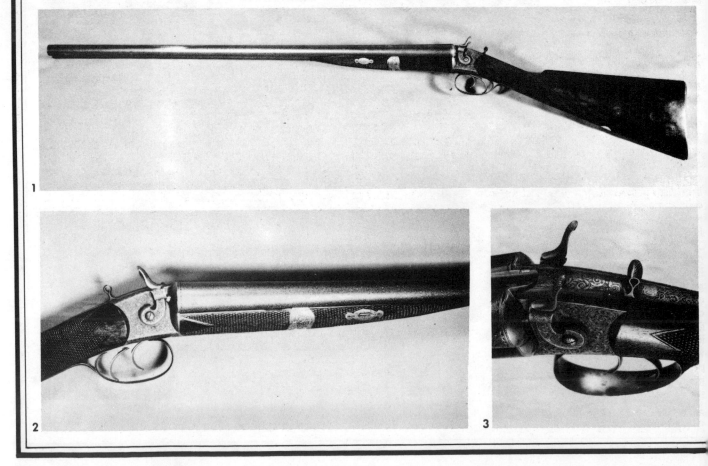

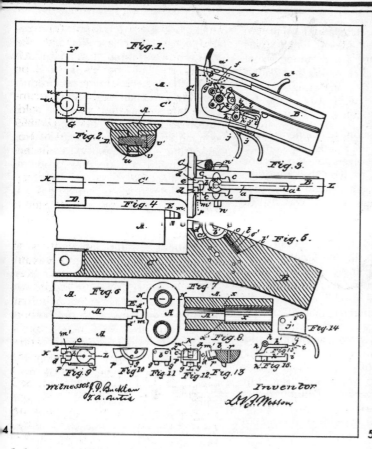

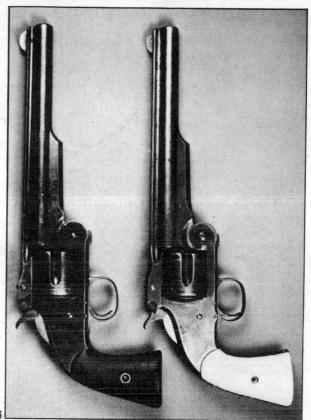

1. Later type "Wesson Shotgun" made by S&W, marked "Smith & Wesson" on rib.

2. Breech and lock detail of later type Wesson Shotgun.

3. Wesson Shotgun, breech area, showing Gustav Young engraving.

4. One of the shotgun patents issued Daniel B. Wesson.

5. First and Second Model Americans. Caliber .44 single action.

rior styling improvements as the No. 1½. There were no changes in lockwork design, however. About 131,000 of this fine little revolver were made until production ceased in 1881. It is interesting to note that the company did not again produce a .22 caliber revolver until the introduction of the First Model Ladysmith in 1902.

The years 1867 to 1869 were important ones for the company. The last of the tip-up models were put in production and work was progressing on a full "army-size" pistol with a completely new cartridge and design. D. B. Wesson, who had become the inventive genius of the firm, was also working on plans for an entirely new product in the firearms line to be manufactured by a separate company set up by himself, Horace Smith and J. W. Storrs. This product was to be a high-grade double-barrel 12 gauge

breechloading shotgun. Price range was $200.00 to $250.00; a high grade piece indeed when the best army-size revolvers sold for about $15.00.

The Wesson Fire Arms Company was formed to produce these guns on May 27, 1867 and most of the patents under which it was produced were held by D. B. Wesson. After considerable difficulties, production was under way in early 1869, but lasted only a short time. Only 216 of these shotguns were made before the venture was terminated. The barrel ribs were marked "WESSON FIRE ARMS COMPANY" and patent dates were stamped on the frame under the breech end of the barrels.

Although the Wesson Fire Arms Company ceased to exist in 1870, a few special-order shotguns were made up in the Smith & Wesson factory over the next five years or so for persons having considerable influence with D. B. Wesson. A few of these were marked "SMITH & WESSON SPRINGFIELD, MASS." Just how many of these special pieces were made is not now known, but it was indeed few.

1870 also brought the introduction of the Model No. 3; the army-size revolver previously mentioned. This was the first of the "break open" models, a term used because the barrel was hinged to the frame at

the front of the bottom strap and latched at the rear of the top strap. When the barrel catch was released and the grip held in one hand and the barrel in the other, the barrel was pushed down and the revolver would break open.

This action also caused one of the major new design features of this totally new gun to operate: the ejection system. This system incorporated an extractor within the cylinder which would force out all six cartridges when the barrel was rotated downward around the hinge; a major step forward over the system used on prior models, and a design which was improved upon and retained until well after 1900.

The model was chambered for a new centerfire cartridge of .44 caliber which was originally known as the .44-100 S&W, but later called the .44 American cartridge to distinguish it from the Russian cartridge of 1871. (About 1000 were chambered for the .44 rimfire Henry cartridge.) The revolver was also to be called the .44 American for the same reason. Collectors now call the original No. 3, which was produced from 1870 to 1871 the First Model American. The standard barrel length was eight inches but some were shortened to as little as six inches. As would be expected, a number of mi-

SMITH & WESSON

nor changes were made during production since the design was the first of a type.

In late 1871 or early 1872 in the serial range of No. 7600 to No. 8000 (serials had begun at No. 1), three fairly prominent changes were made which collectors today use to distinguish the First Model American from the Second Model. The first was the introduction of an interlocking hammer and barrel catch, followed closely by a two-piece hinge pin screw and an increased diameter trigger pin.

Smith & Wesson was fast to try to get government contracts for their new army pistol and submitted a prototype in May of 1870 to the U.S. Small Arms board. This resulted in an order for 1000 for the Army in December. These are rare and highly desirable collectors pieces today.

Several were submitted to foreign governments as well, including one to General Gorloff of Russia. This one resulted in major contracts from 1871 through 1877 involving several models and almost 150,000 revolvers.

The year 1872 saw the Second Model American go into production incorporating the changes mentioned previously. Production continued for

another year and to about serial No. 32,800. Normal barrel length was eight inches, but a fair number have been found in 5½, 6, 6½ and 7-inch lengths. Normal chambering was .44 S&W American with 3014 made for the .44 rimfire Henry.

The submission to General Gorloff resulted in a Russian contract for 20,000 revolvers of the Second Model American type, but modified to chamber a cartridge of slightly different design which was to be known as the .44 S&W Russian. The revolver was called the Russian Model and carried Cyrillic lettering on the barrel rib in the contract version. The wording translates *"Smith & Wesson Arms Factory. Springfield America."* The model was also sold on the commercial market and in this version carried the same barrel marks as the American Model plus the added words "RUSSIAN MODEL." Serials of the contract pieces were No. 1 to No. 20,000. The commercial revolvers were numbered in the same series with the Second Model American with a production run from 1871 to 1873.

Detachable shoulder stocks were available for the Second Model American and the original Russian Model, with a total of 604 being sold. These

stocks are *exceedingly* rare and desirable items for the collector.

There were three Russian Models produced over the years 1871 to 1878, the last two being in production (for Russian contracts) at the same time. This led to some confusion at the factory during production and for some years after when supplying replacement parts. It has also caused considerable problems with collectors.

When the first Russian Model was put into production it was simply called the Russian Model. When the next model started in 1873, and the first model was discontinued, it was called the Ordinetz design after the Russian representative, Captain Kasavery Ordinetz, who was primarily responsible for its exterior design. Matters were further confused in 1874 with the introduction of a third design similar to the second.

This third model was called the New Model to distinguish it from the prior Ordinetz design. Since this third model was the New Model, then the prior one was called the Old Model. This, however, left the original model with a lack of a logical name. In the end it was called the Old Old Model. Thus we have the names by which they are now known: Old Old Model, Old Model

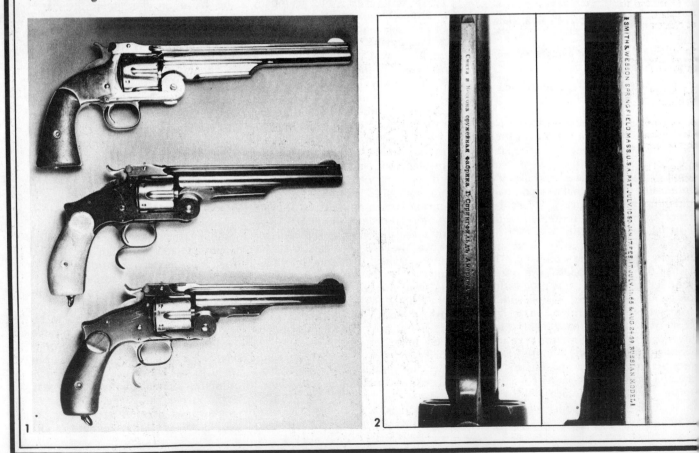

1

2

and New Model. As yet, collectors have not adopted the more logical names of First, Second, and Third Model Russian but perhaps that change will be made.

Late in production of the 00M some suggestions regarding the design of the frame grip, hammer and trigger guard were made by Captain Ordinetz. The barrel length was also to be reduced from eight to seven inches. Terms and design were agreed upon and in 1873 the 00M was replaced as both the Russian contract model and the commercially available model by the 0M. At this same time the Second Model American (identical to 00M but for chambering) was discontinued.

Serial numbers of the commercial OM's picked up where the American and 00M had stopped. Serials of the contract arms ran in a separate series with each contract starting with No. 1. Contracts were usually for 20,000 pieces, although sometimes less. Barrel markings remained the same for both contract and commercial guns as the 00M. A total of about 11,000 commercial and 60,000 contract guns were made. About 1500 were chambered in .44 rimfire Henry (1000 of which were numbered separately from No. 1 to

No. 1000 and sold to the Turkish Government) and the remainder in .44 S&W Russian.

The OM was the first to have the "saw handle" and "hook" trigger guard associated with the Russian Model. Though the Russians liked the hook guard, it was not so appealing to many civilian users. It was not uncommon for it to be removed not long after purchase, if for no other reason than to eliminate the difficulty of finding a holster designed to fit around that rather large protrusion from the bottom of the trigger guard.

In 1874 a third model known as the New Model (NM) was put into production with a redesigned extractor system and cylinder retainer. Both new features were covered in patent No. 158874 of January 19, 1875, taken out by D. B. Wesson. Barrel length was reduced to 6½ inches. This was called (by the Russians) the cavalry model and the OM the infantry model. The NM can be distinguished from the OM by the shorter barrel, shorter extractor housing, and solid rather than pinned front sight.

The Russian Government continued

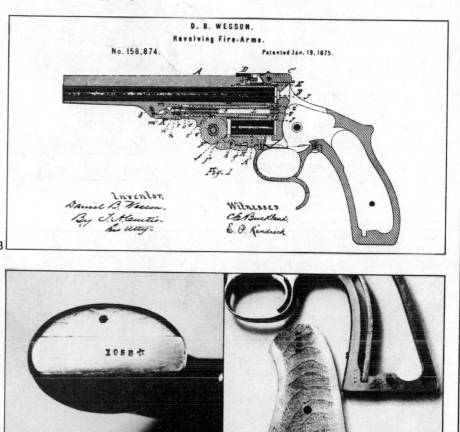

1. From top to bottom: Old Old Model Russian; Old Model Russian; New Model Russian. All caliber .44 Russian.

2. Barrel rib markings found on the Russians can be either Cyrillic or in Roman (English).

3. Patent drawings for the New Model Russian, No. 158,874, Jan. 19, 1875.

4. Star and date marks found on a First Model American, refinished by the factory in March, 1914.

5. Serial and assembly numbers as found on a Model No. 1½, First Issue.

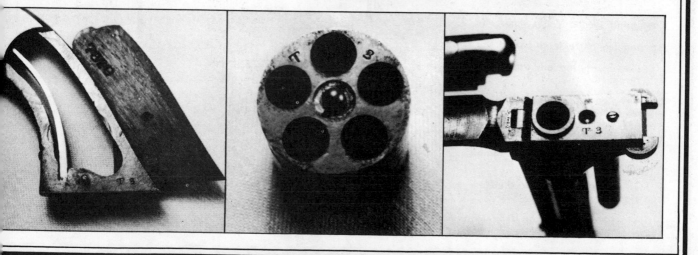

SMITH & WESSON

to contract for the OM as well as the NM with both continuing in production until 1878. From 1874 until late 1877, the OM was not sold on the commercial market and only the NM was available. It picked up in the commercial serial series where the OM stopped and continued to about serial No. 52,000.

A total of 19,000 revolvers were sold on the commercial market, probably no more than 400 of which were chambered in .44 rimfire Henry, the remainder being .44 S&W Russian. A total of 62,386 contract revolvers were made.

Shoulder stocks were available for the OM and NM throughout production with a total of 914 being sold. The same stock would fit both models.

In late 1877, the Russian contracts were terminating and the company was cleaning out the last of the commercial and contract production runs of both the OM and NM in preparation for a completely redesigned No. 3 size single action. As a result of this action the OM was again put on the commercial market, this time serialed in a new series beginning with No. 1. The remaining NMs were also put in this series (intermixed) and the two totaled some 9000 in number. Present information indicates that of the 9000 total, about 3000 were OM and 6000 NM.

On January 1, 1874, Horace Smith retired at age 65 and sold his interest in the company to D. B. Wesson. Profits from the Russian contracts allowed Wesson to pay off this purchase in but a few years. Although for obvious reasons Smith's name was retained, the Wesson family controlled and dominated the firm from then until World War 2.

A mark which often raises a ques-

1. *First and Second Model Schofields.*

2. *Schofield's barrel latch patent.*

3. *"Break open", top, and "tip up" style revolvers.*

4. *Wells Fargo & Co. Express marks on a Schofield revolver.*

5. *From top to bottom: Model No. 1½, Single Action; First Model .38, Single Action (Baby Russian); Second Model .38, Single Action.*

6. *The 1891 Model, top, and the Mexican Model at bottom.*

7. *Original box in which the Baby Russian models were sold.*

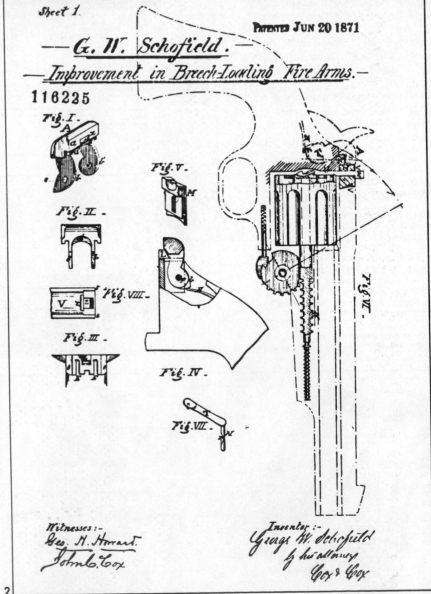

Sheet 1.

PATENTED JUN 20 1871

— G. W. Schofield. —

— Improvement in Breech-Loading Fire Arms.—

116225

Fig. I. Fig. II. Fig. III. Fig. IV. Fig. V. Fig. VI. Fig. VII. Fig. VIII.

Witnesses :—
Geo. H. Howard.
John C. Cox

Inventor :—
George W. Schofield
by his attorneys
Cox & Cox

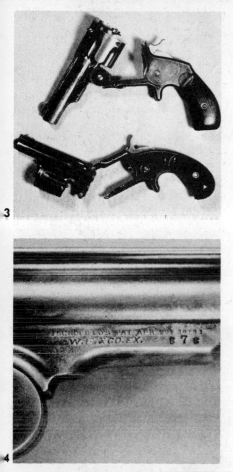

3

4

5

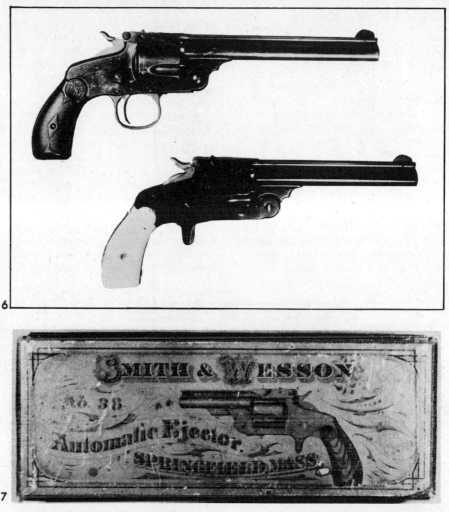

6

7

scrupulous people from selling such factory-reworked guns as new. The star continued in use until 1954. Along with the star will be found on the side of the frame under the left grip a date stamp such as 3.12, indicating March, 1912, as the date the work was done. This date mark remains in use today.

It is also helpful in determining value and originality to know if all major parts of a piece are original to that particular one. With a knowledge of the location and significance of number markings, this can be determined. In early years, major parts were stamped with a combination of serial numbers and fitting or assembly numbers. Beginning in the middle 1870's the assembly numbers were replaced with serial numbers thus giving a single number rather than two.

The two-number system worked like this: The serial number was placed on the butt and grip (usually right one). Thus, the frame was stamped with both numbers. The assembly number was then stamped on the rear of the barrel, front or rear

of the cylinder (dependent on model), and on the barrel catch. With the combination of these two number was placed on the side of the frame under the grip (usually the right one.) Thus, the frame was stamped with both numbers. The assembly number was then stamped on the rear of the barrel, front or rear of the cylinder (dependent on model), and on the barrel catch. With the combination of these two numbers (the assembly number could be either all numbers or a letter-number combination; the serial was always all numbers) the parts can be matched. The all-serial number system worked the same except that no number was stamped on the frame under the grip, and the serial number was used on all locations.

Early in production of the American Model an Army Colonel named Schofield had purchased several of these new cartridge revolvers. The Colonel was very interested in incorporating several improvements invented by himself and having Smith & Wesson manufacture the improved version for contract sales to the

tion is the star sometimes found by the serial number on the butt. The earliest record thus far found of the use of this mark is 1910. It was put there by the factory to indicate some type of major repair work had been done by the factory, generally refinish, but not limited to this work only. Factory parts catalogues indicate this was done to prevent un-

SMITH & WESSON

Army, providing they could persuade proper authorities to issue such contracts to them.

The story of the development and sale of the resultant model is one that cannot be attempted here, though it is surely an interesting one. Let us say the venture was modestly successful and the Army contracted for 3000 of these improved revolvers to be known as First Model Schofield.

Delivery was made in 1875 with only 35 of this model lacking the "U.S." on the butt and other proof marks of the government inspectors. Thus the civilian model is the rare one in this case. The revolver followed closely the design of the Second Model American with the exception of having the barrel shortened to seven inches and the barrel catch and extractor system replaced by one of Schofield's design.

Further contracts were placed in 1876 and 1877 for an additional 5285 revolvers which carried several minor modifications from the First Model, the most obvious of which was a slightly redesigned barrel catch. These are called the Second Model Schofield. A total of 649 of this model were sold on the commercial market. Both this and the First Model were chambered for a .45 caliber cartridge slightly shorter than the .45 Colt and called the .45 S&W.

An interesting and rare variation of the Schofield Models was created when Wells Fargo purchased a fairly large lot (containing some of both models) as government surplus some years later. They were cut back to five inches and stamped on the right side of the extractor housing either W.F. & CO.EX." or "W.F. & CO's. EX." followed by the serial number of the gun. These were issued to various coach, bank and railroad guards for some years later.

The year 1876 brought a new No. 2 size revolver into production which was to replace the No. 2 Army. A new centerfire .38 caliber cartridge was designed and a new revolver to fire it. The extractor system which it used was a scaled down version

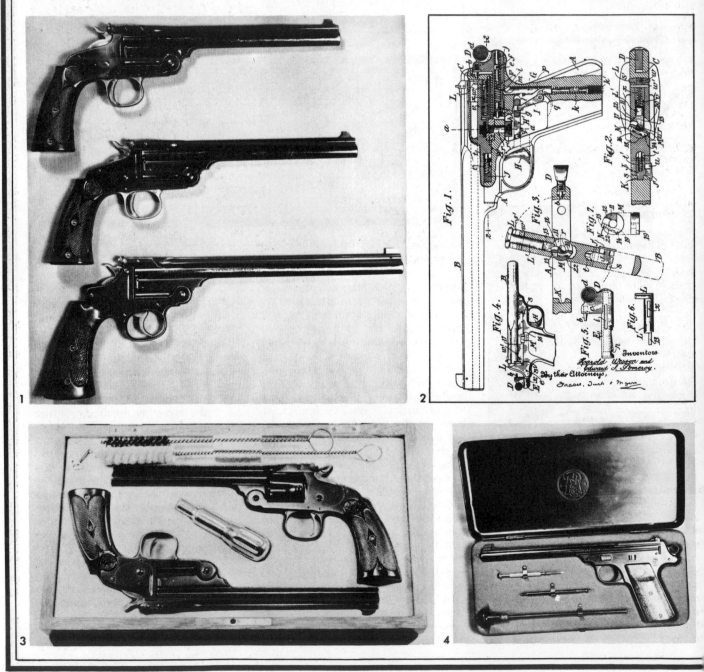

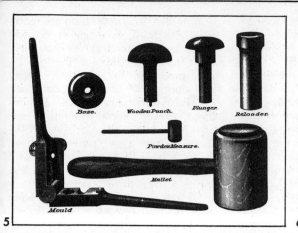

5

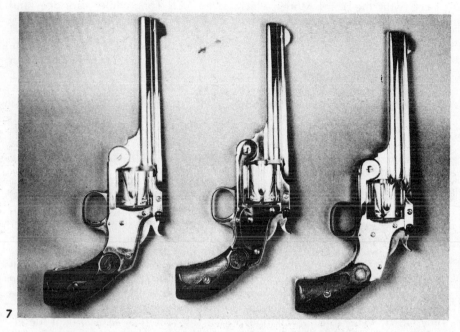

6

1. From top to bottom: First, Second and Third Model Single Shots.

2. Patent drawings for the Straight Line Single Shot.

3. Cased 1891 Model revolver and Second Model Single Shot.

4. Straight Line Single Shot in metal factory box with accessories.

5. Old design reloading tools as illustrated in the 1887 S&W catalog. These tools were offered from 1874 to 1888.

6. New type tools from the 1900 S&W catalog. These were sold from 1888 to around 1915.

7. From right to left: .44 Single Action Frontier; No. 3 Single Action Target; New Model No. 3.

7

of that designed for the New Model Russian. It was a rather complicated system and had a great number of parts. It did not seem to suffer excessively from failure of these fairly delicate parts, however. The cylinder chambered the new .38 S&W cartridges. Barrel lengths were 3¼ and 4 inches.

This model is called the First Model .38 Single Action by many, but more often the Baby Russian because of its great similarity to the New Model Russian. The production run was a short one and a replacement model was introduced in 1877.

This new model is properly called the Second Model .38 Single Action, although it is often mistakenly called the Baby Russian—a name proper only for its predecessor since nothing about this model resembles the Russian Model. Its primary improvement over the prior model was the redesign of the Russian-type extractor system that model had used. The new one was greatly simplified and not only less apt to suffer from parts breakage but much less expensive to produce. The variety of barrel

lengths available for this model was wide with a selection of 3¼, 4, 5, 6, 8 and 10 inches. The 8- and 10-inch lengths are scarce.

Production continued until 1891 when a Third Model .38 Single Action was put on the market. This model is usually called the "1891" Model and was marked on the barrel rib "MODEL OF 91." It and the three Russian models were the only ones ever to be marked with the model name. The primary change from the Second Model was the use of a bow-type trigger guard such as had been used on the No. 3 size revolvers since 1870. The model had only been on the market a short time when the company found they still had sizeable requests for the earlier type spur trigger guard of the prior model. The requests were received primarily from south of the border. To fill these requests, the company made up a group of guard inserts of this type which could be used in place of the removable bow

type guard of the Model 1891. A special narrow spur hammer was also used in conjunction with this spur guard.

Model 1891 revolvers equipped with this hammer and guard were called both the Model of 1880 and Mexican Model by the factory. Collectors call them the Mexican. Exactly how many were made is not known but the model is extremely rare today, perhaps because most were exported. The Model 1891 and the Mexican remained in production until 1911.

The Model 1891 also fostered a single-shot pistol which was built on its frame beginning in 1893 and continuing to 1905. This pistol used the unmodified frame of the Model 1891 with a special single shot barrel mounted on it. The pistol carried target sights and was available with 6-, 8-, or 10-inch barrel in .22, .32, or .38 caliber. The purchaser could either obtain a complete pistol or a barrel to install on his Model

SMITH & WESSON

1891 revolver. He could also purchase a complete revolver with extra single-shot barrel all in a fitted case with accessories.

In 1905, the First Model Single Shot was replaced with the Second Model on which the frame was modified by removing the recoil shields, hand and cylinder stop. It also dropped the .32 and .38 calibre barrels and made .22 calibre 10-inch standard. This model could be used only as a single-shot.

In 1909, the Second Model was replaced with the Third Model which used a completely new frame and lockwork. This Third Model was also called the Olympic Model and was quite popular with shooters, remaining in production until 1923. The name Olympic originated when many of these pieces were used by our Olympic team during competition. A special type of chambering was applied to a very few of these pistols as an experiment to gain even more accuracy. Chambers were bored short so that in order to fully seat the cartridge in the chamber the bullet had to be forced into the rifling. This way the bullet had no gap to jump to start into the rifling. The theory may have had some merit, but in practice it provided no actual betterment in closing up groups.

The company brought out its last single-shot pistol in 1925. Although only 1870 were sold, it continued to be catalogued until 1936. Popularity of the single shot was already on the down swing by 1925 and had

waned to near nothing by 1936.

The pistol was an unusual one. It was made to look and feel like the automatic pistol which was fast rising in popularity. Another design feature was a plunger-like hammer which moved in a straight line parallel to the bore, this theoretically eliminated any tendency for a swing-type hammer to move the barrel when it fell. This hammer design was the reason for the name given to the model, the Straight Line Single Shot. It came in a very nice blued-steel case with screwdriver and cleaning rod. It was chambered for the .22 Long Rifle cartridge and was available in blue finish with 10-inch barrel only.

The last small .32 caliber single action was put on the market in 1878, some three years after the No. 1½ Second Model was removed. This new five-shot centerfire (.32 S&W caliber) revolver was catalogued as the "New Model .32 No. 1½ Single Action" but today's collectors generally call it the No. 1½ Single Action. This little .32 with break-open design and bird's head-shape grip was intended for use as a pocket pistol; 3-, 3½-, 6-, 8-, and 10-inch barrel lengths were available over the years until production was stopped in 1892. The reason for the three longer lengths on such a small revolver is not clear and as one would expect, few were sold in these lengths.

The year 1878 also brought the introduction of the last No. 3 size single action, the New Model No. 3 (NM No. 3). This revolver was un-

doubtedly the most accurate commercially produced single action ever made and in its target version held most target records of the day. It was produced for some 30 years, and during that time was catalogued in six different cartridges. Besides these, it was special-ordered in everything from .22 Long Rifle to .455 Eley. Barrels were available in 4-, 5-, 6-, 6½-, and 8-inch lengths, with special-order lengths of 3½ and 7½ inches known of in small quantities.

Detachable shoulder stocks were available, but few were so equipped. The most famous of those which were are no doubt the "Australian" issue revolvers. These consisted of a lot of 250 with nickel finish, seven-inch barrels and shoulder stocks sold to the Australian Colonial Police in 1881. They were stamped with the British Government's "Broad Arrow" proof on the butt of the revolver and lower tang of the stock.

Besides these there were perhaps 800 additional stocks sold for use on the NM No. 3 and its variations. The stocked S&W single actions of

1. Very rare No. 3 Single Action in caliber .38-40 Winchester.

2. Barrel markings on the late (top) and early New Model No. 3.

3. From top to bottom: A pair of Australian Colonial Police issue New Model No. 3 revolvers (#12299 and #12300); No. 3 Single Action Target; New Model No. 3.

4. A pair of 320 Revolving Rifles.

5. A Revolving Rifle with 16-inch barrel, stock detached.

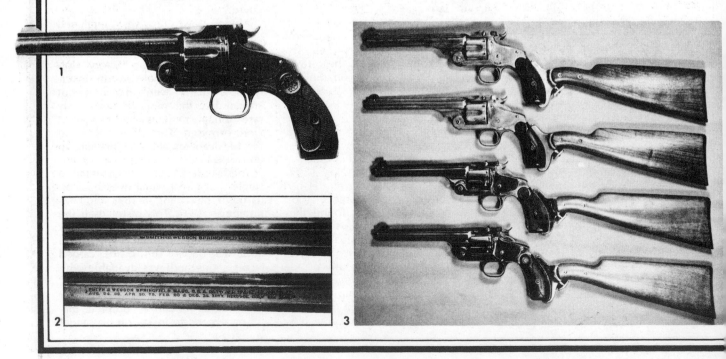

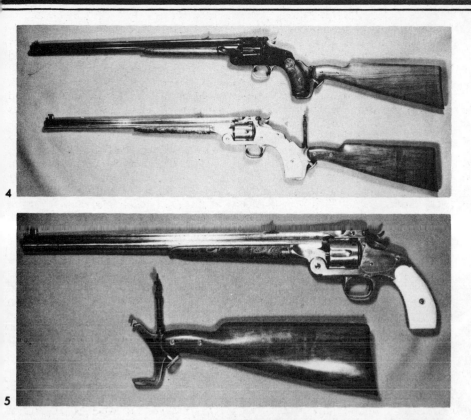

4

5

SMITH & WESSON SINGLE ACTION PRODUCTION CHART			
Model	Serial Range	Dates Catalogued	Produced
Model No. 1 First Issue	1-11671*	1857-1860	11,671**
Model No. 1 Second Issue	11672-126361*	1860-1868	114,690**
Model No. 1 Third Issue	1-131163	1868-1881	131,163
First Model Single Shot	1-28107	1893-1905	3198**
Second Model Single Shot	1-4617	1905-1909	4617
Third Model Single Shot	4618-11641	1909-1923	6949
Straight Line Single Shot	1-1870	1925-1936	1870
Model No. 1½ 1st Model	1-26300*	1865-1868	26,300**
Model No. 1½ 2nd Model	26301-127100*	1868-1875	100,799**
Model No. 1½ SA	1-97594	1870-1892	97,594
Model No. 2 Army	1-88699	1861-1874	88,699
Model No. 3 SA Target	1-4333	1887-1910	4333
320 Revolving Rifle	1-977	1879-1887	977
First Model 38 SA	1-25548	1876-1877	25,548
Second Model 38 SA	1-108255	1877-1891	108,255
Third Model 38 SA (1891)	1-28107	1891-1911	24,000**
38 Single Action Mexican	1-28107	1891-1911	1000**
Model No. 3 SA 38/40	1-74	1900-1908	74
First Model American	1-8000*	1870-1872	8000**
Second Model American	8001-32800*	1872-1873	20,235**
OOM Russian	8001-32800*	1872-1873	4665
(OOM contract guns)	1-20000	1872-1873	20,000
OM Russian	32801-39000*	1873-1878	9200**
(2nd serial series)	1-9000*		
(OM contract guns)	1-20000	1872-1878	60,000
NM Russian	39001-52000*	1874-1878	19,000**
(2nd serial series)	1-9000*		
(NM contract guns)	1-20000	1874-1878	62,386
New Model No. 3	1-35796	1878-1908	35,796
Model No. 3 Turkish	1-5461	1879-1883	5461
Model No. 3 SA Frontier	1-2072	1885-1908	2072
First Model Schofield	1-3035	1875	3035
Second Model Schofield	3036-8969	1876-1877	5934

*—Exact serial numbers are unknown either because of lost early serial
records or overlap in serial range with another model.
**—Exact production figures unknown. Number given is generally accurate to
within 100.

all models are rare and very desirable as collectors items now that they have been ruled as antiques not requiring registration by the AT & F Division of the Treasury Department.

Although during most of its years this gun was catalogued as one model available in several calibers, some of the various chamberings were considered as separate models by the company and were serialed in separate series. The different models, their chamberings and production were: New Model No. 3, .44 S&W Russian and 450 Webley (plus many special order cartridges), 35,796; No. 3 Single Action Frontier, .44/40 Winchester, 2072; No. 3 Turkish, .44 RF Henry, 5461; No. 3 SA Target, .32-44 S&W and .38-44 S&W, 4333; No. 3 SA .38-40, .38-40 Winchester, 74.

A most interesting model which was built on the same frame as the NM No. 3 was the 320 Rifle. This modification was serialed in its own series from No. 1 to No. 977 and catalogued as a separate model. Most were made in 1879 with a few being finished as late as 1887. All were furnished with detachable shoulder stocks and available barrel lengths were 16, 18 and 20 inches. The special barrel had a hard rubber forend piece which was made in a mottled red color as were the pistol grips. The revolver came in a case with cleaning rod. Accessory tang peep sights and globe front were available at extra cost as were loading tools. The piece was chambered for a special .32 caliber cartridge of S&W design which had a case the same length as the cylinder. The bullet was seated entirely within the case.

The last single action was removed from the market in 1911, thus clearing the way for the more modern double-action models. The first of the break-open double actions had been put on the market in 1880 and not many years after 1911, they too would be dropped as obsolete. The first solid-frame swing-out cylinder hand-ejector model was put on the market in 1896, and by 1911 hand ejectors in calibers from .22 to .44 were available. Their exterior design looked much like today's production revolvers.

Thus ended the golden era of the single action revolver of Smith & Wesson manufacture. No other production single action could match it in fineness of finish or fit, nor in accuracy of shooting.

O.F. Winchester [signature]

A COLLECTOR'S GUIDE

WINCHESTER

by Herb Glass

The collector of Winchester products and memorabilia is faced with a dilemma similar to that of the Colt aficionado. Where does one begin? What area should he pick for specialization? Is there enough space in the gun room — and cash in the bank—to house one-each of every major variation of over 75 collectible models? What reference books are in print that will identify the hundreds of variant types?

The answers to these questions do not come easily. Just picking a collecting category presents a problem—and Winchesters are not handgun size, so they do require much more space than Colt six-shooters. Collecting specialties are not so distinct as

in, for example, Colt's, and most Winchester enthusiasts take a general approach. If anything, they use a cut-off date, such as 1898, or may pursue only lever actions or single shots. Some of the better-heeled gentry limit themselves solely to engraved specimens of all models.

Because the approach to Winchester collecting is so varied, the format chosen for the present article is to select the collectible types, and present a primer for collectors. To my knowledge, this is the first such reference history prepared on a rather comprehensive basis. What follows is essentially a complete Winchester collection in pictures and text.

HUNT REPEATING RIFLE

The Winchester firearms story actually begins with the rather ugly

weapon known as the Hunt Repeating Rifle. Inventor Walter Hunt of New York City held U.S. Patent #5701 for a conical lead bullet known as the Rocket Ball. The hollow bullet contained powder and had a disc on its back end with a hole to allow ignition from a separate primer. Hunt designed his rifle to fire the Rocket Ball, and his August 21, 1849 patent (#6663) covered this lever action, repeating, breech loader which he called the Volition Repeater.

From that awkward but highly original beginning evolved the Jennings, Smith & Wesson and Volcanic repeaters and the Henry and Winchester lever action rifles. The number of Hunt rifles produced is extremely limited, and it is a collector's prize of even greater rarity than the Samuel Colt prototypes, which predated the

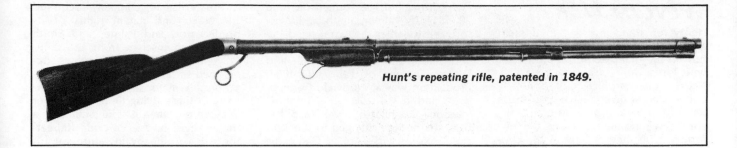

Hunt's repeating rifle, patented in 1849.

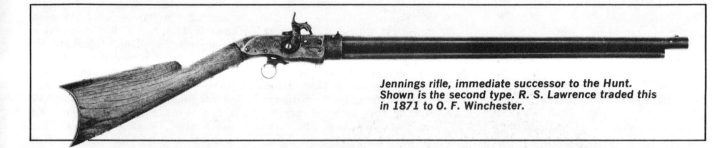

Jennings rifle, immediate successor to the Hunt. Shown is the second type. R. S. Lawrence traded this in 1871 to O. F. Winchester.

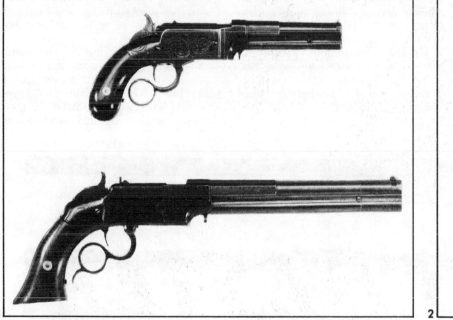

1

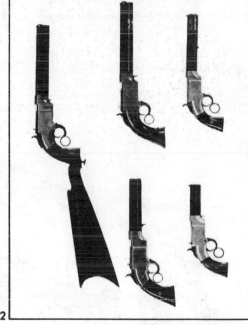

2

1. Smith & Wesson Volcanics. Above, a .30 caliber; bottom a .38 caliber. They were produced in 1854 and 1855. Note spur lever on earliest pistol.

2. A valuable group of Volcanic repeating pistols. The three at left are original Volcanic products, the right-hand two are by New Haven Arms.

Paterson series of firearms. At present the only Hunt rifle known is the one illustrated, from the Winchester Gun Museum collection. Its value: As much as an advanced collector would be willing to pay for it, and that would be a considerable amount.

JENNINGS RIFLES

The Hunt "Volition Repeater" never went into production, and its basic design was quickly improved

upon by a talented gunsmith named Lewis Jennings. The Jennings improvements were covered in a U.S. patent of December 25, 1849. Promoted by entrepreneur George A. Arrowsmith and backed by capitalist C. C. Palmer, the Jennings was manufactured in a run of 5000 rifles at the factory of Robbins & Lawrence, Windsor, Vermont. The foreman at Robbins & Lawrence was B. Tyler Henry, later to develop the Henry Rifle and to figure prominently in the early fortunes of the Winchester Repeating Arms Company.

Horace Smith and Daniel B. Wesson also became involved in the manufacture of the Jennings rifles. Smith held U.S. Patent #8317 (August 26, 1851) which was an improvement on the Jennings design of 1849; the Smith variation is one of the three

basic Jennings Rifle models. These are as follows: The First Model, .54 caliber, made as a breechloading single shot in 1850 and 1851; the Second Model, also in .54 caliber, made in 1851 and 1852 as a repeater and incorporating the improvements of Smith; a third type, .54 caliber, put together by Robbins & Lawrence in 1852, to use up leftover Jennings parts. This latter weapon was a single-shot muzzle loader.

Unfortunately, C. C. Palmer's investment went down the drain, because the Jennings repeating rifles were too complex and lacked sufficient power for commercial success. The failure cut short any further evolution of the magazine type of repeating rifle for the next two years. History indicates, however, that Messrs. Smith, Wesson, Palmer, and

WINCHESTER

Henry remained involved in thought and effort at making a successful return to the manufacture of a repeater type longarm.

The ugly profile and originally poor sales showing have not made Jennings rifles the popular collector's arms they should be. From the historic station they occupy in the evolution of the Winchester repeater, the Jennings is comparable to the Paterson Colt. In effect, the Jennings is the earliest "Winchester" available to collectors, since only one Hunt rifle exists.

SMITH & WESSON AND VOLCANIC REPEATERS

It is an irony of gunmaking that the earliest Smith & Wesson repeaters were lever action magazine handguns. Palmer, Smith, and Wesson remained in alliance following the Jennings Rifle failure. On February 14, 1854, Smith and Wesson were granted U.S. Patent #10535. The new design was quite an improvement over the predecessor types, including the fact that the medium now adopted for their repeater was the handgun rather than the rifle.

A partnership was formed on June 20, 1854, by Palmer, Smith, and Wesson, and together they controlled the original patents of Hunt, Jennings, and Smith, and the new Smith and Wesson patent of February, 1854. Production was at Norwich, Connecticut, and the pistols bore Smith & Wesson markings. In July of 1855, the firm's name was changed to the Volcanic Repeating Arms Company. Among the employees of Smith & Wesson, and later Volcanic, was B. Tyler Henry.

An important detail of the arms made by these firms was the use of a pioneer form of cartridge, in which the primer and powder charge were contained in the hollow base of the lead bullet. The two calibers of handguns made by S&W were .30 and .38.

Here is the interesting, intriguing, and unusual instance of a handgun which fits into the collecting categories of two major fields—the Smith & Wesson specialists, and concentrators on the Winchester. The Volcanic firm had been incorporated by C. C. Palmer, Smith, and Wesson, but among their stockholders was one Oliver F. Winchester. At that time, Winchester was a prospering manufacturer of clothing in New Haven, Connecticut.

The Volcanic company acquired the assets and patent rights of its predecessor, and Palmer and Smith removed themselves from active involvement. Financial difficulties developed as sales were beneath expectations. A major lender to the company in these trying times was Oliver Winchester. In 1857 he acquired a major share of the Volcanic Repeating Arms Company in return for his loans.

Initially, the Volcanic guns were made at the old Smith & Wesson factory in Norwich. But production began at a new plant in New Haven, early in 1856. An ammunition department was also launched in that year.

The variety of Volcanic types was greater than found with the S&W pistols, but they were chambered only for the .38 caliber cartridge. The total Volcanic line was composed of 6- and 8-inch barrel pistols (some with shoulder stocks), a 16-inch barrel shoulder-stocked pistol, and carbines advertised as having 16-, 20- and 24-inch barrels.

The successor to the Volcanic company adopted the corporate name of the New Haven Arms Company. April 25, 1857 was the date that New Haven Arms was organized to take over where its defunct predecessor

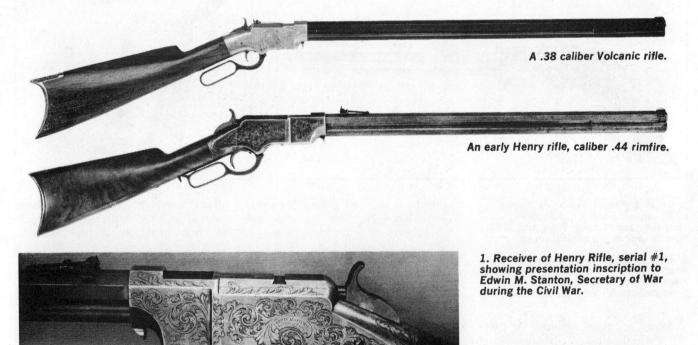

A .38 caliber Volcanic rifle.

An early Henry rifle, caliber .44 rimfire.

1. Receiver of Henry Rifle, serial #1, showing presentation inscription to Edwin M. Stanton, Secretary of War during the Civil War.

2. A Henry Rifle engraved by Louis Nimschke. Note the Mexican Eagle on receiver and position of rear sight.

3. Model 1866 Winchester with factory engraving. The entire receiver has been silver plated after engraving. Engraved Winchesters usually are fitted with fancy wood.

left off. The major change in the new firm's product line was the addition of the special marking: NEW HAVEN CONN. PATENT FEB. 14, 1854. "Volcanic" was still the trade name applied to the firearms.

Volcanic rifles, in .38 caliber, were also manufactured by the New Haven Arms Company. A classic gun collector anecdote exists on these now quite popular weapons. Early in the 20th Century the Winchester factory had several mint, cased specimens of Volcanic rifles. In those days, arms collecting was almost nonexistant. Rather than destroy their stock of mint, boxed Volcanics, the factory offered them for sale to employees at about 50¢ apiece! One of the buyers was a young Yale University graduate and Winchester employee, Edwin Pugsley. Mr. Pugsley would become one of America's most successful collectors of antique firearms and Americana, and this clearance sale of mint Volcanics remains to this day one of his favorite reminiscences from over 60 years as a connoisseur of fine firearms.

THE HENRY RIFLE

Despite their rather modern and efficient outward appearance, the Volcanic arms were limited in sales by the relatively small caliber, the limited power of the "cartridge," and the inefficient seal of gasses at the breech. Success required a major improvement in the cartridge. Fortunately, the rights of the New Haven Arms Company included the use of metallic cartridges without any payments of royalties to the controllers of the patents, Smith & Wesson. B. Tyler Henry, the brilliant mechanic and designer, came through and saved the financial shirts of Winchester and the other investors.

Henry, the company's shop superintendent, took out U.S. Patent #30446 (October 16, 1860) which was entitled: "Improvement in Magazine Firearms." The resultant "Henry Rifle" is one of the most sought-after of all collector's firearms. It is a key item in any collection encompassing the early lever action Winchesters.

All Henry rifles were made in .44 rimfire caliber, with a magazine capacity of 15 cartridges. The dates of production were from 1860 through 1866, with three basic models: The "Iron Frame," of which only a few hundred were produced; the first type Brass Frame, with early style rounded heel butt plate (made in a quantity in excess of about 1500); the standard Brass Frame Model with pointed buttplate.

The total quantity of Henry Rifles made was about 13,000. Serial numbers overlapped into the Model 1866 Winchester, the lowest known number of which is #12476. The Henry's record of Civil War service was outstanding; it was one of the rifles known to the Confederates as "The rifle the Yankees load on Sunday and shoot all week."

The most desirable Henrys are the very rare Iron Frame Model (all having low serials) and engraved and/or mint specimens. A group of early engraved rifles was presented by the company to Civil War leaders in the Union cause. Serial #1 was a gift to Secretary of War Edwin M. Stanton, serial #6 went to President Lincoln, and #9 went to Secretary of the Navy Gideon Welles. The Lincoln rifle is now a national treasure, exhibited in the Smithsonian Institution. The author had the pleasure of owning both the Welles and Stanton rifles, both now in the Richard P. Mellon collection. Stanton's rifle, illustrated with an exhibit award presented by the National Rifle Association, bears the customary serial location on the top of the breech of the barrel, and the simple inscription "EDWIN M. STAN-

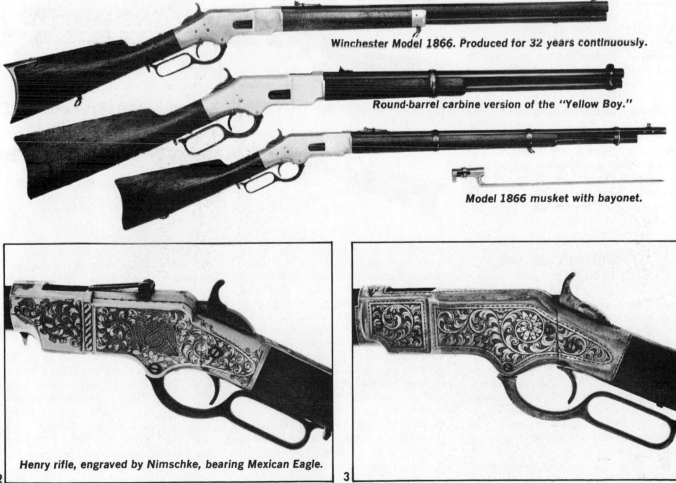

Winchester Model 1866. Produced for 32 years continuously.

Round-barrel carbine version of the "Yellow Boy."

Model 1866 musket with bayonet.

2 Henry rifle, engraved by Nimschke, bearing Mexican Eagle.

3

WINCHESTER

TON Secretary of War", on the left side of the engraved frame.

Engraved decorations on Henry rifles have attracted quite a bit of attention from collectors. Specific factory styles have been identified, and several non-factory designs are also recorded. A standard pattern is on the Stanton rifle, while #4755 from the Ivan B. Hart collection is an excellent example of the work of Louis D. Nimschke (active 1850-1904). Nimschke's own record (published 1964 in a book authored by R. L. Wilson) pictures several Henry rifles which he had personally engraved. The Mexican eagle and large Germanic scroll pattern on rifle #4755 was a favorite Nimschke approach. After engraving, the frame was usually plated in gold or silver.

Inscribed pieces are rare in all Henry and Winchester arms. However, the Henrys as a group boast a greater proportion of these than all other models, due to the use of the gun in the Civil War. Several Henry rifles with wartime inscriptions are known, usually applied rather crudely for the owners by non-factory engravers. A classic example is #9490, inscribed on the frame: *Lieut. Arthur Haine/2nd Infty. C.V.* (California Volunteers). The most exciting factory inscribed Henry is a unique piece, made without serial number, presented by B. Tyler Henry himself to a lawyer, by the lawyer to a friend, and by the third party to still another individual! This prized weapon was only recently purchased by advanced collector Johnie Bassett from the scendents of the recipient of the third presentation. The piece is in excellent condition, with deluxe stocks, and gold-plated frame and buttplate. Bassett was awarded first prize as "Best of Show" at the 1972 Kansas City Gun Show, where his triple presentation Henry rifle was the featured exhibit.

O.F. WINCHESTER AND THE MODEL 1866

Oliver F. Winchester's control of the New Haven Arms Company led eventually to still another corporate reorganization. On July 7, 1865, a charter was granted by the State of Connecticut to the Henry Repeating Rifle Company, an obvious attempt to capitalize on the now-famed Henry name and the popular Henry rifle. But in 1866 the firm's name was changed to the Winchester Repeating Arms Company. As of March 30, 1867, all assets of New Haven Arms had been transferred to the Win-

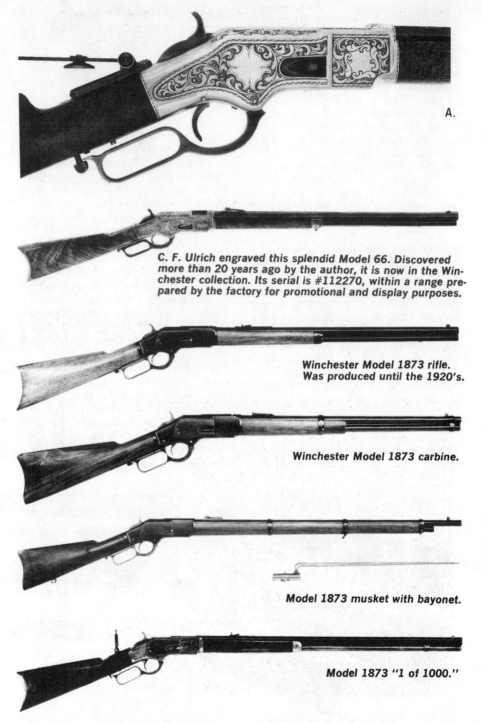

A.

C. F. Ulrich engraved this splendid Model 66. Discovered more than 20 years ago by the author, it is now in the Winchester collection. Its serial is #112270, within a range prepared by the factory for promotional and display purposes.

Winchester Model 1873 rifle. Was produced until the 1920's.

Winchester Model 1873 carbine.

Model 1873 musket with bayonet.

Model 1873 "1 of 1000."

chester firm. For a short while manufacturing was carried out in Bridgeport, Connecticut, with offices remaining in New Haven. The first model made under the Winchester name was the 1866.

With the Model 1866, Oliver Winchester and his employees finally struck pay dirt. The model was so popular that it remained in the Winchester product line through 1898, and approximately 170,101 were produced. The basic configurations were in carbine, rifle and musket types, the latter equipped to take a bayonet. All models 1866s were chambered interchangeably for .44 Flat Rimfire and .44 Pointed Rimfire cartridges.

Collectors are especially fond of the model 1866. With its handsomely contoured brass frame, the rifle has a romantic flavor of antiquity. In appearance and mechanism the "Yellow Boy" is one of the great Winchesters. Another major ingredient in the collector preference of the '66 is its popularity and widespread use in the Wild West and the Indian Wars. John E. Parsons' book "The First Winchester" documents in some detail the rightful claim of the Model 1866 to much of the citation "The Gun That Won the West." Among the frontier owners of the '66 were W. F. "Buffalo Bill" Cody, overland express magnate Ben Holladay, pio-

B.

Two views (A., B.) of an Ulrich-engraved Model 66. Deluxe wood and furniture was used on such pieces. Ivan B. Hart collection.

Barrel markings on a "1 of 1000" rifle.

An early specimen of American currency inspired the bust of Liberty on this 1866 sideplate. Elmer and Gwen Taylor collection.

neer photographer William Henry Jackson, and several astute Indian chiefs and braves. Custer's men did not have them at the Little Big Horn.

The major improvement of the Model 1866 over the Henry was the use of an enclosed tubular magazine loading through a port in the receiver. The Henry's magazine had been tubular, slotted its entire length, and loading from the front. The exposure and weakness of the Henry design was critical. Inventor Nelson King patented the improved design on May 22, 1866 (U.S. Patent #55012). An advantage of these improvements

was the addition of a wooden forearm to the barrel and magazine tube. In other respects the Model 1866 did not differ greatly from the Henry. Basic facts to note in the identification of the '66 are the all-brass frame, the loading port on the right side, the .44 Rimfire caliber, the straight-grip stocks, and the three major configurations of rifle, carbine, and musket.

Engraving was quite popular on the Model 1866, particularly on the rifles. Some of the finest Winchesters ever made were deluxe specimens of the '66, and it was on this model that the famed Ulrich family launched their career as Winchester master engravers. A high proportion of the best grade Winchester guns bore the signature of an Ulrich, applied some-

where on the bottom or side of the lower frame tang with a stamping die. Some extremely rare later pieces have the Ulrich name engraved within frame panel scenes.

The factory pattern engraved on ˙le #27412 in the Ivan B. Hart collection is an unusual combination of scrolls and a sunflower center finial. Finishing was in silver plating on the frame and buttplate. The usual engraved factory coverage on a Model 1866 and on most subsequent lever action Winchesters was the frame, buttplate, and forend cap or barrel/ magazine bands. Barrels were generally left unengraved, as were levers, screws, and hammers. Stock inlays were seldom used.

Winchester engravers quickly developed a selection of standardized patterns and panel scenes, and in the late 1890s the factory published a beautifully illustrated catalogue of engraved designs for their line of longarms. Original copies of this catalogue are now harder to locate than examples of most of the arms decorations pictured therein.

The famed independent engraver L. D. Nimschke is known to have embellished several Model 1866 Winchesters. The most deluxe of these was a profusely decorated rifle having a *sterling silver frame!* One of my own favorite Winchesters is a '66 carbine, scroll engraved, having a solid ivory stock relief carved with a Mexican eagle and snake design. The author recently sold this unique *chef d'oeuvre* of the gunmaker's art for a sum in excess of $50,000. One key factor in its high value was the attribution of original ownership by a high-ranking individual in the Government of Mexico.

THE MODEL 1873

Following the '66 in the company's product line was the famed Model 1873 featured in the James Stewart Western classic, "Winchester '73."

WINCHESTER

The "1 of 1000" version of that rifle garnered widespread publicity for the company through the popular public reception to the motion picture. Enthusiasts can still see the film on TV late shows; it paints a vivid picture of why Winchesters rank high in America's colorful history.

Winchester management in the early 1870s was determined they would not bring out a successor to the Model 1866 rifle unless the new weapon represented a considerable improvement. Among the noteworthy new features claimed by the Model 1873 were a stronger action and chambering for the more powerful centerfire cartridges. Production began in 1873, and continued into the 1920s; about 720,610 of this model were produced. Serial numbering began with #1. The major calibers were .44-40, .38-40 and .32-20. A .22 Rimfire version was also made (1884-1904) and about 19,552 of these were produced. The .22 model is quickly identified by the lack of a loading port on the right side of the receiver.

Several variations appear in the 1873 series, and this model was the first Winchester to offer an array of custom order features. Among the available variants, in addition to the standard carbine, rifle, and musket configurations, were: Special barrel lengths; half-round, half-octagon barrels; extra heavy barrels; half-length magazines; set triggers, shotgun buttplates; engravings and inscriptions; and the legendary "1 of 1000" and "1 of 100" selected barrel series.

Winchester advertised the "1 of 1000" and "1 of 100" types in early catalogues; one of which stated:

The barrel of every sporting rifle we make will be proved and shot at a target, and the target will be numbered to correspond with the barrel and be attached to it. All of these barrels that are found to make targets of extra merit will be made up into guns with set-triggers and extra finish and marked as a designating name, "one of a thousand," and sold at $100.00 The next grade of barrels, not quite so fine, will be marked "one of a hundred" and set up to order in any style at $20.00 advance over the list price of the corresponding style of gun.

Researchers have determined the total number of 1 of 1000 Model 1873 rifles at 136; and 1 of 100s at eight. A total of 54 model 1876 rifles were made as 1 of 1000s; only eight were made as 1 of 100s. Collectors should note that most of these have yet to be found! Besides a documenting letter from the Winchester factory, an original rifle will have the words *"One of One Thousand"* or *"One of One Hundred"* or the numerals "1 of 1000" or "1 of 100" engraved on the top of the barrel at the breech. Exercise caution in purchasing a specimen—many have been faked by unscrupulous individuals.

Part of the enthusiastic devotion of collectors to the Winchester is based on the active role of the product in winning the American West. The major contributions made by the company to that conquest were the

1. An engraving of the Winchester factory, from circa 1871 to 1880. The New Haven site still occupies the present facilities.

2. Model 1876, cased and presented to Colonel Gzowski, Aide de Camp to Queen Victoria, by the Canadian Rifle Association in 1884.

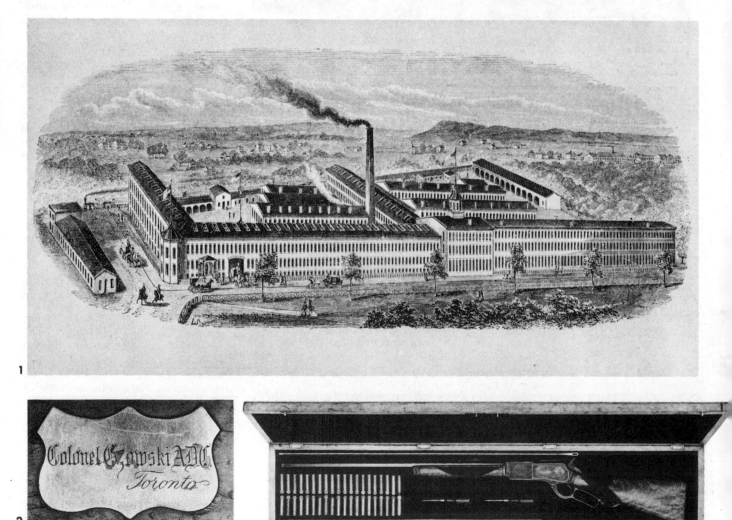

1

2

Colonel Gzowski A.D.C.
Toronto

Models of 1866 and 1873. Buffalo Bill Cody was the foremost champion of the Model 1873. Several photographs exist which show him holding a '73. One of the finest Winchesters the writer owned was a superb .22 rimfire Model 1873, presented by Buffalo Bill to the 12-year-old son of a publisher of Wild West Show pamphlets. The boy must have been thrilled to the extreme by this elegant gift—the finish of which was gold and silver plating over rich scroll engraving and a presentation inscription. Still another exquisite '73 Winchester that passed through my hands was a mint presentation-engraved, inscribed, and cased rifle, given by the Tibbits Veterans Corps of Troy, New York, to the 1st Company, Governor's Foot Guard of Hartford, Connecticut, 1881. The finish on this fine piece was gold and nickel plating, and the stocks were pistol grip deluxe walnut.

In reviewing the entire history of Winchester firearms, the position occupied by the Model 1873 is paramount. This highly successful, popular, and well-designed firearm was not only a key factor in winning the West, but in earning for Winchester a reputation as a quality gunmaker. With that reputation came the very significant ingredient which helps immeasurably to sell any product—prestige.

Few collectors have the opportunity to own an original factory cutaway Winchester. A specimen in the company's Gun Museum was dramatically cut up and shows every conceivable moving and stationary part. The buttstock was cut open to show the mainspring and cleaning rod, and the forend reveals the spring-fed tubular magazine. Beware: Several cleverly machined copies of these cutaways have been produced in recent years. The fact that serial numbers were not always used on factory cutaways is no help in trying to authenticate a suspect specimen. The collector should exercise due caution in making purchase of any cutaway item.

THE MODEL 1876

Although the Model 1876 Winchester was only made in a total of approximately 63,871, this weapon can claim some of the most exciting surviving collector specimens and some of the most colorful of original users. The Model 1876 was a big-caliber version of the 1873. At the request of shooters and hunters, Winchester produced the Model 1876 to handle the hard hitting express calibers of .45-75, .50-95, .45-60, and .40-60. Advanced publicity was given to the new weapon by exhibiting prototypes in Winchester's exhibit at the Philadelphia Centennial Exposition of 1876. As a result, the rifle was often referred to as the Centennial Model.

The Royal Northwest Mounted Police of Canada adopted a special carbine variation of the Model 1876 as their official longarm. Marked with a curved "NWMP" stamp on the buttstock, these weapons can also be identified by their serial ranges (300 in the range #23,801 to #24,100, and 446 in the range approximately #43900 to #44400). The NWMP carbines are highly prized by collectors.

Other popular variations of the Model 1876 are similar to those of the 1873, including special barrels, set triggers, deluxe stocks, engravings and inscriptions, and 1 of 100s and 1 of 1000s. Export sales were large, especially to such United Kingdom

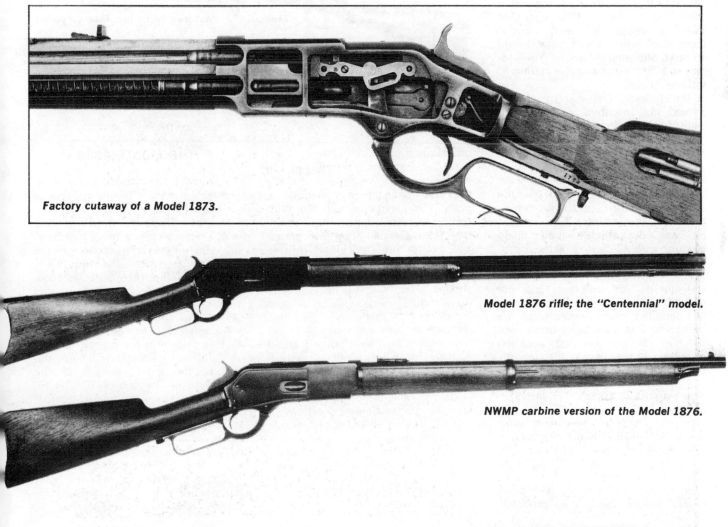

Factory cutaway of a Model 1873.

Model 1876 rifle; the "Centennial" model.

NWMP carbine version of the Model 1876.

countries as India, Africa and Canada. Big game hunters found the Model 1876 a trustworthy and effective companion.

For years a deluxe Model 1876 .45-75 rifle was Theodore Roosevelt's favorite. In his book "Hunting Trips of a Ranchman," T.R. referred to this gun as *"by all odds the best weapon I ever had . . . having killed every kind of game with it, from a grizzly bear to a big-horn."* It is a matter of record that T.R. owned two other Model 1876 Winchesters. One of these was a deluxe .40-60 rifle, and the other an even fancier .40-60 carbine. This latter piece is documented in the illustrated historical letter from descendants of the original owner from whom the author purchased it in 1968. Now in the Richard P. Mellon collection, the carbine is known to have been carried by Roosevelt as a *"saddle gun for deer and antelope"* and was used in his chase after the armed and dangerous boat thieves in the Dakota Badlands in 1886. The letter is illustrated because it is an excellent example of solid documentation for a firearm claiming specific historic significance. Just after purchasing T.R.'s .40-60 carbine the author fired it in his own test range. It shot excellent groups, despite the special short stock which was a bit awkward to hold. Shooting a famous gun adds an extra dimension to appreciating its unique history.

The Colonel Gzowski cased, engraved, and inscribed Model 1876 is one of the finest of all Winchesters. This mint condition half magazine rifle was specially made as a gift from the Riflemen and Rifle Association of Canada (1884) to Gzowski, who was *Aide de Camp* of Canada to Queen Victoria, and a prominent citizen of that country. On the case lid was the shield-shaped inlaid plaque, with Gzowski's name beautifully inscribed. Original cased lever action Winchesters raise the blood pressure of any collector to a full boil of excitement! The Gzowski set has inflicted that condition on the author no less than three times over the past 25 years, on each occasion of which it has passed through my hands enroute to a private collection. The present proud possessor of this extraordinary piece is Jonathan M. Peck.

In my opinion, the finest Winchester of all time was the presentation Model 1876 given to Lt. General Philip H. Sheridan by his friend W. E. Strong. A masterpiece of engraver John Ulrich, and signed by him in several places, the rifle is profusely

General Sheridan's Model 1876 rifle. In the author's opinion, this is the finest Winchester of all time.

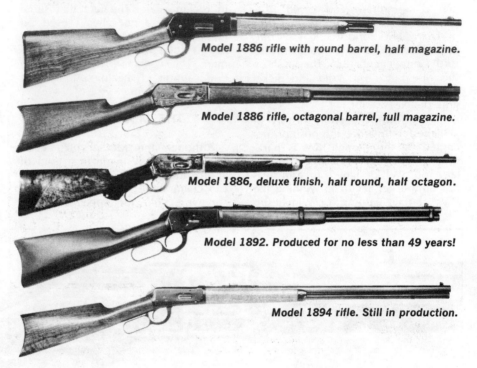

Model 1886 rifle with round barrel, half magazine.

Model 1886 rifle, octagonal barrel, full magazine.

Model 1886, deluxe finish, half round, half octagon.

Model 1892. Produced for no less than 49 years!

Model 1894 rifle. Still in production.

embellished, and its frame, butt-plate, and forend cap are all plated in gold. The stocks were made of finely checkered deluxe French walnut. The author's acquaintance with this Winchester work of art dates back to the late 1940s. General Sheridan's grandson, a resident of the Hollywood area in California, was anxious to acquire a Model 21 Winchester double-barrel shotgun. He wrote to me with pictures of the General's rifle, as an item for trade. In a matter of days I had shipped to him cash and a brand new Model 21. In exchange I could scarcely believe the utter magnificence of this historic presentation Model 1876 rifle.

The Sheridan rifle has since been in three of the finest collections in America, and is now part of James S. Fowler's group of deluxe Winchesters. If a finer Winchester lever action rifle was ever made, we would like to see it. I firmly believe that no piece will ever outshine the General Sheridan Model 1876.

THE MODEL 1886

Following the Model 1876, Winchester turned out several models of long arms in shotgun and rifle configurations. These are covered in separate groupings, since most collectors of Winchesters concentrate on the lever action types. The next lever model after the 1876 was the 1886, also chambered for express cartridges, but capable of handling the .45-70 and several other loads that were too much for the '76. A solid locking system in the breech (known as "sliding vertical locks") was the key to the great strength of the Model 1886. The genius of John M. Browning was an important element in the special design of the 1886. Winchester had obtained patent rights for a lever action mechanism of Browning and his brother Matthew which evolved into the Model 1886.

The new model was so notable an improvement that it immediately slowed down the sales of the '76.

Model 1894 musket with bayonet.

Model 94; Style 7 engraving, Style F checkering. Serial #270282. From the Ivan B. Hart collection.

Another deluxe Model 94 with half magazine, half round, half octagon barrel. Patterns are from the 1897 catalog.

1. Right and left receiver sides of General Philip H. Sheridan's Model 1876 rifle, which was presented to him by a friend, W. E. Strong. The engraving is by John Ulrich, and is superb in design and execution. The author believes this to be the finest Winchester rifle extant.

The Model 1886 remained in production through 1935, and about 159,994 were produced. Serial numbers were marked in an individual series, beginning with numeral #1. This was Winchester's first repeating weapon made in a profusion of calibers. Over a dozen in number, they included the .45-70, .45-90, .38-56, .50-100-450 and the .50-110 Express. A wide variety of barrel lengths, types, and weights were available, as were extras of special stocks, finishes, engravings and single and double set triggers. A takedown model was first advertised in 1894. Only about 350 muskets were made in the '86, so that most of this model's production was in rifle and (to a lesser extent) carbine types.

One of the first outdoorsmen to fall in love with the '86 was Theodore Roosevelt. His deluxe 45-90 rifle, #9205, quickly replaced his favorite Model 1876. In "Ranch Life and the Hunting Trail" (1888) he wrote:
Now that the buffalo have gone, and the Sharps rifle by which they were destroyed is also gone, almost all ranchmen use some form of repeater. Personally I prefer the Winchester, using the new model (1886), with a 45-caliber bullet of 300 grains, backed by 90 grains of powder, or else falling back on my faithful old standby, the 45-75 . . .

T.R. used the Model 1886 as his big game rifle from 1887 to 1894. He took over a hundred head of big game with it, including antelope, elk, moose, mountain goat, mountain sheep, blacktail and whitetail deer, caribou and black and grizzly bear. Not satisfied with factory loads, he handloaded his own, using a 330-grain hollow point bullet backed by

85 grains of smokeless Orange Lightning powder.

THE MODEL 1892

Next in the evolution of the lever action Winchester rifle was the Model 1892. Basically this new weapon was a scaled-down version of the Model 1886, designed to fire the .44-40, .38-40 and .32-20 cartridges then in use with the increasingly antiquated Model 1873 rifle. A later caliber, the .25-20, was added in 1895, and a few were made in .218 Bee in 1936 to 1938.

Approximately 1,004,067 Model 1892 Winchesters were made, from 1892 through 1941; serial numbering was in an individual range, beginning with #1. The two basic Model 1892 styles were rifles and carbines, although muskets were also produced. Some rifles were sold as takedowns. Among the special barrel lengths were 14, 15, 16, and 18 inches on both rifles and carbines. Barrels as long as 36 inches could be ordered at extra cost. Other custom order details included 1/2 and 2/3 magazines, set triggers, deluxe wood, shotgun buttplates,, pistol-grip buttstocks, special sights, and engravings and inscriptions. Of all models of lever action Winchester rifles, the 1892 is the least often found engraved. One of the most desirable of these elaborate specimens was serial number 1,000,000, deluxe engraved and presented to Secretary of War Patrick Hurley in 1932. One of the finest Winchesters of this model was serial #53,614, a deluxe engraved and gold and nickel-plated carbine made for Theodore Roosevelt. Admiral Robert E. Peary carried a '92 carbine on his trips in exploration of the North Pole. According to factory records, the 1892 had an avid following in Australia, South America, and the Far East, as well as in North America. More specimens still remain in use today than are in the hands of private collections and museums.

THE MODEL 1894

The next lever action rifle to appear in the Winchester line is still in production, and as popular as ever—the Model 1894. A design of John M. Browning, the mechanism was the first lever action type in production specifically for smokeless powder cartridges. In excess of 3,000,000 Model 1894s have been made to date in an uninterrupted manufacturing sequence beginning in 1894; serials began with #1.

Chamberings have been for the .32-40, .38-55, .25-38, .30-30 and .32

WINCHESTER

Winchester Special, and the variety of special order features is comparable to the Model 1892 series. A musket variation was experimented with, but the standard configurations have been rifles and carbines. Takedowns were available in the rifles only.

In engraved and inscribed pieces, the Model 1894 offers a larger number than any other model. Most of these deluxe pieces were embellished from designs reproduced in the rare and valuable catalogue of engraved and deluxe stock patterns published by the factory circa 1897.

An elaborately gold-inlaid, deluxe-stocked Model 1894 is in the Winchester Gun Museum collection. It has a shotgun buttplate (hard rubber) pistol grip stock, 2/3 magazine, takedown action, half-round, half-octagon barrel, and stocks and engraving-gold inlay selected from the 1897 design catalogue.

If you seek the finest in historic Model 1894s, try to find the following: #1,000,000, presented in 1927 to President Calvin Coolidge; #1,-500,000, presented to President Truman in 1948; and #2,000,000, a gift from Winchester to President Eisenhower in 1953. One of the finest '94s the author ever owned was an elaborately silver overlaid takedown rifle decorated by Tiffany & Company for the Paris Exposition of 1900. The frame, buttstock, and forend were all partially or wholly sheathed in relief-chiselled sterling silver. For stocks, two richly grained pieces of an exotic South Seas wood were selected. That rifle was featured in the recent best selling book, "The Tiffany Touch," by Joseph Purtell.

THE MODEL 1895

The final major collector's model of Winchester lever action rifle is the 1895. Made in carbine, rifle, and musket variations, and in a total quantity of about 425,881, this box-magazine repeater was sold through 1938. John M. Browning was the major patent holder for the '95, and the thought behind its development was to produce a lever action chambered for the new high-powered smokeless cartridges. Foregoing the use of a tubular magazine as found on all previous lever action Winchesters, the '95 featured a box magazine beneath the receiver. The new model proved to be the first successful rifle featuring the box magazine/lever action combination. Chamberings were for the .30-40 Krag, .38-72, .40-72, .303 British, .35 Winchester,

.405 Winchester, .30 Government M/03 and the .30 Government M/06. One of the more intriguing variations was the U.S. Army National Rifle Association Musket, approved by the NRA for use in their military target competitions. It was this model which served as the inspiration for one variant of the NRA's recent centennial model Winchester commemorative issue.

One style of the 1895 that is avidly sought after by collectors is the so-called "flat side." Approximately 5000 were made; they represent the first production of the Model 1895 rifle, and do not have the long scalloped look of the lower half of the later type receivers. One of the most interesting but rare variations is the 7.62mm Russian Musket, made in a total quantity of 293,816 for the Imperial Russian Government, in 1915 and 1916. The majority of these arms feature a 16-inch sword bayonet, and the whereabouts of most specimens presumably is still in Russia.

In about 1955 the writer was approached by a New York dealer in surplus arms, with an offer of 27 original crates, each holding 10 mint Model 1895 carbines or 1894 carbines —all in .30-40 Krag caliber. This unbelievable cache of guns had been part of the stock of weapons collected by the U.S. Government in answer to appeals by the British home guard for their proposed last-ditch stand against a German invasion. Actually, a total of 50 cases had survived (never having been shipped to Britain), and the dealer only told me of 27. The balance he kept and sold-off in cased and single lots by himself.

I simply could not believe my eyes when the truck pulled in to my warehouse loaded up with the 27 crates. At the time collector interest was not substantial enough to be able to sell each crate as an unbroken lot. So I opened up most of the 27 boxes and sold the mint guns as single pieces. At that time '95s and '94s were selling like hotcakes. But fortunately we held back one crate of each model,

---

HERB GLASS, BULLVILLE, N. Y.

Antique Firearms for Museums and Collectors

FIREARMS CONSULTANT

HONORARY CURATOR
WEST POINT MUSEUM
CONSULTANT — COLT'S
PATENT FIREARMS CO.

PHONE MIDDLETOWN
FOxcroft 1-5031

April 30, 1968

TO WHOM IT MAY CONCERN:

President Theodore Roosevelt presented my Grandfather, John Ryan Washburn, the Winchester rifle that is the subject of this letter. The rifle, a Model 1876 Winchester, serial #45704, had been specially made for Mr. Roosevelt when he lived on his Maltese Cross Ranch in the Dakota Territory. He "used it as a saddle gun for deer and antelope" - as stated in the letter of July 8th 1904, which was part of the presentation to Grandfather. The frame is specially engraved with scroll, animal, and hunting motifs - including a superb elk horn - and the stocks are of fancy wood, checkered, and carved with a large cheek-rest. The barrel is "half round-half octagonal", in a 20" length, 40-60 caliber, with swivels for a carrying strap. The sighting parts are the "African" type, and the magazine is the "1/2" length.

My Great Grandfather, Reverend Henry H. Washburn, had been Mr. Roosevelt's pastor at Oyster Bay, Long Island, New York, the site of the Roosevelt estate, Sagamore Hill. Rev. Washburn was minister at the marriage of Theodore Roosevelt and Edith Carow, and christened each of their children. When Colonel Roosevelt made his triumphant return to Oyster Bay after the Spanish-American War, my Great Grandfather spoke at the welcoming ceremonies. The following year, at a Fourth of July celebration, he predicted that T. R. would someday be President of the United States (two years later he was President).

Great Grandfather was minister to the Roosevelts over a period of some fifteen years, and during this span of time the members of both families formed warm and lasting friendships. T. R. was especially fond of my Grandfather, John R., and certainly a major reason for this affection was their mutual enthusiasm for hunting and the outdoor life.

Grandfather's birthday - his 21st - was early in August of 1904, and the President's Winchester was presented as a most special birthday gift. Grand-dad treasured this gun for the rest of his life. Following his death in 1950, my Father inherited it, and a few years later the rifle was passed on to me. The rifle, President Roosevelt's July 8th letter, and the several papers, photographs, and other relevant memorabilia have long been valued family heirlooms.

(s) Nancy Washburn Winger

State of Maryland
County of Baltimore
Subscribed and sworn to before me, a Notary Public of the State of Maryland, this 14th day of May 1968
my commission expires 7/1/69
Lenore E. Zaccari

Documentation verifying one of most valuable Model 1876's.

and replaced their lids with sheet plexiglass. Today they form unique coffee tables in the Mellon collection gunroom.

From a historic standpoint, the Model 1895 was a popular service arm in the Spanish-American War, and proved to be quite effective in the hands of big-game hunters around the world. The 1895 was the last model of Winchester lever action to be adopted as a favorite by Theodore Roosevelt. He took three '95s along on his great African safari of 1909-1910, and shot lions, hippopotamus, cape buffalo, rhino, and several species of antelope with them. Two were chambered for .405 caliber, and the third was chambered for the .30-40 Krag. The pieces had been custom made by Winchester for the President and his son Kermit. Complete details of T.R.'s negotiations with Winchester, who also assisted in preparations for shipping the President's entire African battery, are published in Larry Wilson's book "Theodore Roosevelt Outdoorsman."

A devoted exponent of the Winchester brand, T.R. was as thoroughly satisfied with his '95s as he was with his Model 1873, 1876, 1886, 1892 and 1894 rifles and carbines. The company could not have asked for a more distinguished enthusiast of its products. For Roosevelt, the Winchester was, as he termed it, "the ace." In honor of his achievements as a sportsman and conservationist, Winchester issued a commemorative

T.R. rifle in 1969. Over 50,000 were sold, and the number would have been twice that figure had not a crippling strike cut the production run short.

SHOTGUNS

Since their first model of 1879, Winchester has marketed a staggering array of shotguns of single-and double-barrel, slide action, semi-automatic, and single-shot types. Basically, only certain of the pre-World War I models are categorized as collector's items, and these alone (with one major addition) are covered here. Winchester's first model was entirely made in England, with sales handled through the company's New York store from 1879 through 1884. All the Model 1879 guns were side-by-side double barrels, with exposed hammers. Among the makers of these arms were W. C. Scott & Sons and C. G. Bonehill. Gauges were 10 and 12, and the first announced variants by grade were the Winchester Match Gun, and Classes A, B, C, and D. Later a Club Gun was added. Winchester markings were placed on the top barrel rib. All told, about 10,000 "Winchester" Double-Barrel guns were imported. The successful merchandising of these weapons led the factory to consider manufacture of a shotgun of their own make, based on the repeating lever action design that had been so widely received and now popularly identified with their name.

In developing a lever action shotgun, the Brownings again held patents which would be purchased by Winchester and put to practical use. The resultant design was the Model 1887 Repeater, made in 10 and 12 gauges, and in a total quantity of about 64,855. Production continued into the year 1901. History records that this series represented the first lever action shotgun of a repeating type made in the United States.

One of the more interesting collector variations of this model is the Riot Gun, having a 20-inch barrel. Variants of the Model 1887 were limited, and are mainly in different barrel lengths (30 and 32 inches standard), chokes, gauges and finishes. Engravings and inscriptions were available as per usual with most of the Winchester line.

Early in the 20th Century, the Model 1887 was succeeded by the Model 1901 Lever Action. This was an improved version of its predecessor, chambered for 10 gauge only and strong enough to handle the new smokeless powders. A quick means of telling one model from another is that case hardening was the standard frame finish on the 1887, and blue was standard on the 1901. Also, the new model commenced with serial #64856, picking up where its predecessor had left off. Only about 13,500 guns were made; production ceasing in 1920.

The Model 1901 was standard in the 32-inch barrel length with choice of full, modified and cylinder-bore chokes. Special-order stocks and engravings were available, but most guns of both the Model 1887 and 1901 were rarely given any deluxe treatments. Serial #1 of the series was recently sold by the author to the Mellon collection.

In slide action or pump shotguns, Winchester again drew on the brilliance of the Browning brothers. With modifications and improvements to a basic Browning patent, Winchester announced their first slide action shotgun in the June 1893 catalogue. The hammer of the Model 1893 was an exposed type, and ejection was through a port on the side of the receiver. Serial numbering began with #1, and continued in sequence through the total of approximately 34,050 guns. The Model 1893 was discontinued in 1897. Standard barrel lengths were 30 and 32 inches, and the gauge was 12 only. Deluxe guns were available on order, but are rarities in Winchester collecting.

Successor to the Model 1893 slide action shotgun was the Model 1897. Quite an improvement over its predecessor, the new scattergun fea-

A famous photo of W. F. Cody holding a deluxe Model 1873.

WINCHESTER

tured basic changes in the action, the chambering (now accepting both the 2⅝- and 2¾-inch cartridge), and in the stock. Among the major variations of the 1897 were the standard 12 gauge solid-frame, 12 and 16 gauge takedown models, and such types as trench and riot guns, and brush, pigeon, tournament, and trap grades.

A generous degree of options and special order features was available on the Model 1897 series. The client could specify his preference in chokes, barrel lengths, matted barrels, pistol- and straight-grip stocks, varying types of slide handles, steel and hard-rubber buttplates, engraving, inscriptions and deluxe finishes.

Serial numbering picked up at #34,151, where the Model 1893 had left off. The total production run was approximately 1,024,700, and the series was discontinued in 1957. Soon after its release, the Model 1897 Winchester had proven a better seller than its competitor arms, the Burgess and Spencer slide actions. Though now out of manufacture for over 15 years, the 1897 is still often seen in the field or at skeet and trap competitions. A major reason for this continued popularity is the exposed-hammer feature of the mechanism.

In 1912 Winchester brought out its most famous slide action shotgun —the Model 12 Hammerless. As a relatively late model, it is less a collector's gun than an excellent design still highly popular with competition shooters and sportsmen. Made in a total of about 1,968,307 guns, production was continuous through 1963. In 1972 the ever-popular 12 was revived by Winchester in response to public demand. Very few of the Model 12 shotguns appear in collections, with the general exception of mint or finely engraved and stocked pieces. It is a type often finely embellished by such modern day craftsmen as John E. Warren and Alvin A. White. The Ulrichs and other Winchester engravers of the 20th Century gave the deluxe treatment to a goodly number of 12s over the 51 years of its first production run.

Winchester's first self-loading (semi-automatic) shotgun appeared in 1911, several years after it should have, and in a design that was comparatively unsuccessful. Although a late model in terms of collector's Winchesters, the gun is important because it was the firm's first shotgun firing on the self-loading principle. The delay in its introduction was due to Winchester's refusal to deal with John M. Browning in his stipulation that payment for his patent rights on a self-loading shotgun be on a royalty basis. In the past, Browning patents had always been purchased outright by the company. On Winchester's rejection, Browning went to Remington Arms, and made a royalty agreement with them (1905). Winchester thus was faced with having to design a semi-automatic shotgun that would circumvent the Browning design. To do this required six years' time for research, design, tooling up and marketing. The new gun never amounted to much; it was weak competition to the Remington product. Only about 82,774 Model 1911 Winchester Self-Loading Shotguns were made, and production lasted just 14 years. All were serial numbered from #1 on up.

In later years Winchester marketed single-shot shotguns (e.g., their first, the Model 20), an over-and-under (the Model 101, introduced in 1963), and added various slide action and semi-automatic types. None of these (as yet anyway) are sought-after collector's items. However, one model of 20th Century shotgun still in production has found its way into the collections of many Winchester enthusiasts—the Model 21 Double-Barrel.

The 21, Winchester's first hammerless double-barrel side-by-side shotgun, was first advertised in 1931. It had been designed as a well-made, sturdy, reliable and attractive shooter that would rank high in its field. To this day the company has maintained the high standards of the 21, and the weapon remains the finest product in the Winchester line. To visit the Custom Shop at the factory, where the new 21s are made and where old ones are refurbished, is to take a nostalgic journey into the grand old days of gunmaking in the finest American tradition.

Quite a degree of variation will be observed in these guns. As a custom product, stocks, engravings, chokes, ejectors, and many other details were subject to customer preferences. The basic grades available were standard, Tournament, Trap, Skeet, Deluxe, Duck, Custom, Pigeon and Grand American. The latter three are still in the Model 21 line. Gauges have been 28, 20, 16, 12, and .410, the latter rarely encountered.

Two of the finest collector guns in the Model 21 series were a .405 double rifle and a presentation gun to the famous pilot, Wiley Post. The double rifle is in the Winchester Gun Museum collection, and is apparently unique. The type was never entered into production, although for African hunters the idea sounds like a good one. Wiley Post's Model 21 shotgun was engraved and inlaid by R. J. Kornbrath, and was inscribed for presentation by Pratt & Whitney Aircraft. On the bottom of the breech was a map of an historic round-the-world flight by Post, and on the sides of the breech were pictures of Post's plane, the "Winnie Mae." Kornbrath was very proud of the engraving, and took several crisp photographs of the gun before it was blued by Winchester.

A number of 21s are being reworked, restocked, and custom en-

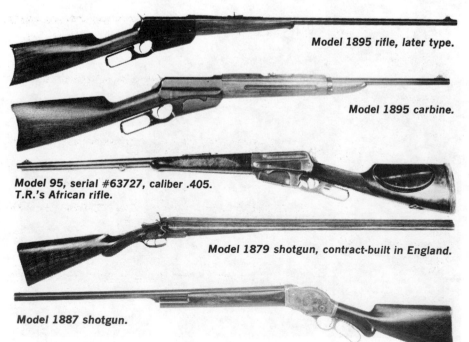

Model 1895 rifle, later type.

Model 1895 carbine.

Model 95, serial #63727, caliber .405. T.R.'s African rifle.

Model 1879 shotgun, contract-built in England.

Model 1887 shotgun.

graved by eminent gun craftsmen of today. Some of the most deluxe pieces have come from the shop of Alvin White, the most recent of which (for Mrs. W. B. Ford III) includes a relief gold-inlaid cartoon motif showing Mr. Ford being closely pursued by a most threatening African lion. The Fords hunt in Kenya every other year and are also collectors of fine Colts and hunting guns.

SINGLE SHOT RIFLES

Some of the finest and most sought-after collector's arms made by Winchester are the single-shot models. The first of these, the High Wall Model of 1885, was a basic design of John M. Browning, U.S. Patent #220271, dated October 7, 1879. After completing negotiations with the Browning brothers, Winchester purchased the rights and all rifles and parts available from the Brownings for the single shot arms. This acquisition, made about 1883, marked the beginning of the Winchester-Browning association, a historic chapter in gunmaking.

Total production of Winchester's Single Shot rifle series was limited to about 139,725, and manufacture ceased circa 1920. The collecting of these guns is rather specialized, and there are enthusiasts who care only for these Winchesters, ignoring even the lever action models. Three of the best references on this subject are actually not Winchester books at all, but are specialty publications for single shot rifle buffs, authored by James J. Grant.

Winchester's single shot rifles covered nearly conclusively all calibers from 22 Short Rimfire to 50 Centerfire. There were three frame sizes and six barrel weights. The lightest-weight gun was a 4¼-pound carbine in .44-40; the heaviest was the Scheutzen-style rifle in .32-40 or .38-55 caliber, tipping the scales at about 13 pounds. Among the major variations were the Winder Musket, various sporting rifles, target models, and even a 20 gauge shotgun. Takedown types were advertised beginning in 1910.

Single Shots were open to special orders for custom sights, stocks, engravings, and inscriptions. A few elaborately engraved specimens were made. However, a high proportion of deluxe single-shot Winchester rifles have been made up by custom gunsmiths years after manufacture ceased around 1920. A collector thus is well-advised to study a piece thoroughly if it purports to have factory original special features.

BOLT ACTION RIFLES

The major classification of Winchesters to collectors is the group of lever action models. Excepting the single shots, only a few enthusiasts specialize in the bolt actions, slide actions, or semi-automatic types. For this reason the information which follows is on selected arms only and is kept at a basic minimum.

Winchester's first bolt action rifle, the Model of 1883, was built on patents held by Benjamin B. Hotchkiss and on improvements patented by Winchester. After nearly eight years

of testing and modification, the rifle was published in the catalogue of January 1, 1884 as the "Winchester Model 1883". The bolt action breech was fed by a tubular magazine in the buttstock. Carbine, musket, and sporting types were produced. The standard caliber was the .45-70-405 U.S. Government. Serial numbering began with #1, and total production was approximately 62,034. Two predecessor types, the First Style of 1879-80, and the Second Style of 1880-83, were made in quantities of 6,419 and 16,102 respectively. Reviewing sales figures for the '83 Bolt Action indicates that the military Musket style sold the best, with the Sporting Rifle overshadowed by the very popular line of Winchester lever action rifles and carbines. In 1889, manufacture of the Model 1883 Winchester was discontinued.

The next bolt action rifle to be made by Winchester was the Lee Straight Pull Model. Winchester had taken on the manufacture of this weapon under contract to the U.S. Navy, in 1895. One of the features of the Lee was a clip-loading magazine, a pioneer use of that feature on an American rifle. Production at first was only for Navy requirements, but the rifle was advertised for sale by the company in their March 1897 catalogue. Its 6mm Lee cartridge, a .236 caliber, proved too light in comparison with the cartridges then favored by American shooters. Thus, the Sporting Model of the Lee had a poor showing on the market. Early in the 20th Century, production was discontinued; only about 18,300 muskets were made, and about 1,700 sporters. Serial numbering began with #1.

Winchester's next venture into manufacture of a high-powered bolt action was in contract orders of the Enfield Pattern 14 rifle for the government of Great Britain. About 245,-866 were produced, in 1915, 1916 and 1917. When America entered World War 1, Winchester purchased from the British the machinery that had been used at the factory to turn out the P-14 rifle. After altering the equipment so that chambering would be for the .30-06 Springfield cartridge, Winchester produced about 545,511 rifles circa 1917-18. The official designation for this weapon was the "United States Rifle, Caliber .30, Model of 1917". Serials were marked beginning with #1, and part of the stamping included numbers which indicated the date of manufacture by month and year. The Model 1917 was a military weapon which was never listed in company catalogues. One specimen is known to

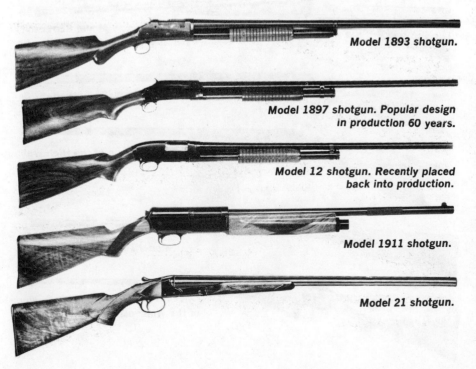

Model 1893 shotgun.

Model 1897 shotgun. Popular design in production 60 years.

Model 12 shotgun. Recently placed back into production.

Model 1911 shotgun.

Model 21 shotgun.

have been used as a presentation from the factory to President Woodrow Wilson.

The first Winchester bolt action chambered for .22 Rimfire cartridges was the Model 1900, a type based on the John M. Browning U.S. Patent #632904 (August, 1899). The company used the Model 1900 as their bid for a share of the market for inexpensive rimfire rifles. Cocking was accomplished simply by pulling back on the firing pin aperture on the rear of the bolt—a type action which in time was copied by several other U.S. arms makers. No serial markings were used on this model, of which about 105,000 were made. In 1902 the rifle was discontinued; its successor (the M1902) was a more expensive looking weapon, right down to the rococco shape of its triggerguard. As with the 1900 model, no variations were available from the one standard design. About 640,-299 rifles of the Model 1902 were made; manufacture ceased in 1931. Again, no serial number markings were used.

A variation of the Model 1902 which has become a novel collector's item is the Thumb Trigger Model 99. Winchester executive T. G. Bennett held the patent on this simple mechanism, the operation of which was based on a thumb release fitting beneath the firing pin knob. No serial numbers were used on this model either. Manufacture began in 1904 and ceased in 1923; approximately 75,433 were produced. No other Winchester weapon has been made employing the thumb trigger mechanism, and it is one of the few .22 caliber single-shot rifles to be a sought-after collector's item.

SLIDE ACTION RIFLES

One of Winchester's all-time most popular rifles was the .22 caliber Model 1890, their first rifle to operate on the slide action principle. Interestingly, Colt's had already beat them to the punch in this mechanism, by introduction of their Lightning series in 1883. John and Matthew Browning designed the Model 1890, at the request of the Winchester factory. Chambering was for the .22 Short, Long, W.R.F., and the Long Rifle—but these cartridges were not interchangeable. Not much variance will be observed in this model, although a few pieces were deluxe engraved and stocked. In 1932, the Model 1890 was discontinued; after a production run totalling 849,000. Many an adult of today has fond

memories of the Model 1890 as his first boyhood firearm.

A cheaper version of the 1890, the Model 1906, was made in a total of 848,000. It too was dropped from the line in 1932. The 1906 had the distinction of being Winchester's first rifle accepting .22 Short, Long, and Long Rifle cartridges interchangeably, as a result of an alteration made in the design circa 1908.

SELF LOADING RIFLES

Still another first from Winchester was their Model 1903 Self-Loading Rifle. It was America's first successful .22 Rimfire blowback action rifle, and the factory's first hammerless repeating rifle, and first self-loading rifle. T. C. Johnson was the designer. Though overshadowed by the more famous John M. Browning, Johnson was a prolific inventor in his own right. To him goes credit for many improvements on Browning's basic designs, before they could be manufactured on a practical basis.

Loading of the Model 1903 was through an aperture in the buttstock; the cartridges used were a special design identified as the .22 Winchester Automatic Smokeless. Made as a takedown weapon, there were two basic production styles: Plain and Fancy. Relatively little variation beyond Plain and Fancy was available, although a few weapons were custom engraved. One deluxe specimen once in the author's collection had cartoons of a card game and an outhouse on either side of the frame; the piece had been custom made

for a wealthy corporation executive, and it was used by him on hunting and camping trips with his pals.

Serial numbering of the Model 1903 began with #1, continuing in sequence through approximately 126,000. Production ceased in 1932; the 1903 was subsequently succeeded by the Model 63, a revised version of its predecessor, chambered for .22 Long Rifle ammunition.

Johnson followed his successful development of the Model 1903 by turning out a similarly structured semi-automatic rifle firing centerfire ammunition. Along with the new rifle, which was given the trade name of the Winchester Self-Loading Rifle Model 1905, two completely new cartridges were developed: .32 Winchester Self-Loading and .35 Winchester Self-Loading. A major difference from the Model 1903 .22 rifle was the use of a detachable box magazine, forward of the trigger. The Model 1905 was the company's first centerfire semi-automatic rifle and their first rifle made with a detachable box magazine. However, the price was high and the cartridges were of a comparatively limited velocity. Sales were slow and manufacture ceased in 1920. Approximately 29,113 were produced; serial numbered from #1 on up. Not much variation will be found in this model, except that deluxe stocks were available, as was custom engraving and inscriptions.

In 1907 an improved variation of the Model 1905 appeared, essentially a heavier rifle to handle a new car-

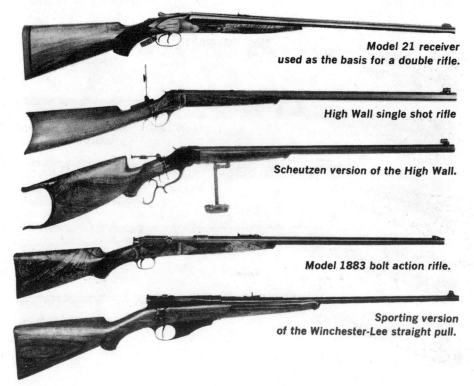

Model 21 receiver used as the basis for a double rifle.

High Wall single shot rifle

Scheutzen version of the High Wall.

Model 1883 bolt action rifle.

Sporting version of the Winchester-Lee straight pull.

tridge (made for this model) known as the .351 Winchester Self-Loading. Three basic styles of the M1905 were made: The Standard, the Fancy Sporting, and the Police. The latter version included a leather sling strap and an optional knife bayonet. The Police Model was made only from 1934 through 1937 and is a rarity in Winchesters. Serial numbering of the Model 1907 began with #1 and continued through the final piece, approximately #58490 (circa 1957).

In 1910, Winchester brought out another semi-automatic rifle of Johnson's design. This was the Model 1910 Self-Loading. Again the purpose of the new weapon was to fire a larger and more powerful cartridge. Chambering was for the new .401 caliber Winchester Self-Loading cartridge. As with its predecessors, the number of variations is limited, and only two styles were made—a Sporting Rifle and a Fancy Sporting Rifle. Special engravings, inscriptions, and stocks could be acquired on order. The M1910 was discontinued in 1936; serial numbers went from #1 on up, and only about 20,786 of these rifles were produced.

None of the three centerfire semi-automatic Winchesters had achieved what could be termed successful sales; they were continually overshadowed by their more popular lever action brethren.

Among the later semi-automatic types made by Winchester were 513,-528 .30 M1 Garand rifles and 818,059 .30 M1 U.S. Carbines. Both were manufactured during World War 2 and were major contributions of the factory to the war effort. Some M2 and T3 Carbine models were also made for the government during the war. These are variations from the standard .30 M1 Model. It was the M1 Carbine which inspired the postwar craze of the '60s for carbine-style small and medium caliber sporting rifles. Bill Ruger, with his .44 Magnum semi-automatic carbine, was a pacesetter in that still-popular movement.

WINCHESTER REVOLVERS

Winchester revolvers are a unique chapter in the company's long and detailed history. Most of the estimated 13 specimens of this experimental series had swingout cylinders. Most were single action, and most were chambered for .44 caliber cartridges. Designers Hugo Borchardt and S. W. Wood were involved in all but one of these experimentals, which were made up circa 1876. The final product was the design of William Mason, and dates from 1883. They represent the earliest swing-out cylinder and cylinder pin ejection revolvers in America—pre-dating the first Colt mass-produced model (the 1889 New Navy) by 13 years. The 1876 series of Winchester revolvers also is important historically for their very early use of .44-40, .44, and .38 caliber cartridge chamberings. Colt's Single Action Army did not use a .44 caliber until circa 1878. The Borchardt-Wood revolvers were created for Winchester in hopes that the company could win handsome production contracts with the U.S. Government (a sample was delivered to the Navy for trials), and with the Russians (another sample went to Colonel Ordinetz of their Ordnance Department). According to tradition, the Wood-Borchardt and Mason revolvers were later used by Winchester executives in the mid-1880s to persuade Colt's that they should drop the Burgess Lever Action rifle from their product line. By doing so Colt's would not face stiff competition from a Winchester line of revolving handguns.

Only one private collector owns a Winchester revolver, and another collector has a patent model of the swingout action. One final piece, the specimen delivered to the Russian Ordnance officer, has yet to be discovered. Though probably still in Russia, someday a lucky collector now reading this article may be able to add this extremely important item to his gun cabinet. Complete details on the Winchester revolvers appeared in the May, 1969 issue of the *American Rifleman*, in an article by R. L. Wilson.

THE WINCHESTER CANNON

From 1903 through 1958, Winchester's product line carried a breechloading cannon, known as the Model of 1898. Fitted with a 12-inch barrel and chambered for a 10 gauge 2⅞-inch blank cartridge, the recommended load was black powder—to give a loud report and a giant cloud of smoke. The cannon was sold for 4th of July celebrations, for starting races, as a yacht gun, and in firing salutes. The noise it makes is devastating, as testified to by the writer's neighbors every July 4th! The first model was made with cast iron wheels; these were modernized by adding rubber tires in 1930. Approximately 18,400 cannon were produced; none of these bear serial number markings. Numbers observed on these curiosities were identification stampings or export markings.

MISCELLANEOUS

Calendars, cartridge boards, and original artwork done for Winchester's advertising department form a category of collecting that the gun enthusiast shares in part with major connoisseurs of American 19th Century art. Among the great painters and illustrators who were commissioned to paint promotional subjects for the company were Frederic Remington, A. B. Frost, and N. C. Wyeth. Not only are these calendars a col-

U.S. Rifle, Caliber .30, Model of 1917, made by Winchester.

Model 1900 rifle.

Model 99 rifle.

Model 1890 rifle.

Model 1903 self-loading rifle.

WINCHESTER

lector's prize, but the original paintings for them could hang in a distinguished gallery such as the Whitney Museum of Western Art, in Cody, Wyoming. Several years ago, while on a trip to the Winchester factory, the author had the pleasant surprise of finding a superb N. C. Wyeth oil painting on the wall of an obscure office. The picture was one of several original advertising paintings then distributed around the plant. Whether original pictures, or published calendars, or cartridge boards, this sphere of Winchester collecting is a specialty worthy of pursuit by the most advanced collector. Several Winchester collectors use these items to liven up their gun rooms. Except for the original paintings themselves, the calendars and cartridge boards are still obtainable at prices in the range of $50.00 on up to about $1500.

Allied with Winchester advertising art, under the general heading of memorabilia, are original documents, letterheads, catalogues, ammunition, and non-gun products. Literally hundreds of thousands of products besides cartridges and firearms have been made with the Winchester imprimatur. These range from ice skates to pocket knives to flashlights to the general run of hardware items. As with the Colt line, one can assemble an excellent collection of Winchester products without owning a single firearm. This avenue is also quite economical, and is as fascinating as any other approach in the Winchester field.

COMMEMORATIVES

Winchester's commemorative program was launched in 1966 with the Centennial Model '66 Rifle. All their issues have been built on the Model 1894 frame, with a series of variations in barrel lengths and shapes, buttstock contours, forend styles, fin-

1. An engraved and gold-inlaid Model 1910 self-loading rifle. Note the harmoniously carved stock and peep sight. Ivan B. Hart collection.

2. Model 1898 cannon, a popular device for starters, etc. Shown is a late version with rubber tires.

3. Experimental Winchester revolver, based around the Borchardt-Wood patents. The swing-out cylinder predates Colt's by 13 years.

4. Winchester revolvers, 1876 series. Finely finished, they are nonetheless experimentals, each showing minor variations. With such designs, Winchester purportedly persuaded Colt to drop the Burgess-design lever action.

ishes, frame markings and stock inlays, sights, and roll or hand engravings. One of the biggest sellers was the Buffalo Bill Model, issued in over 120,000 guns, with a special series of 300 rifles hand engraved and specially cased, priced at $1000 each. At the request of the Buffalo Bill Historical Foundation, the author served as the advisor on the design and promotion of that model.

Unlike nearly all commemoratives my other gunmakers, Winchester has often officially allied their issues with a recognized institution. The Buffalo Bill was authorized by the Buffalo Bill Memorial Association, which built a new museum wing in Cody, Wyoming, with the monies they took in from royalties. Income from the Theodore Roosevelt Commemorative set up an endowment in T.R.'s name for the American Museum of Natural History in New York. The more recent Lone Star (Texas) Commemorative benefitted the cause of big game conservation.

Unlike Colt's and most other makers of commemorative guns, Winchester has generally issued large quantities of each model. Rarely has the total gone below 50,000 pieces per issue, and some of the best sellers have exceeded 100,000 units. Subjects commemorated to date include the Nebraska and Model 1866 Rifle Centennials, and the Lone Star, Theodore Roosevelt, Buffalo Bill, and National Rifle Association models. Profits from the latter issue were generously donated to the NRA by Winchester.

BOOKS

Unlike the Colt collector, whose field of interest has been published

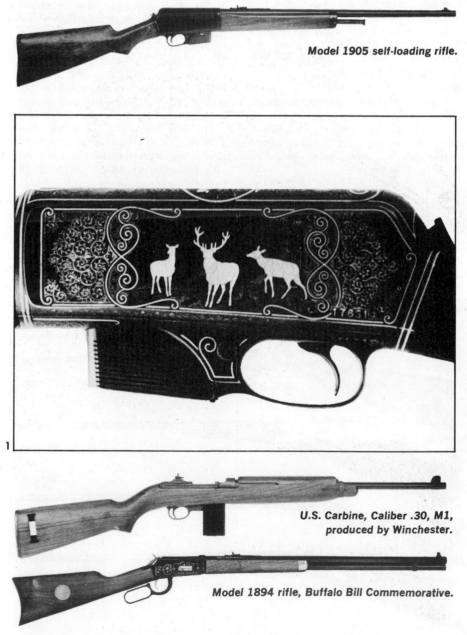

Model 1905 self-loading rifle.

U.S. Carbine, Caliber .30, M1, produced by Winchester.

Model 1894 rifle, Buffalo Bill Commemorative.

rather thoroughly, Winchester enthusiasts do not have large libraries of written material for reference. Only a handful of books are in print, and the true aficionado must complement these by collecting original factory retail catalogues. The two comprehensive, standard texts on Winchesters are George Watrous' "History of Winchester Firearms 1866-1966," and George Madis' "The Winchester Book." Watrous' approach, as edited and revised by the late Pete Kuhlhoff and Winchester Gun Museum Curator, T. E. Hall, covers every Winchester firearm made from the predecessor types (Hunt, Volcanic, etc.) through the current models. Detailed production facts and specimen photographs are presented in an easily used reference format. Madis' book, all 542 pages of it, is a highly detailed, profusely

illustrated specialist's reference. Over 1500 pictures show Winchester firearms up through the period of the early 20th Century. In text and pictures, the Madis book is the most detailed of collector books on Winchesters. Its sole weakness is a lack of an index to enable the reader to find the information so profusely presented in the text. The sole company history of Winchester is Harold F. Williamson's "Winchester the Gun That Won The West." The 494 pages in this volume are of interest to the collector, but deal mainly with company history, and only secondarily with the firm's products. An excellent specialized study is John E. Parsons' "The First Winchester," based on the Henry, Model 1866, 1873, and 1876 rifles. David F. Butler's "Winchester '73 and '76," is a popular title dealing with the same area,

and Bill West's "Winchester" series is another useful and detailed reference. The late Hank Weiand Bowman authored an illustrated booklet entitled "Famous Guns From the Winchester Collection." This is the only volume in print which is based solely on the rich collection of the Winchester Gun Museum.

THE WINCHESTER GUN MUSEUM

Special mention in any article on Winchesters is due to the company's Gun Museum. This unique collection, open to the public, is composed of the original factory reference museum and the Edwin Pugsley arms collection. No Winchester collector is worth his salt until he has seen the factory's Gun Museum. Besides a rich collection of prototype, experimental, engraved, and mint production Winchesters, there is a large group of predecessor types and competitor arms made by a myriad of American, European, and Oriental gunmakers. The collection tells the complete story of Winchester, and at the same time reveals the 500-year history of firearms. Except where otherwise indicated, all pictures in this article were supplied by the Museum.

Museum Curator T. E. Hall, and his assistant Mrs. Anita Sylvia, are extremely helpful in answering the questions of collectors and the general public. Among the Museum's services is answering queries from collectors on specific guns. Although many records no longer exist, production details on the major collectible lever action models are fairly complete. The original shipping point is rarely indicated, but such key factors as engraving, special inscriptions, stocks, sights, and finishes are a matter of record. All that is required is to send a description of your gun, including model and serial number, to The Winchester Gun Museum, 275 Winchester Avenue, New Haven, Connecticut 06504. There is no charge for this service.

The more often the collector finds himself consulting standard reference books, and contacting the Museum for further information and documenting letters, the closer he is to completing a fine Winchester group. Speaking from my own experience, Winchester firearms and related products and memorabilia have enriched my life in guns with the thrill of discovering and studying their historic contributions to America's shooting, hunting, and gunmaking tradition. American history—and the collecting of guns—would not be the same without the major contributions made by the Winchester. 🦅

Facsimile of the 1893 calendar.

COLLECTOR'S CATALOG

On the following pages you will find a catalog of collectable firearms which covers just about every known type and price range. Initially, this section may appear to be just a large collection of pictures, descriptions and prices. However, we have designed this catalog to be far more than that, indeed, more than just a pricing guide. Hopefully, you, the collector, will be able to use this compendium as a complete guide long after the prices are dated —and dated they will become, for collecting is a rapidly advancing hobby and business. Repeated reference to this catalog section will expand your overall knowledge of the subject and permit you to make more rapid identification of different types and groups.

All prices in this catalog reflect current pricing information obtained from gun shops, antique firearms dealers and, to some extent, personal observations at various gun shows. Although prices vary from region to region and depend a great deal on who has what, who wants it and how much the collector is willing to pay for the piece, our price ranges are generally conservative—neither extreme highs nor extreme lows are represented. Why? Simply because such prices would date the catalog much more rapidly, cause it to reflect market extremes and possibly promote justification in some cases for excessive price rise.

The prices given on the individual arms shown on the following pages apply to arms that range from "good" to "fine" condition as promulgated by current National Rifle Association of America (NRA) collectors arms guidelines.

Arms in "poor" to "fair" condition are, unless otherwise indicated, not represented pricewise in this catalog. Certain specimens in the catalog have no prices at all—take a look at them and you'll see why. They are the type of firearm, be they a fabulous wheellock or a crude inventor's prototype, that just can't be evaluated under any fixed system. They are purely subjective in appeal and will bring whatever price a willing buyer and a willing seller can agree upon.

Now that we have established the basic premise of the catalog, we, the editors, hope you will find it a continuing and valuable reference section for a long time to come. May we wish you good luck in your chosen field of collecting and bid you remember the cardinal rule of gun trading: *Caveat emptor!*

AUSTRIA

MILITARY AIR RIFLE Adopted by the Austrian army in 1788. .45 caliber, 32½'' barrel, bright metal finish. Repeater, with 10'' tube magazine. Air chamber in the buttstock. Capable of firing 30 shots a minute. These weapons were declared illegal by Napoleon. When found, they may go for upwards of $800.00.

SPORTING AIR RIFLE 16'' rifled barrel. .47 caliber. Tube-feed magazine. Leather-covered steel buttstock that serves as the air chamber. Engraved and trimmed with gilded brass. This weapon was made by J. Cantriner, a fine Viennese gunsmith of the early 19th Century. This item may sell for over $1000.00.

SCHULHOF MODEL 1883, 11mm, eight-shot, 33'' barrel. This rare martial piece has in its buttstock a magazine holding four cartridges. When the bolt is operated, a rail takes one cartridge at a time through the stock to a position where the bolt can take it into the chamber. Current value about $120.00.

MANNLICHER MODEL 1888/90 8x50 Rmm five-shot Mannlicher clip, barrel 32". Used by Bulgaria, Greece and Chile. Fast action, straight-pull bolt. Was acknowledged to be the deciding factor in the Chilean Civil War of 1891. Fitted with volley-fire sight. Depending on condition, these may go from $40.00 to $60.00.

MANNLICHER MODEL 1895 8x50 Rmm, five shot Mannlicher clip. Principal weapon of Austro-Hungary in WW1. After the war, many were sent as reparations to Italy and Yugoslavia. Many of these were converted to 7.92mm. These will have the letter "M" stamped after M95 on the top of the receiver. These rifles will sell from $40.00 to $60.00.

BELGIUM

FLINTLOCK SMOOTHBORE made by Mathiev Aavbonne 18 gauge, 37½" round barrel. Iron trim, full-length stock with protruding forend. Wing nut on the left-hand side permits quick detachment of the lock. Price ranges on such specimens would be $200.00 to $250.00.

GENDARME CARBINE dating from the late 1840s, .65 caliber, 17½" barrel. This weapon was issued in place of a pistol. The large ring hammer facilitates cocking. Bright metal overall, with a saddle ring on the left side of the stock. Depending on condition, specimens may bring approximately $110.00 to $160.00.

CARBINE altered from flintlock to percussion. Approximately 1842, .69 caliber. Bright metal finish, brass trim with iron trigger plate. Similar to the French pattern 1822. Examples may be found without sling swivels, and a saddle ring bar, in rifled and smoothbore versions. Examples may go for $100.00 to $150.00.

HEAVY TARGET RIFLE .68 caliber rifled, with octagonal barrel. Stock has a cheekpiece. Large peep sight on the tang is adjustable for windage and elevation. Double-set trigger has a screw adjustment. Lock is marked "Bergai Faxkiol. "This specimen might go for between $300.00 and $450.00.

SHOTGUN by N. Vivario Pehmdeer of Liége, 28 gauge, 33½'' damascus barrels, octagonal at the breech. Engravings occur on the edge of the buttplate, locks, and trigger guard. Checkered forend and small of stock The termination of the small is elaborately carved as a boar's head. Examples may be found for between $100.00 and $200.00.

SHOTGUN, 26 gauge, 33'' barrels. Fine checkered stock and forend. Small of stock is carved with an elaborate boar's head. Damascus barrels. Specimens may sell for between $120.00 and $175.00.

REVOLVING RIFLE 12mm, pinfire, six-shot, 26'' barrel. The specimen weighs five pounds, single-action mechanism, engraved. Examples may be found for $175.00 to $250.00.

COLT "BREVET" revolving rifle .36 caliber, six-shot, 23'' barrel A few of these were manufactured experimentally by J.A. Petry of Liége. Based on the 1851 Navy action. When these specimens can be found, they can bring around $1000.00.

BREECHLOADING SPORTING RIFLE Falling-block action with shotgun type takedown. This weapon bears the name ''J.H.Jamer-Smits Fabt-D'Armes A Liége.''Action and barrel bands are scroll engraved. This weapon has a bayonet lug. Caliber .450. This type of piece might go for $125.00 to $175.00.

MAUSER MODEL 1889 7.65mm, 29'' barrel. First smallbore, smokeless powder Mauser production rifle. First Mauser to use a box magazine and the stripper-type clip. One-piece bolt, barrel has a metal jacket surrounding it for better accuracy. Designed by Mauser, produced in Belgium only. Depending on condition these rifles may go from $35.00 to $55.00.

MAUSER MODEL 1889 CARBINE 7.65mm, 22" barrel, ramrods are usually missing from these weapons. A "lightened" version, with a barrel of 18", was used by bicycle troops. This weapon has a turned-down bolt and a catch with a lock on the left side of the stock. Depending on condition, prices are $40.00 to $60.00.

ALTERATION OF MODEL 1917 to 7.9x57mm seven-shot Mauser-type magazine Converted in Belgium, probably for Chinese Government. Cleaning rod was added to the rework, and a thumb slot provided for loading. All British marks were removed. Barrel is marked "B Blindee 7.92mm", indicating, it was proofed for jacketed bullets. Specimens sell for $100.00 to $125.00.

FN 7.62mm FAL Weight, nine lbs. barrel 21", Major European military rifle in wide use throughout the world. Also manufactured in various countries; Mexico, India, South Africa and Canada. There are selective-fire and heavy-barrel versions. This weapon was available in the U.S. in semiautomatic version only. These arms are quite scarce here. Current range, $900.00 to $1200.00.

CHINA

CHINESE MAUSER MODEL 1871 CARBINE, 11mm Mauser, single-shot, 18¾" barrel. These weapons were made for the Chinese, by Mauser and are so marked. Examples may be found for $50.00 to $75.00.

CHINESE-MADE, "HANYANG" RIFLE, Model 1888, 8x57mm, five-shot clip. This weapon has the Japanese-type rear sight and handguard. It does not have the outer barrel jacket. This arm may bring $40.00 to $60.00.

CHINESE-MADE Kar 98k, 8mm with straight bolt handle and early type metal fittings. This weapon is also known as the "Chiang Kai-Shek" Mauser. It is referred to as the Type 79 by the present regime in China. Produced in 1935, it saw considerable service, and was used in Korea. Specimens turn up all over Asia. Examples may be found for $70.00 to $90.00.

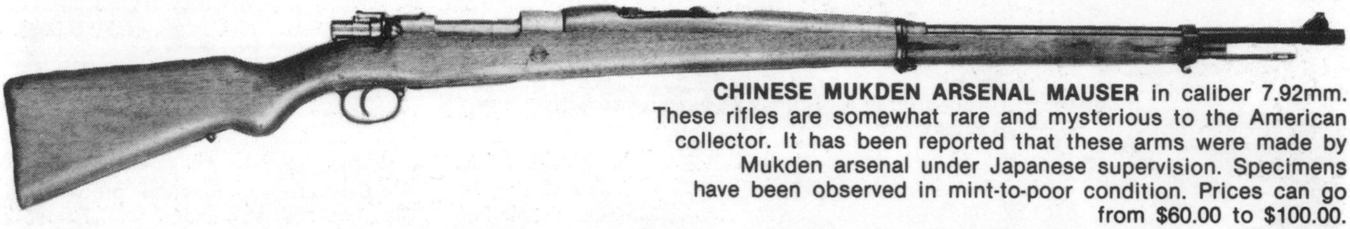

CHINESE MUKDEN ARSENAL MAUSER in caliber 7.92mm. These rifles are somewhat rare and mysterious to the American collector. It has been reported that these arms were made by Mukden arsenal under Japanese supervision. Specimens have been observed in mint-to-poor condition. Prices can go from $60.00 to $100.00.

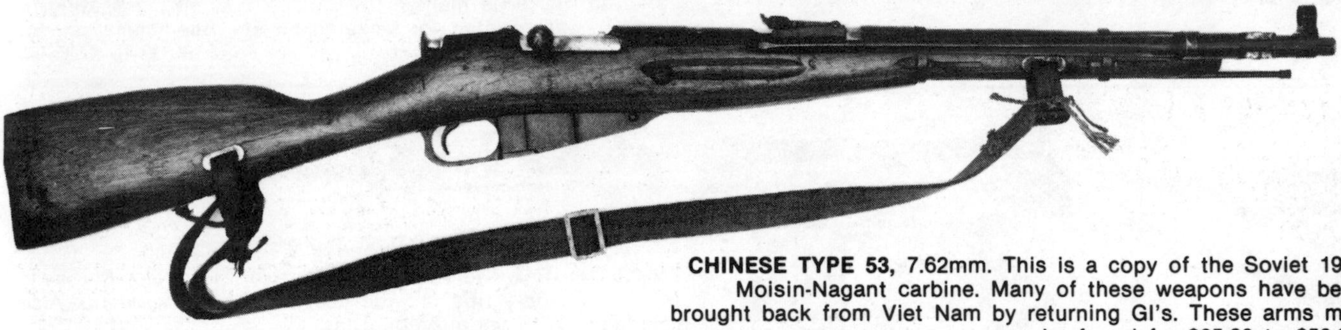

CHINESE TYPE 53, 7.62mm. This is a copy of the Soviet 1944 Moisin-Nagant carbine. Many of these weapons have been brought back from Viet Nam by returning GI's. These arms may be found for $25.00 to $50.00.

CHINESE-MADE SKS TYPE 56 CARBINE This weapon, like its Russian counterpart, is chambered for the M43 7.62 intermediate-sized cartridge. It has a non-detachable 10-round magazine and folding bayonet. This arm, along with the AK-47, is the mainstay of the NVA. Prices may range from $100.00 to $150.00.

DENMARK

UNDERHAMMER RIFLED MUSKET of approximately 1840. .69 caliber, 35" barrel. Ringed hammer is enclosed in the trigger guard. Trigger is a notched spring that engages the hammer. Barrel bands and butt-plate are brass. The weapon is marked with the Danish crown and date 1841. This arm may go for $250.00 to $300.00.

DANISH WALL GUN, MODEL 1848, .69 caliber, with a heavy octagonal rifled barrel. Lock has a pivoting safety to block the hammer. Iron barrel bands, brass buttplate and trigger guard. This arm may go for $300.00 to $375.00.

DOUBLE-BARREL SHOTGUN, 14 gauge 32'' damascus barrels marked "Delcomyn Kobenhaven." Engraved back-action locks. Patent breech is engraved with floral designs. A high quality specimen, such as this, may go for $200.00 to $300.00.

HUNTING RIFLE, by Delcomyn of Copenhagen. .48 caliber, 30'' barrel. It dates from approximately 1850. This specimen may go for $175.00 to $250.00.

HUNTING RIFLE, by Delcomyn of Copenhagen. .60 caliber, 25'' barrel. Engraved lock, buttplate and trigger guard. Double-set trigger has screw adjustment. Current value of such specimens is for $150.00 to $200.00.

BREECHLOADING RIFLE, 11mm, 30'' barrel. The action somewhat resembles the American Hall. The weapon uses a paper cartridge. Front guard circles the hammer. This arm may go for $250.00 to $300.00.

KRAG ARTILLERY CARBINE, MODEL 1889, 8mm Danish, 24'' barrel. This arm has the turned-down bolt handle and a triangular upper sling swivel. It also has a stud on the left side of the stock which was used to hang the carbine from a leather hanger on the gunner's back. This arm is rare, and may sell for $175.00 to $225.00.

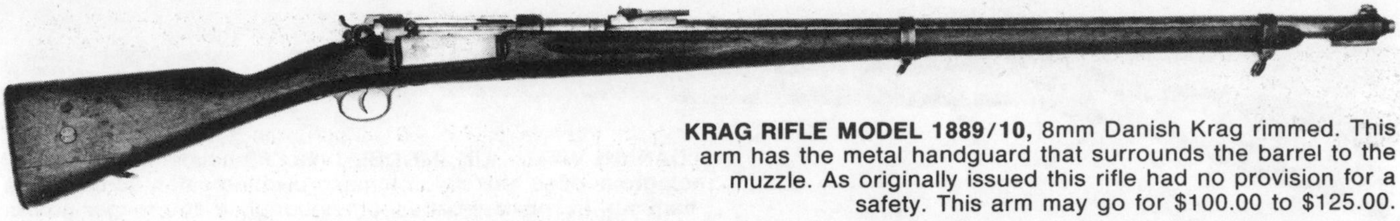

KRAG RIFLE MODEL 1889/10, 8mm Danish Krag rimmed. This arm has the metal handguard that surrounds the barrel to the muzzle. As originally issued this rifle had no provision for a safety. This arm may go for $100.00 to $125.00.

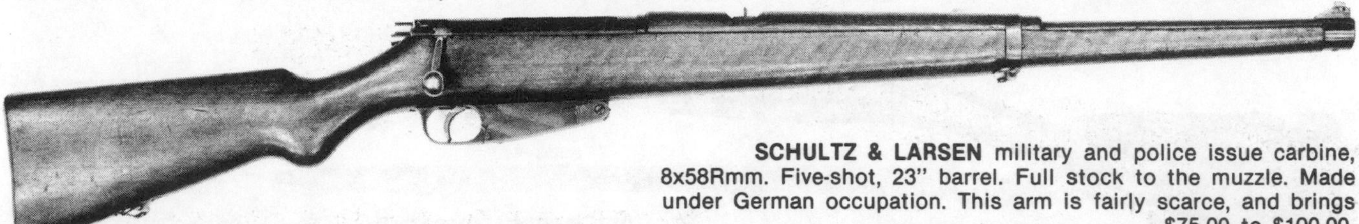

SCHULTZ & LARSEN military and police issue carbine, 8x58Rmm. Five-shot, 23" barrel. Full stock to the muzzle. Made under German occupation. This arm is fairly scarce, and brings $75.00 to $100.00.

FRANCE

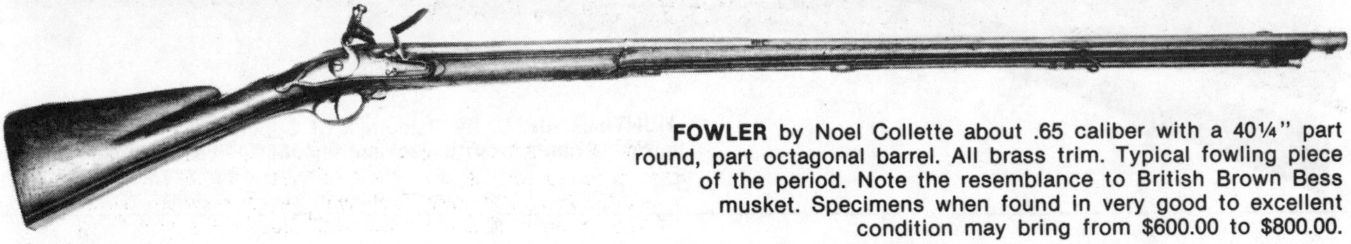

FOWLER by Noel Collette about .65 caliber with a 40¼" part round, part octagonal barrel. All brass trim. Typical fowling piece of the period. Note the resemblance to British Brown Bess musket. Specimens when found in very good to excellent condition may bring from $600.00 to $800.00.

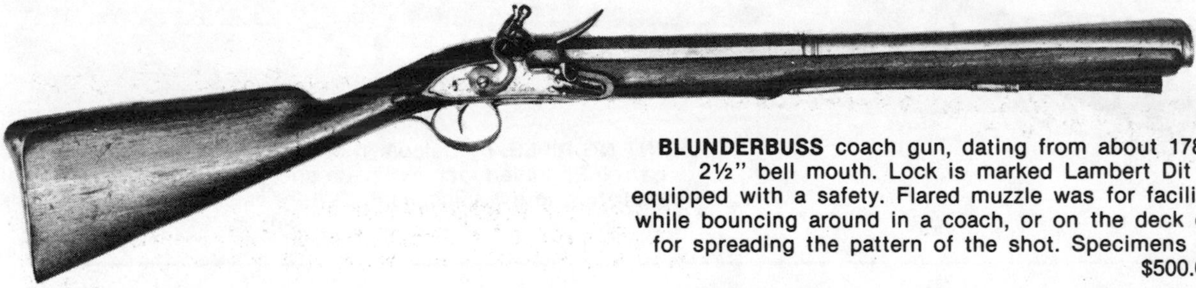

BLUNDERBUSS coach gun, dating from about 1780, 20" barrel, 2½" bell mouth. Lock is marked Lambert Dit Civon, and is equipped with a safety. Flared muzzle was for facilitating loading while bouncing around in a coach, or on the deck of a ship, not for spreading the pattern of the shot. Specimens may run from $500.00 to $800.00.

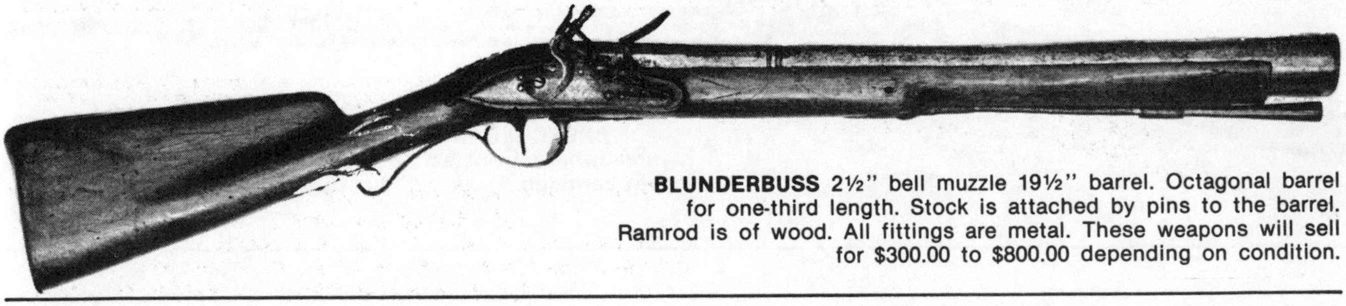

BLUNDERBUSS 2½" bell muzzle 19½" barrel. Octagonal barrel for one-third length. Stock is attached by pins to the barrel. Ramrod is of wood. All fittings are metal. These weapons will sell for $300.00 to $800.00 depending on condition.

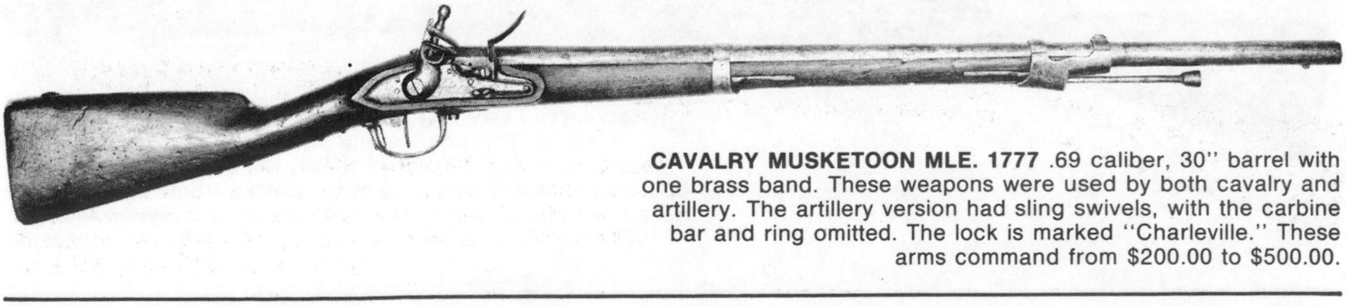

CAVALRY MUSKETOON MLE. 1777 .69 caliber, 30" barrel with one brass band. These weapons were used by both cavalry and artillery. The artillery version had sling swivels, with the carbine bar and ring omitted. The lock is marked "Charleville." These arms command from $200.00 to $500.00.

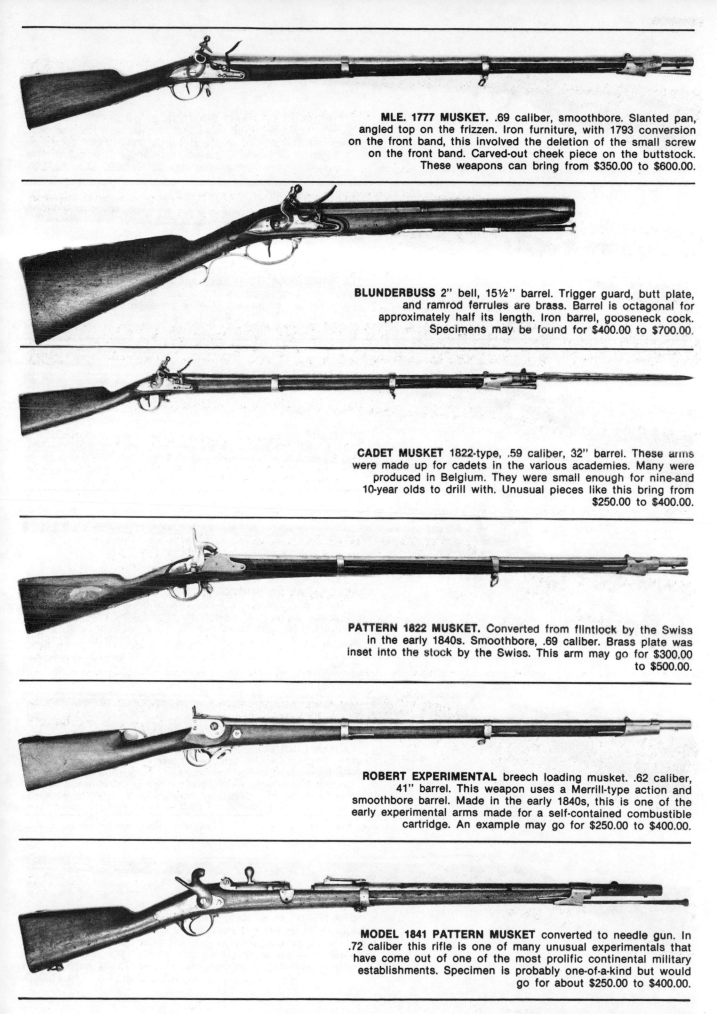

MLE. 1777 MUSKET. .69 caliber, smoothbore. Slanted pan, angled top on the frizzen. Iron furniture, with 1793 conversion on the front band, this involved the deletion of the small screw on the front band. Carved-out cheek piece on the buttstock. These weapons can bring from $350.00 to $600.00.

BLUNDERBUSS 2" bell, 15½" barrel. Trigger guard, butt plate, and ramrod ferrules are brass. Barrel is octagonal for approximately half its length. Iron barrel, gooseneck cock. Specimens may be found for $400.00 to $700.00.

CADET MUSKET 1822-type, .59 caliber, 32" barrel. These arms were made up for cadets in the various academies. Many were produced in Belgium. They were small enough for nine-and 10-year olds to drill with. Unusual pieces like this bring from $250.00 to $400.00.

PATTERN 1822 MUSKET. Converted from flintlock by the Swiss in the early 1840s. Smoothbore, .69 caliber. Brass plate was inset into the stock by the Swiss. This arm may go for $300.00 to $500.00.

ROBERT EXPERIMENTAL breech loading musket. .62 caliber, 41" barrel. This weapon uses a Merrill-type action and smoothbore barrel. Made in the early 1840s, this is one of the early experimental arms made for a self-contained combustible cartridge. An example may go for $250.00 to $400.00.

MODEL 1841 PATTERN MUSKET converted to needle gun. In .72 caliber this rifle is one of many unusual experimentals that have come out of one of the most prolific continental military establishments. Specimen is probably one-of-a-kind but would go for about $250.00 to $400.00.

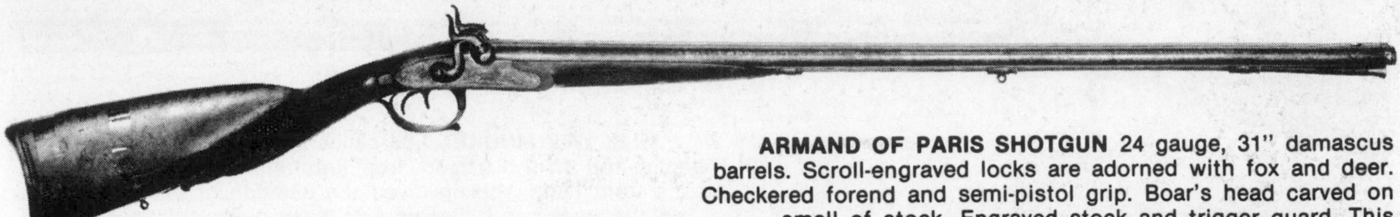

ARMAND OF PARIS SHOTGUN 24 gauge, 31'' damascus barrels. Scroll-engraved locks are adorned with fox and deer. Checkered forend and semi-pistol grip. Boar's head carved on small of stock. Engraved stock and trigger guard. This specimen may go for $200.00 to $275.00.

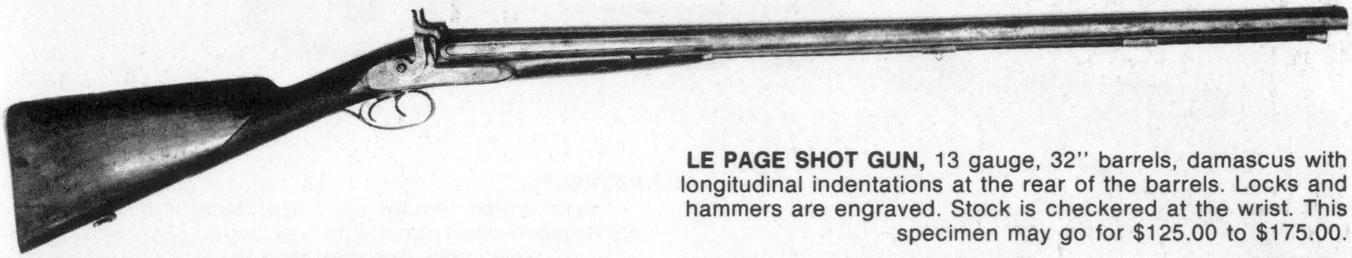

LE PAGE SHOT GUN, 13 gauge, 32'' barrels, damascus with longitudinal indentations at the rear of the barrels. Locks and hammers are engraved. Stock is checkered at the wrist. This specimen may go for $125.00 to $175.00.

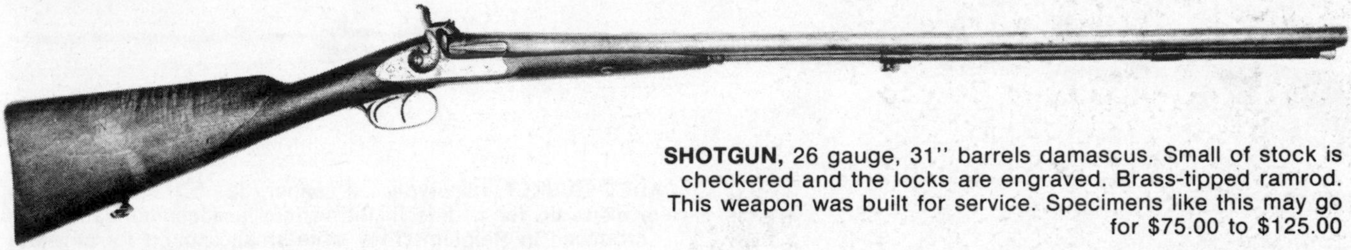

SHOTGUN, 26 gauge, 31'' barrels damascus. Small of stock is checkered and the locks are engraved. Brass-tipped ramrod. This weapon was built for service. Specimens like this may go for $75.00 to $125.00

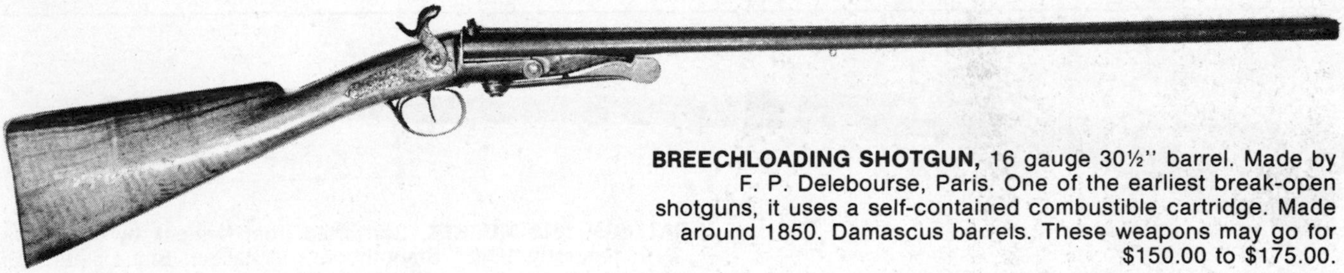

BREECHLOADING SHOTGUN, 16 gauge 30½'' barrel. Made by F. P. Delebourse, Paris. One of the earliest break-open shotguns, it uses a self-contained combustible cartridge. Made around 1850. Damascus barrels. These weapons may go for $150.00 to $175.00.

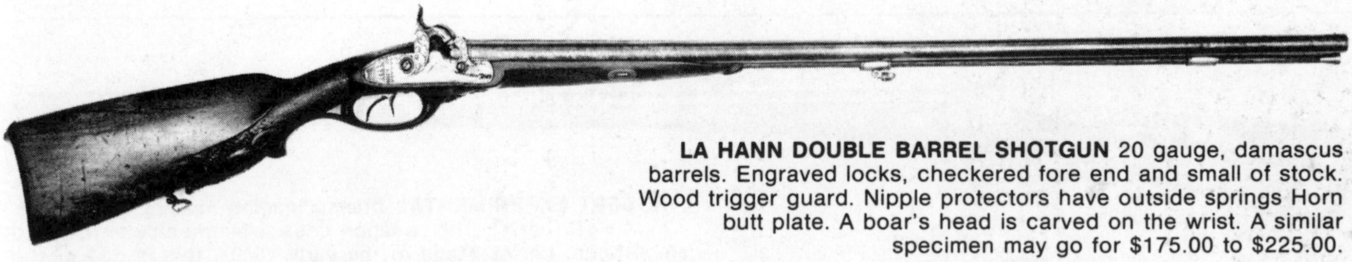

LA HANN DOUBLE BARREL SHOTGUN 20 gauge, damascus barrels. Engraved locks, checkered fore end and small of stock. Wood trigger guard. Nipple protectors have outside springs Horn butt plate. A boar's head is carved on the wrist. A similar specimen may go for $175.00 to $225.00.

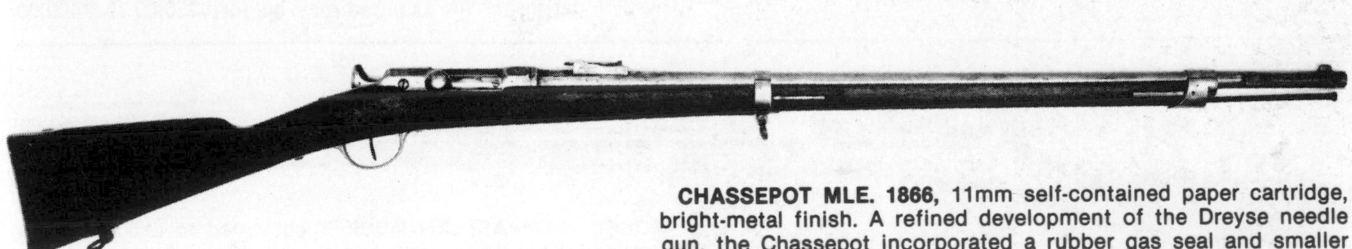

CHASSEPOT MLE. 1866, 11mm self-contained paper cartridge, bright-metal finish. A refined development of the Dreyse needle gun, the Chassepot incorporated a rubber gas seal and smaller caliber. It had almost twice the range of the German arm. A brass-handled sword bayonet was carried. These weapons may be found at $70.00 to $100.00.

GRAS MLE. 1874, 11mm, polished metal bolt, blued barrel and receiver. Converted from the Chassepot system by the insertion of a sleeve in the chamber to handle the 11mm metallic cartridge, a new bolt and new sights. Later models were not conversions. These carried a needle bayonet with a wooden handle and brass butt. This model may go for $50.00 to $75.00.

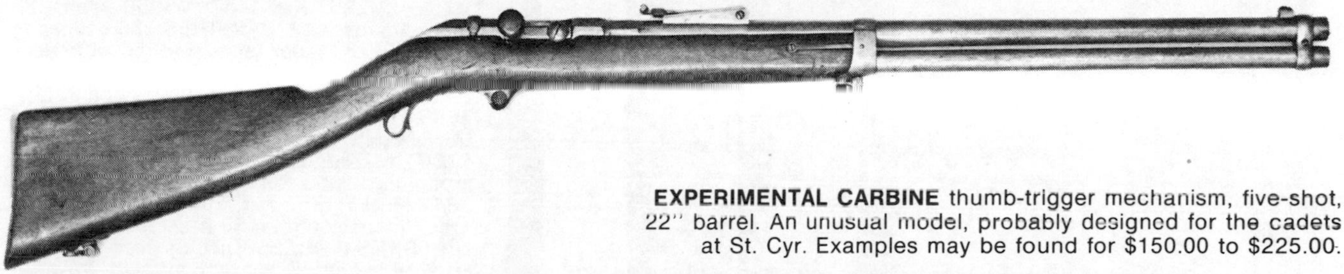

EXPERIMENTAL CARBINE thumb-trigger mechanism, five-shot, 22'' barrel. An unusual model, probably designed for the cadets at St. Cyr. Examples may be found for $150.00 to $225.00.

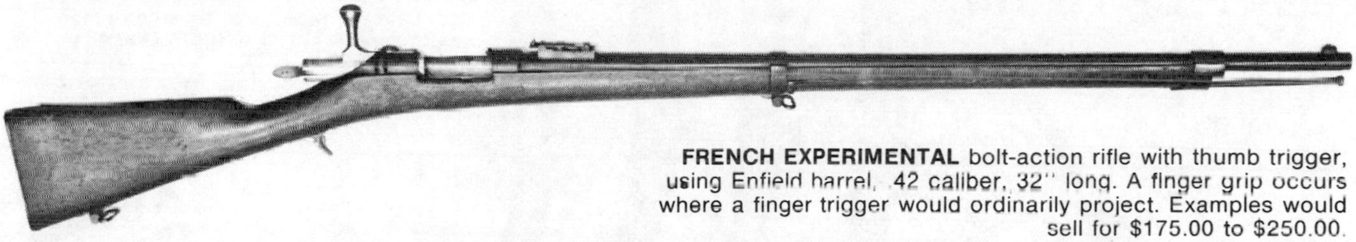

FRENCH EXPERIMENTAL bolt-action rifle with thumb trigger, using Enfield barrel, .42 caliber, 32'' long. A finger grip occurs where a finger trigger would ordinarily project. Examples would sell for $175.00 to $250.00.

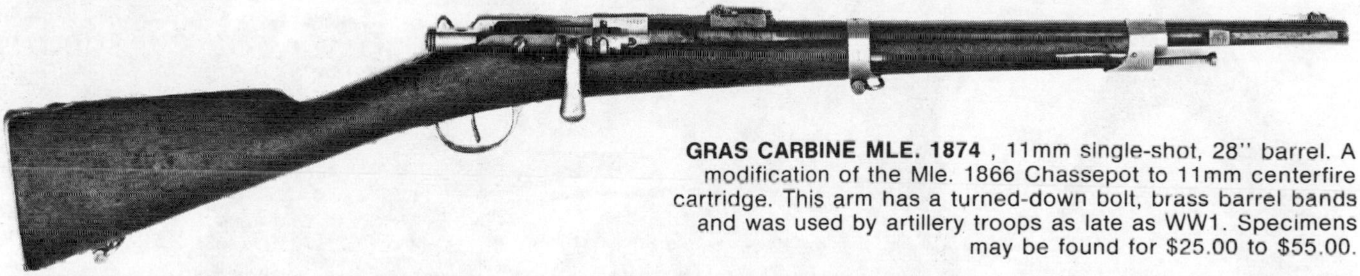

GRAS CARBINE MLE. 1874 , 11mm single-shot, 28'' barrel. A modification of the Mle. 1866 Chassepot to 11mm centerfire cartridge. This arm has a turned-down bolt, brass barrel bands and was used by artillery troops as late as WW1. Specimens may be found for $25.00 to $55.00.

KROPATSCHEK MARINE RIFLE MLE. 1878 11mm, seven-shot, 32'' barrel. This model was issued in bright metal finish. Many were manufactured at the Steyr factory in Austria. Ramrod was placed along the left side of the stock. Specimens may go for $30.00 to $50.00.

LEBEL RIFLE MLE. 1886/93, 8mm Lebel eight-shot, 31'' barrel. The first successful military rifle designed for small-bore, smokeless powder. Its proven feasibility started an armaments race that swept over all Europe. Specimens may be found in the $60.00 to $90.00 price range.

1780-1880

The height of greatness achieved by the British Empire is typified by these weapons

England has had a long and honorable military history filled with pageant and glory. The arms and uniforms of the United Kingdom tell quite a bit about those who served King and Country. BAYONETS: Brown Bess bayonet; Pattern 1853 rifle-musket; Pattern 1854 Sword bayonet. SWORDS: Pattern 1822 Light Cavalry officer's model; Pattern 1854 Cavalry Trooper's model from the IV Light Dragoons of Light Brigade fame; Pattern 1797 Hussar's officer sabre. PISTOLS and REVOLVERS: Pat. 1844 Naval Pistol; 3rd Model .442 Tranter; .442 Wedge frame Webley; M1857 Kerr .442; M1856 Beaumont-Adams .442. CARBINES: .56 caliber Terry breech loader (shown to left of handguns); Sergeant's Pattern Snider mosqueton; Pat. 1856 Enfield cavalry model; Pat. 1858 Artillery model (atop of uniform). LONGARMS: India Pattern Brown Bess c. 1786 (marked "Leicestershire Militia"); 1st Model Pat. 1853 Rifle Musket .577"; Pat. 1842 Musket .75"; Pat. 1860 Westly-Richards "monkey tail" .450 breechloader. UNIFORMS & ACCESSORIES: Boer War tropical helmet; Officer's bear skin, Royal Highland Fusiliers; Officer's cocked hat c. 1854; Busby, Royal Horse Aty.; Kilt Gordon Highlanders; Sporan, Clan Innes; 12th Lancers; jacket and waistcoat, Monmouthshire R. F. c. 1808; 6th Dragoon Guards helmet c. 1902.

1896 Mauser

This unusually fine piece is the rare transitional model. The gold Damascene was done in Spain on special order. Mauser did not offer factory engraving although there are some exceptions to this rule. The pistol was made around the turn of the century but the Damascening was applied at a later date.

No. 200,000

This unusual piece was made to mark a milestone in production at Mauser Werke. Normally pistols were not factory engraved. This piece features inlay work of pure silver. The grip panels are of walnut with silver wire inlays and a tasteful diamond inlay of ivory.

Bolo Mauser

This 10-shot Bolo Mauser pistol was made up as a promotional piece, not for sale to the public, by the firm of Von Lengerke & Detmold. This company was the sole agent for the products of Mauser Werke in the United States, before World War 1. After World War 1 this pistol fell into private hands. The piece is profusely engraved with an oak leaf motif in the Germanic style.

DAUDETEAU M1896 TYPE "B" in caliber 6.5mm Daudeteau. This cavalry carbine was manufactured at St. Denis. Although superior to the 8mm Lebel cartridge the 6.5 Daudeteau was not adopted by France as the rifles and ammunition in 8mm caliber were already in full production. Daudeteaus were adopted by El Salvador, Portugal, and Uruguay. These sell for $50.00 to $75.00.

REMINGTON MLE. 1907/15, Caliber 8mm Lebel. Practically identical to the French made Mle. 1907/15 except made by Remington in the U.S. and so marked. Bayonets for these weapons were also produced by Remington. These arms sell for $60.00 to $100.00

MANNLICHER-BERTHIER CARBINE MLE. 1892, 8mm Lebel, three-shot, 18" barrel. Mannlicher system. Nearly all the 1890, 1892, and 1916 models were modified in 1927 by the removal of the cleaning rod and the addition of a stacking swivel. These rifles may command $30.00 to $50.00.

MANNLICHER-BERTHIER MLE. 1892/1916 CARBINE, 8mm Lebel, five-shot 18" barrel. This is the same weapon as the Model 1892, but was modified in 1916 to hold a five-shot clip. These weapons may be found for $30.00 to $50.00.

RIFLE MLE. 1917 in caliber 8mm Lebel. These rifles were issued in small quantities. The action is crude but effective. Gas is tapped off the barrel and serves to push the operating rod back which in turn forces the bolt, through cam-action to unlock. A very advanced action for its time it was copied by U.S. and Swiss ordnance establishments. Uses a special five-shot clip. Both clip and rifle are scarce specimens in very good plus condition sell for about $200.00 to $250.00.

RIFLE MLE. 1918 in caliber 8mm Lebel. This rifle is quite rare as very few were made at the end of WW I. These rifles take the standard Mle. 1916 five-round clip. Extremely scarce specimens may sell for from $250.00 to $350.00.

SHORT RIFLE MLE.1907/15/34 7.5x54mm, M29 MAS. This is a arsenal revision of the 1907/15. This includes a new barrel chambered for the 7.5mm cartridge, and a five-shot Mauser-type magazine. These weapons are some what scarce in the U.S. and may go for $35.00 to $75.00.

LEBEL CARBINE, MLE. 1886/93 R35, 8mm Lebel, five-shot, 18" barrel. These weapons were modified in the 30s as a result of the rise of Adolf Hitler. The modification involved a shorter magazine, and different furniture. Model number is on the receiver. These weapons may be found for $40.00 to $60.00.

MAS MLE. 1936, 7.5mm, five-shot, 23" barrel. Standard French service rifle during WWII. This weapon has a recessed bolt head for rimless cartridges, a peep sight, and a Mauser-type magazine with a quick-detachable floorplate. The bayonet fits into the rifle's upper forend. These rifles are around for $45.00.

MODEL 98 MAUSER in caliber 7.92mm as made at Mauser Werke after World War 2 for the French occupying forces. These arms were used by the French Gendarmere as well as the Foreign Legion. Specimens sell for about $40.00 to $75.00.

MAS 1949 MLE., gas-operated semi-automatic, uses a tilting bolt with a direct gas impingement system. 7.5mm, 10-round box magazine. Two piece stock, no provision for a bayonet. These weapons sell at about $125.00 to $150.00.

Swiss Military Arms

Switzerland's arms, both antique and modern, have quality and originality. Most are found in superb condition and with sufficient variations to make them eminently collectable.

As a result of stalwartness and fierce individuality Swiss military arms have been as unique and distinguished as the Swiss people. In Switzerland the shooting sports have been heavily stressed. This tradition dates back to the time of the legendary William Tell and his famous feat of marksmanship with the crossbow. The arms pictured here represent over 100 years of shooting prowess. Muzzle loading rifles, early bolt action rifles, the famous Schmidt-Rubin straight-pull rifles have all played a part in keeping Switzerland free and independent in a changing world set with violent upheavals. Starting from the top with the long arms is the K31/42 Zielfernrohr Karabiner. This arm was developed for Swiss sharpshooters. The telescope on this piece is permanently built into the left wall of the receiver. The objective lens is actually inside the scope tube not in the swinging arm, which acts as a periscope. The next piece in line is known as a "Cantonal Stutzer". The rifle, in caliber 23mm, was made for Canton Zoug about 1842. The next piece is also a Cantonal rifle as made for Canton Fribourg. The first rifle has a bayonet which strongly hints at its Germanic origins as it is more of a hunting sword than a bayonet. Below the two "Cantonals" is the Milbank-Amsler conversion of the 1853 .41 caliber Federal Rifle to the then new .41 rimfire cartridge. Next is the Vetterli Model 1869. It has the distinction of being the first repeating rifle developed in Europe. It is in caliber 10.4mm also known to American collectors as the .41 Swiss. The Model 1869 featured ejection port cover and the King loading gate. These features were dispensed with on later models. The changes can be seen on the next piece, the Model 81. With the coming of smokeless powder the Swiss went on to design a unique, straight-pull military rifle known to collectors as the Schmidt-Rubin. In Switzerland it is known simply as the Model 89. The Model 89 introduced the 7.5mm Swiss cartridge, a round known for its high accuracy. By 1911, the basic Schmidt-Rubin action had been much improved. The specimen Model 1911 rifle featured a six round magazine as opposed to the 12 round magazine of the Model 89 and the bolt was strengthened. In all 428,000 Model 89s, 89/96s and 1911s were built. By 1931 Swiss ordnance decided that the Schmidt-Rubin action was a bit dated and developed a rifle with frontal locking lugs. The basic design for the K31 was devised by Colonel Furrer of Waffenfabrik Bern. The carbine shown below the K31 was really the first frontal locking straight-pull arm adopted by Switzerland. This piece was made in Switzerland by S.I.G. based on Ferdinand Mannlicher's design but with Swiss modifications. Needless to say the Model 1893 Karabiner was not successful as very few were made. The bayonets shown are the Engineers bayonet Model 14 for the Karabiners 11 and 31, the Engineers bayonet for the Model 78, 78/81 and 81 Vetterli, the dagger bayonet Model 18 for the K31 and two dress daggers, the one on the right is the Officer's model; the piece in the sheath is the enlisted man's model. The pistols shown are the Model 49 S.I.G. pistol, currently used by the Swiss army in 9mm Parabellum; the Pistol Parabellum Model 06/29; the Pistol Model 06/24; and the Revolver, System Schmidt Model 1882. The Parabellums fire the 7.65mm (.30 Luger) cartridge and the revolver the 7.5mm M82 cartridge. All handguns are shown with standard holsters. ⚜

MILITARY MATCHLOCK, dating from approximately 1600, 10 gauge, 45" barrel, half round, half octagonal. The pan is equipped with a cover. The match holder (cock) is lowered by pressure on the trigger rather than spring activated. These weapons are quite rare and will sell for at least $700.00.

MILITARY MATCHLOCK, dated approximately 1600, .76 caliber, 44" barrel, octagonal at the breech. The pan is covered; the serpentine pivots ahead of the pan and the trigger is enclosed in a trigger guard. Lock assembly is removeable as a unit. Specimen can command $700.00 to $900.00.

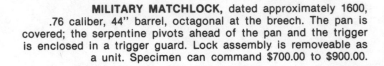

WHEELLOCK SPORTING RIFLES, approximately 1600, .36 caliber 30" octagonal barrel. The lock plates are engraved with elaborate hunting scenes. Trim is brass. Wheellocks in any form are quite expensive, this specimen could go for $1200 to $1500.00.

WHEELLOCK, dating from approximately 1600, .55 caliber, 28" octagonal barrel. The weapon bears handsome inlays of ivory and ebony. Floral engraving on the lock. Specimens may go for $1500.00 to $2000.00.

FLINTLOCK HUNTING RIFLE, converted form wheellock, .57 caliber, 28" barrel. The large wheellock lockplate remains, bearing the name, F.D. Hall. A stag horn adorns the patch box, and another appears on the forend tip. Trim is brass. This piece may go for $900.00 to $1200.00.

GERMAN JAEGER RIFLE, built by E.D. Tanner. .60 caliber, octagonal barrel. Brass buttplate, trigger guard, and ramrod pipes. Patchbox and wrist of stock are checkered. The lock is engraved. Double-set trigger has a screw adjustment. The Jaeger rifle formed the prototype of the Kentucky. Such a specimen could sell for $400.00 to $700.00.

JAEGER RIFLE, circa 1725, .64 caliber (rifled), 30" barrel (octagonal). Engraved brass buttplate, trigger guard, side plate, and ramrod pipes. Light carving appears on the stock and patch-box. This piece is worth $300.00 to $600.00.

JAEGER FLINTLOCK HUNTING RIFLE .59 caliber, 31" octagonal barrel. Full stock is highly carved and inlaid with ivory Brass trim. One-leaf rear sight. This specimen would sell for $500.00 to $900.00.

JAEGER FLINTLOCK rifle by Ascha of Vienna. .50 caliber, 27" octagonal barrel, partially blued. Brass trim, with patchbox, checkpiece and checkering on the forend and small of the stock. This weapon might sell at $500.00 to $900.00.

FLINTLOCK FOWLER, dating approximately 1780, by Gottschalk, 18 gauge, 32" barrel half-octagonal, half round barrel. Brass trim. Horn trigger guard. Ivory inlays occur in the stock, and an ivory spacer in the trigger guard. This specimen may go for $400.00 to $600.00.

JAEGER RIFLE, by Fischer of Hanover, .60 caliber, 25" octagonal barrel. Full-stocked to the muzzle. Semi-pistol grip. Light engraving on the butt, and lockplate. This weapon could bring $400.00 to $600.00.

SMITH & WESSON

Smith & Wesson has been the pioneer in the development of the metallic cartridge revolver as we know it today. Starting with the Model No. 1 First Issue in .22 Short caliber to the Model 29 .44 Magnum, probably the most powerful double action revolver in the world, Smith & Wesson has led the way in firearms technology. Smith & Wesson's single action handguns with top break actions were very popular in the "old days," and fortunately for collectors many have survived the ravages of time. (Left, top to bottom) The .38 caliber Single Action Mexican, serial number range 1-28107. Actually only 1000 were made but the serial range fell into the Third Model 38 SA (1891) number range, produced from 1891 to 1911. The Model No. 3 SA Target in

.32-44 caliber; 4333 of these were sold between the years 1887 and 1910. The New Model Russian—approximately 98,182 Second serial series and New Model contract guns were produced. (Right, top to bottom) The Model No. 1½ 1st Model sold between 1865-1868. During that time approximately 26,300 were produced, a very popular revolver in its time. The First Model Schofield, shown in the catalog for 1875. It was replaced by the Second Model; 3035 of these were made. The First Model American was sold between 1870 and 1872 with approximately 8000 being made. The Second Model Single-Shot was sold between 1905 and 1910. (Bottom) The S&W 12 ga. Shotgun, Monogram Grade, circa 1872.

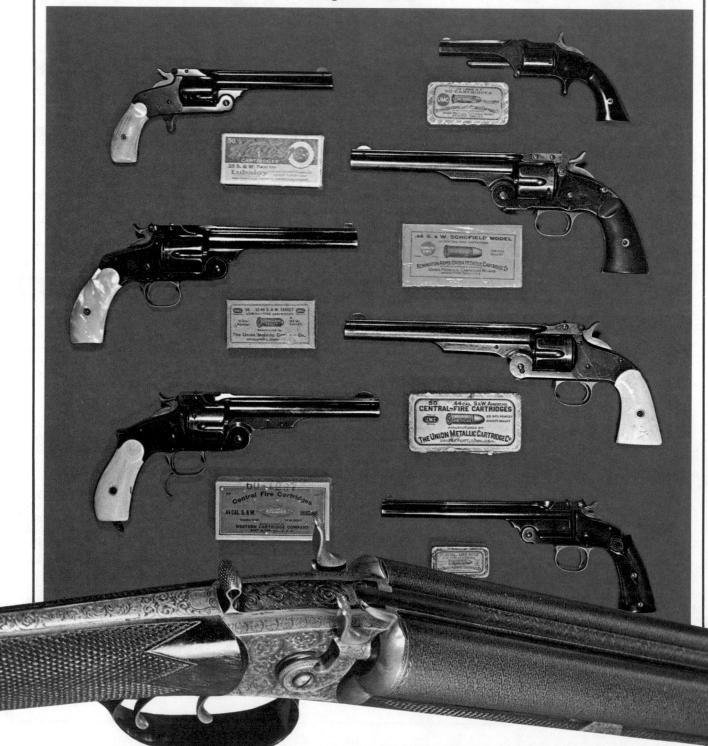

SHARPS

The Sharps rifle was perhaps foremost among firearms which opened up the West. These simple but finely-made arms went on buffalo hunts, fought off marauders, stopped (and started) range wars, participated in some of the West's most infamous gun battles and served unstintingly on both sides during the Civil War. The Sharps' fame as a long-range hunting rifle for big game went unequaled until the demise of the buffalo herds—a case of unplanned obsolescence! From left to right: A Sharps Model 1853 Sporter, No. 8163, caliber .38 percussion with 25½-inch barrel. Barrel is browned with blue sights, case-hardened action. Shipped from Hartford in December of 1855; New Model '69 Sporter, No. C49271, caliber .44-2¼" Berdan shell, 28-inch-long barrel. It is 71st rifle shipped from the Hartford plant during the metallic cartridge era. Rifle is unfired! Model 1874 Sporter, No. C53915, caliber .50-2½" with 30-inch barrel, piece is representative of true "Buffalo Bill" used by hunters of the early 1870s. It weighs 14½ pounds. Its stock is oil finished, not varnished! Model 1874 Sporter, in caliber .44, has 30-inch barrel and is standard in all respects. It has the original globe front and tang peep sight. Forend tips on all rifles shown are of pewter.

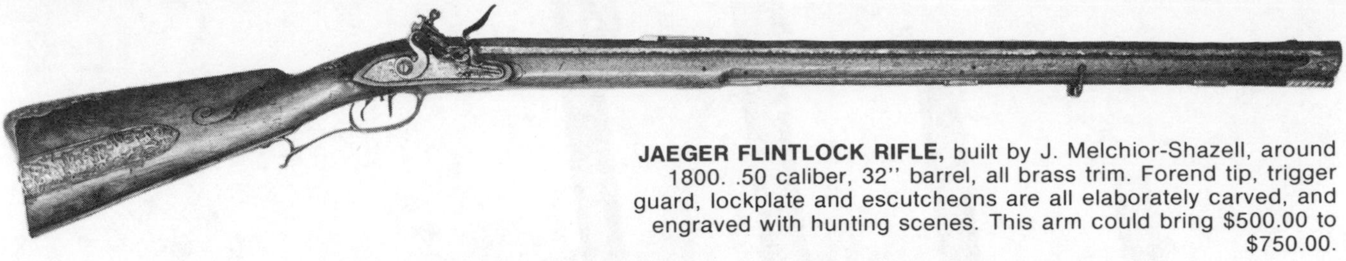

JAEGER FLINTLOCK RIFLE, built by J. Melchior-Shazell, around 1800. .50 caliber, 32'' barrel, all brass trim. Forend tip, trigger guard, lockplate and escutcheons are all elaborately carved, and engraved with hunting scenes. This arm could bring $500.00 to $750.00.

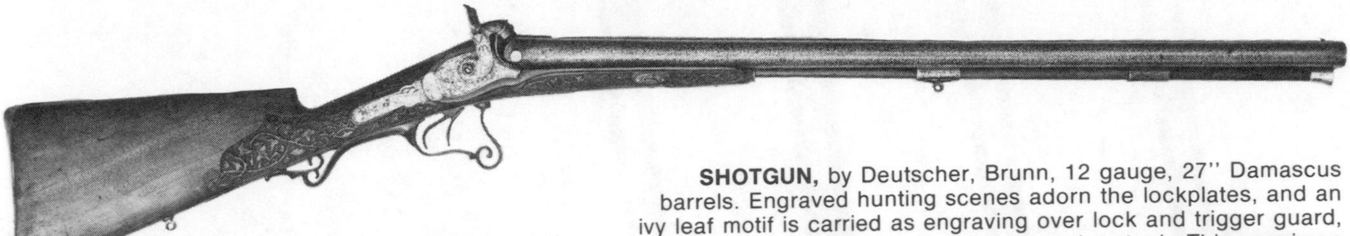

SHOTGUN, by Deutscher, Brunn, 12 gauge, 27'' Damascus barrels. Engraved hunting scenes adorn the lockplates, and an ivy leaf motif is carried as engraving over lock and trigger guard, the same leaf pattern is carved into the stock. This specimen may go for $250.00 to $400.00.

HEAVY JAEGER RIFLE by F. Schlosser of Budingen, .60 caliber, 30'' barrel, octagonal. Double set triggers. Patch box and cheekpiece are wood. Heavy brass trigger guard and butt plate. Specimen weighs 10½ lbs. An example may go for $300.00 to $500.00.

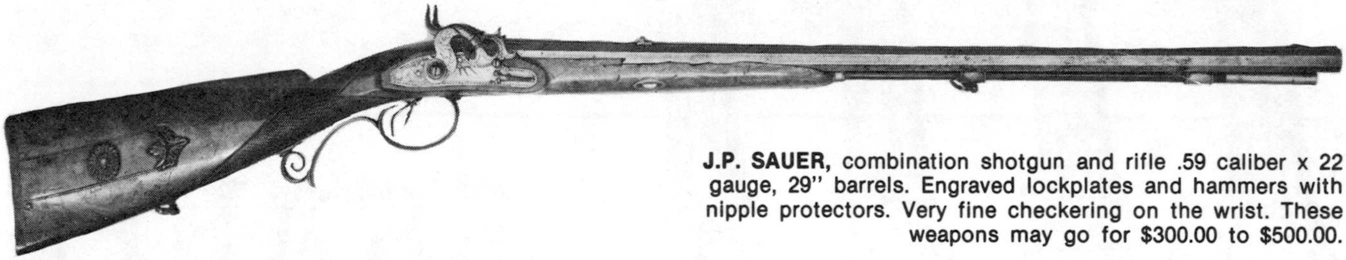

J.P. SAUER, combination shotgun and rifle .59 caliber x 22 gauge, 29'' barrels. Engraved lockplates and hammers with nipple protectors. Very fine checkering on the wrist. These weapons may go for $300.00 to $500.00.

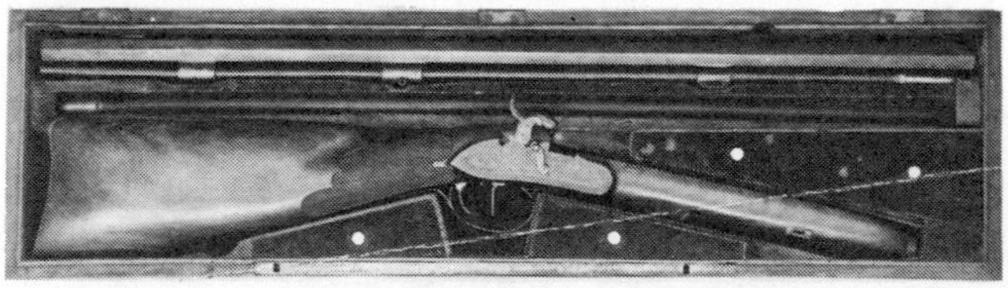

ULRICH SPORTING RIFLE, .62 caliber, 30'' barrel. This is a half-stock cased, muzzle loader. The stock is high grade walnut. Enclosed hammer with highly engraved lock, cased weapons tend to command high prices on today's market. This arm could bring from $750.00 to $900.00.

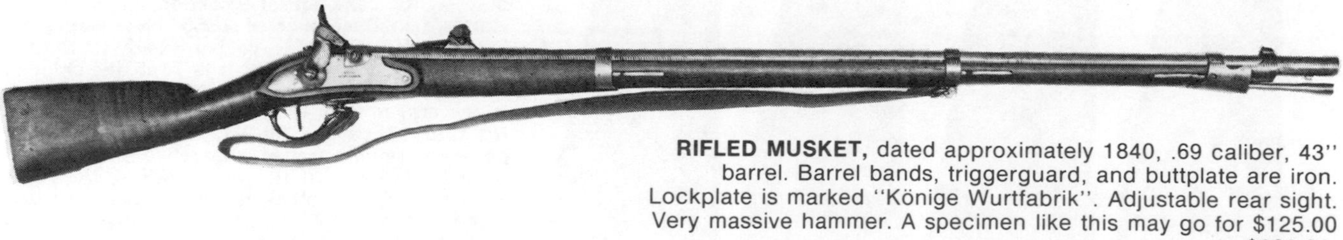

RIFLED MUSKET, dated approximately 1840, .69 caliber, 43'' barrel. Barrel bands, triggerguard, and buttplate are iron. Lockplate is marked ''Könige Wurtfabrik''. Adjustable rear sight. Very massive hammer. A specimen like this may go for $125.00 to $200.00.

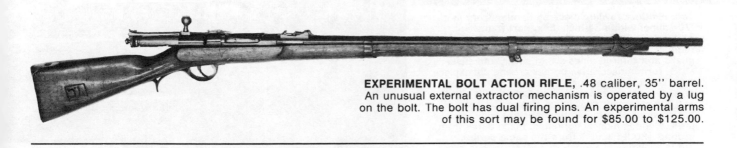

BAVARIAN LINDNER'S PATENT, BREECHLOADING RIFLE, .56 caliber, 36'' barrel. Bolt action has interupted-screw locking threads. Bolt face is tapered to fit into the cone of the barrel, thus forming a gas seal. Weapon uses a paper cartridge with a percussion cap. The standard weapon of the Bavarian Army in the Franco-Prussian War. These weapons may go for $150.00 to $225.00.

PRUSSIAN DREYSE NEEDLE GUN CARBINE, .65 caliber, 15'' barrel. Stock extends to the muzzle, and the nose cap forms the sight guard. Used by the Uhlan cavalry, this arm became the prototype for a whole series of saddle carbines, characterized by full-length stocks and guards to prevent the sight from catching in the saddle scabbard. Specimens may command $150.00 to $250.00.

PRUSSIAN DREYSE NEEDLE GUN, MODEL 1868, .60 caliber, 35'' barrel. The bolt-action mechanism is designed solely for sealing the cartridge in the chamber. Cocking piece in the rear of the bolt must be pulled back manually, and the needle cocked by hand after the bolt is closed. Although heavy and clumsy and prone to fouling, it was superior to the muzzle loaders of the day. Specimens go for $175.00 to $300.00.

EXPERIMENTAL BOLT ACTION RIFLE, .48 caliber, 35'' barrel. An unusual external extractor mechanism is operated by a lug on the bolt. The bolt has dual firing pins. An experimental arms of this sort may be found for $85.00 to $125.00.

MODEL 71 MAUSER, 11mm, single shot. This was the first metallic cartridge rifle adopted by the German Army and has a split-bridge receiver. This model used a removable bolt. Specimens may be found for $60.00 to $90.00.

Guns that reflect a heritage of craftsmanship from the past

ANTIQUES

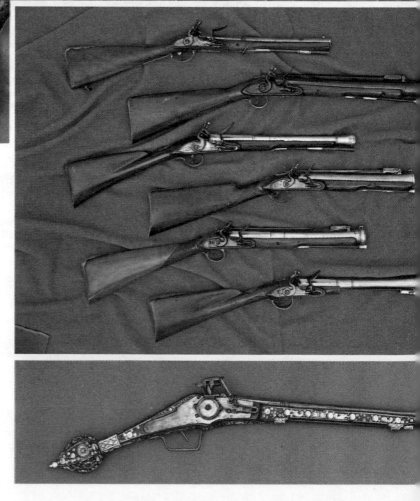

Top: Flintlock fowling piece by Sanderstrom in
.70 caliber with a 34-inch-long, part round
part octagonal, barrel. The piece has been
reblued, but the reblue is an old job. Trigger
guard and ramrod pipes are of silver, and silver
studs form a decorative border around cheekpiece
pad. The arm is unusual in that two ramrods are
provided; one rammer is wood tipped with silver
and the other rammer, same size as the bore, is
felt covered. Reinforced hammer has wide, square
jaws. Wood is heavily darkened. Piece dates from
around 1800. Pistol is from the same period,
but is probably of French manufacture, has silver
furniture and inlays in the stock. Middle: The
Blunderbuss has been the object of attention by
many collectors. Here is an excellent sampling of
the blunderbuss art as produced in England. Most
of these arms were used to ward off highwaymen
and the like. Locks were basically the same as on
muskets and fowling pieces of the 18th Century.
Barrels are of iron or brass. Bottom: German wheellock (circa 1595) boasts exquisite mother-of-pearl
and ivory inlay. Most of these fine pieces are in
museum collections. However, a few still are to
be found by private collectors, but prices are
high. Overall length of this piece is 22½ inches
with bore diameter of approximately .50 caliber.
It is rifled! The pear-shaped butt ending in a
beautifully carved ivory plug gives this piece
individuality. Piece is representative of the
quintessence of the early gunmaker's art.

刀 SAMURAI SWORDS 劍

Top: Two Tachi-type ceremonial swords with the finest quality fittings and lacquer. Rosewood stand is inlaid with silver wire. Bottom left: Sword guards (tsubas) fashioned from thick pieces of iron as these were meant for wartime use. Tsubas are decorated with inlays of precious metals, especially gold. Shown with the tsubas are utility knives (tozuka), a hair arranger (kojai) and little figures (menuki) which are set under the hilt wrapping to cause bulges along the hilt for a better grip. Bottom right: Sword hilts. Top piece displays over 100 tiny solid gold family crests of the Tokugawa family. Middle sword has manta ray skin stretched over handle and ornamented. Bottom sword's pommel depicts Phoenix bird, symbol of the Empress. This indicated sword was carried by general in charge of guarding women's quarters in the palace.

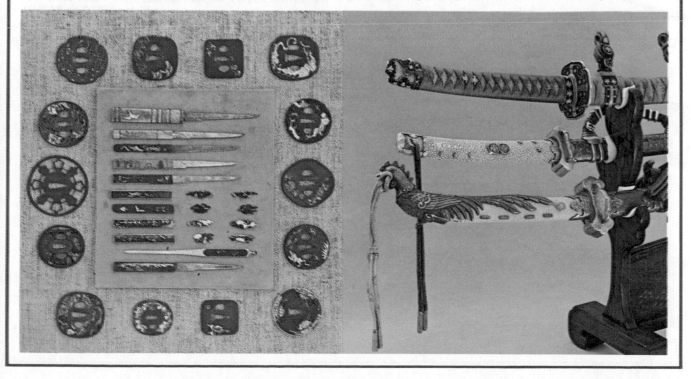

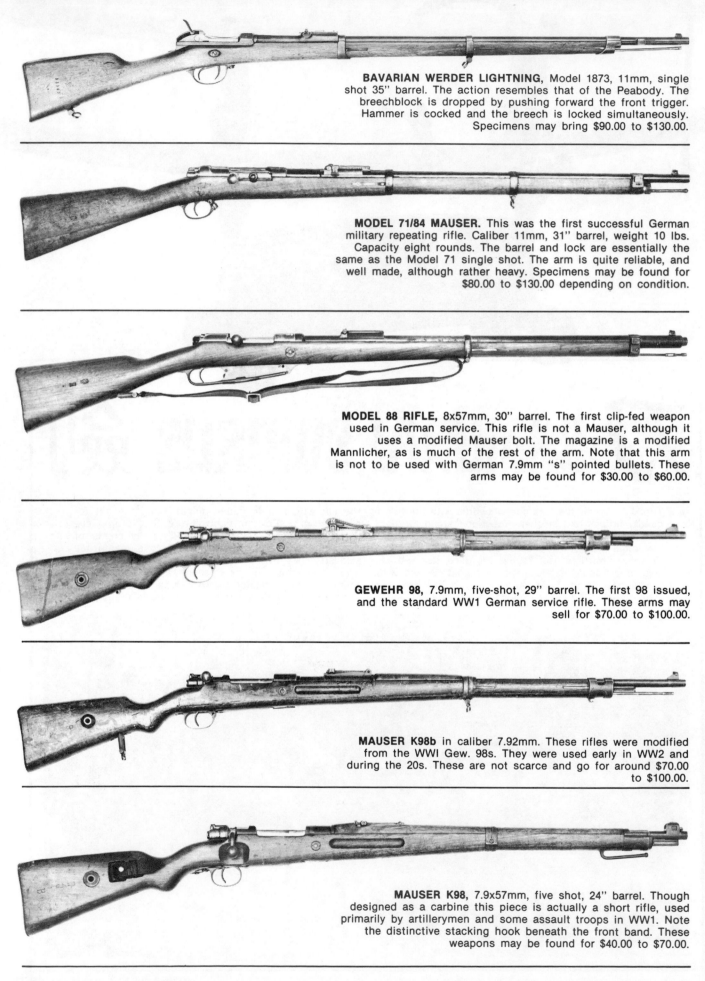

BAVARIAN WERDER LIGHTNING, Model 1873, 11mm, single shot 35" barrel. The action resembles that of the Peabody. The breechblock is dropped by pushing forward the front trigger. Hammer is cocked and the breech is locked simultaneously. Specimens may bring $90.00 to $130.00.

MODEL 71/84 MAUSER. This was the first successful German military repeating rifle. Caliber 11mm, 31" barrel, weight 10 lbs. Capacity eight rounds. The barrel and lock are essentially the same as the Model 71 single shot. The arm is quite reliable, and well made, although rather heavy. Specimens may be found for $80.00 to $130.00 depending on condition.

MODEL 88 RIFLE, 8x57mm, 30" barrel. The first clip-fed weapon used in German service. This rifle is not a Mauser, although it uses a modified Mauser bolt. The magazine is a modified Mannlicher, as is much of the rest of the arm. Note that this arm is not to be used with German 7.9mm "s" pointed bullets. These arms may be found for $30.00 to $60.00.

GEWEHR 98, 7.9mm, five-shot, 29" barrel. The first 98 issued, and the standard WW1 German service rifle. These arms may sell for $70.00 to $100.00.

MAUSER K98b in caliber 7.92mm. These rifles were modified from the WWI Gew. 98s. They were used early in WW2 and during the 20s. These are not scarce and go for around $70.00 to $100.00.

MAUSER K98, 7.9x57mm, five shot, 24" barrel. Though designed as a carbine this piece is actually a short rifle, used primarily by artillerymen and some assault troops in WW1. Note the distinctive stacking hook beneath the front band. These weapons may be found for $40.00 to $70.00.

MAUSER M1914 in caliber 7.92mm, a most unusual military rifle from the WW1 era. This piece was originally to be made for the Chinese Government in 6.8mm. When the war broke out all foreign orders were cancelled and production was geared-up strictly for domestic needs. These rifles are quite rare and are identified by the short upper band and tangent-curve rear sight, unlike the "Lange"-sighted Gew. 98. Specimens should bring at least $100.00 to $130.00.

MAUSER MODEL 98K in caliber 7.92mm this rifle served as the standard infantry rifle of the Wehrmacht during World War 2. Specimens can be found in varying conditions and for widely fluctuating prices. Some rifles have special unit markings which increase their value. Base price for one in very good condition is about $70.00 to $150.00.

STEYR WERKE M29 (660-code) in caliber 7.92mm. These rifles were made up at Steyr for the Wehrmacht but were originally produced for use by the Austrian Army. The "Anschluss" changed the picture. These rifles then went to arm the joint German/Austrian Armies. Some of these rifles were almost shipped to Colombia but WW2 interceded. Note cupped butt plate and unusual upper band/nose cap. Specimens sell for about $60.00 to $80.00.

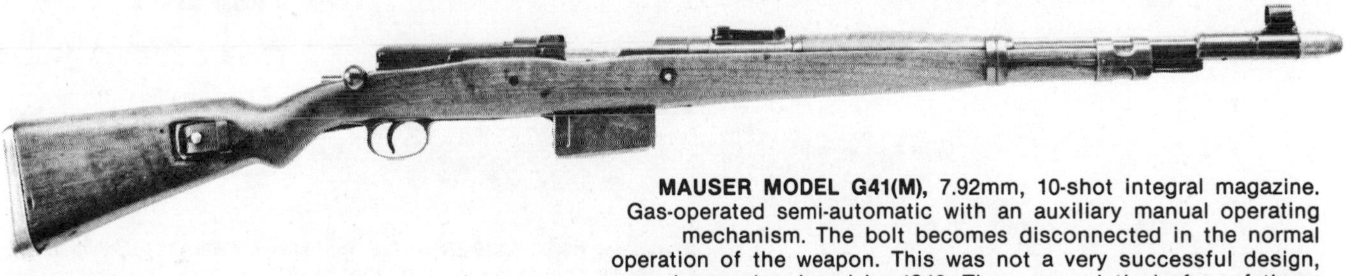

MAUSER MODEL G41(M), 7.92mm, 10-shot integral magazine. Gas-operated semi-automatic with an auxiliary manual operating mechanism. The bolt becomes disconnected in the normal operation of the weapon. This was not a very successful design, and was abandoned by 1943. There are relatively few of these weapons in the U.S. Examples may be bought for $250.00 to $400.00.

GEW. 41(W) 7.9x57mm, semi-automatic. 10-round magazine. This weapon employs a unique gas system in the form of a gas cone at the front of the barrel which directs the gas backwards to a circular gas piston. This system was not very successful as these weapons saw only limited use before the adoption of the G43. These weapons may go for $175.00 to $300.00.

MODEL G43, 7.92mm, 10-round detachable magazine. Gas operated, semi-automatic. This weapon is constructed largely of stampings, the finish is quite crude, however they are reliable and function very well. Many were brought into the country after the war. These weapons may go for $100.00 to $200.00.

VOLKSTURM GEWEHR VG 2, 7.9mm, with 10 shot G43 magazine. 21" barrel with no provision for a bayonet. This is a cheaply made, last-ditch defense weapon of unusual design. Barrel is from an MG-13 altered to fit. Receiver housing is a U-shaped stamping, action is a crude bolt type, with two locking lugs. These weapons are rare and may go for $250.00 to $350.00.

MAUSER GEW. 98 SNIPER RIFLE this piece is an extremely rare bird. Most German sniper equipments were destroyed by the sniper before capture and after the armistice. This piece was made up from the "Radfahrer Gewehr" and sports a Voigtlander scope offset to the left to provide clip loading. Specimens are worth at least $500.00 to $650.00.

MAUSER K98K SNIPER RIFLE in caliber 7.92mm. Shown is the early sniper model with the ZF 41/1 scope. The scopes are fairly common, rifles with mounts for them are not. Specimens with scopes are valued at $200.00 to $350.00.

MAUSER 98K, 7.9x57mm, five-shot Mauser action, 23" barrel. Sniper model with a 4X Hensoldt scope. Special telescope safety, external winter trigger and checkered steel buttplate are unusual features. This weapon may go for $400.00 to $600.00 with scope.

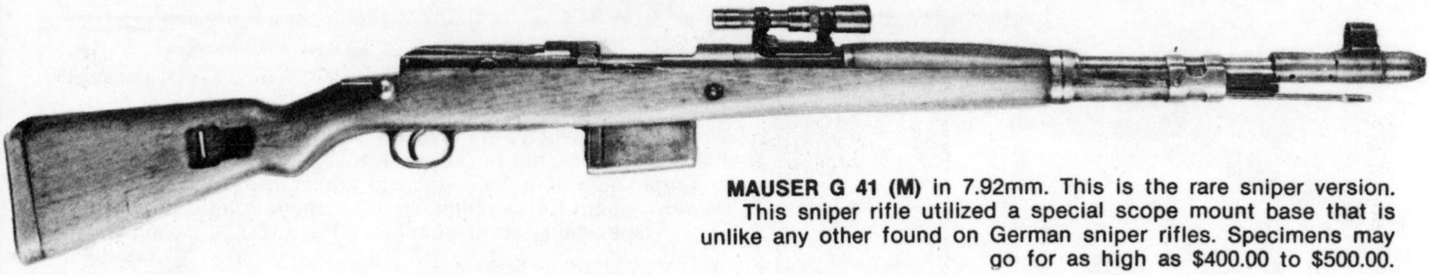

MAUSER G 41 (M) in 7.92mm. This is the rare sniper version. This sniper rifle utilized a special scope mount base that is unlike any other found on German sniper rifles. Specimens may go for as high as $400.00 to $500.00.

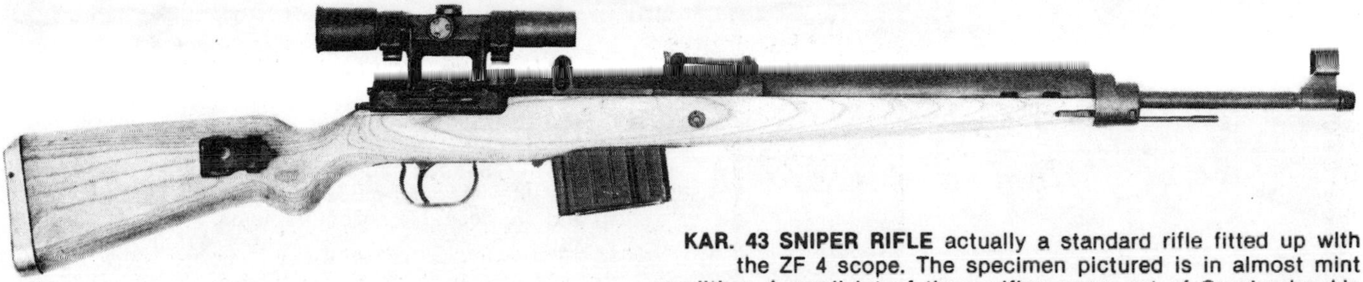

KAR. 43 SNIPER RIFLE actually a standard rifle fitted up with the ZF 4 scope. The specimen pictured is in almost mint condition. A small lot of these rifles came out of Czechoslovakia shortly after WW 2. Scopes and rifles do not match and never did. Specimens sell for at least $275.00 to $400.00.

GERMAN G3 (CETME) ASSAULT RIFLE, 7.62mm, Delayed blowback action. Weight 11.3 lbs with bipod. This weapon was developed in Spain being based on the German StG 45M. It was adopted by the West German Army and given the designation G3. Semi-automatic versions are available in the U.S. These arms sell from $300.00 to $350.00.

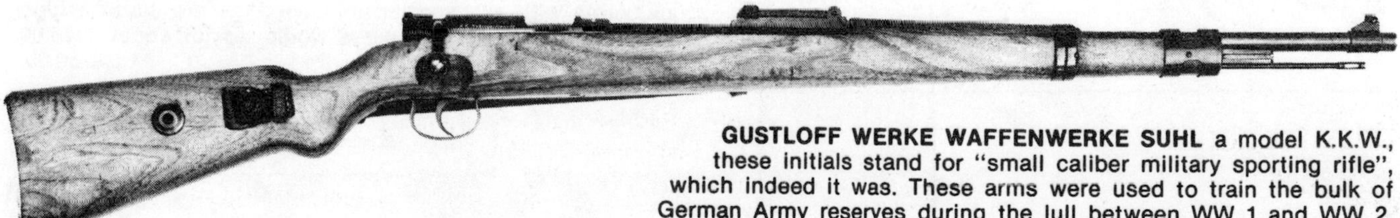

GUSTLOFF WERKE WAFFENWERKE SUHL a model K.K.W., these initials stand for "small caliber military sporting rifle", which indeed it was. These arms were used to train the bulk of German Army reserves during the lull between WW 1 and WW 2. Note the stout M98-type bayonet lug, definitely meant for more than just show. Specimens are found in excellent condition and bring about $100.00 to $150.00.

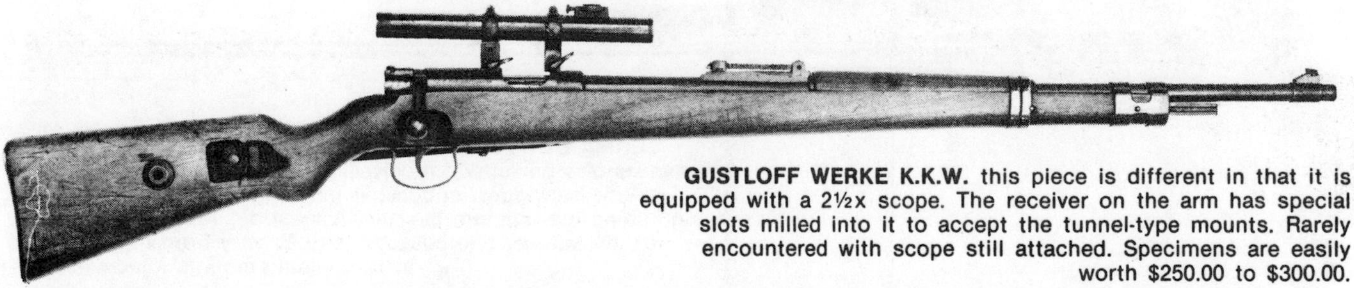

GUSTLOFF WERKE K.K.W. this piece is different in that it is equipped with a 2½x scope. The receiver on the arm has special slots milled into it to accept the tunnel-type mounts. Rarely encountered with scope still attached. Specimens are easily worth $250.00 to $300.00.

GERMANIAWAFFENWERK A.G. in 4mm long caliber. An interesting piece not unlike the K.K.W. in outward appearance. The 4mm-calibered arms are not to common but they are not as widely sought for as ammunition for them is hard to come by. Specimens bring from $75.00 to $150.00 depending on condition.

MAUSER WERKE DSM-34 in caliber .22 Long Rifle. Arms made by this manufacturer are most often encountered by the collector. Other manufacturers are Waffenfabriks Suhl, Herm, Gustloff and Walther. Mauser-made arms show a high degree of finish and are desirable collectors items. Prices range from $75.00 to $150.00.

HAENEL SPORT MODELL 33 a 4mm air rifle, this interesting trainer was made as per Hugo Schmeisser's patent. It utilizes a five round box magazine which is similar to a regular .22 rifle magazine but has a smaller cross-section. The bolt handle, when turned goes up at a vertical angle and serves as a lever when pulled back. Arms in mint condition are worth $100.00 to $150.00.

WALTHER DEUTCHES SPORTMODELL This specimen in .22 rimfire caliber was at one time used to train some poor marksmen in an SS unit as noted by the SS runes on the butt stock. Arms with any special unit markings are worth a high premium to collectors, this piece would go for about $175.00 to $250.00.

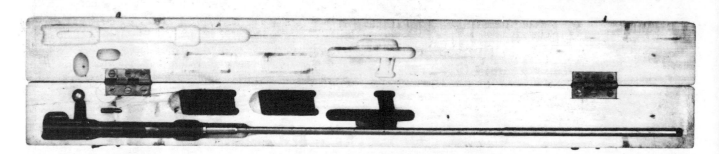

ERMA CONVERSION UNIT made for the M98k service rifle consists of a barrel and receiver group, magazines for .22 Long Rifle cartridges, subcaliber magazine adapter, and tool for tightening the unit into the rifle. A most desirable '98-accessory for the Mauser rifle collector. Prices vary from reasonable to astronomical amounts for these units.

HOLLAND

DUTCH DOUBLE-BARREL SHOTGUN, lock marked Rotterdam on the left-hand and Tomson on the right-hand, 32'' watered-steel barrels. Forend tip, trigger guard, and buttplate are brass. This weapon might go for $200.00 to $350.00.

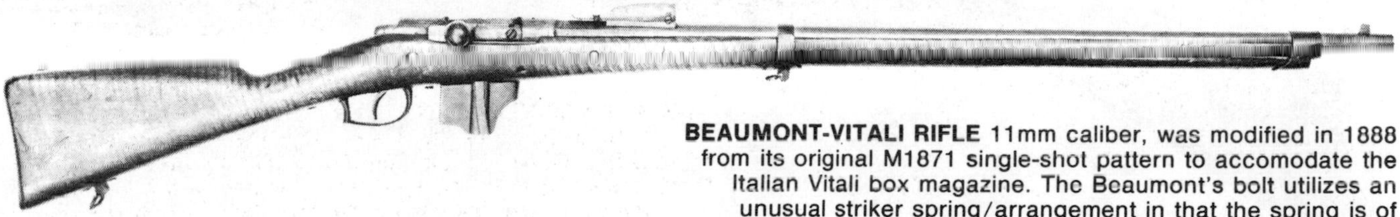

BEAUMONT-VITALI RIFLE 11mm caliber, was modified in 1888 from its original M1871 single-shot pattern to accomodate the Italian Vitali box magazine. The Beaumont's bolt utilizes an unusual striker spring/arrangement in that the spring is of "V"-type and located in the bolt handle. While somewhat scarce these arms sell for only $30.00 to $50.00.

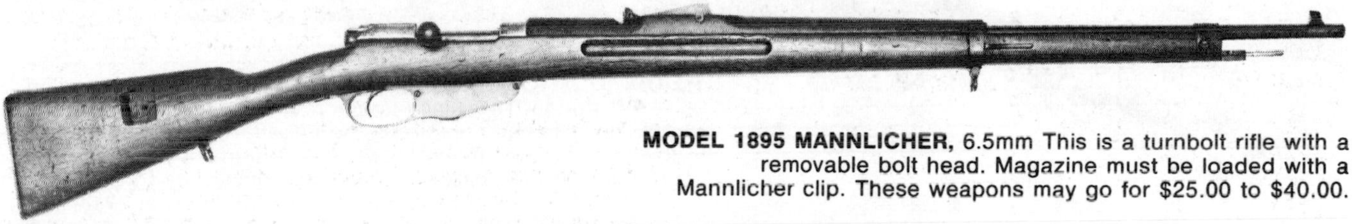

MODEL 1895 MANNLICHER, 6.5mm This is a turnbolt rifle with a removable bolt head. Magazine must be loaded with a Mannlicher clip. These weapons may go for $25.00 to $40.00.

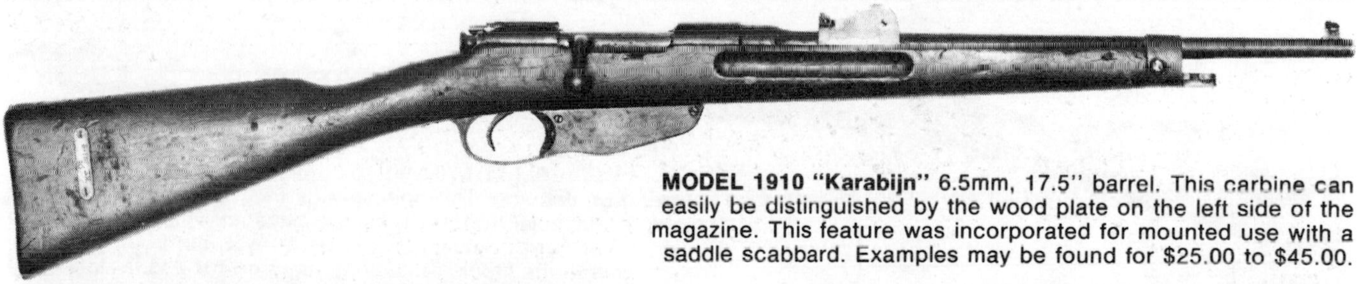

MODEL 1910 "Karabijn" 6.5mm, 17.5'' barrel. This carbine can easily be distinguished by the wood plate on the left side of the magazine. This feature was incorporated for mounted use with a saddle scabbard. Examples may be found for $25.00 to $45.00.

ITALY

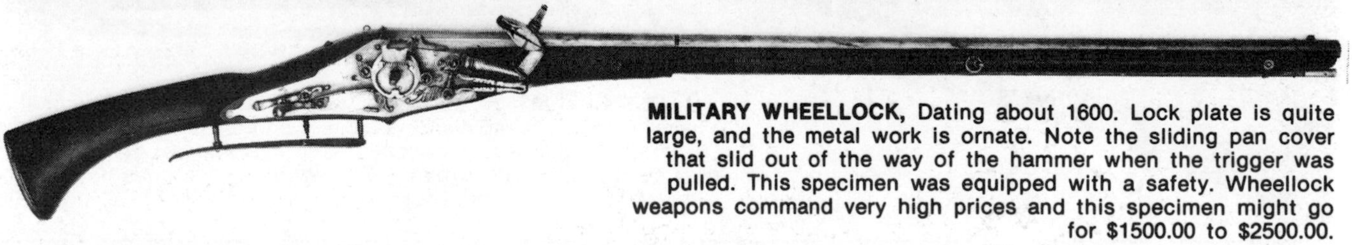

MILITARY WHEELLOCK, Dating about 1600. Lock plate is quite large, and the metal work is ornate. Note the sliding pan cover that slid out of the way of the hammer when the trigger was pulled. This specimen was equipped with a safety. Wheellock weapons command very high prices and this specimen might go for $1500.00 to $2500.00.

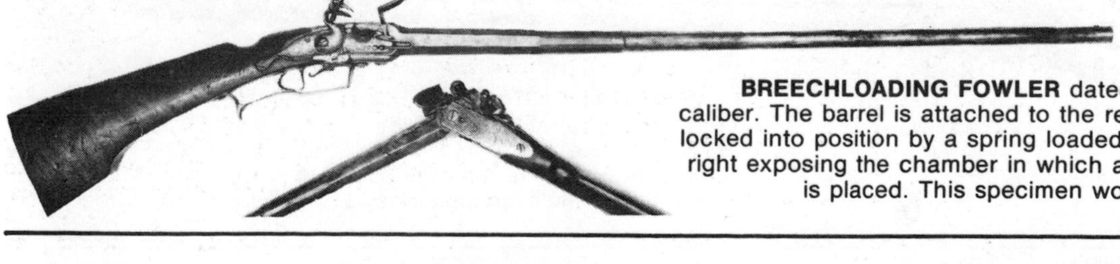

BREECHLOADING FOWLER dated approximately 1740, .62 caliber. The barrel is attached to the receiver by a large pin and locked into position by a spring loaded stud. Barrel pivots to the right exposing the chamber in which a metal cartridge chamber is placed. This specimen would go for over $1000.00.

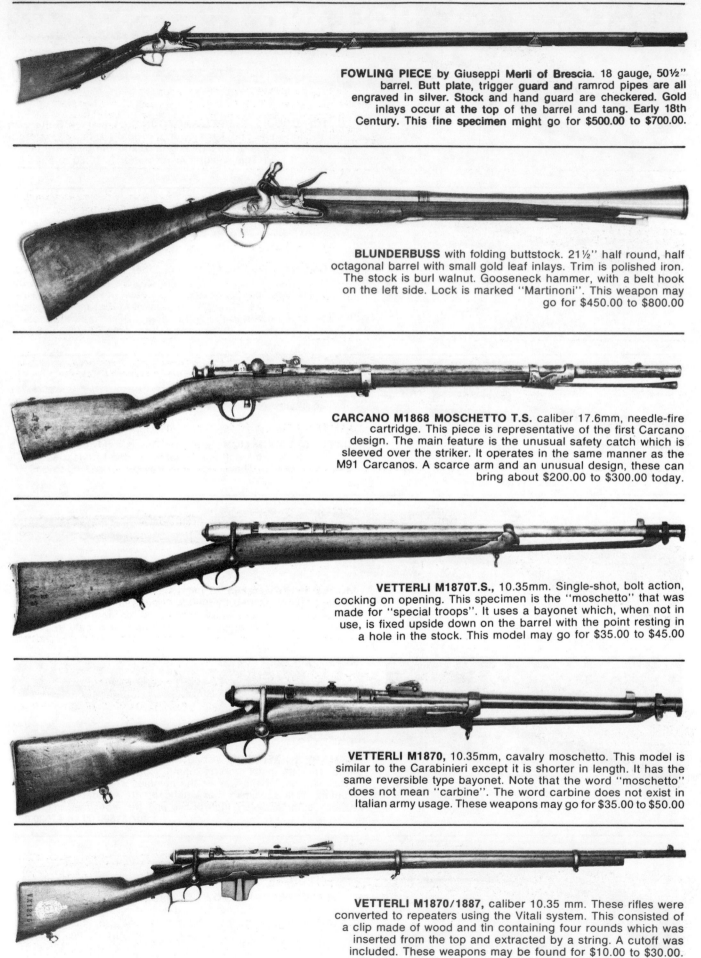

FOWLING PIECE by Giuseppi **Merli** of **Brescia**. 18 gauge, 50½" barrel. Butt plate, trigger **guard and** ramrod pipes are all engraved in silver. Stock and hand guard are checkered. Gold inlays occur at the top of the barrel and tang. Early 18th Century. This fine **specimen might** go for $500.00 to $700.00.

BLUNDERBUSS with folding buttstock. 21½" half round, half octagonal barrel with small gold leaf inlays. Trim is polished iron. The stock is burl walnut. Gooseneck hammer, with a belt hook on the left side. Lock is marked "Martinoni". This weapon may go for $450.00 to $800.00

CARCANO M1868 MOSCHETTO T.S. caliber 17.6mm, needle-fire cartridge. This piece is representative of the first Carcano design. The main feature is the unusual safety catch which is sleeved over the striker. It operates in the same manner as the M91 Carcanos. A scarce arm and an unusual design, these can bring about $200.00 to $300.00 today.

VETTERLI M1870T.S., 10.35mm. Single-shot, bolt action, cocking on opening. This specimen is the "moschetto" that was made for "special troops". It uses a bayonet which, when not in use, is fixed upside down on the barrel with the point resting in a hole in the stock. This model may go for $35.00 to $45.00

VETTERLI M1870, 10.35mm, cavalry moschetto. This model is similar to the Carabinieri except it is shorter in length. It has the same reversible type bayonet. Note that the word "moschetto" does not mean "carbine". The word carbine does not exist in Italian army usage. These weapons may go for $35.00 to $50.00

VETTERLI M1870/1887, caliber 10.35 mm. These rifles were converted to repeaters using the Vitali system. This consisted of a clip made of wood and tin containing four rounds which was inserted from the top and extracted by a string. A cutoff was included. These weapons may be found for $10.00 to $30.00

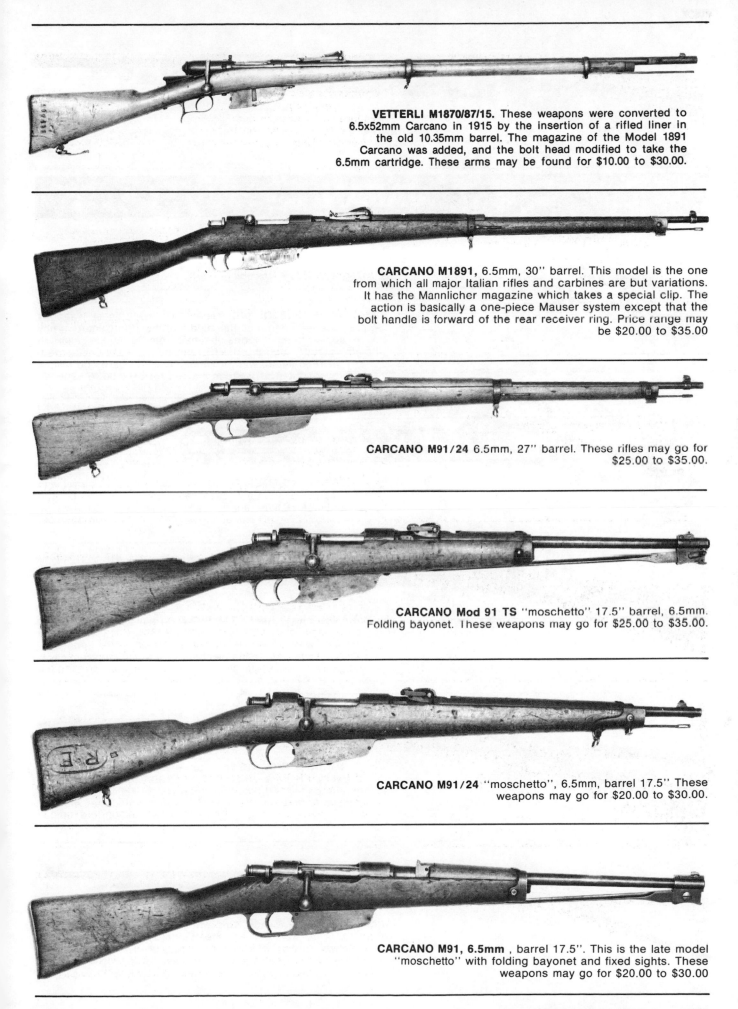

VETTERLI M1870/87/15. These weapons were converted to 6.5x52mm Carcano in 1915 by the insertion of a rifled liner in the old 10.35mm barrel. The magazine of the Model 1891 Carcano was added, and the bolt head modified to take the 6.5mm cartridge. These arms may be found for $10.00 to $30.00.

CARCANO M1891, 6.5mm, 30'' barrel. This model is the one from which all major Italian rifles and carbines are but variations. It has the Mannlicher magazine which takes a special clip. The action is basically a one-piece Mauser system except that the bolt handle is forward of the rear receiver ring. Price range may be $20.00 to $35.00

CARCANO M91/24 6.5mm, 27'' barrel. These rifles may go for $25.00 to $35.00.

CARCANO Mod 91 TS ''moschetto'' 17.5'' barrel, 6.5mm. Folding bayonet. These weapons may go for $25.00 to $35.00.

CARCANO M91/24 ''moschetto'', 6.5mm, barrel 17.5'' These weapons may go for $20.00 to $30.00.

CARCANO M91, 6.5mm , barrel 17.5''. This is the late model ''moschetto'' with folding bayonet and fixed sights. These weapons may go for $20.00 to $30.00

CARCANO M 38 rifle, 7.35mm, 21.5'' barrel. These may go up to $30.00

JAPAN

MATCHLOCK PISTOL. .46 caliber, 13'' barrel. These weapons were used in Japan until the middle of the 19th Century. They were copied from weapons obtained from Portugese sailors in the 15th century, and the design remained virtually unchanged. In 1868 Japan went from matchlock to cartridge almost overnight. This weapon may go for $100.00 to $200.00.

JAPANESE MATCHLOCK PISTOL. .52 caliber, 14½'' barrel with flared, cannon muzzle. It has a pivoted pan cover. The serpentine lockplate, and trim are in brass. Ramrod is wood. This weapon may go for $150.00 to $250.00.

JAPANESE EXPERIMENTAL RIFLE. 11mm. This weapon was made in Belgium by A. Francotte in 1876. It is a bolt action percussion system that was apparently tested by the Japanese. Except for the bolt-action mechanism the rifle is essentially a Belgian percussion musket. One known, it sold for $175.00.

MURATA TYPE 20, 8mm, tube magazine with eight-shot capacity. This rifle was adopted in 1887 and was the major infantry arm during the Sino-Japanese War of 1894. These rifles are difficult to find in good condition. When found they may go for $60.00 to $100.00.

ARISAKA TYPE 30, 6.5mm. This arm was introduced into service in 1897, and was the standard army rifle during the Russo-Japanese War. It is basically a Mauser-type design. In the U.S. it is often referred to as the ''Hook Safety'' rifle. This arm may go for $30.00 to $40.00.

ARISAKA TYPE 30 CARBINE, 6.5mm, 19" barrel. This is the carbine version of the Type 30 rifle. This version may go for $40.00 to $60.00.

MURATA SHOTGUN. These arms were produced in the 1920s primarily for export trade. Many went to Japanese settlers in Brazil and Argentina. These arms may go for $35.00 to $40.00.

JAPANESE, "SIAMESE MAUSER", 8x52Rmm. These weapons were built in Japan in the early 1920s for the Siamese Government. They are essentially a Mauser 98 action with a dust cover and modified magazine. These arms may go for $30.00 to $45.00.

ARISAKA TYPE 38 CARBINE, 6.5mm modified for paratroop use by the addition of a hinge to the wrist of the stock. Other than this it is a standard Type 38 carbine. This gun may bring $125.00.

ARISAKA CARBINE TYPE 44. This version was adopted in 1911. 6.5mm 19" barrel with a non-detachable folding bayonet. For some reason, this version is sought after, and this is reflected in the price, which may go for $45.00 to $85.00.

ARISAKA TYPE 99. 7.7mm, 31" barrel. Five-shot Mauser-type magazine. Scarce "long barrel" models are non-standard. This model was also equipped with a bolt cover which was usually discarded by the troops because of its tendency to rattle. This arm may go for $20.00 to $35.00.

ARISAKA TYPE 99 RIFLE .7mm, 25'' barrel. This arm was the standard version of the Type 99 rifle. These arms may go for $20.00 to $35.00.

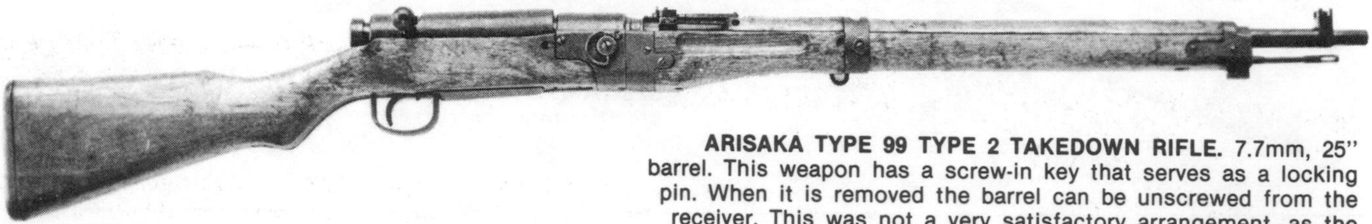

ARISAKA TYPE 99 TYPE 2 TAKEDOWN RIFLE. 7.7mm, 25'' barrel. This weapon has a screw-in key that serves as a locking pin. When it is removed the barrel can be unscrewed from the receiver. This was not a very satisfactory arrangement, as the receiver is weakened and accuracy is affected. These arms may go for $75.00 to $125.00.

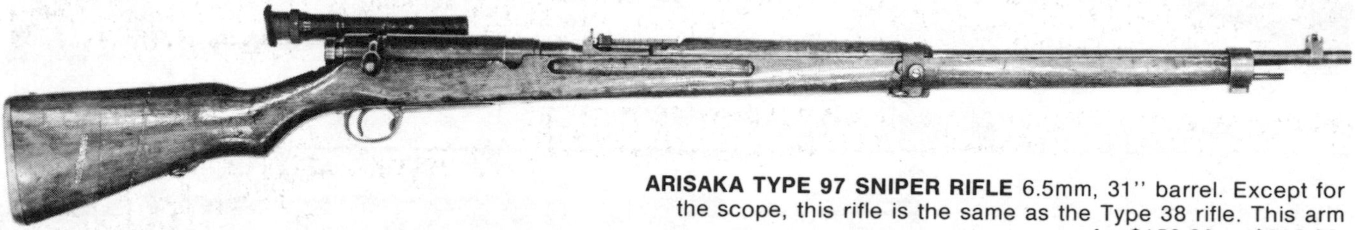

ARISAKA TYPE 97 SNIPER RIFLE 6.5mm, 31'' barrel. Except for the scope, this rifle is the same as the Type 38 rifle. This arm may go for $150.00 to $200.00.

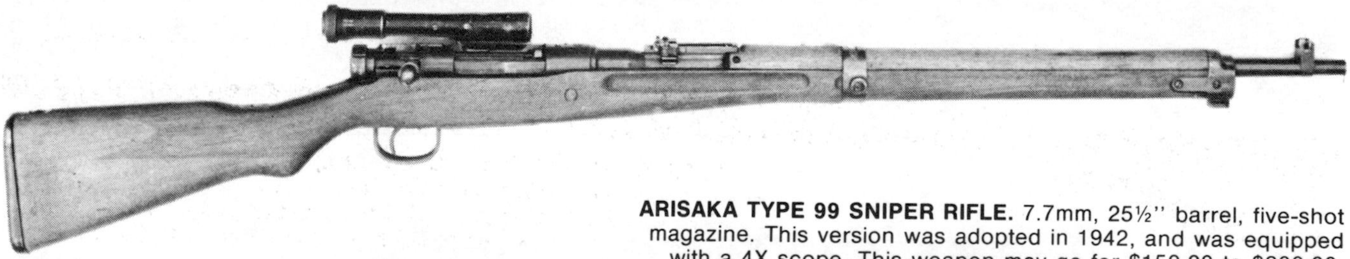

ARISAKA TYPE 99 SNIPER RIFLE. 7.7mm, 25½'' barrel, five-shot magazine. This version was adopted in 1942, and was equipped with a 4X scope. This weapon may go for $150.00 to $200.00. The scope and scope mount, should have the same number.

JAPANESE EXPERIMENTAL SEMIAUTOMATIC RIFLE, 6.5mm, built on the Pedersen principle. The bolt functions much like a Luger's. The weapon has a 10-shot rotary magazine, which is loaded by strip clips. It was tested during the 1920s at the same time as the American and British tests. This arm was found in the Tokyo Arsenal in 1945. This arm would probably go for well into the thousands on today's market.

NORWAY

KRAG-JORGENSEN CARBINE MODEL 1895, 6.5x55mm, 20½''
barrel. This arm has no provision for a bayonet. It is basically
similar to the U.S. Krag carbine in appearance. The weapon was
issued to cavalry and mountain troops.
Valued at $75.00 to $125.00.

KRAG-JORGENSEN CARBINE MODEL 1912, 6.5mm, 24'' barrel.
This weapon is stocked to the muzzle with a full length hand
guard. The bayonet lug is mounted on the combination barrel
band and nose cap. Six-shot Krag-type magazine. The weight is
7½ lbs. A few of Norwegian Krags were produced after WW II.
These scarce rifles sell at $50.00 to $100.00.

PORTUGAL

MODEL 1885 GUEDES-CASTRO, 8mm, single-shot rifle. This is a
modification of the Martini-Henry action, and is the last military
design based on the falling-block system. The rifle was
manufactured at Steyr in Austria. This caliber was adopted at a
time when most European Powers were using 11mm, cartridges.
These arms may go for $75.00 to $125.00.

PORTUGUESE KROPATSCHEK MODEL 1886 in caliber 8mm. This
arm is essentially a Mauser 71/84 with a magazine cut-off. It was also
made in a carbine version. These arms are scarce in the U.S. but are
available in Europe. Specimens may sell for $45.00 to $75.00.

MAUSER-VERGUEIRO MODEL 1904 6.5mm, 29'' barrel. This
weapon is like a Mannlicher in that it has a split-bridge receiver
with the bolt locking down forward of the receiver bridge. This
rifle is worth $35.00 to $50.00.

**MAUSER-VERGUEIRO
MODEL 1904.** During the 1930s many of
the Model 1904s were converted to 7.92x57mm Mauser.
Specimens sell from $35.00 to $50.00.

SPAIN

PERCUSSION SHOTGUN. This weapon dates from approximately 1840. The lock, while resembling a Miquelet converted to percussion, is actually made as a percussion lock. The weapon is very ornate and has the traditional Spanish stock. This arm may go for $400.00 to $600.00.

MODEL 1893 MAUSER, 7x57mm. This was the principal weapon of Spanish forces during the Spanish-American War. It proved quite costly in American lives when our forces were armed with single-shot 45/70s. Our rather poor showing in that war led the Germans to greatly miscalculate our military potential for WW 1. These weapons may be found for $35.00 to $45.00.

MAUSER CARBINE MODEL 1916, 7mm, 21'' barrel. This weapon is actually a Model 1893 receiver and action, combined with a tangent rear sight. Nearly all the parts were hand made. Markings on the receiver ring read "INDUSTRIAS DE GUERRA DE CATALUNA 1938." These weapons may be found for $35.00 to $50.00.

MAUSER MODEL 1916, short rifle 7x57mm. Many of these weapons were converted to 7.62mm NATO for issue to reserve forces. They may go for $40.00 to $60.00.

MAUSER RIFLE MODEL 1943, 7.92mm. This is the Spanish version of the German 98K used from WW II to the present. Production continued until the middle 1950s. This weapon may be found for $30.00 to $45.00.

"DESTROYER" MILITARY POLICE CARBINE. Model 1921, 9mm Bayard, seven-shot, 20'' barrel. This bolt-action rifle uses the Bayard pistol cartridge. The weapon is quite unusual, and is sought after by collectors of military weapons. This arm may go for $50.00 to $65.00.

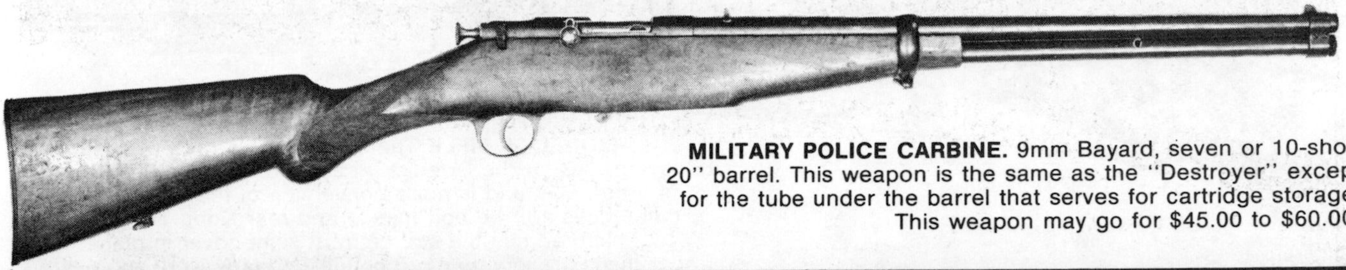

MILITARY POLICE CARBINE. 9mm Bayard, seven or 10-shot, 20'' barrel. This weapon is the same as the ''Destroyer'' except for the tube under the barrel that serves for cartridge storage. This weapon may go for $45.00 to $60.00.

SWEDEN

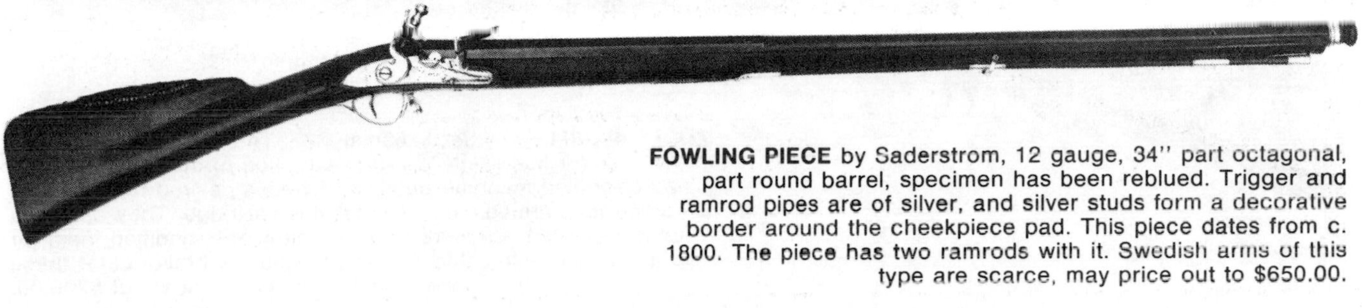

FOWLING PIECE by Saderstrom, 12 gauge, 34'' part octagonal, part round barrel, specimen has been reblued. Trigger and ramrod pipes are of silver, and silver studs form a decorative border around the cheekpiece pad. This piece dates from c. 1800. The piece has two ramrods with it. Swedish arms of this type are scarce, may price out to $650.00.

SWEDISH MODEL 94 CARBINE Caliber 6.5x55mm. A very popular arm on the surplus market until recently, the M94 is now scarce in its original military livery. Some specimens are found in new condition. The specimen pictured is arsenal new but had its barrel lengthened to conform to an early U.S. Federal requirement for rifle barrel lengths to be over 18''. Mint carbines sell for around $85.00.

MODEL 94/17 CARBINE similar to the regular M94, this piece was either converted from M94s or built from the ground up to take a knife bayonet. This pattern was issued to artillery or engineer troops. Specimens in mint condition are hard to find. Most will be found in very good to excellent. Most of these carbines were sporterized. Average price $60.00.

MODEL 96/38 RIFLE Actually a standard Model 96 rifle that was converted to the later M38 pattern. Originally, barrel was 29.9'' long. This piece still retains the straight bolt handle (for infantry use). Most specimens are usually in good condition as they were used extensively. Most found in the U.S. came in from Denmark. Average price $45.00 to $65.00.

MODEL 38 RIFLE The specimen pictured was made by Husqvarna AB for the Swedish Army in 1942. This rifle was built as a true M38 and is not a conversion of the M96. The major differences are the bolt handle and rear sight. The specimen pictured has the scarce front sight cover in place. Most specimens are in very good condition, many were sporterized. $45.00 to $75.00.

MODEL 40 RIFLE Caliber 8x63mm M37. This was a round issued for use in the Swedish variation of the Colt-Browning water-cooled machine gun. The Swedes desired to have their MG-troops armed with rifles for this cartridge. They bought a quantity of M98k Mausers from Germany and modified them for a four-shot magazine and fitted a muzzle brake. Later these were sold to Israel. Value about $200.00.

MODEL 96/41 SNIPER'S RIFLE A finely made rifle with a rugged scope and mount. Some are still available. Specimen has the AGA 3x M42 scope, rail-type side mount. Made from selected M96 rifles. Leather lens covers are not common, strap-on cheek rests were also issued. Specimens vary from good to excellent condition. Scopes and rifles do not match. $80.00 to $100.00.

MODEL 96/41 SNIPER'S RIFLE is basically the same as other sniper model illustrated, but for a scope which is a later pattern (M44) featuring adjustments for elevation in a turret as opposed to a ring on the early model. As mentioned before, conditions vary from good to excellent, but scopes and rifles are not matching. Prices generally run from $80.00 to $100.00.

LJUNGMAN MODEL AG 42B This is quite a rare bird in this country as very few were ever released by the Swedish Government as surplus. In caliber 6.5x55mm, this rifle has been reputed to be one of the most accurate semi-automatic military rifles ever issued. Action is operated by the direct gas principle as in the M16A1. A very scarce arm, it may sell for $400.00.

SWISS MILITARY MUSKET .72 caliber. 39'' barrel. Four barrel bands with a funnel-like front ramrod pipe. This piece dates approximately 1750 and may sell for $250.00 to $400.00.

SWISS CADET MUSKET, This specimen is very close to the English Brown Bess pattern musket (India Pattern) as the barrel is held to the stock with pins, the hammer is a goose-neck type, and the ramrod ferriols, butt plate, and trigger guard are all pinned to the stock. Bayonet is a British pattern. This specimen may sell for $200.00 to $350.00.

SWISS MILITARY RIFLE .72 caliber, 38¼'' barrel. Note the finger-grips on the wrist of the stock. The barrel on this specimen was reblued about 1830. This specimen may sell for $300.00 to $450.00.

SWISS WALL GUN .75 caliber (rifled) 42'' barrel, 56¼'' over-all. Weight 24½ lbs. Furniture is brass. This specimen may sell for $400.00 to $600.00.

SWISS FLINTLOCK FOWLER .64 caliber. This specimen dates from approximately 1730. Part octagonal, part round barrel measures 36''. Engraving occurs on the brass buttplate, sideplate, trigger guard and ramrod pipes. This specimen may sell for $350.00 to $500.00.

SWISS JAEGER RIFLE .72 caliber, 40'' barrel. Full stock to the muzzle. Brass trim. Two-leaf rear sight. Double-set trigger. Weight 11½ lbs. This specimen may sell for $300.00 to $350.00.

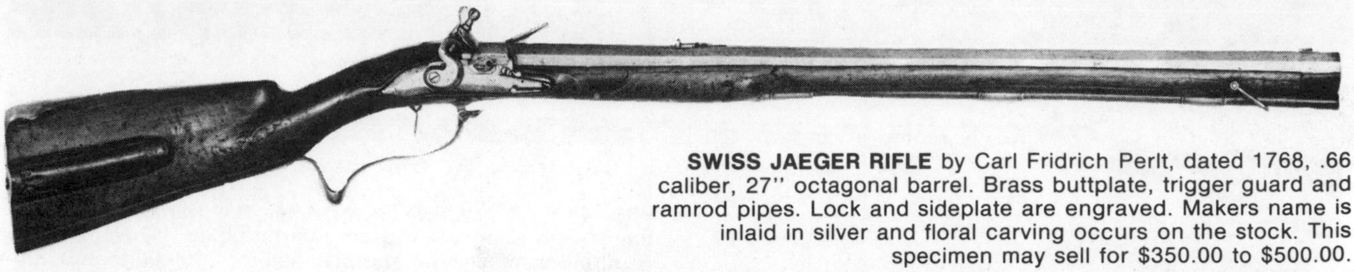

SWISS JAEGER RIFLE by Carl Fridrich Perlt, dated 1768, .66 caliber, 27'' octagonal barrel. Brass buttplate, trigger guard and ramrod pipes. Lock and sideplate are engraved. Makers name is inlaid in silver and floral carving occurs on the stock. This specimen may sell for $350.00 to $500.00.

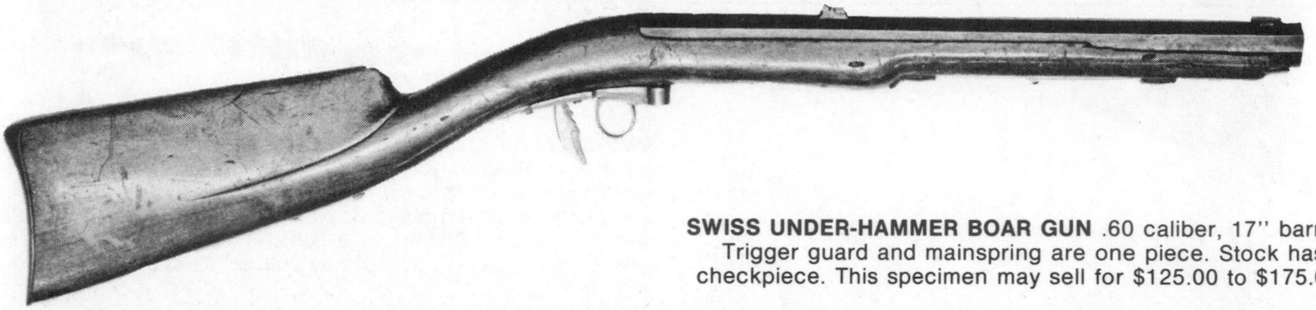

SWISS UNDER-HAMMER BOAR GUN .60 caliber, 17'' barrel. Trigger guard and mainspring are one piece. Stock has a checkpiece. This specimen may sell for $125.00 to $175.00.

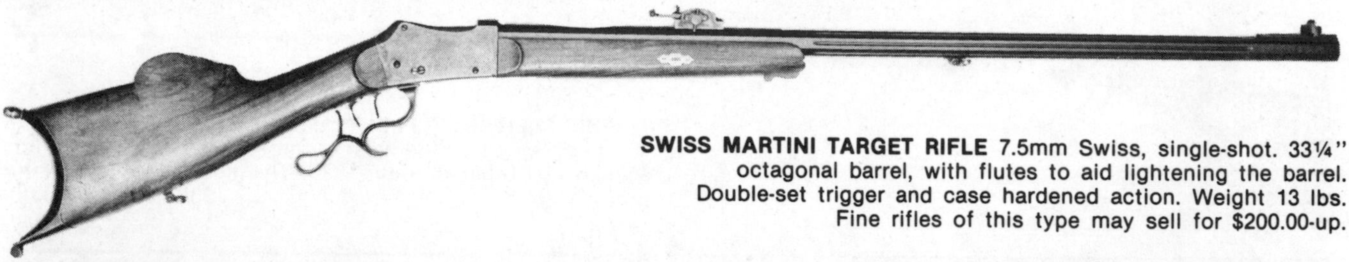

SWISS MARTINI TARGET RIFLE 7.5mm Swiss, single-shot. 33¼'' octagonal barrel, with flutes to aid lightening the barrel. Double-set trigger and case hardened action. Weight 13 lbs. Fine rifles of this type may sell for $200.00-up.

UNITED KINGDOM

DOGLOCK MUSKET, produced around 1640. Note the pivoted hook (dog) attached to the rear of the lockplate. This served as a safety. Records indicate that arms of this type were used by the Puritans, contrary to popular pictures showing blunderbusses. Specimens ranging from $1200.00 to $1500.00.

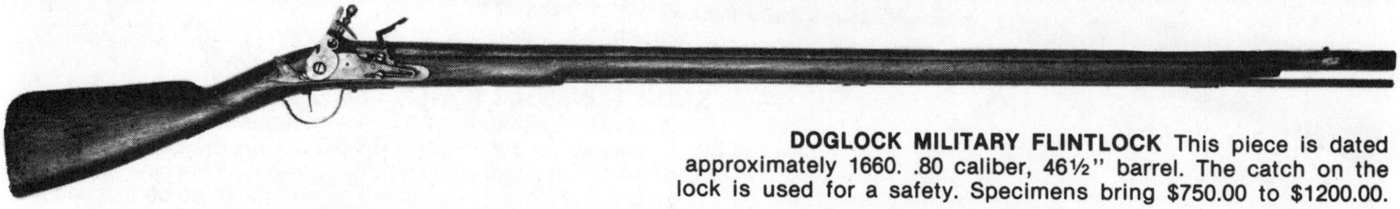

DOGLOCK MILITARY FLINTLOCK This piece is dated approximately 1660. .80 caliber, 46½'' barrel. The catch on the lock is used for a safety. Specimens bring $750.00 to $1200.00.

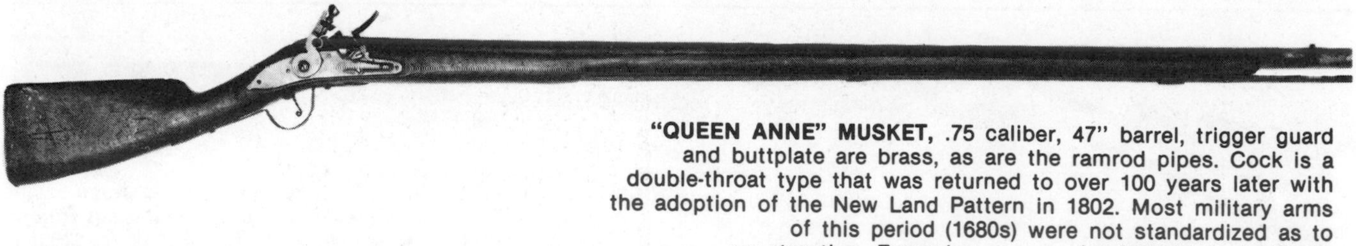

"QUEEN ANNE" MUSKET, .75 caliber, 47'' barrel, trigger guard and buttplate are brass, as are the ramrod pipes. Cock is a double-throat type that was returned to over 100 years later with the adoption of the New Land Pattern in 1802. Most military arms of this period (1680s) were not standardized as to construction. Examples may go for $700.00 to $1000.00.

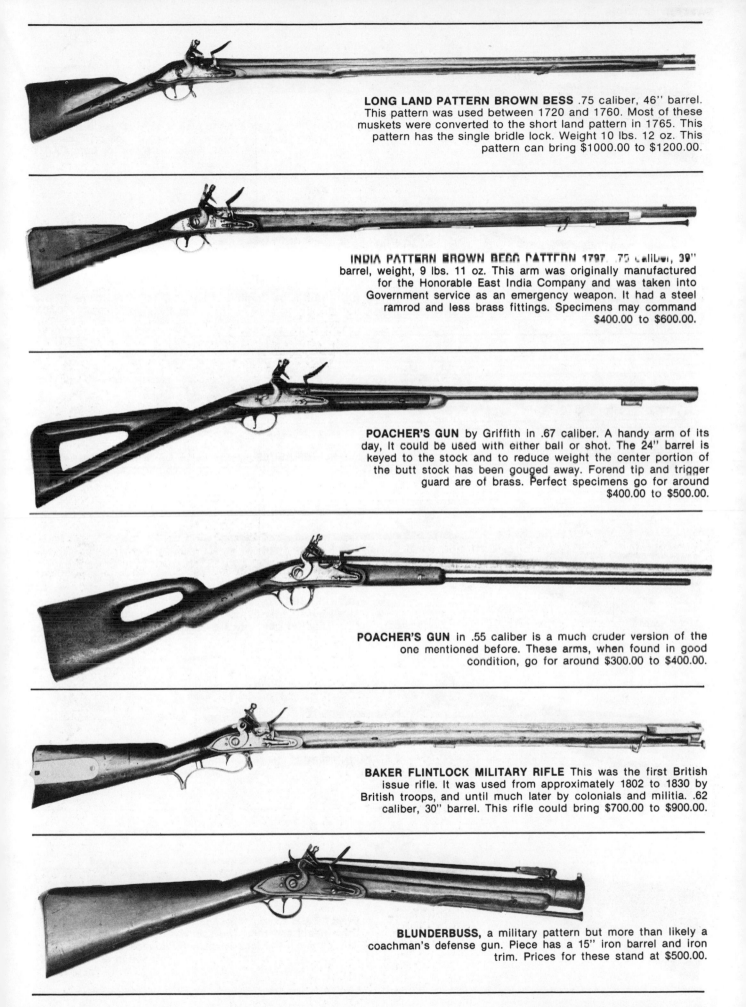

LONG LAND PATTERN BROWN BESS .75 caliber, 46" barrel. This pattern was used between 1720 and 1760. Most of these muskets were converted to the short land pattern in 1765. This pattern has the single bridle lock. Weight 10 lbs. 12 oz. This pattern can bring $1000.00 to $1200.00.

INDIA PATTERN BROWN BESS PATTERN 1797 .75 caliber, 39" barrel, weight, 9 lbs. 11 oz. This arm was originally manufactured for the Honorable East India Company and was taken into Government service as an emergency weapon. It had a steel ramrod and less brass fittings. Specimens may command $400.00 to $600.00.

POACHER'S GUN by Griffith in .67 caliber. A handy arm of its day, It could be used with either ball or shot. The 24" barrel is keyed to the stock and to reduce weight the center portion of the butt stock has been gouged away. Forend tip and trigger guard are of brass. Perfect specimens go for around $400.00 to $500.00.

POACHER'S GUN in .55 caliber is a much cruder version of the one mentioned before. These arms, when found in good condition, go for around $300.00 to $400.00.

BAKER FLINTLOCK MILITARY RIFLE This was the first British issue rifle. It was used from approximately 1802 to 1830 by British troops, and until much later by colonials and militia. .62 caliber, 30" barrel. This rifle could bring $700.00 to $900.00.

BLUNDERBUSS, a military pattern but more than likely a coachman's defense gun. Piece has a 15" iron barrel and iron trim. Prices for these stand at $500.00.

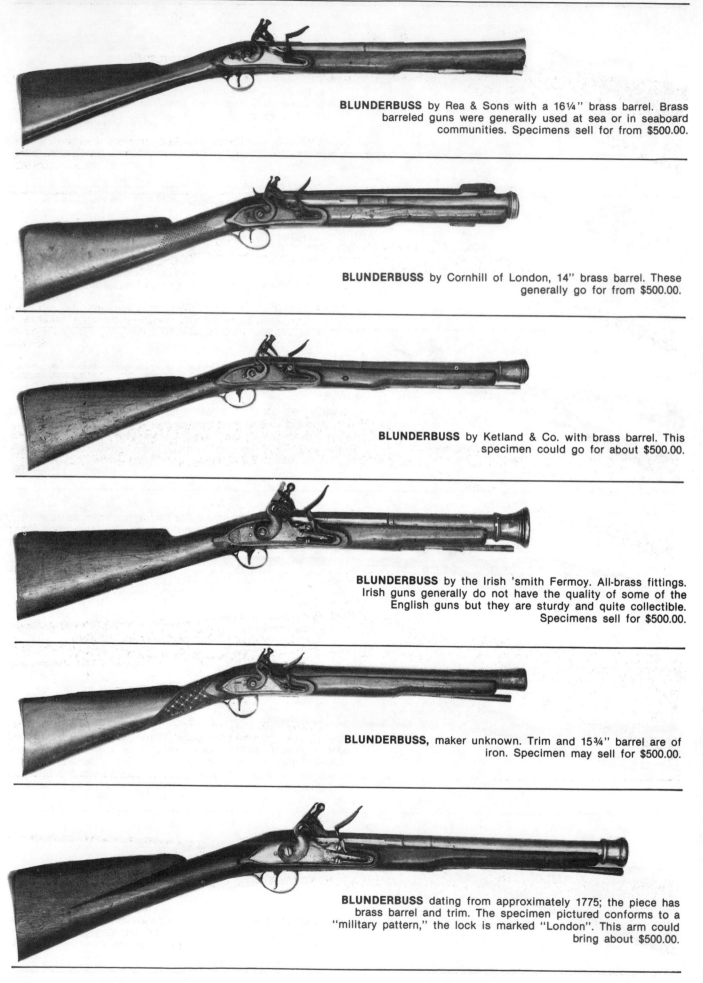

BLUNDERBUSS by Rea & Sons with a 16¼" brass barrel. Brass barreled guns were generally used at sea or in seaboard communities. Specimens sell for from $500.00.

BLUNDERBUSS by Cornhill of London, 14" brass barrel. These generally go for from $500.00.

BLUNDERBUSS by Ketland & Co. with brass barrel. This specimen could go for about $500.00.

BLUNDERBUSS by the Irish 'smith Fermoy. All-brass fittings. Irish guns generally do not have the quality of some of the English guns but they are sturdy and quite collectible. Specimens sell for $500.00.

BLUNDERBUSS, maker unknown. Trim and 15¾" barrel are of iron. Specimen may sell for $500.00.

BLUNDERBUSS dating from approximately 1775; the piece has brass barrel and trim. The specimen pictured conforms to a "military pattern," the lock is marked "London". This arm could bring about $500.00.

BLUNDERBUSS by Dobson & Baker, marked "London". Barrel and trim are of brass. Abbreviated forend. Specimens bring about $550.00.

BLUNDERBUSS by Bolton. This fine piece from the early 19th Century is quite massive, weighing almost 11 pounds. Is brass-trimmed with gooseneck hammer. Piece could go for $550.00.

BLUNDERBUSS by Wogdon & Barton, dating from approximately 1770. Trim is of brass, barrel is iron. This piece could bring about $500.00 to $600.00.

BLUNDERBUSS by Tomlinson, 15" barrel, trim of brass, iron barrel. Lock is marked "Dublin". This fine specimen could sell for from $400.00.

BLUNDERBUSS by Osborne & Jackson with a 16" iron barrel. This piece is representative of the late English blunderbuss. Specimens go for around $300.00.

TERRY CARBINE, .56 caliber. Adopted as provisional issue in 1854, these arms were used by only one or two regiments. They saw only limited use in the Civil War. They were also made in a double-barrel hunting model. These arms may bring $150.00 to $300.00. A cased version may go as high as $650.00.

ENFIELD PATTERN 1853 2nd MODEL. .577 caliber. This model does not have the band springs for the barrel bands and the ramrod is straight. This was the second most widely used musket in the Civil War. It was the finest rifled musket of its day. Arms of this type bring from $125.00 to $350.00.

ENFIELD ARTILLERY MUSKETOON PATTERN 1853, used by the Royal Artillery, and to a limited extent during the Civil War. It was equipped with a sword bayonet. Examples may go for $175.00 to $350.00.

ENFIELD PATTERN 1853 RIFLED MUSKET .577 caliber. This was the first pattern Enfield with band springs for the barrel bands and a swelled ramrod. This was the weapon used in The Great Indian Mutiny and in the Crimea. Specimens can bring $200.00 to $450.00.

SNIDER ENFIELD CARBINE, .577 caliber. An American invention by Jacob Snider, it was adopted as an intermediate arm until a suitable design could be produced. This weapon filled the gap until the Martini was adopted. They are quite common in this country and may be found for $40.00 to $75.00.

ENFIELD PATTERN 1856 .577 caliber. This weapon has a swivel ramrod and a carbine ring and slide on the left hand side. These weapons saw limited use in the Civil War. Of course, every military weapon from 1800 on saw some use in that debacle. This specimen may go for $175.00 to $300.00.

BEASLEY WHITWORTH, military target rifle, made under license by Beasley Bros. This weapon fired the hexagonal Whitworth bolt. .450 caliber, they were very accurate but difficult to load. Specimens may sell for $400.00 to $500.00.

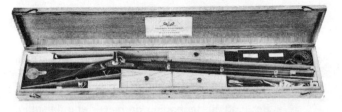

WHITWORTH This cased version has two packages of bullets plus all the original tools and accessories. Cased weapons, complete, bring considerably more than an uncased one. This specimen may go for $1500.00 to $2000.00.

DEANE, ADAMS & DEANE REVOLVING RIFLE .50 caliber, five-shot, 23" barrel. The double-action mechanism with shrouded hammer was designed so that the hammer spur would not become entangled with the clothing when withdrawn from a saddle boot. This weapon may sell for $250.00 to $350.00.

WESTLEY RICHARDS PATTERN 1860 "MONKEY TAIL" .450 caliber. This weapon went through several modifications but when finally perfected it was too late to see active service on any large scale. It was used mostly by militia. Specimens may sell for $90.00 to $125.00.

WESTLEY RICHARDS "MONKEY TAIL" CARBINE. .450 caliber, 20" barrel with Whitworth rifling. Lever on the breech lifts up for loading. Gas seal is achieved by a greased wad in the base of the cartridge, which expands when fired. The next round pushes the wad out, when fired, greasing bore. Specimens may command $100.00 to $150.00.

SHOTGUN by John Manton in 18 gauge with 29½" Damascus barrels. A fine piece for the English double gun collector, it may bring about $350.00 to $500.00.

DOUBLE RIFLE by Westley-Richards in .65 caliber with 30" barrels. This piece sports an unusual "squeeze"-type safety device. Prices for these fine old muzzle loaders run in the vicinity of $400.00.

SHOTGUN by Westley-Richards in 16 gauge. A beautiful specimen with engraved locks, hammers and trigger guard. These exposed-hammer guns are becoming quite the thing to collect of late and command reasonable prices such as $200.00 to $500.00 depending on maker and finishing.

SHOTGUN by Tatham of London. A fine cased set made about 1850 with 30" Damascus barrels, patent breech, and engraved bar action locks. This set is complete. When found these arms can go for at least $400.00 to $600.00.

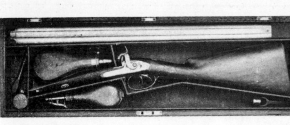

SHOTGUN, also by Westley-Richards with 26" barrels in 12 gauge. A beautiful cased set it could sell for from $400.00 to $600.00 depending on condition.

SHOTGUN by Westley-Richards in 14 gauge. A fine cased set complete with accessories that would make a collector drool. Specimens of these fine arms, cased and complete are now $600.00-up.

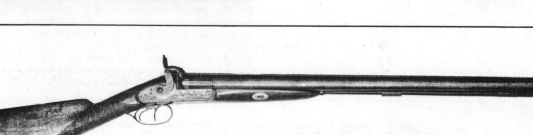

SHOTGUN by Fifield & Richardson in 10 gauge. The piece sports 28" barrels and is extensively engraved in the fine English manner. Specimens such as this which have Damascus barrels make fine collector's items but are definitely not "shooters." Prices vary, run from $300.00 to $500.00.

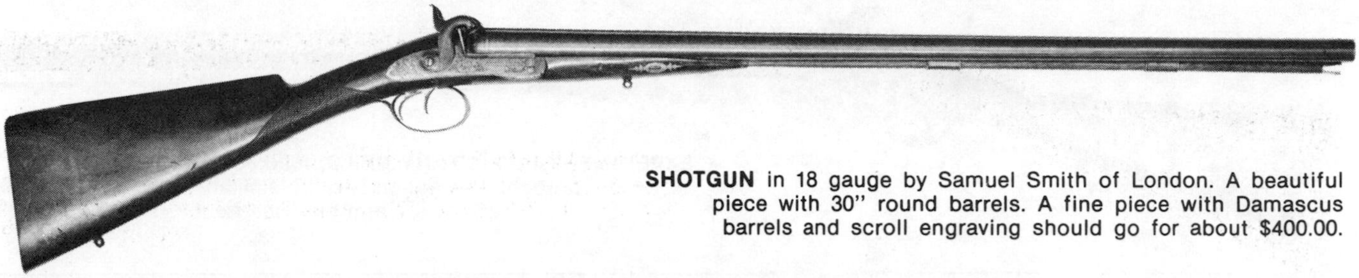

SHOTGUN in 18 gauge by Samuel Smith of London. A beautiful piece with 30" round barrels. A fine piece with Damascus barrels and scroll engraving should go for about $400.00.

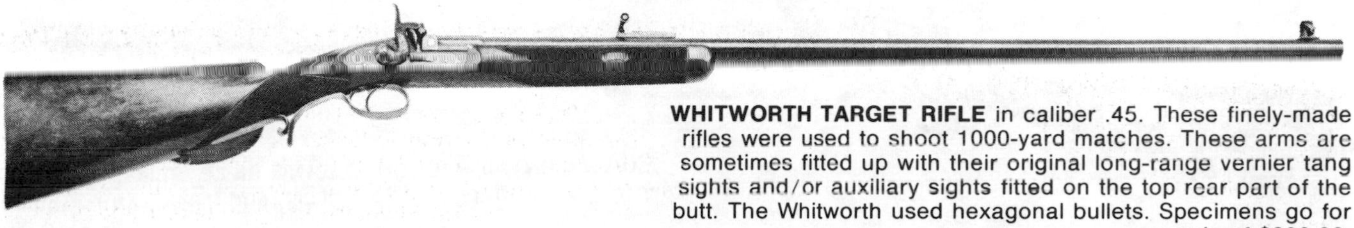

WHITWORTH TARGET RIFLE in caliber .45. These finely-made rifles were used to shoot 1000-yard matches. These arms are sometimes fitted up with their original long-range vernier tang sights and/or auxiliary sights fitted on the top rear part of the butt. The Whitworth used hexagonal bullets. Specimens go for upwards of $800.00.

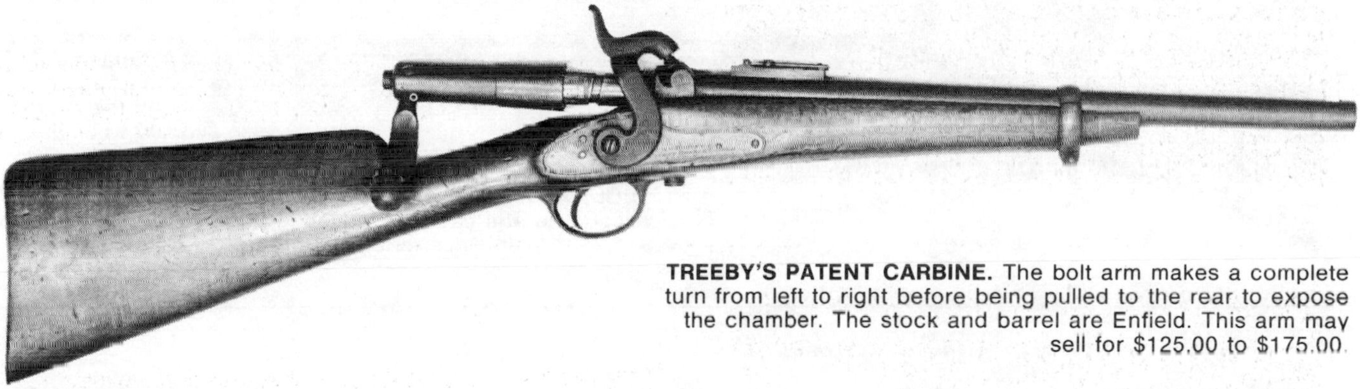

TREEBY'S PATENT CARBINE. The bolt arm makes a complete turn from left to right before being pulled to the rear to expose the chamber. The stock and barrel are Enfield. This arm may sell for $125.00 to $175.00.

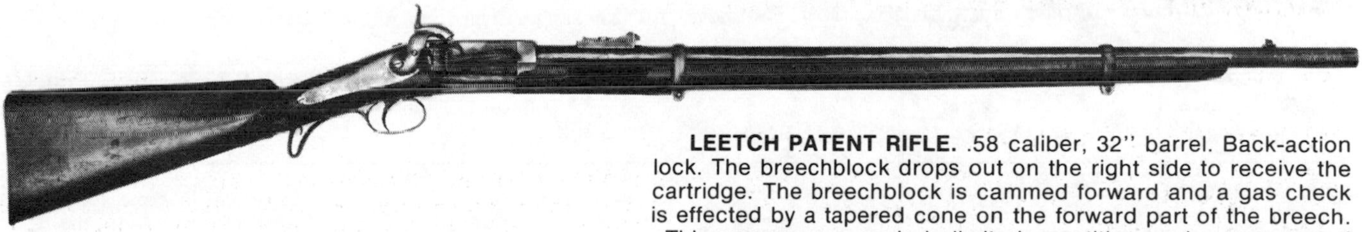

LEETCH PATENT RIFLE. .58 caliber, 32" barrel. Back-action lock. The breechblock drops out on the right side to receive the cartridge. The breechblock is cammed forward and a gas check is effected by a tapered cone on the forward part of the breech. This weapon was made in limited quantities, and was accepted by the British Army. Such a piece would sell for $400.00 to $600.00.

STORM'S PATENT RIFLE. It is built on a standard Enfield musket and is one of the many attempts at converting muzzle loaders to breechloaders. This arm uses paper cartridges with percussion cap seperate. Prices may go from $150.00 to $225.00.

EXPERIMENTAL MILITARY RIFLE, marked THOMAS SHEDDENS on the breech. The action is quite similar to the Sniders. This arm may sell for $150.00 to $200.00.

EXPERIMENTAL BREECHLOADING RIFLE. This arm is quite similar to the U.S. trap-door Springfield, and may sell for $125.00 to $175.00.

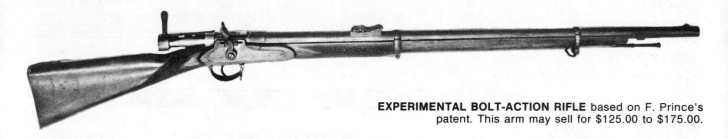

BOLT-ACTION CARBINE made by Carter & Edwards in .58 caliber. The arm has one locking lug and an outside cocking lever. Price may be between $150.00 and $200.00.

EXPERIMENTAL BOLT-ACTION RIFLE based on F. Prince's patent. This arm may sell for $125.00 to $175.00.

EXPERIMENTAL BREECHLOADING RIFLE marked MAJOR FOSBERY'S PATENT #425. Caliber .58. This arm is built on an Enfield type stock and barrel with a trap-door type action. Price may range from $150.00 to $200.00.

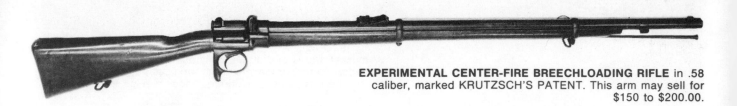

EXPERIMENTAL CENTER-FIRE BREECHLOADING RIFLE in .58 caliber, marked KRUTZSCH'S PATENT. This arm may sell for $150 to $200.00.

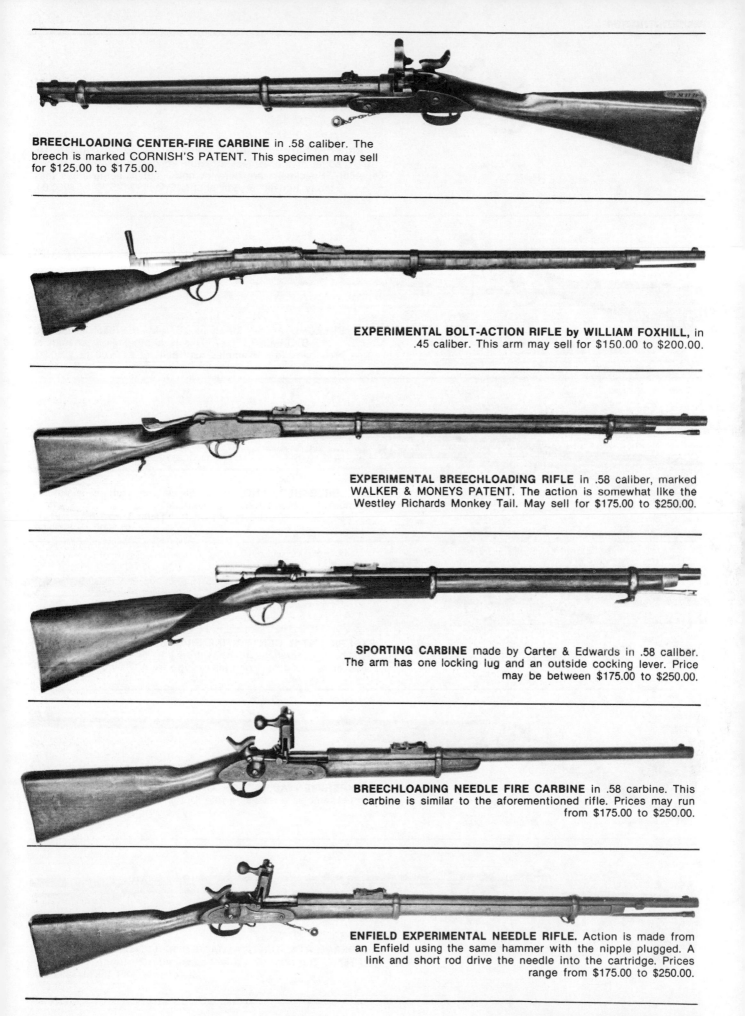

BREECHLOADING CENTER-FIRE CARBINE in .58 caliber. The breech is marked CORNISH'S PATENT. This specimen may sell for $125.00 to $175.00.

EXPERIMENTAL BOLT-ACTION RIFLE by WILLIAM FOXHILL, in .45 caliber. This arm may sell for $150.00 to $200.00.

EXPERIMENTAL BREECHLOADING RIFLE in .58 caliber, marked WALKER & MONEYS PATENT. The action is somewhat like the Westley Richards Monkey Tail. May sell for $175.00 to $250.00.

SPORTING CARBINE made by Carter & Edwards in .58 caliber. The arm has one locking lug and an outside cocking lever. Price may be between $175.00 to $250.00.

BREECHLOADING NEEDLE FIRE CARBINE in .58 carbine. This carbine is similar to the aforementioned rifle. Prices may run from $175.00 to $250.00.

ENFIELD EXPERIMENTAL NEEDLE RIFLE. Action is made from an Enfield using the same hammer with the nipple plugged. A link and short rod drive the needle into the cartridge. Prices range from $175.00 to $250.00.

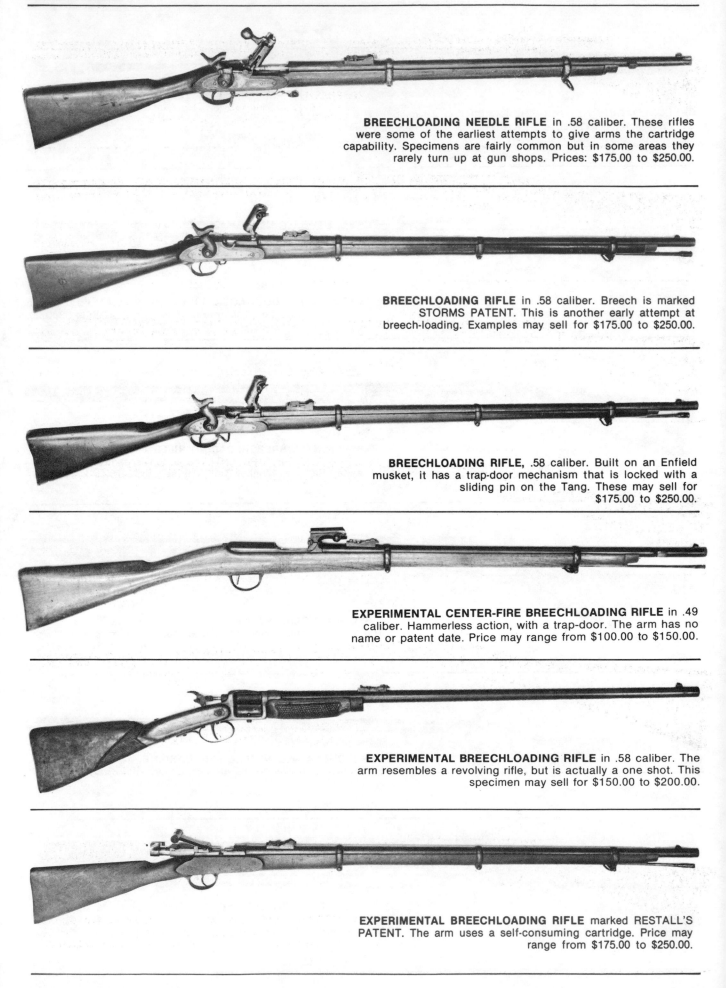

BREECHLOADING NEEDLE RIFLE in .58 caliber. These rifles were some of the earliest attempts to give arms the cartridge capability. Specimens are fairly common but in some areas they rarely turn up at gun shops. Prices: $175.00 to $250.00.

BREECHLOADING RIFLE in .58 caliber. Breech is marked STORMS PATENT. This is another early attempt at breech-loading. Examples may sell for $175.00 to $250.00.

BREECHLOADING RIFLE, .58 caliber. Built on an Enfield musket, it has a trap-door mechanism that is locked with a sliding pin on the Tang. These may sell for $175.00 to $250.00.

EXPERIMENTAL CENTER-FIRE BREECHLOADING RIFLE in .49 caliber. Hammerless action, with a trap-door. The arm has no name or patent date. Price may range from $100.00 to $150.00.

EXPERIMENTAL BREECHLOADING RIFLE in .58 caliber. The arm resembles a revolving rifle, but is actually a one shot. This specimen may sell for $150.00 to $200.00.

EXPERIMENTAL BREECHLOADING RIFLE marked RESTALL'S PATENT. The arm uses a self-consuming cartridge. Price may range from $175.00 to $250.00.

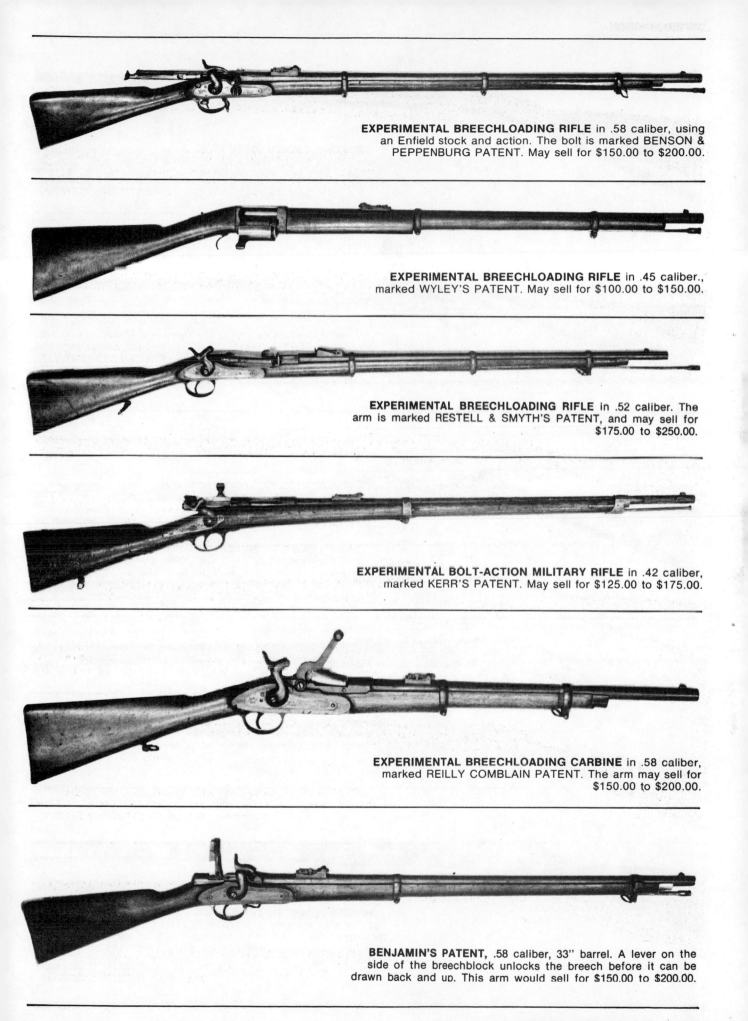

EXPERIMENTAL BREECHLOADING RIFLE in .58 caliber, using an Enfield stock and action. The bolt is marked BENSON & PEPPENBURG PATENT. May sell for $150.00 to $200.00.

EXPERIMENTAL BREECHLOADING RIFLE in .45 caliber., marked WYLEY'S PATENT. May sell for $100.00 to $150.00.

EXPERIMENTAL BREECHLOADING RIFLE in .52 caliber. The arm is marked RESTELL & SMYTH'S PATENT, and may sell for $175.00 to $250.00.

EXPERIMENTAL BOLT-ACTION MILITARY RIFLE in .42 caliber, marked KERR'S PATENT. May sell for $125.00 to $175.00.

EXPERIMENTAL BREECHLOADING CARBINE in .58 caliber, marked REILLY COMBLAIN PATENT. The arm may sell for $150.00 to $200.00.

BENJAMIN'S PATENT, .58 caliber, 33'' barrel. A lever on the side of the breechblock unlocks the breech before it can be drawn back and up. This arm would sell for $150.00 to $200.00.

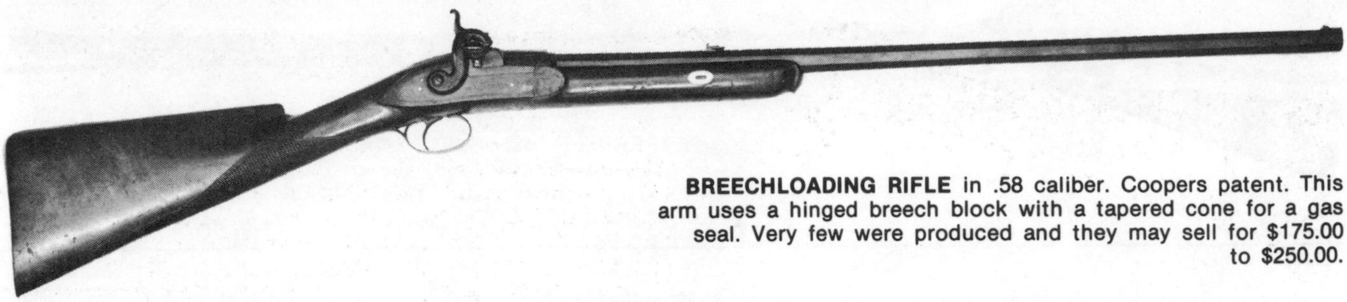

BREECHLOADING RIFLE in .58 caliber. Coopers patent. This arm uses a hinged breech block with a tapered cone for a gas seal. Very few were produced and they may sell for $175.00 to $250.00.

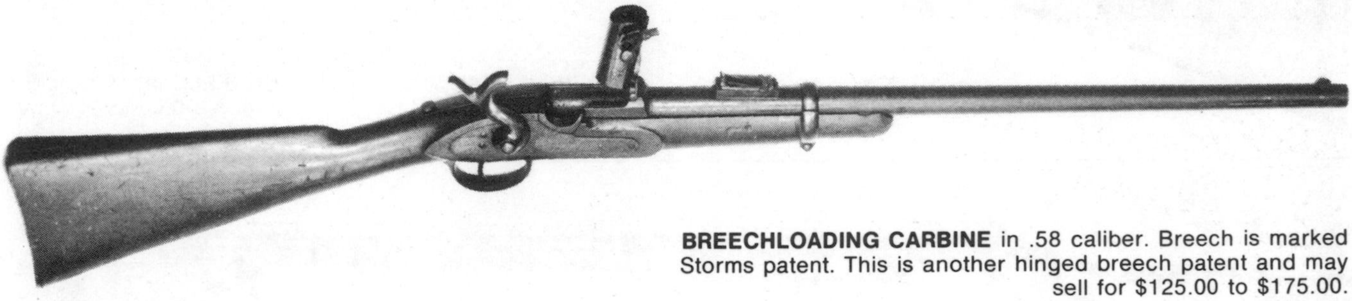

BREECHLOADING CARBINE in .58 caliber. Breech is marked Storms patent. This is another hinged breech patent and may sell for $125.00 to $175.00.

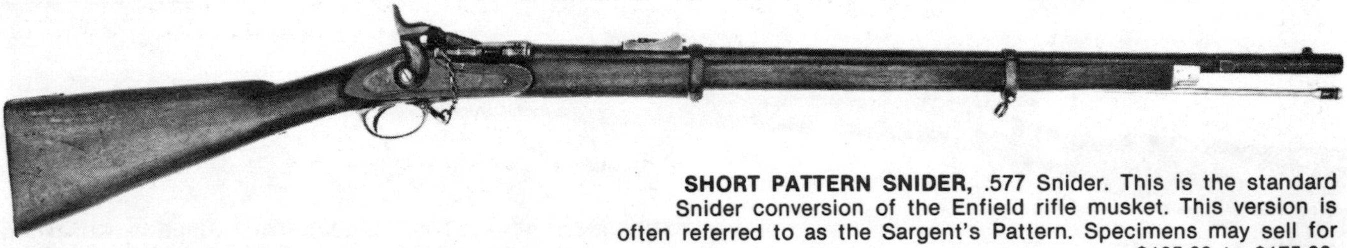

SHORT PATTERN SNIDER, .577 Snider. This is the standard Snider conversion of the Enfield rifle musket. This version is often referred to as the Sargent's Pattern. Specimens may sell for $125.00 to $175.00.

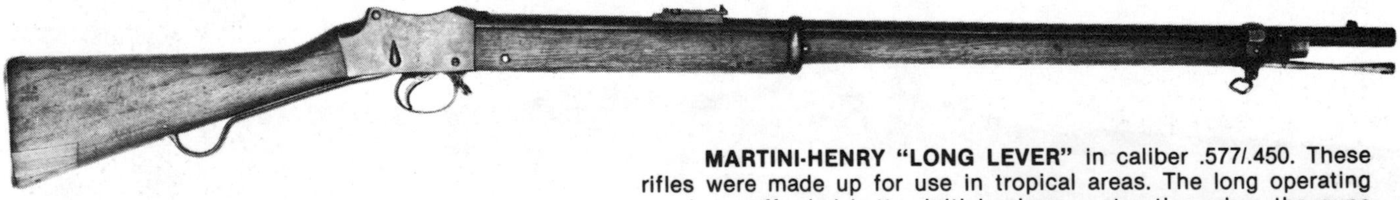

MARTINI-HENRY "LONG LEVER" in caliber .577/.450. These rifles were made up for use in tropical areas. The long operating lever afforded better initial primary extraction when the guns heated up. Specimens are found in fair condition and sell for about $60.00 to $100.00.

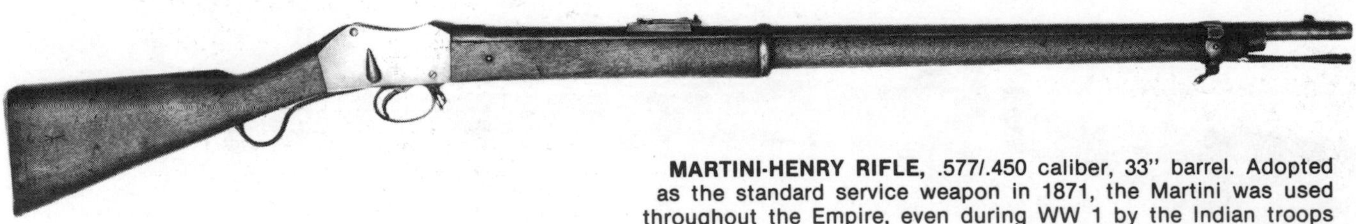

MARTINI-HENRY RIFLE, .577/.450 caliber, 33'' barrel. Adopted as the standard service weapon in 1871, the Martini was used throughout the Empire, even during WW 1 by the Indian troops in Africa. Due to its strong action many have been cut up into sporters, and as a result the military versions are becoming quite scarce. Specimens bring from $60.00 to $100.00.

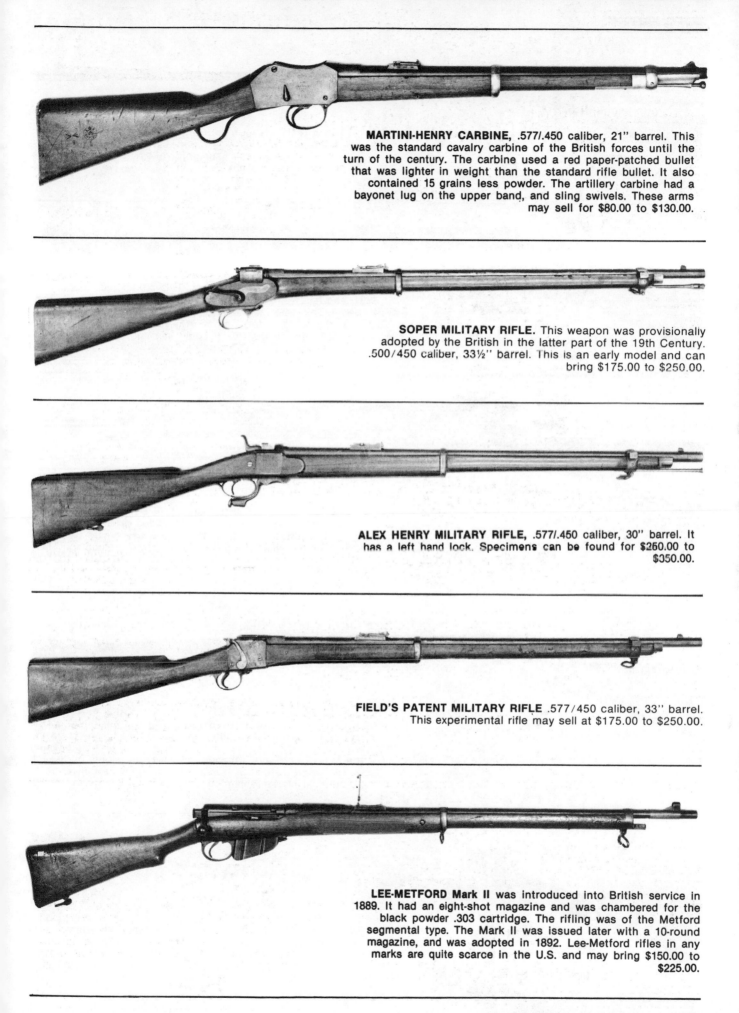

MARTINI-HENRY CARBINE, .577/.450 caliber, 21" barrel. This was the standard cavalry carbine of the British forces until the turn of the century. The carbine used a red paper-patched bullet that was lighter in weight than the standard rifle bullet. It also contained 15 grains less powder. The artillery carbine had a bayonet lug on the upper band, and sling swivels. These arms may sell for $80.00 to $130.00.

SOPER MILITARY RIFLE. This weapon was provisionally adopted by the British in the latter part of the 19th Century. .500/450 caliber, 33½" barrel. This is an early model and can bring $175.00 to $250.00.

ALEX HENRY MILITARY RIFLE, .577/.450 caliber, 30" barrel. It has a left hand lock. Specimens can be found for $260.00 to $350.00.

FIELD'S PATENT MILITARY RIFLE .577/450 caliber, 33" barrel. This experimental rifle may sell at $175.00 to $250.00.

LEE-METFORD Mark II was introduced into British service in 1889. It had an eight-shot magazine and was chambered for the black powder .303 cartridge. The rifling was of the Metford segmental type. The Mark II was issued later with a 10-round magazine, and was adopted in 1892. Lee-Metford rifles in any marks are quite scarce in the U.S. and may bring $150.00 to $225.00.

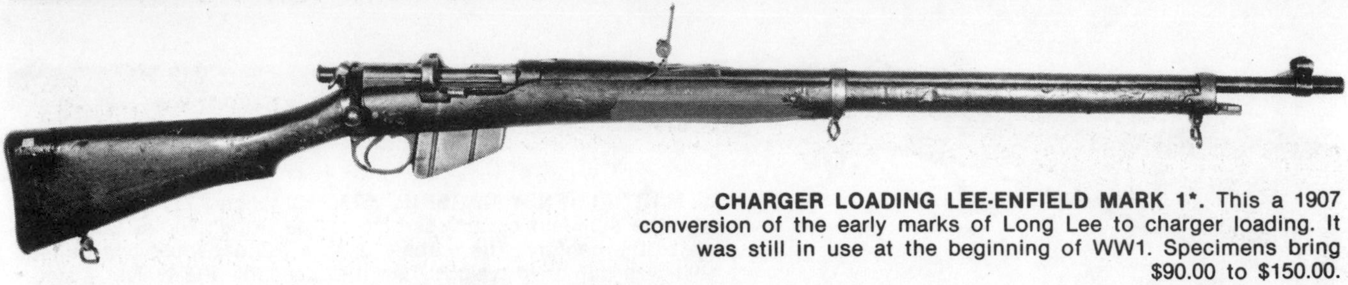

CHARGER LOADING LEE-ENFIELD MARK 1*. This a 1907 conversion of the early marks of Long Lee to charger loading. It was still in use at the beginning of WW1. Specimens bring $90.00 to $150.00.

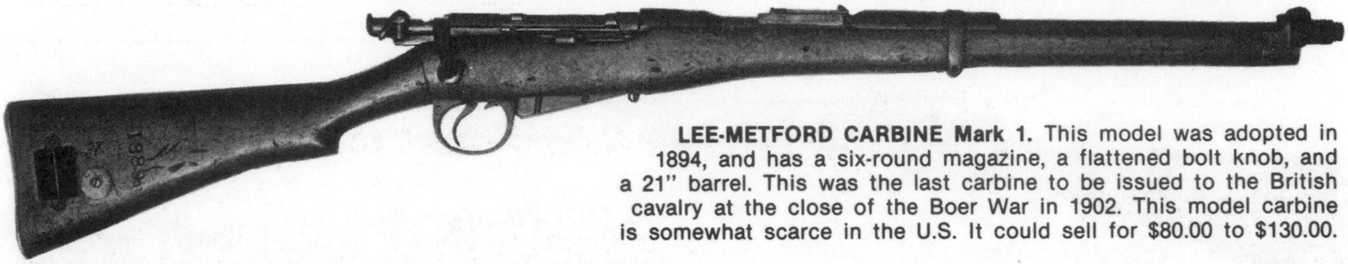

LEE-METFORD CARBINE Mark 1. This model was adopted in 1894, and has a six-round magazine, a flattened bolt knob, and a 21" barrel. This was the last carbine to be issued to the British cavalry at the close of the Boer War in 1902. This model carbine is somewhat scarce in the U.S. It could sell for $80.00 to $130.00.

LEE-ENFIELD CARBINE Mark 1* This model carbine was adopted in 1900. Nose cap/bayonet lug piece from earlier pattern rifles was fitted to enable a bayonet to be used. Specimen pictured was issued the Royal Irish Constabulary. This model may go for $70.00 to $100.00.

SHORT MAGAZINE, LEE ENFIELD No. 1 MARK 1. Adoped in 1902. This was the first of the SMLE's. The charger guide on the right is fixed to the bolt head, and the left hand one is on the receiver. Full stocked to the muzzle, it has a windage adjustment on the rear sight. It also retained the volley-fire sights on the left side. These rifles are scarce as most of them were converted to the later Marks. This model could go for $35.00 to $65.00.

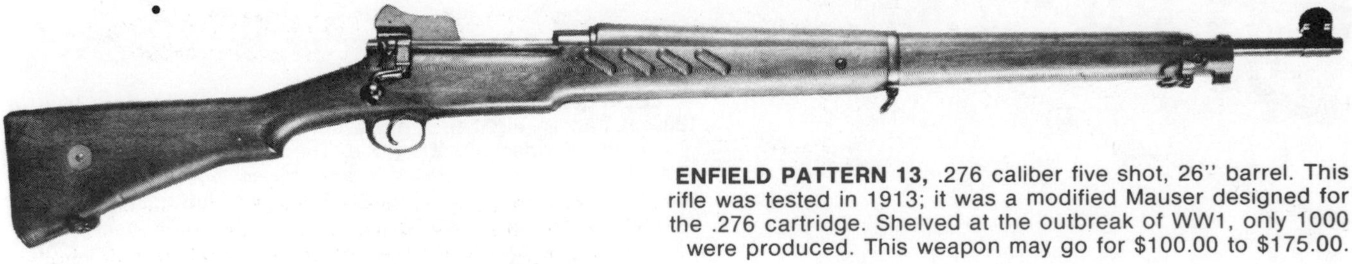

ENFIELD PATTERN 13, .276 caliber five shot, 26" barrel. This rifle was tested in 1913; it was a modified Mauser designed for the .276 cartridge. Shelved at the outbreak of WW1, only 1000 were produced. This weapon may go for $100.00 to $175.00.

PATTERN 14 RIFLE, .303 caliber. This weapon was made in the U.S. during WW 1. The rifle was classified as limited standard in the British Army. It was used mainly for sniping. After the war the P-14 was designated as the Rifle No. 3 Mark 1*. These weapons may go for $45.00 to $75.00.

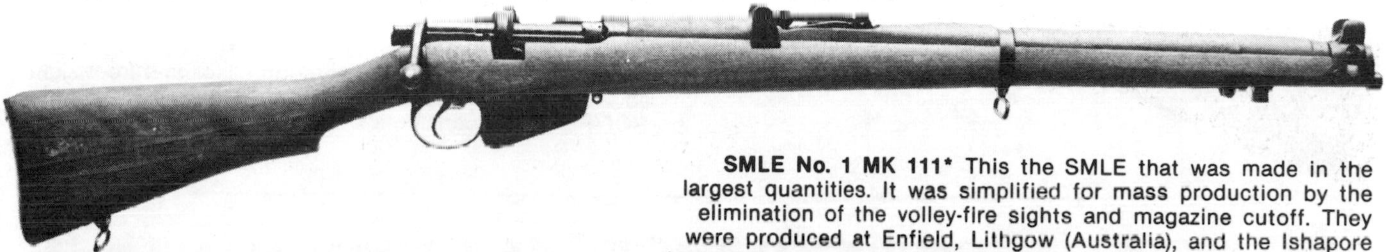

SMLE No. 1 MK 111* This the SMLE that was made in the largest quantities. It was simplified for mass production by the elimination of the volley-fire sights and magazine cutoff. They were produced at Enfield, Lithgow (Australia), and the Ishapore Arsenal in India. This model Enfield may go for $35.00 to $70.00.

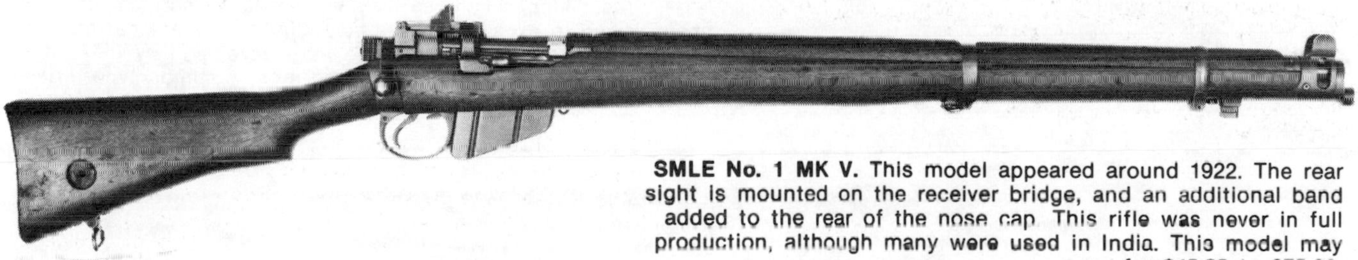

SMLE No. 1 MK V. This model appeared around 1922. The rear sight is mounted on the receiver bridge, and an additional band added to the rear of the nose cap. This rifle was never in full production, although many were used in India. This model may go for $45.00 to $75.00.

LEE-ENFIELD No. 4 Mark 1* This model appeared in 1931, and was redesigned for mass production in 1939, utilizing stamped bands and other shortcuts. Later versions may be found with simple "L"-type sights. The No. 4 version was manufactured in Canada, England and the U.S. Generally speaking any No. 4 can bring $25.00 to $45.00.

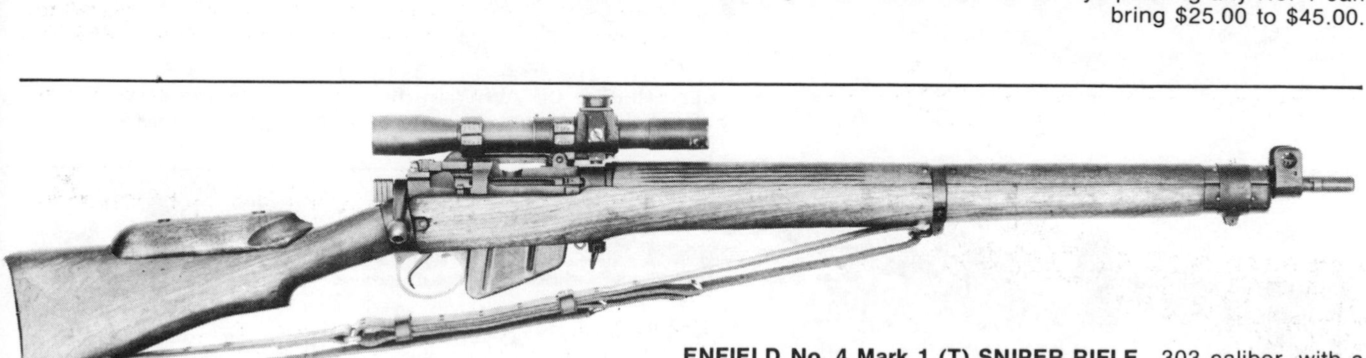

ENFIELD No. 4 Mark 1 (T) SNIPER RIFLE, .303 caliber, with a 3X No. 32, Mk. III scope. British sniper rifles were issued with U.S. slings. These weapons sell for $100.00 to $150.00.

JUNGLE CARBINE NO. 5 MK I in the old reliable .303 Mk VII caliber. These rifles served British, Australian and New Zealand troops well in the tropics. Most of these handy guns have been used for hunting. Mint specimens are hard to find now. Prices range from $45.00 to $65.00.

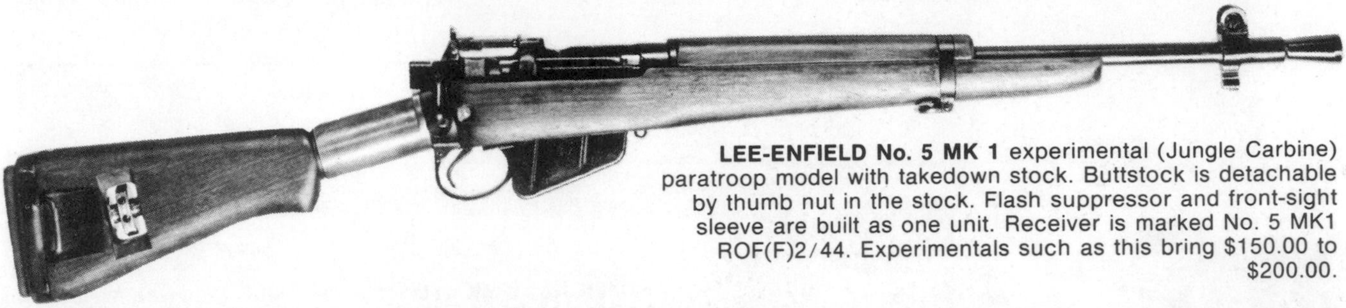

LEE-ENFIELD No. 5 MK 1 experimental (Jungle Carbine) paratroop model with takedown stock. Buttstock is detachable by thumb nut in the stock. Flash suppressor and front-sight sleeve are built as one unit. Receiver is marked No. 5 MK1 ROF(F)2/44. Experimentals such as this bring $150.00 to $200.00.

LEE-ENFIELD No. 2 Mk IV* in .22 Long Rifle caliber these rifles are quite common here as they were sold as surplus for some years. When in excellent to mint condition they are desirable as collectors items. Many "marks" were developed by the British but the specimen pictured here is the most common type. Prices run from $70.00 to $90.00.

LEE-ENFIELD No. 7 RIFLE in .22 rimfire caliber, these rifles were made up for use by the Royal Air Force as trainers. The .22 caliber conversion of the No. 4 to No. 7 was first attempted by Long Branch Arsenal in Canada. Prices range from $70.00 to $90.00.

LEE-ENFIELD CUTAWAY of the Long Lee-Metford rifle. This is a rather unusual demonstration piece and could go for $45.00 to $70.00.

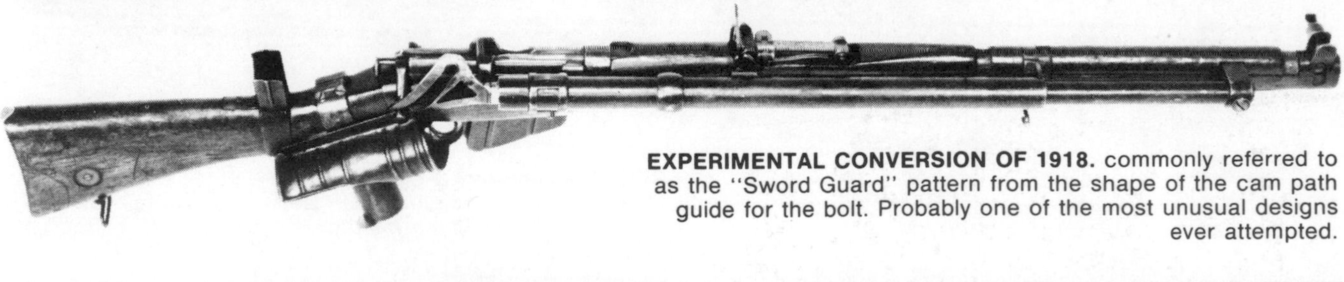

EXPERIMENTAL CONVERSION OF 1918. commonly referred to as the "Sword Guard" pattern from the shape of the cam path guide for the bolt. Probably one of the most unusual designs ever attempted.

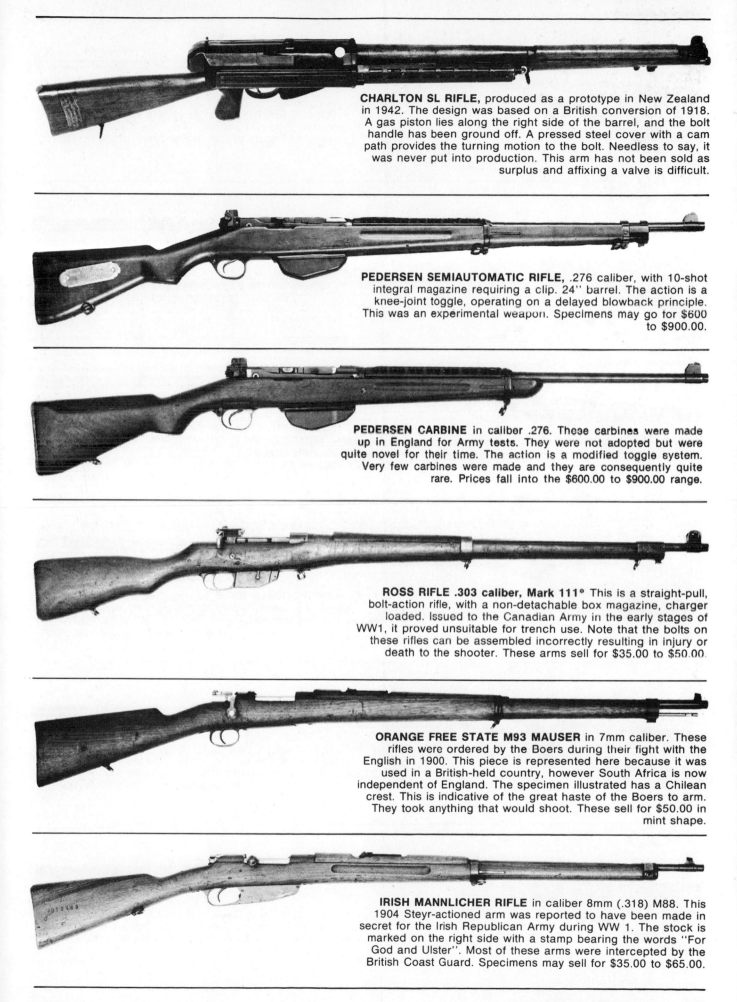

CHARLTON SL RIFLE, produced as a prototype in New Zealand in 1942. The design was based on a British conversion of 1918. A gas piston lies along the right side of the barrel, and the bolt handle has been ground off. A pressed steel cover with a cam path provides the turning motion to the bolt. Needless to say, it was never put into production. This arm has not been sold as surplus and affixing a valve is difficult.

PEDERSEN SEMIAUTOMATIC RIFLE, .276 caliber, with 10-shot integral magazine requiring a clip. 24'' barrel. The action is a knee-joint toggle, operating on a delayed blowback principle. This was an experimental weapon. Specimens may go for $600 to $900.00.

PEDERSEN CARBINE in caliber .276. These carbines were made up in England for Army tests. They were not adopted but were quite novel for their time. The action is a modified toggle system. Very few carbines were made and they are consequently quite rare. Prices fall into the $600.00 to $900.00 range.

ROSS RIFLE .303 caliber, Mark 111* This is a straight-pull, bolt-action rifle, with a non-detachable box magazine, charger loaded. Issued to the Canadian Army in the early stages of WW1, it proved unsuitable for trench use. Note that the bolts on these rifles can be assembled incorrectly resulting in injury or death to the shooter. These arms sell for $35.00 to $50.00.

ORANGE FREE STATE M93 MAUSER in 7mm caliber. These rifles were ordered by the Boers during their fight with the English in 1900. This piece is represented here because it was used in a British-held country, however South Africa is now independent of England. The specimen illustrated has a Chilean crest. This is indicative of the great haste of the Boers to arm. They took anything that would shoot. These sell for $50.00 in mint shape.

IRISH MANNLICHER RIFLE in caliber 8mm (.318) M88. This 1904 Steyr-actioned arm was reported to have been made in secret for the Irish Republican Army during WW 1. The stock is marked on the right side with a stamp bearing the words ''For God and Ulster''. Most of these arms were intercepted by the British Coast Guard. Specimens may sell for $35.00 to $65.00.

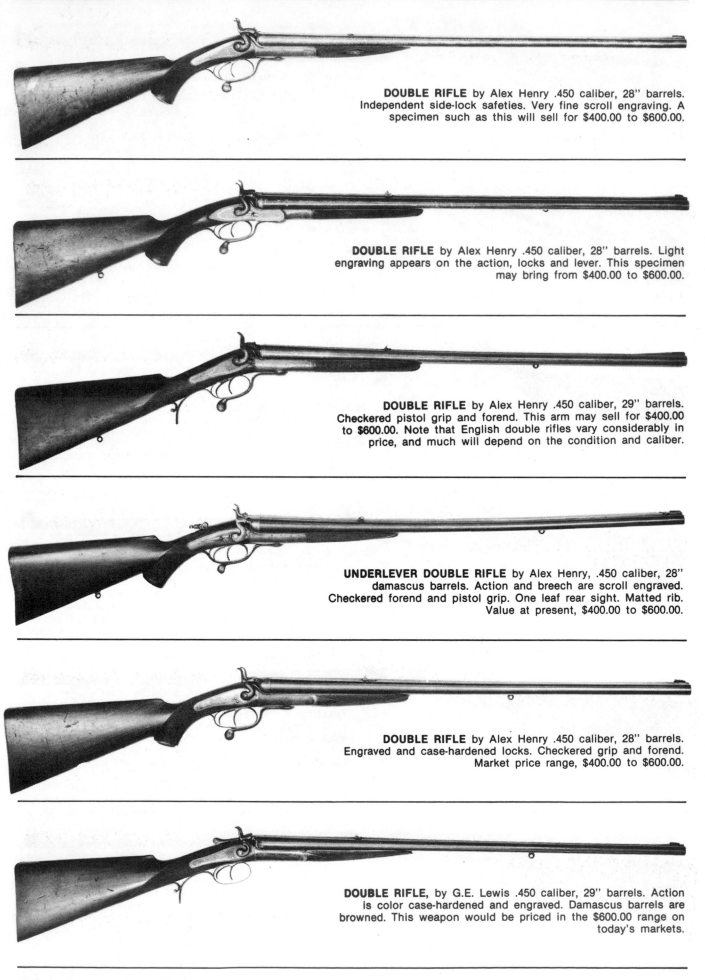

DOUBLE RIFLE by Alex Henry .450 caliber, 28" barrels. Independent side-lock safeties. Very fine scroll engraving. A specimen such as this will sell for $400.00 to $600.00.

DOUBLE RIFLE by Alex Henry .450 caliber, 28" barrels. Light engraving appears on the action, locks and lever. This specimen may bring from $400.00 to $600.00.

DOUBLE RIFLE by Alex Henry .450 caliber, 29" barrels. Checkered pistol grip and forend. This arm may sell for $400.00 to $600.00. Note that English double rifles vary considerably in price, and much will depend on the condition and caliber.

UNDERLEVER DOUBLE RIFLE by Alex Henry, .450 caliber, 28" damascus barrels. Action and breech are scroll engraved. Checkered forend and pistol grip. One leaf rear sight. Matted rib. Value at present, $400.00 to $600.00.

DOUBLE RIFLE by Alex Henry .450 caliber, 28" barrels. Engraved and case-hardened locks. Checkered grip and forend. Market price range, $400.00 to $600.00.

DOUBLE RIFLE, by G.E. Lewis .450 caliber, 29" barrels. Action is color case-hardened and engraved. Damascus barrels are browned. This weapon would be priced in the $600.00 range on today's markets.

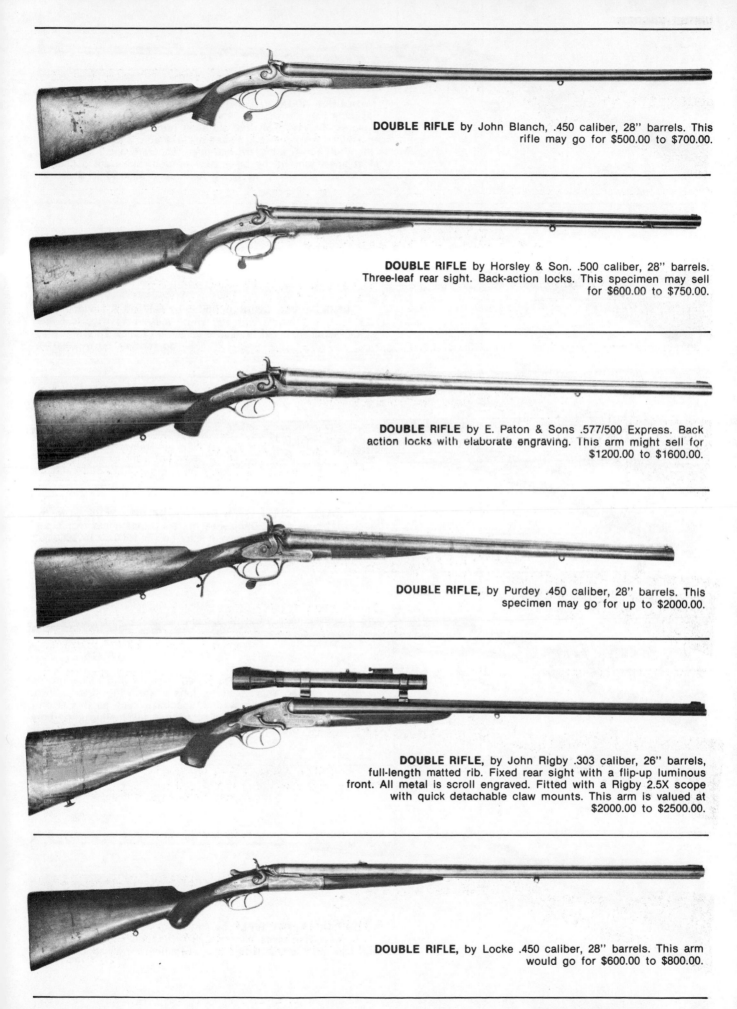

DOUBLE RIFLE by John Blanch, .450 caliber, 28" barrels. This rifle may go for $500.00 to $700.00.

DOUBLE RIFLE by Horsley & Son. .500 caliber, 28" barrels. Three-leaf rear sight. Back-action locks. This specimen may sell for $600.00 to $750.00.

DOUBLE RIFLE by E. Paton & Sons .577/500 Express. Back action locks with elaborate engraving. This arm might sell for $1200.00 to $1600.00.

DOUBLE RIFLE, by Purdey .450 caliber, 28" barrels. This specimen may go for up to $2000.00.

DOUBLE RIFLE, by John Rigby .303 caliber, 26" barrels, full-length matted rib. Fixed rear sight with a flip-up luminous front. All metal is scroll engraved. Fitted with a Rigby 2.5X scope with quick detachable claw mounts. This arm is valued at $2000.00 to $2500.00.

DOUBLE RIFLE, by Locke .450 caliber, 28" barrels. This arm would go for $600.00 to $800.00.

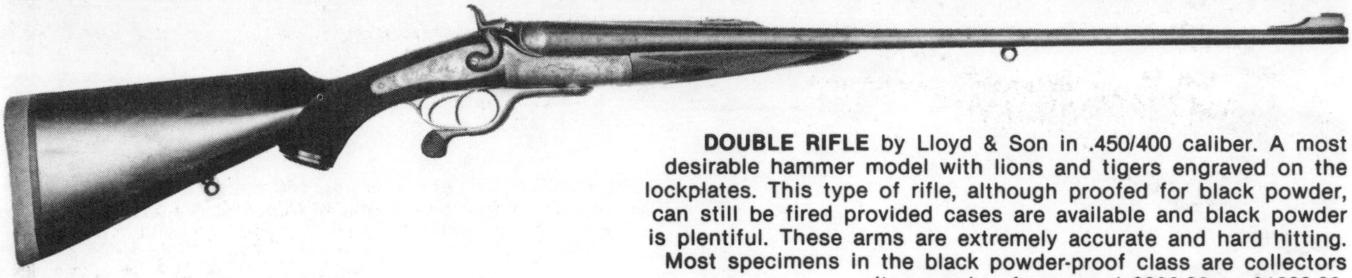

DOUBLE RIFLE by Lloyd & Son in .450/400 caliber. A most desirable hammer model with lions and tigers engraved on the lockplates. This type of rifle, although proofed for black powder, can still be fired provided cases are available and black powder is plentiful. These arms are extremely accurate and hard hitting. Most specimens in the black powder-proof class are collectors items going for around $900.00 to $1200.00.

UNDERLEVER DOUBLE RIFLE by Holland & Holland, .360 Express, 27" barrels with full-length matted rib. Two leaf rear sight. Scroll-engraved breech. Back-action locks. This arm may go for $400.00 to $600.00.

ENGLISH BOLT ACTION DOUBLE BARREL SLUG GUN, by Bacon. 12-bore rifled. Damascus barrels. Folding-leaf rear sight with four leaves. This weapon may go for $600.00 to $800.00.

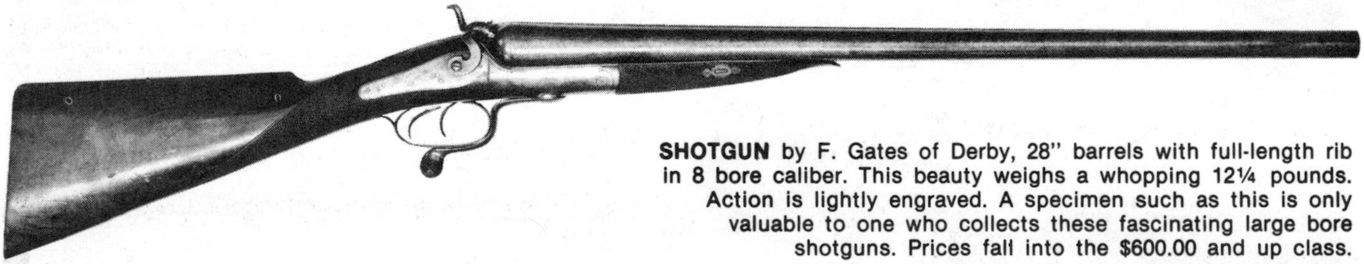

SHOTGUN by F. Gates of Derby, 28" barrels with full-length rib in 8 bore caliber. This beauty weighs a whopping 12¼ pounds. Action is lightly engraved. A specimen such as this is only valuable to one who collects these fascinating large bore shotguns. Prices fall into the $600.00 and up class.

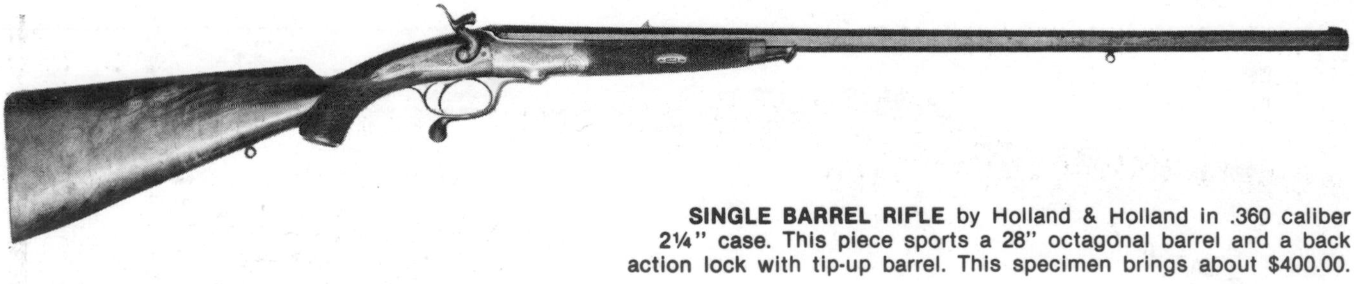

SINGLE BARREL RIFLE by Holland & Holland in .360 caliber 2¼" case. This piece sports a 28" octagonal barrel and a back action lock with tip-up barrel. This specimen brings about $400.00.

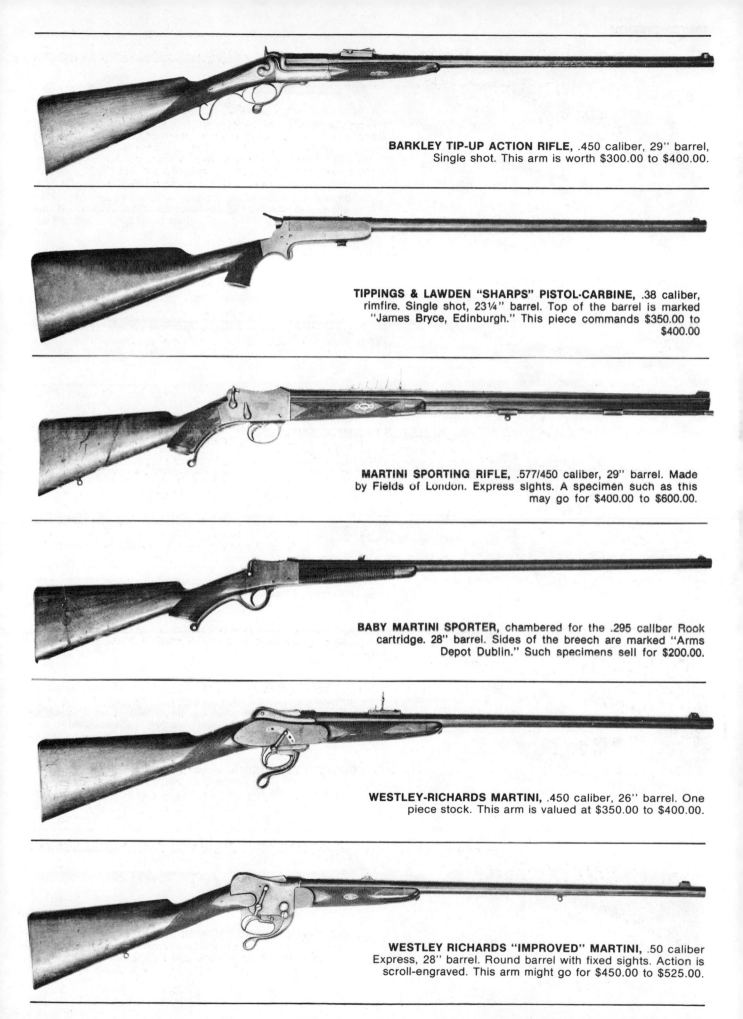

BARKLEY TIP-UP ACTION RIFLE, .450 caliber, 29'' barrel, Single shot. This arm is worth $300.00 to $400.00.

TIPPINGS & LAWDEN "SHARPS" PISTOL-CARBINE, .38 caliber, rimfire. Single shot, 23¼'' barrel. Top of the barrel is marked "James Bryce, Edinburgh." This piece commands $350.00 to $400.00

MARTINI SPORTING RIFLE, .577/450 caliber, 29'' barrel. Made by Fields of London. Express sights. A specimen such as this may go for $400.00 to $600.00.

BABY MARTINI SPORTER, chambered for the .295 caliber Rook cartridge. 28'' barrel. Sides of the breech are marked "Arms Depot Dublin." Such specimens sell for $200.00.

WESTLEY-RICHARDS MARTINI, .450 caliber, 26'' barrel. One piece stock. This arm is valued at $350.00 to $400.00.

WESTLEY RICHARDS "IMPROVED" MARTINI, .50 caliber Express, 28'' barrel. Round barrel with fixed sights. Action is scroll-engraved. This arm might go for $450.00 to $525.00.

RIGBY RIFLE in .22 caliber. This is a custom-made arm for an invalid that is confined to a wheelchair. Oddities such as this can bring $75.00 to $125.00.

ALEX HENRY SPORTING RIFLE, .450 caliber, 28'' barrel. This specimen has a takedown action somewhat similar to the Sharps. Case hardening on the breech and lock. Very fine checkering on the grip and forend. Presently valued at $600.00 to $700.00.

SOPER SPORTING RIFLE, .450 caliber, 28'' barrel, single-shot. Fully ribbed barrel. This specimen would sell for $300.00 to $375.00.

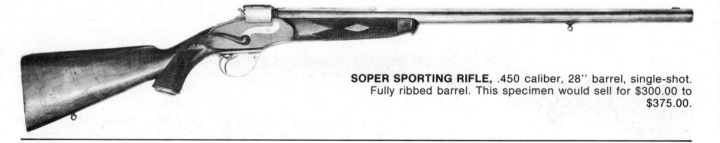

BOLT-ACTION CARBINE, maker unknown, .40 caliber rimfire. 18'' barrel. The action is locked by a interrupted screw. Two-piece bolt. This specimen is valued at $85.00 to $125.00.

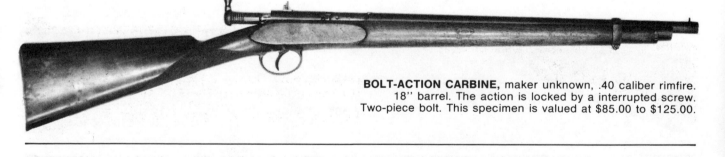

EXPERIMENTAL BOLT-ACTION SPORTING RIFLE, .52 caliber, 26'' barrel, enclosed bolt. Forend cap and barrel band are brass. All metal parts are white. This specimen may go for $100.00 to $150.00.

GREENER EXPERIMENTAL SPORTING RIFLE, .45 caliber, 24" barrel. Engraved and checkered. Rear sight folds down to cover the breech opening. Rotary magazine. This arm is valued at $250.00 to $400.00.

CERTUS RIFLE, .303 caliber, 27" barrel. Four-shot clip. This specimen was manufactured by Cogswell & Harrison. Rear receiver has a double track, on top of which the bolt body slides. This arm may go for $300.00 to $450.00.

CERTUS SPORTING RIFLE by Westley-Richards, .450 caliber single shot, 33" barrel with Metford rifling. Bolt action with three locking lugs on the bolt head. Walnut stock with checkered wrist and forend. This arm may go for $300.00 to $450.00.

JEFFERY sporting rifle built on a Dutch Mannlicher action and barrel. 6.5mm Dutch. Current value $175.00 to $225.00.

BRITISH SPORTER built on a Dutch Mannlicher action. This arm is fitted with a Fraser patent trigger. 6.5mm Dutch 26" barrel. This weapon features a takedown that is locked by a screw in the breech. Such arms go for $150.00 to $200.00.

BISLEY MATCH RIFLE built on a Dutch Mannlicher action, with a special BSA barrel. .303 "Magnum", 30½" barrel. This arm would sell for $85.00 to $100.00.

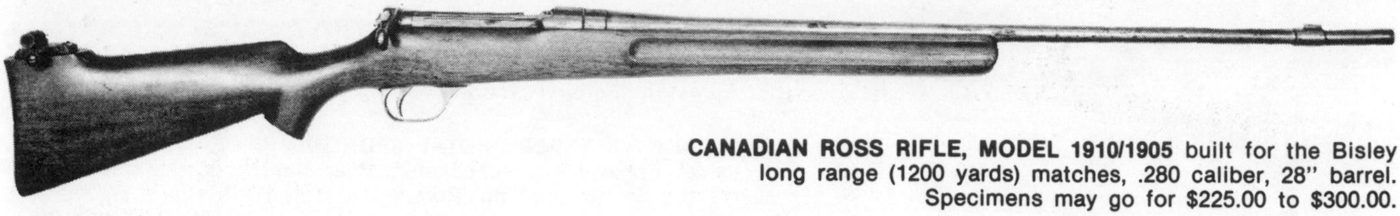

CANADIAN ROSS RIFLE, MODEL 1910/1905 built for the Bisley long range (1200 yards) matches, .280 caliber, 28" barrel. Specimens may go for $225.00 to $300.00.

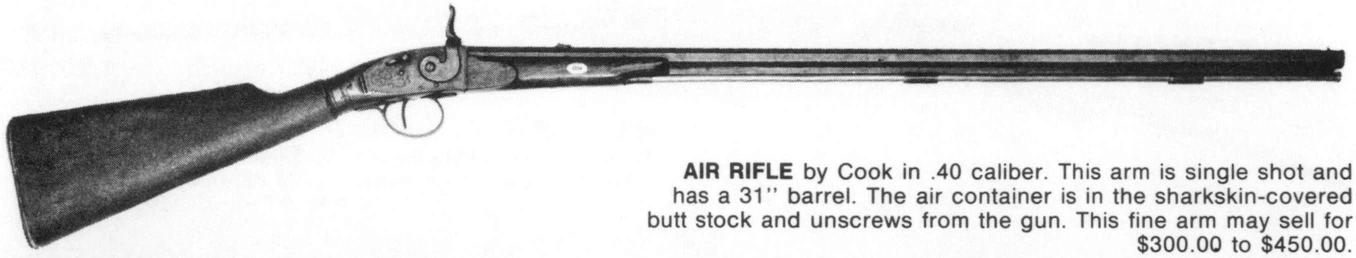

AIR RIFLE by Cook in .40 caliber. This arm is single shot and has a 31" barrel. The air container is in the sharkskin-covered butt stock and unscrews from the gun. This fine arm may sell for $300.00 to $450.00.

UNITED STATES

DOGLOCK MUSKET, dated approximately 1650. It has a full-length walnut stock, and a wooden ramrod. These weapons were used by the early American settlers. This specimen could command $2000.00 and up.

SPRINGFIELD MODEL 1812 in .69 caliber, these muskets are also known as the "first pattern". Very few were used in the War of 1812 due to low production and the newness of the pattern. Later on these were used in the Seminole Wars in Florida. Specimens may sell for from $800.00 to $1200.00.

SPRINGFIELD MODEL 1816 Specimens of this musket made before 1818 are found with pans made of iron; those produced after 1818 have brass pans similar to the French Mle. 1777. Specimens made after September 27, 1821, will be found to have browned barrels and furniture. The lock plates of these are case hardened. Specimens sell for from $800.00 to $1200.00.

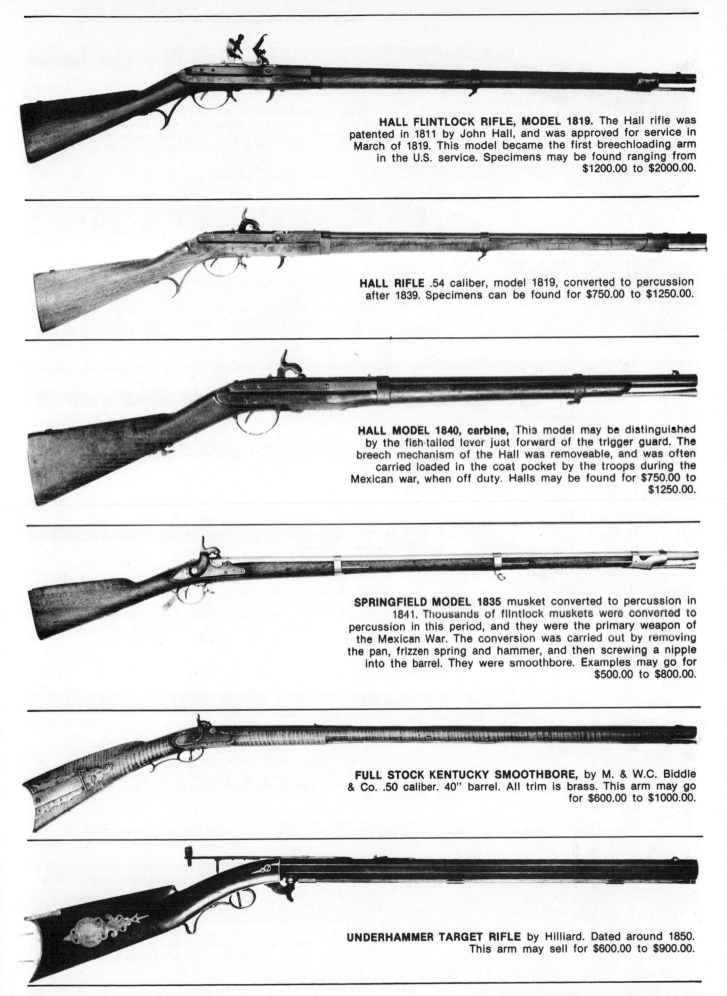

HALL FLINTLOCK RIFLE, MODEL 1819. The Hall rifle was patented in 1811 by John Hall, and was approved for service in March of 1819. This model became the first breechloading arm in the U.S. service. Specimens may be found ranging from $1200.00 to $2000.00.

HALL RIFLE .54 caliber, model 1819, converted to percussion after 1839. Specimens can be found for $750.00 to $1250.00.

HALL MODEL 1840, carbine, This model may be distinguished by the fish-tailed lever just forward of the trigger guard. The breech mechanism of the Hall was removeable, and was often carried loaded in the coat pocket by the troops during the Mexican war, when off duty. Halls may be found for $750.00 to $1250.00.

SPRINGFIELD MODEL 1835 musket converted to percussion in 1841. Thousands of flintlock muskets were converted to percussion in this period, and they were the primary weapon of the Mexican War. The conversion was carried out by removing the pan, frizzen spring and hammer, and then screwing a nipple into the barrel. They were smoothbore. Examples may go for $500.00 to $800.00.

FULL STOCK KENTUCKY SMOOTHBORE, by M. & W.C. Biddle & Co. .50 caliber. 40" barrel. All trim is brass. This arm may go for $600.00 to $1000.00.

UNDERHAMMER TARGET RIFLE by Hilliard. Dated around 1850. This arm may sell for $600.00 to $900.00.

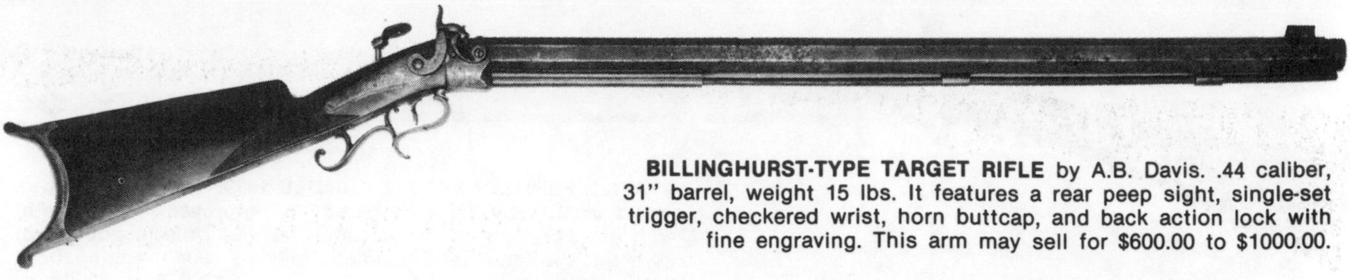

BILLINGHURST-TYPE TARGET RIFLE by A.B. Davis. .44 caliber, 31" barrel, weight 15 lbs. It features a rear peep sight, single-set trigger, checkered wrist, horn buttcap, and back action lock with fine engraving. This arm may sell for $600.00 to $1000.00.

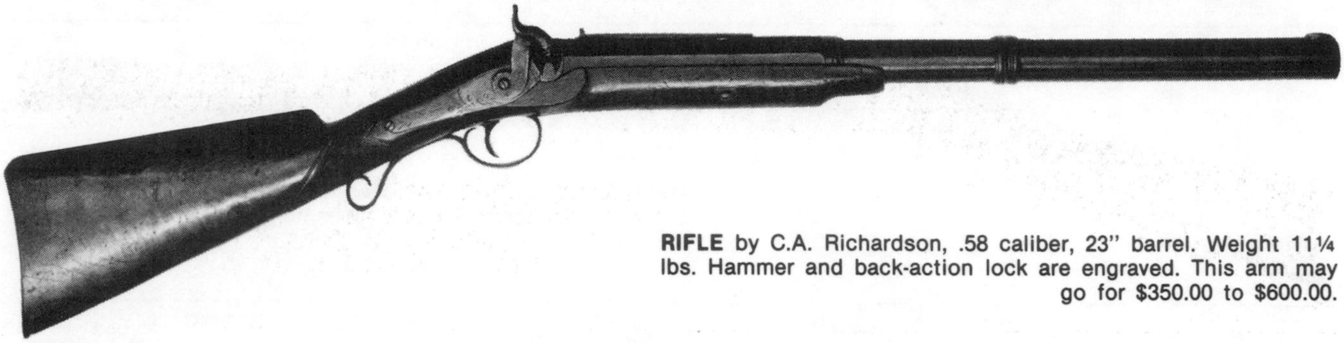

RIFLE by C.A. Richardson, .58 caliber, 23" barrel. Weight 11¼ lbs. Hammer and back-action lock are engraved. This arm may go for $350.00 to $600.00.

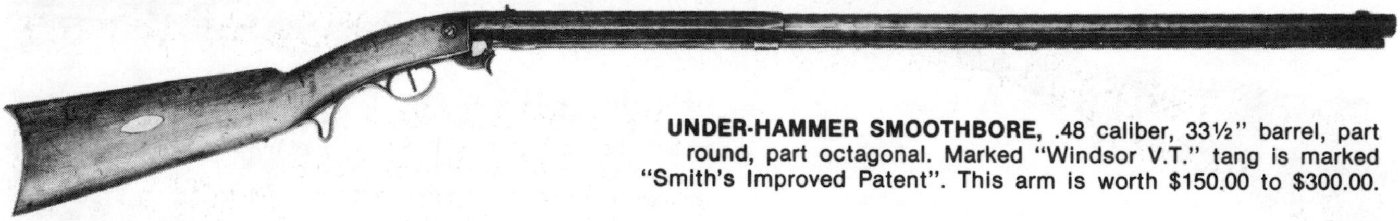

UNDER-HAMMER SMOOTHBORE, .48 caliber, 33½" barrel, part round, part octagonal. Marked "Windsor V.T." tang is marked "Smith's Improved Patent". This arm is worth $150.00 to $300.00.

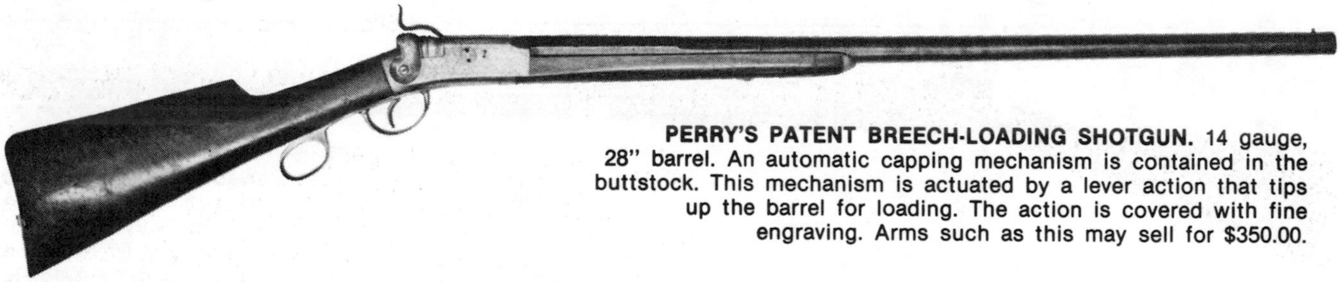

PERRY'S PATENT BREECH-LOADING SHOTGUN. 14 gauge, 28" barrel. An automatic capping mechanism is contained in the buttstock. This mechanism is actuated by a lever action that tips up the barrel for loading. The action is covered with fine engraving. Arms such as this may sell for $350.00.

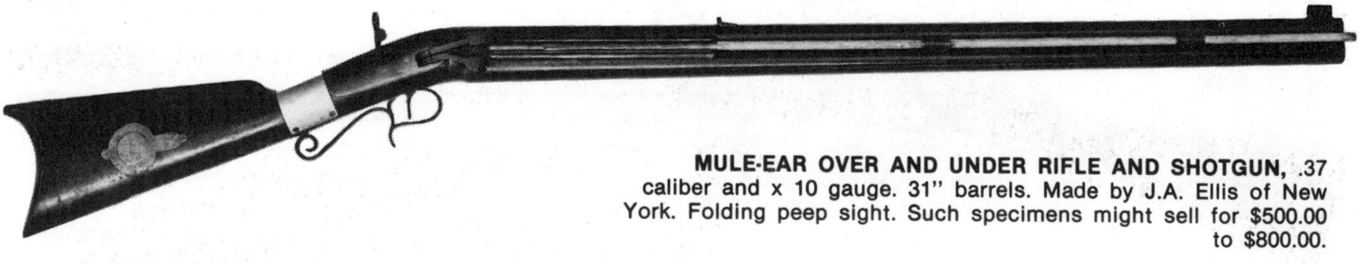

MULE-EAR OVER AND UNDER RIFLE AND SHOTGUN, .37 caliber and x 10 gauge. 31" barrels. Made by J.A. Ellis of New York. Folding peep sight. Such specimens might sell for $500.00 to $800.00.

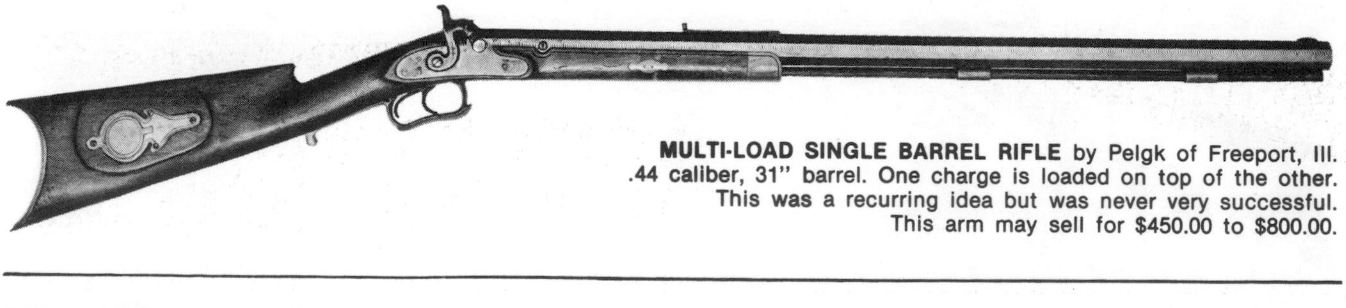

MULTI-LOAD SINGLE BARREL RIFLE by Pelgk of Freeport, Ill. .44 caliber, 31" barrel. One charge is loaded on top of the other. This was a recurring idea but was never very successful. This arm may sell for $450.00 to $800.00.

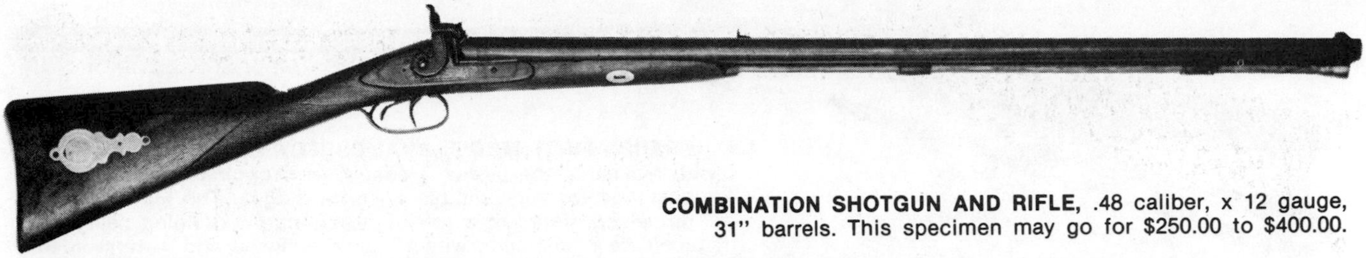

COMBINATION SHOTGUN AND RIFLE, .48 caliber, x 12 gauge, 31" barrels. This specimen may go for $250.00 to $400.00.

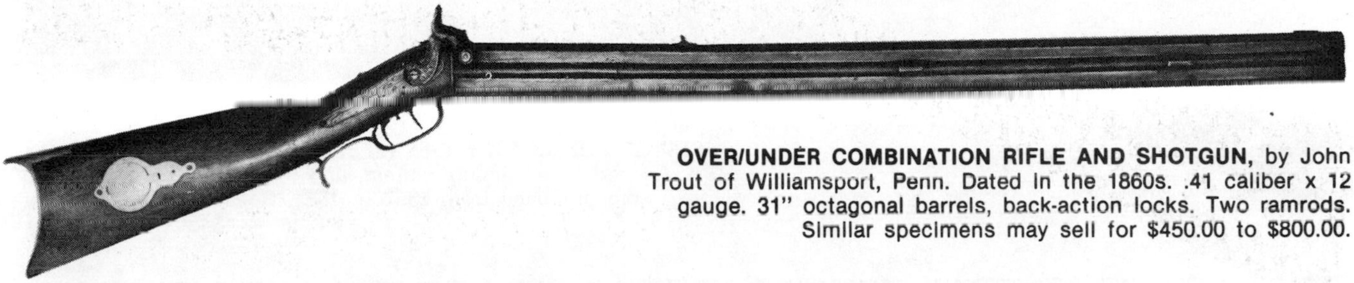

OVER/UNDER COMBINATION RIFLE AND SHOTGUN, by John Trout of Williamsport, Penn. Dated in the 1860s. .41 caliber x 12 gauge. 31" octagonal barrels, back-action locks. Two ramrods. Similar specimens may sell for $450.00 to $800.00.

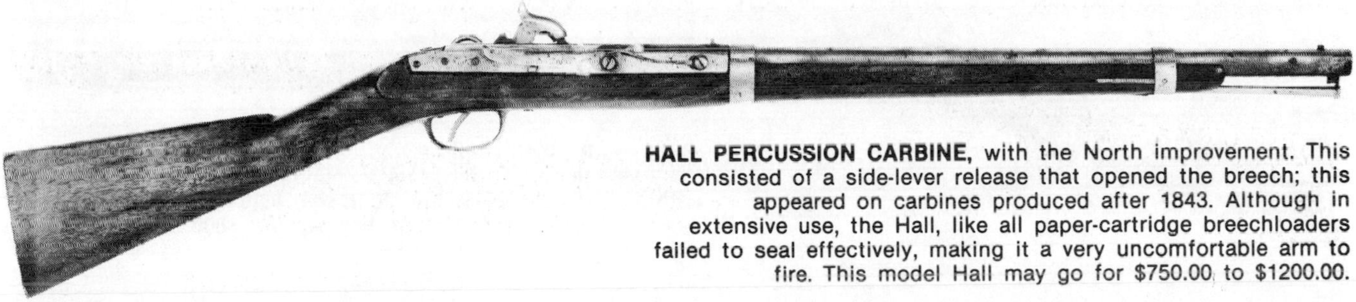

HALL PERCUSSION CARBINE, with the North improvement. This consisted of a side-lever release that opened the breech; this appeared on carbines produced after 1843. Although in extensive use, the Hall, like all paper-cartridge breechloaders failed to seal effectively, making it a very uncomfortable arm to fire. This model Hall may go for $750.00 to $1200.00.

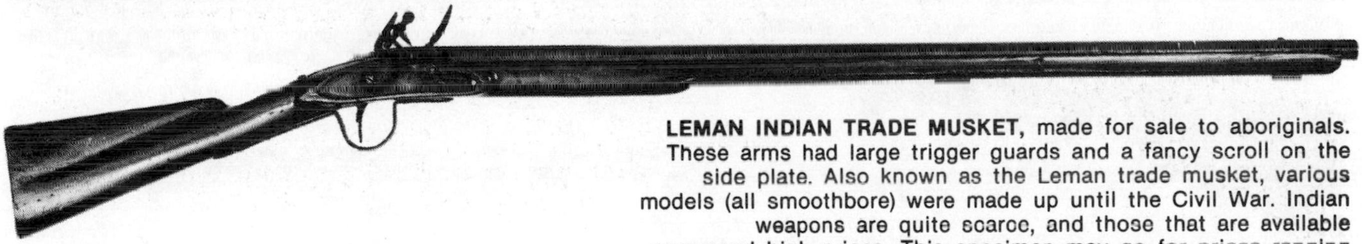

LEMAN INDIAN TRADE MUSKET, made for sale to aboriginals. These arms had large trigger guards and a fancy scroll on the side plate. Also known as the Leman trade musket, various models (all smoothbore) were made up until the Civil War. Indian weapons are quite scarce, and those that are available command high prices. This specimen may go for prices ranging from $700.00 to $1000.00.

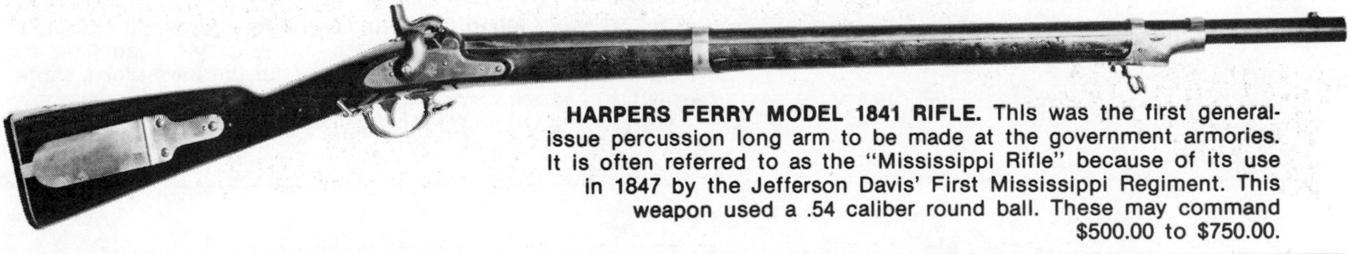

HARPERS FERRY MODEL 1841 RIFLE. This was the first general-issue percussion long arm to be made at the government armories. It is often referred to as the "Mississippi Rifle" because of its use in 1847 by the Jefferson Davis' First Mississippi Regiment. This weapon used a .54 caliber round ball. These may command $500.00 to $750.00.

U.S. SPRINGFIELD ARMORY MODEL 1816 CONVERSION. This .69 caliber musket was rifled and converted to percussion in 1856 to 1859. The stock bears the inscription "Gettysburg July 3, 1863". Arms with legitimate inscriptions on them will bring perhaps $450.00 to $750.00.

SHARPS FIRST MODEL OVAL-BREECH CARBINE. .52 caliber, with Maynard tape primer. Under lever dropping block action is designed for combustable linen cartridges. The Maynard tape primer consisted of a roll of paper tape containing pellets of fulminate of mercury, which was shellacked and waterproofed. This early model Sharps may command $2000.00 up.

SPRINGFIELD ARMORY 1855 RIFLE MUSKET Equipped with the Maynard tape priming system, and in .58 caliber, over 47,000 were produced from 1857 to 1861. Specimens may sell for $450.00 to $850.00.

CIVIL WAR PICKET RIFLE, .45 caliber. The Union forces used many varieties of target rifles for sniping. Most were equipped with a long tube telescope sight and were fitted with bayonet lugs. This specimen may sell for $800.00 to $1200.00.

SPENCER NAVY MODEL as chambered for the .56-50 cartridge. Only 700 of this rare variation were made. They are identified by a permanent bayonet lug mounted under the barrel for a sabre bayonet. Prices will vary on those variations (of which only a few are known). Obviously this would command a premium price.

ENFIELD MUSKET, MODEL 1861, SERGEANTS PATTERN, U.S. marked. Many Enfield muskets were manufactured in the U.S. before the Civil War. During the war both the North and South imported Enfields. This specimen has the British crown and a U.S. Eagle over it. These arms may go for $250.00 to $450.00.

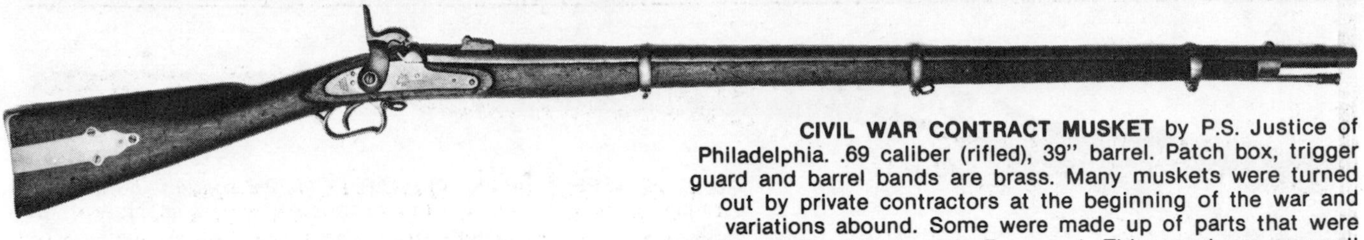

CIVIL WAR CONTRACT MUSKET by P.S. Justice of Philadelphia. .69 caliber (rifled), 39" barrel. Patch box, trigger guard and barrel bands are brass. Many muskets were turned out by private contractors at the beginning of the war and variations abound. Some were made up of parts that were available at the time (mostly European). This specimen may sell for $350.00 to $600.00.

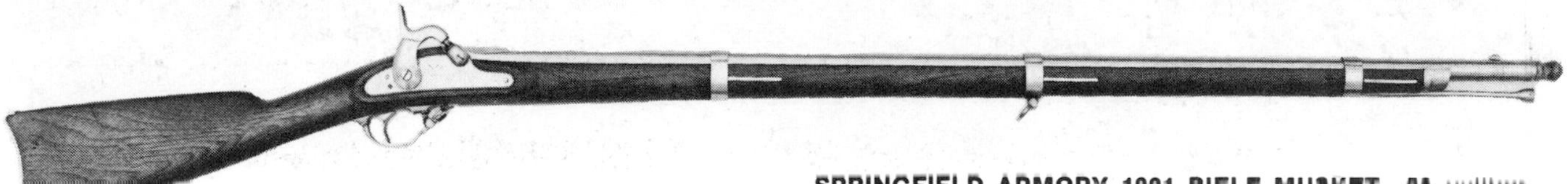

SPRINGFIELD ARMORY 1861 RIFLE MUSKET. .58 caliber, muzzle loading. Produced from 1861 to 1863, this was the most commonly used musket during the Civil War. Over 265,000 were made. These weapons, once quite common, are now increasing in price. Depending on condition, one may find examples for $350.00 to $700.00.

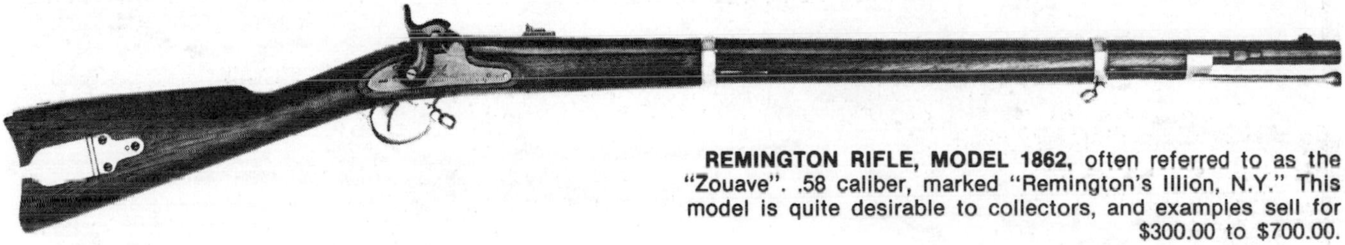

REMINGTON RIFLE, MODEL 1862, often referred to as the "Zouave". .58 caliber, marked "Remington's Illion, N.Y." This model is quite desirable to collectors, and examples sell for $300.00 to $700.00.

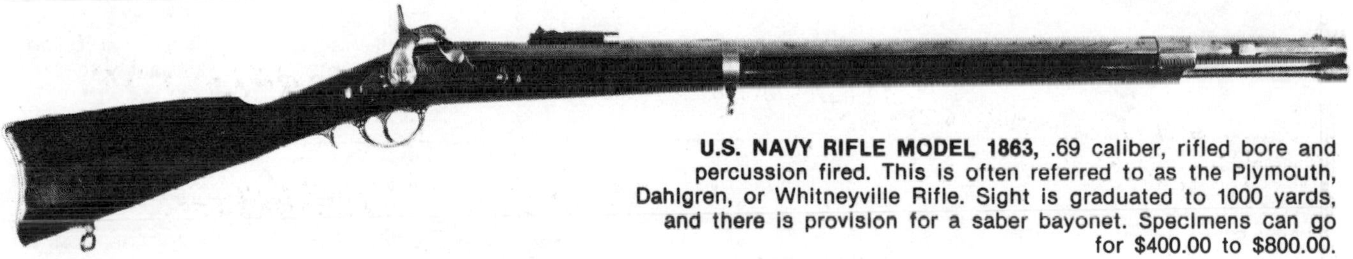

U.S. NAVY RIFLE MODEL 1863, .69 caliber, rifled bore and percussion fired. This is often referred to as the Plymouth, Dahlgren, or Whitneyville Rifle. Sight is graduated to 1000 yards, and there is provision for a saber bayonet. Specimens can go for $400.00 to $800.00.

CONFEDERATE HALL CONVERSION This has been converted into a muzzleloader by the use of an entirely new barrel and lock system. Most of the Confederate Hall conversions simply involved welding shut the action. This specimen is quite rare with prices falling into the $1500.00 to $3000.00 range.

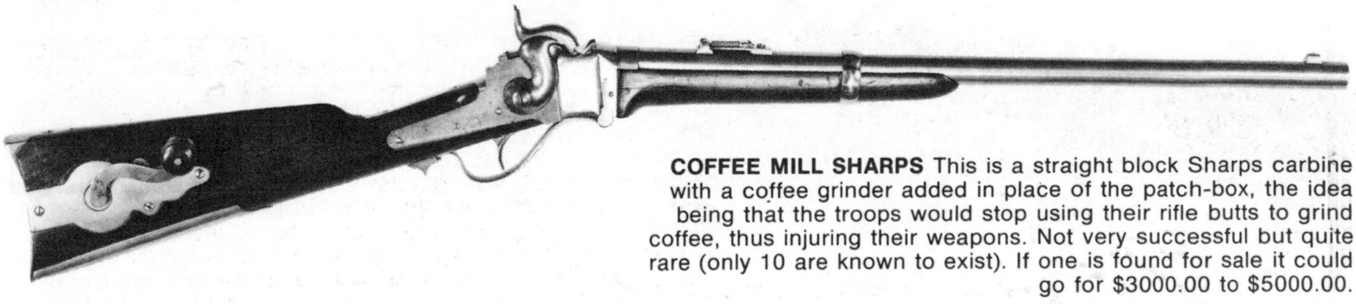

COFFEE MILL SHARPS This is a straight block Sharps carbine with a coffee grinder added in place of the patch-box, the idea being that the troops would stop using their rifle butts to grind coffee, thus injuring their weapons. Not very successful but quite rare (only 10 are known to exist). If one is found for sale it could go for $3000.00 to $5000.00.

SHARPS RIFLE, CIVIL WAR PATTERN Straight breech, .54 caliber. This arm used a linen cartridge that was sheared off by the breech when it was closed, thus exposing the powder. The breech assembly contained a hollow cavity over which a metal gas ring fit. When the charge was fired, the expanding gas forced the ring forward forming a tight gas seal. This arm may go for $400.00 to $800.00.

LINDSAY DOUBLE MUSKET, Model 1863, .58 caliber, marked "Lindsay Patent Oct. 9, 1860." This weapon was designed with two hammers, and one barrel. Two charges were loaded on top of one another and in theory the two percussion caps would set them off, one at a time. It was not very successful. These arms may command $300.00 to $500.00.

SMITH CARBINE. This weapon fired a hard-rubber cartridge by a separate percussion cap. The arm has a breakopen, tilt-down barrel that is activated by a lever inside the trigger guard. These weapons are very well made. Approximately 30,000 were produced during the Civil War. Smith carbines may go for $250.00 to $475.00.

MAYNARD PERCUSSION CARBINE. Ths weapon was introduced into U.S. service in the late 1850's, and at the outbreak of the war in 1861 it was put into mass production. It uses a brass cartridge that is identical in appearance to modern rimmed types, except that it uses a separate percussion cap. Many versions were produced. They may be found for $200.00 to $400.00.

SPENCER CARBINE, .52 caliber. This is commonly referred to as the "Indian Model." It was used by the cavalry in the Indian campaigns after the Civil War. This model is distinguished by the addition of the Stabler cut-off forward of the trigger. The General Staff was still worried about the expenditure of ammunition, thus the reason for the cut-off. These arms may go for $200.00 to $350.00 on today's market.

MERRILL CARBINE, .56 caliber, 20" barrel. This weapon was designed for a combustible cartridge, fired by a percussion cap. A lever that folds flat on the top of the barrel exposes the loading chamber when lifted and pulled back. Manufactured in Baltimore. These arms can command $250.00 to $450.00.

MAYNARD CARBINE, .50 caliber, 19" barrel. Weight 6½ lbs. Lever action trigger guard tilts barrel up for loading. The cartridge is a wide-rimmed, brass-cased unit that except for the absence of a primer, is identical to a modern rimmed cartridge. This weapon saw extensive use during the Civl War. Examples may be found for $200.00 to $400.00.

BURNSIDE CARBINE, .54 caliber, 21" barrel. This weapon incorporates an unusual dropping breech mechanism that tilts up like the Hall. It uses a reverse-taper cartridge fired by a percussion cap. It was quite popular with the Federal cavalry. Examples may be found for $250.00 to $500.00.

GALLAGHER CARBINE, .50 caliber, 22" barrel. This weapon uses a special brass-foil cartridge, fired by a standard musket cap. When the lever was depressed the barrel moved forward and tips up for loading. Examples may be found for $200.00 upwards to $450.00.

U.S. EXPERIMENTAL breechloading alteration of Model 1855 musket. Caliber has been reduced from .58 caliber to .50 by the addition of a liner with ratchet type rifling. The breech and receiver are milled out of a single block of steel, and has a hinged breechblock that opens to the right for loading. Internal hammer. When found these arms may command at least $600.00.

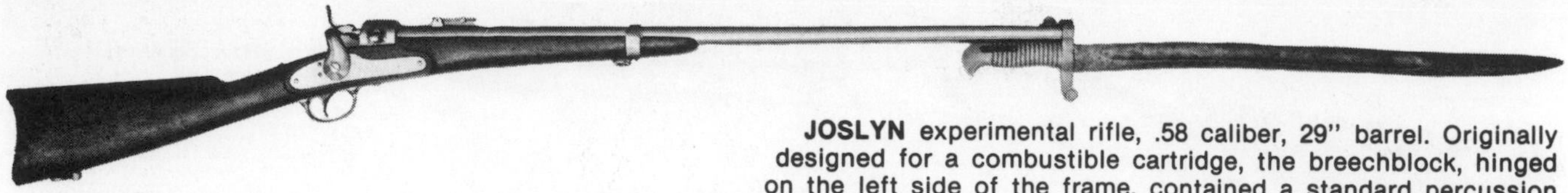

JOSLYN experimental rifle, .58 caliber, 29" barrel. Originally designed for a combustible cartridge, the breechblock, hinged on the left side of the frame, contained a standard percussion nipple. The design was changed at the beginning of the Civil War to metallic cartridge. This involved modifying the breechblock for a firing pin and extractor. This weapon may go for $250.00 to $500.00.

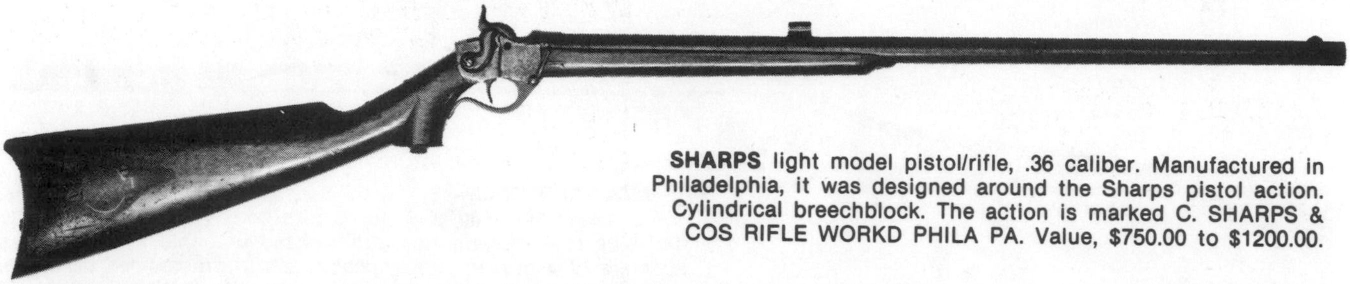

SHARPS light model pistol/rifle, .36 caliber. Manufactured in Philadelphia, it was designed around the Sharps pistol action. Cylindrical breechblock. The action is marked C. SHARPS & COS RIFLE WORKD PHILA PA. Value, $750.00 to $1200.00.

MERRILL, breech-loading system for the alteration of the U.S. 1821 musket. Tail of the breechblock folds down and locks into the comb. This arm was made for official army tests, but was never adopted. One of a kind. Such experimental specimens may sell for upwards of $800.00.

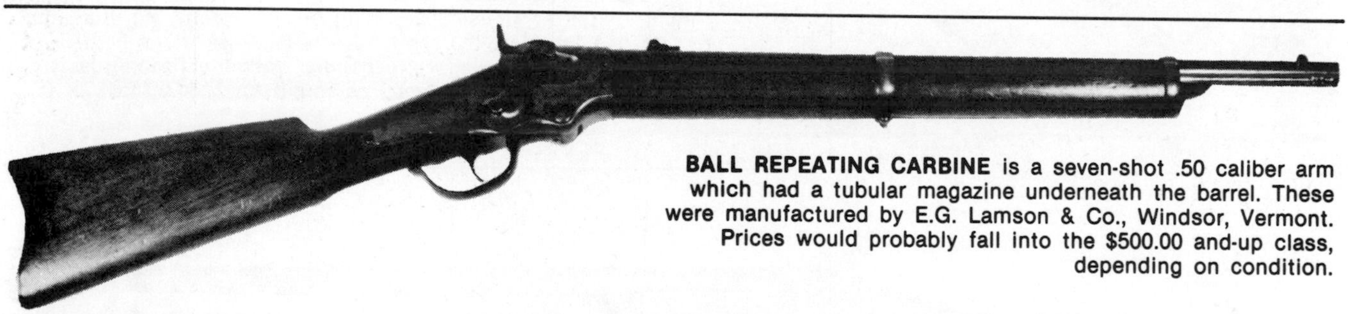

BALL REPEATING CARBINE is a seven-shot .50 caliber arm which had a tubular magazine underneath the barrel. These were manufactured by E.G. Lamson & Co., Windsor, Vermont. Prices would probably fall into the $500.00 and-up class, depending on condition.

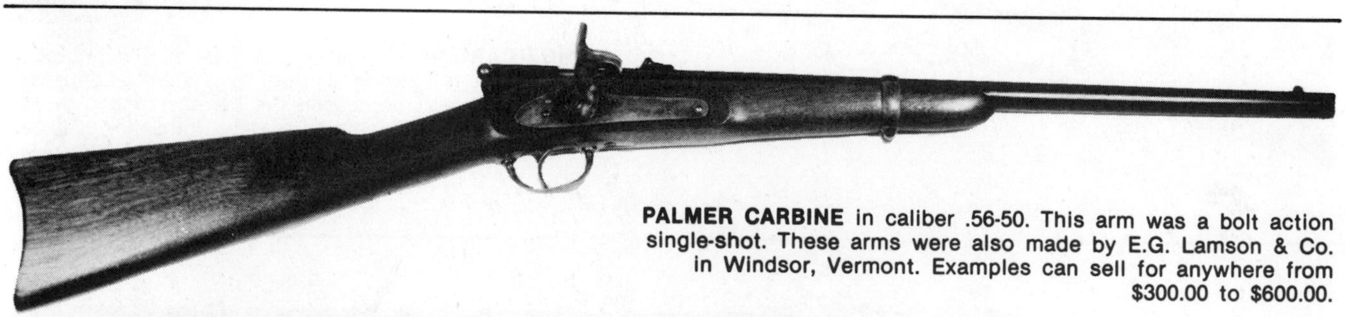

PALMER CARBINE in caliber .56-50. This arm was a bolt action single-shot. These arms were also made by E.G. Lamson & Co. in Windsor, Vermont. Examples can sell for anywhere from $300.00 to $600.00.

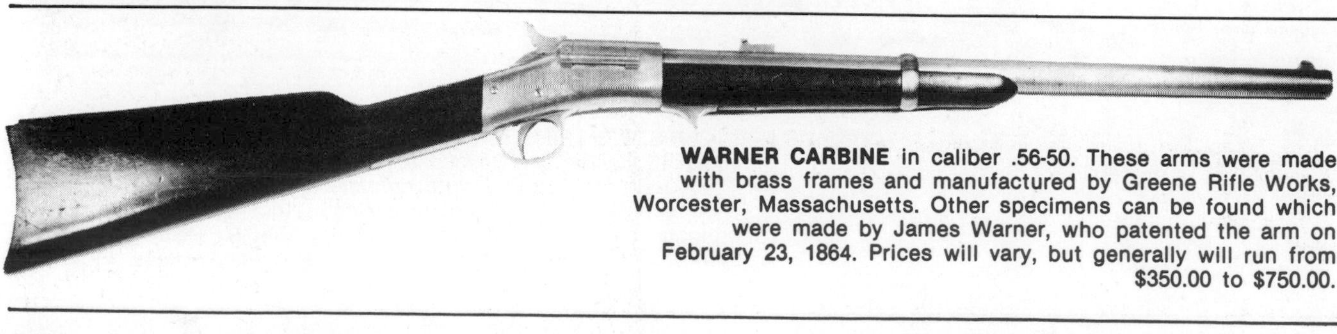

WARNER CARBINE in caliber .56-50. These arms were made with brass frames and manufactured by Greene Rifle Works, Worcester, Massachusetts. Other specimens can be found which were made by James Warner, who patented the arm on February 23, 1864. Prices will vary, but generally will run from $350.00 to $750.00.

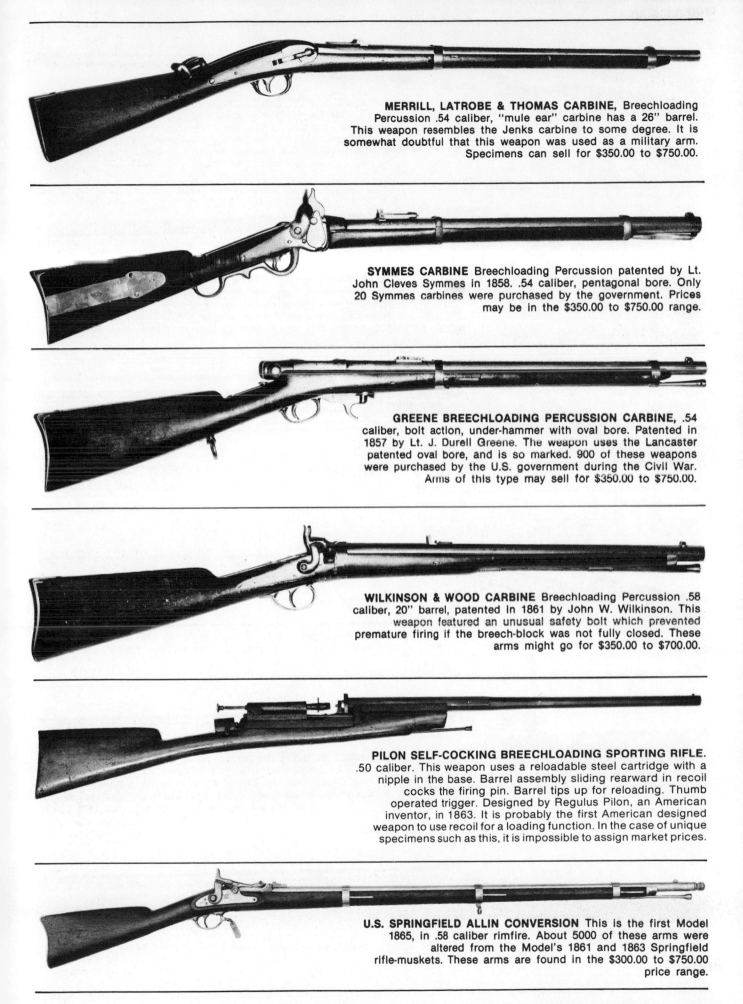

MERRILL, LATROBE & THOMAS CARBINE, Breechloading Percussion .54 caliber, "mule ear" carbine has a 26" barrel. This weapon resembles the Jenks carbine to some degree. It is somewhat doubtful that this weapon was used as a military arm. Specimens can sell for $350.00 to $750.00.

SYMMES CARBINE Breechloading Percussion patented by Lt. John Cleves Symmes in 1858. .54 caliber, pentagonal bore. Only 20 Symmes carbines were purchased by the government. Prices may be in the $350.00 to $750.00 range.

GREENE BREECHLOADING PERCUSSION CARBINE, .54 caliber, bolt action, under-hammer with oval bore. Patented in 1857 by Lt. J. Durell Greene. The weapon uses the Lancaster patented oval bore, and is so marked. 900 of these weapons were purchased by the U.S. government during the Civil War. Arms of this type may sell for $350.00 to $750.00.

WILKINSON & WOOD CARBINE Breechloading Percussion .58 caliber, 20" barrel, patented in 1861 by John W. Wilkinson. This weapon featured an unusual safety bolt which prevented premature firing if the breech-block was not fully closed. These arms might go for $350.00 to $700.00.

PILON SELF-COCKING BREECHLOADING SPORTING RIFLE. .50 caliber. This weapon uses a reloadable steel cartridge with a nipple in the base. Barrel assembly sliding rearward in recoil cocks the firing pin. Barrel tips up for reloading. Thumb operated trigger. Designed by Regulus Pilon, an American inventor, in 1863. It is probably the first American designed weapon to use recoil for a loading function. In the case of unique specimens such as this, it is impossible to assign market prices.

U.S. SPRINGFIELD ALLIN CONVERSION This is the first Model 1865, in .58 caliber rimfire. About 5000 of these arms were altered from the Model's 1861 and 1863 Springfield rifle-muskets. These arms are found in the $300.00 to $750.00 price range.

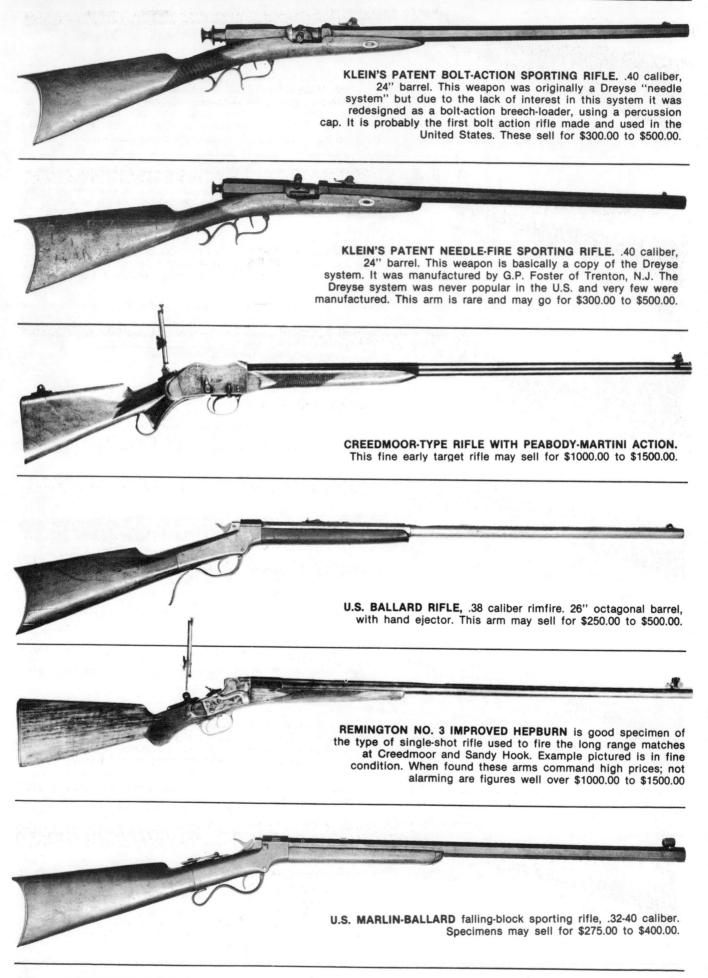

KLEIN'S PATENT BOLT-ACTION SPORTING RIFLE. .40 caliber, 24" barrel. This weapon was originally a Dreyse "needle system" but due to the lack of interest in this system it was redesigned as a bolt-action breech-loader, using a percussion cap. It is probably the first bolt action rifle made and used in the United States. These sell for $300.00 to $500.00.

KLEIN'S PATENT NEEDLE-FIRE SPORTING RIFLE. .40 caliber, 24" barrel. This weapon is basically a copy of the Dreyse system. It was manufactured by G.P. Foster of Trenton, N.J. The Dreyse system was never popular in the U.S. and very few were manufactured. This arm is rare and may go for $300.00 to $500.00.

CREEDMOOR-TYPE RIFLE WITH PEABODY-MARTINI ACTION. This fine early target rifle may sell for $1000.00 to $1500.00.

U.S. BALLARD RIFLE, .38 caliber rimfire. 26" octagonal barrel, with hand ejector. This arm may sell for $250.00 to $500.00.

REMINGTON NO. 3 IMPROVED HEPBURN is good specimen of the type of single-shot rifle used to fire the long range matches at Creedmoor and Sandy Hook. Example pictured is in fine condition. When found these arms command high prices; not alarming are figures well over $1000.00 to $1500.00

U.S. MARLIN-BALLARD falling-block sporting rifle, .32-40 caliber. Specimens may sell for $275.00 to $400.00.

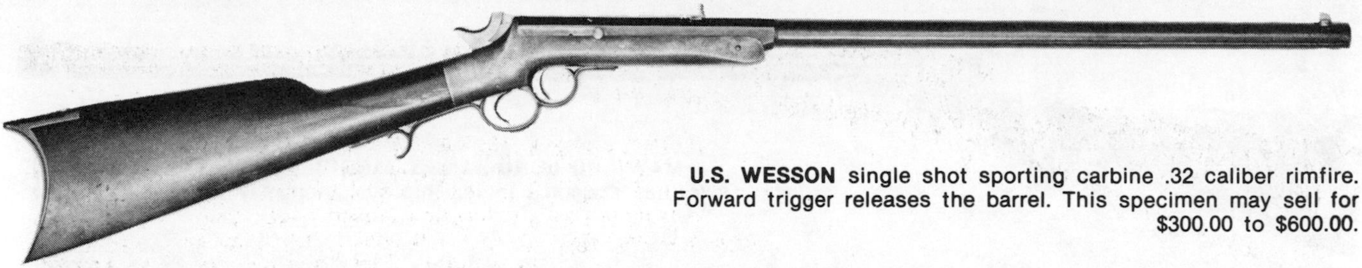

U.S. WESSON single shot sporting carbine .32 caliber rimfire. Forward trigger releases the barrel. This specimen may sell for $300.00 to $600.00.

SPENCER SPORTING CARBINE is a very early piece with a frame smaller than normal. Such unusual specimens, when found in fine condition command premium prices.

REMINGTON HEPBURN NO. 3 SPORTING RIFLE. This arm may sell for $500.00 to $700.00.

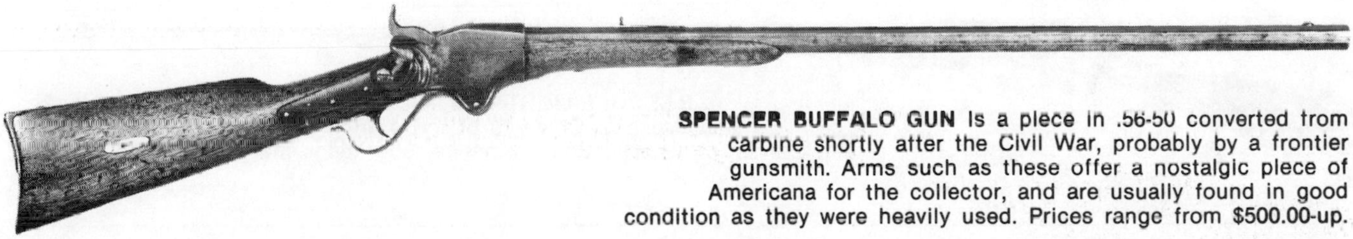

SPENCER BUFFALO GUN is a piece in .56-50 converted from carbine shortly after the Civil War, probably by a frontier gunsmith. Arms such as these offer a nostalgic piece of Americana for the collector, and are usually found in good condition as they were heavily used. Prices range from $500.00-up.

BUFFALO SHARPS in caliber .45/70 were massively built hunting rifles which helped to open the frontier. The rifles in .45/70 were most popular as they could use the "Army" cartridge in a pinch. Most of these are well used, but in spite of their worn condition can still be fired with a modicum of accuracy. Specimens bring around $600.00 and up.

WINCHESTER M1886 was an arm rated as a true workhorse of the outdoorsman. It was offered in a host of calibers. The specimen pictured is in .45/70, and is in worn, but excellent mechanical condition. These arms, when found in calibers still available, demand (and get) some high prices. Ordinary specimens sell for from $250.00 to $450.00.

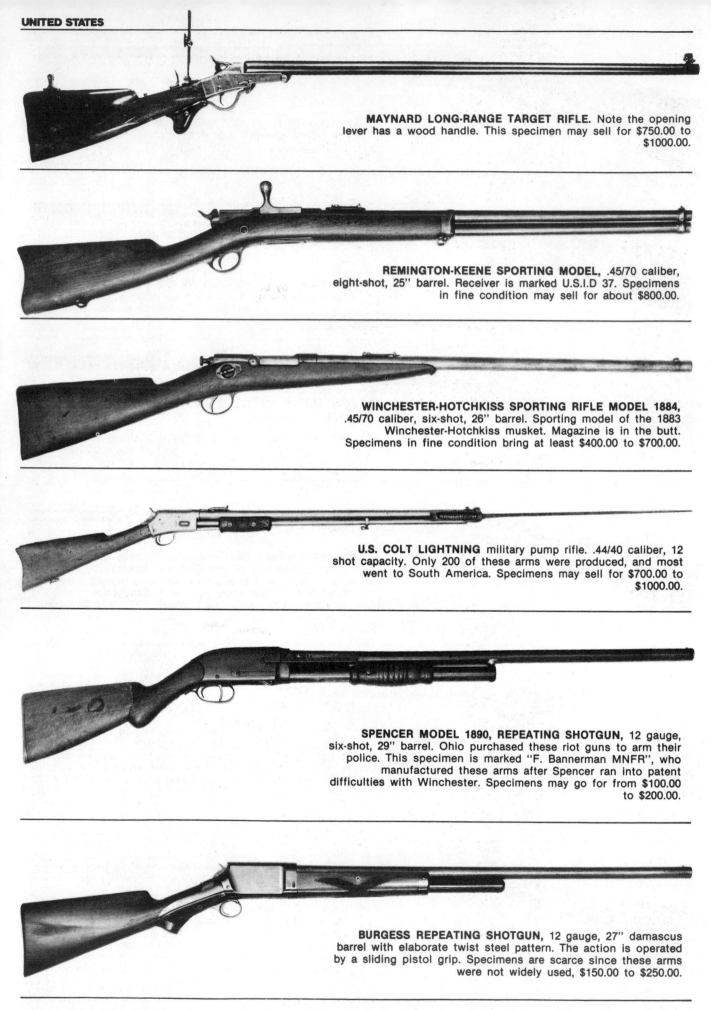

MAYNARD LONG-RANGE TARGET RIFLE. Note the opening lever has a wood handle. This specimen may sell for $750.00 to $1000.00.

REMINGTON-KEENE SPORTING MODEL, .45/70 caliber, eight-shot, 25" barrel. Receiver is marked U.S.I.D 37. Specimens in fine condition may sell for about $800.00.

WINCHESTER-HOTCHKISS SPORTING RIFLE MODEL 1884, .45/70 caliber, six-shot, 26" barrel. Sporting model of the 1883 Winchester-Hotchkiss musket. Magazine is in the butt. Specimens in fine condition bring at least $400.00 to $700.00.

U.S. COLT LIGHTNING military pump rifle. .44/40 caliber, 12 shot capacity. Only 200 of these arms were produced, and most went to South America. Specimens may sell for $700.00 to $1000.00.

SPENCER MODEL 1890, REPEATING SHOTGUN, 12 gauge, six-shot, 29" barrel. Ohio purchased these riot guns to arm their police. This specimen is marked "F. Bannerman MNFR", who manufactured these arms after Spencer ran into patent difficulties with Winchester. Specimens may go for from $100.00 to $200.00.

BURGESS REPEATING SHOTGUN, 12 gauge, 27" damascus barrel with elaborate twist steel pattern. The action is operated by a sliding pistol grip. Specimens are scarce since these arms were not widely used, $150.00 to $250.00.

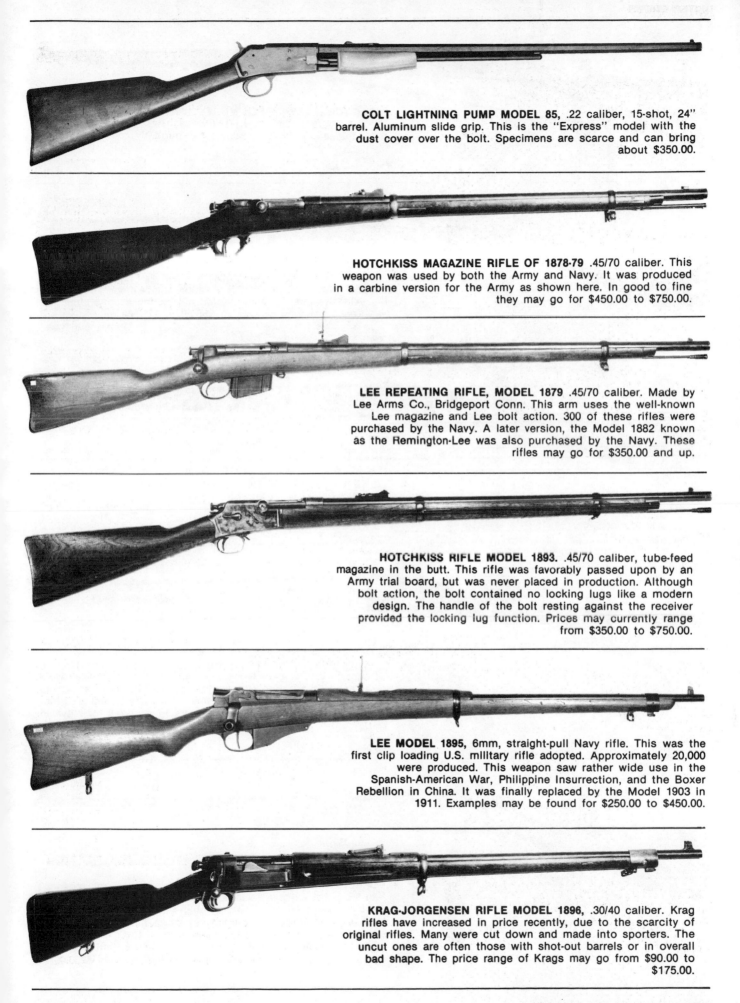

COLT LIGHTNING PUMP MODEL 85, .22 caliber, 15-shot, 24" barrel. Aluminum slide grip. This is the "Express" model with the dust cover over the bolt. Specimens are scarce and can bring about $350.00.

HOTCHKISS MAGAZINE RIFLE OF 1878-79 .45/70 caliber. This weapon was used by both the Army and Navy. It was produced in a carbine version for the Army as shown here. In good to fine they may go for $450.00 to $750.00.

LEE REPEATING RIFLE, MODEL 1879 .45/70 caliber. Made by Lee Arms Co., Bridgeport Conn. This arm uses the well-known Lee magazine and Lee bolt action. 300 of these rifles were purchased by the Navy. A later version, the Model 1882 known as the Remington-Lee was also purchased by the Navy. These rifles may go for $350.00 and up.

HOTCHKISS RIFLE MODEL 1893. .45/70 caliber, tube-feed magazine in the butt. This rifle was favorably passed upon by an Army trial board, but was never placed in production. Although bolt action, the bolt contained no locking lugs like a modern design. The handle of the bolt resting against the receiver provided the locking lug function. Prices may currently range from $350.00 to $750.00.

LEE MODEL 1895, 6mm, straight-pull Navy rifle. This was the first clip loading U.S. military rifle adopted. Approximately 20,000 were produced. This weapon saw rather wide use in the Spanish-American War, Philippine Insurrection, and the Boxer Rebellion in China. It was finally replaced by the Model 1903 in 1911. Examples may be found for $250.00 to $450.00.

KRAG-JORGENSEN RIFLE MODEL 1896, .30/40 caliber. Krag rifles have increased in price recently, due to the scarcity of original rifles. Many were cut down and made into sporters. The uncut ones are often those with shot-out barrels or in overall bad shape. The price range of Krags may go from $90.00 to $175.00.

KRAG-JORGENSEN RIFLE MODEL 1898 .30/40 caliber, with the 1901 rear sight. This weapon was modified, (arsenal reconditioned) in 1902. Examples can currently command $90.00 to $175.00.

SPRINGFIELD M1903, .30/06 caliber, 24" barrel. The basic model 1903 used in WW1 is a rather scarce item, because of the extensive modifications carried out on these arms after the war. These weapons can go for $65.00 to $250.00 depending on make and type.

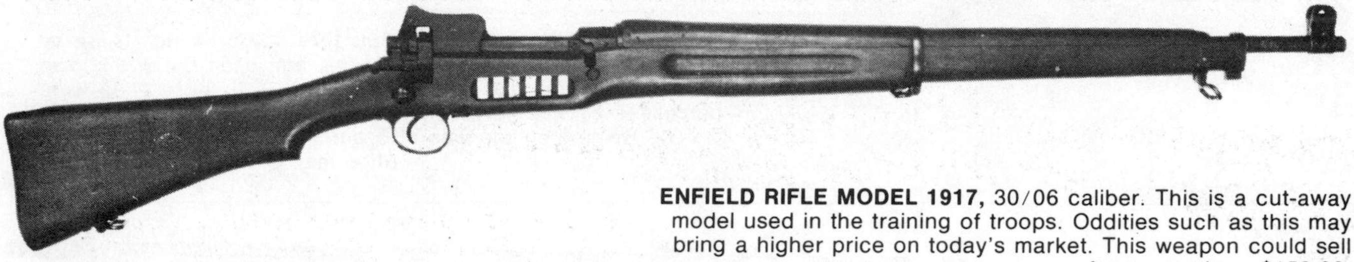

ENFIELD RIFLE MODEL 1917, 30/06 caliber. This is a cut-away model used in the training of troops. Oddities such as this may bring a higher price on today's market. This weapon could sell for as much as $150.00.

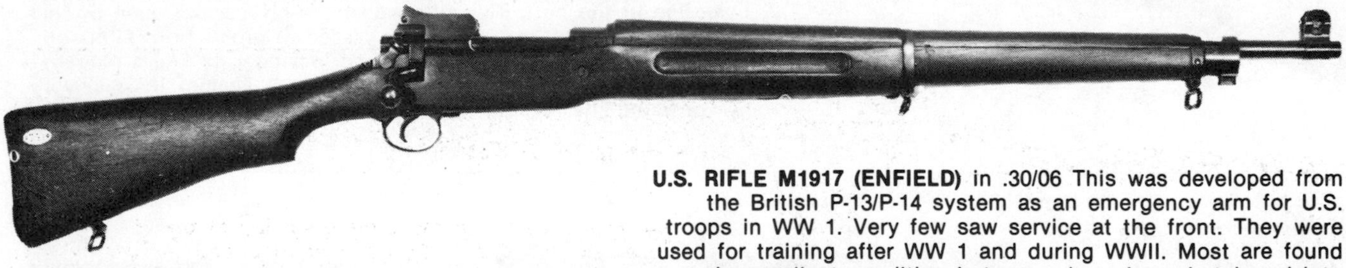

U.S. RIFLE M1917 (ENFIELD) in .30/06 This was developed from the British P-13/P-14 system as an emergency arm for U.S. troops in WW 1. Very few saw service at the front. They were used for training after WW 1 and during WWII. Most are found in excellent condition but many have been butchered into sporters. An excellent to mint uncut version may sell for between $70.00 to $100.00.

SPRINGFIELD .22 M2 in .22 Long Rifle caliber. First appearing in 1922 these finely made .22 trainers were quickly praised by the Army. These arms went through various modifications and are known by model designation changes. The most common of the .22 Springfields is the last modification, the M2. Prices vary the first model, the 1922 may bring $350.00 in mint shape the M2s could bring from $175.00 to $250.00 and up.

SPRINGFIELD MODEL 1903A4, This the sniper version of the '03 rifle. A full pistol grip stock was fitted, the bolt handle cut away to clear the M73B1 scope. No iron sights were fitted. The M82 scope by Lyman was also fitted. When available this goes for $175.00 to $250.00.

GARAND RIFLE, .30/06 caliber. Eight-shot enbloc clip loading. The standard weapon of U.S. troops in WWII and Korea. Garands have recently started to go up in price, which may vary from $175.00 to $300.00 depending on condition.

JOHNSON SEMIAUTOMATIC RIFLE, .30/06 caliber, hesitation-locked breech, firing from a closed bolt. Barrel partially recoils to begin unlocking phase. 10-round rotary magazine. The Johnson saw limited service as a front-line weapon in WWII. It was also adopted by the Dutch for use in the East Indies. Many were rebarreled in different calibers after the war. Prices may range from $150.00 to $250.00.

U.S. M14, 7.62mm. A modernized version of the M1 rifle. This weapon has a 20-round box magazine, and the gas cylinder shortened. Built in full-automatic versions as well as semi-automatic, the M14 cannot be owned by civilians. Several versions using M1 cutdown receivers have been available, selling for $300.00 and up.

UNION OF SOVIET SOCIALIST REPUBLICS

RUSSIAN FLINTLOCK probably military. The lock is marked "Tula 1841," .70 caliber, 33½" barrel dated 1842 on the top in front of the rear sight. Bright-metal finish, brass butt plate and trigger guard. Ramrod is completely concealed within the stock. Note the sling escutcheons, and narrow barrel bands. Flintlock Russian weapons are quite rare and this one could go for as much as $600.00

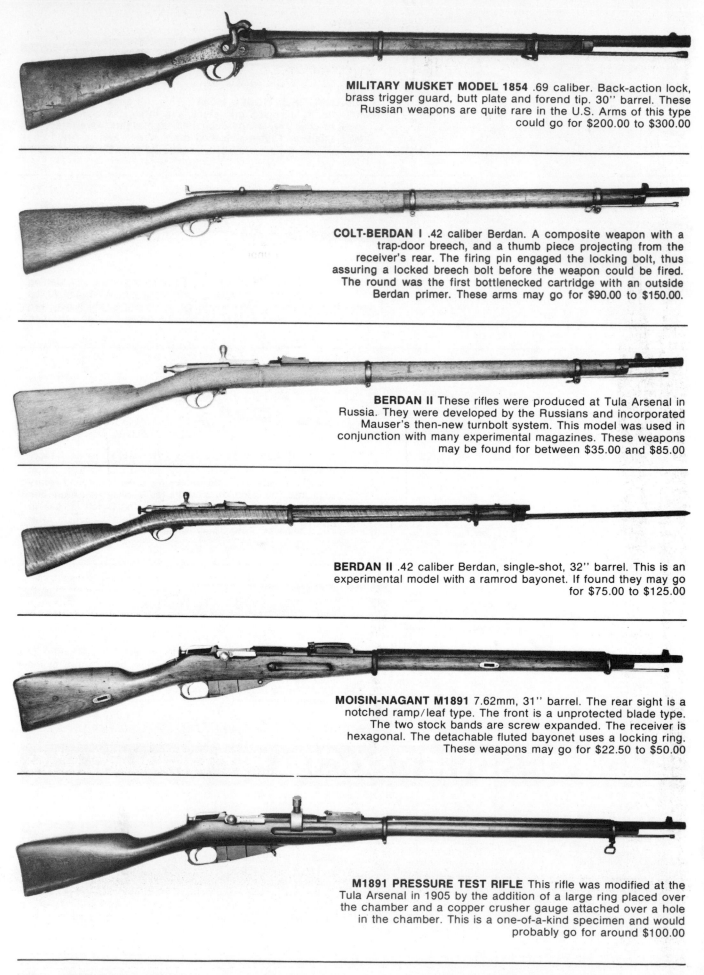

MILITARY MUSKET MODEL 1854 .69 caliber. Back-action lock, brass trigger guard, butt plate and forend tip. 30'' barrel. These Russian weapons are quite rare in the U.S. Arms of this type could go for $200.00 to $300.00

COLT-BERDAN I .42 caliber Berdan. A composite weapon with a trap-door breech, and a thumb piece projecting from the receiver's rear. The firing pin engaged the locking bolt, thus assuring a locked breech bolt before the weapon could be fired. The round was the first bottlenecked cartridge with an outside Berdan primer. These arms may go for $90.00 to $150.00.

BERDAN II These rifles were produced at Tula Arsenal in Russia. They were developed by the Russians and incorporated Mauser's then-new turnbolt system. This model was used in conjunction with many experimental magazines. These weapons may be found for between $35.00 and $85.00

BERDAN II .42 caliber Berdan, single-shot, 32'' barrel. This is an experimental model with a ramrod bayonet. If found they may go for $75.00 to $125.00

MOISIN-NAGANT M1891 7.62mm, 31'' barrel. The rear sight is a notched ramp/leaf type. The front is a unprotected blade type. The two stock bands are screw expanded. The receiver is hexagonal. The detachable fluted bayonet uses a locking ring. These weapons may go for $22.50 to $50.00

M1891 PRESSURE TEST RIFLE This rifle was modified at the Tula Arsenal in 1905 by the addition of a large ring placed over the chamber and a copper crusher gauge attached over a hole in the chamber. This is a one-of-a-kind specimen and would probably go for around $100.00

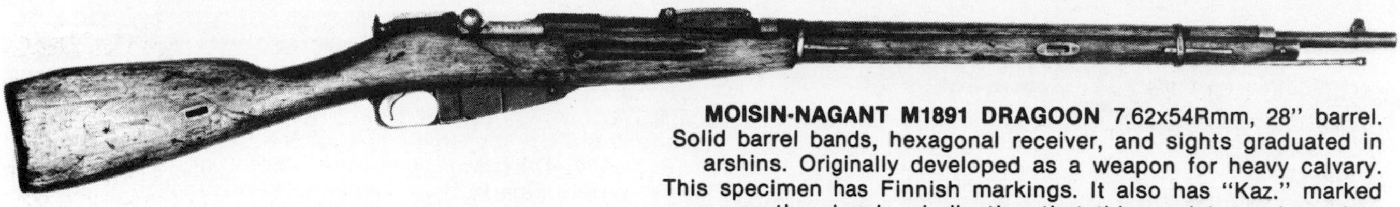

MOISIN-NAGANT M1891 DRAGOON 7.62x54Rmm, 28" barrel. Solid barrel bands, hexagonal receiver, and sights graduated in arshins. Originally developed as a weapon for heavy calvary. This specimen has Finnish markings. It also has "Kaz." marked on the chamber indicating that this model was issued to Cossack units. This model may be found for $30.00 to $50.00.

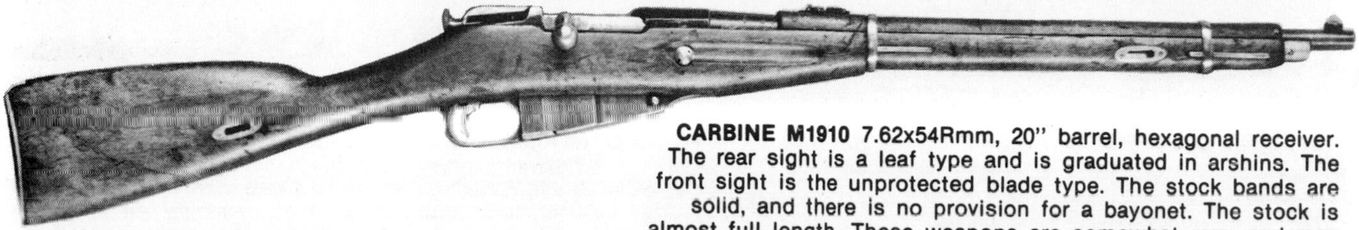

CARBINE M1910 7.62x54Rmm, 20" barrel, hexagonal receiver. The rear sight is a leaf type and is graduated in arshins. The front sight is the unprotected blade type. The stock bands are solid, and there is no provision for a bayonet. The stock is almost full length. These weapons are somewhat rare, and may go for $60.00 to $80.00.

M1938 CARBINE 7.62x54Rmm, 20" barrel. Hooded front sight mounted on a barrel band, graduated from 100 to 1000 meters. Stock bands are held by retaining springs. There is no provision for a bayonet. These arms may be found for $30.00 to $45.00

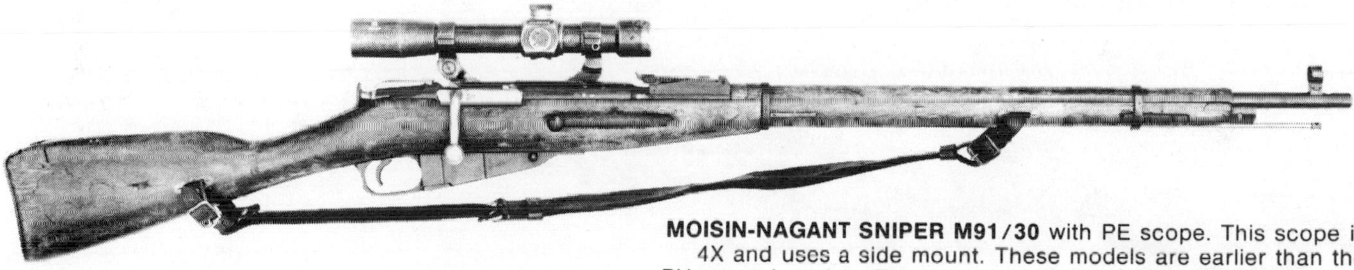

MOISIN-NAGANT SNIPER M91/30 with PE scope. This scope is 4X and uses a side mount. These models are earlier than the PU-scoped models. There are two mount variations. When found these weapons may go for $200.00 to $250.00

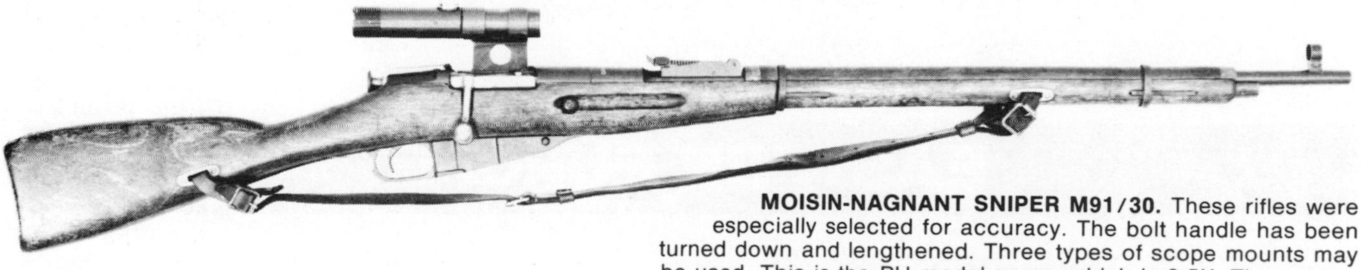

MOISIN-NAGNANT SNIPER M91/30. These rifles were especially selected for accuracy. The bolt handle has been turned down and lengthened. Three types of scope mounts may be used. This is the PU model scope which is 3.5X. The scopes should be numbered to the arms. These weapons are somewhat rare and could go for $175.00 to $225.00.

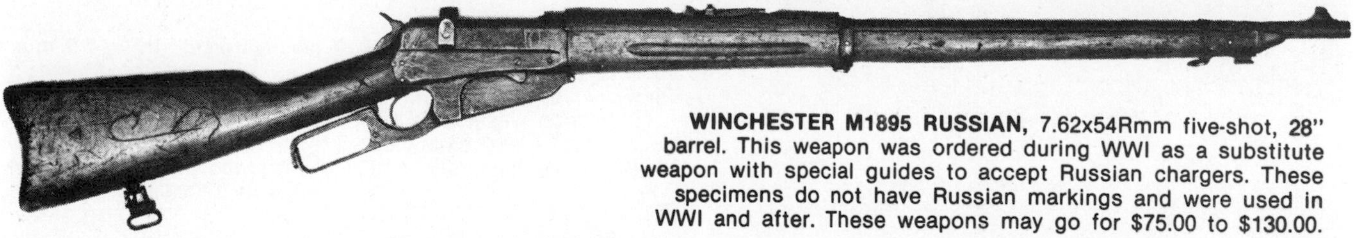

WINCHESTER M1895 RUSSIAN, 7.62x54Rmm five-shot, 28" barrel. This weapon was ordered during WWI as a substitute weapon with special guides to accept Russian chargers. These specimens do not have Russian markings and were used in WWI and after. These weapons may go for $75.00 to $130.00.

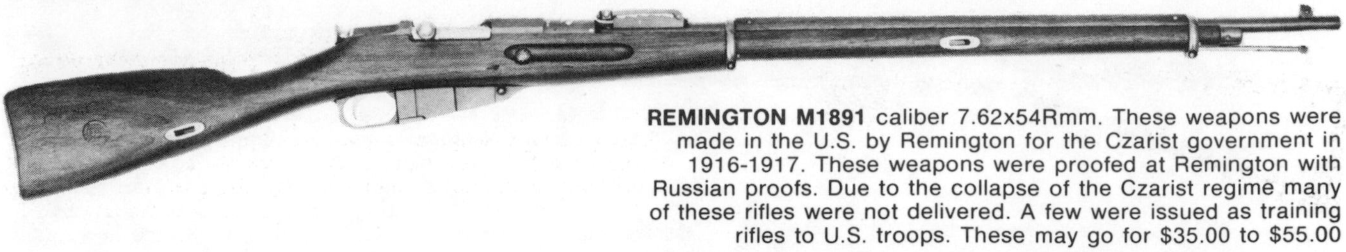

REMINGTON M1891 caliber 7.62x54Rmm. These weapons were made in the U.S. by Remington for the Czarist government in 1916-1917. These weapons were proofed at Remington with Russian proofs. Due to the collapse of the Czarist regime many of these rifles were not delivered. A few were issued as training rifles to U.S. troops. These may go for $35.00 to $55.00

TOKAREV MODEL 1938 semiautomatic, gas operated action in the 7.62mm rimmed cartridge caliber. 10-shot magazine, two-piece stock, cleaning rod inletted into right side of stock. This was the first model of the Tokarev series but was not successful and was replaced by the M1940 Tokarev. Most specimens encountered are in good condition, prices are from $75.00 to $110.00.

TOKAREV M1940 7.62mm, 24.6" barrel, semiautomatic. 10-shot magazine box. These weapons are well made, although they proved to be somewhat prone to breakage when in military use. The action is quite similar to the Belgian FN. These weapons may be found for $70.00 to $100.00.

RUSSIAN SKS 7.62x39 M43 cartridge, 20" barrel, gas-operated semi-automatic, with a non-detachable box clip holding 10 rounds. The Soviets refer to this weapon as a carbine because of its barrel length. It is not intended to be a replacement for the pistol as with the U.S. carbine. Prices currently fluctuate from $90.00 to $200.00.

EASTERN EUROPE

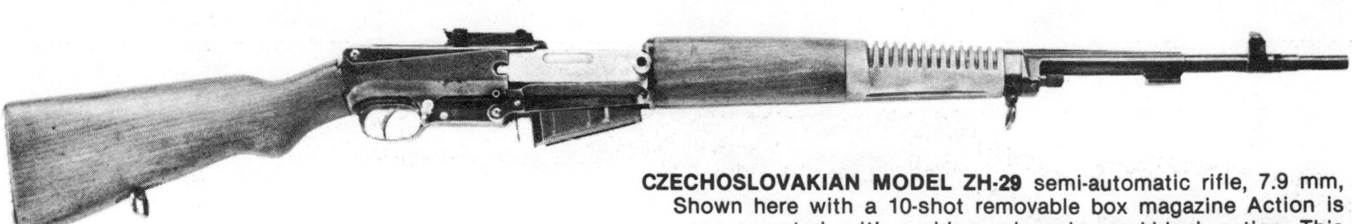

CZECHOSLOVAKIAN MODEL ZH-29 semi-automatic rifle, 7.9 mm, Shown here with a 10-shot removable box magazine Action is gas operated, with a side-moving claw-and-block action. This weapon was extensively tested abroad. It was issued in Czechoslovakia and examples with various crests are reported. This weapon is quite rare in this country and prices may go as high as $800.00 to $1000.00.

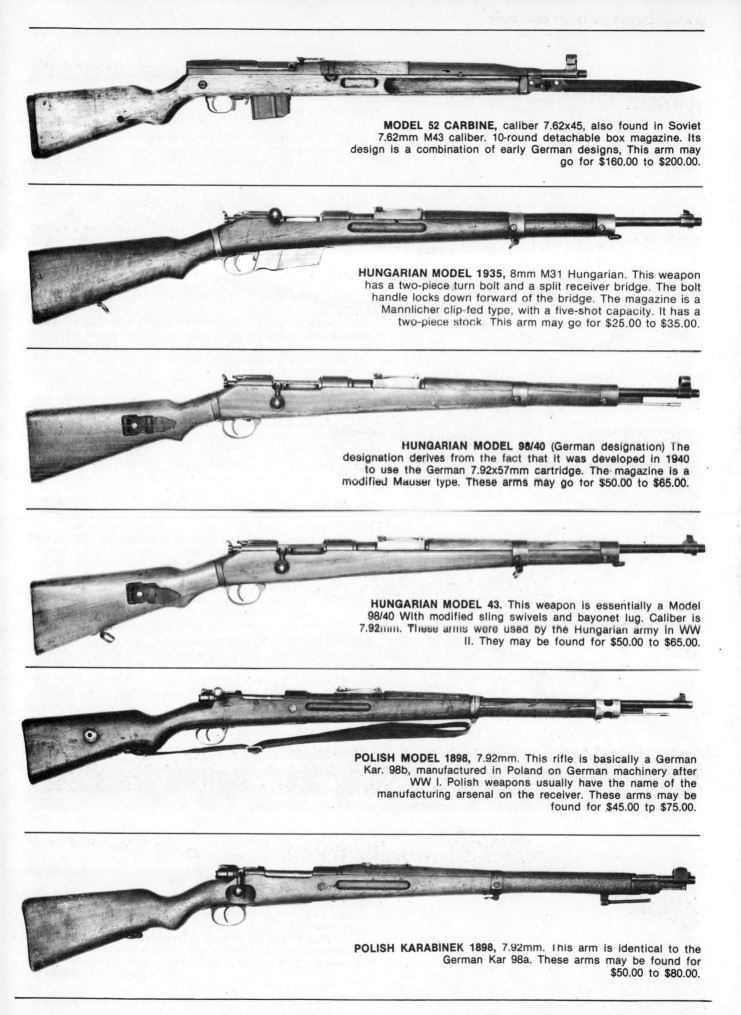

MODEL 52 CARBINE, caliber 7.62x45, also found in Soviet 7.62mm M43 caliber. 10-round detachable box magazine. Its design is a combination of early German designs, This arm may go for $160.00 to $200.00.

HUNGARIAN MODEL 1935, 8mm M31 Hungarian. This weapon has a two-piece turn bolt and a split receiver bridge. The bolt handle locks down forward of the bridge. The magazine is a Mannlicher clip-fed type, with a five-shot capacity. It has a two-piece stock. This arm may go for $25.00 to $35.00.

HUNGARIAN MODEL 98/40 (German designation) The designation derives from the fact that it was developed in 1940 to use the German 7.92x57mm cartridge. The magazine is a modified Mauser type. These arms may go for $50.00 to $65.00.

HUNGARIAN MODEL 43. This weapon is essentially a Model 98/40 With modified sling swivels and bayonet lug. Caliber is 7.92mm. These arms were used by the Hungarian army in WW II. They may be found for $50.00 to $65.00.

POLISH MODEL 1898, 7.92mm. This rifle is basically a German Kar. 98b, manufactured in Poland on German machinery after WW I. Polish weapons usually have the name of the manufacturing arsenal on the receiver. These arms may be found for $45.00 tp $75.00.

POLISH KARABINEK 1898, 7.92mm. This arm is identical to the German Kar 98a. These arms may be found for $50.00 to $80.00.

POLISH KARABINER 29, 7.92mm. This arm is a minor variant of the Czech Model 24. The sights are graduated from 300 to 2000 meters. This arm may go for $35.00 to $50.00.

ROMANIAN MAUSER, 7.92mm. This arm is essentially a Czech Model 24, with the crest of King Carol on the receiver. Note the front sight guard, which is usually missing from examples found in the U.S. This specimen may be found for $40.00 to $60.00.

YUGOSLAVIAN MODEL 1924 MAUSER SHORT RIFLE, for mounted troops. 7.92mm, 24" barrel. This Mauser action features a cocking piece cut so that the safety can be "on" with the cocking piece in the fired position, a design peculiar to this model. Coat of arms appears on the receiver. These weapons may be found for $40.00 to $60.00.

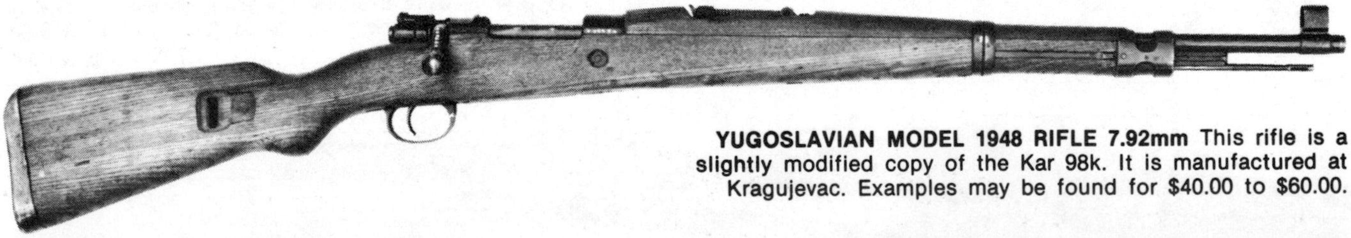

YUGOSLAVIAN MODEL 1948 RIFLE 7.92mm This rifle is a slightly modified copy of the Kar 98k. It is manufactured at Kragujevac. Examples may be found for $40.00 to $60.00.

MIDDLE EAST

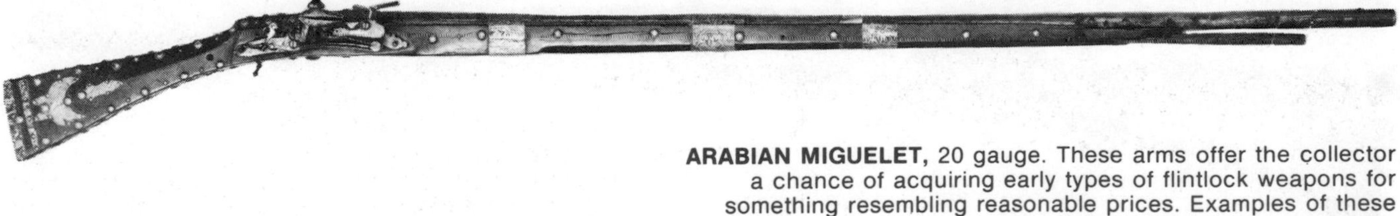

ARABIAN MIGUELET, 20 gauge. These arms offer the collector a chance of acquiring early types of flintlock weapons for something resembling reasonable prices. Examples of these arms may go for $65.00 to $150.00.

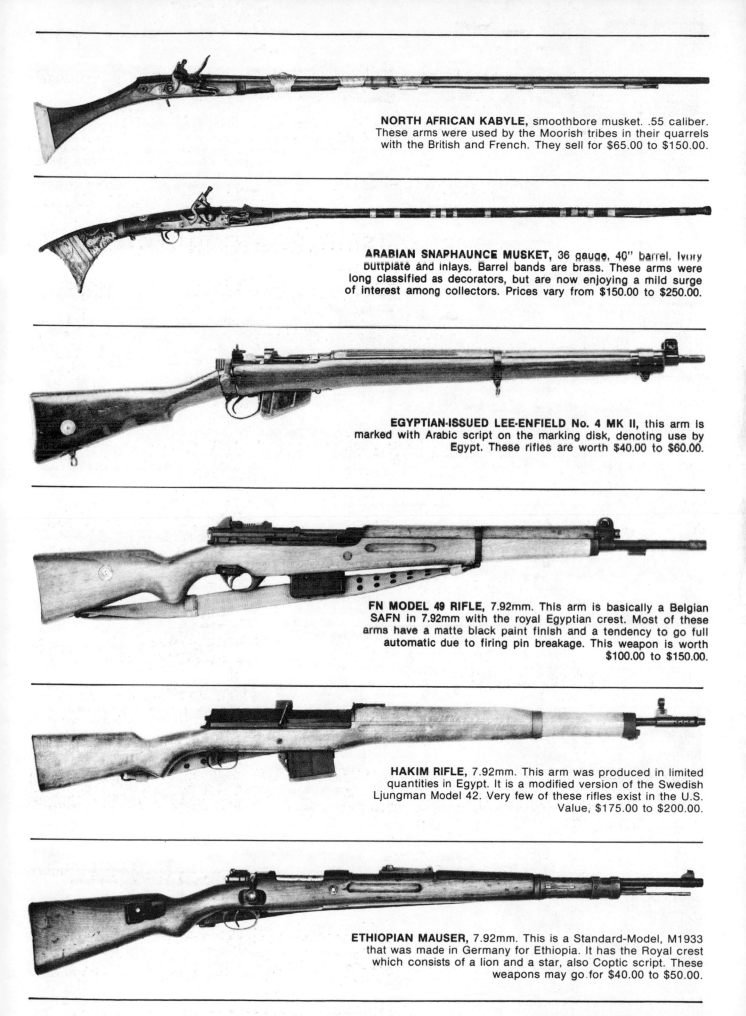

NORTH AFRICAN KABYLE, smoothbore musket. .55 caliber. These arms were used by the Moorish tribes in their quarrels with the British and French. They sell for $65.00 to $150.00.

ARABIAN SNAPHAUNCE MUSKET, 36 gauge, 40" barrel. Ivory buttplate and inlays. Barrel bands are brass. These arms were long classified as decorators, but are now enjoying a mild surge of interest among collectors. Prices vary from $150.00 to $250.00.

EGYPTIAN-ISSUED LEE-ENFIELD No. 4 MK II, this arm is marked with Arabic script on the marking disk, denoting use by Egypt. These rifles are worth $40.00 to $60.00.

FN MODEL 49 RIFLE, 7.92mm. This arm is basically a Belgian SAFN in 7.92mm with the royal Egyptian crest. Most of these arms have a matte black paint finish and a tendency to go full automatic due to firing pin breakage. This weapon is worth $100.00 to $150.00.

HAKIM RIFLE, 7.92mm. This arm was produced in limited quantities in Egypt. It is a modified version of the Swedish Ljungman Model 42. Very few of these rifles exist in the U.S. Value, $175.00 to $200.00.

ETHIOPIAN MAUSER, 7.92mm. This is a Standard-Model, M1933 that was made in Germany for Ethiopia. It has the Royal crest which consists of a lion and a star, also Coptic script. These weapons may go for $40.00 to $50.00.

INDIAN MATCHLOCK MUSKET .58 caliber, smooth-bore, 50″ barrel with flared muzzle. The full-length wooden stock is held to the barrel by 68 engraved brass barrel bands. This type weapon was made up into the 20th Century by native 'smiths. These weapons, along with the Arabian camel muskets, have started to go up in price. This specimen might go for $90.00 to $150.00.

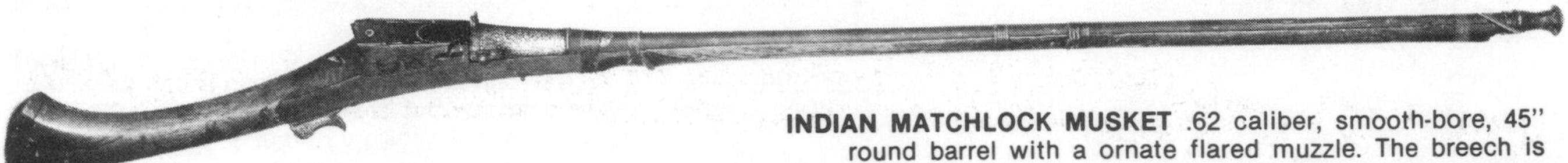

INDIAN MATCHLOCK MUSKET .62 caliber, smooth-bore, 45″ round barrel with a ornate flared muzzle. The breech is damascened with gold, and the stock has small ivory inlays. Due to the inlays and gold work, this weapon might go for $125.00 to $175.00.

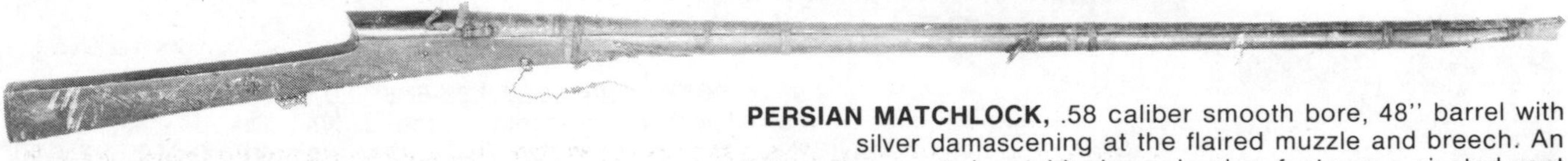

PERSIAN MATCHLOCK, .58 caliber smooth bore, 48″ barrel with silver damascening at the flaired muzzle and breech. An internally mounted matchlock mechanism features a pivoted vent cover. An ornate vent pick is attached to the stock by a chain. This specimen may go for $100.00 to $150.00.

MODEL 98/29 Short Rifle, made for Iran by Czechoslovenka Brno works before the outbreak of World War 2. The specimen pictured is for all outward appearances a Vz. 24 Mauser. Iranian rifles are chambered for the 7.92mm Mauser cartridge. Specimens with front sight guards are scarce. Prices range from $60.00 to $75.00.

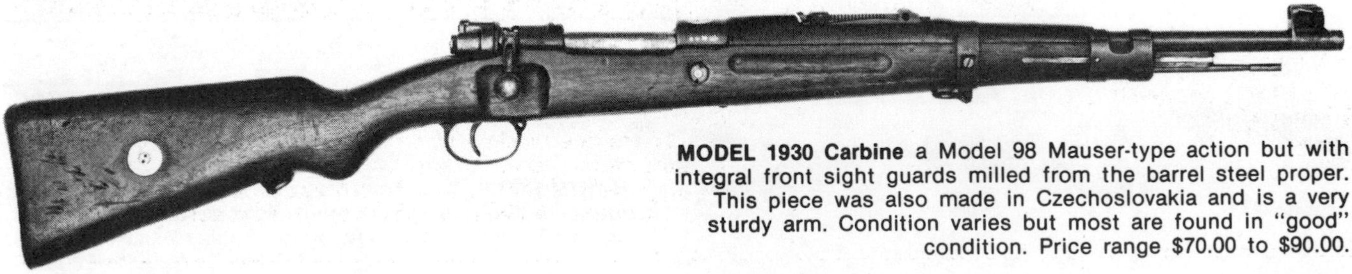

MODEL 1930 Carbine a Model 98 Mauser-type action but with integral front sight guards milled from the barrel steel proper. This piece was also made in Czechoslovakia and is a very sturdy arm. Condition varies but most are found in "good" condition. Price range $70.00 to $90.00.

IRANIAN-MADE MODEL 49 CARBINE This handy carbine was produced entirely in Iran. These arms have come into the United States in small numbers and are very well made. Most specimens are in near mint condition. Prices will vary from piece to piece but usually fall in the $70.00 to $90.00 range.

ISRAELI MAUSER in caliber 7.62mm NATO, this rifle was one of the thousands smuggled into Israel from Czechoslovakia to help the Israelis maintain their viability as a nation. Sometime after 1948 these arms were converted from 7.92mm to 7.62mm by replacing the barrel and blocking the magazine box for the shorter round. Quite scarce in this country and still issued to Israeli reserves they should bring at least $90.00 to $130.00.

TURKISH MAUSER MODEL 87 RIFLE 9.5mm cartridge of Mauser design. Except for changes required to handle the smaller cartridge, and a smaller trigger guard, this arm is the same as the German Infantry Rifle M71/84. These are quite rare in the U.S., and may go for $100.00 to $150.00.

TURKISH MODEL 1893 MAUSER, 7.65mm This is similar Model 93 Spanish Mauser in 7.65mm Mauser with a magazine cutoff Incorporated. These weapons may go for $75.00 to $90.00.

LATIN AMERICA

ARGENTINE "MODELO ARGENTINO 1879" in caliber 11mm (.43 Spanish) is a rifle that gained great popularity in South America during the late blackpowder/early smokeless era. These reliable, sturdy arms served to arm both government and rebel troops well into "smokeless" times. Most of these have been converted to other calibers. Originals go for from $90.00 to $125.00.

ARGENTINE M1891 "ESCUELA" MODEL is a very unusual piece as it was made for the National Military college. These rifles have, in addition to the Argentine crest, a special crest over the chamber of the school insignia and a special serial number range. Once considered common they are quite rare, most are found in mint condition. Specimens sell for $100.00.

ARGENTINE M1909 CARBINE in caliber 7.65mm this variation is quite uncommon, but recently there have been some imported in small numbers. These arms are in very good to excellent condition and are still available. The specimens made in Argentina at the Fabrica Militares are scarce and prime collectors items. They may command from $80.00 to $125.00.

ARGENTINE M1891 CARBINE in caliber 7.65mm, a potent little package. Most specimens are found in good to very good condition. These arms came in with crests intact and in large quantities. Quite common they may soon become scarce. Prices run from $40.00 to $60.00.

ARGENTINE M1909 CARBINE in caliber 7.65mm this variation is quite uncommon, but recently there have been some imported in small numbers. These arms are in very good to excellent condition and are still available. The specimens made in Argentina at the Fabrica Militares are scarce and prime collectors items. They may command from $65.00 to $85.00.

ARGENTINE M1909 in caliber 7.65mm, this piece was the last major action variation adopted by Argentina. Most are found with crest intact, however a few came through "ground". These are "commercial quality" guns and many have been butchered into sporters. Mint, unmodified ones go for $80.00 to $125.00.

BRAZILIAN MAUSER M1908 CARBINE in caliber 7mm. These rifles were imported in small quantities during the late 50s and early 60s. Most were butchered into minimum sporters and forever ruined as collectors items. Mint specimens are hard to find. Prices range from $60.00 to $90.00.

BRAZILIAN MAUSER M1908 RIFLE in caliber 7mm. The long rifle version of the Brazilian contract is hard to find. These pieces show fine workmanship and careful finishing but they were used in terribly humid areas and are usually in good or worse condition. Prices range from $50.00 to $75.00.

BRAZILIAN MAUSER M1894 in 7mm caliber these rifles are somewhat common, more so than their 98-actioned antecedents. Identified by "Star Crest" on the receiver ring, specimens are usually found in fair condition. Prices range from $40.00 to $60.00.

CHILEAN MAUSER M95 ARMY MODEL in caliber 7mm these arms were used by Chile for many years and served well. Most of these are in good to very good condition, some are found in almost mint condition. Basically they are still available from surplus arms dealers. Prices go from $40.00 to $75.00.

CHILEAN MAUSER M95 NAVY MODEL in caliber 7mm these rifles feature an "anchor crest" indicative of Naval usage. Most are found in very good condition, some are mint, these, like most South American rifles are found with mis-matched bolts, however a few are found "matching". Prices range from $40.00 to $75.00.

COLOMBIAN MADSEN in caliber .30/06. This rifle saw limited service in the Columbian Armed Forces. This piece has an unusual rear-locking action. Probably the last effort of the Madsen factory to capture sales from a rapidly dwindling military market. Specimens usually are found in mint or excellent condition at $50.00 to $75.00.

COSTA RICAN MAUSER M1910 in caliber 7 x 57mm. This piece is scarce. Specimens are found in fair to good condition. Bayonet lug similar to M95 type Mauser rifles. Tangent curve rear sight in lieu of the Gew. 98 sight prevalent for that time, is fitted. Specimens can be found for from $40.00 to $60.00.

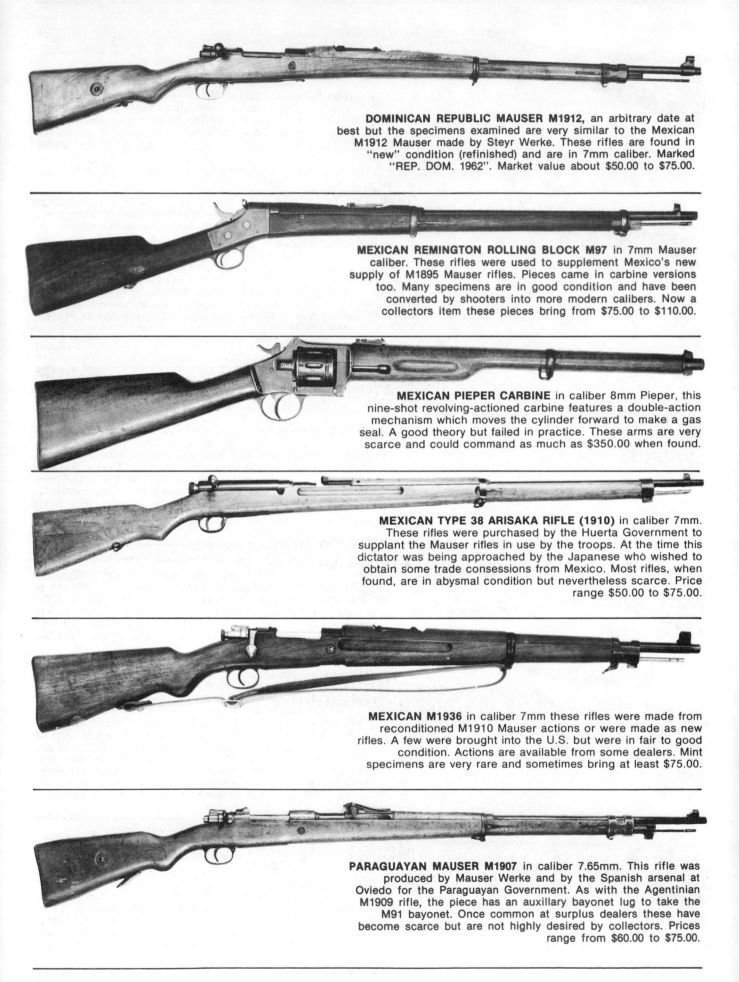

DOMINICAN REPUBLIC MAUSER M1912, an arbitrary date at best but the specimens examined are very similar to the Mexican M1912 Mauser made by Steyr Werke. These rifles are found in "new" condition (refinished) and are in 7mm caliber. Marked "REP. DOM. 1962". Market value about $50.00 to $75.00.

MEXICAN REMINGTON ROLLING BLOCK M97 in 7mm Mauser caliber. These rifles were used to supplement Mexico's new supply of M1895 Mauser rifles. Pieces came in carbine versions too. Many specimens are in good condition and have been converted by shooters into more modern calibers. Now a collectors item these pieces bring from $75.00 to $110.00.

MEXICAN PIEPER CARBINE in caliber 8mm Pieper, this nine-shot revolving-actioned carbine features a double-action mechanism which moves the cylinder forward to make a gas seal. A good theory but failed in practice. These arms are very scarce and could command as much as $350.00 when found.

MEXICAN TYPE 38 ARISAKA RIFLE (1910) in caliber 7mm. These rifles were purchased by the Huerta Government to supplant the Mauser rifles in use by the troops. At the time this dictator was being approached by the Japanese who wished to obtain some trade consessions from Mexico. Most rifles, when found, are in abysmal condition but nevertheless scarce. Price range $50.00 to $75.00.

MEXICAN M1936 in caliber 7mm these rifles were made from reconditioned M1910 Mauser actions or were made as new rifles. A few were brought into the U.S. but were in fair to good condition. Actions are available from some dealers. Mint specimens are very rare and sometimes bring at least $75.00.

PARAGUAYAN MAUSER M1907 in caliber 7.65mm. This rifle was produced by Mauser Werke and by the Spanish arsenal at Oviedo for the Paraguayan Government. As with the Agentinian M1909 rifle, the piece has an auxillary bayonet lug to take the M91 bayonet. Once common at surplus dealers these have become scarce but are not highly desired by collectors. Prices range from $60.00 to $75.00.

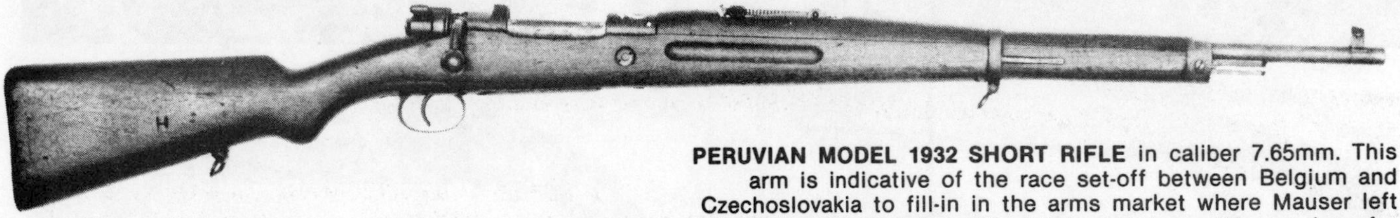

PERUVIAN MODEL 1932 SHORT RIFLE in caliber 7.65mm. This arm is indicative of the race set-off between Belgium and Czechoslovakia to fill-in in the arms market where Mauser left off. These arms are found in fair to good condition and go for about $60.00 to $75.00.

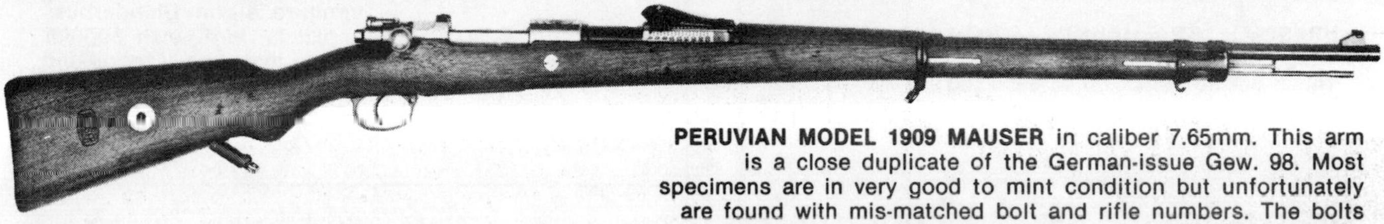

PERUVIAN MODEL 1909 MAUSER in caliber 7.65mm. This arm is a close duplicate of the German-issue Gew. 98. Most specimens are in very good to mint condition but unfortunately are found with mis-matched bolt and rifle numbers. The bolts were taken out and placed in one armory and the rifles in another. This was done to prevent unauthorized target practice at the Presidential Palace. Specimens sell for $75.00 to $90.00.

URUGUAYAN ROLLING BLOCK in caliber 11mm, an unusual item to be found in "del Norte". This rifle was made by Francotte of Belgium and has crossed cannons over the breech, indicative of this piece's issuance to artillery troops. Barrel is marked "Republica Oriental" an early name for Uruguay. A very scarce gun easily worth $150.00.

URUGUAYAN MAUSER M1894 in caliber 7mm. This arm is unusual in that it was produced by Fabrique Nationale after WW I for Uruguay. The piece pictured is in excellent condition and is serial number 1. Indeed a rare find! Most specimens are found in good condition and command about $50.00.

VENEZUELAN MAUSER M24/30 in caliber 7mm, these were made after WW 2 by Fabrique National of Belgium. Most of these rifles are found in excellent to mint condition and are extremely well made. Quite a few have been butchered into economy sporters. Any that are found in their original military livery and in mint shape are premium guns. Prices range from $45.00 to a good specimen to $95.00 for a mint gun.

VENEZUELAN SAFN M1949 in caliber 7mm, most of these semi-automatic rifles are found in mint condition, however, some have come through in worse shape. Well made and interesting design-wise these make for ideal collectors items in the semi-auto field. Prices range from $90.00 to $125.00.

BRESCIAN SNAPHAUNCE PISTOLS
These date from 1640 to 1650. These sell for $1500.00 to $2500.00.

BLUNDERBUSS PISTOL, 5½" barrel of nearly .95 caliber. This arm has a belt hook on the left side, and the furniture is iron. Blunderbuss pistols were never popular due to their heavy recoil and tendency to blow up. This piece may sell for **$350.00** to **$500.00.**

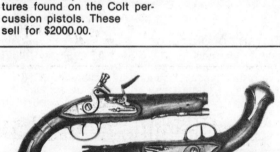

AMERICAN FLINTLOCK REVOLVER
pre-revolutionary-war design, by Thomas Pim. This unique arm has many of the features found on the Colt percussion pistols. These sell for $2000.00.

COAT PISTOL, 4" barrel. Early-type lock has no bridle on the frizzen pivot. Action is engraved with floral designs. This specimen may sell for $200.00 to $250.00.

GERMAN POCKET PISTOLS
dating around 1725, .47 caliber. Rifled barrels, half round, half octagonal, with cannon muzzles. Note that the early locks do not have a pan bridle. These arms may sell together for $600.00 to $700.00.

BLUNDERBUSS POCKET PISTOLS, .75 caliber, 3" barrels of brass. Locks are engraved, "Palais" on the right side, and "Goffart" on the left. Hammer and frizzen safeties. This pair might sell for $500.00 to $700.00.

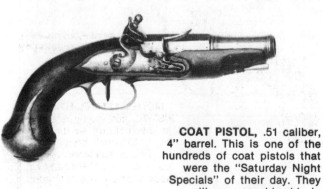

COAT PISTOL, .51 caliber, 4" barrel. This is one of the hundreds of coat pistols that were the "Saturday Night Specials" of their day. They will vary considerably in quality. This specimen may sell for $175.00 to $200.00.

COAT PISTOLS, dating about 1740. .50 caliber, 7½" barrels half round, half octagonal. Locks are marked "Loggia" Trim is iron. These pistols may sell as a pair for **$600.00** to **$800.00.**

HORSE PISTOL, dating about 1750. Brass trigger guard and buttcap, iron barrel. .65 caliber. This specimen may sell for $350.00 to $450.00.

MIQUELET PISTOL, .69 caliber 8½" barrel. All trim is brass with floral engravings. Barrels are half round, half octagonal, with armorer's mark and proofs in gold. This specimen may sell for $400.00 to $600.00.

HORSE PISTOLS, .58 caliber, 8" barrels. Silver furniture. Carved walnut stock is inlaid with silver wire. Barrels are inlaid with gold. Lockplates are marked "A PARIS." These specimens when sold as a set may bring **$800.00** to **$1200.00.**

SWISS PISTOL .47 caliber, 5½" barrel. Barrel, trigger guard and buttcap are brass. A bear's face appears on the buttcap. This specimen dates about 1770. and may sell for **$200.00 to $300.00.**

BLUNDERBUSS PISTOL, 7" barrel. dating from approximately 1760. Oval bore. This specimen may sell for **$400.00 to $500.00.**

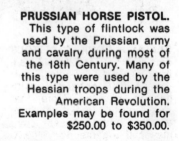

PRUSSIAN HORSE PISTOL. This type of flintlock was used by the Prussian army and cavalry during most of the 18th Century. Many of this type were used by the Hessian troops during the American Revolution. Examples may be found for $250.00 to $350.00.

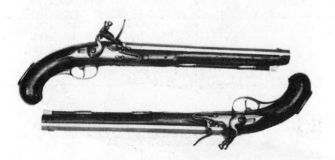

HORSE PISTOLS .52 caliber 13" barrels, octagonal. Hammer safeties. These pistols are fitted for shoulder stocks, a habit unique to the German States in this period. These arms may sell together for $700.00 to $900.00.

MODEL 1777 FLINTLOCK PISTOL, commonly referred to in this country as the "St. Etienne" pistol. This particular specimen is the common or enlisted man's weapon. The officer's model is slightly thinner in the wrist. This arm may sell for $250.00 to $400.00.

MIQUELET, .67 caliber, 9½" barrel with maker's name and proof. Engraved brass trim. Iron parts are engraved also. Belt hook. This piece may sell for $400.00 to $600.00.

OFFICER'S PISTOL, .58 caliber, smoothbore, 10¼" barrel, part round, part octagonal, bearing the makers name "Argviano" and a gold armorer's mark. The cock has features of the miquelet. Lock, buttcap, and trigger guard are engraved. This specimen could bring $300.00 to $500.00.

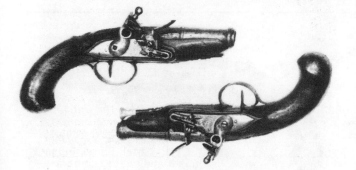

COAT PISTOLS dated about 1800. .52 caliber, 3½" barrels. Bright metal barrels, military type hammers. These arms would probably sell for $200.00 to $250.00 a piece.

OFFICER'S PISTOL, dating about 1810. This type of arm was made up for individual officers by private gunmakers. They were of military caliber, usually .69, and were built on the lines of a dueler. This specimen is rifled with multi-groove rifling, and has a rain-proof pan. This arm may sell for **$350.00** to **$450.00.**

PERCUSSION

MODEL 1822 PATTERN PISTOL converted to percussion in 1854, and rifled in 1860. Most French weapons of Pattern 1822 went through these conversions. Ramrod contains a powder-measure. This specimen may sell for $100.00 to $150.00.

BELGIAN CENTER-HAMMER PISTOL. .46 caliber, 7¼" barrel. This is a belt style weapon of rather inexpensive manufacture. These arms can be found in all sizes. Specimens may be found for $125.00 to $175.00.

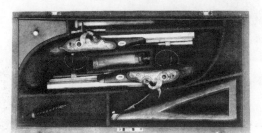

BRITISH SYKES of OXFORD cased horseman's pistols. .54 caliber. This set may sell for $800.00 to $1200.00.

AUSTRIAN DRAGOON PISTOL, .64 caliber, 9½" barrel. Originally a flint doglock, it was converted to percussion in the 1840s. This specimen with shoulder stock sell for **$150.00** to **$250.00.**

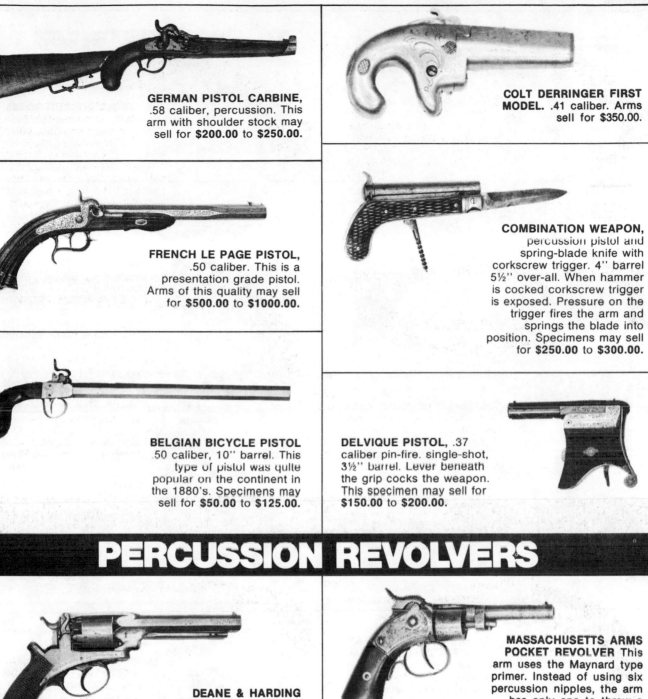

GERMAN PISTOL CARBINE, .58 caliber, percussion. This arm with shoulder stock may sell for **$200.00** to **$250.00**.

COLT DERRINGER FIRST MODEL. .41 caliber. Arms sell for **$350.00**.

FRENCH LE PAGE PISTOL, .50 caliber. This is a presentation grade pistol. Arms of this quality may sell for **$500.00** to **$1000.00**.

COMBINATION WEAPON, percussion pistol and spring-blade knife with corkscrew trigger. 4'' barrel 5½'' over-all. When hammer is cocked corkscrew trigger is exposed. Pressure on the trigger fires the arm and springs the blade into position. Specimens may sell for **$250.00** to **$300.00**.

BELGIAN BICYCLE PISTOL .50 caliber, 10'' barrel. This type of pistol was quite popular on the continent in the 1880's. Specimens may sell for **$50.00** to **$125.00**.

DELVIQUE PISTOL, .37 caliber pin-fire. single-shot, 3½'' barrel. Lever beneath the grip cocks the weapon. This specimen may sell for **$150.00** to **$200.00**.

PERCUSSION REVOLVERS

DEANE & HARDING REVOLVER, .44 caliber. Specimens may sell for **$150.00** to **$300.00**.

MASSACHUSETTS ARMS POCKET REVOLVER This arm uses the Maynard type primer. Instead of using six percussion nipples, the arm has only one to throw a flash through a touch hole over each chamber. Specimens sell for **$175.00** to **$250.00**.

STARR REVOLVER, Navy Model. .36 caliber. Models sell for **$200.00** to **$400.00**.

ROGERS & SPENCER REVOLVER, .44 caliber. Arms may sell for **$200.00** to **$400.00**.

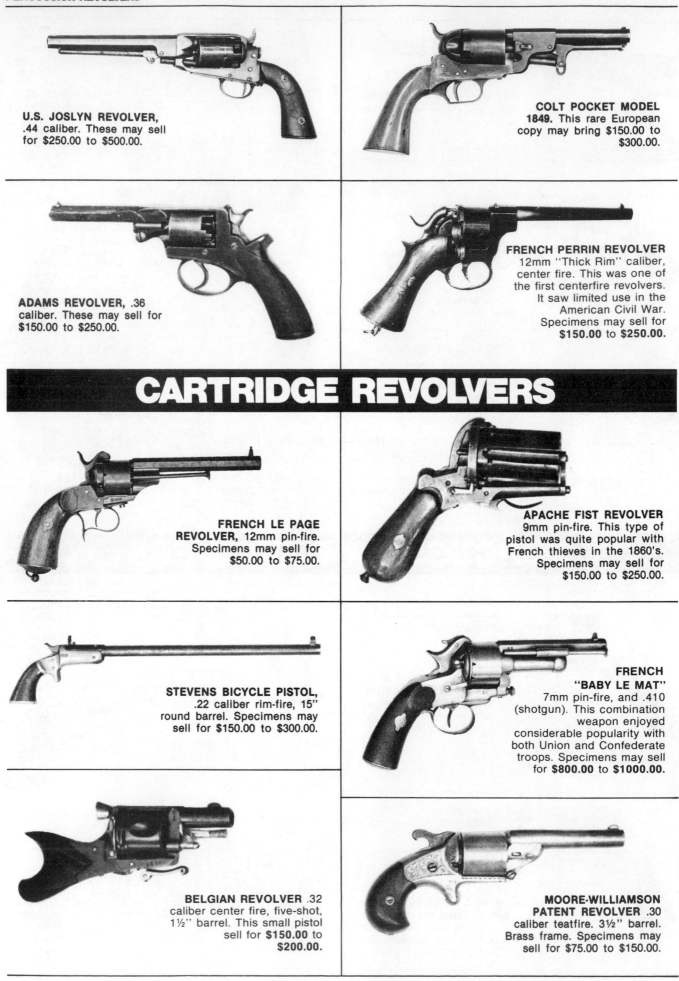

U.S. JOSLYN REVOLVER, .44 caliber. These may sell for $250.00 to $500.00.

COLT POCKET MODEL 1849. This rare European copy may bring $150.00 to $300.00.

ADAMS REVOLVER, .36 caliber. These may sell for $150.00 to $250.00.

FRENCH PERRIN REVOLVER 12mm "Thick Rim" caliber, center fire. This was one of the first centerfire revolvers. It saw limited use in the American Civil War. Specimens may sell for **$150.00 to $250.00.**

CARTRIDGE REVOLVERS

FRENCH LE PAGE REVOLVER, 12mm pin-fire. Specimens may sell for $50.00 to $75.00.

APACHE FIST REVOLVER 9mm pin-fire. This type of pistol was quite popular with French thieves in the 1860's. Specimens may sell for $150.00 to $250.00.

STEVENS BICYCLE PISTOL, .22 caliber rim-fire, 15" round barrel. Specimens may sell for $150.00 to $300.00.

FRENCH "BABY LE MAT" 7mm pin-fire, and .410 (shotgun). This combination weapon enjoyed considerable popularity with both Union and Confederate troops. Specimens may sell for **$800.00 to $1000.00.**

BELGIAN REVOLVER .32 caliber center fire, five-shot, 1½" barrel. This small pistol sell for **$150.00** to **$200.00.**

MOORE-WILLIAMSON PATENT REVOLVER .30 caliber teatfire. 3½" barrel. Brass frame. Specimens may sell for **$75.00** to **$150.00.**

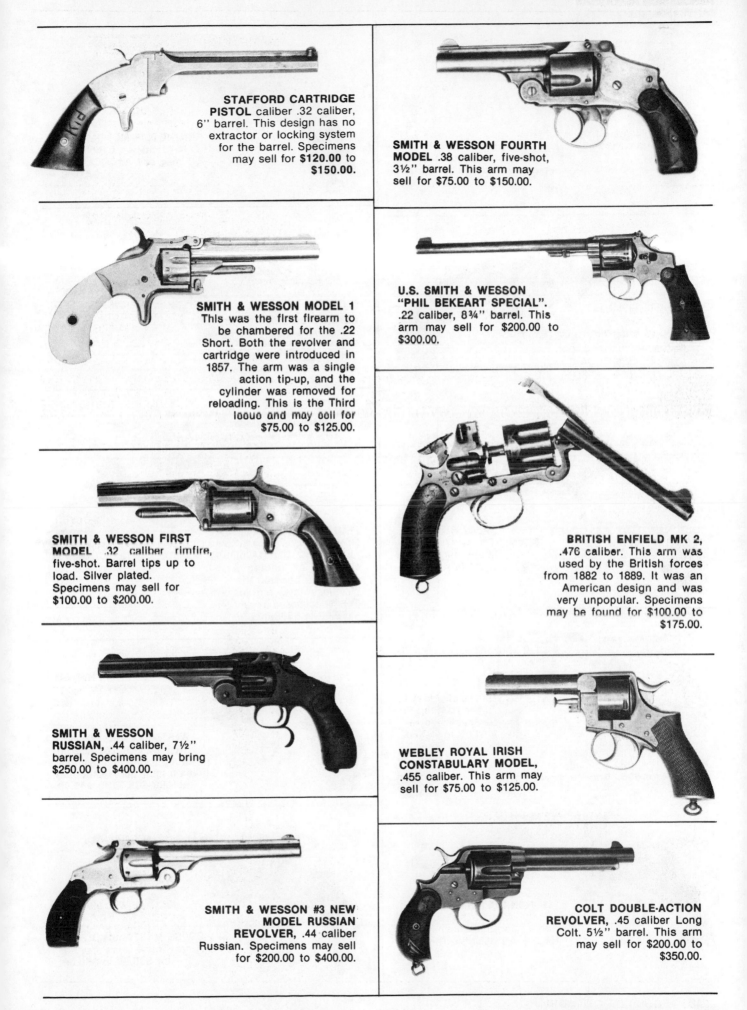

STAFFORD CARTRIDGE PISTOL caliber .32 caliber, 6'' barrel. This design has no extractor or locking system for the barrel. Specimens may sell for **$120.00** to **$150.00.**

SMITH & WESSON FOURTH MODEL .38 caliber, five-shot, 3½'' barrel. This arm may sell for $75.00 to $150.00.

SMITH & WESSON MODEL 1 This was the first firearm to be chambered for the .22 Short. Both the revolver and cartridge were introduced in 1857. The arm was a single action tip-up, and the cylinder was removed for reloading. This is the Third Issue and may sell for $75.00 to $125.00.

U.S. SMITH & WESSON "PHIL BEKEART SPECIAL". .22 caliber, 8¾'' barrel. This arm may sell for $200.00 to $300.00.

SMITH & WESSON FIRST MODEL .32 caliber rimfire, five-shot. Barrel tips up to load. Silver plated. Specimens may sell for $100.00 to $200.00.

BRITISH ENFIELD MK 2, .476 caliber. This arm was used by the British forces from 1882 to 1889. It was an American design and was very unpopular. Specimens may be found for $100.00 to $175.00.

SMITH & WESSON RUSSIAN, .44 caliber, 7½'' barrel. Specimens may bring $250.00 to $400.00.

WEBLEY ROYAL IRISH CONSTABULARY MODEL, .455 caliber. This arm may sell for $75.00 to $125.00.

SMITH & WESSON #3 NEW MODEL RUSSIAN REVOLVER, .44 caliber Russian. Specimens may sell for $200.00 to $400.00.

COLT DOUBLE-ACTION REVOLVER, .45 caliber Long Colt. 5½'' barrel. This arm may sell for $200.00 to $350.00.

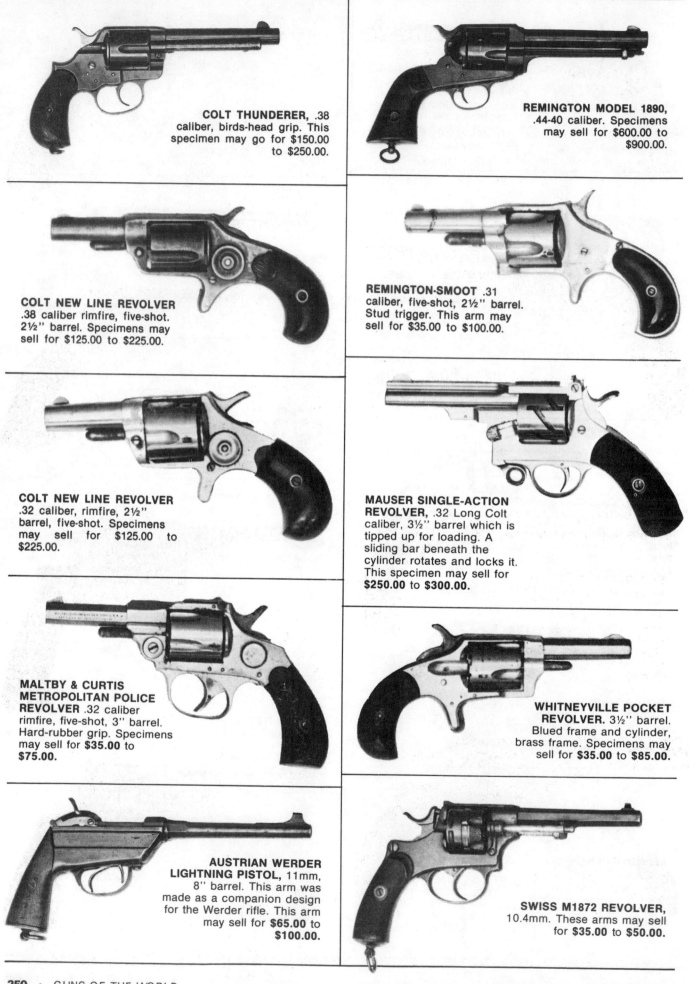

COLT THUNDERER, .38 caliber, birds-head grip. This specimen may go for $150.00 to $250.00.

REMINGTON MODEL 1890, .44-40 caliber. Specimens may sell for $600.00 to $900.00.

COLT NEW LINE REVOLVER .38 caliber rimfire, five-shot. 2½" barrel. Specimens may sell for $125.00 to $225.00.

REMINGTON-SMOOT .31 caliber, five-shot, 2½" barrel. Stud trigger. This arm may sell for $35.00 to $100.00.

COLT NEW LINE REVOLVER .32 caliber, rimfire, 2½" barrel, five-shot. Specimens may sell for $125.00 to $225.00.

MAUSER SINGLE-ACTION REVOLVER, .32 Long Colt caliber, 3½" barrel which is tipped up for loading. A sliding bar beneath the cylinder rotates and locks it. This specimen may sell for **$250.00** to **$300.00**.

MALTBY & CURTIS METROPOLITAN POLICE REVOLVER .32 caliber rimfire, five-shot, 3" barrel. Hard-rubber grip. Specimens may sell for **$35.00** to **$75.00**.

WHITNEYVILLE POCKET REVOLVER. 3½" barrel. Blued frame and cylinder, brass frame. Specimens may sell for **$35.00** to **$85.00**.

AUSTRIAN WERDER LIGHTNING PISTOL, 11mm, 8" barrel. This arm was made as a companion design for the Werder rifle. This arm may sell for **$65.00** to **$100.00**.

SWISS M1872 REVOLVER, 10.4mm. These arms may sell for $35.00 to $50.00.

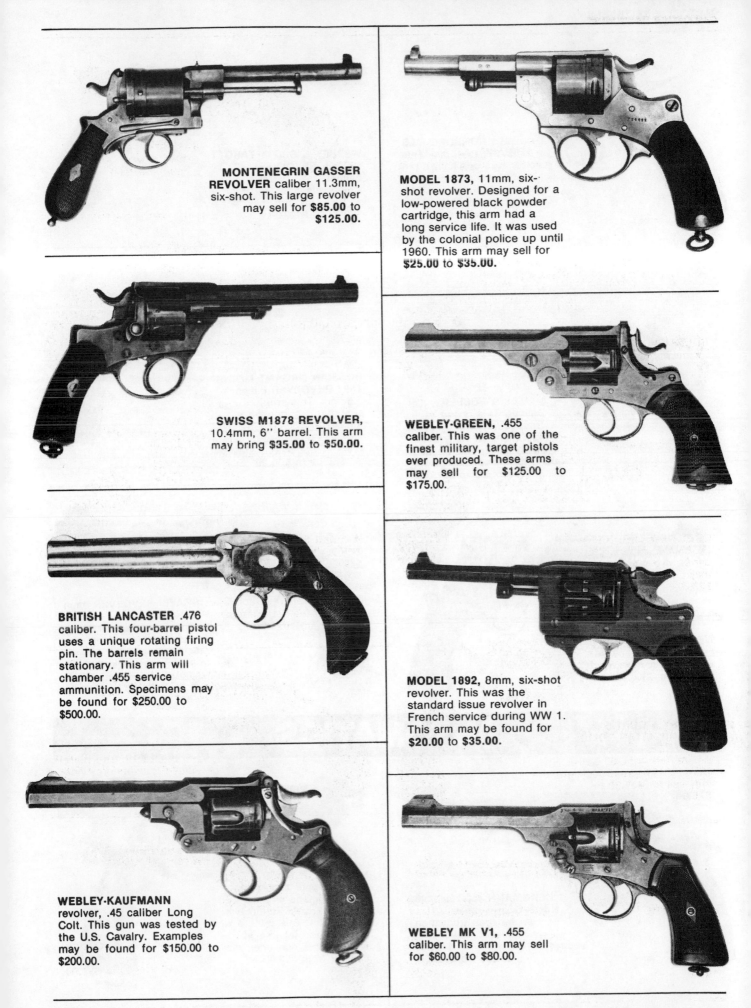

MONTENEGRIN GASSER REVOLVER caliber 11.3mm, six-shot. This large revolver may sell for **$85.00** to **$125.00**.

MODEL 1873, 11mm, six-shot revolver. Designed for a low-powered black powder cartridge, this arm had a long service life. It was used by the colonial police up until 1960. This arm may sell for **$25.00** to **$35.00**.

SWISS M1878 REVOLVER, 10.4mm, 6'' barrel. This arm may bring **$35.00** to **$50.00**.

WEBLEY-GREEN, .455 caliber. This was one of the finest military, target pistols ever produced. These arms may sell for **$125.00** to **$175.00**.

BRITISH LANCASTER .476 caliber. This four-barrel pistol uses a unique rotating firing pin. The barrels remain stationary. This arm will chamber .455 service ammunition. Specimens may be found for **$250.00** to **$500.00**.

MODEL 1892, 8mm, six-shot revolver. This was the standard issue revolver in French service during WW 1. This arm may be found for **$20.00** to **$35.00**.

WEBLEY-KAUFMANN revolver, .45 caliber Long Colt. This gun was tested by the U.S. Cavalry. Examples may be found for **$150.00** to **$200.00**.

WEBLEY MK V1, .455 caliber. This arm may sell for **$60.00** to **$80.00**.

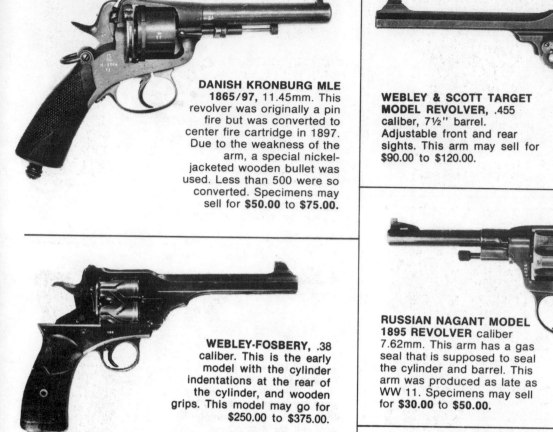

DANISH KRONBURG MLE 1865/97, 11.45mm. This revolver was originally a pin fire but was converted to center fire cartridge in 1897. Due to the weakness of the arm, a special nickel-jacketed wooden bullet was used. Less than 500 were so converted. Specimens may sell for **$50.00** to **$75.00**.

WEBLEY & SCOTT TARGET MODEL REVOLVER, .455 caliber, 7½" barrel. Adjustable front and rear sights. This arm may sell for $90.00 to $120.00.

WEBLEY-FOSBERY, .38 caliber. This is the early model with the cylinder indentations at the rear of the cylinder, and wooden grips. This model may go for $250.00 to $375.00.

RUSSIAN NAGANT MODEL 1895 REVOLVER caliber 7.62mm. This arm has a gas seal that is supposed to seal the cylinder and barrel. This arm was produced as late as WW 11. Specimens may sell for **$30.00** to **$50.00**.

WEBLEY-FOSBERY, .455 caliber. This is the late version, and may sell for $200.00 to $300.00.

ISRAELI REVOLVER 9mm Parabellum. This a copy of the Smith & Wesson Military and Police model. It was slightly modified to chamber the 9mm cartridge in half-moon clips. It bears Israeli Military Industries markings. Specimens may sell for **$250.00** to **$350.00**.

AUTOMATICS

BERGMANN MODEL 1896 No. 3. 6.5mm rimless. This was the first production pocket automatic. This specimen may go for $400.00 to $600.00.

ROTH-STEYR M1907, 8mm, stripper clip loading, semi-automatic with an unusual double action type trigger pull. This feature was incorporated for use by cavalry. This specimen may sell for from $90.00 to $150.00.

ITALIAN GLISENTI, MODEL 1910, 9mm, (8.9mm). This arm should not be used with 9mm Parabellum cartridges. Glisentis may sell for **$85.00** to **$135.00**.

AUSTRIAN STEYR-HAHN MODEL 1911 in 9mm Steyr. This was the standard side arm of the Austro-Hungarian Empire during WW 1. It is loaded by means of a stripper clip. The barrel rotates to unlock the slide. During WW11 the Germans rebarreled many of them to 9mm Parabellum. These arms are marked ''08'' on the left side of the slide. Specimens may sell for **$45.00** to **$75.00**.

MAUSER 1910 MODEL .32 caliber. This is straight blow-back pistol was extensively used during WW I and WW II by the German forces. It also saw wide commercial distribution. In 1934 the pistol was simplified for ease of manufacture. This arm may sell for $90.00 to $150.00.

WEBLEY & SCOTT MODEL 1913 MK 1, Navy. Examples may sell for $125.00 to $175.00.

DANISH MODEL 1910 9mm Bergmann-Bayard. This was one of the strongest and most powerful pistols ever designed. Specimens may sell for $175.00 to 250.00.

WEBLEY & SCOTT MODEL 1913 MK 1 No. 2, .455 Webley automatic. This version has adjustable rear sights and a safety located on the hammer. It may sell for **$200.00** to **$300.00**.

DANISH MODEL 1910/21 caliber 9mm Bergmann-Bayard This is a conversion of the 1910 model and may sell for $150.00 to $250.00.

ITALIAN BRIXIA PISTOL, 9mm. This is the early model of the Glisenti and may sell for **$100.00** to **$200.00**.

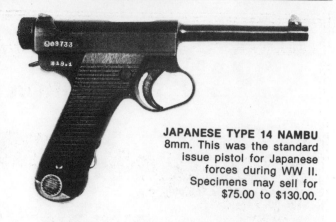

BROWNING MODEL 1922, .380 caliber. This specimen bears the Yugoslavian coat of arms. Examples may sell for **$65.00** to **$100.00**.

JAPANESE TYPE 14 NAMBU 8mm. This was the standard issue pistol for Japanese forces during WW II. Specimens may sell for **$75.00** to **$130.00**.

SWEDISH LAHTI MODEL 1940 PISTOL caliber 9mm. Specimens may sell for $135.00 to $175.00.

JAPANESE TYPE 94 caliber 8mm. This pistol was thought to have been produced for export. Early arms were well finished. Specimens may sell for **$45.00** to **$65.00**.

MAUSER MODEL 1934, "NAVAL MODEL" This is a standard 1934 model witht the addition of a large eagle with the letter M beneath it, denoting naval issue. Because of the scarcity of the marking this increases the value considerably. A legitimate naval model may bring $150.00 to $200.00.

JAPANESE NAMBU "BABY NAMBU" caliber 7mm. This basically is a scaled down 1904-type pistol. It was thought to have been introduced as a result of European military preference for small pistols by upper-echelon personnel. This arm has always been a sought after collectors item and may sell for $400.00-up.

MAUSER HSc .32 caliber. The arm pictured here is a post-war French occupation variant, as denoted by the small stamp on the left side and at the rear of the trigger guard. HSc's were used throughout WW II by the German military and police forces. Depending on model the HSc may go for $125.00 to $175.00.

TOKAREV MODEL 1933, 7.62mm. This was the standard side-arm of the Russian forces during WW 11. It has been manufactured in several variations by the Communist satelite countries. The Russian version may sell for **$55.00** to **$95.00**.

THE 30S REMINGTONS WHERE ARE THEY NOW?

by Harris R. Bierman

The usual question when one pulls out a 30S Remington hunting rifle on the range and at a gun shop is, "Hey, whatcha got there, a sportsterized Pattern 1917 Enfield?" The usual reply is, "No, this is a Model 30 Remington." Finally the interrogator asks, "What's that?" The purpose of this article will be to give those interested a short appraisal of the Models 30 and 30S.

The Model 30 had its initial start after World War I. Remington had fulfilled its military contracts by providing the U.S. and British Armies with both the Pattern 14 and the U.S. Model 1917 rifles. These variations have been generally known to collectors and amateur gunsmiths as the Enfields, probably because of the noteriety of the design's eminence from the Enfield Lock "think-tank."

Remington had large amounts of unfinished '17 parts on hand and nothing to do with them. World War I had started many would-be hunters out on the bolt-action rifle. This action type had already been used extensively in Europe, but in the United States our nimrods were still diehard "cowboy-gun" types and for the most part the good old crank action was still "king."

With the coming of the roaring 20s, bolt-actioned rifles started to find favor. The M1903 Springfield was being sold to target shooters and many of these were also used to make those almost flawless sporters by Griffin & Howe, Hoffman, Neidner, Owen, Pachmayr and the like. The Models 30 and 30S fit into the picture about 1920. Remington decided to develop its raw capital into a more salable product: Enter the Model 30.

Needless to say, the first Model 30s were worked over Model 1917s. Remington smoothed out the unusually high rear receiver ring "ears," took off the hump from the trigger guard/floorplate assembly, and turned out a most unusual sporter stock with an extremely long pistol grip wrist on the stock and a shapely, but less than utilitarian schnabel forend tip. These features were coupled with the same old, irritating cock-on-closing feature of the striker assembly as with its predecessor, the M1917. In fact, if one finds a Model 30 with an unsightly hole in the rear receiver ring, and its markings are correct, he may be the proud possessor of one of

1. Page from the Remington catalog of 1938. Shown here is the Model 30A or the "Standard Grade", made in .30/06 only the 30A was not fitted with the Lyman 48R receiver sight but its receiver was drilled and tapped for it.

THE 30S REM.

the first of the Model 30s. Other identifying features are its five-groove barrel, its caliber, 30/06, for the very first rifles, and its rear sight, attached to the barrel by means of a ring band, which in turn was used to hold the barrel to the forend by way of a sling swivel screw as featured in the later Model 54 Winchester. Receivers were also drilled and tapped for either the Lyman 48R or Redfield No. 102 rear sights.

Later, other calibers were added to the list and the striker mechanism was modified to cock on opening. The new calibers offered were: .25 Remington, .30 Remington, .32 Remington, and .35 Remington. But the stock design remained unchanged much to the disappointment and vitriolic comments of the shooting pundits of the day. To say the least, E. C. Crossman, a well read writer of the times, waxed demonic over the poor fit and utterly painful effects of shooting the "new" Remington rifle in .30/06. He never got off this tack, even when Remington modified its stock design. Crossman also nit-picked about the trigger pull of the rifle he tested, which was in all probability one of the early military parts/cum-sporter pieces.

Remington modified the stock design around 1930 to a full-rounded forearm and shortened the pistol grip wrist, widening it and lowering the comb in the process. The trigger pull was modified to give a neat let-off without take-up slack. The Remington-series of rimless calibers was dropped and instead arms were offered in .30/06, 7mm Mauser, 7.65mm Mauser, 8mm Mauser, and the new .257 Roberts cartridges.

Rifles were also changed to incorporate the new stocking-up changes and the crude on-the-barrel buckhorn sights and simple front sight were changed over to a full ramp front sight base, and a choice of Lyman or Redfield rear sights. Model 30s were offered in carbine lengths with 20-inch barrels, while rifles had 24-inch barrels. Stock had checkering fore and aft with the coming of the 30S models, but the stocks of the carbines were left uncheckered. The sights on the 30A were left as on the early Model 30s, but the stocks were brought up to the Model 30S design standard.

Buttplates of the early rifles were crescent-shaped and due to the poor stock design, were reported as being extremely uncomfortable to take in full recoil. Later on in the 1930's, these were changed to shotgun types, some with simple horizontal lines in lieu of checkering, and some with a fine to coarse diamond-shaped checkering pattern. Some of the last Model 30S rifles to be produced also had beefed-up wrists in the pistol grip and heavier buttstocks, which of course increased the weight of the piece from an original weight of 7¼ pounds to a heavy-to-tote nine pounds!

There was a military model of the 30S made, this piece was called the Model 40, in order not to confuse it with another Remington model. Mr. S. M. Alvis, Manager of Ilion Research Division, has communicated with the author concerning these military versions. As it stands, these arms were made for the Government of Honduras in 7mm Mauser caliber from 1934 to 1935. Approximately 3000 were made and are marked "Model 34." The stock is of the Model 1917/Pattern 14 design but sports a barrel-mounted rear sight and an unprotected front sight. It has been reported that the Model 40 was made in 7.65mm Mauser for Argentina, but no production records for this caliber have been unearthed.

The Models 30 and 30S were somewhat ahead of their time. The '30 antedated the Winchester 54 and really was the first bolt-actioned sporter made available to the U.S. market from an American manufacturer after World War I and unlike the pre-War, Newton sporters had a modicum of success. Many of these arms were restocked and rebarreled

by their owners and became much improved as hunting arms. Today, however, they are quite scarce in their original livery.

The total production of the Model 30 and 30S stood at 22,728 units, ending in 1939. One of the reasons for their demise was that the Winchester 70 swept the boards clean with its immediate popularity in 1937, cutting into the Model 30 sales figures drastically. The '70 was a lighter arm and supposedly had a much smoother action. What many aficionados of the '70 fail to realize is that Winchester continued to use the front bedding screw, a feature detrimental to accuracy, where the 30S had discarded it in about 1930. Also, the M70's safety catch, in its first pattern, precluded the low mounting of a scope and also was noisy in the woods, giving out a loud clicking noise when operated. The 30s retained the M1917 safety which was placed close to the thumb and could be easily tripped in and out of engagement without a sound. As far as functioning goes, the 30S rifles were first class. As was reported when they first came out, many writers thought them sticky and not very smooth. However, upon examination of over 10 post-1930 specimens, the author has found them extremely smooth and positive in operation.

By 1940, some four years after the introduction of the Model 70, Remington introduced the Model 720. Production of this rifle only went on for about one year, for in 1941 production ceased when Remington tooled up for war.

The 720 was the quintescence of the Model 30S. It had the same basic features of the 30S except for its modified bolt handle. This design did away with the "S" curve of the 1917/30S bolt handle producing a straight, low-slung lever, a design which has been similarly carried on with the new Ruger Model 77 bolt rifle. The 720 was produced in only three calibers; .30/06, .270 Winchester, and .257 Roberts. Very few are around and, though unrecognized, would rate a premium price if they have not been butchered by some modern-day improvement artist. Design elements incorporated into the Model 720 are to be found in today's 700 series bolt-action rifles produced by Remington.

All in all, the 30S and its successors are "sleepers" as far as collectors arms go, and if found unaltered in excellent condition in the common calibers or in any condition above "good" in the Remington "rimless" line or in the metric calibers, they would and should merit the attention of the serious pre-World War 2 sporter collector.

1. The Pattern 13, great grandaddy of the 30S Remington rifles. This facinating rifle was produced in 1910 for British service trials as a replacement for the SMLE. Its caliber, .276 was excellent but hot due to powders used. While rifles were well thought of, British Ordnance felt that expense of retooling offset benefits of adopting arm.

2. The Pattern 14 rifle was a direct offshoot of the P13. Produced in the United States for the British in their .303 MK VII caliber these rifles were some of the most modern variations of the Mauser-type design for their time. Remington, Eddystone and Winchester produced the rifle. When United States entered the war, rifle was redesigned to fire the .30/06 becoming the U.S. Rifle Model of 1917 in our service.

3. One of the earliest production models of the Model 30 rifle. This piece is serial number 370, its features include a cock-on-closing striker mechanism and a milling cut in rear receiver ring. Inset shows the early marking denoting the transition from Remington-UMC to Remington Arms Co.

4. Early, middle production Model 30 in .30/06, note crescent shaped butt plate and combination bedding screw/sling swivel in forend.

5. The Model 30R carbine is quite a rare bird. These arms were made with 20" barrels. Known as the "Carbine" Grade in the catalog these arms were made without checkering on the pistol grip or forend. They weighed in at 7¼ lbs. The specimen shown has finger grooves in the forend and a scnabel forend tip. The butt plate has been changed to the flat shotgun-type and the rear sight base does not double as a barrel bedding device.

6. The Model 30S was known earlier as 30 Special. 30 Special was made in 1930 and introduced new modifications promoted by Whelen's specifications as to what constituted the N.R.A. Sporter. Note the full forend with ample checkering pattern, pistol grip stock and shotgun-type butt, Lyman rear sight, full ramp front sight base.

7. One of the later models of 30S, this piece in .257 Roberts. Note increased depth in the butt stock especially around the pistol grip.

8. Remington's Model 720 was slated to take the place of 30S but the coming of World War 2 changed the picture. These are now quite rare.

9. Later models of Remington rifles still retain the characteristics of their older cousins. The 725 still has the old safety catch but the outside extractor is gone.

10. The Model 725 ADL.

THE JAPANESE SWORD

A BASIC GUIDE FOR COLLECTORS By W. M. Hawley

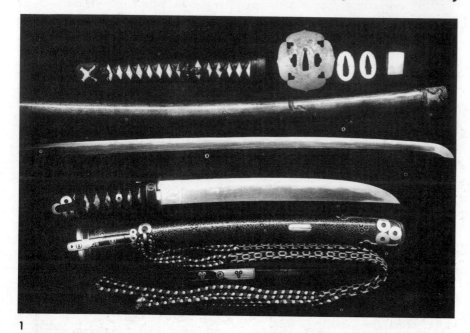

1

Nearly everybody who is weapon conscious has heard about Japanese Samurai swords and perhaps wondered why all the fuss! The word Japanese seems to give some dealers visions of Instant Wealth though they couldn't for the life of them tell the difference between a sword worth $10.00 and one worth $10,000.00! But the difference is there and reading this article will tell you why but won't make anybody an *Instant Expert*. It takes long study and the viewing of many blades together with someone who can point out the fine points of good, bad, and indifferent workmanship.

An iron army issue scabbard almost always contains an army issue blade, but about one in a hundred has an old family keepsake blade that some officer carried along for luck. This blade may be anything from a poor quality to medium but seldom anything extra good. Nobody risked a fine blade for modern war use.

Age alone is not the determining factor in a blade. Every 'smith had to start and it would be stupid to place a high value on a poor first attempt even if the man became famous. So, some men's blades are rated early, middle, and late with a wide variation in value.

1. Top: A katana, blade isn't signed but comes from Namino hira group in Satsuma. Piece was made some time in 15th or 16th Century. It shows a good example of straight grain forging and the shallow temper line is typical of that group. Gold lacquer scabbard, handachi mounts. Bottom: A heavy tanto, akikuchi style (no guard), blade by Kanekage c. 1650. This piece has a custom-made mounting featuring two family crests, circles and arrow feathers in finest quality gold, silver and shakudo inlay with lacquered scabbard.

So, it is the skill that went into an otherwise routine procedure that makes the difference. Many blades that are 600 years old are worth very little because of poor workmanship or condition, or having been sharpened so many times the outside laminations have been worn away exposing the inner soft steel. These last are called "very tired." Also, fires were frequent in Japan and many famous blades were rendered useless this way. They might be cleaned up and polished and retain a genuine famous signature but have only slight curiosity value. Then there are fake signatures to contend with. Of the thousand or so big names in swords, nine out of ten that you run across are fakes, although some may be very good blades.

People collect Japanese blades because they have heard that these arms are the best (of swords) in the world, both from functional qualities and artistic merit. Why this is so involves many questions, not the least of which is how could blacksmiths of the 12th and 13th Centuries produce things of such high technological excellence that we can not duplicate them today with all our skill and research. To explain this, the author will start, step by step, with the construction of blades from iron

ore to iron to steel to the finished blade.

Iron occurs in Japan in two forms: Basic mined ore as found all over the world, and sand iron, which is the same iron eroded from deposits in the mountains, washed down in streams where it is ground to sand consistency among boulders in stream beds over uncounted centuries. Both kinds are used in sword making, but the sand iron is the easiest to work with as it is already reduced to almost pure iron by the crushing, washing,

and oxidation of impurities that has taken place in nature. It is recoverable from stream beds, but 1000 years of sword making has exhausted many deposits. Modern sword makers are scrounging for old broken tea kettles, nails, and old iron fittings that were made from the once-plentiful sand iron.

Plain iron does not make good weapons or tools as it will bend on impact and will not hold an edge. To produce good steel, carbon has to be added in controlled quantities

and thoroughly distributed through the iron.

For sword making, it is desirable to have an assortment of different grades of steel which later can be laminated together to make a stronger blade.

In order to reduce either kind of ore to usable iron, it has to be melted. This is most efficiently done in large quantities. Thus, in the old days, several 'smiths would get together. A large pit was dug and air ducts constructed to the bottom of

JAPANESE SWORD

same. The pit was often 10 feet long by four or five feet wide, and eight feet deep. A bed of charcoal was put in first, then alternate layers of iron ore and charcoal were added until several hundred pounds of iron filled the hole. Next, vents were added at the top and the pit was covered with clay and dirt. Then a fire was started and air was forced into the pitbottom from huge bellows operated by six to ten men who sometimes worked around the clock for a month straight. Actual time required depended on the size of the pit.

When the pit was opened there would be irregular masses of iron mixed with charcoal ash in the bottom. These were subsequently broken up, re-melted into smaller quantities, poured out on a smooth mud floor and then quenched by poured on water. This formed very brittle plates about 1/8-inch thick; brittle because of too-much natural carbon picked up from the charcoal smelting process. These sheets were then broken with a hammer into small pieces the size of coins. After one more heating, the iron would be suitable for casting objects like tea kettles. The 'smiths were now ready to start the steel making process.

The small broken pieces were stacked on a four-by-six-inch plate to which a handle had been attached. This two-inch-high pile was wrapped in mud-soaked paper to hold it together during its tenure in the forge. Once heated to a welding temperature, it was withdrawn and the hammering begun. While the master held onto the plate by that two-foot-long handle, two or three "hammer men" beat the metal into a solid slab and at the same time drew it out to twice its original length. Once more it was folded back to the original size, reheated and drawn out again. All the hammering and folding compacted the metal, worked out impurities, and at the same time incorporated just the right amount of carbon. The unwanted coarse carbon particles were broken up and forced out by the pounding; new fine carbon particles were introduced by dipping the slab into a pot of mud to which had been added a small quantity of finely powdered pine charcoal with each return to the fire. By this method, the early 'smiths were able to control, to a remarkably exact degree, the carbon content of their steel. They learned by trial and error. The drawing out and folding served to double the layers each time, making them half the thick-

ness of the previous condition. For the best blades, three kinds of steel were required—the hardest, for the edge, would be folded 15 times, this producing 32,800 layers in the one-inch thick block. There was no chance for impurities to remain in such thin layers.

But such a high carbon steel would not be suitable for the whole blade, only the edge needed to be that hard. Some 'smiths experimented with folding the thing 20 to 30 times with nothing gained, as too much material was lost in the working. Consequently, fifteen became the standard number of folds.

For a blade to have stamina and not be brittle, a softer steel was needed. A steel folded five times could be used for a shock-absorbing core that could not be hardened, having only 32 layers and about one third the carbon of the edge steel, yet very tough. This was encased in a medium hard steel on the sides and back (folded about 10 times, roughly

1000 layers with two thirds the carbon of the edge steel). This corresponded to spring steel—flexible but very resistant to cutting by an enemy's blade.

Now, to produce a blade from these assorted steels, small bars of each steel were assembled in a block which would be welded together, then drawn out the full length of the sword. At the point, various tricks were employed to turn the edge steel to follow around to the point.

Up to now, I have described only one method of lamination using four or five pieces of steel. A simpler method much used in Mino province and for tantos that required no great strength entailed the wrapping of a hard steel around a medium steel. Several other arrangements by various schools of 'smiths also produced very good blades. Imported steel picked up the name *Namban* (Southern Barbarian), which was a general term for foreigners. Most of it came from China, Malay, or India. Some

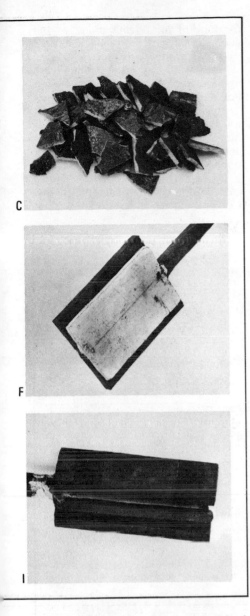

1. (A) Natural sand iron ore. (B) Sand iron after smelting (tamagahane). (C) Second melting, poured out thin and chilled, then broken up with a hammer. (D) Broken pieces piled up and heated preparatory to forging to convert iron into steel. (E) Folding and drawing out process started to refine iron and convert it into steel of varied carbon content. Five folds produced mild steel for core metal of sword; 10 folds made spring quality steel for back (top of blade) and sides; 15 folds produced high carbon steel for edge. (F) Assembled block to be folded sideways with soft core (white piece) surrounded by 15-times folded steel. (G) Hard steel wrapped around soft core. (H) Four piece lamination, white is soft, sides are spring steel and small bottom piece is for the edge. (I) Five piece lamination, similar to former but with medium hard back piece added. Forging set courtesy of the Japanese Sword Collectors Club of Los Angeles.

Masamune blade breaking in action, or getting dull so it actually had to be sharpened? Apparently not. Then there were many secrets which the master only revealed (if he didn't die first) to his sons or best pupils. These lost secrets prevent our duplicating the old techniques. There were many different methods of laminating blades other than the five piece Soshu style described above.

The second method eliminated the medium hard back piece; the third dropped out the center soft shock absorber allowing the hard edge steel to form the center core with only the edge hardened; the fourth wrapped hard and medium steel around the soft core; the fifth (the most common method), wrapped the hard steel around a soft or medium core; while the sixth reversed this by wrapping a medium steel partly around a hard edge and core piece. The seventh and final method was not often used for long blades, although it would do for theatrical blades. It called for inserting the hard edge piece into a slot in the medium steel back piece. This was the cheapest method, but not too satisfactory as it lacked the stiffening effect of the sandwich methods and it was hard for the craftsman to be sure that the welding was perfect. Such swords, easily bent, would only be good for daggers.

In the first, second, and third methods, the final sword shape was achieved by scraping and grinding to uncover the edge steel, as forging to final shape would result in a skin of medium steel covering the edge portion which should be hard.

In most of these procedures, the point is formed by turning the end so that the edge steel follows around to the back. This is done in the forging. However, with the third method it could be done by grinding.

As the hammering frequently distorts the blade, it is necessary to correct the curvature. This is done by heating a block of copper or brass that has a groove in it. By laying the blade in the groove, the back or edge can be expanded slightly. If it were stretched by hammering, the blade would become thinner in places, perhaps ruining it.

Great skill is necessary in drawing the blade out, as uneven heating and hammering can cause internal distortion in which the soft core steel is forced to one side in spots, parts of which might even become exposed when the blade is ground and polished. This would greatly weaken it.

Regardless of the forging method employed, the newly forged blade is rough and has to be finished by scraping, filing, and grinding. A drawshave is used first. This tool needs to be very hard and tough and would be fabricated in the same way that a sword is forged. Or it could be made by adding handles to a broken section of sword blade.

Next the 'smith does a rough grinding on stones. This allows a better look at the surface to see if any flaws are present. Assuming that the blade is in good order, the 'smith shapes the tang and adds the file marks.

Next, the edge must be hardened without affecting the body of the blade. to do this, the blade is coated with an eighth of an inch of clay. The 'smith then scrapes it thin along the edge so that the edge will get hotter than does the body. This is the most critical operation of all. The smithy is darkened so the 'smith can judge the exact shade of redness of the edge when it is plunged into a tank of water maintained at a certain temperature. Water taken from certain streams in spring or fall is considered best for this.

The water chills the edge where the clay is thin, forming a whitish crystalline surface called yakiba—literally—fired edge. If the hardening comes out just right, no tempering will be necessary, but usually an additional heating is needed to reduce the hardness a little and prevent the edge from being too brittle. The first quenching produces a line of coarse crystals called nie, separating the yakiba from the rest of the surface. The tempering, if required, is done at a lower temperature and produces another line of very fine darker crystals called nioi. The presence of both indicates a very good blade. Skips in the line of nioi are bad flaws.

was very good quality, and we find inscriptions on swords stating that the 'smith used imported iron.

Basically, sword making followed the pattern described above, but the skill of the 'smith still counted for much. Swords by Masamune bring many thousands of dollars, while copies made of the same steels using the same methods, may be worth only $25.00. Why this difference? Skill and integrity would be the answer. Did the master or his apprentices really fold the steel 15 times? Was the master skillful enough in drawing out the blade to insure that none of the laminations came unstuck in the process? A flaw of this nature could be completely hidden and only show up after many tests in battle. In combat, if your sword failed you were dead! Many tests were used to make sure a sword was strong, but there was always the chance that it might have broken on the next one. So you had to trust the reputation of the 'smith. Has anyone ever heard of a

JAPANESE SWORD

In the old days, the 'smith made the peg hole in the tang with a punch while the blade was hot. This is seldom done today since power drills have become available and it is easier to spot the hole exactly where you want it in case you are going to use an existing handle.

The blade is next signed and then sent to a polisher, who in a series of 12 to 15 operations grinds the blade to its final shape. Minor errors in curvature and thickness are corrected here. The process consists of honing with successive stones from rough (which cuts fast but leaves deep scratches), to finer and finer stones, each of which removes scratches left from the previous stone. The final work gives such a smooth surface that the texture of the steel becomes plainly visible, and the colors and crystalline structure of the temper line stand out. This cannot be duplicated by machine and is the focal point in judging many of the characteristics of the blade. The final polish is done with thin slivers of stone pasted on paper. These are manipulated by thumb or finger. Powders used to bring out the colors of the steel also make the crystals in the temper line stand out. On poorer quality blades, these last operations are slighted: Not so on a higher quality blade, especially if it carries a famous name. The master 'smiths each had their own secret alchemy. Certain of these tricks are known but

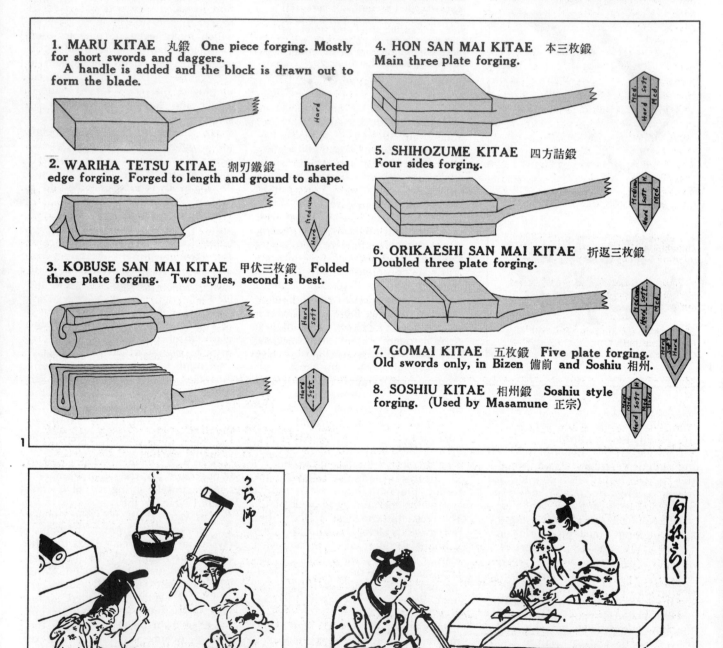

1. MARU KITAE 丸鍛 One piece forging. Mostly for short swords and daggers.
A handle is added and the block is drawn out to form the blade.

2. WARIHA TETSU KITAE 割刃鐵鍛 Inserted edge forging. Forged to length and ground to shape.

3. KOBUSE SAN MAI KITAE 甲伏三枚鍛 Folded three plate forging. Two styles, second is best.

4. HON SAN MAI KITAE 本三枚鍛 Main three plate forging.

5. SHIHOZUME KITAE 四方詰鍛 Four sides forging.

6. ORIKAESHI SAN MAI KITAE 折返三枚鍛 Doubled three plate forging.

7. GOMAI KITAE 五枚鍛 Five plate forging. Old swords only, in Bizen 備前 and Soshiu 相州.

8. SOSHIU KITAE 相州鍛 Soshiu style forging. (Used by Masamune 正宗)

others have defied all attempts at re-discovery. Some show up accidentally, but can't be produced at will. Many such secrets are lost.

The nature of these effects (most of which occur in the temper line area) can be judged by their names: golden streaks; sand floating lines; rainbow hues; reflections; wet spots; and coarse or fine crystals. In addition to the effects consistently found in one man's work, there are accidental results like double temper lines or occasional spots of temper away from the edge; these can be caused by the clay flaking off in the fire.

Flaws that mar the quality may occur at all stages of the forging process. These may consist of cracks, blisters, carbon pockets, wrinkles, and lines that indicate a separation of laminations. Any one takes away from the value of a sword. Some are fatal as no one wants a sword that might bend or break in action. Even the presence of slight flaws usually resulted in a 'smith leaving a blade unsigned. It is these blades that often

1. Details of the forging processes showing the various types of steels used and edges formed from them.

2. Woodcut showing the 'smith and his apprentices drawing the steel out to begin forming the blade.

3. Blades were filed before final hardening operation was performed on the edge.

get fake signatures added on later. Sometimes carvings are added to a blade to cover up flaws. If you see a dragon carving that looks awkward, beware, because it may hide a number of bad defects. Usually these carvings are easy to spot because of their poor workmanship.

Other flaws could be the result of too many grindings and polishings where the outer layers may be ground away in spots, thus exposing the soft core. We call this condition "very tired," and it makes the blade practically worthless as such a blade has lost the strength and stiffness given it by the laminations. Even if made by a famous 'smith, it will have little value.

We have now covered the steps in producing a finished blade by various general methods. These methods apply to all types of long blades—*tachi*, *katana*, and *wakizashi*, and to a certain extent to *tanto* and *yari* points. Because the short dagger and short spear points do not require the strength of the longer blades, they can be made by simpler methods like the two piece *kobusei*, or even one piece construction. Long spear points of one to three foot lengths would require a laminated technique—one that provides hard steel for both edges.

Types of weapons used underwent changes as time went on, and for a variety of reasons. The earliest swords found in the burial mounds in Japan have some Chinese char-

acteristics. They were long, straight, or very slightly curved and one or both edges were sharp. These gave way to long, slim, curved *tachi* blades which had a good slicing action against the padded cloth or boiled leather armor worn in those early times. The *tachi* was a good weapon for horsemen as it had a long reach and its light weight made it easy to handle. A long tanto of 10 to 14 inches was worn with the *tachi*.

When iron armor came in, a heavier blade was needed, although chopping away at steel helmets probably went out when warriors discovered what it could do to a sword blade! This changed the style of fencing to a series of feints and pulled strokes until someone made a mistake and left an opening for a thrust to a vital spot. Clashing of swords would be accidental.

Horses were killed in battle faster than they could be replaced, so eventually only generals and their aides were mounted.

With most fighting being done on foot, the *tachi* slung scabbard got in the way and required two hands to draw. It was also too long for foot soldiers. So, the shorter *katana* came into being with its companion *wakizashi*, both being thrust through the sash to which the scabbards were tied so they could be drawn with one hand. These were worn edge-up so that they came out in fighting position. At this time, many favorite *tachi* blades were shortened by cutting the

TYPES OF SWORDS		
TACHI 太刀 A slung sword	尺	2.0 - 7.3
DAI KATANA 大刀 Long sword		2.5 & up
KATANA 刀 Standard fighting sword		2.0 - 2.5
CHI ISA KATANA 小刀 Short katana		1.85 - 2
WAKIZASHI 脇差 Short sword		1.65 - 1.85
KO WAKIZASHI 小脇差 Short sword		1.2 - 1.65
TANTO 短刀 Dagger		.3 - 1.2
(Tanto used to commit Hara-kiri measured .8)		
AIKUCHI 匕首 Dagger without guard		.3 - 1
HEYAZASHI 部屋差 Tanto carried in the clothing		
HIMOGATANA 紐刀 Stilleto		
HAN-DACHI 半太刀 Katana with part tachi mounts		
KEN or TSURUGI 剣 Old straight 2 edged		1 - 4
HOKEN 寶剣 Ken shaped temple sword		
RYOBA 兩刃 or MOROHA 諸刃 Double edged		
YOROI TOSHI 鎧透刺 Armor piercing tanto		.75 - 1
YAGEN DOSHI 薬研 A short heavy armor cutter		
NAGINATA 長刀 Curved blade on 6.5 handle		1.6
CHIKUTO 竹刀 Bamboo fencing sword		
(Blades are measured from Point to Back Notch)		

FORGING PROCESSES

Smiths generally had five grades of steel on hand or available. These had been prepared by laborious hand processes, consisting of melting, chilling, breaking, re-melting, forging, folding, and re-forging until the texture and carbon content were as desired.

THE FIVE BASIC STEELS

1. SEN 鑄の熔鐵 Pure or nearly pure malleable iron. This contained 0 to .1 percent carbon and could be re-worked into almost any kind of steel.

2. HOCHO 鉋丁 Soft steel, .1 to .3 carbon. Was generally re-worked to contain .5 to .7 carbon.

3. JAMI 熔鐵 Medium steel, .3 to .4 carbon. This was worked over to .7 or .8 carbon.

4. CHIGUSA 千草 Hard steel, .7 to .8 carbon.

5. DEWA 出羽 Tool steel, .8 to 1 percent carbon.

These were refined to suit the personal taste of the 'smith, after which they were combined in various ways to form the different grades of steel for edge, center, sides and back of the blade.

The repeated forgings caused a loss of from 60 to 80 percent of the material started with.

The resulting bars were combined and drawn out to sword length according to one of the following systems or schools. In latter times, any 'smith could use any system his customer desired or could afford.

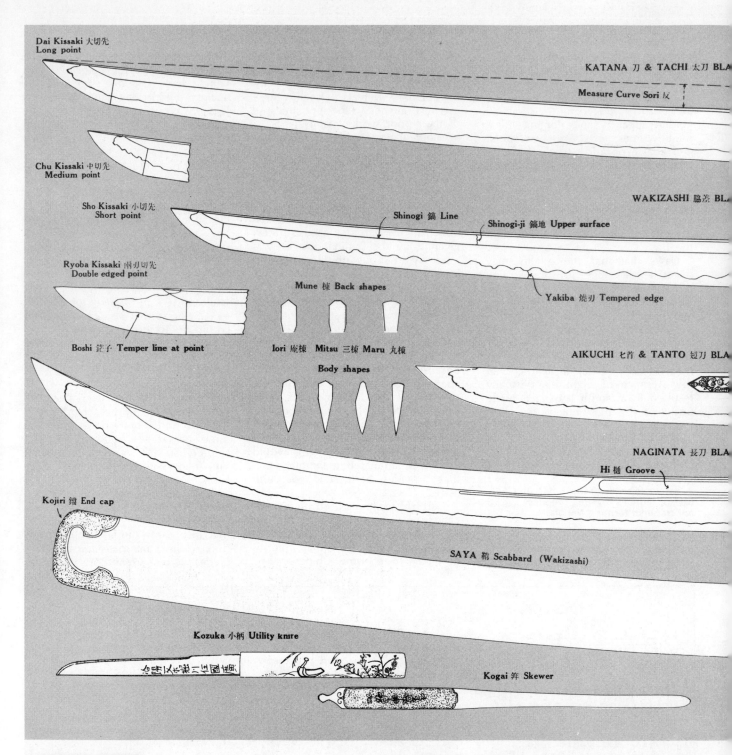

Dai Kissaki 大切先
Long point

KATANA 刀 & TACHI 太刀 BLA

Measure Curve Sori 反

Chu Kissaki 中切先
Medium point

WAKIZASHI 脇差 BL

Sho Kissaki 小切先
Short point

Shinogi 鎬 Line

Shinogi-ji 鎬地 Upper surface

Ryoba Kissaki 雨刃切先
Double edged point

Mune 棟 Back shapes

Yakiba 焼刃 Tempered edge

Boshi 鋩子 Temper line at point

Iori 庵棟　Mitsu 三棟　Maru 丸棟

AIKUCHI 匕首 & TANTO 短刀 BLA

Body shapes

NAGINATA 長刀 BLA

Hi 樋 Groove

Kojiri 鐺 End cap

SAYA 鞘 Scabbard　(Wakizashi)

Kozuka 小柄 Utility knife

Kogai 笄 Skewer

JAPANESE SWORD

tang; the result is that many famous swords lost their signatures.

The *katana* was supposed to fit the wearer. When held point down it should clear the ground by about two inches, and thus avoid hitting rocks that might break the point on a downswing. A broken point could ruin a sword.

Because of the metal armor, two changes came about in swords. The blade had to be heavier in case it was necessary to cut metal, and as fencing techniques evolved from

chop to thrust, an almost straight blade made it easier to keep track of where your point was for a thrust.

At all times, the curved *naginata* blade on a long six to eight foot handle was popular especially by and against horsemen. A variation of this was the *nagamaki*, which had a straighter, heavier blade on a four foot handle, although this never reached popularity.

Spears also were used from earliest times when armies of peasants were armed with sharpened bamboo poles. Regular spears had steel points from four inches to three feet or more in length, mounted on long poles.

Eventually, cross bars were added, sometimes on the poles below the point—but later forged in one piece with the point. These were to prevent a too-deep penetration and subsequent difficulty in withdrawing the spear—especially from horses. Many variations exist, ranging from a short spur on one side to curved hooks designed to pull a man off a horse.

Bows and arrows saw wide use and armor came to be worn mainly as protection against the steel pointed arrows. Later, when guns were introduced, the armor helped shield against bullets. The makers of *Hineno*-type armor sometimes dis-

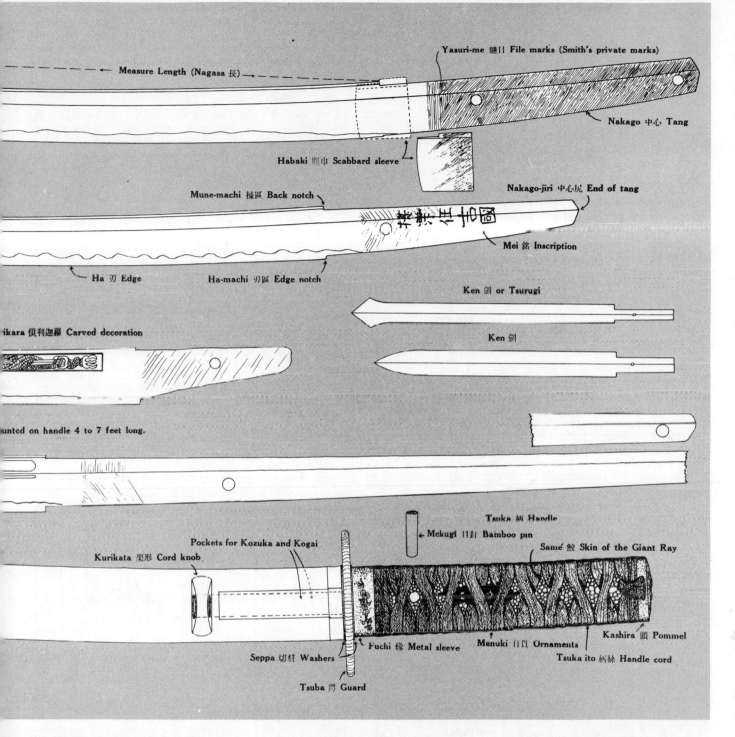

Measure Length (Nagasa 長)

Yasuri-me 鑢目 File marks (Smith's private marks)

Nakago 中心 Tang

Habaki 鎺巾 Scabbard sleeve

Mune-machi 棟區 Back notch

Nakago-jiri 中心尻 End of tang

Mei 銘 Inscription

Ha 刃 Edge

Ha-machi 刃區 Edge notch

Ken 劔 or Tsurugi

Ken 劔

Kurikara 倶利迦羅 Carved decoration

Mounted on handle 4 to 7 feet long.

Kurikata 栗形 Cord knob

Pockets for Kozuka and Kogai

Tsuka 柄 Handle

Mekugi 目釘 Bamboo pin

Same 鮫 Skin of the Giant Ray

Fuchi 縁 Metal sleeve

Menuki 目貫 Ornaments

Kashira 頭 Pommel

Tsuka ito 柄絲 Handle cord

Seppa 切羽 Washers

Tsuba 鍔 Guard

played their wares with bullet dents as proof of strength.

Sword construction during the *Koto* or Old Sword period was as described just previous, with each 'smith or group of 'smiths making their own steel in all the various grades needed. This gave the master absolute control over every step in the forging. But toward the end of that time (from about 1530 to 1596), a long civil war created such a demand for blades that most 'smiths went into a production line operation in which less skilled apprentices did the minor operations, with the master only holding the blade for the drawing-out

and tempering processes. It was during this era covering three generations of 'smiths that the secrets which had made their ancestors' swords so great were lost. Nobody had time for frills or to practice the master's secrets (which would have to be done when nobody was around), as the old masters were not about to divulge their secrets to poorly-trained students. By the third generation, all these tricks were completely lost!

At the end of the civil war, with the country unified and the fighting virtually ceased, many 'smiths lacked for work and thus were obliged to go

to ordinary blacksmithing. Some of these, however, specialized in making steel for sale to swordsmiths who could then concentrate on making blades.

This change from old to new methods and to peace time demands represented the change from *Koto* (old sword) to *Shinto* or New Sword times. However, the ability to buy ready-made steel had its drawbacks, as you could not tell by looking at it whether it had indeed been folded 15 times or what the ingredients were. This, along with the loss of the old secrets made *Shinto* blades inferior to any *Koto* blades, with the exception, perhaps, of some of the production line blades. This is not to say that *Shinto* blades were poor quality—a few were very fine blades that just lacked some of the fine points of the old masters. Any *Shinto* blade made by the lamination process was far superior to any foreign blade.

Around 1780 when Masahide attracted many students to his school by advocating a return to *koto* methods, a new period was born called *Shinshinto* or New-new sword. All attempts to duplicate the best of the great masters failed, although again some very fine swords were produced. By this time, the techniques of the main schools of sword making were common knowledge and almost any good 'smith could turn out blades by any method.

Naotane was especially adept in several schools and shared top honors for the period with Kiyomaro. Both made top quality swords, but neither could match the early *koto* masters. Probably the secrets of the early masters lay in the production of the various steels more than anything else, although tempering tricks undoubtedly contributed much to their perfection.

What may be classed as a special type of sword is the oversize blade.

These were made by many 'smiths on special order for customers big enough to handle one, but mostly they were demonstration pieces presented to temples where they would be displayed as advertisements for the maker. These would be pretty good for display purposes. They were never expected to be used in any kind of combat.

Another type of extremely long blade, this for theatrical use, was generally of very poor quality. It was very dramatic for an actor to stride on stage brandishing a sword so long he probably couldn't even draw it. Usually they're found in poor quality scabbards with cheap brass fittings, but sometimes (usually in bad condition) they'll appear in *Shirasaya*. One other type of "sword" should be mentioned—the blacksmith iron imitations found in gift swords, notably in the carved bone or even ivory scabbards made for sale to tourists.

HOW TO STUDY THE BLADE

It is interesting to note how closely 'smiths and groups followed certain patterns, especially during *Koto* times. The general shape of *Koto* blades were long, slim, curved, tapered. They were lightweight, had small points, bold grain patterns, and were well-balanced and graceful.

copied in later times, there were always differences, although they might be slight. Usually the grain is not so pronounced, and the color of the steel is different. Also, the tangs have not had time to acquire the depth of dark brown rust of 600 years of use.

Before we take up individual characteristics, one by one, and determine which were used by which groups or individuals, we will list the points to be covered and how to go about studying them.

1. The shape. This includes curvature, point, cross-section, weight, tang, and general gracefulness and balance, each having many variables.

2. Visible fine points. Texture of steel, color, temper patterns, file marks and rust conditions of the tang, inscriptions, grooves and carvings.

3. Bad points. Waviness of blade or surface, rust pits, nicks, broken point, shortening, sand-papering, and other aberrations due to abuse or neglect.

Now we can take up these general points as applied to the longer swords and break them down into sub-groups. *Tantos* and *yari* come later.

CURVATURE

Deep curve—Early tachi types and naginatas of all periods.

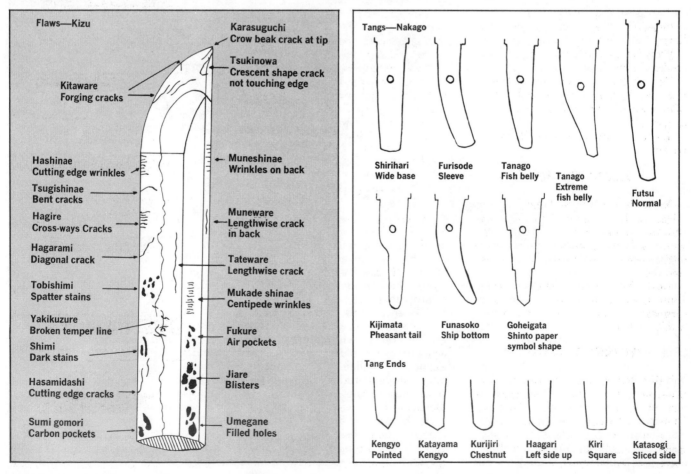

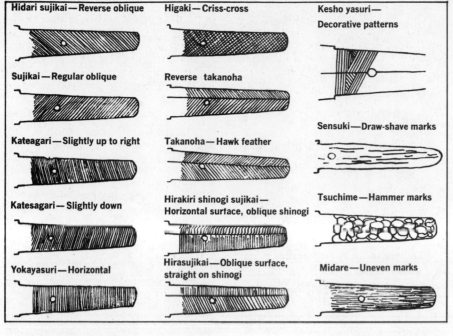

Hidari sujikai — Reverse oblique

Sujikai — Regular oblique

Kateagari — Slightly up to right

Katesagari — Slightly down

Yokayasuri — Horizontal

Higaki — Criss-cross

Reverse takanoha

Takanoha — Hawk feather

Hirakiri shinogi sujikai — Horizontal surface, oblique shinogi

Hirasujikai — Oblique surface, straight on shinogi

Kesho yasuri — Decorative patterns

Sensuki — Draw-shave marks

Tsuchime — Hammer marks

Midare — Uneven marks

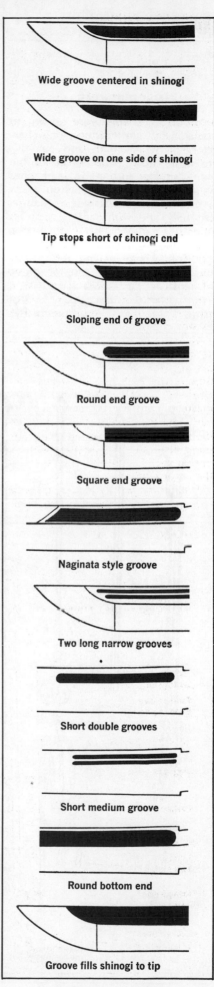

Wide groove centered in shinogi

Wide groove on one side of shinogi

Tip stops short of shinogi end

Sloping end of groove

Round end groove

Square end groove

Naginata style groove

Two long narrow grooves

Short double grooves

Short medium groove

Round bottom end

Groove fills shinogi to tip

Two types—*Torii-zori*—even curve with greatest depth in center. *Koshi-zori*—greatest depth nearer tang or at the notches.

Less curve—even but not so deep

Slight curve—late *Shinto* and *Shinshinto* times.

Slight curve but more pronounced near the point—some *nagamakis*.

POINTS

Small, stubby—early *tachi*.

Regular shape—small, medium, large—various schools.

Very long—*naginatas*, fancy short *wakizashi* and *tanto* types.

No dividing *yokote* line—flat surface blades and some special shapes that have *shinogi* surfaces, and some *nagamakis*.

Re-shaped points—see under flaws, below.

CROSS-SECTION

Body—Flat surfaces taper to the edge. Parallel surfaces with edge cut to one side like *kozuka*. *Shinogi* type with surfaces parallel or slanting either way—called high, flat, or low *shinogi*.

Meat—No meat—flat surface; with meat—convex surface, various degrees of fatness or partial when *yakiba* is flat.

WEIGHT & WIDTH

Light weight and narrow—mostly *Koto* or copies of *koto*. Normal average weight and width—late *Koto* to *Shinshinto*. Heavy solid blades mostly *Shinshinto*. A characteristic of some *Masahide* student experiments. Awkward and unbalanced.

TANG

Many shapes—identifiable with schools.

Tang Tips—Square, round, V-shape (*ken*), slanted to either side. Original or shortened—holes give a clue.

Holes—Punched hot (somewhat irregular) or drilled. Locations of holes. Several holes indicate shortening or pseudo shortening or refitting to existing handles.

One punched hole—most likely original.

One drilled hole—greatly shortened or late Shinshinto to modern.

Small added hole at tip—early tachi mounting or copy of same.

If hole cuts through a signature, check for burrs in the hole indicating signature added at a later date —phony!

Rust in hole redder than tang— hole added later or drilled out.

FILE MARKS

Study angle of slant; plain or fancy. Hammer marks or scraper marks instead of file marks.

RUST CONDITION

Rust should never be removed unless necessary to read signature or ease removal of handle, and then only enough to accomplish the purpose. Remove very carefully by light tapping.

No rust to light red rust—modern to 75 years old. Firm dark rust but not deep—file marks plainly visible —100-300 years old.

Deeply corroded dark rust—400 to 600 years old if not faked. Faking of old rust may be hard to detect.

JAPANESE SWORD

Clean but pitted tang may have been treated with Naval Jelly—never use it!

INSCRIPTIONS

About 50 'smiths were known to occasionally sign with only one character, of which *Ichi*—and *Sa* are best known. Almost all of the older 'smiths and many later ones signed with two characters on a few swords. Three character signatures generally end with *saku* or *tsu kura* (made) or start with a clan name like *Minamoto* *Taira* etc. Four character inscriptions are most often clan + name or group + name—*Fujiwara Masayiko NioKiyotsune* or name + *sakukore* (made by).

Signatures were supposed to be on the side of the tang away from the body, so we speak of *tachi-mei* or *katana-mei* to indicate which side. Where inscriptions are on both sides, one is usually the date. However, many long inscriptions violate all rules.

When a blade has been shortened several possibilities exist:

1. Signature left attached and folded up into slot cut for it.

2. Signature cut out and inlaid in a slot. (May not be genuine!)

3. Signature "moved up"—copied by the man who shortened the blade with statement like "Original *mei* so-and-so."

4. Appraiser puts the 'smith's name in gold (inlaid, damascened, or lacquer) with or without his own name and *kakihan*. This should be accompanied by a certificate. Red lacquer sometimes.

5. Signature cut by anybody to enhance the value. May be on a genuine blade or on any blade he thinks might get by!

GROOVES

Grooves were not for blood but to balance or lighten a blade, or to hide flaws, or often just for decoration.

CARVINGS

Decorative carvings were mostly Buddhist symbols consisting of Ken plain or with a simple or elaborate dragon coiled around it. *Bonji* or priest characters are invocations to Buddhas. Early carvings were mostly

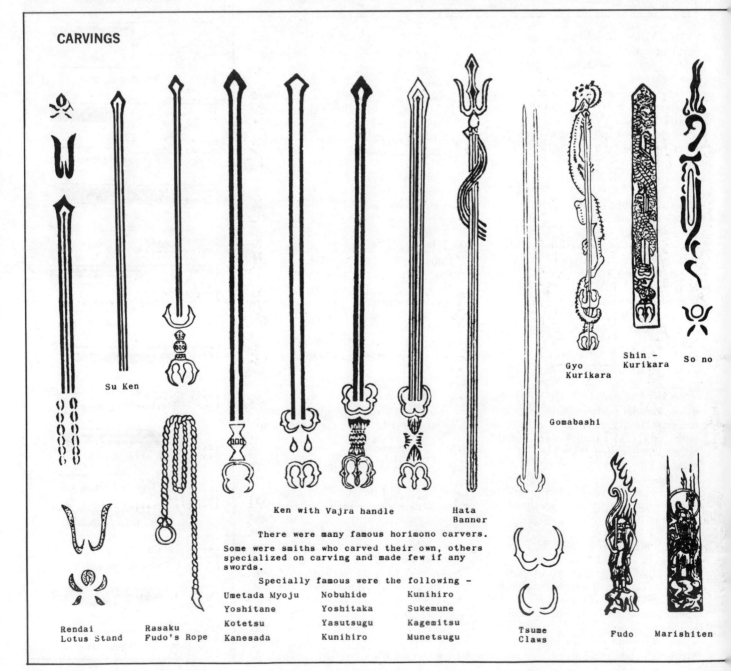

CARVINGS

Su Ken

Rendai
Lotus Stand

Rasaku
Fudo's Rope

Ken with Vajra handle

Hata
Banner

There were many famous horimono carvers. Some were smiths who carved their own, others specialized on carving and made few if any swords.

Specially famous were the following —

Umetada Myoju	Nobuhide	Kunihiro
Yoshitane	Yoshitaka	Sukemune
Kotetsu	Yasutsugu	Kagemitsu
Kanesada	Kunihiro	Munetsugu

Gomabashi

Gyo
Kurikara

Shin -
Kurikara

So no

Tsume
Claws

Fudo

Marishiten

simple; elaborate ones came in peace times when decorations helped sell blades. Judge by workmanship— crude work often hides flaws.

BAD POINTS

Examine every blade for straightness. Look lengthwise, if surface is wavy or bumpy, it has been badly polished by taking out pits or flaws where they occur without bringing the entire surface down equally. If the edge is not an even curve, nicks have been taken out locally. If point has been broken, then reshaped, boshi temper line may be thin or disappear, going off into space. Flaws from forging. Some affect the strength and some do not. All cut the value. Core metal shows—too "tired."

SIGNATURES—GENUINE OR FAKE?

It is one thing to read the characters on a sword tang and something else again to say for sure who made it! It is generally assumed that 90 percent of all big name signatures are fakes, as well as a good percentage of lesser 'smiths.

This was possible because many 'smiths left those blades unsigned which did not turn out well enough to suit them. Often they are very superior blades compared to those made by average 'smiths, but lacking verification of a signature, their origin may be doubtful. Then, of course, there are the out and out fakes and copies imitating the style but seldom the quality of those of the great masters. So, the problem is to be able to recognize a fake signature.

Signatures cut with a chisel exhibit as many or more characteristics than those written with a pen or brush. The variables are as follows:

1. The chisel. Each 'smith had his own favorite chisel for cutting a signature. Now—what shape point? Was it V-shaped or U-shaped and what angle V or how wide a U? A wide angle V-point held at a low angle to the work would cut a shallow groove the same width as a narrow V shape that was hit harder at a steeper angle, producing a much deeper groove. The depth of the groove would not show up on an *oshigata* rubbing, only the width. Neither would the roundness of a U shape of the same width. The difference between a V and a U might be apparent in a photograph but not

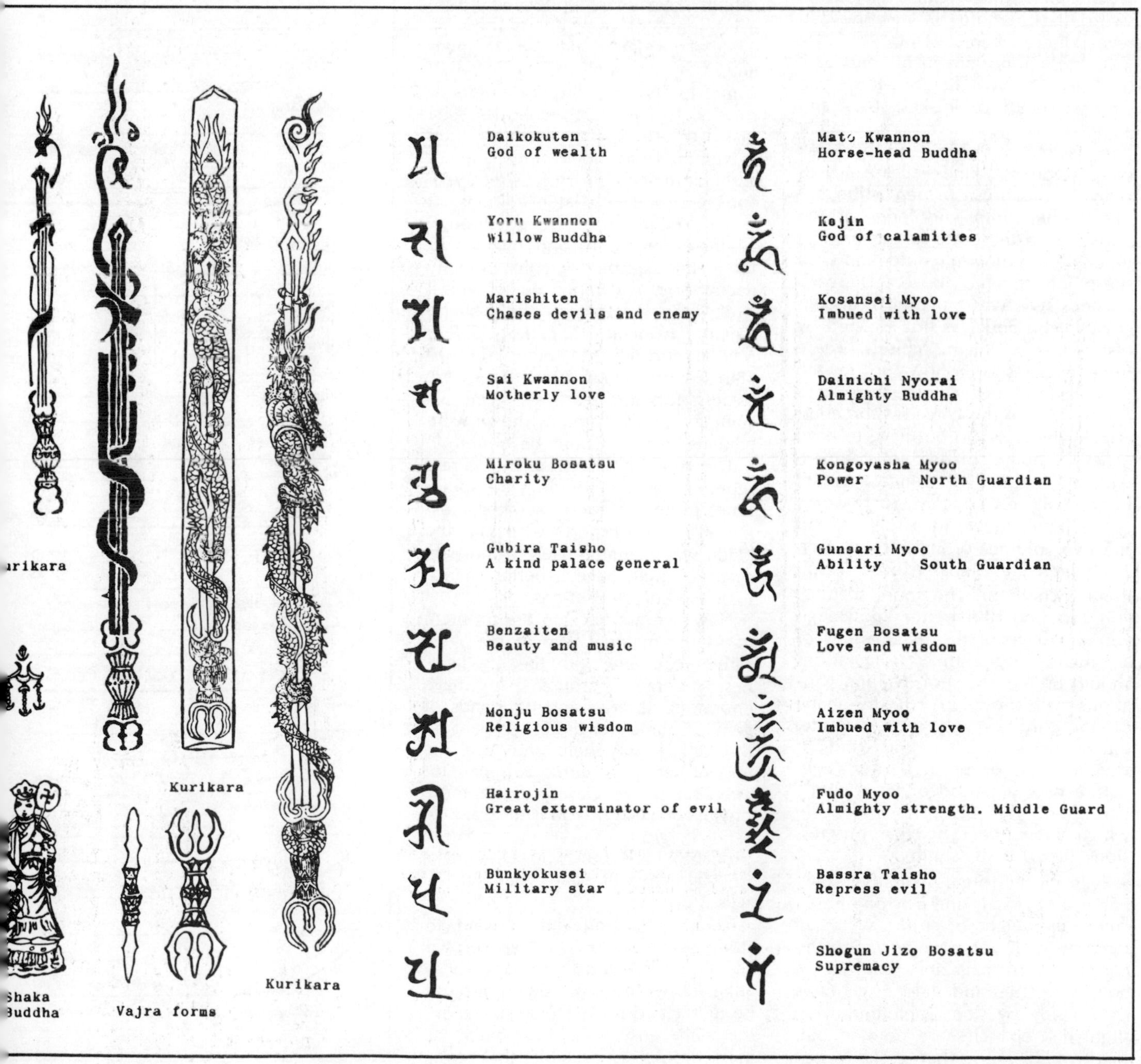

Daikokuten
God of wealth

Yoru Kwannon
Willow Buddha

Marishiten
Chases devils and enemy

Sai Kwannon
Motherly love

Miroku Bosatsu
Charity

Gubira Taisho
A kind palace general

Benzaiten
Beauty and music

Monju Bosatsu
Religious wisdom

Hairojin
Great exterminator of evil

Bunkyokusei
Military star

Mato Kwannon
Horse-head Buddha

Kejin
God of calamities

Kosansei Myoo
Imbued with love

Dainichi Nyorai
Almighty Buddha

Kongoyasha Myoo
Power   North Guardian

Gunsari Myoo
Ability   South Guardian

Fugen Bosatsu
Love and wisdom

Aizen Myoo
Imbued with love

Fudo Myoo
Almighty strength. Middle Guard

Bassra Taisho
Repress evil

Shogun Jizo Bosatsu
Supremacy

Kurikara

Kurikara

Shaka Buddha

Vajra forms

Kurikara

the depth of the cut. In badly rusted old tangs, you would not be able to see either. Direct comparison with a genuine blade would be necessary to prove this point. So here we have a number of characteristics that would not be in hand writing or show up in a rubbing: The depth and shape of the cut.

2. At what angle did the 'smith hold the chisel and how hard did he tap it with what weight hammer? We don't have to know these three variables but they would definitely affect the cuts. How many taps with the hammer did he use to cut a line a half inch long? If the strokes were heavy this might show up on an *oshigata*, but if light it probably would not. A magnifying glass on the sword itself would be necessary to reveal these characteristics.

3. Most important of all, and easy to see, is how did he form the strokes? Length of strokes, shape and angle of dots, curved or straight lines, shape and angle of the hook on the end of a line—all are just as individual as brush or pen writings— as are the width and taper of the strokes, and these are just as hard to imitate even if you could know all the points covered above. Also, each master's style was a matter of unconscious habit and was not affected by his age or changing chisels. These little nuances all show up in the *oshigata* and are ample enough to expose all but the cleverest forgeries. For this part, we do not have to have actual genuine blades to compare with, as pictures of *oshigata* in the books will serve nicely. Such works as the Juyos, the various Taikans, and the two volumes of Fujishiro's *Nihon Toko Jiten* are available even if you don't own them. The more pictures you can find, the better knowledge you will have of the peculiarities of a man's signature. Irregularities should be easy to spot. Natural variations will show up but the shape of the strokes will remain pretty much the same. For the kind of changes that occur in a man's signature over a period of years, study Part 2 of the *Osaka Shinto Zufu* which shows year by year progressions of a lot of 'smiths.

Even clever forgers had their own habits and chisels and a wrong hook, curve, or weight of stroke will give them away. If you have access to the current sword magazines from Japan, note the true and false signatures shown side by side. Sometimes very slight discrepancies are pointed out.

It would seem that certain men specialized in forging signatures of certain 'smiths as the forger's own characteristics may show up in several fakes. A study of true and false signatures of Kiyomaro and Naotane bear this out. In the big work *Minamoto Kiyomaro,* huge blow-ups of his signatures show an even swelling or tapering of his horizontal strokes, while all the fakes show bumps at the end of each stroke. Fake signatures of Naotane are extremely close to the genuine except in the *kakihan,* where the top zigzag lines of the genuine are crowded together but appear much more open on the fakes.

In order to research signatures, you need as many examples as possible that can reasonably be expected to be genuine. Disagreement among experts is mostly confined to unsigned blades and a few Juyo certifications have been repudiated. However, some of the very old books, while considered reliable in general, are completely useless when it comes to checking the fine points of strokes. This is because the *oshigata* first had to be copied by brush, then carved in wood blocks, then printed, and ultimately recopied, recarved, and reprinted for later editions. It would be impossible to go through all these operations and retain anything like a photographic quality necessary for comparison of chisel strokes. Such works as the *Honcho Kajiko, Honcho Gunkiko, Shinto Meijin,* and all the other 16th to 18th Century wood block books are useless for this purpose, even assuming that all examples shown were genuine (which would be doubtful).

The modern books give accurate reproductions, leaving only the sometimes pertinent question of how expert was the "expert" who said the blade was genuine? Here again, signatures would have a better chance than *mumei* attributions.

Now, we are back to the problem of source material. We of the West cannot compete with the big Japanese appraisal groups who have enormous libraries and thousands of genuine blades for direct comparison. But still, it will help and save the cost of sending swords to Japan for appraisal if we can spot the more obvious fakes. If you still want to send it, you can state "signature probably false but who DID make it?"—which will save your face if it is a phony!

Certainly we all should want to study, regardless of whether we own an almost "National Treasure" or a Sukesada we can't pin down because he didn't add his personal name. So, the only answer is to acquire as many books as possible that show

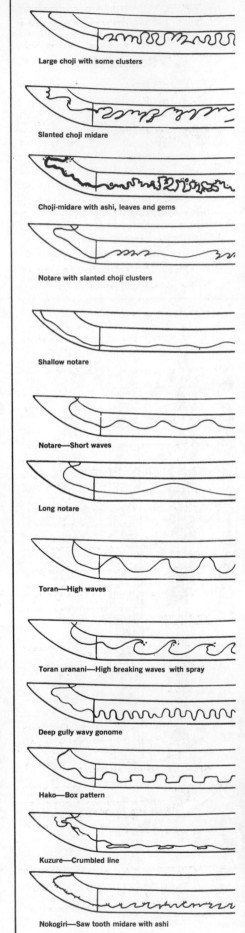

Large choji with some clusters

Slanted choji midare

Choji-midare with ashi, leaves and gems

Notare with slanted choji clusters

Shallow notare

Notare—Short waves

Long notare

Toran—High waves

Toran uranani—High breaking waves with spray

Deep gully wavy gonome

Hako—Box pattern

Kuzure—Crumbled line

Nokogiri—Saw tooth midare with ashi

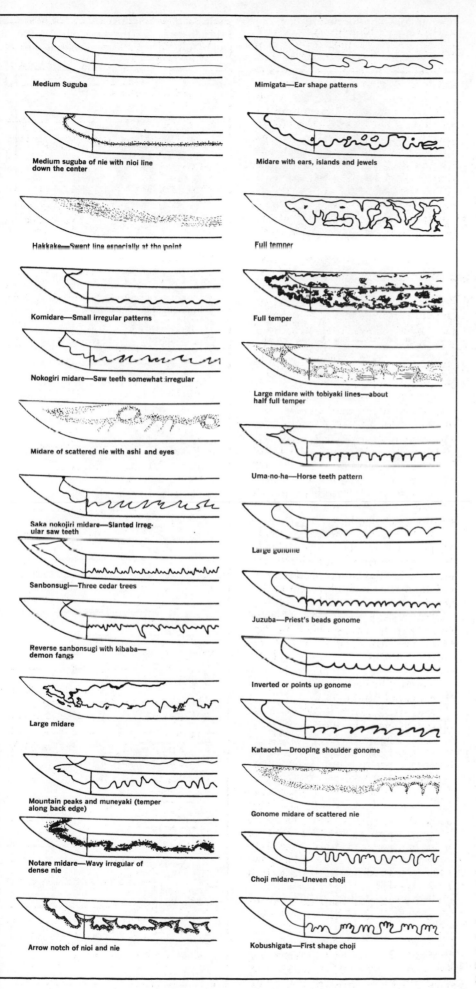

Medium Suguba

Medium suguba of nie with nioi line down the center

Hakkake—Swept line especially at the point

Komidare—Small irregular patterns

Nokogiri midare—Saw teeth somewhat irregular

Midare of scattered nie with ashi and eyes

Saka nokojiri midare—Slanted irregular saw teeth

Sanbonsugi—Three cedar trees

Reverse sanbonsugi with kibaba—demon fangs

Large midare

Mountain peaks and muneyaki (temper along back edge)

Notare midare—Wavy irregular of dense nie

Arrow notch of nioi and nie

Mimigata—Ear shape patterns

Midare with ears, islands and jewels

Full temper

Full temper

Large midare with tobiyaki lines—about half full temper

Uma-no-ha—Horse teeth pattern

Large gonome

Juzuba—Priest's beads gonome

Inverted or points up gonome

Kataochi—Drooping shoulder gonome

Gonome midare of scattered nie

Choji midare—Uneven choji

Kobushigata—First shape choji

pictures of tangs. Some are certainly expensive but there are a lot of inexpensive ones also being turned out in Japan that are in the $5.00 to $10.00 bracket. Assuming that you have acquired some of these, there is still the problem of finding the picture you want without a knowledge of Japanese, or a whole day of searching. Indexes are the answer. An index is being prepared for "Tanto," but many more are needed. For those of you owning some volumes of the *Juyo Token nado Zufu* or the two volumes of the *Nihon Toko Jiten*, these are indexed in the author's book, Japanese Swordsmiths. The author is indexing, one by one, all of his library that contains pictures by using a code letter for each work, and noting each picture of a tang opposite the man's name in the book. Anyone who can figure out names and dates well enough to use such a reference should be able to do this to almost any modern book.

Two good sources are the *Koson Oshigata* and the *Umetada Meikan* which reproduce the scrap books of *oshigata* gathered by those two men who were such experts in earlier days. Both need indexing.

Now back to reading and evaluating inscriptions. We have to remember that there are genuine swords to which the name was added later by someone who recognized the work, and added the name with or without trying to imitate the signature (in order to make the blade easier to sell). Properly, such attributions should have been done in gold by a recognized appraiser and signed with his name and/or *kakihan*, but many tried to counterfeit the signature. Certification of these has to ignore the fake signature.

Signatures added at a much later date often exhibit a different color of rust in the chisel marks. Another thing to watch is a hole through a character of a signature. Generally, new holes were added when the blade was shortened, but a blade with signature and only one hole right through a character is obvious nonsense! Or even several holes if the lowest one pierces a character. When blades were shortened, the new holes (always drilled, not punched) had to be higher, not lower. When a hole pierces a character, use a glass to see if burrs from the chisel were pushed into the sides of the hole; this is a dead giveaway.

For the most part, fake signatures were intended to upgrade the value of a blade, so these tended to indicate the most famous man if several generations existed. However, later generations sometimes thought they were good enough to pass off a blade as that of a famous predecessor and cut an inscription that was only recorded to him. Generally the blade itself will give this away and a check of signature characteristics will confirm it. So the wording of an inscription does not always pin it down to the only one listed in the books. Always check the other generations.

A signature badly encrusted with rust may require some cleaning, but don't disturb it if it is obviously very, very old. First lay the tang on a hard wood block. Lay a piece of thin leather or thick cloth over the inscription and tap lightly with a small hammer . . . not hard enough to distort the metal but enough to break up the layers of rust. A chisel made of bone or bamboo may help to lift off the layers of rust. New red rust often indicates a deliberate attempt to make a tang look old. It won't stick very tight and usually comes off with a wire brush or coarse steel wool. After cleaning, oil or wax the

tang to prevent further rusting.

One final word, a signature is a lot easier to fake than the blade itself, so a thorough study of the blade should precede the research on the signature. Then, if the school and

1. *Various representations of the tsuba (sword guard). Note the beautiful, but understated work of these carvings in metal. Yen values in chart below are pre-War gold Yen and are equivalent to $.50 per Yen.*

2. *Swords were "proof" tested on convicted criminals or their corpses. Shown is a "test" chart.*

3. *Portrait of the most famous of all Japanese 'smiths, Masamune.*

FAMOUS SWORDSMITHS

Name	Province	Value Yen 圓	Period
Amakuni 天國	Yamato 大和	35,000	AD 701
Shinsoku 神息	Buzen 豊前	20,000	708
Yasutsuna 安綱	Hoki 伯者	30,000	806
Sanemori 眞守	"	20,000	851
Yukihira 行平	Buzen 豊前		985
Munechika 宗近	Yamashiro 山城	30,000	987
Tomonari 友成	Bizen 備前	25,000	987
Yoshiiye 吉家	Yamashiro 山城	15,000	1004
Norimune 則宗	Bizen 備前	20,000	1206
Nobufusa 信房	"	"	1207
Muneyoshi 宗吉	"	18,000	1207
Sukemune 助宗	"	"	1207
Kuniyasu 國安	Yamashiro 山城	"	1207
Kunitomo 國友	"	"	1207
Tsunetsugu 恒次	Bitchu 備中	15,000	1207
Yoshimitsu 吉光	Yamashiro 山城	20,000	1264
Kuniyuki 國行	"	8,000	1259
Kuniyoshi 國吉	"	"	1232
Nagamitsu 長光	Bizen 備前	"	1264
Yukimitsu 行光	Sagami 相摸	5,000	1264
Kunimitsu 國光	"	7,000	1278
Masamune* 正宗	"	20,000	1288
Sadamune 貞宗	"	5,000	1319
Kaneuji 兼氏	Mino 美濃	"	1319
Muramasa 村正	Ise 伊勢	2,000	1322
Kanemitsu 兼光	Bizen 備前	7,000	1329

(*Masamune was best; Muramasa was second but his blades were considered unlucky.)

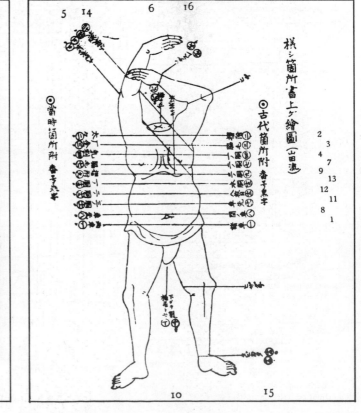

probable date are compatible with the inscription, it is time to go to work on the signature. Of course, study is the key to understanding swords in general and the same applies to the peculiarities of signatures. Start with the swords you own and check out every stroke of every character in the whole inscription. Then read up on the man, making notes of everything pertaining to him. Then go on to other generations of the line, then to pupils, and finally pay special attention to the outstanding points of difference in the signatures. Sometimes one line or dot will be enough to identify a generation.

On your sword record sheet enter a reference to every book and page that shows one of his swords. It will surprise you how soon you will have a fund of knowledge about that beautifully elusive blade. ♛

All drawings copyright © W. M. Hawley 1967 from the book "Japanese Swordsmiths" Vol. I & II. Published by W. M. Hawley, 8200 Gould Ave., Hollywood, Ca. 90046.

PORTRAIT OF MASAMUNÉ. *(Gioku Seki Zasshi.)*

CARE OF SWORDS

Never handle the blade. Wipe off finger prints immediately with a soft cotton cloth and fine talcum powder. Never attempt to polish a good sword.

The Japanese use fine stones to bring out the grain of the steel which would be hidden by buffing. Raw rust spots may be removed by crocus paper.

Examine blades frequently and wipe carefully. Japanese polishers charge from 2 to 5 Yen per inch.

JAPANESE SWORDS
WORKS IN ENGLISH

JAPANESE SWORDSMITHS
by W. M. Hawley
Largest list ever compiled—18,000 names listed, where and when they worked, how they signed in Japanese and Romanization, value index and many tables. Two volumes, 5½x8½ inches. 750 pages.

JAPANESE SWORD BLADES
by A. Dobree
Revised by W. M. Hawley 1967. A good short introduction. Paperback, 5½x8½ inches. 80 pages.

SWORD AND SAME
by Joly and Inada
A translation of two old Japanese works. A vast amount of information. Clothbound 6½x10 inches. 250 pages.

ART OF THE JAPANESE SWORD
by Robinson
A good general work on swords and fittings, well illustrated. 1961, 6¼x10 inches. 110 pages, 100 plates.

A PRIMER OF JAPANESE SWORD-BLADES
by B. W. Robinson
Lists of important 'smiths. 1955 Paperback, 96 pages.

THE SAMURAI SWORD
by John Yumoto
A good general introduction. Clothbound 6x8½ inches. 191 pages.

ORIENTAL CULTURE CHARTS
by W. M. Hawley
Two sizes: 17x22 inches and 27x35 inches. No. 7—Japanese Phonetic Symbols (Kana); No. 11—Japanese Swords—Nomenclature; No. 21—Japanese Crest Designs (Mon); No. 23—Japanese Chronology.

WORKS IN JAPANESE (all illustrated)

NIHON TOKO JITEN
by Fujishiro
A valuable reference work. Contains pictures of tangs of about 1000 important 'smiths. Kotohen—before 1600. Shintohen—1600 to 1870. Two volumes.

NIHON TO NO OKITE TO TOKUCHO
by Honami Koson
Best Japanese textbook. 6¼x8½ inches. 470 pages, 16 plates.

SHUMI NO NIHON TO
by Okoshi
Very useful reference. Illustrations of forging, polishing, etc. 7½x10½ inches. 300 pages.

SHINSHINTO NYUMON
by Shibata
Excellent! Swords made since 1785. 6x8½ inches, 240 pages mostly plates.

TANTO by Suzuki
Devoted to daggers. 6x8½ inches. 270 pages well illustrated.

WAKIZASHI NO MORYOKU
by Shibata
Very useful. Famous short swords. 5¼x7½ inches, 235 pages mostly illustrations.

KOGATANA
by Shibata
Devoted to the kozuka blades found in a pocket in the scabbards of short swords. 6x8½ inches. 175 pages mostly illustrations.

BOOKS ON SWORD FITTINGS

NIHON TSUBA NO MEI
Church Collection
Reprinted with English and Japanese. 10½x12½ inches, 168 pages plus 40 plates.

SUKASHI TSUBAS
by Shibata
Openwork sword guards, 7¼x10½ inches, 285 pages mostly plates.

Note: Hundreds of books are available from Japan on swords and fittings. All in-print items are available from the author. Address all book and sword inquiries to W. M. Hawley, 8200 Gould Avenue, Hollywood, California 90046.

SWISS MILITARY ARMS

WITH THE BOOM IN EUROPE OF COLLECTING OLD MILITARY WEAPONS, ONCE EASILY OBTAINABLE ITEMS ARE SLIPPING FROM UNDER THE NOSES OF AMERICAN COLLECTORS

by Hans Tanner

The collecting of Swiss military rifles has been a long neglected subject. This is probably due to the large numbers of Schmidt-Rubin straight pull rifles that flooded the market in the past 15 years—rifles of a type that were unorthodox and for which shooting ammo was almost unobtainable. However, the time has come when collectors are beginning to realize that there is a great appeal in collecting Swiss military rifles; not only are they extremely well made but they also have a reputation second to none for accuracy.

Perhaps the greatest interest for the collector is the fact that a far greater number of variations exist than anyone (except the Swiss) ever imagined and many of the best pieces are rapidly making their way back across the water to Europe. (where collecting of old military weapons is blossoming at a tremendous rate).

Prices in Europe for Swiss items are consistently higher than in the U.S., and many of the once easily obtainable items are slipping out from under the noses of American collectors.

The Swiss have always been thrifty in their arms procurement, despite national insistence on having the most efficient and advanced weapons available for their citizens army. Many of the available but obsolescent weapons were modified and transformed to keep them moving in a continuous upgrading cycle.

This is the main reason why original Swiss items are scarce and why there are so many variations on the originals. The majority of the conversions were carried out by Federal establishments or authorized suppliers and the work is of a truly professional nature.

The few unofficial modifications that one occasionally comes across are hardly worth the collector's time and have very little interest value.

This does not of course include the many and greatly varied Swiss target rifles built on military actions, for the Swiss are great enthusiasts of target shooting. As a result, a large number of exceptionally fine personalized target rifles have been produced in Switzerland.

For the purpose of this article the Swiss flintlocks will not be discussed, as Federal coherence in firearms procurement thinking really began in the percussion era.

PERCUSSION CONVERSIONS

On the 13th of April, 1842, the Swiss War Council issued orders to convert the flintlocks then in use to a percussion system.

The conversions were made on the following models:

French Infantry Model 1777, modified according to the "Swiss experience"

French Voltigeur Model 1822, modified according to the "Swiss experience"

French Infantry Model 1822, modified according to the "French experience"

At the same time two new models of percussion weapons were introduced:

Infantry Musket Model 1842

Sappers, Engineers and Park Artillery Musket Model 1842; both of these being in 17.5mm caliber.

CANTONAL SHARPSHOOTER STUTZERS

These fine rifles vary in detail from Canton to Canton and calibers vary from 15 to 16.5mm. The majority of these were conversions ordered on the 20th of August, 1842 for the "Heavy Ball Rifle" flintlocks issued in 1817.

FEDERAL RIFLES

In 1848 the decision was made that the arming of Switzerland was to become a Federal affair rather than being left in the hands of the indi-

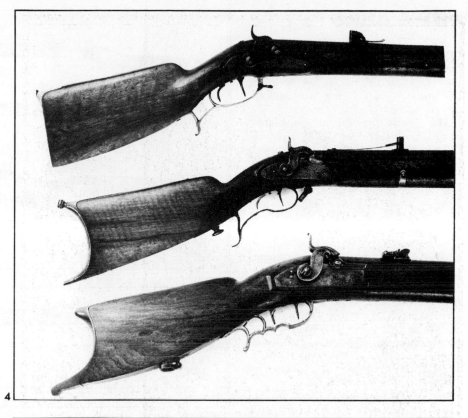

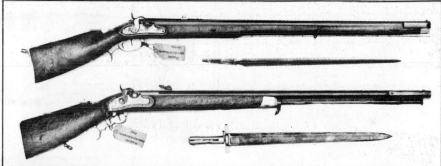

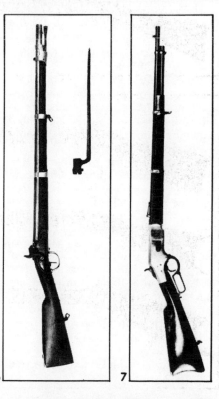

1. Swiss fusiliers at field maneuvers armed with the venerable Model 1889 rifle, the first Swiss rifle to use a smokeless powder cartridge.

2. Top: A French percussion musket used by the Swiss to a great extent and given the designation Model 1822 in Swiss service. Bottom: The superbly accurate, small bore (.41 caliber) Swiss "Federal Rifle" in use from 1856 to 1867.

3. Sharpshooter's rifles from top to bottom: Canton Glarus' Model 1842 converted from flint, about .72 caliber; Canton Waadt (Vaud) c.1840; Canton Bern converted in 1842.

4. Lock details of the Sharpshooter's rifles shown in photo 3.

5. Two more "Cantonal" sharpshooter's rifles. Top: Canton Freiburg. Bottom: Canton Zug (Zoug). These arms were made in small quantities for Cantons.

6. A representative of typical Swiss Cadet musket is a scaled-down version of the musket patterns.

7. The Model 1866 Winchester test piece sent to Switzerland in .44 Henry Flat.

SWISS ARMS

vidual Cantons. A proposal was also made to establish a national arms factory, but this was not adopted as the costs would be higher than if the arms manufacturing was left to private industry.

The first of the new weapons produced under Federal authority was the Model 1851 Federal Stutzer, the caliber of which was reduced to 10.5mm. As a result this was the first "small caliber" rifle produced in Europe. This was followed by the Jager Rifle Model 1853 and the Jager Rifle Model 1856.

In 1859 it was decided to convert all old smoothbore percussion weapons to the Prelaz-Burnand system of rifling. The weapons converted were the Infantry Rifle Model 1842 and a series of German Infantry rifles, 66,000 of which were purchased by Switzerland. The majority of these were converted at the Thun Central Workshops. These rifles were in caliber 18mm.

In 1863 a new infantry rifle in caliber 10.5mm was introduced, and altogether 80,000 were produced between 1863 and 1869.

MILBANK-AMSLER

In April of 1867 the Swiss Government decided to establish a program of converting the service muzzle loaders to breechloaders using the system developed by Professor Amsler of Schaffhausen. The design was a further development of patents held by the American, Milbank.

The Government contracted 24 private companies to undertake the job; the major supplier being Schweizerische Industrie-Gesellschaft (SIG) of Neuhausen.

Up to 1869 a total of 133,000 long arms were converted and these conversions are known by collectors as Milbank-Amslers. Both small caliber (10.4mm) and large caliber (18mm) were modified, and it is a popular misconception that the 18mm conversions predated the 10.4mm conversions. In fact, the decision to convert the small caliber to breechloaders was made on the 24th of April, 1867, while the decision to convert the large caliber weapons came down on the 29th of April, 1867. The 18mm conversions are scarcer than the 10.4s, and the 18mm cartridges are much rarer than the 10.4mm as the smaller caliber was retained through the Vetterli bolt action period.

The small caliber (10.4mm) conversions were:

Jager Rifle Model 1856, converted 1867

1

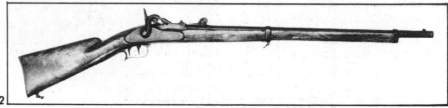

2

3

1. In 1867, Peabody rifles were ordered in .41 Rimfire, 15,000 were delivered and issued to sharpshooter troops. Gradually the bores wore out and these were rebarreled and given the designation M1877.

2. The Milbank-Amsler, a trap-door breech locking system was introduced in 1867, shown is an example of the Stutzer version.

3. The Vetterli-system rifles from top to bottom: Model 69, with receiver cover and King loading gate; Model 71; Stutzer Model 71 with Thury trigger system; Stutzer Model 81 with Rubin trigger system; Model 81; Frontier Guard carbine officially cut-down from a Model 71; Cadet rifle, type 1.

4. Offhand with the Vetterli.

5. A special target rifle using the Vetterli system is a single shot, with a 34" octagonal barrel. Receiver appears to be handmade.

6. Various marking styles common to Vetterlis. Manufacturers were WF Bern, S.I.G. Neuhausen, W. V. Steiger and Montier Werkestadte, Bern.

4

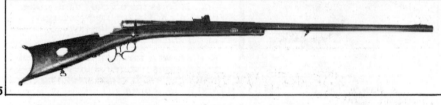

5

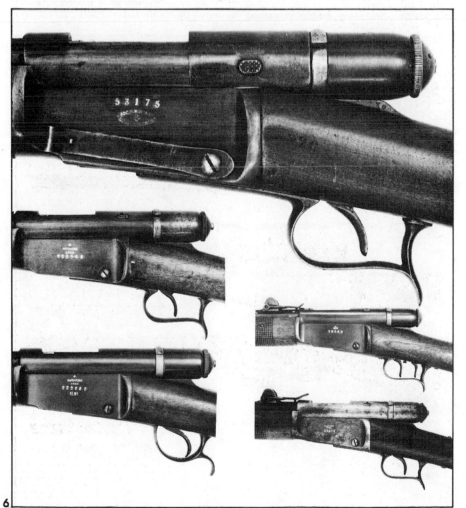

6

Infantry Rifle Model 1863, converted 1867

Stutzer Model 1851, converted 1867

Stutzer Model 1864, converted 1867

The large caliber conversions (18mm) were:

French Infantry Rifle Model 1840, converted 1867

Infantry Rifle Model 1842, converted 1867.

It should be remembered that both the Model 1840 French Infantry Rifle and the Infantry rifle Model 1842 had already undergone a previous modification from a smoothbore to the Prelaz-Burnand system of rifling.

PEABODY

The decision to convert to the Milbank-Amsler breechloading system caused the withdrawal of a large number of rifles from the troops. The Swiss Government felt that the situation was leaving the country vulnerable in view of the constant turmoil and threat of war in Europe and consequently placed an order in 1867 in the U.S. for 15,000 Peabody (Patented 1862) single shot breechloading rifles in .41 caliber Swiss (10.4mm).

The Peabodys were issued in the first instance to the sharpshooters, with the balance being maintained in the arsenals as reserve. Later they were issued to the service troops.

Because there were problems with extraction, a number of the Peabodys were modified by the Eidgenossiche Waffenfabrik to accept a wider-based extractor. At a later date, as the barrels wore out, Peabodys were rebarreled and renamed the Model 1877. Rebarreled Peabodys had a barrel length of 32.36 inches instead of the 32.75 inches of the originals.

TESTS

During the years 1865 and 1866, Switzerland commenced the testing of breechloading systems of other nations. The rifles tested were the Dreyse Needlefire Carbine in caliber 15.43mm; the Winchester Model 1866 in caliber 11mm (.44 Henry "Flat"); and the Chassepot Model 1866 in caliber 11mm.

As a result of these tests it was decided to arm the country with a breechloading repeating rifle.

VETTERLI

Professor Friderich Vetterli began experimenting at SIG Neuhausen. His first experimental breechloader was made in 1866, followed in 1867 by

SWISS ARMS

one based on the Terry System.

By 1869 Vetterli's breechloading repeating rifle reached the development stage.

It has been stated that the Austrian Fruwirth carbine was the first European repeater to go into service. This is not so: The Vetterli was adopted on the 8th of January, 1869, and the Fruwirth on May 22nd, 1872. By the time the Fruwirth was adopted, over 49,000 Vetterlis had already been produced.

The basic models of the Vetterli were:

Vetterli Rifle Model 1869
Vetterli Rifle Model 1869/71
Vetterli Cadet Rifle Model 1870
    Type I
Vetterli Cadet Rifle Model 1870
    Type II
Vetterli Carbine Model 69/71
Vetterli Police Carbine Model 1870
Vetterli Stutzer Model 1871
Vetterli Stutzer Model 1878
Vetterli Carbine Model 1878
Vetterli Frontier Guard Carbine
    Model 1878
Vetterli Stutzer Model 1881 Type I
Vetterli Stutzer Model 1881 Type
    II.

Vetterlis will be found with a number of different manufacturers markings on them. SIG Neuhausen was the main producer, thus the SIG marking is the most common. The Vetterlis were also manufactured by Eidgenossische Montier Werkstatte, Bern; Cordier & Cie, Bellefontaine; W. von Steiger, Thun; Ostschweizerische Buchsenmacher, St. Gallen; Rychner & Keller, Aarau; V. Sauerbrey, Basel; and Zeughaus, Zurich.

Stutzers were manufactured by SIG and Eidgenossiche Montier Werkstatte and carbines were manufactured by Rud. Pfenniger, Buchsenmacher, Stafa.

Markings can be found in both the German and French languages.

SCHMIDT-RUBIN

On June 19th, 1889, the Swiss Government, in view of the advances made by other European states, decided to go to a true small-caliber rifle. The matter had been studied since 1882, and in 1886 a commission had been created to generate further information.

In 1881, Major Rubin (later elevated to Colonel), director of the munitions factory at Thun had proposed a copper-jacketed 9mm bullet. Further research revealed that it would probably be appropriate to go to a 6mm or 7.5mm caliber.

The well-known ballistician, Pro-

1

1. A Swiss reservist on his way to drill armed with a Model 81 Vetterli.

2. The Model 1893 Cavalry carbine was based on the Mannlicher system but utilized a detachable double-row magazine. Bolt was complicated.

3. Schmidt-Rubin rifles from top to bottom: Model 89, Model 89 trainer in 4mm caliber, loading port in bottom of upper forestock; Model 11; Model 11 carbine; Model 97 Cadet rifle.

4. Oberst Schmidt

5. Oberst Furrer

6. Two experimental rifles: piece pictured on top is a developmental model of the 89/96, a rather short lived variation of the '89. The second rifle is a Carbine 11 converted at sometime after World War I to fire semiautomatically. This conversion is remarkably similar to the "sword guard" pattern used by the British with their 1918 conversion of the Short Magazine Lee-Enfield.

7. The incomparable K 31. Its design was set forth by Col. Furrer of the Federal Arms Factory at Bern. These rifles were used by the Swiss until 1956 as the official infantry rifle, presently K 31s are used for target shooting and remain the favored target arm of Swiss shooters.

8. K 31s were made up for sharpshooters. The rifle pictured is the K 31/42 which has a 1.8x scope graduated from 100 to 1000 meters.

9. An experimental K 31 match rifle made by Hammerli in 1946.

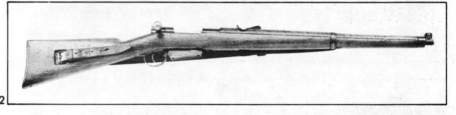

2

3

fessor Hebler of Zurich, proposed a steel-jacketed round that would be less expensive to produce, but in tests the Rubin Tombac-jacketed round was preferred.

A number of new rifles were tested and the contest boiled down to two rifles, one produced by SIG Neuhausen and the other by Colonel Schmidt of Bern.

Eighty test pieces were made up and sent to the Marksmanship Academy at Wallenstadt. After tests were completed, the Schmidt design was considered the better of the two.

In 1889 the System Schmidt Model 1889 was adopted. This is commonly known to collectors as the Schmidt-Rubin.

The following is a compilation of the Schmidt-Rubins produced. They are listed by their official designation.

  Repeater Rifle System Schmidt
    Model 1889
  Repeating Rifle Model 1889/96
  Cadet Rifle Model 1897
  Short Rifle Model 1889/00
  Cavalry Carbine Model 1905
  Infantry Rifle Model 96/11
  Carbine Model 00/11
  Carbin eModel 05/11
  Infantry Rifle Model 11
  Carbine Model 11
  Carbine Model 11 Special.

MANNLICHER CARBINE

Until 1931, the only variation from the Schmidt-Rubin was the Model 1893 Carbine produced by SIG Neuhausen. This firm was given an order for a cavalry carbine based on the Mannlicher System as the 1889 rifle was too long for mounted troops. These Model 93s were not popular and their service life was brief.

KARABINER MODELL 31

On June 16th, 1933, a new rifle was adopted by the Swiss Government to replace the Model 11 rifle and carbine; this was the Karabiner Modell 31. It was a straight pull type like the Schmidt-Rubin but had a new locking system designed by Colonel Furrer. The K31 was the standard rifle, the K31/42 and K31/43 were sniper rifles as was the K31/55. These straight-pull bolt action rifles were the last of the straight-pull line before the advent of the SIG-designed automatic assault rifle Model StG. 57 which was adopted in December of 1956.

The K31 is a superbly accurate rifle and is still in use by the reserve troops in Switzerland. The "Karabiner" is universally held in high regard by Swiss high-power rifle target shooters.

THE MOISIN-NAGANT IN FINNISH SERVICE

A CLASSIC CASE OF MILITARY ADAPTABILITY

by Harris R. Bierman

1

To collectors of military rifles the M91 Moisin-Nagant rifle, better known as the "Russian rifle" is undesirable. Aesthetically it is ugly and crude in appearance, even when finished to Western standards of metal and wood work. But the exigencies of war and lack of arms and munitions to carry on the battle cause aesthetic considerations and careful workmanship to give way to the desperate throes of war.

The M91 has served to equip the Russian and the Finnish armies in their times of greatest need. The Russians, during the wars carried on by the Czarist Government and the Soviets, used this design (as did the Finns) in defense of their homeland from a mighty and omnipresent neighbor.

Until recently, Finland has been a "twilight land" to most of the world, cut off from the mainstream, keep-

ing very much to herself. Modern-day Finland has had to endure four major incursions on her soil in the 20th Century and stands ready to repel yet another if that unfortunate circumstance should arise. The Finnish Army's utilization of the Russian M91 design has played an important role in maintaining Finnish freedom.

Before getting into the discussion of the Finnish experience with the M91 it is best to have a short discussion of Finnish military history.

As previously discussed, Finland has been involved in conflict four times since her Declaration of Independence in 1917. Her defense forces have been instrumental in maintaining her independence and territorial integrity for over 55 years.

Finland's military history goes back in time to when Finland was a border land between the two great empires of Sweden and Russia. Finland, from

medieval times up to the beginning of the 19th Century was fought over time and again; practically each generation experienced war. Finnish men came to regard participation in the defense of their country as an implied requisite of being a citizen. Many present day Finnish army units were assault regiments who can trace their origins back to regiments founded on a regional level in the Swedish period, with a record of battles fought deep in Central Europe and Russia and a tradition of original military maneuver especially suited to guerrilla warfare.

Soon after the Finnish Declaration of Independence in December of 1917, the country was caught up in a civil war. Although the Soviet Government had recognized Finland's sovereignty, Russian troops still stationed in Finland refused to leave. These troops joined the Finnish revolutionary worker's movement which,

2

of Finnish adaptability and improvement on Russian equipment had its real beginnings in the early 1920s.

The development of a "true" Finnish modification of the M91 came in with the development of the Model 1924. This rifle for all appearances was identical to the Russian M91, but with one important difference: Its barrel. The Finns discarded the relatively light barrel of the M91 and replaced it with a heavy barrel approximately one pound heavier than the Russian barrel. Rifles so modified had the barrel channel expanded in the forestock to accommodate the larger diameter of the barrel. The barrel also was made with steps along its length. These steps occur just behind the rear sight base and about one-inch in front of the rear sight base. The front band was pinned to the forestock and the take-up screw of the band was left loose. This was to allow the barrel to float free of the stock and not be bound by the forend, a feature crucial to accuracy. The foresight was changed from the issued Russian barleycorn-type to the Finnish stepped-notch blade from sight, 2.5mm in width. The bore diameter of the Model 1924 was nominally set at .3095

1. A squad of the famous, hard fighting Finnish ski troops moving up to the Petsamo front.

2. Representative arms showing the Finnish progression in developing M91 to its fullest potential. (A) A M91 but with special sling swivels added. This piece was produced by Remington and has an unusual serial number range, dated 1918. (B) Russian Dragoon, Istvesk Arsenal manufacture c. 1899, modified upper handguard, of type used by the Finnish Cavalry. (C) A shortened M24, work probably done at Valmet. Note additional step in front of rear sight base on barrel, no provision for bayonet. (D) M27, showing the radical change from the M91, note new upper handguard, nose cap/bayonet lug, new rear band. (E) M27 Cavalry carbine (musketoon) with turned down bolt handle, clearance cut in stock for bolt operation with gloved hand, 24" barrel, rotating rear sling swivel, sling cut-out in butt as on K98, aperture added to rear sight notch. (F) M28 showing changes made in 1927 but with a one piece nose cap/bayonet lug setup. (G) M28/30 also showing changes of the Models 27 and 28 but with a completely redesigned rear sight and a front sight which incorporates lateral adjustment for windage. (H) M39 changes in upper band and lower band, new hand guard, pistol grip stock and a lighter barrel than the M28/30. Note the changed cleaning rod tip. (I) Finnish rework of M91 Dragoon. Note the modified front sight blade, regraduated rear sight base, modified sling swivels and two piece stock put together at the balance (as can be seen by a line just under the front of the rear sight base.)

encouraged by the Bolshevik take-over in Petrograd (Leningrad), attempted to seize power. The Finnish moves to disarm the Russian garrisons turned into a civil war between the Whites and the Reds. Battles raged from January to May of 1918. Finally government troops, partly with the aid of a German division, suppressed the insurrection.

In these, the formative times of the Finnish defense forces, the shoulder rifle issued to the troops was the standard Russian Model 1891 in its rifle, dragoon and carbine versions. From this experience the Finns decided to adopt the Russian shoulder rifle and cartridge.

After the Civil War period, the development of the defense forces of independent Finland began in earnest. Thousands of concerned Finns joined voluntary defense organizations like the Finnish Voluntary Guards (known as the Sk.Y. Organization). Gradually, Finland's defensive capabilities were improved. Much was done to improve military tactics and army organization. Great mobility was the answer and proved to be the most effective *modus operandi* during the Winter War of November, 1939 and the Continuation War

which began in 1941 (known to us as World War 2).

During the post-Civil War time and the time of the Winter War Finnish Army ordnance was hard at work to improve the venerable M91 rifles in service with the army.

The Finnish decision to retain the standard M91 action and the Russian 7.62 x 54mm rimmed cartridge was a sound one, for by this retention of the Russian rifle/cartridge combination the Finns had a ready-made supply of munitions left over from the occupying army which they could improve upon.

Presently, the Finnish army still follows the principle of keeping abreast of its western neighbor. The adoption of the Assault Carbine M62 and its 7.62mm M43 cartridge is a direct result of earlier Finnish experience. Although the Finnish M62 uses the same design principles embodied in the Russian Avtomat Kalashnikov 47 (AK 47) the Finnish product is better made and more accurate than its Russian counterpart. The Finns also produce a cartridge that uses a brass case instead of the Russian steel case and utilizes a non-corrosive priming composition.

But the aforementioned discussion

MOISIN-NAGANT

inches when measured groove-to-groove.

A specimen of the M24 has been examined by the author and appears to be an arsenal cut-down version of this variation. The work was done by the Finnish military arsenal, Valmet. The trigger mechanism is set up to utilize an auxiliary spring to give a crisp let-off of only four pounds; the barrel has been shortened from the standard 31-inch length to a musketoon length of 24 inches. The front sight was modified to a later pattern that will be discussed further on in the text.

Needless to say the Model 1924 with its heavy 31-inch barrel was not the most advantageous rifle for an army basing its tactics on swift movement. This fact led to the adoption of a further modification of the M91 design. This came with the issuance of the Model 1927 Rifle and Musketoon (i.e. Cavalry Carbine).

The modifications of 1927 consisted of shortening the barrel to approximately 27 inches, adding protecting ears to the front sight and affixing the front sight base around the barrel instead of brazing it to the top of the barrel as on the Russian rifles. The use of the Russian quadrangular bayonet was dispensed with and a new knife-type bayonet and forend nose cap arrangement for same was adopted. The nose cap/bayonet stud assembly on close examination is not unlike the design used on the German Kar. 98a of World War 1, except for the fact that the bayonet and bayonet stud are of Model 1895 Mauser-type patterns.

In addition to the aforementioned modifications, the Model 1927 also featured extensive modifications to the rear sight, stock, and in the case of the Musketoon the barrel and bolt handle. The rear sight leaf remained the same as on the Russian 91 except that in place of the U-notch sighting

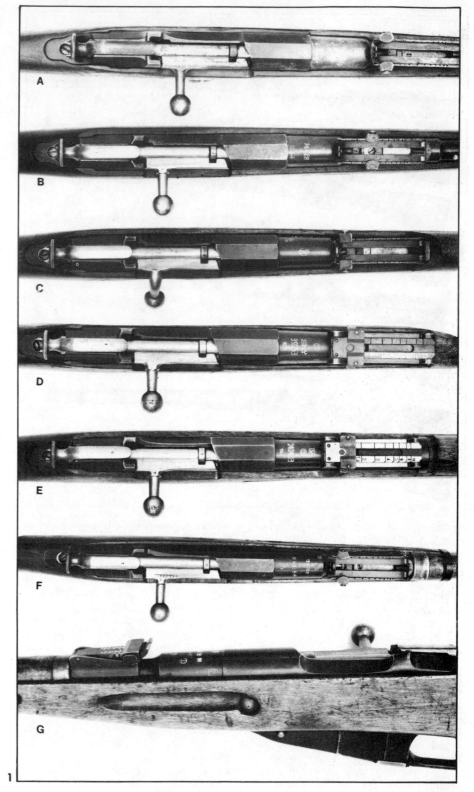

1. Markings as found on Finnish arms. (A) M91 made by Remington with unusual five-digit number, possibly a secret aid weapon sent during the time of Russian Revolution and corresponding Finnish Civil War. (B) M24, reworked in 1934 at Valmet. (C) M27 Musketoon, the "S" with three fir sprigs was symbol of Finnish Army, note "SA" property mark. (D) M28/30 marked with S-in-the-gear denoting manufacture by SAKO and the Sk.Y. marking, initials of Finnish Guards organization, disbanded after 1944. (E) M39 also made by SAKO but with Army markings only, dated 1944. (F) Rework Dragoon, note hammer and sickle mark struck out over the date. (G) A captured M38 Russian carbine with Army property markings.

groove an aperture was fitted for better sighting. The range graduations on the sight base were changed from the Russian arshin system to that of the metric system.

The stock went through a complete redesign. As discussed before, the nose cap and bayonet lug were set up for the knife bayonet, but the most important modification aside from this was the use of two pieces of wood to make up the stock. The stock was joined at the balance (just in front of the finger grooves) by interlocking fingers of wood, and glued together. This was supposedly done to prevent the stock wood from warping in excessively cold temperatures. The stock furniture was also changed. The Cavalry/Musketoon variation was fitted up with a rear band upon which a wire loop was welded to the left side to form the upper sling swivel and the butt stock

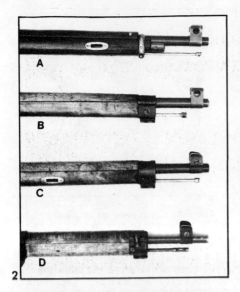

2. Details of the progression of variations in forend modifications: (A) Modified M24 Carbine, note "projecting ear" front sight feature plus addition of keeper pin through upper band and forestock, note also that upper sling escutcheon is unchanged. (B) M27 with hinged nose cap feature similar to K98, also bayonet lug. (C) M28/30 has a slide-on nose cap which fully covers forend tip. (D) M39, change back to hinging cap.

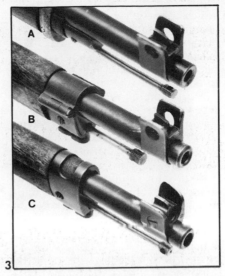

3. Front sight details: (A) M24, sight blade could only be moved by drift punch, front band was left loose to allow barrel to float freely. (B) Model 27, front sight setup similar to M24, note details of nose cap. (C) M28/30 shows greatest change to come with these rifles. Front sight blade much thicker, "ears" incorporate lateral wind adjustment.

was inletted for a Mauser-type sling/frog arrangement. Near the toe of the butt a revolving swivel was fitted. The stock was hollowed out to provide clearance for the turned down bolt handle of the Musketoon, and the inner side of the bolt knob was heavily checkered to provide a sure grip on the knob by the user. The barrel of this rifle was shortened to 24 inches.

The trigger mechanism was also modified to give a crisp four-pound let-off. This modification involved heightening the sear engagement, thereby speeding up the lock time of the trigger mechanism.

Most of the features of the Model 27 were carried over to later variations of the Finish service rifle.

The Model 1928 came soon after the Model 1927, so much so that it may be assumed that modifications to the new standard were made on Model 27 rifles which came in for ordnance repair.

The most interesting features of the Model 28 to the collector are its new barrel bedding system and stock furniture. The barrel bedding system used in the construction of the Model 1928 was similar to the Swiss system of barrel bedding embodied in the Swiss Model 1911 Schmidt-Rubin rifles. These arms and the Model 28 both utilized copper alloy tubes fitted around the barrel at the forestock to allow the barrel to vibrate freely, and to elongate without being

affected by the wood of the forend. The rest of the barrel was free-floated its entire length except for the reinforce at the chamber and of course at the forend. The front nose cap of the Model 28 was also changed to affect the new bedding system. The cap, instead of being made in two pieces with a hinging top piece as on the Model 27, was made in one piece and was slipped onto the forestock, where it was held in place by a fixing screw fitted horizontally through the forend tip.

With the new modifications of the Model 28 the Finns accomplished what they had set out to do: Make an accurate, serviceable rifle. However, as most military establishments are wont to do, still more modifications were made.

By 1930, the Model 28 was again redesigned and became the Model 28/30. The Model 28/30 retained the previously mentioned modifications but introduced a much heavier barrel than the Models 27 and 28. The interior dimensions of the 28/30's barrel were also changed from .3095-inch bore diameter to .3082 inches. The twist rate was also increased from the previous 1 in 9½ inches to 1 in 10 inches for the heavier 185 grain, Finnish-designed boat-tailed bullet.

The rear sight of this model was completely changed from the braised-on-the-barrel type of the previous models to a more solid type that had its base sleeved over the barrel just in front of the chamber reinforce. The new rear sight featured a stouter leaf that was graduated from 200 to 2000 meters and adjusted by way of an elevation slide with spring loaded catches to hold the adjustment. The sight also featured a battle sight adjustment of 150 meters. With the leaf raised, graduations could be effected from 1200

to 2000 meters.

The Model 28/30's front sight also went through a major redesign. Unlike the previously discussed Models 24, 27, and 28; the front sight of the 28/30 is adjusted for windage by means of two screws in the front sight base.

Adjustment is made by loosening these dual opposed lateral locking screws. On the left ear of the front sight there is an eight-point scale. This scale is graduated to give a change in impact from a six o'clock hold to five centimeters-per-click (or point) on the target at 300 meters. The earlier model's front sights could only be adjusted by way of a drift punch, a crude adjustment at best.

The Model 28/30 was well liked by those who used it. It was the most accurate rifle then in use by the Finnish armed forces. The use of a heavy barrel and a sighting system that gave fine adjustment capability to the user made for a rifle that was hard to beat in international competitions. The 28/30, when used in international military competitions, acquitted itself very well. This rifle was used by one of Finland's celebrated marksmen, Olavi Elo, to garner a world's record and at the same time win the International Army Rifle matches of 1937.

The last modification of the Model 91 design to be officially used in the Finnish service was the Model 1939 rifle. This piece went to a lighter barrel configuration than used with the Model 28/30. The barrel not only was lightened, but its bore diameter was increased from .3082-inch to .310-inch to conform to the increased bullet and bore diameters of its Russian counterparts. The rifling twist was changed back to 1 in 9½ inches from the 28/30's 1-in-10-inch twist.

The interrupter, a part that allows the feeding of only one round at a time through to the bolt way, was made in two parts (as with the Russian M91/30 modification) instead of the one-piece interrupter of the original M91 design.

The stock and furniture were completely changed from previous models. The forend cap/bayonet stud went back to the hinged, two-piece design of the earlier Model 27, but this piece featured a built-up rib in the nose cap that fitted into an inlet-

THE MOISIN-NAGANT

ted portion of the forend to alleviate the chances of the nose cap moving forward under recoil, thereby affecting the bedding at the forend. The stock also featured a pistol grip, similar in configuration to the Model 98k Mauser's grip. The stock, made of Arctic Beech, was also constructed from two pieces of wood in similar manner to the earlier patterns. The barrel is left entirely free floating in the forend except for approximately 1.3 inches at the forend bearing. Here the barrel is gripped tightly between the upper handguard and the forend tip. Finnish manuals stress that the barrel be firmly held down at the forend or accuracy will suffer.

The upper hand guard and furniture are also completely new in configuration. With previous patterns the rear stock band was used to hold down the hand guard at the rear, (leaving it free of the rear sight base) with stock escutcheons serving as swivel strap retainers. In the Model 39's design, the front of the rear sight base has an overhanging lip milled in it under which the rear lip of the handguard is placed. This modification was made to leave the rear band free to take the pressure of the carrying sling. The rear band is fitted with two swing swivels, on the left side and on the bottom, and the butt stock has a swivel just behind the pistol grip and inlet into the left side of the butt.

The front and rear sights of the Model 1939 are basically unchanged from the Model 28/30, having the same graduations and adjustment capabilities.

CAPTURED RUSSIAN RIFLES AND AID WEAPONS

During the conflict that raged between Russia and Finland, the Russians took very heavy losses in men and equipment. Wherever possible, the Finnish Army pressed every serviceable captured Russian M91 into service. Gradually these rifles came into repair shops and were stamped with Finnish ordnance and property stamps. Some of these rifles were extensively modified. One such specimen examined is a post-Russian Revolution Dragoon model with a Tula Arsenal-manufactured receiver (manufacturing date 1931 on receiver tang) which had been extensively overhauled by the Finns even to the point of remaking the stock in the interlocking joint pattern at the balance! This rifle had the hammer and sickle struck out, probably to give graphic evidence of its new ownership. The sling swivel escutcheons have been

replaced by metal plates through which sling swivel screws are fitted, and the horseshoe-shaped sling swivels are fitted around the stock. This is an unusual modification and has been observed on a number of captured Russian rifles used in Finland.

Most captured rifles, however, just received a Finnish Army property stamp "SA" in a round-cornered square and were reissued, but not all captured rifles and carbines were so-marked.

The Finns captured and used to some extent the Russian semiautomatic rifles. Quite a few Model 38 and 40 Tokarev rifles have appeared bearing Finnish Army property stamps. The Finns did not go over to an official self-loading rifle until the adoption of the Model 60 and later 62 Assault Carbine.

During the Continuation War Finland received aid from Italy and Sweden. Suffice it to say, certain rear echelon troops were equipped with the 7.35mm Model 38 Carcano short rifle and some troops, front line or otherwise, were issued the Swedish Model 1896 rifle in 6.5x55mm. As German involvement in Finland increased, some German small arms

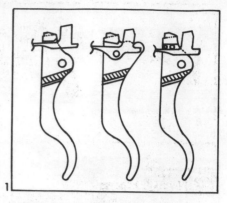

1. The Finns improved on original M91 trigger mechanism to such an extent that rifles came up to standards reached by pre-war '03 Springfield, i.e. a 4- to 4½-lb. trigger pull. Trigger groups center and right show the change in rear angles and engagement surfaces which made this possible.

2. Bayonets: (A) Standard Russian M91 bayonet with German issued scabbard. (B) M91/30, used on captured rifles and reworks. (C) Russian "sight-guard" model, this piece pre-dated the 91/30 type featuring its own front sight hood. (D) "first type" knife bayonet with smooth scabbard body, fits M27 to M39 model rifles. (E) "second type" with corrugated scabbard body, drainage hole in pommel, fits only M28/30, M39 models. (F) M62 Assault Carbine.

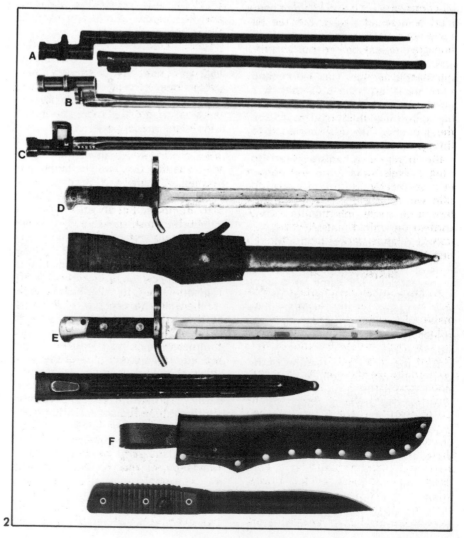

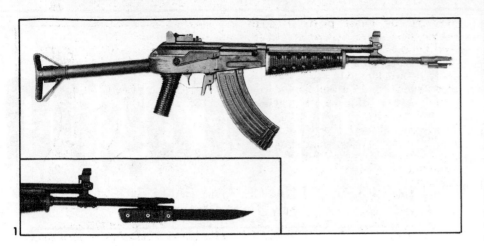

1. Finland's newest infantry rifle the M62 Assault Carbine. This piece takes its design heritage from the days of the Molsin-Nagant. It is a Russian design (Kalashnikov) improved as to fittings and sights but still retaining Russian caliber of 7.62 x 39mm M43. Courtesy Interarms.

were probably used to a small extent between 1940 and 1944. One Finnish Army source states that the 33/40 carbine was used. However, none have turned up with Finnish property markings.

One particularly fascinating piece has turned up in a private collection that dates from the period of the Finnish Civil War (1917-1918). This rifle is a standard Model 91 rifle but made by Remington Arms in 1918. Supposedly all production of the Russian rifle stopped in the United States after the overthrow of the Czarist Government, but it appears that some kind of a secret deal was made between our government and the fledgling government of Finland. The rifle does not have the usual six-digit number common to the contract rifles made up for the Russian Government. The specimen piece instead has a five-digit number. The date on the piece is 1918 and its additional fittings are distinctly Finnish, especially in regard to its early form of sling swivels which are also shown in a very early Finnish manual. This rifle will continue to remain a mystery until more information is unearthed on United States/Finnish military assistance pacts made after the first World War.

MANUFACTURE

As far as it can be ascertained, Finland has used (in the main) Russian-made M91 actions to make their own indigenous modifications. While most Finnish issue rifles are found with actions made at Russian arsenals, actions made by Remington, New England-Westinghouse, Schweitzerishe Industrie Geselshaft and possibly Chatellerault were used. It has been reported that the Finns have produced various replacement parts or their M91-based rifles. These parts are hard to identify as they were confined to bolt bodies, various springs, firing pins and the like. All stocks and metal furniture for the rifles were made in Finland by small work

shops, or "feeder industries" for the major arsenal (Valmet) and factories.

As to actions, the Finns, (it seems), endeavored to utilize the best possible actions when building their rifles. On the specimen rifles encountered by the author, receivers by both New England-Westinghouse and Remington have been observed, these being the early "hexagonal" pattern which antedated the rounded receiver of the Russian M91/30. It has been said that these American-produced rifles were among the best as far as quality was concerned and were considered to be "premium" candidates for conversion. Exclusive use of the "hex" receiver seems to have continued up to the end of the war, but this fact has not been fully verified. Generally Finnish-reworked arms have matching bolt-body and rifle numbers, but it is not unusual to find Finnish rifles where these numbers do not match.

As discussed before, Finland's official arsenal has been, and still is, Valmet. Most modifications made to Finnish service rifles and repairs to them and to captured rifles were made at this arsenal. However, due to the emergency of the Civil War and the strong feeling in Finland to get moving with defense preparedness, a repair shop was opened in a building owned by the Helsinki Technical School. This factory was operated by the Finnish Voluntary Guards organization and became known as *Suojeluskuntien Ase-ja Konepaja* or SAKO. By 1921, the shop became an independent firm and by 1927 relocated to its present premises at Riihimaki. In 1928, the firm began production of ammunition for the government and had become heavily involved in pro-

duction of both rifles and ammunition. In 1944, under the peace terms forced on the Finns by the Russians, (the Moscow Treaty) SAKO had to be closed down and the Voluntary Guard disbanded. To get around this, the factory was signed over to the Finnish Red Cross in order to save it from being dimantled. Thus SAKO was saved.

BAYONETS

Finnish bayonets are quite uncommon in this country, as are the rifles. It has been reported that the Finns adopted a knife bayonet, however what has not been brought out is the fact that there were two distinct variations of same. The Finns originally used the Russian quadrangular bayonet, and continued to do so throughout the service life of the M91 and M91/30 rifles pressed into Finnish service. The Finnish bayonet for their modification of the M91 was first adopted for use with the Model 27 rifle. This bayonet had a knife blade approximately 11$^{7}/_{8}$ inches long, with a polished blade and blued crossbar, wooden grip plates, a Mauser-type release button and a blued metal scabbard with a smooth body. This, the earliest model of knife bayonet may be designated "first type." The carrying frog for this bayonet was made of rough finished undyed leather and incorporated a hold-down strap on the frog reaching across the cross guard and slipping over a button on the front of the frog.

The next change in the bayonet came with the bayonet for the Model 28. This bayonet has a dirt escape hole just behind the grip panels and has a wider point on the blade. The entire bayonet is polished bright. The later pattern of bayonet will not fit on Model 27 rifles, as their bayonet studs are too large. The frog for this "second type" bayonet is not unlike an M98 Mauser frog and does not have a cross strap as on the earlier pattern. The scabbard for the M28 has a ribbed body and is not blued, but painted olive drab.

The major manufacturers of bayonets for the Finnish forces were Fishars and Hackman. Bayonets may also be marked with the Finnish Guards abbreviation of "Sk.Y."

The author wishes to thank the following people for helping him in the presentation of this article: Mr. William Piznak; Mr. Ted Komula; Col. T. Olavi Lehti, Military Attache, Embassy of Finland; Mr. A. Patanen, Attache, Embassy of Finland; Mr. James H. Helms; Mr. Jack T. Y. Harker, Mr. Warren W. Odegard; Mr. Martin B. Retting and Mr. H. Pohjolainen.

Mondragon

MEXICO'S ORDNANCE AND BALLISTICS GENIUS
by Hans Tanner

The name Mondragon is not new to the dedicated cartridge collector. The mention of the name, however, induces controversy and stimulates conversation among collectors concerning the legendary 5.2mm piston cartridge which bears this Mexican general's name. For this reason alone his name would remain forever famous among the international weapons cognoscenti, but the fascinating story does not end there. Naturally, as with all legendary characters, misinformation often clouds the picture. Therefore it is our purpose to attempt to clarify some facets of the achievements of a man who was Mexico's ordnance and ballistics genius.

Manuel Mondragon was born in 1858 in Ixtlahuaca, Mexico. As a teenager he was enrolled in the Military College of Mexico at Chapultepec Castle, specializing in the study of artillery. At that time, the Mexican academy organized its courses along similar lines to those adopted by the French Army and some of the texts were actually in French to familiarize future officers with that language.

After his graduation from Chapultepec, Mondragon was sent to France where he graduated from the famous French military college at St. Cyr. His European excursions served him in good stead for his future activities and while there he made many useful contacts.

After his return to Mexico he was placed in charge of war materials procurement for the Mexican Army. In the course of the presidency of Porfirio Diaz, he was made commander-in-chief of the Department of Artillery and appointed professor at the military academy of Chapultepec. During this time he wrote a book on coastal defense and translated the book "El Arte de Mandar" from the French. Mondragon spent some time in Europe investigating the military arts for his government. In Paris he resided at 205 rue de Becon Courbevoie. He began an association with Swiss authorities which led to the design of the Mondragon "automatic" rifles.

While in France, he designed the Mexican 75mm field gun. Mondragon has often been credited also with the design of the French 75; this is not so. The French 75 was mainly the work of Colonel DePorte and the Puteaux Arsenal, while Mondragon's design was the Mondragon/St. Chamond. The Mexican gun was actually superior to the French 75, and ac-

cording to M. Damancier, the director of artillery service at St. Chamond, was the first of its type, the prototype having been built in 1891. Thus Mondragon's design predated the French 75 by two years. It had the added advantage that its breech was semi-automatic, a system which had been used on light naval guns by Vickers-Maxim, Elswick and Coventry Ordnance Works in England.

But Mondragon was the first to apply it to field artillery and received U.S. Patent No. 787,528 for the device.

The first guns were produced at the Societé Forges et Acieries of the navy at St. Chamond. The Mondragon/St. Chamond underwent a competitive test in Mexico against the 75s manufactured by Schneider/Canet and Krupp.

After the tests were over it was

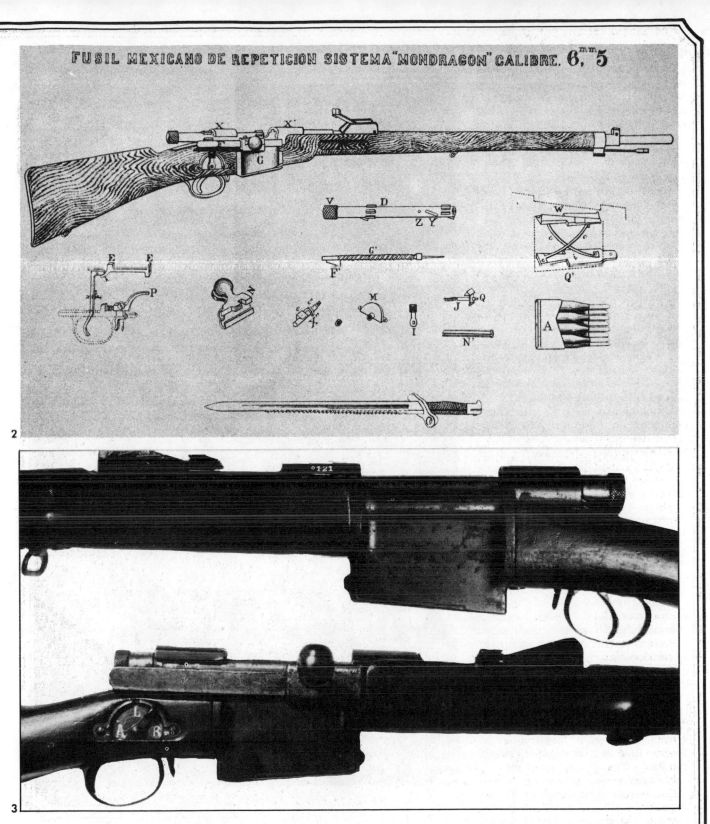

FUSIL MEXICANO DE REPETICION SISTEMA "MONDRAGON" CALIBRE. 6^{mm},5

ascertained that the Mondragon/St. Chamond had an effective rate of fire at 21 rounds-per-minute while the rates of fire for both the Schneider/Canet and the Krupp were 18 rounds-per-minute. The Schneider/Canet proved more stable on even ground than the other two, but the Mondragon/St. Chamond proved its superiority in rough terrain. The Krupp proved to be the least stable of the three. Consequently, due to Manuel Mondragon's efforts, Mexico had the best 75mm gun in the world at the turn of the century. Mondragon also designed the Mexican 70mm Mountain Gun which was also initially built at St. Chamond. Later, production of guns and ammunition took place in Mexico. Some sources indicate that Mexico's industry was incapable of producing such

1. **General Manuel Mondragon, brilliant designer of rifles and field guns to which his name is associated. He was a major military figure in Mexico.**

2. **Drawing of Model 1893 from manual. Swiss sawtooth bayonet was issued.**

3. **Model 1893 in 6.5mm. This used the famous piston cartridge. Switch controls fire modes. Bolt knob is very similar to Swiss Schmidt-Rubin. Swiss influence in construction is evident.**

Mondragon

equipment, but this is not so. The Mexican machinist displays a skill and patience in basic craftsmanship that is equalled by few others in the world, and the Mexican arms factory was exceptionally well outfitted for the task.

Mondragon's brother, Lt. Colonel Enrique Mondragon was responsible for the opening of the National Powder Factory extension at Santa Fe, near Mexico City and wrote a book on high explosives entitled "Los Principios Rudimentarios Sobre Cruerpos Explosivos y su Fabrication."

U.S. War Department Document 499C, 1910 "Diaz War, Estimate of Situation Report" quotes: "The regiment of field artillery contained two battalions and each battalion two batteries. The peace organization contained two regiments of mountain artillery, one of horse artillery and two of light artillery; total 20 batteries. Batteries each have six guns, except the horse batteries, which have four. The plan was to have each mountain artillery regiment doubled in wartime, and the other regiment increased by two additional batteries." From this report, Konrad F. Schreier estimates that there were in first-line service 48 mountain guns, 16 horse guns and 48 light guns, for a total of 112 guns—all of Mondragon design, while the second line of older breechloaders comprised 80 pieces.

In 1907, at the time of the construction of the port of Salina Cruz in the state of Oaxaca, the Mexican government named several groups of artillery experts to study the placement of artillery for the defense of the port. Since this was before the Panama Canal, Mexico was concerned about the possible invasion from the Pacific by the Japanese in an attempt to secure control of the Isthmus of Tehuantepec as a land route between the Pacific and Atlantic oceans.

A group of military experts led by General Antonio Flores y Paz installed coastal artillery batteries on either side of the port. At this time, eight very large coastal guns were built at the Santa Fe factory under the supervision of General Mondragon. These enormous guns had a barrel length of 40 feet, being a product of the studies made by Mondragon while in Europe.

Because of his French connections Mondragon was also responsible for the introduction of the Hotchkiss machine gun into the Mexican Service.

While in Europe Mondragon associated himself with SIG (Schweizerische Industrie Gesellschaft) at Neuhausen, Switzerland and with this company he began to develop a line of Mondragon rifles.

The Model 1893 was the first rifle designed by Mondragon. Its design was completed in 1891 at the request of President Porfirio Diaz, and the first rifle was produced the following year. Diaz gave orders that it undergo a series of tests to be carried out by the Fabrica de Armas on October 18, 1892.

The tests were completed and a report submitted on February 2, 1893. On September 27, 1894, 50 Mondragon rifles were issued for field tests to the 25th Infantry battalion. The results of these tests were apparently successful.

The Mexican Government exhibited one of these rifles at the 1893 Columbian International Exhibition in Chicago. In "Mexican Military Arms"

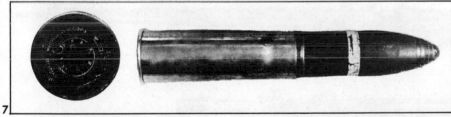

1. National powder factory at Santa Fe, near Mexico City as it appeared in the era of President Porfirio Diaz. It was opened by Lt. Col. Enrique Mondragon, brother of Manuel.

2. Interior of National Arms Factory, showing large lathes for artillery.

3. Manufacture of shells for the Mondragon/St. Chamond 75mm gun at the Santa Fe works.

4. Huge Salinas Cruz coastal defense gun manufactured by Mondragon.

5. Mondragon/St. Chamond 75mm field in use by Federal troops against the army of Emiliano Zapata. The crew is armed with Mauser carbines.

6. Books written by, or associated with Mondragon, from left: his translation of "Arte de Mandar" by Cavet; report of tests between Schneider/Canet and Mondragon/St. Chamond field guns; his brother's work on explosives.

7. Complete shell with projectile for the 75mm Mondragon/St. Chamond. Headstamp found on the 75mm shell, indicating Mexican manufacture.

James B. Hughes quotes from a translation of a report taken from the Mexican Defense Ministry's Archives:

"The weapon was a Mondragon system 6.5mm caliber rifle for both repeating fire action and for automatic rapid fire when desired. The barrel is enclosed in a wood casing attached to the chamber below and fastened above with the ramrod housing ring. The chamber (receiver) is screwed on to the barrel at one end, and at the other end being attached to the lower part of the casing. The bolt encloses a needle (firing pin) with its spring, and is moved by a knob. The trigger is connected inside and protected by a trigger guard. A half-disc holds the devices to control the type of fire desired. Quadrant sights are attached by a bolt. The total number of parts is 54. This model is the lightest in use today, equal in weight only to the German Mauser. A multiple number of cartridges can be loaded and automatically passed from the clip to the chamber. The bolt moves longitudinally by means of the knob at the right, sliding over a track. The body of the bolt is 16cm long and consists of a tube with two crowns with lugs; diameter of

Mondragon

the tube is 18mm, and of the lug crowns 23mm, the chamber (magazine) that receives the clip has a false bottom supported by two crossed springs. On opening the bolt, this bottom stays below the lower lug, at the same level with it, and the clip is placed upon the bottom, by the pressure of the thumb, the clip is depressed until it catches in place. The clip is small in volume and weight, similar to the Swiss rifle, with the cartridges arranged in two rows, to avoid the magazine protruding in front of the trigger guard. The quadrant and half disc at the right side of the plate above the trigger guard contains the safety lock, the control for ordinary

fire, and for rapid fire. Rapid fire is arranged to produce the discharge in the same moment as the mechanism closes; the trigger lug does not catch and the needle (firing pin) strikes forcefully against the cartridge primer, cancelling the action of the releasing lug upon the needle catch. The safety mechanism is complete, recoil small, detonation insignificant with smokeless powder. 32 cartridges were fired at 500 yards, all of them hits. Of 78 cartridges fired at 1200 yards, 31 bullets hit the target, or only 40%. The total average of hits was 45%. The desirability of the rapid fire feature is doubtful, although it works smoothly. The weapon is sufficiently solid to stand rough handling in service. Only two

movements are required to produce a discharge. The knife bayonet in a steel scabbard has a serrated back to use as a saw. Its blade measures 26cm of a total length of 41cm. The cartridge case is brass, with a groove at the bottom for extraction; the bullet is of hardened lead with a white metal jacket; the charge is smokeless powder manufactured in Germany. The clip weighs 26 grams; eight cartridges 176 grams. The issue of 160 cartridges per man weigh 4 kg. as compared to the 11mm Remington ammunition of which 160 rounds weigh 13 kg. Handling is very easy, loading is fast."

So concludes a rather superficial report.

Apparently, the correct method of using the weapon in its "automatic"

form was to place the stock under the left elbow, waist high, and operate the bolt with the right hand while supporting the front with the left hand. This method of fire could only have value for very close-range purposes and during barrage fire where sighting is not necessary. Only one type of the Model 1893 is listed with the following characteristics: length, 48 inches; barrel, 29 inches; weight 7.5 pounds. Fixed box magazine with "en bloc" clip taking eight rounds. Front sight: Inverted "V" (barleycorn). Rear sights: Adjustable leaf, 200 to 2600 meters. However, two different dimensions of cartridges are known—a 6.5 x 48mm and a 6.5 x 52mm. The latter could possibly have been as a result of the 1200-yard tests mentioned in the report in an attempt to provide a more powerful cartridge. This

6.5mm ammunition has been found packaged by the Societé Francaise des Munitions at 30, Rue Notre Dame des Victoires in Paris.

It should be noted that the Mondragon "en bloc" clip predates the Pedersen Garand clip (c. 1925) by 34 years. The knife-type bayonet had a length of 16.15 inches and a blade length of 10.25 inches. It is similar to the Swiss engineers' bayonet adapted to the Swiss Vetterli repeating rifle, not surprising as they were probably manufactured in Switzerland either by SIG Neuhausen or a SIG subcontractor. The only markings on the Model 1893 are the serial numbers on the various parts and FAB.D'ARMES NEUHAUSEN, which is the French-language rendition of SIG Neuhausen.

Mondragon's Model 1894 resembles the Model 1893. Like the earlier

model, it has a switch plate to control the type of fire required. In the "A" position the rifle fires as the bolt is closed, in the "L" position the rifle is on safety and in the forward "R" position it acts as a conventional bolt-action type.

It is a straight-pull rifle with a rotating bolt provided with three sets of locking lugs. Five of the lugs are located at the rear of the bolt and another five at the front with five supplemental lugs being fitted on the gas shield. According to the H. P. White Laboratory files, the rifle inspected by them had the following features: "A"—lever to the rear is "safe," bolt locked in closed position trigger cannot be depressed. "L"— lever in the mid-position; piece functions as a normal bolt-action rifle and is fired by depressing the trigger. "R" lever forward. In this position,

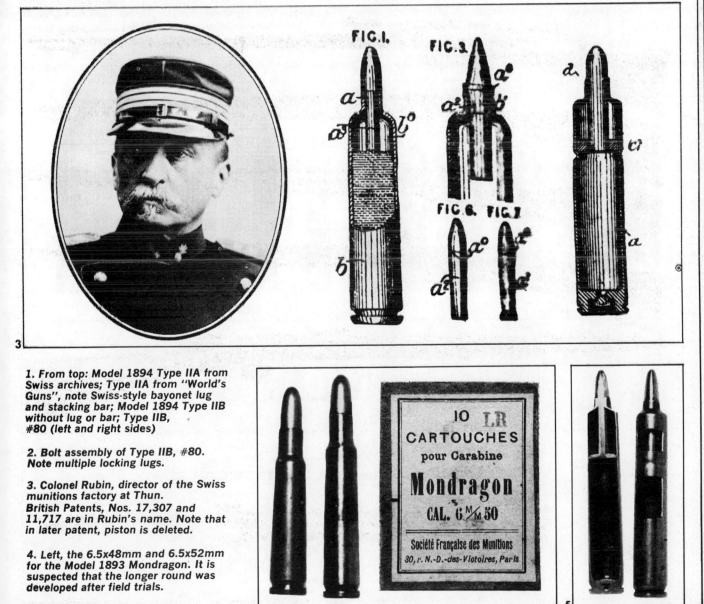

1. From top: Model 1894 Type IIA from Swiss archives; Type IIA from "World's Guns", note Swiss-style bayonet lug and stacking bar; Model 1894 Type IIB without lug or bar; Type IIB, #80 (left and right sides)

2. Bolt assembly of Type IIB, #80. Note multiple locking lugs.

3. Colonel Rubin, director of the Swiss munitions factory at Thun. British Patents, Nos. 17,307 and 11,717 are in Rubin's name. Note that in later patent, piston is deleted.

4. Left, the 6.5x48mm and 6.5x52mm for the Model 1893 Mondragon. It is suspected that the longer round was developed after field trials.

5. Sectioned 5.2x68 cartridges.

as soon as the bolt reaches the forward location and the locking lugs turn into position, the firing pin falls. This latter description is questionable. It either indicates that the gun was misassembled, or it was put together this way experimentally. This is borne out by the fact that "A" stands for "Automatique" and "R" for "Repetition," while the "L" is as yet undeciphered.

The various types of the Model 1894 Mondragon so far recorded are the following:

Type I: Length 54 ins. Bbl. 34.5 ins. Wt. 7 lbs. 11 oz.

Type IIA: Length 48 ins. Bbl. 29.5 ins. Wt. 7 lbs. 6 ozs.

Type IIB: Length 48 ins. Bbl. 29.5 ins. Wt. N/A.

Type III: Length 45.5 ins. Bbl. 27 ins. Wt. N/A.

Type IV: Length 40.25 ins. Bbl. 21.75 ins. Wt. 7 lbs.

It should be noted that the "type" allocations are those made strictly by the author and do not represent an official classification, and are merely done in the absence of any such official classification.

The "Type II" seems to be the most common. Serial #121 is in the Robert N. Green collection, and serial #202 is in the Mexican Defense Department's museum. H. P. White has a report on Serial #80.

It will be seen that the Type II has two sub-types. Rifle #121 has a typically Swiss bayonet lug and stacking bar. This is Type IIA. Rifle #80 has neither bayonet lug nor stacking bar. This is Type IIB. Another Type IIA rifle was illustrated in "World's Guns", but its serial number was not recorded. A further illustration of a Type IIA came from the SIG archives, but again the serial number was not recorded. The Type IIB Model 1894 Mondragon also illustrated in the first edition of "World's Guns" was the same serial #80 recorded by the H. P. White Laboratory.

A carbine version, the Type IV, is illustrated in James B. Hughes "Mexican Military Arms."

Calvin Darst in "Guns & Ammo" Magazine (May, 1967) describes a Type II with a 27-inch barrel. Although the rifle found by him in Mexico was in poor shape with the forestock missing, the Darst rifle had serial #76 on the receiver and #123 on the bolt actuator. In the same article he refers to another Model 1894 examined by H. P. White, this being a Type I with a 34½-inch barrel. H. P. White recorded that the rifling was four-groove right-hand twist with one turn in 4½ inches. Bore diameter was .1973-inch and groove diameter .2183-inch. The serial number of this rifle was #72. While developing the Model 1893, Mondragon came into contact with Colonel Rubin, the director of the Swiss Munitions Factory at Thun. Rubin was the most brilliant cartridge designer of his time, being responsible, amongst many other things, for the development of the 7.5mm Swiss cartridge and the .303 British cartridge. The two designers must have seen "eye to eye" at once and as a result a revolutionary cartridge for the Model 1894 Mondragon rifle was proposed—the famed 5.2-mm high velocity piston cartridge. That the basic design of this Mondragon cartridge was the work of Rubin is borne out in the fact that both British patents on the piston

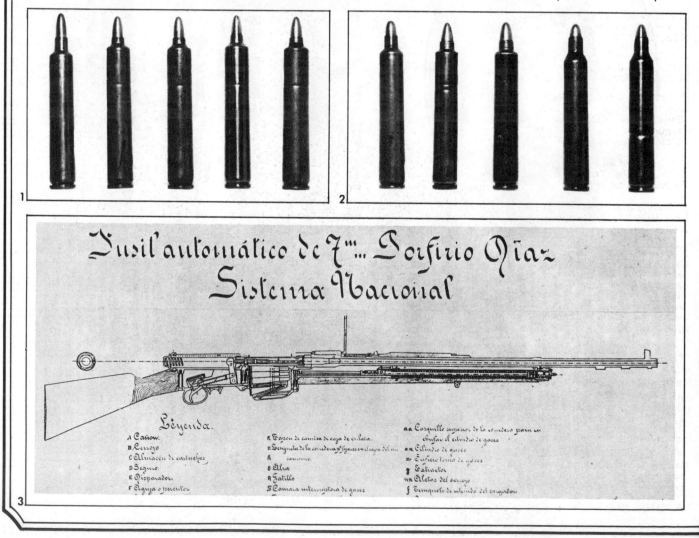

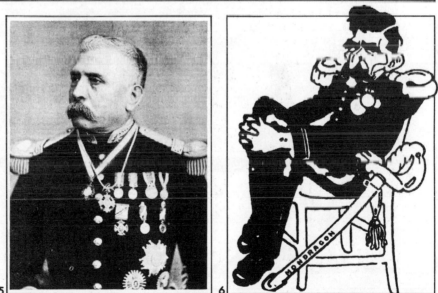

1. From left: 5.2x67.7mm (Polte);
5.2x68mm (Polte); 5.2x68mm (Thun);
5.2x68mm; 5.2x68mm.

2. 5.2x71mm (Polte); 6.1x68mm
(Thun); 6.3x68mm (Thun); 5.9x71mm
(Thun); 5.9x71mm (Thun) dummy.

3. Cutaway of the Model 1908 Mondragon. It was generally known as the
"Fusil Porfirio Diaz Sistema Mondragon", but here it is labelled
"Sistema Nacional".

4. Closeup of Mondragon rifle, Model
1908 in caliber 7mm Mauser.
Patent drawing of Mondragon.

5. Porfirio Diaz, President of Mexico
until 1910. Under his patronage, the
Mondragon designs evolved.

6. A contemporary cartoon drawing of
General Mondragon. He played a very
prominent role in Mexican history
of the early 20th Century.

system, No. 17,307 of September 11,
1899 and No. 11,717 of May 29,
1896 are taken out in Rubin's name.
That the 1894 Mondragons were in
effect experimental rifles is indicated
by the variations of types, but when
one examines the cartridges this
theory begins to jell as the following
types of Mondragon cartridges have
been identified:

5.2 x 68mm with cannelure 90-
grain bullet, headstamped: POLTE
MAGDEBURG; 5.2 x 68mm with cannelure 105-grain bullet, headstamped: POLTE MAGDEBURG;

5.2 x 68mm with cannelure, headstamped: T 12 A 94 indicating assembly by the Thun munitions factory
in Switzerland with components
from Altdorf in December, 1894.
There is also a 5.2x67.7mm manufactured by Polte of Magdeburg in
the Woodin collection; this is mentioned as the other cases measure
the full 68mm.

During the same period the Thun
factory manufactured a 6.1x68mm
version with the headstamp "T 12
A 94" which indicates that it was
produced during the same month

of 1894 and with components by
Altdorf as with the 5.2x68mm.

The 6.1x68mm comes in two versions with a different ogive on the
bullet. There are also two case variations—one with no cannelure and
the other with a double cannelure,
the former type case having a slightly longer neck.

The 5.2x68mm also exists in specimens without a cannelure on the
case. Then there is the 5.2x71mm
with the headstamp POLTE MAGDEBURG and the 5.9x71mm with the
headstamp "T 4 T 97" and "T 6

Mondragon

T 99" which indicate total manufacturing by the Thun factory in the years 1897 and 1899. These also show variations with a sloping shoulder and long neck contrasting to the very sharp shoulder normally found on the Mondragon cartridges.

Yet another type is the 6x71mm with the headstamp "T 9 T 99" indicating manufacture by Thun at the end of 1899.

The final Mondragon rifle design was the Model 1908. Mondragon obtained a United States Patent No. 853,715 on May 14, 1907, although the late Julian Hatcher in the "Book of the Garand" states that Mondragon obtained a patent for this gas-operated model on August 8, 1904. (This was actually the date of application for the patent.) The introduction of the 1907 patent reads: "Be it known that I, Manuel Mondragon, a citizen of the Republic of Mexico, residing at Tacubaya, in the Federal District, Mexico, have invented certain new and useful improvements in firearms, of which the following is a specification.

"My present invention pertains to improvements in automatic firearms and relates more particularly to that class generally known as or styled gas-operated, though the arm is equally adapted to be operated manually, either as a single-loader or as a repeater."

A prototype rifle was produced that differed from the final "production" types. This rifle was specially inlaid with the initials of President Porfirio Diaz, the crest of the republic and the words "Modelo Mondragon". The piece was presented to Porfirio Diaz and is at present in the Museo del Ejercito Mexicano. It is in the familiar .30-30 caliber(!) and has an overall length of 42½ inches with a barrel length of 21½ inches; this differs from the "production" model which has a length of 43 inches and a barrel length of 24 inches.

Another presentation piece, one of the "production" rifles, has the stock inscribed with the initials of General Joaquin Amaro. This is also in the Museo del Ejercito and bears the serial #10. The "production" rifle weighed nine pounds and used an eight-round en bloc clip and was in 7x57mm Mauser, the then standard caliber of the Mexican Army. It was issued to Mexican troops in 1908 and became the *first* semi-automatic rifle adopted by any army. Markings

on these rifles were FUSIL PORFIRIO DIAZ SYSTEMA MONDRAGON MOD 1908 FABRICA DE ARMAS DE NEU-HAUSEN SUIZA. For Mexican service the rifle was fitted with a bipod and a spade bayonet, also made in Switzerland. A sheet-metal scabbard was provided for the bayonet which also held two cleaning rod sections. All the blades were deeply stamped "Madera" (wood) and "Hierro" (iron). The reason for these marks are unknown. Some bayonets are numbered on the wood handle and all bear Swiss proof marks as well as "Republica Mexicana" on the cross guard. Blade length is 10.75 inches, blade width 2.5 inches, and overall length is 15¼ inches.

The British tested prototypes of the 1908 rifle as early as July, 1903, when field trials took place with Mondragon and three other representatives. Two weapons were presented, a rifle with a 28-inch barrel weighing nine pounds, 10 ounces, a muzzle velocity of 2149 fps (the rifle had already fired 5000 rounds); and a carbine with a 26-inch barrel weighing eight pounds, 13 ounces, giving a velocity of 2061 fps. It can be seen from the above weights and dimensions that the test pieces differed from the later "production"

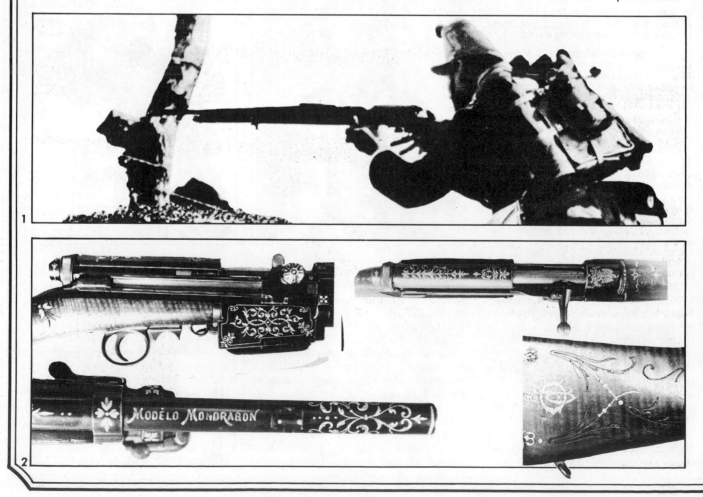

rifles. Tests conducted were the firing of 20 rounds as a magazine rifle (which disclosed hard extraction), and 30 rounds as a self-loading rifle—at which time the mechanism functioned well. Cartridges supplied by the Mauser Werke in 7x57mm were supplied for special trials, but these did not develop enough pressure to operate the self-loading mechanism.

The July tests having been unsatisfactory, Mondragon resubmitted his rifle for a test at Enfield in September of 1903. A breakage stopped testing on the fourth round firing and the rifle was submitted once more later in the same month. It did not pass the sand test and was difficult to clean, although when clean it functioned well as a self-loading rifle. It showed a penetration of one-inch elm boards spaced one-inch apart to be 28 to 31 at 25 yards. It was also found that the clips were hard to insert, and as a result, the British Committee recommended that the rifle was not durable enough for service needs . . . no additional tests were carried out.

Some of the Model 1908 rifles reached Mexico before World War 1, but others were diverted and saw limited service with the Germans during the war. They were used as aircraft guns and fitted with special 30-round "snail drum" magazines similar to those used for the Luger pistol. In this form, the rifle was known as "Aviators Self Loading Carbine Model 1915."

SIG Neuhausen tested the Mondragon in various calibers, including 7.5mm Swiss. Two of these rifles in 7.5 Swiss have been examined—one was serial #1158 with an unmarked receiver, and the other had the Mexican crest on top of the receiver. In the April, 1958, issue of the "American Rifleman" there was an illustration of a cutaway of the Model 1908 Mondragon.

The era of Porfirio Diaz ended in 1911. Mexico was cast into a turmoil that did not end until 1920. Diaz was succeeded by Madero, and after the subsequent deposing of Madero, General Mondragon was appointed Minister of War of Mexico. The continuous revolution turned the tides of fortune once more and Manuel Mondragon retired to Spain where he died in 1922 at the age of 74.

Author's Note:

In compiling this article the author wishes to thank the following persons who contributed materially to the research of the project.

General Hermenegildo Cuenca Diaz, Secretary of National Defense of the Republic of Mexico for the photos of the Mondragon rifles in the collection of the Museo del Ejercito Mexicano; General Somuano, Secretary of the Department of Archives, Correspondence and History; Manual Gonzales Cosio, advisor to the President of Mexico; Manual Mondragon, Jr., son of General Mondragon; Susana Mondragon, granddaughter of General Mondragon; Gustavo Mondragon, nephew of General Mondragon; Robert N. Green of Mexico City who coordinated the Mexican research; James B. Hughes Jr. of Houston, Texas for permission to quote from his book, "Mexican Military Arms—The Cartridge Period 1866-1967" published by Deep River Armory Inc., 5700 Star Lane, Houston, Texas 77027; Konrad F. Schreier, Technological Historian, Los Angeles, California; Roberto Cabello of the Chicano Library, University of California, Los Angeles; Fred A. Datig, Lucerne, Switzerland; William H. Woodin, Tucson, Arizona; Frank Wheeler, Osborne, Kansas; the late Colonel Berkeley R. Lewis, Vista, California, Kearney Bothwell, Los Angeles, California and J. R. Schmitt of Greensburg, Ohio.

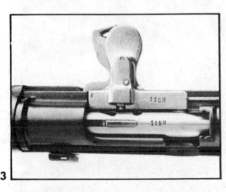

1. A photo of a Federal trooper firing a Model 1908. Federal troops were much better equipped than revolutionaries.

2. Details of the prototype Model 1908 presented to Diaz and currently in the Museo del Ejercito Mexicano. It is in caliber .30-30 Winchester.

3. The Model 1908 was further developed in Switzerland in caliber 7.5mm.

4. This particular piece bears serial #1158.

5. Model 1908s issued in Mexico had bipods. Wicked appearing bayonet actually doubled as trowel.

6. Bayonet for the 1908 was made in Switzerland. It had a metal sheath and storage for two-piece cleaning rod. The inscriptions "madera" (wood) and "hierro" (iron) on the blade have not been clarified as to purpose.

MILITARY RIFLE MARKINGS

by Hans Tanner

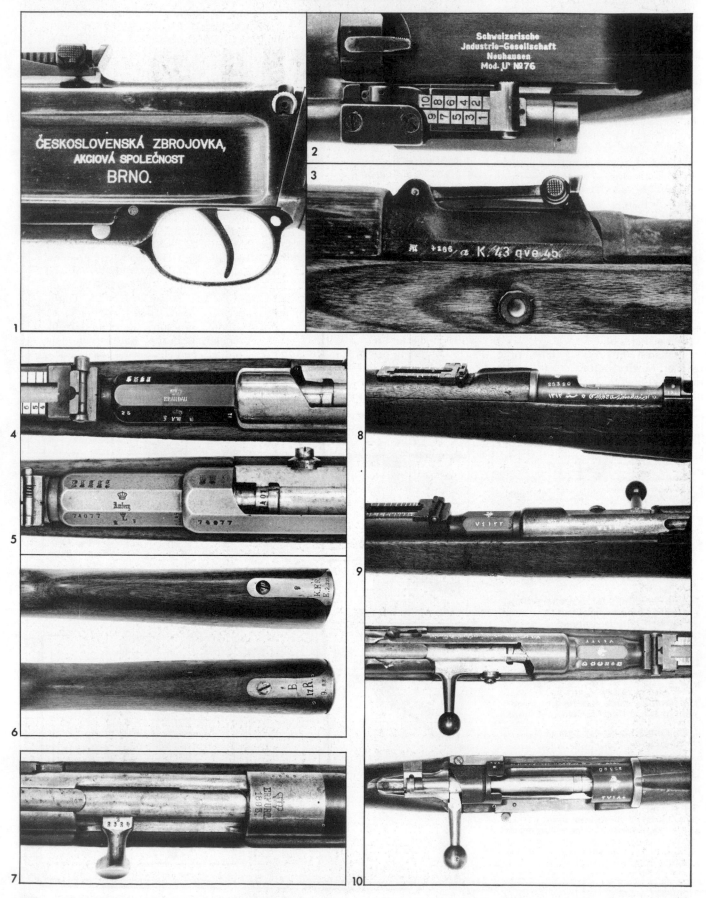

1. Czech Model ZH-29 rifle, piece is in 7.92mm caliber. Some rifles were ordered by Ethiopia.

2. S.I.G. Model "U" equipped with a Model 42 scope, 1.8x. Reportedly not more than 100 were made.

3. A standard Kar. 43, code "qve 45" stands for Carl Walther, piece was made in 1945, previous code was "ac."

4. Model 71/84 Mauser in 11mm (.43 Mauser). This piece is representative of 71/84s made by arsenals other than Spandau.

5. Predecessor to 71/84, the 71 was made as a single shot, note changes in sights and receivers of the two.

6. Unit markings commonly found on pre-World War I issue German arms, markings also found elsewhere.

7. German Model 88 carbine, note position of marking on receiver ring and reduced range rear sight affixed to barrel jacket. Spoon handle on bolt.

8. Model 1893 Turkish Mauser in caliber 7.65mm.

9. Model 1887 Turkish Mauser in 9.5mm caliber.

10. Above Model 1887 Turkish Mauser, the last black powder military rifle to be produced, it has been reported that only 10,000 were made.

11. Portuguese Mauser-Verguiero Model 1904 in caliber 6.5x58mm. These rifles were made by DWM.

12. Top view of above showing the crest of King Carlos the First.

13. Swedish Model 94 carbine in 6.5x55mm M94 as made for Sweden by Mauser Oberndorf, these were first production of Swedish variation, 10,000 were made by Mauser.

14. Model 29 Mauser as made by Steyr Werke of Austria. These rifles bear early code for Steyr "660".

15. Thai Mauser in 8x52mm Rimmed. These fascinating rifles have 98-type actions, were made by Tokyo Arsenal.

16. Royal Iranian crest atop a Czech-produced Model 1930 carbine in caliber 7.92x57mm.

17. Portuguese Mauser-Verguiero in caliber 7.92mm. A conversion carried out in Germany for Portugal during World War 2. Carlos the First crest.

18. Model 1924 Bruno-produced Mauser as made for Romania with the crest of King Carol.

19. Polish made Kar. 98a Mauser, produced by Warsaw Arsenal.

20. Polish Model 29 as made by the arsenal at Radom followed design and fittings of Czech Model 24. Polish Mausers are in 7.92mm caliber.

21. Czech-made Model 1932 Mauser in 7.65mm had a limited production.

22. Chinese Hanyang Arsenal-made Model 88 Mauser (Commission Rifle). Many of these rifles were sold to China in the 1900s. Receivers could be Chinese-made or refinished originals.

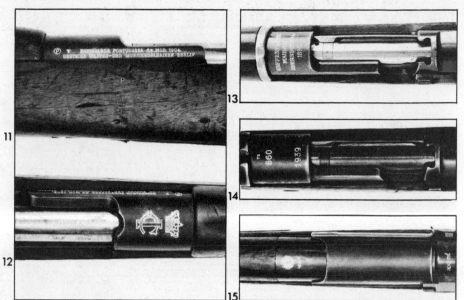

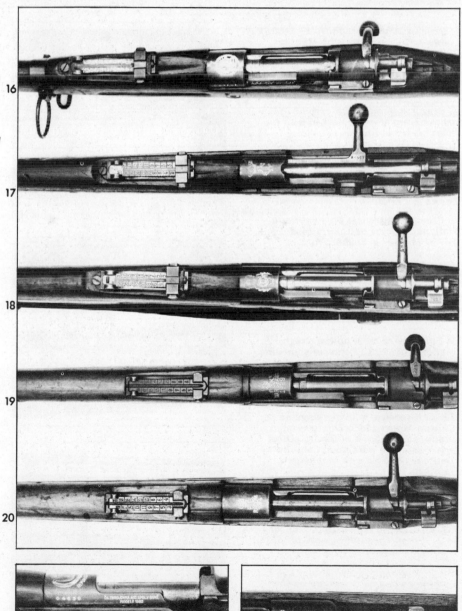

MILITARY RIFLE MARKINGS

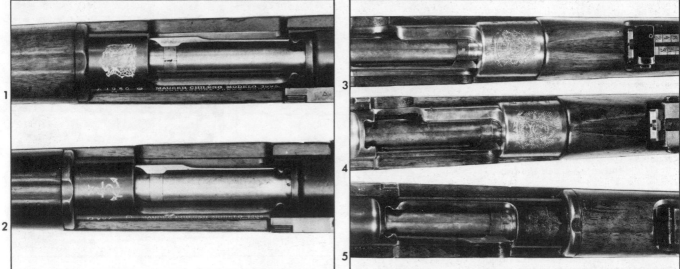

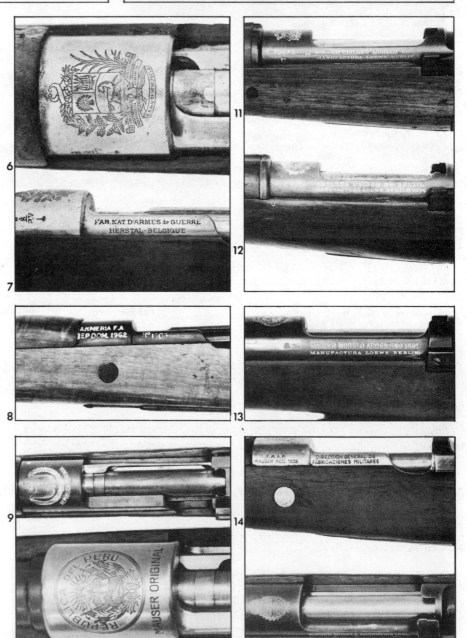

1. Chilean Mauser produced by Ludwig Loewe & Co. Known as the Mauser Chileno Modelo 1895. This is the army issue model.

2. Chilean Model 1895, naval issue. Chilean rifles are in 7x57mm caliber.

3. Brazilian Model 1908 carbine in caliber 7mm Mauser marked with the "star crest" of Brazil.

4. Brazilian Model 1908 rifle, a 98-type action made at Mauser, Oberndorf.

5. Brazilian Model 1894, a 93-type action in 7mm caliber made by Ludwig Loewe in Berlin.

6. Crest of Venezuela on a Fabrique Nationale Armes de Guerre Model 24/30 Mauser in caliber 7mm.

7. FN's manufacturer's stamp on the Model 24/30 Venezuelan Mauser. Note placement of proof marks.

8. Dominican Republic Model 1912 Mauser, arsenal refinished in 1962.

9. Full view of crest on the Czech-made Model 1932 Peruvian short rifle.

10. Peruvian Model 1909 Mauser in caliber 7.65mm as made by Mauser Oberndorf and so noted on receiver.

11. Left receiver wall markings on Chilean Model 1895. This specimen produced by Loewe of Berlin, others are found that were manufactured by Deutches Waffen und Munitions-fabriken.

12. Left receiver wall markings of Brazilian Model 1894. Portuguese spelling of Berlin is "Berlim."

13. Argentinian Model 1891 Mauser in 7.65mm. These rifles were produced mainly by Loewe.

14. Argentine-produced Model 1909 carbine as can be discerned by the markings on receiver ring and sidewall.

15. Argentine Model 1891 carbine. These arms came through with their crests intact due to a change in Argentine laws regarding sales of military arms.

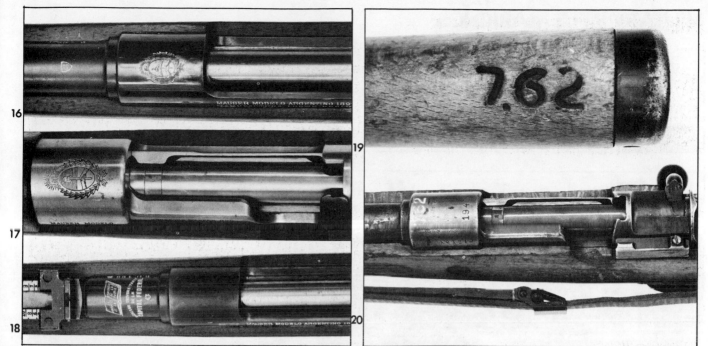

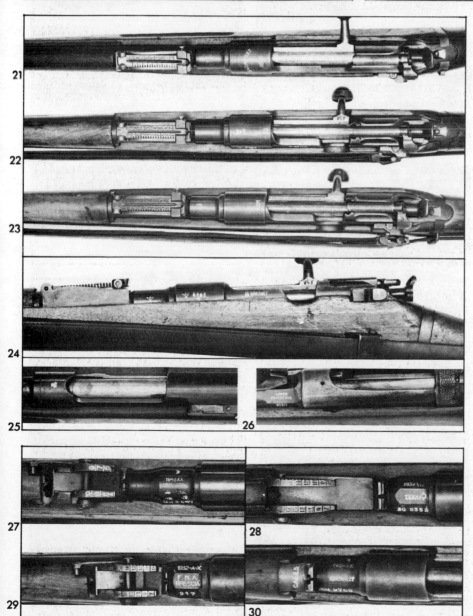

16. Argentine Model 1891 rifle with crest intact. To find a 91 rifle with crest is a rare occurrence.

17. Argentine Model 1909 with crest. Early imports of this model had the crest ground, with later ones it's intact.

18. Argentine "escuela" Model 91, this arms, although its crest is ground, still retains the insignia of the Argentine Cadet Corps. Has its own serial number range.

19. Butt stock marking of the Israeli conversion of the Model 98 Mauser to 7.62mm NATO caliber.

20. Marking on receiver ring of Israeli 7.62mm NATO conversion. These were converted by Ha'as, generally only the bolt and receiver numbers match.

21. Hungarian Model 35 in 8x56R note receiver ring markings and range graduations on sight leaf.

22. German issued variation of the M35, the 98/40, in caliber 7.92mm Mauser. Magazine changed to Mauser type. Takes German bayonet.

23. Hungarian Model 43. Retains the characteristics of German variation but is fitted for Hungarian bayonet.

24. Left sidewall markings of the 98/40. Note Waffenamt stamps.

25. Austrian Model 88/90 straight pull in 8x50R. Long range volley fire sight extended.

26. Italian Vetterli Model 70/87 in 10.4mm. The four round magazine was added in 1887.

27. Italian Model 27 rifle made in 1943. Has rear sight graduated to 1000 meters.

28. Italian M91 made in 1934 at Terni.

29. Model 91 carbine made by the State Arms Factory at Brescia.

30. Model 91 carbine with fixed rear sight made at Gardone in 1942.

MILITARY RIFLE MARKINGS

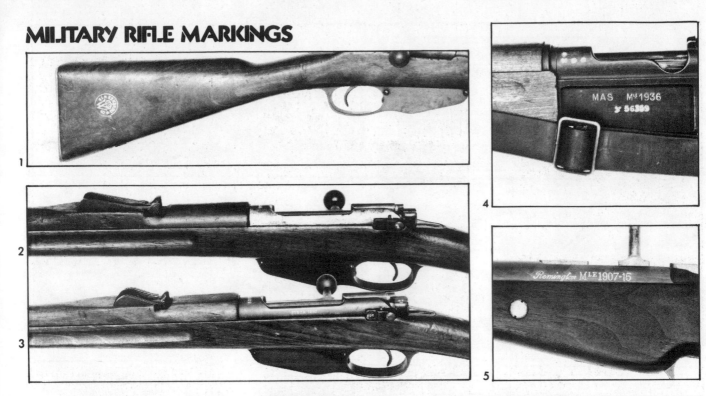

1. **Dutch M95 Carbine No. 4** butt stock marking denoting arsenal overhaul at Hembrug in 1940 during the reign of Queen Wilhelmina.

2. **Dutch Model 95 rifle** made at Hembrug in 1918.

3. **Dutch carbine,** receiver made at Steyr in 1897.

4. **French MAS Mle. 36,** in 7.5x54mm caliber. "MAS" stands for Manufacture de Armes St. Etienne.

5. **Markings on the Remington-produced Mannlicher-Berthier Mle. 07-15** in 8mm Lebel caliber.

6. **Swedish 96/41 Sniper rifle.** Note turned down bolt handle and placement of scope mount base. These rifles were made up from issued Model 96s.

7. **Standard Model 96 Swedish Mauser rifle** as made at Carl Gustav Stads Gevarsfaktori. Note modification to rear sight leaf for fine elevation adjustment.

8. **Swedish Model 94 carbine/receiver** made in 1907, however this does not mean the arm was produced in that year as a carbine or a rifle. Swedish Ordnance has stated that some M94/96 receivers have been rebarreled at least 10 times without showing signs of wear.

9. **Danish Krag** in 8x58mm Rimmed. This piece is the artillery carbine. The piece has an "A" suffix to its serial number, turned down bolt handle and a stud to fit into leather carrying plate on gunner's back.

10. **Danish Krag rifle** receiver made in 1910, rifle built in 1911.

11. **Trajectory reading disc and plate** on butt of a Swedish 96/41 Sniper rifle.

12. **Portuguese Guedes** caliber 8mm Guedes.

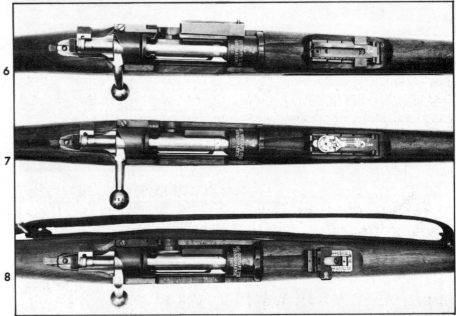

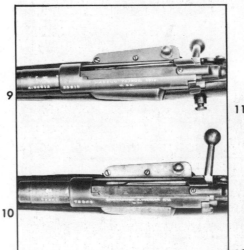

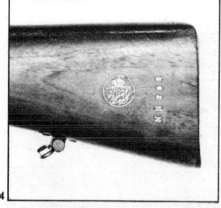

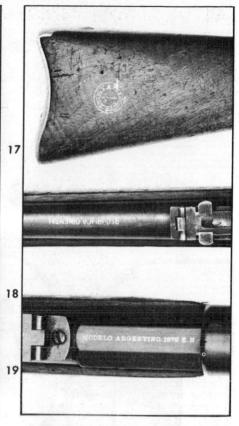

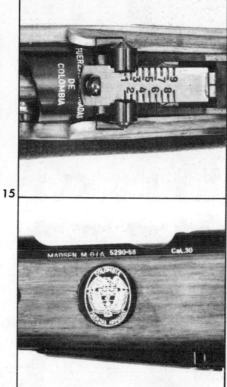

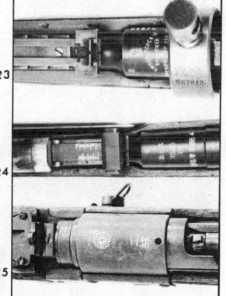

13. Portuguese Kropatchek Model 1886. Made at Steyr Werke in 1889 for Portugal in caliber 8mm Kropatchek.

14. Left side of Portuguese M1886 Kropatchek showing the Portuguese crest.

15. Danish Madsen rifle made in caliber .30/06 for the Colombians.

16. Left side view of receiver and stock crest markings of the Madsen.

17. A Francotte produced rolling block in .43 Spanish as made for the Uruguayan Government.

18. Marking on barrel of the Francotte rolling block.

19. Argentine rolling block Model 1879 made by Remington in .43 Spanish.

20. British SMLE No. 1 Mk 1. Note the "EY" marking on the receiver ring denoting for emergency use only.

21. Above rifle again, note date, 1907 and the three asterisks which denote arsenal modifications of the arm.

22. Russian Model 91 Dragoon rifle as made for Cossack regiments. Istvesk Arsenal manufacture.

23. Russian M91 rifle converted to pressure test gun in 1916 to be sent to Remington Arms Co. to develop ammunition for contract sales. Rifle made at Tula in 1905. Old style sight.

24. Chinese variation of Soviet M1944 carbine known as the Type 53.

25. Japanese Type 2 Paratroop takedown rifle, caliber 7.7x58mm.

26. Swedish Ljungman AG 42B in 6.5mm.

THE GRAY GHOST P.38

THE MOST MYSTERIOUS OF THE WALTHERS HAS AN INTRICATE AND FASCINATING HISTORY. by Warren H. Buxton

During the early 1960s, the firm of Interarmco in Alexandria, Virginia imported a group of extremely interesting P. 38 pistols bearing the code "SVW". They were, up to that time, generally unknown among collectors, and in particular the so-called "star-proofed" specimens were the least known or understood of the entire shipment. Since then the SVW-coded guns in general have become an enigma to many collectors of the P. 38.

A historical outline of these pistols and a compilation of their variations follows, however a sketch of the events leading up to the incorporation of the SVW-code will be presented first to give the reader a better understanding of the "SVW" pistols themselves.

A Walther-designed and produced locked-breech, short-recoil, double-action semi-automatic pistol was adopted in 1938 by the German Wehrmacht as a standard issue to all service branches (therefore the designation "P. 38", i.e. pistol adopted in the year 1938). It was destined to replace the expensive, unreliable and complicated P. 08 or Parabellum (Luger) pistol.

Early issues bore the Walther Banner (trademark of the Walther firm) and no attempt was made at concealing the identity of the manufacturer or his quantity of production. This type of marking for the P. 38 was very short lived.

1. Slide from the Police Issue version of the SVW-45. Note the eagle-over-N proof forward of the serial number.

2. Military version of the SVW-45, all German gray finish. The other military version is identical except for a blue barrel. Note WaA stamp.

Several years before 1938 it was decided to change the method of marking military-procured equipment with the manufacturer's name or trademark and assign a "code" designation, which was to be kept secret, and was to be affixed on the item of equipment in place of a factory name. The exact reasons for the decision to issue these codes and their evolution does not concern us here, but codes were issued to all manufacturers of Wehrmacht-procured arms including Walther and Mauser. Walther's code, for example, first consisted of the number "480" but was later changed to "ac".

The Mauser firm was initially engaged in producing the Luger, but production was halted in the latter quarter of 1942 in favor of the P. 38. Mauser's code, in 1942, used the lower-case letters "byf", and all P. 38s manufactured by them up to the end of 1944 bore the "byf" code. The last two digits of the year of manufacture were also included with all "byf"-coded P. 38s and were placed below the "byf" letters. At the beginning of 1945, Mauser's code was changed to the capital letters "SVW" with the year designation "45" below these letters. The exact reason for this change is unknown but it is plausible that in late 1944 a list of the secret codes fell into Allied hands thereby prompting the code change.

The "SVW" pistols manufactured by Mauser for issue to German troops are found in three basic variations. The first two are distinguished primarily by their finishes, the third mainly by its markings. These three variations were not produced in any definite sequence with respect to each other but were manufactured at random, being mixed together throughout their production run.

The basic finish found on all of these pistols is a smooth gray texture that will vary from a light gray to a darker green/gray as opposed to the standard military dull blue seen on most of the "byf"-coded pistols. It will be designated as the "German gray" for reasons which will become apparent in a following section. Experiments had taken place in 1944 at Mauser with various finishes in order to find a cheap and more durable replacement for the military dull blue. This gray type of finish seems to have been the final solution, and it approximated the parkerized finish as used on the U.S. Colt M1911A1 pistol among others.

The first of these "SVW" variations to be discussed will bear the German gray finish on all components except those normally left unfinished which are the locking block, sear, and all pivots and pins.

As for markings, this variation will bear, in addition to the usual "P.38" and "SVW 45" on the slide's left forward side, the German Waffe-namt (Ordnance Office) acceptance stamps which consist of an eagle over WaA135. The WaA indicates Waffenamt, the 135 indicates the specific Waffenamt office assigned to the Mauser factory. This office was responsible only to the Waffenamt and not to the factory. (These stamps have definite meanings and form a story all their own. A detailed discussion of them is unfortunately beyond the scope of this article.) The stamps will appear as follows:

On the right side of the slide (two such stamps separated by another, different stamp).

On the left of the frame (one).

On the left of the barrel (one).

On the right side of the locking block (one).

A pressure/stress proof mark consisting of an eagle over swastika will appear between the two acceptance stamps on the slide's right side (one). On the left, rear of the barrel (one).

On the left of the locking block (one).

This description concerning markings will also apply to the other two German issue "SVW" pistols discussed below. That is to say, this marking pattern is the standard German pattern for the 1945 "SVW" pistols.

The second "SVW" variation, German issue, is exactly the same as the first, described above, except that it has a blued barrel. These blue barrels were still in the bins when the German grey finish was first put into production in late 1944 and were used on a random basis into the 1945 "SVW" series. Barrel production far exceeded frame and slide production, thus the reason for a surplus of these in 1945.

The third "SVW" variation German issue, could be, and sometimes is, designated a "commercial" piece due to the presence of a "commercial" proof mark. However this is a somewhat misleading, although not entirely incorrect term, and requires something of an explanation. As we shall see, a more correct designation for these "commercial" "SVW" pistols is "police issue", consequently the latter term will be used here.

There were no commercial sales of firearms in Nazi Germany as we understand the meaning of the term here in the United States. Most civilians were simply not allowed to purchase firearms in general, especially after Hitler obtained the authority to suppress such sales.

The Nazi "commercial" proof, consisting of an eagle over an "N", was used to designate those weapons that were to be used by non-military

3. *Right side of a Police Issue slide. Note the police procurement stamp consisting of an eagle adjacent to an upper-case F.*

4. *Right side view of a typical military issue SVW pistol. It has the characteristic three-stamp pattern.*

or pseudo-military organizations who did not procure their weapons directly from Wehrmacht orders or supplies. The term "commercial" is correct, with respect to this Nazi proof mark, since it is merely a modification of a pre-Nazi, standard commercial proof mark. It is also a correct term in the sense that it denotes arms destined for purposes other than purely military, but this proof was never meant to imply a direct or "commercial" sales outlet to civilians in general.

Used in conjunction with the Nazi "commercial" proof mark for the "SVW" pistols, will be one of two other stamps. These will consist of an eagle-over-swastika — the swastika is enclosed in a circle—and to the immediate right of the swastika will be either, never both, the upper-case letters "F" or "L". This stamp is properly referred to by the designation "eagle with F" or "L" as the case may be. This terminology is used to avoid a mixup with the eagle-over-swastika military proof mark mentioned above, even though the style of eagle used with these two stamps is radically different from that used with the acceptance stamp or the military proof mark.

The presence of one of these stamps on an "SVW" P. 38, in addition to the commercial proof mark, indicates that the pistol was procured for use by one of the German police agencies and not by the Wehrmacht. The letters "F" and "L" indicated departments assigned for the procurement of "police-issue" pistols. These departments were responsible to the Interior Ministry and not the factory. They were only indirectly responsible to the Waffen-amt. Unlike the 135 seen in the Waffenamt eagle over WaA135 acceptance stamp, the letters were not assigned to a specific KW factory.

The reason for the preference of the term "police issue" over "commercial issue" is now obvious.

The "police issue" "SVW" P. 38s can have either of the two basic finishes described for the first and second German issue Wehrmacht procured "SVW" variations described above. Markings will also be the same with these exceptions:

Slide left; the commercial proof mark (one) will appear between the end of the safety lever's thumb spur and breech face.

Slide right; Waffenamt acceptance stamp (one), police procurement stamp (one), either the eagle with "F" or "L", but never both.

Barrel left front; the commercial proof mark (one).

Locking block, left; the commercial proof mark (one).

Round portion of the barrel, bottom, immediately forward of the front flat; the caliber designation, in millimeters, will take the form for example, 8,83 (8.83mm) and will vary from 8,80 to 8,90. The commas seen in these caliber designations are correct. The Germans use a comma where we use a period.

Another stamp may also be seen on all three of these variations which was used by Mauser on some of their "byf"-coded P. 38s plus numerous other guns. It is the small inspector's stamp consisting of the intertwined letters "RW" which are about 3/32-inch in height. This will usually appear on the slide, barrel and frame, although it is not uncommon to find it stamped in only one place on the weapon or be completely absent.

Grip panels should be either a glossy black semi-hard plastic or steel (not aluminum). During early 1945 Mauser began producing these steel grips in place of the plastic variety. Plastic material was in too short supply late in the war to be used on an extensive basis for non-critical items such as grip panels, thus the reason for the switch to the steel pattern. If steel, they must have the German gray finish. No markings will be found on these two types of panels. However, due to subcontract purchases, repairs, it cannot be considered incorrect to have panels of other colors or made from plastic compositions on these K.W. pistols.

Mauser-manufactured magazines will have the eagle over WaA135 acceptance stamp on their spine and these would be correct for the "SVW" guns. Finish may be either blue or German gray, as with the grip panels, though it cannot be considered incorrect to find magazines

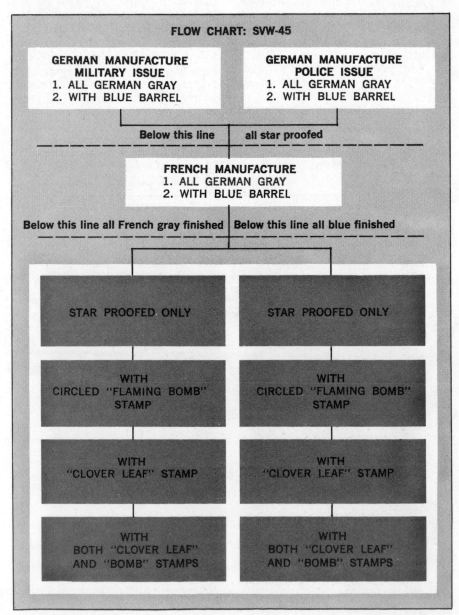

bearing other markings, or none at all in these pistols.

There were no German-issue "SVW" P. 38s that were all-blue finished from the factory.

Serial number locations for all three variations are:

Slide, left side between the safe lever's thumb spur and breech face.

Frame, left side above front of trigger guard.

Barrel, front flat.

Locking block, last three digits and letter suffix (explained below) on bottom. In the case of one-, two-, or three-digit numbers the entire number was placed on the block.

The German military system of serial numbering consisted of, for the most part, numerical and alphabetical sections with the numerical portion limited to a maximum of four digit blocks. For example: Numbering started at 1 and progressed sequentially to 9999. The numbering then reverted back to 1 but with a letter suffix, namely "a", and progressed sequentially to 9999a, then back to 1b and on to 9999b, back to 1c, and so on. This process was continued until the alphabet was exhausted. Various methods were used to avoid duplicating numbers when the alphabet was started over but this does not concern us here. It may be noted that the letter suffixes have *absolutely nothing* to do with the month of manufacture, and never did have, even though this has been reported to be the case in some areas.

A detailed discussion of the serials associated with these German issue "SVW" P. 38s would go far beyond the text of this article due to influences of other models and production difficulties. Therefore this subject will be only touched upon, but a basic understanding will still be possible.

Serial numbering started at 1 and ended in the low "f" range. The "police issue" pistols were mixed in with this range and did not have a separate block. A range of 1 to 2500f implies a total production run of approximately 69,996 units. This is not the case however. Some of the letter blocks were, it appears, skipped and some were not assembled into complete pistols even though they were used. The influence of a foreign power in the immediate postwar era (to be explained) also contributed to the confusion that surrounds these early serial ranges. Of the total production range, not over 15,000 units were completed within it. The majority of these will fall into the high "d" to low "f" range, or from approximately 8000d to 2500f with the remaining pistols placing in the no-letter to high "d" ranges.

Very, very few "police issue" "SVW" pistols were made—possibly less than 100. Judging from the few known specimens, they fall into the mid no-letter block but it would not be unusual to find an example with a serial ranging anywhere from 1 to the high "f" range.

These guns were produced under trying conditions due to lack of suitable manpower, equipment and material. Consequently production was slow and the time left for Nazi Germany was limited. Nevertheless the German-produced "SVW" 45 was in every way a quality military pistol. With the appearance of Russian troops at the Mauser Works production ceased in early April, 1945, and more likely several weeks before that time.

For a very short time the Russians had control of Mauser and proceeded to strip it of all machinery that could be easily loaded on trains or trucks and be shipped east. However they had no idea of how long they would be at Mauser and were concerned with confiscating only useable machinery and tools. No assembly or production of P. 38s was attempted by them, then or at any time later, using "SVW"-coded parts. Their interest was not in the small arms *per se*; they had an abundance of them, but in machines, tools, drawings, personnel and blueprints that would serve to produce more war materials later on.

Therefore, at 3:00 p.m. on April 20, 1945 the Mauser Works fell into the French sector when temporary boundaries were laid out and established. In fact, the French were probably present at Mauser at the same time the Russians were, or very shortly thereafter.

France became involved in Southeast Asia during mid-1945 and needed weapons, including handguns. Enough of Mauser was left intact to

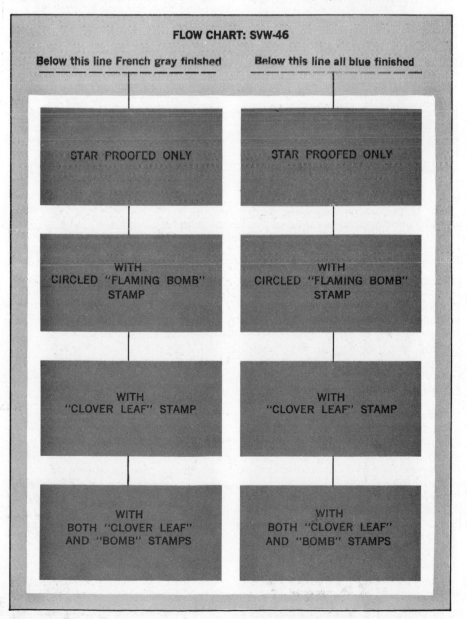

FLOW CHART: SVW-46

Below this line French gray finished	Below this line all blue finished
STAR PROOFED ONLY	STAR PROOFED ONLY
WITH CIRCLED "FLAMING BOMB" STAMP	WITH CIRCLED "FLAMING BOMB" STAMP
WITH "CLOVER LEAF" STAMP	WITH "CLOVER LEAF" STAMP
WITH BOTH "CLOVER LEAF" AND "BOMB" STAMPS	WITH BOTH "CLOVER LEAF" AND "BOMB" STAMPS

assemble and produce pistols, namely P. 38s and HSCs. It is very unlikely that any attempt was made to manufacture complete arms from basic raw materials. There was a drastic shortage of raw materials to begin with, to say nothing of technical help and plans. There were however, an abundance of parts in various states of manufacture within the factory.

The French retained the German code of "SVW", the serial system, and dating method. The various Waffenamt acceptance stamps and military proof marks were not disturbed, that is to say, defaced or removed, if already present. Occasionally though, one will find a French-made "SVW" P. 38 that has defaced German stamps. This was the result of individual acts and not French policy. In fact, the small "RW" inspector's stamp was taken over by the French for their own use and this, one may recall, was strictly a German stamp.

Identification of a French-produced "SVW" P. 38 is quite easy since they applied their own pressure/stress proof. This proof mark consists of a five-pointed star which indicated "Ordinary Smokeless Proof (Powder 'T') Pressure—850 kg/cm²". Location of this star was as follows:

On the slide's right (one).
Left rear of the barrel (one).
Left of the locking block (one). All French-produced "SVW" P. 38s will bear this star.

Due to the various stages of production some of the components were found in, any one given component may or may not carry a Waffenamt stamp. For that matter the usual three-stamp pattern seen on the slide's right side (eagle over WaA135, eagle over swastika, eagle over WaA135) may be incomplete or completely absent. More often than not the barrel will have a Waffenamt stamp. Frames and slides though, come in "you-name-it" Waffenamt stamp configurations.

There are three finishes associated with these French P. 38s. First is the original German gray. Second is a very dark gray—in some cases almost black—which is a true parkerized finish. Other than the color, the distinguishing feature between this French gray (as we will term it) and the German gray, is that the metal surfaces of the French pistols have a definite sandblasted appearance. The third finish is the standard military dull blue.

A French P. 38 with the German gray on all major components or with a blue barrel is quite a scarce

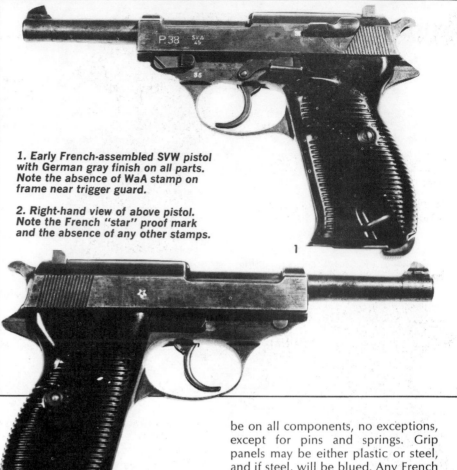

1. Early French-assembled SVW pistol with German gray finish on all parts. Note the absence of WaA stamp on frame near trigger guard.

2. Right-hand view of above pistol. Note the French "star" proof mark and the absence of any other stamps.

item. These pistols represent those few guns that were in the factory and far enough along in assembly to have been finished by the Germans. They were merely assembled by the French. Grip panels will be either the semi-hard glossy black plastic, or the steel variety, and if steel should have the German gray. Magazines may be blue or German gray.

The vast majority of the French guns will have the French gray. These pistols represent those parts that required some additional amount of work to be done on them to complete their manufacture which, obviously, included parkerizing them. The French gray will be found on all parts, no exceptions, other than pins and springs. Grip panels will usually be the steel variety, although existing stores of plastic panels were used up in this period and will be encountered from time to time.

Those pistols with the German or French gray were for issue to French military (army) forces and saw duty in Southeast Asia and North African areas.

The third finish, the dull blue, will

be on all components, no exceptions, except for pins and springs. Grip panels may be either plastic or steel, and if steel, will be blued. Any French P. 38 with an all-blue finish is quite hard to come by. These were for issue to police and border guards inside France and occupied Germany. The French military needed more arms than did police and border units, consequently few all-blue specimens were produced.

Production continued during the remainder of 1945, after resuming production in May, with the "SVW" 45-code. At the beginning of 1946 the code was changed to "SVW" 46 and ran to May 2, at which time production was terminated. The reason for the termination was twofold. One of the agreements made between the Allies relating to the German surrender and occupation terms was that no armaments would be made by any of the Allies on German soil using captured German facilities. The French either pointedly ignored this provision or their position in the terms was vague enough, in their opinion, to allow them to utilize Mauser. The Soviets did not see it this way and put up a continuous string of protests against the French/Mauser operation. These protests may have had little immediate effect on the French but they did strengthen the Soviet position. Also definite boundaries had not been established between the various Allied occupation zones until around

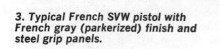

3. Typical French SVW pistol with French gray (parkerized) finish and steel grip panels.

4. Right side view of above pistol showing the French "star" proof.

3

4

April, 1946. When all was settled and definite boundaries were established, Mauser fell into the Soviet zone. The earlier Soviet protests may have had some influence on these final events.

In any case the French had to leave. Before their departure they saw to it that the Mauser Works would be of no use to the Russians or East Germans. All machinery and anything else that could be moved was sent into France. Some items were routed to other Allied nations and possibly to a few other countries whose political faith was between the French and Soviet viewpoint. The buildings and all that could not feasibly be moved were razed to the ground. For some unknown reason any and all records were destroyed promptly when the French first took over Mauser, and those few remaining records were subsequently destroyed when they left. Mauser Werke, which had survived three major conflicts intact; who had become one of the largest small arms producers the world had ever seen; who had influenced poli-

tical and military decisions; whose name had become synonymous with a product (any bolt-action rifle was a "Mauser" as any lever action rifle was a "Winchester" or any revolver a "Colt" or any automatic small arm a "Browning"), literally ceased to exist in a few weeks time. Mauser was no more.

Up to this point, the discussion of these French P. 38s has been of a general nature. Let us now examine these in greater detail.

The three basic finishes, German gray, French gray, and all blue, will be found in only the "SVW" 45 pistols. The German gray units were assembled first and because of the low number of parts bearing this finish they were quickly exhausted and did not extend into 1946. The French gray and all-blue guns were made in both the "SVW" 45 and "SVW" 46 codes. The vast majority of the P. 38s made will have the French gray; the all-blue weapons are very scarce especially in the "SVW" 46 codes.

The serial numbering system used for these pistols is the same as the German; in fact, the older German serials were used, and the French did not initiate separate or special blocks for their pistols. As mentioned previously a detailed discussion of the serials pertaining to these "SVW" pistols, the French weapons included, is far beyond the context of this article, and they will be treated in a very general fashion.

However the reader will still have a basic understanding of what took place and when as well as being adequately informed as to variation identification.

Most of the German-gray specimens fall into one general block, this being the early no-letter range. A very few are known in the "d" to "f" ranges and none in the "a", "b" or "c" ranges. As for the predominate no-letter range, not all of this was used for the French pistols. Total production of these P. 38s probably did not extend over 200 to 300 completed units.

A general pattern is first seen here which will apply to those French pistols which have serials in the same ranges as the German serials. The French used those German numbers which the Germans themselves did not have recorded as being on completed and issued pistols. The reason for these "gaps" scattered among the German serials is tied up in other areas outside the scope of this article, but one reason is quite obvious. If a completed or almost completed, but numbered, pistol failed to pass the various tests it was set aside. Normally its useable parts and therefore its number would be recycled into the assembly lines and be issued if at all possible. In 1945 there was no time for this and the pistol, or numbered parts, were shelved in the hopes that time and sufficient workmen would be available later to put it into service. The war ended too quickly to implement this policy which resulted in serial "gaps" with respect to the German records. Those numbered parts which were available were taken over by the French authorities. This means then that through the entire German production run, to the low "f" range, one will find French-made pistols with serials mixed in with the German serials.

Although P. 38s with numbered parts were being assembled, it is apparent that all parts of the French assembled unit would not be matching. The assemblers were quite careful about renumbering, or matching components with respect to the numerical portion of the number only. Thus, some of these French P. 38s will be seen to have matching numbers but the letter suffix may not match. The frame number with its suffix was the controlling serial in these cases. To match the barrel and slide serials to the frame's, the frame numbers were stamped over the former two.

The French gray and all-blue units start rather abruptly where the German production run was halted, this

1. Typical French-made SVW with all-blue finish.

2. Typical French SVW-46 with all-blue finish. French gray specimens are the same in detail except for the differences in finish.

THE GRAY GHOST

being in the low "f" range. A few French gray units are known which fall into the German serial ranges though. At the end of 1945, the mid-"k" range had been reached. These 1945 numbers placing between the low-"f" and mid-"k" ranges are of course new numbers that were never utilized by the Germans, being merely a continuation of the original German series.

The all-blue units were mixed in with the French-gray pistols, and no special or separate blocks were allotted to them. Very few were produced, probably not over 100 to 200 pistols.

Total production in 1945 of the French-gray and all-blue P. 38s combined was approximately 51,000 finished units.

The "SVW" 46 serials were a continuation of the 1945 series and progressed sequentially to the high-"k" range. A few oddballs have been seen with serials that place them at random in the 1945 ranges. These were simply parts found here and there in 1946 that had been missed in 1945. Both the French gray and all-blue finishes were turned out in 1946. As in 1945, the all-blue pistols were mixed in with the French gray varieties and no special or separate block was set aside for them.

Total production of "SVW" 46 pistols was around 4000. Of these very, very few were the all-blue variations. A rough estimate of the number produced would be not over 100.

A grand total of "SVW" 45 and "SVW" 46 French P. 38s, all variations, is approximately 55,000 units. Most of these disappeared into the

African and Asian sink holes before France was able to extract herself from those areas. The remaining stocks, warehoused in France, were eventually declared as surplus material and sold to Interarms who imported them into the U.S. The import total was around 3000 pieces.

All the variations of the French P. 38s so far presented have been based on the three styles of finish found among them. No mention has been made of variations in markings except for the code change in 1946. There are certainly some interesting marking variations and they can now be discussed. The marks that are to concern us now may be found on any of the French P. 38s with the possible exception of the early types having the German-gray finish. This does not mean that the marks will never be or cannot be found on these early pistols, but it is very doubtful that they will be due to their early assembly date and the fact that the marks appear to have been utilized after these guns were assembled.

The first is the "RW" German inspector mark. Available information indicates that the French used this for some phase of barrel production. It will often be found on the bar-

rel's left side and will appear from one to four times on a barrel.

The second is a stylized "flaming bomb" so named because of its general appearance. This ⅛-inch diameter stamp is not actually a true flaming bomb, but consists of two concentric circles with the inner circle topped by three half-circles, or more properly half-ovals, since their elongated shape allows the center one to tower slightly above the other two. Location of this mark is on the left of the frame, either under or directly to the rear of the takedown lever, or to the front of the serial number. It may also appear on the left, front of the trigger guard. This "flaming bomb" may appear in either one or both locations on the same pistol.

The next and last mark is conveniently termed a "clover leaf," approximately ⅜-inch high, and has but one location. This is on the left of the frame in the vicinity of the sear and is always covered by the left grip panel when present.

The "flaming bomb" and "clover leaf" stamps may appear alone or together on the same pistol. Any French P. 38 with these stamps, in any combination, is quite hard to come by, but those specimens bearing both stamps are especially difficult to find. The meaning or significance of these two stamps is unknown.

The preceding discussion of the "SVW"-coded P. 38s has presented 22 variations of this pistol type! The problem now becomes akin to a game such as "what 22 variations?" or "how to find the rabbit in the picture." The details, in other words, obscure the story, yet without them there would be no story. Flowcharts have been provided to alleviate this problem and display the variations in a manner which will clearly point them out. Basically the charts are self explanatory. The dots in various sections indicates those variations that are definitely known to exist. Those without dots certainly can exist, and in all probability will be found as time passes.

Those "SVW"-code P. 38 pistols were the last ones of their kind manufactured by their original masters. They were also the final segment in a line that stretched back to the early 1930's and which would emerge once again as one of the three major pistol systems in the free world to survive the second world war. The other two systems are the Colt M1911A1 and Browning GP-35 Hi-Power. Therein lies a portion of their interest and historical significance.

P.38 VALUE CONSIDERATIONS

Generally speaking, the Walther P.38 has stepchild status with collectors of automatic pistols because it is still considered to be a modern design. In spite of this, the Walther has collectors' appeal. More and more variations of the arm are being turned up and gradually, collectors are consolidating the variations into well-defined groupings wherein we find a definite beginning and end to P.38 production from 1938 to 1945.

Presently, the design is still going strong in Germany as the official military sidearm (P1) and is the official police arm. The modern-day P.38 has been exported to the United States in moderate quantities, and is currently being marketed by Interarmco.

After World War 2, the P.38 was still being used by countries west and east of the Iron Curtain. The source of many wartime P.38s has been from the surplus sales of these arms from the various countries that used them for military and police service. They are, to mention a few: Bulgaria, Czechoslovakia, Denmark, East Germany, Finland, France, Israel, Greece, Norway, Rumania, Sweden, Turkey and in some cases, the Arab countries.

Some of these pistols were marked with the property markings of the aforementioned countries, others were used as-issued and form a crazy-quilt of non-Third Reich marking styles.

Prices given here will pertain to mint, matching examples of the various P.38 types unless otherwise indicated.

Walther Armee, caliber 9mm	N.A.
Walther Armee, caliber .45 ACP	N.A.
Walther HP (Heeres Pistole), Square Pin	$450.00
Walther HP (Heeres Pistole), Round Pin, a most common type among the HP-series (Pre-WW 2 commercial	$250.00
Walther HP (wartime production)	$175.00
Walther HP, 7.65mm	$350.00
Walther HP, m/39, Swedish Contract	$350.00
Walther "O" Series (c. 1938)	$250.00
Walther 480 (c. 1939)	$300.00
Walther ac 40	$200.00
Walther ac 41	$150.00
Walther ac 42 (change in exterior finish, rough)	$ 95.00
Walther "police issue" c. 1943	$125.00
Walther ac 43	$ 95.00
Walther ac 44	$ 90.00
Walther ac 45	$ 90.00
Mauser byf 42 (only made for last three months of '42)	$ 95.00
Mauser byf 43	$ 95.00
Mauser byf 44	$ 95.00
Mauser svw (German issue)	$125.00
Mauser svw 45 (French issue)	$ 95.00
Mauser svw 46 (French issue)	$110.00
Spree Werke cyq (c. 1944-45)	$ 90.00
Turkish Copy (four known to exist)	$1000.00

Other variations of the post-War Mauser-produced P.38s have been discussed in this publication but as yet prices have not been determined for these and will not be included here.

LUGERS, HOLSTERS AND ACCESSORIES

A COLLECTOR'S GUIDE TO VALUES
by Jim Helms and Bill Evans

Is Luger collecting really dead? Some collectors are fed-up with paying the stupendously high prices commanded for the Luger and have turned to other fields saying that Lugers have "dried-up." True, it is very frustrating to go to a collector's meeting, find a piece that fits in one's collection and then find out that this fine piece is selling for an outlandish price. Nevertheless, the cult of the Luger goes on. This brings to mind the old cliche, "Hope springs eternal in the human breast."

The Luger design holds fascination for the design enthusiast. The fine workmanship displayed with most Lugers brings to the aficionado the feeling of the "good-old-days" when time meant very little and mass production meant quality first, plus a lot of fine hand work. In other words, a lot of hands doing a lot of operations, expertly and with precision. This type of production philosophy was the boon and the bane of the Luger. The German Army found that the modern age of arms-making had caught up with them, and the fine, old, well-finished P.08 had to make way for more modern weaponry.

Much has been written about the "Luger." Some writings have great importance; other writings are quite useless to the researcher. It is not the intent of the authors to "beat-a-dead-horse," we want to impart to the reader new information on one of the most popular gun-collecting subjects of the last two decades. We feel that combining previous research with new information will accomplish two most important purposes: It will furnish the advanced collector some new insights and approaches to the field; and it will give new collectors a general view of what is available and collectible in the Luger field.

The foregoing material has been gathered and put together by the authors after many years of research including reams of correspondence and hours of observation and discussions with other collectors.

When dealing with a subject where so much primary source material has been lost and destroyed, much information has to be based on personal recollection combined wtih a cer-

1. The Swiss still use the Parabellum for target shooting. Here an officer (on right) and an enlisted man (on left) are at shooting practice with their 1929s.

2. Artillery Parabellum shown with complete kit including holster, stock, snail drum, dust cover, loading tool (drum), cleaning rod, magazine pouch, sight adjusting tool, WW 1-issue cartridges, extra 8-round magazines.

3. Finnish Model 1923 in caliber 7.65mm Parabellum. Note dull finish, Army property stamp, DWM trademark on toggle, black plastic grips.

4. First issue German Army/Parabellum made in 1908. Note absence of stock lug, and grip safety (a feature common to earlier models). About 20,000 of these were made. Hold-open catches were added later.

5. Simson rework, unmarked, in 9mm.

6. 1908 Bulgarian, 10,000 were made.

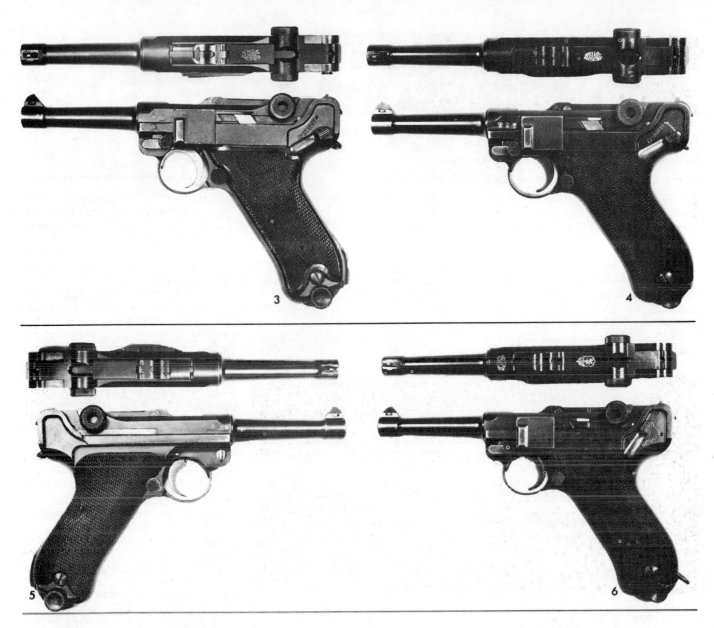

VALUES OF PARABELLUM PISTOLS

tain amount of "suppose this" or "maybe that." We realize that there are bound to be inaccuracies and take this opportunity to request any useful comments or corrections from the readers.

The cost (buying or selling) of a Luger can be influenced by a number of factors. The amount of money one is willing to spend is not always *the* determining factor. Geographical location, source of the pistol, condition, rarity, buyer's attitude, seller's attitude, demand by collectors and/or shooters, and change in supply as dictated by the laws of any number of countries are influences that anyone interested in purchasing a Luger must take into account.

Let us follow the imaginary trail of an excellent condition 1900 Luger. Suppose it has been in the estate of the original owner, who died, and

now his wife wants to dispose of the pistol. Let us imagine a nephew has a vague interest in Lugers—one of those "I've always wanted one" varieties of aficionados. The wife gives the pistol to him outright as a gift, or perhaps there is a nominal cost involved in the transaction—say $25. After a time, the nephew tires of his toy, thinking that he should buy a .22 automatic pistol that is easier to handle (and cheaper to shoot). He goes to a local dealer and explains what he has and what he wants. He has $25.00 in the pistol, the dealer puts it out for $125.00, and the piece is bought for that price. The new owner might realize that the pistol is worth more than he paid for it, so he searches out someone who knows a little more about Lugers and the price goes up to $250.00. Depending on the location of these imaginary transactions, the price of the 1900 could go up to between $550.00 and $600.00.

It would be ideal to be in on the

ground floor of such goings on, but unfortunately one cannot be where all the good deals are at the time they are happening.

Again, let us suppose that a dealer in a small town somewhere has acquired a World War I or World War 2 Luger of the garden variety. This "dealer" might be the owner of the general store. He is not a collector, but has seen a few Lugers over the years (very few!), consequently the piece he has for sale is a "scarce" or "rare" item, and he prices it accordingly.

Take the case of a World War 1 or 2 veteran who brought a P.O8 home as a souvenir and stored it ever since he took off his uniform for the last time. Not being a shooter or collector, he might feel indifferently about the pistol. It's just a piece of steel he picked up and brought home, and the past has dimmed the memories of his service —making the Luger a not too important possession. In this case (should

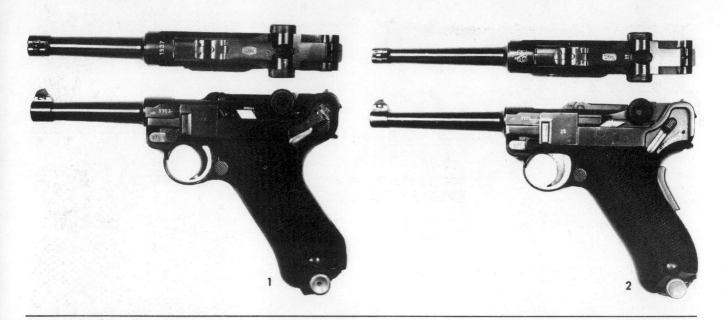

1

2

LUGERS, HOLSTERS

someone evince interest in buying his Luger) the price would probably be quite reasonable. Then there's the veteran who brings home a Luger and gathers a little knowledge from his "expert" friends and perhaps from a little casual reading. He might hear about (or see) a rare Luger that looks like his (but happens to be marked Kreighoff S while his war stamped byf41). The rare one is perhaps worth several hundred dollars, so why isn't his? It would be quite an experience trying to get this fellow's Luger for a fair price!

The buyer's attitude is also a factor in determining the price of Lugers. If he says to himself, "I've got to have that piece," and he has the money at the time, he gets the pistol regardless of cost. On the other hand, the cautious and knowing buyer will control his "impulse buying" and evaluate the situation cooly. Of course, there are instances where the prospective purchaser might realize the piece he wants is a terribly scarce and desirable variation, and the chance of finding another one like it is almost nil—in that case, an impulse purchase is the only reasonable solution.

Government legislation has recently become a part of the military weapons collecting game. The 1968 Gun Control Act stopped importation of surplus military weapons to the United States (including some P.08 types of military issue). This law was instrumental in forcing prices up steeply for a time, but fortunately the spiral began its natural downward trend about 18 months ago—even with the increase of Luger collectors. There are, of course, some variations that are so rare that the ordinary ups

and downs of the Luger market have little or no effect on their value. For instance, the .45 caliber test piece, authenticated presentation pieces, Iranian, and Russian variations.

Condition is also a large factor in determining the worth of a Luger. The better its condition, the more it is worth (except in the case of an extremely rare variation).

Our listing of values does not include all variations—only those a collector might run into in the ordinary course of plying his hobby.

Two of the little known variations of Parabellum pistols are the Finnish-issued P.08 and the Spandau Arsenal P.08. Some new light has been brought to bear on these subjects, and the authors feel that the reader will find this new information to his benefit.

THE FINNISH P.08

Finland purchased a quantity of P.08s from Germany in the '20s and '30s. These pistols are still used today in the armed forces of Finland. The pistols purchased were the "standard" P.08 type with a four-inch barrel, stock lug and short sear bar. In Finland the P.08 is called "MODEL 1923." It's in caliber 7.65mm.

The Air Force, Army and Navy use the same model of pistol, consequently there is not an "Air Force Luger" or "Navy Luger" (and so forth) known in Finland. The only distinction between the services is a brass disc placed on the wooden grip, which gives the unit to which the pistol was issued. The majority of Finnish Lugers have been refinished one or more times. When this happens, the wood grips are replaced with black plastic ones like the late World War 2 Mauser type. The brass disc is not put back on, and the guns

1. Dutch Contract of 1934 by Mauser Werke. Approximately 1000 pistols were made with chamber dates running from 1936 to 1940.

2. Portugese "GNR" with 4¾" barrel in caliber 7.65mm Parabellum. "GNR" means "Garde Nationale Republicanie" specimen shown is serial number 1921v the first piece produced under the contract specifications.

3. 1920 Carbine with 11¾" barrel in 7.65mm Parabellum (some reported in 9mm). An unknown quantity of these were manufactured, is easily distinguished from the 1902 by "new" toggle and stock lug.

4. 1902 Carbine in caliber 7.65mm Parabellum.

5. Deutches Waffen und Munitionsfabriken armorer's cutaway, used to train apprentice gunsmiths.

are never matching after the refinish.

The Finnish M1923 P.08 shown in the photo is of DWM manufacture. This piece has been redone in a black Parkerized type of finish with only ont straw-colored part—the ejector. The trigger, sear bar plunger, sear bar safety catch and the coupling link are white, the rest of the pistol is parkerized. The "new" finish is much more serviceable than the original blue, and in a country with a climate such as Finland's, one can be sure that their weapons are not reworked with an eye towards beauty.

None of the part numbers match on the specimen pistol, not even the Finnish rework number! The frame has been restamped "40" while the barrel is numbered "20." There is still a "Crown N" proof on the receiver. The Finnish Army mark "SA" is surrounded by a round-cornered square under the "Crown N" proof on the left side of the piece. The magazine is a late type, but with a wooden bottom piece, also numbered —but not matching anything else.

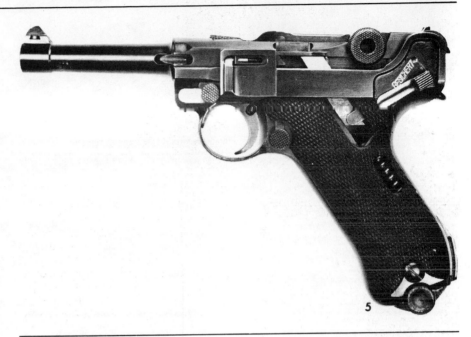

3

4

5

The firing pin is blued, and of late type, with the characteristic four grooves cut into the front part of the pin.

FINNISH P.08 HOLSTERS

Generally, Lahti holsters are used for Lugers after the guns are refinished. Some German holsters left in Lapland have been put to use also, but most Finnish Luger holsters were made in Finland and resemble World War 1 German types for the four-inch barrel. They are flatter-looking, being made of thinner leather than their German counterparts. They are sometimes marked with the leather factory's stamp (a reindeer, or crocodile). A great many were worn out and thrown away, so about 95 percent of Finnish Lugers are without holsters.

A rare Finnish holster for the Luger was made in extremely limited numbers which resembles the Lahti holster, but has straps on the back of it to carry a shoulder stock.

The Finnish Army still uses the P.08, Lahti, Browning Hi-Power, CZ 52, and the Beretta M1934 in .32 ACP. No pistols are being manufactured or procured for the armed forces, as the assault rifle M62 will gradually replace the pistol in most instances. The Finnish police use mainly F.N.-made pistols in .32 ACP of various models.

The Finns also modified a very small quantity of P.08s to .22 Long Rifle caliber. These are known as the "Salobellum" pistol.

It is very doubtful that Finnish Lugers will ever see the surplus market, as there was an incident in Finland which caused the Army to stop selling any surplus weapons except absolute junk and bayonets. The trouble began when deactivated machine guns were being sold to the public. Such a furor was raised by the press and various groups that the government was pressured into not selling *any* surplus weapons. Even the export by Finland to the United States of the semiautomatic version of the current Finnish assault rifle (M62) has caused problems inside Finland. Thus, even if it were possible to import military surplus weapons into the United States today, there would be

little chance of Finnish Lugers becoming an item on the collector's lists.

THE SPANDAU P.08

The existence of a P.08 made at the Spandau Arsenal has long been a point debated among collectors. Several examples have been reported and some examined, but the examiners felt that the pieces were not correct.

There is now a bit more conclusive evidence that the Spandau P.08 is indeed not fiction. One of the authors of this article is in touch with a man in Germany who is a veteran of World War 2 and was on the Russian front for some time before being wounded and sent to other areas. He is not a collector, but is still interested in weapons used during the time he was in the Wehrmacht.

At no time in the correspondence were there any specific questions raised regarding markings on P.08s, but in one letter he mentioned (recalling his service time) that the P.08 he had at the time was marked "SPANDAU." This remark, of course, aroused our interest and our friend was questioned further regarding his P.08. In a later letter he replied, "- - - Miene 08 auf dem Kniegelenk gestempelt war mit "SPANDAU" daruber eine Krone." —(" - - - My 08 had "SPANDAU" stamped on the

knee joint (toggle) and also a crown above the Spandau." He recalls the serial number as being 7732—which was his foreign field post number divided by three. The weapon had belonged to a sergeant killed in action, and the pistol was then registered to the new owner. The gun was stolen from him while he was recuperating in a hospital in Lowitsch, Poland.

He told us that Spandau-marked P.08s were considered scarce (almost rare) at the time he was in the service, and recalls that the magazine had a wooden bottom piece. The other details of the pistol are hazy, as he has not seen a P.08 since the end of the war. He feels that if he had any P.08, he could remember much more concerning the Spandau P.08.

This information is just another small piece in the Spandau puzzle, and is offered in the hope that somewhere, someone else might be able to contribute another bit or piece of material that will help to clear up the "Spandau P.08 Mystery."

LUGER ACCOUTREMENTS

In spite of all the collecting fever associated with the acquisition of the Parabellum pistol and its unending variations, the discussion and dissemination of information regarding holsters and accessories for same is sketchy and at best downright inaccurate. The authors have presented in this section a survey of Luger holsters and accessories, a list that is probably by no means complete, but one that is at least as accurate as the unkind sands of time permit.

The literal translation of the German word for holster is "Tasche," which also means pocket, purse, handbag, satchel or pouch. A holster is nothing more than a pouch into which a pistol fits so that it may be more conveniently carried by the owner. For clarity's sake, P.08 holsters will be divided into two broad categories: Military and Commercial.

From these major categories come the subcategories best described as: German Military (including Police issues); Military Contract (excluding Swiss); Swiss issues (both Military and Commercial); Commercial (European and non-European manufacture.)

GERMAN MILITARY HOLSTERS 1908-1945

The German Army adopted the Pistole Parabellum in 1908 (hence the official designation P.08). The holster designed and made for the four-inch barrel model remained essentially unchanged during the 37 years the P.08 was in service.

These holsters were made of an excellent grade of leather, well sewn and finished. The flap was kept closed by a buckle/strap arrangement which did a good job of keeping out dust and foul weather; but it was not exactly a quick-draw holster. From information received from the son of an old German holster manufacturer, P.08 holsters were for the most part made by hand—especially in the "old days." The great amount of handwork would account in part for the longevity of a P.08 holster, as it is not unusual to see an example 50 or 60 years old that is still tightly sewn, and with leather that is not cracked or otherwise in poor condition.

There were three minor manufacturing changes in the four-inch P.08 holster which may be enumerated as follows:

The early pouch is fastened to the body of the holster (back side) by one line of thread, the pouch is curved around and sewn to the front part of the holster (inside). With the late pouch a back piece of the holster is extended so that the pouch can be "double stitched" onto it, thus affording more strength to the pouch itself. The flap of the early type has a leather "hinge" onto which the flap is sewn. This hinge is then sewn onto the body of the hol-

ster a total of three pieces of leather. Later on, the flap is attached directly to the body of the holster, providing more strength and less chance of the flap parting from the holster by ordinary wear.

The early leather lining that covers half the inside of the holster is held in place by the thread of the belt loops and pull-up strap as well as being stitched between the front and back pieces.

The later lining is thicker and is sewn across the bottom as well. The stitching for the belt loops and pull-up strap are also covered by the lining.

Both early and late types have a magazine pouch on the leading edge of the holster, a small pouch under the flap for the loading/stripping tool, two separate belt loops on the back, and a pull-up strap attached to the inside of the holster, put there to help the user extract the pistol from the holster more easily.

The exact date of the changes noted above cannot be pinpointed,

1. Markings: (A) 1917-dated Artillery. **(B)** DWM double-date 9mm, Erfurt examples are also found, date and cut in front of the new date shown that an artillery receiver was used. **(C)** 1920 Police/Military, 9mm with 4" barrel. Generally reworked WW 1 pieces. **(D)** Simson & Co., Suhl, made or reworked by Simson for military or commercial sales from 1922 to 1932. **(E)** K-date, actually made in 1934 by Mauser, no grip safety, but with stock lug. First coded P. 08 made under Nazi control, approximately 10,500 made. **(F)** Krieghoff S-date (1935 3rd series) approximately 1600 to 1800 made reportedly for the Luftwaffe. **(G)** Mauser 42-code made between 1939 and 1940, made strictly for the Wehrmacht, approximately 50,000 produced.

2. Swiss ski troops armed with the Parabellum Model 1929 note how the holster is slung off the shoulder.

3. Model 1929 Swiss-made Parabellum with holster, belt, shoulder straps, and enlisted man's dress dagger which was generally worn for festive, dress or parade occasions. Switzerland is one of the few countries that still issue dress daggers to its troops.

2

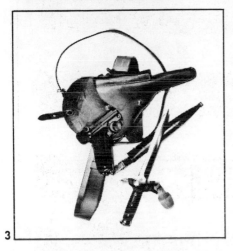

3

but from holsters that have been observed, it was between the years 1926 and 1929. The 1926 dated holster is of the early type, the 1929 of the late type. Of course, it is possible the changes could have occurred in 1927 or 1928, but until holsters from these years are examined, it will be impossible to give the *exact* year when the manufacturing changes were implemented.

LAMINATED PAPER HOLSTERS

A very few late Nazi (1943) police holsters have been examined that are made of a stiff laminated paper, combined with leather. An inquiry to Germany revealed that the paper holsters were known there to collectors, but the survival rate was not too great. These holsters are black.

THE GERMAN NAVY
1904-1918

The German Navy adopted a six-inch barrel version of the P.08 in 1904, and two types of holsters were issued with this pistol.

The early type was issued with a wooden shoulder stock magazine pouch (two magazines), cleaning rod,

loading tool and shoulder straps. The flap was closed by a stud placed in the body of the holster over which the flap was placed. The holsters were black smooth leather, usually rather thin.

The late version was made of brown leather, much thicker than the early type. The closure was of the buckle/strap type (like the four-inch version). There was no provision for a shoulder stock, instead the standard loops were used. A loading tool and cleaning rod were issued with this holster.

Naval holsters of either type are rather scarce but hardly what one would call rare. The early types are generally in worse condition than the late types.

ARTILLERY HOLSTERS
1914-1918

Holsters for the Artillery model were issued with the shoulder stock, extra magazine pouch (held two magazines), cleaning rod, loading tool, 32-round snail drum, loading tool for the snail drum, carrying bags for the snail drums, and shoulder straps for the holster/stock combination. As pictured in the 1917 instruction manual (Deutsche Waffen Journal reprint) for the Artillery model P.08, the soldier is shown carrying the holstered gun on the right side (over the shoulder), and on the left side are two canvas bags containing the snail drums. A small chest is also shown which contains five snail drums, one loading tool and 12 boxes of ammunition (16 rounds each). The photos of the drum itself are of the old type (round handle). The pistol is shown as having both the long and short sear bar. Not shown in the manual are the leather pouches for the snail drums, and the unloading tool for the drums.

Artillery holsters were issued in

various shades of brown, but sometimes a black one is seen. Again, these are dyed holsters. These holsters are fairly common pieces, though frequently some will be seen that have been shortened to accommodate a pistol with a shorter barrel, and quite a number were reworked into holsters for the four-inch P.08.

THE GERMAN POLICE
1919-1945

It is not known if the German police used the P.08 before or during World War 1, but there is enough evidence to substantiate the use of the P.08 by the German Police from 1919 to 1945. Holsters used by the police differed only in the method of latching the holster. The police holsters used a pull-down strap and stud, whereas the military used the buckle and strap closure. This "pull-down" was not a Nazi innovation, but can be noted in photos taken during the 1920s in which the Weimar police can be seen wearing P.08 holsters of this type. Many World War 1 military holsters were converted to pull-down police types during the early period of the Weimar Republic. Early police holsters were some shade of brown (as noted before) but some early police conversions have been examined that were black—obviously an old dye job. Frequently, the pistol number is stamped on the back of the holster, and sometimes a matching loading tool can be found with the holster.

FOREIGN CONTRACT HOLSTERS
PORTUGAL

A few years ago, Portugal released the M2 and GNR pistols, along with the holsters, cleaning rods, pin punches, and magazine pouches.

The holster for the GNR (1935) is the same type as the M2 with the exception of the belt loops. GNR holsters and magazine pouches will be dated (1936), while the M2 holsters are almost always unmarked except for an "AE" on the back or inside. Many of each type were new or nearly new, while a great number were in ratty condition.

The four-inch Naval pistol and holster rig is an extremely rare piece, never having been released by the Portuguese Government. However, an outstanding specimen of the four-inch Naval pistol is owned by Mr. Reinhard Kornmayer, a noted Parabellum collector in Germany.

HOLLAND

Holsters for the Dutch Lugers are a scarce item (as are most Dutch

LUGERS, HOLSTERS

leather goods). Two types were equipped with loading tool, pin punch, and cleaning rod. There is also a double magazine pouch sewn on them. The tools for Dutch pistols were also numbered to the gun.

BULGARIA

Generally the countries of the Balkans have their own methods of equipping their troops. The Bulgarians have produced many variations of holsters for the P.08. Most of the Bulgarian types are made without rhyme or reason and generally out of poor leather. The Yugoslavians, when their troops were equipped with ex-Nazi issue P.08s, either kept the German-issued holster or made up leather to suit the individual unit's fancy.

U.S. 1900 TEST PIECE

The United State's brief fling with the Luger came with the Ordnance Trials of 1900. When the Ordnance Department found that DWM did not furnish holsters, Rock Island Arsenal made up a requisite amount to fulfill requirements for in-service tests. These "test piece" holsters are almost non-existent and quite desirable.

Other countries that ordered the P.08 include Sweden, Latvia, Iran (Persia), Russia, possibly Turkey, and Brazil; but some of these are unknown at this time. A well-known collector in Finland has in his collection a Russian contract piece with holster which hopefully will be photographed for print in the not too distant future.

SWISS PARABELLUM HOLSTERS

During the 47 years the Pistole Parabellum was the official service

PARABELLUM AUTOMATIC PISTOL VALUE CONSIDERATIONS

YEAR	MODEL	EXCELLENT	GOOD	FAIR
1900	Commercial	$375	$225	$150
	Swiss Military	400	275	200
	Swiss Commercial	425	300	225
	Eagle	350	200	150
	Eagle Test Piece	500	325	275
	Bulgarian	650	475	375
1902	Commercial	575	375	300
	Eagle	525	350	275
	Carbine	950	700	400
	Test	650	475	300
1904	Navy	950	675	425
1906	Commercial	375	250	150
	Swiss	350	225	135
	Eagle	300	200	125
	Brazilian		185	125
	Portuguese	250	165	125
	Dutch	375	300	225
	Portuguese Navy	750	475	275
	German Navy	500	300	175
1908	Commercial	275	225	145
	Military (1st-2nd issue)	175	150	75
	Dated Military (1910-1913)	155	100	55
	Navy	500	300	175
	Bulgarian		225	145
1914	Military (1914-1918)	150	125	75
	Navy	350	225	165
	Artillery	200	150	100
1920	Commercial	165	125	80
	Carbine	575	375	175
1923	Commercial	185	155	85
	Dutch	325	250	125
	Stoegers	300	225	100
	Simson	275	175	100
	Vickers	275	200	75
	1906 Bern	325	275	100
1929	Swiss	350	275	125
MISC.	Mauser (K date)	275	225	100
	S/42 (G date)	225	175	85
	S/42 (dated)	165	125	75
	42 (dated)	165	125	75
	BYF (dated)	165	125	75
	Portuguese GNR	250	175	85
	Banner (dated)	225	155	90
	Kreighoff (early)	275	225	145
	Kreighoff (dated)	250	175	100

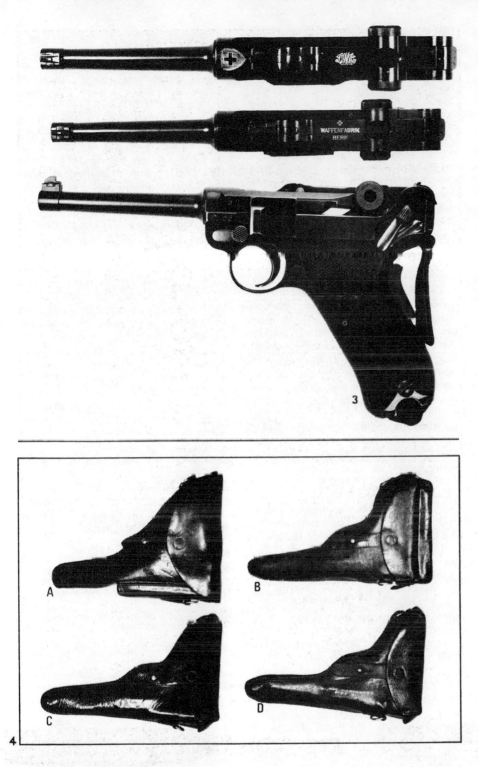

1. Swiss Model 1900 of the commercial and military type. Approximately 3000 military and 2000 commercial guns were manufactured. Caliber 7.65mm.

2. Swiss Model 1929 (or 06/29) made in both a military series (50001 to 77941) and a commercial series (P25001 to P26600; P77942 to P78258).

3. Swiss Model 1906 10,125 made serial numbers running from 5001 to 15215, of these pistols number 5001 to 9000 have "Cross-in-Sunburst" crest, 9001 to 15215 have "Cross-in-Shield" crest. Shown at top is the later. Later "06s" were made at WF Bern in 1917, no crest. 17,874 were produced.

4. Swiss leather: (A) 1929. (B) 1906. WF Bern. (C) 1900. (D) 1906.

and the belt loops were riveted on instead of sewn. Shoulder straps were also issued with this holster.

The holster for the 1906 pistol (erroneously called the "06/24") was simply the 1900 or 1906 holster with a magazine pouch added to the top and issued with shoulder straps.

The 1900/1906 Police and Commercial Swiss will not have the maker's name or year of manufacture on them, and will be a much darker color than the other holsters. They will be found in both the 1900 and 1906 types.

The 1929 model is totally different from the earlier models, having the much bulkier appearance, partially due to the addition of a magazine pouch on the leading edge, and the generally large configuration of the holster. Issued with shoulder straps.

The 1929 is currently available. It is exactly like the military style (and as well made) but comes in a dark chocolate brown color, with shoulder straps. Military examples of the 1929 type have been dated as late as 1967. The commercial holster is not dated or marked with the maker's name.

COMMERCIAL HOLSTERS (NON-EUROPEAN)

Although large numbers of commercial Lugers were manufactured and sold, the commercially manufactured holsters for the pistols are difficult to find these days and the reasons for this are quite simple: Most people who buy a pistol, even today, don't plan on carrying it around with them, so they don't buy a holster. Also, commercial holsters were generally not as well made as the military holsters, therefore they deteriorated rapidly.

The famous sporting goods house of Abercrombie and Fitch in New York reports that most holsters for the pistols they sold (including Lugers) were made to a customer's individual requirements, so a great variety of A&F holsters were put out. Abercrombie and Fitch dealt with two firms who produced their holsters: 1) Heiser of Denver, Colorado (out of business); 2) K. Leather Products, Inc., New York (still in business).

THE IDEAL HOLSTER

The Ideal Holster Company was located at 254 South Broadway, in Los Angeles, California. Little is known of this company today, except that they described themselves in their patent applications as "Manufacturers and Dealers in Attachments for Guns." In addition to the stock/holster for the P.08, the same type

pistol of Switzerland, five types of holsters were used (actually two types with minor variations on one type).

The first type of Swiss Parabellum holster, the Model 1900, was a form-fitting piece made of the finest leather. At first glance, it would seem too small to hold the pistol, but it does, and without an extra centimeter to spare. There was no magazine or tool pouch, and the holster was issued with shoulder straps.

The 1906 holsters were the same design as the 1900 holster, but generally the leather was a little heavier,

LUGERS, HOLSTERS

were manufactured for at least three other pistols—Colt Bisley 5½" barrel, Smith & Wesson M1889 .38, and the Colt .22 caliber Woodsman automatic.

In the company's British patent application (dated November 9th, 1901) an "improved revolver" is also mentioned, but no details are known of this pistol.

Any of the Ideal holsters are desirable and rather hard to come by.

LUGER SHOULDER HOLSTERS

So far as is known, there was never an *issue* military shoulder holster for the P.08. However, there are some examples of shoulder holsters which individuals had made for themselves, as well as a few commercially manufactured examples.

P.08 MAGAZINE POUCHES

The Artillery and Navy model Parabellums were issued with a magazine pouch (leather) that held two extra magazines. Two types of loops are found on the backs of these pouches: The standard bell loop, and the small loop through which the straps of the artillery or navy holster were passed. These pouches were also sold with the pre-World War 1 Navy rigs, and post-World War 1 Artillery and Naval rigs.

Two very common magazine pouches are the Portuguese M2 and GNR. The M2 type is often found in new condition (as are the holsters), while the GNR types are generally much more worn.

The German pouches were some shade of brown, the Portuguese

black. The German pouches will have the maker's name and so forth, generally under the flap. Occasionally there will be a unit mark, and some have no marks at all. The M2 Portuguese pouches are unmarked except for the same "AE" found on the holsters. There have been a couple of exceptions to the previous statement where some sort of unit mark was present, but one can safely say that the "no mark" statement applies easily to the vast majority of M2 pouches one is likely to encounter. The GNR pouch will have the same type of markings as the holster.

MARKINGS

On the early four-inch, the manufacturer's name, city, and date of manufacture will be found stamped on the body of the holster next to the pull-up strap, or on the underside of the flap. Infrequently, the name will appear on the back of the holster. Sometimes the stamps were done with ink (under the flap), and if the holster was well used it might be difficult to decipher the marks. The owner's name and unit might also be found scratched or inked-in somewhere on the holster. Unit marks done by the unit itself will be found quite often also. A few early holsters carry only the maker's name and city—no date of manufacture. Possibly these holsters were commercial pieces that were taken over by the army, or perhaps the year of manufacture was not a "regulation" strictly enforced at this early period. Once again, we find a minor point that probably is not even worth investigating.

From the year 1929, late four-inch P.08 holsters were marked with the name, city, and date on the back of the holster, between the belt loops. This practice continued until 1940, when military holsters began to be stamped with the manufacturers' codes that were in vogue at the time. The date was still used. Police hol-

sters continued to be stamped with the maker's full name, location, and date. There are exceptions to this, but the above remarks apply to probably 99 percent of the observed holsters.

Late type military holsters are not found with unit marks, but from time to time a police holster is seen that has some sort of unit designation on it, generally on the back. In 1940, P.08 holsters had an additional marking stamped on the back, next to the right belt loop: "P.08." This mark was probably added in order to more easily distinguish between the P.08 holster and the P.38 holster—which have a "family" resemblance.

In an effort to track down details of German holster manufacture and distribution, letters were written to as many firms as could be contacted in West Germany, but for one reason or another, the firms declined to give any information. There may well be more of the companies on the list still in business, but located in East Germany, which is, of course, a dead end. Some of the firms also might be thriving under different names in East or West Germany.

The information that was received regarding firms no longer in business came from the *Industrie Und Handelskammer* (Chamber of Commerce) of various cities, and they were most cooperative in searching for whatever information still existed on the firms in question.

1. American commercial holster for a 4¾" barreled pistol. Dates around the late 20s early 30s. Dyed black.

2. Dutch Air Force rig complete with tools, spare magazines.

3. World War 2 Bulgarian issue.

4. Dutch Army issue, all tools are numbered to the pistol, also note position of auxiliary pouches on holster as compared to Air Force model.

5. Danish World War 2 Naval model, no pouches or pull-up, black leather, inside flap are the markings, "Oplagte skibe i Nordhaven," indicating use by the Danish Harbor Guard Corps.

P-08 HOLSTER VALUES

P-08 holsters are graded here in three conditions:
1) **Excellent**—no appreciable wear, no restitching, no replaced parts, no cracks in leather.
2) **Very Good**—Average wear, might need a good polish, no restitching or replaced parts, no cracks in leather.
3) **Fair**—More than average wear, few cracks in leather, might need some restitching, no replaced parts.

	EXC.	V.G.	FAIR
1) WORLD WAR I (or before) 4"	$15.00	10.00	6.00
2) ARTILLERY (no shoulder stock)	$30.00	20.00	15.00
3) NAVY (early or late)	rarely found in this cond.	23.00	15.00
4) EARLY COMM. GERMAN (like military 4" or ¾")	$25.00	18.00	12.00
5) ARTILLERY REWORKS	$15.00	10.00	6.00
6) MILITARY 4" REWORKED TO POLICE	$15.00	10.00	6.00
7) 1900 U.S. TEST PIECE	$50.00	40.00	30.00
8) 1908 BULGARIAN (early)	$12.00	8.00	5.00
9) 1908 BULGARIAN (late)	$12.00	8.00	5.00
10) WW2 BULGARIAN (either type)	$ 8.00	5.00	3.00
11) POSTWAR BULGARIAN	$ 8.00	5.00	3.00
12) DUTCH (either type)	$30.00	20.00	15.00
13) 1906 M2 PORTUGUESE (any of the three types)	$10.00	7.00	5.00
14) GNR PORTUGUESE	$12.00	9.00	7.00
15) SWISS 1900/1906	$15.00	10.00	7.00
16) SWISS 1906 W.F. BERN	$15.00	10.00	8.00
17) SWISS 1929	$15.00	10.00	8.00
18) SWISS 1900/06 POLICE/COMMERCIAL	$15.00	10.00	8.00
19) 1919-1932 GERMAN POLICE/MILITARY	$17.00	12.00	8.00
20) NAZI ERA 1933-1945	$15.00	10.00	6.00
21) ABERCROMBIE & FITCH (any)	$30.00	25.00	15.00
22) 1902 CARBINE LEATHER (any)	Whatever you feel is fair.		
23) EARLY (Pre-WW2) COMMERCIAL	$25.00	18.00	12.00
24) IDEAL STOCK/HOLSTER	$75.00	65.00	55.00

From time to time a Nazi era four-inch P-08 holster will appear bearing markings *in addition to* the standard marks. Naval "M"s, Kreighoff and Simson proofs, SS Runes, and so forth, will sometimes be found. The prices of holsters so marked depends on how much one is willing to pay for a couple of extra letters. True it is that these "extraordinary" marks do not show up too often, thus we can put this holster in the category of "scarce but common." The buyer should know (by reputation if nothing else) the seller of such an item. There is not a great deal of travail

LUGERS, HOLSTERS

involved in adding a couple of marks or letters to a piece of leather. SS marked equipment is especially popular these days, but documentation of such marks on P.08 holsters is lacking, and the number that have shown up in the hands of collectors do not add any credence to the idea that the SS used specially stamped holsters for the P.08. This is not to say that such things do not exist, but it's a *Caveat Emptor* world for the purchaser. There are photos of SS troops wearing P.08 holsters (police style as well as military), but no photos or descriptions of how they are marked. There is less doubt concerning Naval marked P.08 holsters, as holsters so marked for other types of pistols are rather common (Mauser 1934, HSc, and so forth).

Cartridge pouches for the 98k rifle with the Marinen "M" are also well known. There are also many .32 caliber pistol holsters stamped with various Kreighoff proofs and stamps, so the P.08 Kreighoff holsters are much less subject to doubt regarding authenticity. Simson proofed leather goods are hard to come by, but there is little doubt as to the Simson proofed P.08 holsters.

The only exception observed regarding the coding of Nazi P.08 military holsters (after 1940) was a black military style (buckle/strap) dated 1942, marked with the maker's full name: Otto Koberstein, Landsberg A.W. The "P.08" was also stamped in the usual place.

Whenever one is offered something out of the ordinary in P.08 holsters as far as the markings are concerned, the best thing to do if there is any question is to consult someone who *does* know the field. Even the knowledgeable can be fooled, but at least the odds will be in your favor. If the consensus is that the piece is authentic, then you must decide how much the extra marks are worth to you. As a rule of thumb, figure out the price of the "regular" holster, then add 30 to 50 percent for the extras, depending on the condi-

tion. This is a fair markup for the holster, but remember: No one ever said the world was fair!

Holsters for the four-inch model P.08 were always some shade of brown or beige up until the very early 1930s. Occasionally one will see a black holster from this era, but if examined closely, it will be discovered that the holster has been dyed. Usually the inner lining is still the original color, and sometimes under the belt loops the original color will be still present. This "dye job" does not necessarily lessen the value of the holster to a collector (unless it is obviously a very recent job) as the holster is still a Luger holster which was simply transferred from army service to police use.

The variations in original shades of brown is enormous—from a very natural looking finish in every gradation to a dark cordovan. As mentioned previously, the quality of leather is for the most part excellent, but sometimes one will find an early holster made of a thin, almost paperlike leather. The majority, however, exhibit the excellent standards of material and workmanship expected of the period.

Brown was the "in" color for P.08 holsters up until the early thirties, just before the Nazi takeover of Germany. At this time black holsters began to make their appearance. Both police and military holsters were made in brown and black. It is not known if there was a specific reason for the crossover of the two colors in police and army use. Not as many variations in shades of brown are seen in holsters of the late Weimar/

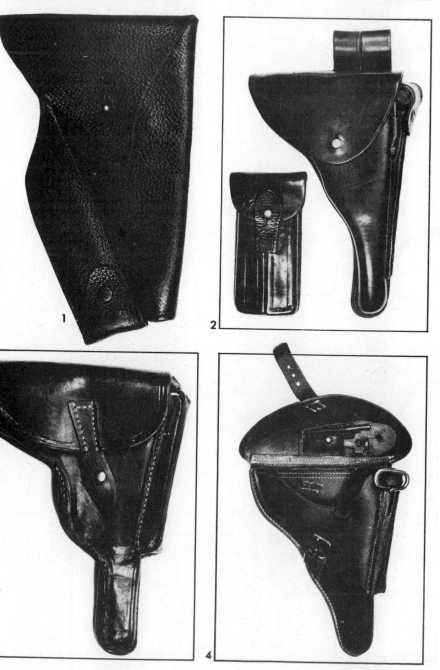

1. World War 2 Yugoslav partisan manufactured holster, note unusual arrangement for the magazine pouch. Holster is of soft pebbled-grain leather.

2. Portugese GNR 1935 holster and magazine pouch, dyed black at factory. Note unusual configuration of belt loops.

3. World War 1 Turkish.

4. Early German commercial for 4" barreled models. Note location of cleaning rod and pin punch.

P-08 HOLSTER MANUFACTURERS

By far the majority of holsters made for the P-08 in its various forms were made by German firms. The holsters for the Portuguese P-08s were made by a German firm, but it has been impossible, at the time of this writing, to find out which firm it was.

The list presented below of German holster manufacturers is not complete by any means, but it will (hopefully) spur those who are interested in this particular area of Luger collecting on to a greater surge of "research fever."

The names of some of these companies may be found today on the West German Police holsters for the Hi Power, Astra 600, Star Model "B," and the Bundeswehr P-38 holsters.

An asterisk (*) following the name indicates the firm is still in business. The letters in parenthesis (hjh) are the code letters used by that company during the Nazi era.

1) Ackva, Karl* (hjh)
2) Auwaerter Bubeck K.G. (cdg)
3) Barth, Karl (dla)
4) Becker & Co. (hft)
5) Bierenoreier, F.
6) Billep, C.
7) Bocker, Karl (eqp)
8) Brand, Wilh. (jvf)
9) Burghard, C.N.
10) Cobau, Franz
11) Conte, Rudolph, Nachfg. Theo. Siebod (gjh)
12) Clemen, H.
13) DanzigerLeder Industrie
14) Deuter, Hans
15) Ehrhardt, Richard (bdr)
16) Elder, H., & Linde
17) Estellman, L.
18) Fischer, A.
19) Fockler, J.
20) Genschow, Gustav* (Trademark: GECO) (Berlin-cxm/Alstadt-Hachenburg-jhg)
21) Grosse, F.
22) Heinichen, Karl (joa)
23) Kellendorfer, S.
24) Kern, Klager & Cie (cdc) (went out of business in 1959)
25) Kimmach & Brunn (hjg)
26) Kind, Albrecht* (trademark—AKAH w/ crossed rifles)
27) Klinge, Gebruder (gxy)
28) Koberstein, Otto
29) Kuhn, Reinhold
30) Larsen, Robert* (dde)
31) Leuner, E.G. (bla)
32) Lieferungsgenossenshaft der Sattler, Nurnberg (This was a leather makers guild formed on March 3, 1915 in Nurnberg, which existed under various names until 1969)
33) Maury & Co. (blv)
34) Meckart, J.
35) Meier & Abitzsch
36) Moll, Joseph* (cxb)
37) Nagel, R. (went out of business in 1937)
38) Reichel, C.
39) Reichel, Otto/Jnh. Rudolph Fischer (eue)
40) Richter, Julius
41) Ritzman, Ferd.
42) Romer, Hans* (bml)
43) Rytel & Dorns
44) Sattlerinnung-Esileben
45) Schambach & Co.
46) Schaefer & Reiche
47) Schiedbrand, A.
48) Schneider-Briegl
49) Schutz, F.
50) Siegemund, Ernst
51) Sindel, Otto (cvb)
52) Stecher, Moritz (jwa)
53) Thieme, F.H.
54) Ver. Sattlemeister GMBH
55) Voegels, Franz & Carl (cwx)
56) Vogel, curt
57) Vogel & Koln
58) Waldhausen, A. /Jnh. N (dta)
59) Weiss, Carl (cww) (went out of business in 1969)

Nazi period, and holsters from this time assume a generally bulkier appearance.

The leather used in P.08 holsters was always a smooth type with these exceptions: Some Nazi era holsters were made of pigskin (black and brown); and one early type observed (undated) has the magazine pouch, inner lining and tool pouch made of pebbled leather. It is not a "rework," so the reason for the different grain of leather remains unknown at this time. (As with many of the small "variations" seen in pistols and holsters, the reason is probably unimportant and meaningless.)

SWISS MARKINGS

Swiss holsters of the 1900, 1906, 1906 W.F. Bern-type can be found in almost any shade of brown, beige or cordovan. The leather is always the finest, as is the finish on the leather. Some will be seen in a natural finish, while others might have the color and finish of a fine piece of luggage. The 1929 holsters are always a natural finish, though the darkening of the leather through handling and polishing might make it appear as though it had been dyed. As mentioned before, the 1900/06 Police and Commercial holsters are always a dark cordovan.

Swiss holsters will be marked on the back with the name of the maker, location and date of manufacture. Sometimes the shoulder straps will also bear the maker's name, date; but not too frequently. There are many variations in the shoulder straps, simply due to the different manufacturers. Widths, lengths, buckles, etc. will vary. Straps made for the 1929 Parabellum are issued today with the new holsters made for the current Swiss service pistol, the SIG.

AVAILABILITY

With World War 1 and before issues, the standard holster is a very common item, even today, over 50 years after the end of World War 1. The most common are those made during the period 1914-1918; but it is not difficult to find pieces dated from 1910-1913. They can be found in conditions varying from nearly new to poor.

Holsters dated between 1919 and 1933 are more scarce than the earlier ones, but not impossible to find. Those dated towards the end of the 1920s seem to be more readily available, and on arriving at the early 1930s, many more examples make their appearance.

Nazi holsters dated 1936 through

LUGERS, HOLSTERS

1942 are more common than the World War 1 types. Police and military versions should present no problem to the collector seeking a holster for his P.08. The latest date observed on a Nazi holster was the 1943 date on the paper police holster mentioned previously. Many Nazi holsters are in excellent to new condition.

Naval holsters of either early or late types are rather scarce in any condition, and should be picked up regardless (almost) of condition. Artillery holsters are much easier to come by, and can be found in excellent shape. The collector should not have a great deal of difficulty in locating a good, solid artillery holster for his collection.

Leather for contract Lugers is much harder to come by generally, as the contracts were not large compared to the numbers of P.08s made for the Germans, consequently the number of holsters made was not as great. It is possible to ferret out some of these holsters without too much trouble, (i.e.—Portuguese) while others are ridiculously hard to find (Russian).

Once a rather scarce piece of leather, Swiss Parabellum holsters are now rather easy to come by for the collector. The 1900, 1906, and 1929 types are the most common, while the 06 W-F Bern (Magazine pouch added) and the 1900/06 Police/Commercial types are not quite as numerous. As with the majority of Swiss surplus military goods, the conditions of the holsters are, by and large, very good to excellent.

ACCESSORIES

Luger accessories are without a doubt most collectible. It seems that they are in more abundance and are more readily available to most collectors. An accessory may be defined as anything (other than the pistol itself) that was issued with the piece, or sold as an addition to a commercial pistol (being manufactured especially for the arm). As an off-shoot of the definition, one may consider accessories as holsters, military and commercial; instruction manuals; cleaning rods and kits; original packing containers; sub-caliber conversion units (.22 rimfire or 4mm Ubungsmunition calibers); magazines and magazine pouches.

Cartridges and cartridge boxes that have been specifically manufactured for use in P.08 pistols are almost an entire field in themselves. The 9mm Parabellum and 7.65mm Luger cartridges have had wide use the world

over. Both types of cartridges present myriad variations of headstamps and bullet designs. A collector would be wise to accumulate either single specimens or complete boxes of ammunition to accentuate his collection, as they do make colorful additions.

Original and reprint manuals on Luger pistols are available and make for an interesting sub-collecting category. Most of these publications are found in the original German. However, Stoeger's still sells a reprint of a turn of the century instruction booklet in English on the American export model.

Cleaning rods present another wild and woolly collecting sub-category. They were made either for issue with the pistols or were issued/sold separately. If one has a question as to originality, seek out an advanced collector for his opinion and/or a comparison of pieces.

Cleaning kits for most firearms, as issued, are extremely hard to come by. If one does find a complete kit, then one has indeed been lucky. However, some kits are incomplete and "part of the fun" as one might say, is to complete the kit. The two most common types of kits found are those issued with the Portuguese GNR and M2 P.08s and the Swiss-issued kits, both military and comercial. Dutch and complete German kits are more difficult to find as a result of the vagaries of war and time.

Since Swiss kits are more easily obtained, a short discussion about them is in order. Each Swiss Parabellum pistol was issued with a compact cleaning kit and a small can of grease. When the 1900 Parabellum

1

2

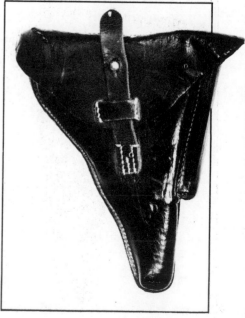

3   4

P-08 ACCESSORY VALUES

	EXC.	V.G.	FAIR
1) ARTILLERY STOCK (w/ or w/o iron)	$40.00	30.00	20.00
2) NAVY STOCK (w/ or w/o iron)	$50.00	35.00	25.00
3) DRUM MAGAZINE (early or late)	$75.00	65.00	55.00
4) DRUM LOADING TOOL	$75.00 (any condition)		
5) 1902 CARBINE STOCK	$85.00	70.00	45.00
6) DRUM MAG DUST COVERS	$ 4.00	3.00	2.00
7) DRUM MAG M.G. ADAPTORS	$ 3.50	2.50	2.00
8) COMMERCIAL CLEANING ROD (non-oiler type)	$10.00	7.00	5.00
9) CLEANING ROD (comm. and Portuguese brass or steel oiler type)	$ 5.00	3.50	2.50
10) ARTILLERY CLEANING ROD	$15.00	10.00	7.00
11) NAVY CLEANING ROD	$15.00	10.00	7.00
12) DUTCH CLEANING ROD	$15.00	12.00	9.00
13) LOADING/STRIPPING TOOLS (originals)	$5.00	3.50	2.50
14) PIN PUNCHES		2.00	
15) SWISS CLEANING KITS (any var.)		8.00	
16) PORTUGUESE M2 (1906) MAG POUCHES	$ 4.00	3.00	2.00
17) PORTUGUESE GNR (1935) MAG POUCHES	$ 5.00	4.00	3.00
18) WORLD WAR I TYPE MAG POUCHES	$ 8.00	6.00	5.00

5

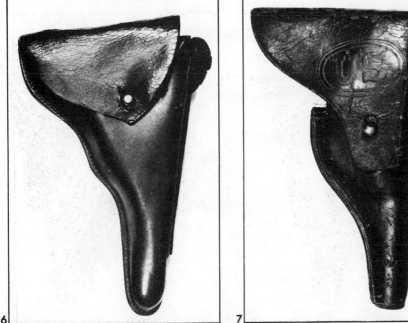

6   7

pistol was issued, the Swiss continued to use the same cleaning kit used for the 1882 Ordnance Revolver. Since the Swiss do not believe in throwing anything useful away, they reasoned that since the 1882 Revolver barrel was the same length and bore diameter of the ''new'' pistol (7.65mm) it would be advantageous to retain the old kits. By World War 2 the last Parabellum kit was issued, but with a Parkerized steel storage case instead of the usual brass.

Conversion units are without a doubt a most desirable item for the Luger. Most units that have been observed are the World War 2 and post-war Erma types. The Swiss have made a few sub-caliber units, and there is presently available from West Germany a commercially produced unit.

Last but not least, magazines for the P.08 are numerous and go beyond the scope of this article. Suffice it to say that throughout the years, the Germans went through various manufacturing changes. The earlier patterns of magazines were polished and featured wooden bottom pieces. These features were continued during the '20s and up to the Nazi-produced arms. During World War 2, however, the Germans went over to plastic or aluminum bottom pieces and did away with folded metal magazines. They adopted extruded magazine boxes and matte finishes in lieu of nickeled and/or polished blued metal surfaces. 🙶

1. Standard Wehrmacht-issued holster for the P. 08 used during World War 2. This piece is of cordovan leather and is marked inside as being used by Sgt. Willi Schieferstein, Luftwaffen-Sturm Regiment.

2. Holster made for use with the Benke-Thiemann Extension Stock (c. 1926). The piece is of German manufacture with no pull-up and tool pouch fitted to the outside of the body. Of heavy brown leather with belt loops.

3. World War 1 or before P. 08, undated with magazine pouch and tool pouch made of pebble grain leather; main body made of brown leather. Lining is also of pebbled grain leather.

4. 1943-dated police issued holster made of laminated paper and leather.

5. Ideal stock/holster combination for 1900/1906 models. Grips were backed with a metal plate into which the claw of the stock was fitted.

6. German Imperial Navy early type with stud used to hold down flap.

7. 1900 American Test Piece holster as made at Rock Island Arsenal. Most of these, if found, are in well used condition as they were service tested.

Mauser Pistols

THE MAUSER NEVER ENJOYED THE DEGREE OF ACCEPTANCE THAT THE LUGER AND BROWNING GUNS DID AS A FIRST-LINE MILITARY PISTOL OF ANY OF THE MAJOR COUNTRIES, BUT THE FACTORY DID FIND SALES FOR OVER A MILLION PIECES

By John E. Plimpton

PHOTOGRAPHS COURTESY MARIO PANCINO

To any person interested in the history or the collecting of automatic pistols it is abundantly clear that many basic designs and thousands of models and variations of these designs are to be found. Most of these pistols are of a more limited interest because many were not particularly successful or their designs were incorporated into more advanced and/or successful pistols.

Quite a few of these autoloading pistols were manufactured only for a limited period of time and/or were used by only one or two countries. Out of all these pistols, a few arms which originated in the early days before the turn of the century managed to keep pace with later developments. They survived to earn themselves a permanent place in the history of autoloading pistols. Of those that were successful, only a few designs can equal the history of the *Mauser Modell 1896 Selbstlader.*

Its history is even more remarkable when one considers that two of the major competitors of Paul Mauser's design were the Luger, based on Hugo Borchardt's pistol, and the many models and variations based on John Browning's patents. The Mauser did not possess the worldwide popularity or superb balance and good looks of the Luger, nor did it have the simple construction and inexpensive design which made the Browning guns so successful. Both the lack of gracefulness and simplicity were inherent in the design of the pistol, yet the Mauser had an indisputable reputation for reliability and rugged serviceability shared by few other automatic pistols of its time. The Mauser never enjoyed the degree of acceptance that the Luger and Browning guns did as a first-line military pistol of any of the major countries, but the factory did find sales for over a million pieces.

Except for a few years in the early 1920s, when the Treaty of Versailles was in effect, the Mauser was in continuous production for more than 40 years. During that entire time the basic features of the design went unchanged. The Mauser factory did follow a policy of continual modifi-

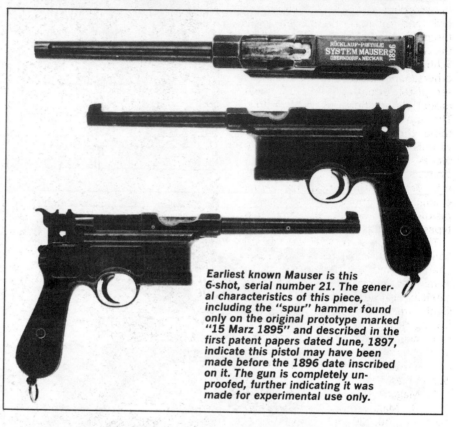

Earliest known Mauser is this 6-shot, serial number 21. The general characteristics of this piece, including the "spur" hammer found only on the original prototype marked "15 Marz 1895" and described in the first patent papers dated June, 1897, indicate this pistol may have been made before the 1896 date inscribed on it. The gun is completely unproofed, further indicating it was made for experimental use only.

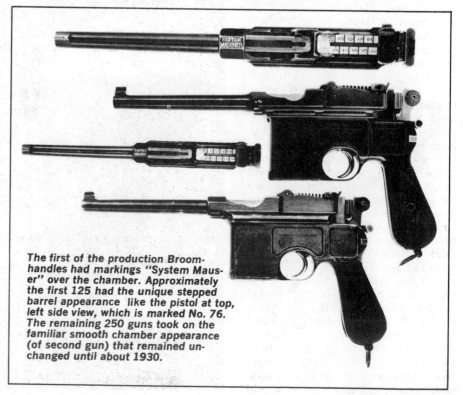

The first of the production Broomhandles had markings "System Mauser" over the chamber. Approximately the first 125 had the unique stepped barrel appearance like the pistol at top, left side view, which is marked No. 76. The remaining 250 guns took on the familiar smooth chamber appearance (of second gun) that remained unchanged until about 1930.

cation both to improve the system so far as safety, reliability, and ease of manufacture were concerned, but also to satisfy either military or civilian markets. Most of these changes were gradual and of a minor nature. These modifications, however, serve the serious collector in his attempt to chronologically identify the many variations and contract pieces he may possess or come across.

According to available factory records and catalogs, there were only three basic models; the Model 1896, the Model 1930, and the Model 1932 Schnellfeuer (rapid fire). Of course, other countries which used the Mauser pistol often applied their own model designations to their pistols. The modifications and contracts of these three basic models, plus the various experimental and prototype pieces, has created as much confusion among collectors as it has interest. Before going into the actual changes that appear in the Mauser pistols, a brief description of the two types of changes is necessary.

The first, and most interesting to collectors, are changes in the basic characteristics of the pistol. Such things as barrel length, magazine capacity, caliber, grip size and rear sights are in this category. The following list shows those characteristics which make up over 99 percent of the variations encountered.

1. Barrel lengths—3.9, 4.75, 5.2, 5.5 inches.
2. Magazine capacity (fixed)—6, 10, 20. Magazine capacity (detachable)—6, 10, 20, 40.
3. Calibers—7.63mm Mauser, 7.65-mm Luger, 8.15mm, 9mm Parabellum, 9mm Mauser, 9mm Largo (Spanish copies only) and .45 ACP (Chinese copies only).
4. Grip frame size—small and large. Grip type (small)—grooved or checkered wood, checkered or floral hard rubber. Grip type (large)—grooved or checkered wood, checkered hard rubber.
5. Rear sight—fixed or adjustable.

The second type of change, and usually the least noticeable, are those which are of a somewhat permanent nature. That is, any modification which was not reverted back to at a later date. Hammer shape, safety mechanism, frame milling, markings and serial number location are of this type. The chart will show the year and approximate position in the overall serial number range of the changes of this type. The exact point of some of the early changes is not known because of the rarity of pistols in that range. Later changes were sometimes spread over a wide serial number range as stocks of old

SERIAL # RANGE	DATE	NATURE OF CHANGES
before #25	1896	The cone hammer used in place of spur hammer.
#50	1896	"SYSTEM MAUSER" marked on top of the chamber.
before #200	1897	The locking system changed from one to two lugs. —The barrel contour at the chamber is tapered instead of stepped.
#390	1897	"WAFFENFABRIK MAUSER OBERNDORF A/N" marked on top of the chamber.
#975	1897	The center section of the rear panel on the left side of the frame is not milled out (this feature appears earlier on a few 20-shot pistols). This area is sometimes used for special markings on contract pieces such as the Turkish and Persian.
#12,200- #14,999	1898	The large ring hammer replaces the cone hammer.
#21,000	1899	There is no panel milling on either side of the frame. —A single lug bayonet type mount adopted for retaining the firing pin instead of the dovetail plate. —The trigger is mounted directly to the frame by two integral lugs rather than attached to a removable block. —The position of the serial number moved from the rear of the frame above the stock slot to the left side of the chamber.
#22,000	1900	Two integral lugs used to mount the rear sight instead of a pin.
#29,000	1902	Very shallow panels milled into the frame on both sides.*
#31,200	1903	"WAFFENFABRIK MAUSER OBERNDORF A NECKAR" added to the right rear frame panel.*
#34,000	1904	The depth of the frame panel milling increased.*
#35,000	1904	The barrel extension side rails lengthened about a half inch.* —An additional lug for mounting added to the firing pin.* —The hammer changed to the small ring pattern.* —The safety mechanism altered to require that the lever be pushed up to engage it instead of down.* —The center of the safety lever knob is no longer milled out.*
#38,000	1905	The short extractor with two ribs replaces the long thin extractor.*
#100,000- #130,000	1910 to 1911	The rifling changed from four groove to six groove.
#270,000	1915	"NS" (Neues Sicherung or New Safety) appears on the back of the hammer. The hammer must be moved back beyond the cocked position to engage the safety.
#440,000	1921	The lanyard ring stud is rotated 90 degrees.
#501,000	1923	The Mauser "banner" appears on the left rear frame panel.
#800,000	1930	The Mauser banner is enlarged. —A step is added to the barrel contour just ahead of the chamber. —The safety is changed to allow the hammer to be dropped from a cocked position, without danger, by pulling the trigger (called Universal Safety). —The front of the grip frame widened to equal the rear part where the stock slot is.
#850,000	1932	"D.R.P.u.A.P." (Deutsches Reich Patenten und Anderes Patenten) added below the inscription on the right rear frame panel.
#860,000	1932	The lettering in the frame inscription is slanted forward.
#900,000	1934	The serial number is moved to the rear of the barrel extension behind the sight. —The two grooves in each side of the barrel extension side rails are eliminated.

*These nine changes appear out of sequence (either early or late) on three small batches of guns (29,000 to 29,900, 40,000 to 41,000, and 42,600 to 43,900). Most of these pistols are of the "bolo" style, that is they have 3.9-inch barrels, small grips, six- or 10-shot magazines and fixed or adjustable rear sights. A few of these pistols show non-standard barrel contours, barrel extension milling and hammer safety devices. Apparently the factory withheld these numbers from the regular production series and reissued them at later dates.

Mauser Pistols

parts were used up concurrently with the introduction of new parts.

Collectors will often encounter pistols that carry crests, issue markings or non-standard proofs. The following is a list of the countries that contracted or issued Mauser pistols. The figures in parentheses indicate the quantities involved:

1. Turkey 1897—(1000)
2. Italy (Navy) 1899—(5000)
3. Siam (police) 1911—(?)
4. Persia 1912—(1000)
5. German (Army) 1916 to 1918—(135,000)
6. Austria 1917 to 1918—(?)
7. Finland 1920 to ?—(?)
8. German (Navy) 1920 to 1945—(?)
9. Norway 1930 to 1934—(?)

Mausers will also be found marked with the names and addresses of the many dealers (mostly U.S., English, Scottish, and Irish) who sold the pistol.

The *Modell 1932 Schnellfeuer* is probably the most exotic of all the more common models of Mausers. It saw limited service in World War 2 by German troops (mostly SS and Navy). Many were brought back to this country by returning servicemen. The selective fire idea is of limited value due to the pistol's heavy recoil and high rate of fire. The idea must have been popular, though, because all the Spanish copies have fully automatic variations along with the Mauser, and most were sold in fairly large quantities in the Orient. Slightly less than 100,000 Model 1932s were manufactured and they

were numbered in their own group from 1- to 100,000.

Commercial production and sales of Model 1930 and Model 1932 ceased with the beginning of World War 2, although the Model 1932 was produced in limited quantities for the military up to the end of the war.

The war itself saw the destruction of many of the vital records and the dispersion of most of the factory personnel. Someday enough information will be gathered together from what is left so that an accurate and fairly complete story will be available to those who are interested in this part of the Mauser mystique.

Any inquiries or additional information from our readers may be sent to Mrs. Mario Pancino, Box 345, La Canada, Ca. 91011.

Once Mauser production stabilized, the number of variations grew along with the sales force, which initially included the excellent merchandising of Westley-Richards & Co. in London who maintained the exclusive sales distributorship for the British Empire for many years. A) a scarce 10-shot variation, #9209 with fixed rear sight and 4⅞" barrel. B) A typical 10-shot. C) rare 6-shot variation #14437 with short barrel. D) unusual 20-shot slab side, #43 made on special order.

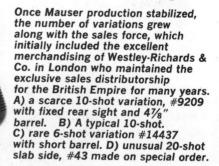

Just prior to the last of the cone-hammer variations (approximately #15,000) and following the Italian Navy order for 5000 pistols (which filled the gap from 15,000 to 20,000, although these had their own range of #1 to #8000) are found a few scarce Broomhandles known as the Large Ring Transitionals. B) An early example #13288 with a late type rear sight graduated from 50 to 500 meters and Von Lengerke & Detmold markings. A) A late example, #20507, with the later type rear sight and factory experimental "view slots" cut into the magazine well.

With the successful completion of
the Italian Navy contract of 1899,
the smooth milled frame (slabside)
went "public" and for a little over
a year enjoyed limited sales on
the commercial market. Probably
among the first to appear was the cutaway test model (A) which has no
proofs or serial number. B) A patent
model made, undoubtedly for securing
foreign patents. The specimen, #330
bears Austrian proofs as well as German proofs. C) and D) These exem-
plify full scale production of the slabside, but did not sell well in either
10- or 6-shot variations.

With the exit of the slabside came
a return of the earlier milled frame
pattern with the exception that the
depth of the milling was now much
shallower than before. This variation
also marked the end of the large
ring hammer types. Probably among
the first to appear in this group
is the 6-shot #M (A) which was probably sent to V L & D, the U.S. dis-
tributor prior to WW 1, as a promotional
sales piece. This was followed by
several 10-shot variations (B) and
the long and short Bolos (C) and (D).

In the 1902-1905 period, the Mauser factory was busy trying to improve on the pistol's hammer mechanism, at last finalizing on the small ring hammer, push-up safety lever system (as opposed to the push-down lever previously used). Alternate systems were used but abandoned. A) and B) The interspersed cocking lever, 1902 pattern, where the hammer is cocked by pushing down with the thumb on the cocking lever, and is on "safe" when lever is at rest between the bolt and the hammer. C) and D) Another design is illustrated wherein matching notches are machined on the left of the hammer and inside face of the safety lever so that pulling back on the hammer when gun is on safe releases the safety in one motion.

With the introduction of the improved small ring hammer and safety, a number of prototype and limited-production pieces were developed. A) a cutaway demonstrator, #7. B) and C) samples proffered to the military as test pieces, #10 and #37. Undaunted by the German Army's non-acceptance of the Mauser design and their acceptance of the Luger (P. 08), Mauser continued to experiment with the design. D) is an example of such experimentation as it features an improved floorplate release.

Even if pistol sales were not all Mauser had hoped for in the decade preceding World War 1, rifle sales were soaring. With an appropriate de-emphasis on radical pistol design changes, Mauser, for the most part supplied the market with standard production items such as the A) 10-shot, standard type. A temporary departure in markings occurred on about 10,000 pistols in the 80,000 to 90,000 range. Instead of the usual three-line inscription over the chamber, the Mauser "banner" trademark was used as on (B) and (C). D) A British army-proofed Bolo, probably one of many Mauser pistols that found its way into unofficial military use.

Seldom encountered and quite sought after are custom examples of the continental European gunmakers art such as this engraved, pre-World War 1 commercial Mauser, with a 12" barrel by the Austrian firm of Gebr. Bohler. A feature of this piece is its fully adjustable rear sight.

Prompted by the increasing demands of war and recalling the prior military tests by the German Army, the German Government, in 1916, let a contract to Mauser Werke for 150,000 pistols. These arms were to be chambered for the 9mm Parabellum cartridge and the grips of these arms were to be marked with a large red numeral "9" to differentiate them from the 7.63mm calibered pistols already pressed into service. A) A typical specimen of "Red 9." B) A post-war rework (1920) of the issue pistol to comply with the Versailles Treaty weapons limitations on Germany. These were issued to German police.

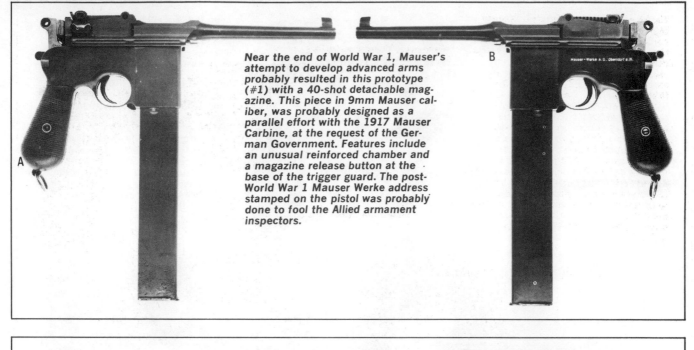

Near the end of World War 1, Mauser's attempt to develop advanced arms probably resulted in this prototype (#1) with a 40-shot detachable magazine. This piece in 9mm Mauser caliber, was probably designed as a parallel effort with the 1917 Mauser Carbine, at the request of the German Government. Features include an unusual reinforced chamber and a magazine release button at the base of the trigger guard. The post-World War 1 Mauser Werke address stamped on the pistol was probably done to fool the Allied armament inspectors.

Variations of the Broomhandle issued for use by German Navy personnel. A) A World War 1 7.63mm calibered piece, but with barrel shortened to 4″ and a Luger-type front sight added. Naval property marks stamped in left panel. B) Another 7.63mm caliber piece re-issued during the late Weimar—early Nazi period, grip strap marked "N809." C) A late pre-World War 2 Bolo with unusual M over an anchor marking on receiver with property marking #606692. Property marking "N69a."

The decade following the first World War found Mauser again stressing the commercial market. It was during this time that the Bolo model (named after the Bolsheviks who were rumored to favor them during the revolution) reached its peak of popularity. The first models were basically similar to the standard pre-War commercial model except for a shorter barrel and a more compact grip as with (A) #445957. As production progressed, the location of the serial number was relocated on the receiver and the now famous Mauser trademark was added to the left panel of the frame, (B) is such an example. C) This arm features the final form of the changes near the final production for this model (about #700,000), the finish was changed to a faster hot dip blue.

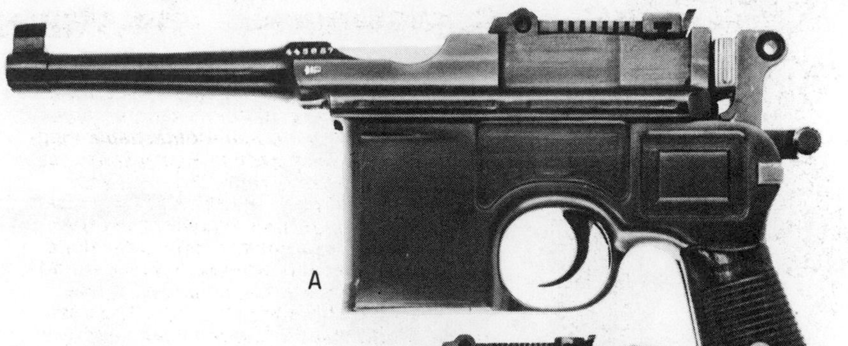

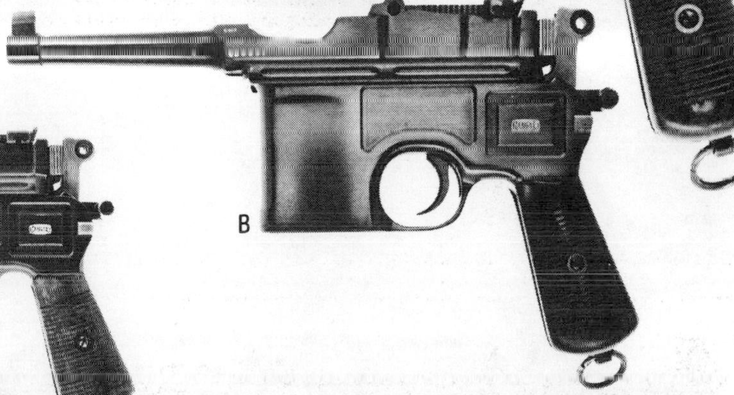

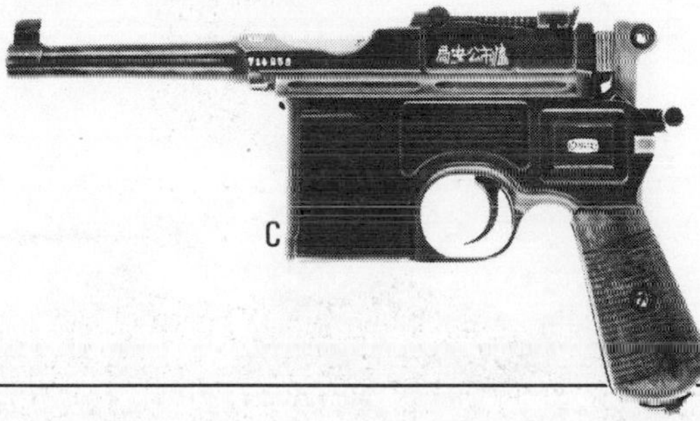

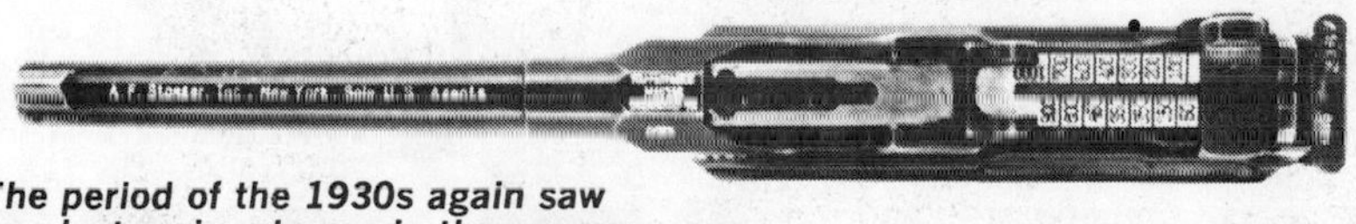

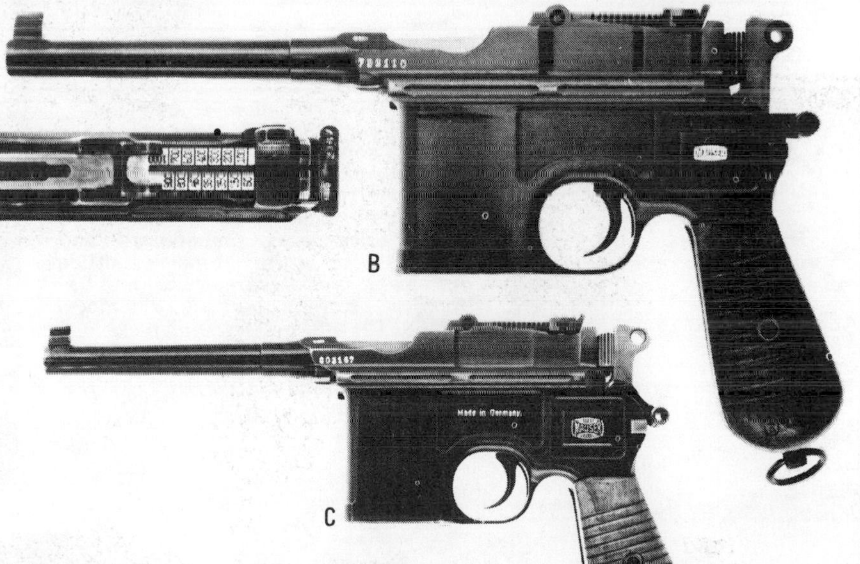

The period of the 1930s again saw one last major change in the appearance of the Broomhandle pistol. The factory nomenclature was changed from Model 1896 to Model 1930. These pistols are best recognized by the "step" in the barrel and the "banner" trademark on the left panel of the frame. The "Universal" safety was fitted to these models, a mechanism which allowed the hammer to be dropped when the safety is engaged. Examples shown are: B) An early transitional model (#732110) with small banner. A) and C) Special U.S. export model (#803187) sold exclusively for a short time by the firm of A. F. Stoeger Inc., New York. D) Special Chinese contract model (#881653) marked "Made in Germany" in Chinese. E) Norwegian contract (#919994).

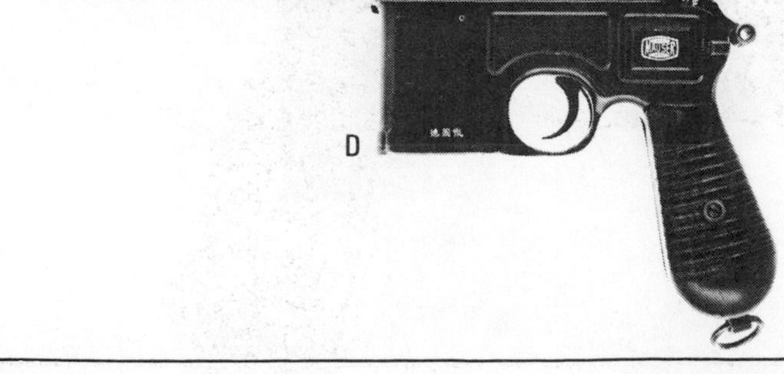

As with the earlier models, the Mauser factory in the 1930s also produced a small group of promotional, experimental and special order guns. These are quite rare today. Known examples include: A) and B) Unusual factory sales pieces, #868600, with an attempt again at the flat milled slabside frame and special markings. C) and D) A prototype of the standard 1930 model (#868610) with a detachable magazine. E) and F) A special order semi-automatic version of the famous "Schnellfeuer" purportedly made for the personal use of Mr. A. F. Stoeger.

Several specific foreign military contracts were filled by Mauser during the pistol's production lifetime. Examples of contract sales include: A) Turkish contract (1896-7) identified by the Turkish crest in the left rear panel, the five-pointed star proof, cone hammer and Farsi markings on rear sight, and serial number in Farsi lettering. B) Italian Navy contract of 1899, identified by its slabside, serial range (1-5000). Example shown is #4895. Note Italian "DV" and crown over "AV" proofing. C) Purported French Gendarme contract (#423304) identified by the short barrel, large checkered plastic grips and serial range (430,000-440,000). D) Persian (or Iranian) contract (#154719) identified by the royal crest of Iran, the "Sun Lion" and serial range (154,000-155,000). E) Finnish Army contract (#22117) identified by the round-cornered square with "SA" (Suomi Armeija) property stamp. F) Turkish 1930 contract (#889915) identified by the Turkish crest in left panel instead of the "banner" mark, is very scarce as only one example is known in the U.S.

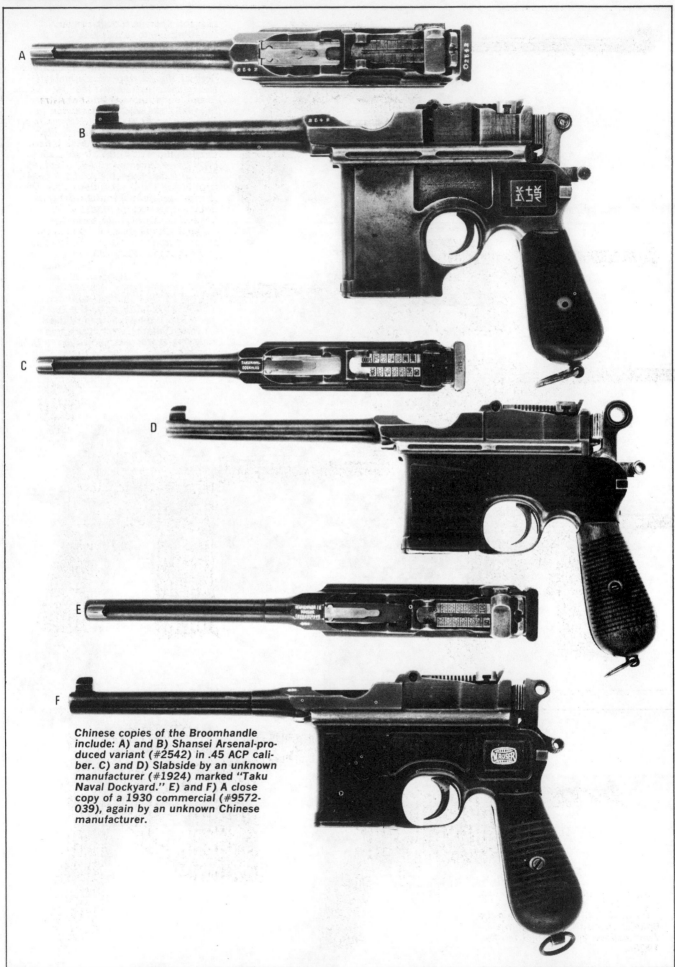

Chinese copies of the Broomhandle include: A) and B) Shansei Arsenal-produced variant (#2542) in .45 ACP caliber. C) and D) Slabside by an unknown manufacturer (#1924) marked "Taku Naval Dockyard." E) and F) A close copy of a 1930 commercial (#9572-039), again by an unknown Chinese manufacturer.

Like the Chinese the Spaniards were also great believers in the mystique of the Broomhandle, but unlike the Asiatic copies, which were made for indigenous consumption, the Spanish copies were widely marketed and to some extent hurt Mauser's sales. Examples include: A) 20-shot Astra Model 902 (#12604), semiautomatic. B) Astra Model 900 (#27615) made for Asiatic customers. C) Royal 10-shot with Bolo frame (#160). D) Standard size Royal (#2054). E) 20-shot, detachable magazine Azul (#31745). F) 20-shot fixed magazine Azul (#27264); both D and E are semiautomatics. In general, the semiautomatic versions of the Astra (except Model 900), Royal, and Azul had selective fire capability, thus they are considered machine guns and illegal to possess without proper authorization.

Largest and smallest of the Mauser look-a-likes is the Chinese-made copy in .45 ACP caliber (A) and the Spanish-made Charolla y Anitua in 7mm caliber, both dating from the 1920s.

Mauser Pistols

1

The Genuine
MAUSER
Automatic pistol with wood holster stock
Cal. 7.63 mm (300")
MODEL 1930
Mauser=Werke AG
(formerly: Waffenfabrik Mauser AG.) Oberndorf a. N. (Germany)

2

The
Mauser Automatic Pistol
with wood holster stock

Mauser-Werke A.-G.
Oberndorf a. Neckar
(Germany)

Cal. 7.63 mm (.300")

MAUSER PISTOLS AND ACCESSORIES

(Table of approximate values based on Models in NRA Very Good to Excellent condition (as normally found for sale on today's market).

Guns in new condition or with factory original special features will generally bring more, but the overall scarcity of such pieces on today's market makes accurate pricing very difficult.

1. Average Conehammer — $300 up
2. Conehammer, Turkish Contract — $500 up
3. Large Ring Transitional — $300 up
4. Italian Navy Slabside — $350 up
5. Average Slabside — $250 up
6. Large Ring Shallow Milling — $250 up
7. Early Small Hammer — $250 up
8. Standard Pre-War Commercial — $200 up
9. Banner over Chamber — $300 up
10. Persian Contract — $400 up
11. WWI Commercial — $200 up
12. WWI Army (.30cal.) — $175 up

13. WWI Army Issue (9 mm) — $225 up
14. 1920 Police Rework — $175 up
15. French Gendarme — $350 up
16. Post-War Bolo — $250 up
17. Model 1930 (.30 cal.) — $250 up
18. Model 1930 (8.15mm) — $400 up
19. Spanish Copies (Astra, Royal, Azul, etc.) — $250 up
20. Chinese (hand-made) copies — $200 up
21. Chinese .45 ACP (Shanshei) Copy — $450 up

MAUSER ACCESSORIES

1. Stripper Slips — $ 1-2
2. Wooden Stock/Holsters — $35 up
3. Leather Carriers for Above — $15 up
4. Standard Leather Holster — $20 up
5. Bolo Holster — $30 up

6. Naval Proofed Holster — $40 up
7. Chinese .45 ACP Holster — $40 up
8. Conversion Units (Single Shot) — $100 up
9. Cleaning Rod (Reg.) — $10 up
10. Cleaning Rod (Bolo) — $20 up
11. Putzstock (combination tool/cleaning rod) — $20 up
12. Manuals — $10 up

1. Frontspiece from a Mauser catalog circa 1930 for the English and American markets.

2. An interesting cover depicting the Bolo Mauser.

3. One of Mauser's more popular imitators was the Spanish Astra.

4. Cover of a rare catalog on the Royal, another imitator of Mauser.

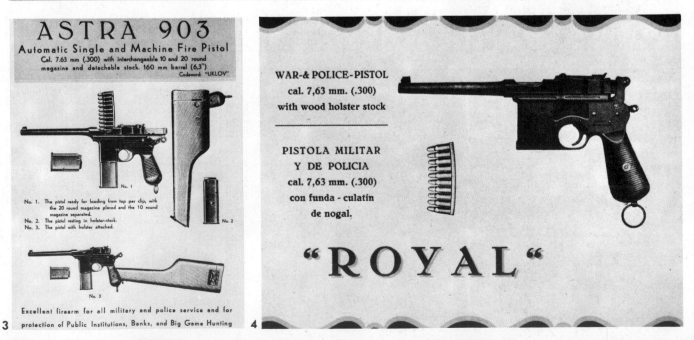

ASTRA 903
Automatic Single and Machine Fire Pistol
Cal. 7.63 mm (.300) with interchangeable 10 and 20 round magazine and detachable stock. 160 mm barrel (6,3")
Codeword "UKLOV"

No. 1. The pistol ready for loading from top per clip, with the 20 round magazine placed and the 10 round magazine separated.
No. 2. The pistol resting in holster-stock.
No. 3. The pistol with holster attached.

Excellent firearm for all military and police service and for protection of Public Institutions, Banks, and Big Game Hunting

3

WAR-& POLICE-PISTOL
cal. 7,63 mm. (.300)
with wood holster stock

PISTOLA MILITAR Y DE POLICIA
cal. 7,63 mm. (.300)
con funda - culatín
de nogal.

"ROYAL"

4

PRICE LIST, 1903-04

MILITARY ARMS, EQUIPMENTS
AND ORDNANCE STORES

M. HARTLEY CO.
313 and 315 Broadway, New York, N. Y.

AGENTS: REMINGTON ARMS CO.   AGENTS: THE UNION METALLIC CARTRIDGE CO.

BREECH LOADING MILITARY ARMS

REMINGTON NEW MODEL SMALL-BORE MILITARY RIFLES

FOR SMOKELESS POWDER

UNEQUALED FOR SIMPLICITY, STRENGTH, DURABILITY AND RAPIDITY OF FIRE.

The production of these arms is to meet the urgent demand for high power rifles of the simple Remington System, with which the National Guard and Armies of South and Central America are so perfectly familiar.

MODEL 1897.

These Arms are adapted for the following small-bore cartridges and smokeless powder:

7 M-M. CALIBRE MAUSER, MODELS SPANISH AND BRAZILIAN.   30 CALIBRE U. S. GOVERNMENT.

No. 6. Remington Military Rifles, without knife bayonet, length of Barrel 30 inches, full length 45 ½ inches, weight 8 ½ lbs. **$18** 00
Knife bayonet with leather scabbard. **4** 00
Remington Military Carbine, length of barrel 20 ½ inches, full length 36 inches, weight, 6 ¾ **16** 00

Contents of case, 20. Special Quotations on application.

U. S. SPRINGFIELD BREECH LOADING RIFLES

STANDARD ARMS OF THE UNITED STATES

No. 70. Military Rifles, 45 Cal., Brown Finish, Open Springfield Sight, Two Notch Tumbler, Stacking Swivels, Angular Bayonet, length 52 inches, weight, 9 lbs.. $7 50

" 71. Military Rifles, 45 Cal., Brown Finish, Buckhorn Wind Gauge Sight, Three Notch Tumbler, Stacking Swivels, Angular Bayonet, length 52 inches, weight, 9 lbs.. 9 00

" 75. Military Rifles, 50 Cal., Bright Finish, refinished, Angular Bayonet, length 56 inches, weight, 9 ½ lbs.................. 4 50

" 74. " Carbines, 45 Cal., Brown Finish, Two Notch Tumbler, Cleaning Rod in Butt, length 41 ½ inches, weight, 7 ½ lbs. 7 50

" 76. " " " " " " " " length 41 ½ inches, weight, 7 lbs........................ 6 50

SPRINGFIELD CADET RIFLES

No. 7. Springfield Cadet Rifles, U. S. Army and West Point System, 45 Cal., Brown Finish, Buckhorn Wind Gauge Sight, **Three** Notch Tumbler, Stacking Swivels, Angular Bayonet, length 49 inches, weight 8 ¼ lbs..................... $9 50

No. 7P. Springfield Cadet Rifles, U. S. Army and West Point System, 45 Cal., Brown Finish, Open "Springfield" Sight, Three Notch Tumbler, Stacking Swivels, Angular Bayonet, length 49 inches, weight, 8 ¼ lbs............................ 7 50

" 8. Springfield Cadet Rifles, 50 Cal., Brown Finish, **Angular Bayonet, length 45 inches, weight,** 8 ¼ lbs 6 00

BREECH LOADING MILITARY ARMS

REMINGTON RIFLE

No. 1. Military Rifles, 43 Cal., Brown Finish, Angular Bayonet, length 51 inches, weight 9 ½ lbs.......................... $12 50

" 2. " " 43 " " " Sabre " " 51 " " 9 ½ lbs.......................... 15 00

" 5. " " 50 " " " Angular " " 51 " " 9 ½ lbs.......................... 12 50

REMINGTON CARBINE.

No. 80. Military Carbine, 43 Cal., Brown Finish, length 36 inches, weight 7 ½ lbs.. $10 00

" 81. " " 50 " " " 36 " " 7 ¼ lbs.......................... 10 00

" 83. Military Baby Carbine, 44 " " " 35 ½ " " 5 ¾ " 10 00

" 84. " " " 44 " Nickel " " 35 ½ " " 5 ¾ " 10 50

THE CELEBRATED SPANISH MODEL REMINGTON RIFLES. OVER 1,600,000 ALREADY SOLD.

SPECIAL LIST OF CADET RIFLES

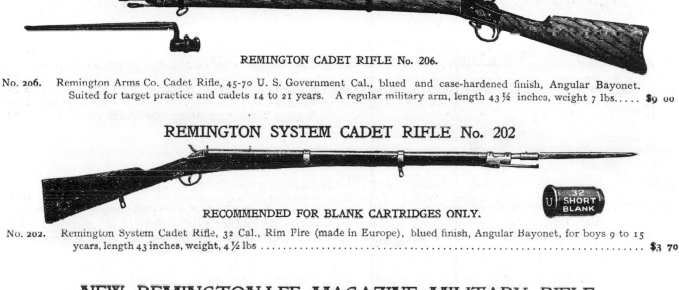

REMINGTON CADET RIFLE No. 205.

No. 205.   Remington Cadet Rifle, 50 Cal., Central Fire Short Cartridge, Brown Finish, perfectly proportioned, Angular Bayonet,
for boys 10 to 20 years, length 42 ½ inches, weight, 6 lbs. $6 00
The best moderate price cadet rifle ever offered.   Made from obsolete material by the Remington Arms Co. especially for us.   Entirely new, serviceable and attractive.   5,000 of these arms now in use by the best Military Schools and Cadet Corps.

REMINGTON CADET RIFLE No. 206.

No. 206.   Remington Arms Co. Cadet Rifle, 45-70 U. S. Government Cal., blued and case-hardened finish, Angular Bayonet.
Suited for target practice and cadets 14 to 21 years.   A regular military arm, length 43 ½ inches, weight 7 lbs. $9 00

REMINGTON SYSTEM CADET RIFLE No. 202

RECOMMENDED FOR BLANK CARTRIDGES ONLY.

No. 202.   Remington System Cadet Rifle, 32 Cal., Rim Fire (made in Europe), blued finish, Angular Bayonet, for boys 9 to 15
years, length 43 inches, weight, 4 ½ lbs $3 70

NEW REMINGTON-LEE MAGAZINE MILITARY RIFLE

MODEL 1899.

29-inch special steel barrel.   Five shots.   Total length, 49 ½ inches.   Weight, 8 ½ lbs.

This arm is of the well-known bolt type, adopted by military organizations throughout the world on account of its simplicity, durability and ease of manipulation.   The celebrated Lee rifle, formerly in use by the Navy Department, has been altered and adapted to
the modern smokeless, high power ammunition, giving great penetration, velocity and flat trajectory with extreme accuracy.

In addition to the bolt locking mechanism on the large calibre Lee, this arm has double-locking shoulders on the bolt head, and is
arranged to load with a filler or clip, whereby five cartridges can be placed in the magazine in the same space of time as is ordinarily
consumed by the insertion of one cartridge in magazine arms of other types.

List price. $35 00
Knife bayonet and scabbard. 4 00

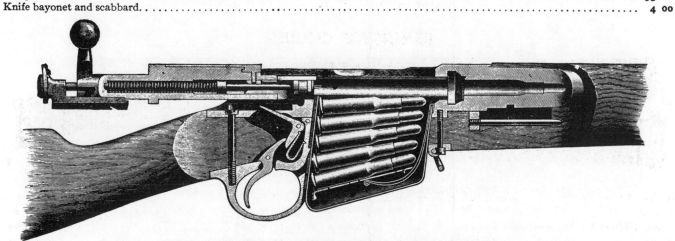

SECTIONAL VIEW, MAGAZINE CHARGED AND IN POSITION.
Made for the following cartridges: 30 Calibre Gov't. 6 M/M. U. S. Navy. 7 M/M. Spanish Mauser.

MISCELLANEOUS BREECH LOADING CADET RIFLES

No. 209. 18 only, Remington, 50-70 Cal., Brown Finish, Angular Bayonet, length 45 ½ inches, weight, 8 lbs. $6 00
"   220. 12 only, Miller, 58 Cal., bright, refinished, Angular Bayonet, 48 inches, weight, 8 ½ lbs.. .... 5 00

MUZZLE LOADING CADET RIFLES

No. 219. 28 only, West Point Model, 58 Cal., with Bayonet, refinished, 54 ¾ inches, weight, 8 lbs. $4 00
"   210. 149 only, Springfield pattern, 58 Cal., with Bayonet, length 47 inches, weight, 7 lbs. 3 50

REMINGTON-LEE MAGAZINE MILITARY RIFLE

WITH DETACHABLE MAGAZINE —SERVICE ARM OF THE U. S. NAVY AND GREAT BRITAIN

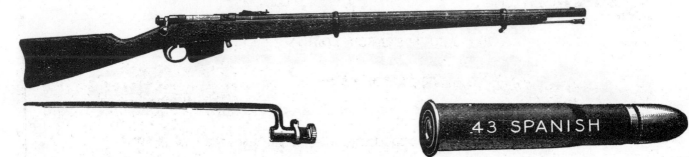

No. 56. Military Rifles, 43 Cal., South American Model, Angular Bayonet, length 52 inches, weight, 9 ¼ lbs. $18 00

EACH ARM IS PROVIDED WITH FOUR MAGAZINES.

No. 31.   7 only, Ballard Carbines, 56/56 Cal., R. F., refinished, length 38 inches, weight 7 ½ lbs $3 50
" — 468 " Remington Carbines, N. Y. S. Model, 50 Cal., c. f. length 37 inches, weight, 7 lbs., Second hand 4 50
" — 171 " Sharps B. L. Carbines, 52 Cal., linen, length 39 inches, weight, 7¾ lbs., refinished 2 00
" — 13 " Smith's B. L. Carbines, 50 Cal., linen, Blued, length 39 inches, weight, 7¾ lbs., new 3 00
" — 451 " Spencer B. L. Carbines, 52 Cal., r. f. length 39 inches, weight, 9¼ lbs., blued, refinished 4 00
" — 49 " Balls B. L. Repeating Carbines, 50 Cal., r. f., length 37½ inches, weight, 7¾ lbs., blued barrel, case
           hardened mountings, new 6 00
" — 40 " Burnside B. L. Carbines, 54 Cal., linen, Bright, length 39 inches, weight, 7½ lbs., refinished 2 50
" — 21 " Starr B. L. Carbines, 54 Cal., linen, length 37½ inches, weight, 7½ lbs., Second hand 2 50
" — 14 " Maynard B. L. Carbines. 50 Cal., linen, blued, length 36½ inches. weight, 6 lbs., *new* 2 00

"QUAKER."

No. 215. "Quaker" Muskets for Boys' Brigades. Genuine Rifles, except they have stained wooden Barrels. Metal parts are
       bright, Angular Bayonet. **Well finished and substantial,** length 48 inches, weight, 4 ½ lbs. $2 50
" 216. Same as No. 215, but better finished. Length 49 inches, weight, 6 lbs. 2 75
    These muskets are made from genuine Springfield Rifle parts, and are superior in every way to the roughly put together "Quakers"
usually supplied.

BREECH LOADING MILITARY ARMS

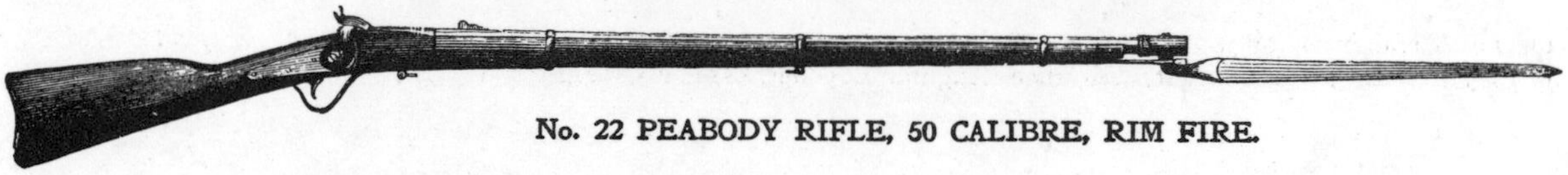

No. 22 PEABODY RIFLE, 50 CALIBRE, RIM FIRE.

MISCELLANEOUS BREECH LOADING MILITARY RIFLES

These arms are entirely serviceable, but are more or less obsolete in pattern. For drill or defence purposes are equal to modern arms.

No. 28.	3 only	Roberts Transformed Springfield Rifles, 58 Cal., Rim Fire, Angular Bayonet, bright refinished, length 36 inches, weight, 9 lbs.	$4 00
" 49.	90 "	Sharps Rifles, '74 Model, 50-70 Cal., Brown Finish, Angular Bayonet, length 52 inches, weight, 10½ lbs.	5 00
" 10.	4 "	Peabody-Martini Rifles, 45 Cal., Turkish Model, Quadrangular Bayonet, length 49 inches, weight, 9 lbs.	12 00
" 11.	20 "	Spencer 7-Shot Magazine Rifles, 56/52 Cal., R. F., Angular Bayonet, length 47 inches, weight, 10 lbs., refinished .	6 00
" —	88 "	Hall's Flint Lock B. L. Rifles with Bayonets, 52 Cal., Brown, length 52 inches, weight, 11¼ lbs., *new* .	10 00
" —	33 "	Hall's Percussion Lock B. L. Rifles with Bayonets, 52 Cal., linen, brown, length, 52 inches, weight 10½ lbs., *new* .	6 00
" —	20 "	Merrill B. L. Rifles, .58 Cal., linen, Brown Barrel, Brass Mountings, lengeh 49 inches, weight 10¼ lbs., No Bayonets, refinished	4 00
" —	274 "	Sharps B. L. Rifes with Angular Bayonets, 52 Cal., linen, length 47 inches, weight with bayonet 10 lbs., Second Hand.	4 00

MISCELLANEOUS BREECH LOADING CARBINES

No. 24. PEABODY MILITARY CARBINE, USING 50 CALIBRE RIM FIRE CARTRIDGES.

No. 33.	57 only,	Palmer Carbines, 50 Cal., Rim Fire, length 37 inches, weight, 5½ lbs.	$4 00
" 27.	27 "	Sharps Carbines, '74 Model, 50 Cal., Central Fire, refinished like new, length 39 inches, weight, 7½ lbs.	4 50
" 23.	55 "	Peabody " 50 Cal., Central Fire, new, length 39 inches, weight, 6¾ lbs.	5 50
" 24.	500 "	" " " 50 " Rim " " " 39 " " 6¾ "	4 00

MUZZLE LOADING MILITARY MUSKETS

AS USED IN WAR OF THE REBELLION. ALL ARE IN PERFECT CONDITION, CLEANED AND READY FOR USE

No. 35.		U. S. Springfield Model '64, 58 Cal. Bright Finish, Angular Bayonet, new, length 56 in., weight, 8½ lbs.	$3 00
" 36.		" Plymouth, " '64, 69 " " " Sabre " almost new, length 50 in., weight, 9½ lbs.	3 00
" 37¾.		U. S. (22 P. B.), Model '40, 69 Cal. Bright Finish, Angular Bayonet, refinished, length 58 inches, weight, 9¼ lbs.	2 30
" 38.		U. S. Model '42, 69 Cal. Bright Finish, Angular Bayonet, refinished, length 58 inches., weight 9 lbs.	2 50
" 39.		U. S., Model '42, 69 Cal. Bright Finish, Angular Bayonet, new, length 58 inches, weight, 9 lbs.	2 60
" 37.	128 only,	U. S. Harper's Ferry, 58 Cal. Bright Finish, Sabre Bayonet, refinished, length 49 inches, weight 9¼ lbs.	2 75
" 40.	13 "	British Enfield, long, 58 Cal. Brown Finish, Angular Bayonet, 2d hand, length 57 inches, weight 9½ lbs.	2 75
" 41.	30 "	British Enfield, short, 58 Cal. Brown Finish, Sabre Bayonet, 2d hand, length 48½ inches, weight, 8½ lbs.	3 00
		U. S. Springfield "Colts," 58 Cal., Bright, Angular Bayonet, length 55 inches, weight with bayonet 9¾ lbs., refinished	2 50
" —	65 "	Austrian M. L. Rifled Muskets and Triangular Bayonets, 58 Cal., length 52 inches, weight with bayonet 10 lbs., Second hand.	2 00
" —	24 "	U. S. Model, 1822, Flint Lock, M. L. Rifles, 54 Cal., brown, length 51 inches, weight 10 lbs., no bayonets, *new*	12 00
" —	198 "	U. S. M. L. Rifles, '40, 54 Cal., Brown, Brass mountings, length 48½ inches, weight 9¾ lbs., no bayonets, refinished	2 25
" —	105 "	U. S. M. L. Rifles, '40, 54 Cal., with Sabre Bayonets and leather Scabbard, Bright, Brass mountings, lentgh 48½ inches, weight with bayonet 12¼ lbs., refinished.	2 75
" —	42 "	U. S. M. L. Rifles, '40, 54 Cal., with Angular Bayonets, Brass Mountings, length 48½ inches, weight with bayonet, refinished.	2 50

BAYONETS, SABRES AND CANTEENS

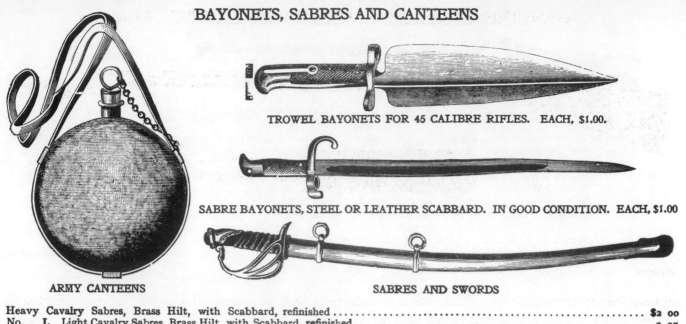

TROWEL BAYONETS FOR 45 CALIBRE RIFLES. EACH, $1.00.

SABRE BAYONETS, STEEL OR LEATHER SCABBARD. IN GOOD CONDITION. EACH, $1.00

ARMY CANTEENS

SABRES AND SWORDS

Heavy Cavalry Sabres, Brass Hilt, with Scabbard, refinished			$2 00
No. J.	Light Cavalry Sabres, Brass Hilt, with Scabbard, refinished		2 25
" K.	U. S. Army Canteens, 1 Quart, Cloth or Canvas Covered, per doz.		3 70
" L.	Valises, Canvas or Rubber Flaps, with Slings, per doz.		7 00
Old rusty triangular Bayonets for decorating purposes, each.			10
Army Haversacks, Canvas, with Leather Sling, Brass Hooks for Adjusting length, per doz.			5 00
Army Haversacks, Canvas, with Canvas Adjustable Sling, per doz.			7 00
Hand Grenades with Fliers and Plungers	1lb. $1 00, 3lbs. $1 50, 5lbs.		2 00
119 only, U. S. Artillery Sabres, with Steel Scabbards, Brass Hilts, light			3 00
863 " Musicians' Swords with Brass Mountings, Leather Scabbards, and Brass Hilt, refinished			1 75
497 " Non-Commissioned Officers' Swords, Brass Mountings, Brass Hilt, refinished			2 00

PRICES ON APPLICATION FOR BALL OR BLANK CARTRIDGES, CANNON PRIMERS, TENTS, ETC.
PRICES IN THIS LIST ARE NET, EXCEPT FOR QUANTITIES.

MILITARY EQUIPMENTS, BELTS AND CARTRIDGE BOXES

FOR CARRYING METALLIC AMMUNITION

SETS OF
EQUIPMENTS

No. A.	For Muzzle-loading Muskets, including Cartridge Box, Cap Pouch, Bayonet Scabbard, Waist Belt, U. S. Plate, good as new, 58 or 69 Cal., per set.		$1 00
" AA.	For Quaker Muskets, including Cartridge Box and Plain oval Plate, Swivel Bayonet Scabbard, Waist Belt with Plain oblong Plate, good quality, per set.		1 10
" AB.	For Quaker Musket, including Pouch and Plain oval Plate, Bayonet Scabbard, Waist Belt with Plain oblong Plate, good quality, per set.		75
" B.	For Cadet Rifles No. 202. Belt with Plain oblong Plate, Cartridge Box and Bayonet Scabbard on Swivel, new, per set.		1 25
" C.	For Remington Cadet Rifles. Belt with Plain oblong Plate, Cartridge Box, Bayonet Scabbard on Swivel, new per set.		1 25
" D.	For Springfield and other Breech Loaders, Waist Belt with Eagle Plate, Hanger Cartridge Box and Bayonet Scabbard, good quality, per set.		1 50
" DD.	Same set with Steel Bayonet Scabbard.		1 85
" E.	For Springfield and other Breech Loaders, Waist Belt with Eagle Plate, McKeever Patent U. S. Army Cartridge Box, Steel Bayonet Scabbard with Swivel, good quality, per set.		2 25
" F.	Rifle Slings, Russet, White Buff, or Black Leather, each.		$0 30
" G.	Carbine Slings and Swivels, Black Buff Leather, each.		1 00
" H.	Cavalry Sabre Belts and Eagle Plates, Black Buff Leather, each.		75

GENUINE SPANISH MAUSER REPEATING ARMS

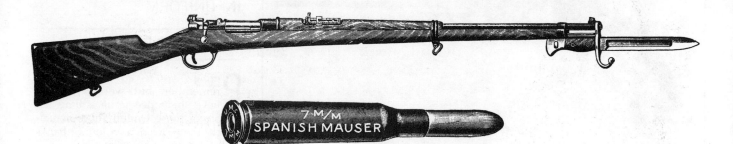

We are prepared to furnish specimens of Mauser Rifles and Carbines, same as used by the Spanish and Cuban Armies. Having secured a limited quantity of each, entirely new.

Spanish Mauser Repeating Rifles, 7 M/M. Calibre, complete with Knife Bayonet and Scabbard.. . . . .$25 00
Spanish Mauser Repeating Carbines, 7 M/M. Calibre . . . . : 23 00

CAPTURED WAR RELICS

The U. S. Government sold at Auction, a limited number of Mauser Rifles and cartridges captured from the Spanish at Santiago, Cuba.

We own a few of these and offer them for sale.

Mauser Rifles and Carbines (boxed), each. $12 00
Mauser Cartridges per box of 15. 75

A Certificate of genuineness, signed by us, will be supplied with each arm.

PISTOLS AND REVOLVERS

Allen P. & B. Revolvers, 44 Calibre, 7½ inch Barrel, First Class . . . . .each $2 00
Colt P. & B. Revolvers, 44 Calibre, 7½ inch Barrel, Second Class . . . . " 1 50
Remington P. & B. Revolvers, 44 Calibre, 7½ inch Barrel, First Class. . . . . " 2 00
Remington P. & B. Revolvers, 44 Calibre, 7½ inch Barrel, Second Class . . . . " 1 50
Starr P. & B. Self-Cocking Revolvers, 44 Calibre, 6-inch Barrel, Second Class. . . . . " 1 50
Adams' P. & B. Revolvers, 44 Calibre, 6-inch Barrel, Second Class. . . . . " 3 00
Remington Breech Loader, Single Shot Army Pistol, 50 Calibre, Center Fire Blued Barrel, Case Hardened Frame, New . . . . " 3 00

CARTRIDGE BELTS, ETC.

Genuine Anson Mills Cartridge Belts, 45 Cal., grey, for Cadets $2 00
Web Cartridge Belts, woven in one piece, 45 Cal., blue. 2 00
Web Cartridge Belts, 45 Cal., grey 1 50
Web Cartridge Belts, 30 Cal., brown 1 50

M. HARTLEY CO.

313 and 315 Broadway, New York, N. Y.

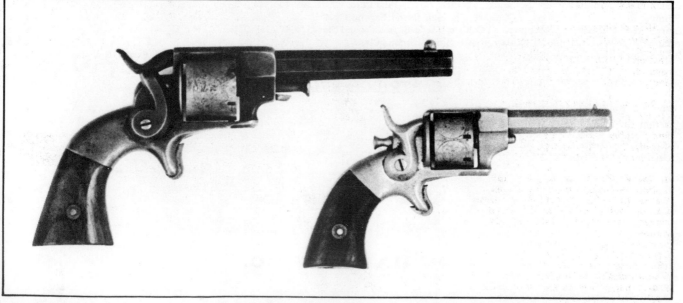

A TOKEN OF THE TIMES

THE PEOPLE OF THESE UNITED STATES FELT THEY OWED A VOTE OF THANKS TO THEIR MEN IN UNIFORM

By Rick Saccone

Perhaps you're all too young to remember, but would you believe that once upon a time the people of these United States actually felt they owed a vote of thanks to their men in uniform. Sometimes these "thank you's" took the form of housekeeping items which would enable the soldier to better endure the hardships imposed by the military life. Most, however, were the result of concern for the safety of the individual and took the form of edged weapons or firearms that would in effect somewhat supplement the "issue" firepower. Some town councils voted funds for the purpose of providing each newly mustered recruit with a dress dirk or similar token. Sweethearts gifted their departing swains with arms, as well as love tokens. Parents, seeking to insure their son's safe return, provided them with a little "extra" something. And fellow workers chipped in for a lethal little companion to accompany their stalwart steward off to war.

When the question is raised as to which particular arm was the most popular choice, the determinate factors which provide the answer must be the contemporary photographs, written accounts of usage, and surviving examples of type. Taking first the contemporary photograph, we must consider the circumstances under which the photo was taken. There are two general areas to consider

here. The first is the portrait photo which sometimes incorporated "prop" weaponry lent by the photographer to glamorize the subject, and the second is the "casual" photo taken of an individual or group generally equipped only with their actual possessions. The ultimate in photo research would be to be able to compare all the results of a typical photographer's average week's work. However, the passage of 108 years has caused the dispersal or destruction of this outlay, rendering the ideal an impossibility. Thus, a researcher must weigh gravely each singular example that comes his way.

Under written accounts, there are again two areas to research; personal accounts, such as letters, and published accounts such as contemporary newspapers and official records. The third and seemingly most vital area for investigation is the surviving arm itself. Researching martial or contracted arms, and being confronted and confounded by incomplete or missing records and correspondence, is difficult enough. But, many makers of sub-martial caliber arms left little if any trace of their activities (other than the arms themselves). Once having fathomed the reasoning behind each maker's serial number system, we arrive at a logical involvement, *supply* countering *demand*. Considering the attrition rate, a safe assumption is that a weapon made in large numbers is more likely to

have survived than its antithesis. With this, we can arrive at some idea as to what items, in their time, achieved the greatest popularity.

Experience tells us that something doesn't have to be practical to be popular. One of the era's least practical, but most popular, pocket revolvers was the Smith and Wesson Model One, Second Issue. Reports of

its lack of stopping power were legion. The only incident of usage mentioned in the official records concerns a quarrel between two Union officers. The argument ended when the junior officer fired his Model One point blank into the forehead of his adversary. The bullet pierced the skin and following the curve of the skull, exited the scalp at the top.

1. Smith & Wesson Model No. 2 6-shot, .32 caliber rimfire revolver. Sometimes called the "Old Issue Army Revolver," it was produced from June of 1861 to 1874 with a total production of 66,502 units. The Smith & Wesson Model No. 1, second issue, 7-shot, .22 caliber rimfire. This piece was the first breechloading revolver to use fixed ammunition as it is known today.

2. Allen & Wheelock, 6-shot, .32 caliber rimfire revolver, patented September 7, and November 9, 1858. The next one is the Allen & Wheelock revolver in .22 rimfire, patented September and November, 1858.

3. Remington-Elliot ring trigger, .22 caliber rimfire, 5-shot double-action derringer, patented May, 1869 and October 1861. The Sharps No. 1, 4-shot, .22 rimfire caliber derringer patented in 1859.

4. Warner .28 caliber, single action, 6-shot, percussion revolver. James Warner managed the Springfield Arms Co., the output of which was based on his patents. The E. Whitney, .31 caliber revolver. This model was a product of Whitney's New Haven, Connecticut factory. Colt's Model of 1862, New Police, .36 caliber, 5-shot percussion revolver. This arm is also known as Model of 1862 Pocket, or Officer's Model Pocket Pistol.

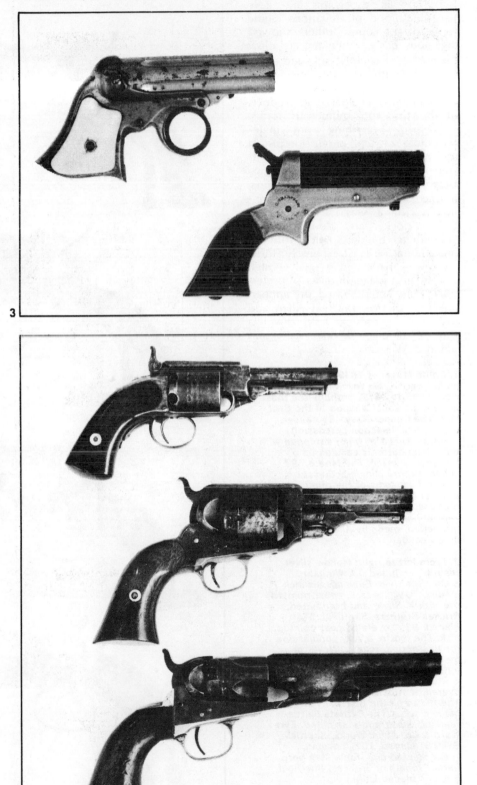

3

4

The total damage done? A slight loss of blood and a severe headache. Nevertheless, the compactness of the seven-shot arm with its newly developed self-contained ammunition was novelty enough to induce the sale of 126,430 units of the Second Issue and its predecessor, the First Issue, which had been superceded in 1860.

The popularity of this arm gave rise to a flood of imitations. Some were blatant copies, others showed ingenious enough thinking to allow them to stand slightly aside and apart. One of Smith and Wesson's most successful competitors was the firm of Allen and Wheelock. The products of this firm took numerous forms. They made everything from single-shot muzzle-loaded percussion pistols to large-caliber revolvers which utilized the latest in self-contained cartridges. Yet the most popular sellers, if one can judge by the aforementioned criteria, was the sub-martial-caliber pocket arm designed as a "confidence builder." Aside from being among the least expensive, these were well made and rugged enough for practical usage. In order of preference, one could, based on appearances in photos, say that Allen and Wheelock's products held down a firm third place behind Colt and Smith & Wesson.

1. Colt's Model of 1849, .31 caliber, 5-shot percussion revolver produced from 1849 to 1872, perhaps the most popular personal weapon of the Civil War. The Cooper Navy, .36 caliber, 5-shot, double-action percussion revolver. This arm when equipped with the 6-inch barrel is considered a primary martial. The Moore, .32 caliber rimfire, single-action revolver. Like some of the other popular arms of the period, the Moore was produced in a number of barrel lengths. Typical percussion, boot pistol of the period, made by Allen & Thurber in .36 caliber.

2. From left to right: Hollow silver resin filled, hilted C.I. Wingaard & Co., Sheffield, England. Six-inch bladed, 10⅛" overall, spear pointed dress dirk. Silver and horn hilted, Crickes Brothers, Sheffield, 5¾" bladed, 9⅝" overall, spear pointed dirk. The motto, a very popular one for this period, reads, "Never draw me without reason nor sheath me without honor." Slab horn hilted, A. Fiest & Co., England, 9⅞" bladed, 14⅝" overall, mottoed, spear pointed dirk. The motto on the unusually large blade reads, "The Patriots Selfdefender." Silver and stag hilted. Eyre Ward & Co. Sheaf Works, Sheffield, 6 3/16" bladed, 10⅜" overall, spear-pointed dirk. Slab, stag horn hilted, Jonathan Crookes, Sheffield, 6 5/16" bladed knife.

3. Showing to good advantage the precise workmanship done on knives of the period.

The Colt story is so often told that the word, Colt, became synonymous with the word revolver. Even early accounts of hostile action generally refer to an individual defending himself with his "Colt," while in fact the arm may have been a trusty Whitney, or perhaps even a Moore, or Cooper. As was the case with the impact of Smith & Wesson's bored-through cylinder chambers and self-contained ammunition, Colt too, by virtue of the success of their percussion designs, spawned a crop of imitators. Some design elements are so similar that frames, barrel assemblies, loading levers, cylinders and even internal parts appear to be

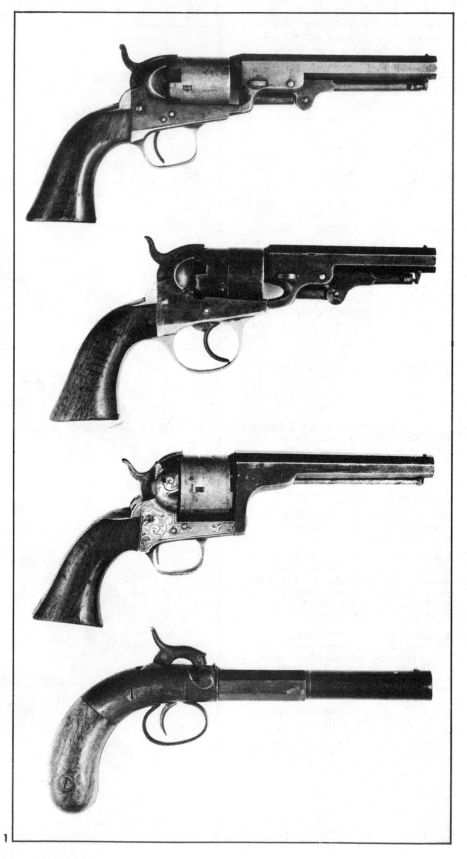

1

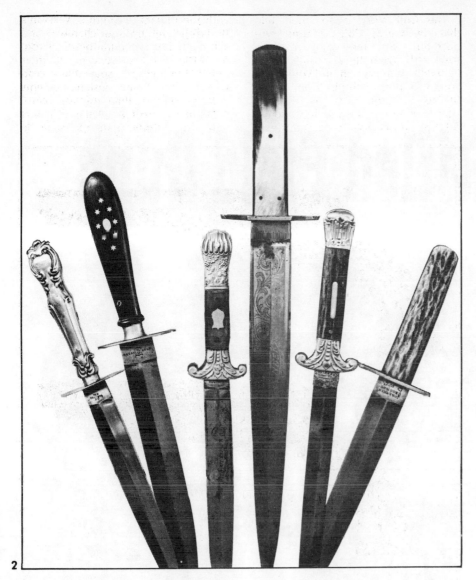

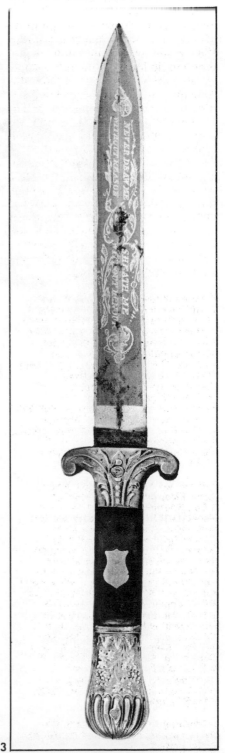

were used to create handles which could almost be regarded as minor works of art. This, combined with a mottoed blade, which echoed the sentiments of the purchaser, became a highly desirable and much appreciated gift.

Federal uniform regulations of the Civil War period specified that things be exactly that, uniform. But, if contemporary photographs were the only record, an observer would assume that subscription to regulations was almost the exception, rather than the rule. ♔

interchangeable. Colt did sell more guns than any of their imitators or competitors. The very fact that Colt had been producing arms for 25 years prior to the war, accounts for a good percentage of the frequency with which they show up in photographic studies of the period.

Someone once said that, ''at the start of the war there were more Colts south of the Mason-Dixon line than north.'' Ambro-types and tin-types of Confederate soldiers, proudly displaying their "49" Pockets or "51" Navies, echo the fact.

Utilizing the criteria developed so far, we can progress to the last step and judge that the title of most popular pocket revolvers of the Civil War period should be bestowed on Col. Colt's Model of 1849, not only because of the vast numbers produced or sold, but also because elements of its design as embodied in competitors' products made them desirable substitutes.

You don't have to reload a knife, and this fact alone sold lots of dirks and Bowies. The drawbacks to own-

ing a percussion arm were the weight of loading accessories or trying to obtain the fragile prepared loads. Cartridge guns were totally useless if the owner ran out of cartridges, and in the field ,the new novelties were almost impossible to obtain once the initial supply was used up. The owner of a fine knife only worried about losing his shiny companion, and as they traveled alone together, he found that its capability for odd jobs made it an indispensable part of his equipment.

The style most sought after by collectors is the classical Bowie form, yet the spear-point dirk style accounted for an exceptionally large part of the market. Early in the 1860s, manufacturers developed designs specifically for the newly established market. Since each firm produced basically the same article, each sought to achieve a larger share of the market by producing a knife that was superior in finish and design to those produced by the competition. Such materials as silver, brass, German silver, mother of pearl, ivory and horn

CIVIL WAR Rifled Field Guns

1

FORERUNNERS OF MODERN ARTILLERY.
by Konrad F. Schreier, Jr.

The culmination of the Battle of Gettysburg came on its third day: July 3, 1863. Confederate Maj. Gen. George E. Pickett was scheduled to make one more effort to crack the Union lines, and to make way for his charge, the battle opened with an artillery bombardment of the Union lines by massed Rebel artillery. The barrage began at about 10 minutes past 1:00 p.m. on that hot summer afternoon.

The Union troops on the receiving

end of the Confederate cannon serenade could only hunker down behind what cover there was and listen to the music. The bass was played by the deep thunder of Rebel batteries of smoothbore, muzzle-loading field guns, and a melody line was played by the continuous cracking of exploding case shot and shell. Another theme was played by the distinctive whistling of the shells from the high-powered Confederate rifled field guns, and this had its own bass melody of solid shot, unexploded case, and dud rounds thumping into the ground. Above all this there was a soloist whose daemonical howl punctuated the music every

so often—everybody knew it was the Whitworth field gun.

There were two Confederate Whitworth guns, which were the only ones on the Gettysburg Battlefield, and they kept popping off from about the same place where the two Whitworth guns are parked on the Gettysburg Battlefield today. The Rebel bombardment ended about 3:00 p.m. that deadly afternoon, and Pickett's Charge failed shortly thereafter. It is remarkable to read the accounts of the veterans of that afternoon and find that almost every one of them had something to say about those two Whitworth guns! That pair seems to have scared every man in the Union lines, and encouraged every Rebel in the process. Scream though the Whitworth did, most of the projectiles fired by the guns were solid shots called "bolts," producing very few casualties.

The lack of combat effectiveness was more or less the report on all rifled cannon used by both armies in the Civil War, but nonetheless both sides used rifled field guns extensively. Of course most of these guns were U.S. Army models since most of the Rebel artillery weapons came from captured Union stocks. Of the several types of rifled field guns used, the Parrott was the one most usually deployed.

The U.S. Army procured 587 10-pounder (3-inch) Parrotts and 338 20-pounder (3.67-inch) Parrotts during the Civil War, the loyal states bought a few more, and the Confederate Army arsenals made a few copies of it. The Parrott was designed by Robert P. Parrott, superintendent of the West Point Foundry at Cold Spring,

1. The 3-inch (10 pounder) Ordnance or Rodman field gun. It was considered to be the finest muzzle loading rifled field gun ever built.

2. A 3-inch (10 pounder) Parrott with full crew in drill pose.

3. A 2.56-inch (6 pounder) Wiard rifle was very modern looking for the Civil War period. Notice the globe front sight on the muzzle.

New York in the late 1850s, and he was awarded a U.S. Patent for the design about 1860. The Parrott was nothing more than a simple rifled muzzle-loading barrel, a cast-iron tube similar to the contemporary cast-iron muzzle-loading, smoothbore field guns. It was, however, reinforced by a sleeve of wrought iron shrunk over the powder chamber portion of the barrel to strengthen it for the increased pressures inherent in a rifled design. The Parrott was a relatively simple gun to make, a 10-pounder running about $2000, while the 20-pounder cost some $4000. The carriages for the Parrott guns, and all Civil War field guns

for that matter, was simply a variation of the single stock-trail wooden field carriage of the period.

The Parrott was very extensively used during and after the Civil War, however it was never the standard regulation rifled field gun of the U.S. Army. The Parrott was what would be called a "substitute standard" weapon today, and that means it was a weapon issued in place of the regulation model because there weren't sufficient numbers of the prescribed gun to fill the requirements. The Parrott was dangerous because the breech end of its brittle cast iron barrel would blow out every so often. Even though Parrott guns

Rifled Field Guns

were still in limited use in the 1890s, the Parrott cannoniers were always cautioned against its tendency to blow out at the breech. Fortunately the force of these breech failures was usually directly to the rear of the gun, and the crew could protect themselves by standing to either side.

The regulation rifled field gun of the U.S. Army was the 3-inch (10-pounder) Ordnance Rifle, a gun far superior to the Parrott. A total of 925 of these rifled muzzle loaders were made during the Civil War at a cost of about $3500 each. The 3-inch rifle was designed and manufactured by the U.S. Army Ordnance Department, and named for Gen. Thomas J. Rodman, who had much to do with the design of Civil War period artillery weapons. The 3-inch Ordnance Rifle was constructed in a most unusual manner. A tube of sheet wrought iron was wrapped in several layers around a mandrill, then the tube was forge-welded into a solid gun barrel, subsequently a solid breech was installed. After forging and installing the solid breech, the tube was lathe turned, bored, and rifled.

The 3-inch Ordnance Rodman Rifle was a very strong field piece, and probably the most effective rifle of the muzzle-loading field gun era. There is no record of one bursting,

although a few did crack after many thousands of shots; a very unusual record in the muzzle-loading days. The 3-inch Rodman barrels were actually so well made that some were used to make the first experimental breech-loading field guns of the U.S. Army in the late 1870s.

Another rifled muzzle loading field gun used in the Civil War was the James Rifle developed by Gen. Charles T. James of the U.S. Army. A James Rifle was simply an old bronze muzzle-loading gun which had been rifled, however 162 new 6-pounder (2.56-inch) James Rifles were fabricated during the Civil War. Because they were bronze, a relatively soft metal, the James Rifles

wore out very quickly, so most of them were either bored out smooth or re-cast to make new cannon.

There were other muzzle-loading rifled field guns used in the Civil War, including 25 6-pounder (2.56-inch) Wiard rifles, 10 12-pounder (3.40-inch) Wiard rifles purchased by the U.S. Army. Defects in the Wiard's metal kept them from seeing much use. Both the Union and Rebel armies acquired 12-pounder (2.75-inch) Whitworth, 12-pounder (3.40-inch) Blakely, and 3-inch (10-pounder) Armstrong muzzle-loading rifles from England, but the numbers of these guns in use were so small they were of no importance.

There were two breechloading

2

3

4

1. The 3-inch (12 pounder) Armstrong Breech Loading Rifled Field Gun at the factory in England. Although a rare weapon in the Civil War, reports indicate both sides used it.

2. This engraving of the Armstrong gun was made from the above photograph. People sometimes doubt the authenticity of old engravings.

3. An engraving of the Whitworth rifle with breech open. The "pipe cap" construction forced use of a cartridge.

4. This 12-pounder Whitworth gun was captured from the Confederate States Army during the Civil War.

rifled field guns which both armies procured from England in very small numbers. The less common and important of these was the 3-inch Armstrong Breech Loading Rifle designed by Sir William Armstrong, a famous British engineer. The Armstrong barrel was made from several pieces of steel somewhat like a modern field gun. Its breech-block traveled through a transverse hole in the breech and was locked in firing position by a large hollow screw entering the tube behind it. The breech of the Armstrong rifle was its chief fault because the breech-block and its seat were easily damaged when the block was pulled out of the barrel for reloading. Although both armies had Armstrong breech-loading rifles, they were so little used that they left no record.

And then there was the 12-pounder (2.75-inch) Whitworth Breech Loading Rifle, the gun which struck

terror at Gettysburg. Designed by British steelmaker Sir Joseph Whitworth, this gun was a very unusual pioneer breech loader. To say it was rifled is really somewhat of an understatement, because it had a hexagonal-shaped bore and fired hexagonal-profile projectiles called "bolts" because they were so different from any other artillery shells. The Whitworth breech was a cap which screwed over the breech like a pipe cap, requiring a cartridge case to seal against gas leakage. The strange hexagonal zinc- or tin-plate cartridge case for the Whitworth Rifle is a virtually unknown Civil War relic today, even in museum collections. Should anyone doubt the need for this Whitworth cartridge case, a look at the construction of the gun's breech will show that it couldn't have been safely fired without one. Evidently the Whitworth cartridge case isn't mentioned in any of the

contemporary publications about the gun, because it was overlooked in the discussion of the gun's extremely unusual hexagonal bore. Also, details are lacking from most descriptions of rifled field gun ammunition.

The Whitworth gun had a serious problem which made its life as a military weapon very short. It had a tendency for the projectiles to jam in its bore when the barrel was a bit dirty and the projectiles were not heavily lubricated with grease. When a projectile stuck, the breech could blow off or the barrel burst. This dangerous malfunction tendency prejudiced practical artillerymen against the Whitworth, although it was a very powerful gun. After the Civil War it dropped out of sight as more practical rifled field guns came into use.

All the early rifled muzzle-loading and breechloading field guns including the Whitworth were much more powerful weapons than the old style smoothbore muzzle loaders. A smoothbore 12-pounder (4.62-inch)

Rifled Field Guns

Napoleon field gun fired a 12.3-pound projectile 5280 yards at about seven degrees elevation, while a 3-inch Ordnance Rifle or a 10-pounder Parrott could fire their projectiles 5280 yards at only five degrees elevation; about 30 percent less. The maximum range of the 12-pounder smoothbore Napoleon was reckoned at 2000 yards, while the maximum range of either the Ordnance or Parrott rifles was about 4000 yards. The Whitworth breech loader could easily reach to over 5000 yards range. All the rifled field guns could hit a point target about the size of a pickup truck at about half their maximum range, and a target the size of a massed infantry batallion at their maximum range, however the smoothbore Napoleon couldn't hit a pickup with every shot at 500 yards, and it could miss the infantry batallion at 1000 yards! The potential of the rifled field gun was great, but there were unsolved problems which kept it from being realized during the Civil War.

Gun sights and artillery fire direction systems were still very underdeveloped. The rifled field gun was only about 15 years old when the Civil War began, and it was still using the crude sights of the smoothbore muzzle loader. The gunner's quadrants issued to measure the guns elevations were only accurate to $1/4$-degree, and the line-of-fire sights were put on and taken off the gun for every shot, so they weren't good for more than $1/4$-degree of accuracy. Modern artillery sights measure these critical angles within thousandths of a degree. The guns also had tangent sights like an

infantry rifle, but these sights were more or less useless beyond the 1000-yard range. This lack of adequate sights made long-range fire with rifled field guns almost impossible and unheard of in the Civil War.

Another factor which compromised the utility of the rifled field guns during the Civil War was the projectiles they fired. In the muzzle-loading rifles, some sort of provision was made to cause a portion of the projectile to expand into the rifling when the gun was fired. At their best, these systems worked some 95 percent of the time, and at their worst they wouldn't work at all. When a projectile didn't take the rifling, it always fell far short of the target, and this could prove disas-

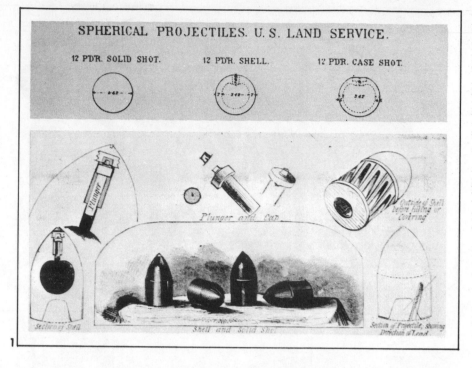

SPHERICAL PROJECTILES. U. S. LAND SERVICE.

12 PDR. SOLID SHOT.   12 PDR. SHELL.   12 PDR. CASE SHOT.

1. At the top of the photo are drawings of smoothbore projectiles. Balls inside the case shot are omitted. Below is the general construction of the James Rifle projectile. This gun and its ammunition were withdrawn from service before the end of the Civil War.

2. Engravings of the Armstrong (above) and Whitworth rifled field guns. The pipe cap construction is clearly seen on the Whitworth.

3. Drawing of the Whitworth case and projectile. The projectile is similar to the famous Whitworth rifle bullet.

4. Six common rifled field gun shell systems; solid, cannister, case, shell.

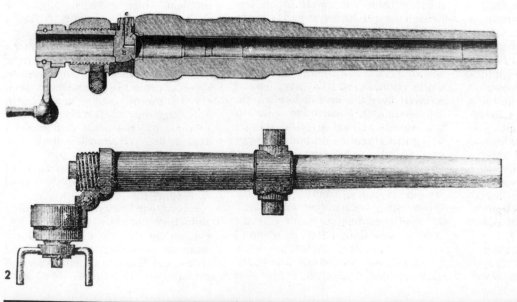

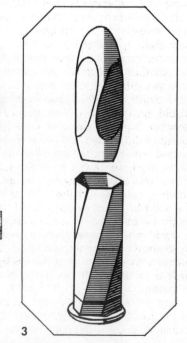

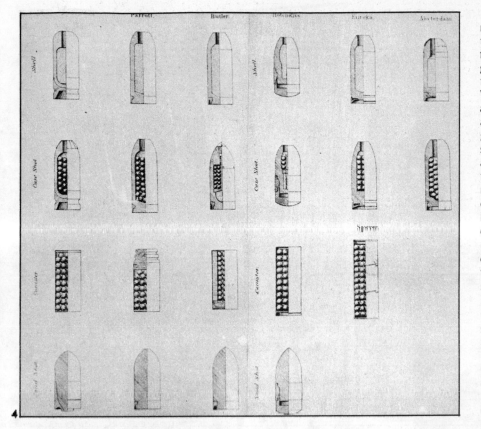

terous when firing over the heads of friendly troops because a "short round" could hit them. This problem was so acute that Civil War rifled field artillery didn't fire over the heads of its own troops unless it was a dire emergency.

The various types of projectiles fired in Civil War rifled field guns were also of doubtful effectiveness. Canister could be fired in a smoothbore or rifle with equal expectations according to contemporary reports, but the 3-inch rifle canister only fired two-thirds the weight of canister shot in the charge for the 12-pounder Napoleon. This meant that the shotgun effect of the rifle was only two-thirds that of the smoothbore. Solid shot fired in a rifled gun would bury itself in the ground or ricochet high in the air, while the round, solid shot fired in a muzzle loaded smoothbore would bounce along the ground and have the same effect on massed enemy troops a bowling ball has on the pins. While the solid ball shot of the smoothbore might be effective on massed troops, it could nowhere near equal the effectiveness or penetration of the rifled cannon shot on a hard target such as a well-built building or fortification.

Another projectile commonly used in the Civil War field guns was case (canister) shot—shrapnel in modern terminology—which was a hollow projectile filled with a mixture of gunpowder and balls. Fitted with a time fuse, the gunner set it to make the case shot burst when it reached its target. The time fuse was a powder train type which was ignited by the flash from the gun firing, and they worked quite well in smoothbore guns, but the fire couldn't seem to be able to flash by the rifled projectile to light the fuse. Some 80 percent of the case shot fired in smoothbores would detonate, but only 40 to 50 percent of the time fuses fired in rifled guns would function. If the time fuse failed to ignite, the effect would be the same as if solid shot had been fired.

The last type of field artillery projectile commonly fired in the Civil War was the "shell" which was simply a hollow projectile filled with gunpower. In the smoothbore, shell was fired with the time fuse, and it had about the same effect as case shot. In rifled guns, shells could be fired wtih either a time fuse or a percussion fuse which would cause the shell to explode on impact with its target. While the time fuse was still only 40 to 50 percent effective with rifled shell, the percussion impact fuses would function some 80 percent of the time. Shell was the most effective projectile fire in Civil War rifled field guns.

The record shows, however, that most Civil War soldiers considered the smoothbore cannon a more effective weapon than the rifled field gun. Gen. Henry J. Hunt, Chief of the U.S. Army Artillery in the Civil War and a man of proven judgment and intelligence, considered the adoption of the rifled field gun the great mistake of the Civil War. Hunt said the 3-inch caliber was too small, and his opinion was borne out by the adoption of 3.5-inch rifles by most armies shortly after the end of the Civil War, and still in service long after the adoption of high-explosive shell made the 3-inch caliber practical. Because of the novelty of rifled cannon at the time of the Civil War there were not only several types of rifled guns in service, but no less than seven designs of ammunition to be fired in them. Each of these ammunition types had something wrong with it, and Gen. Hunt bitterly complained about both the effects and diversity of types of ammunition for rifled field guns during the Civil War. The problem of the general effectiveness of rifled field guns in the Civil War was made even more dubious by the tactics used by both armies—a bastard combination of the old mass formations of Europe and the modern extended order formations still used today. Gen. Hunt, however, tempered his remarks on Civil War rifled field artillery with comments on the results of rifled artillery in another war.

Gen. Hunt was of the opinion that the reason the Germans adopted rifled field guns in 1866 was because of their observations of rifled field artillery in the Civil War. The German's rifled, breech-loading field artillery was the deciding factor leading to the defeat of the French in the Franco-Prussian war of 1870 when the French were still armed with muzzle-loading field guns. Modern field artillery is said to have been born in the Civil War and the Franco-Prussian War.

As a footnote to the history of the U.S. Army's field artillery it should be noted that some elements of the Army were still using Civil War vintage field guns when the Spanish-American War broke out in 1898. The Army had long since adopted a breech-loading rifled field gun, but the Congress did not see fit to provide enough money to build enough of the new guns to completely replace the old Civil War field guns in service.

TINTYPES PROVIDE AN INSIGHT TO THE EQUIPMENT OF THE SOLDIER

by Rick Saccone

CIVIL WAR SAMPLER

Federal uniform regulations of the Civil War period specified that things be exactly that, uniform. But, if contemporary photographs were the only record, an observer would assume that subscription to regulations was almost the exception, rather than the rule.

The men who wrote the Uniform Regulations for the Confederate Army were as optimistic as their Federal contemporaries. They, too, indicated standards that should universally be met, but, obviously couldn't be or weren't.

A sampling of 100 tintypes and ambrotypes of armed troops provided insight into what a typical cross section of actually used equipage might have been. Notwithstanding the mixture of Militia and Regular Army equipments, it is interest-ing to note that a number of soldiers seemed to prefer elements of civilian costume. In the case of weapons, however, it was not prefer-ence which was the important fac-tor, but availability. At the outset of the War both sides scrambled to arm the swelling ranks. Stocks of obsolete arms in both European and local arsenals were obtained and distrib-uted. In the south, arsenals and private contractors could not meet the demand for the new regulation patterns and the authorities, in des-peration, called upon the civilian populace to give up their private arms so that they might be recondi-tioned and issued to virtually weapon-less regiments of newly mustered militia. And so, shotguns, squirrel rifles, flintlock pistols, family heir-looms . . . all were poured into the hopper of war.

1. What every well-dressed Union infantryman was supposed to wear. A totally typical campaign uniform as issued early in the war.

2. Two dashing Confederates in their colorful battle shirts posed for this circa 1861 tintype. The battle shirt was a mark of distinction in the espirit-loaded Rebel calvary.

3. This full-plate tintype was taken a few days before the outbreak of war. This Maine Militiaman with his flintlock musket and horn-hilted dirk looks fit and able to fight . . . within three months he was dead of dysentary.

4. A classic ambrotype—a Confederate cavalryman sits next to his captor. For purposes of record and to give the Union soldier's friends at home an idea of the fierceness of his foe, the luckless Rebel still displays his Model 1849 Colt revolver.

5. When this Confederate major stood before the camera, he wore a non-regulation coat, sword and sword belt. Taken late in the war, the coat is probably a home-tailored replacement, and lacks the bullion galloons from the sleeves. His belt buckle is of the interlocking type, but bears no unit designation or state seal. His sword is a French pattern dating back to the first part of the 19th Century.

6. Colt Pocket Model in the hand of this Confederate 1st lieutenant must be, by virtue of its small caliber, considered a personal weapon.

7. Younger brother of the C.S. officer pictured above, evidently borrowed his brother's Model 1849 Colt to establish the fact, that though only an enlisted man, he was ready to fight.

5

6

7

CIVIL WAR SAMPLER

1. Here is a classic half-plate ambrotype depicting a very non-regulation Confederate artilleryman. Clad in a fine velvet-collared civilian coat, he sits astride an English "Jennifer" style saddle. He is holding a double-barrel shotgun, identical to the one illustrated above and below his picture. This specimen was made by C. Park, Birmingham, circa 1855, and imported by F. Glassick, Memphis, Tennessee.

2. Almost too young to be a soldier, this infantryman is swallowed up by a magnificent pair of cavalryman's boots. His Springfield is almost taller than he.

3. Extremely colorful Confederate militiaman's uniform embodies elements of pre-Civil War uniforms along with wartime regulations. He is armed with a Model 1840 Militia Officer's sword and a Model 1851 Colt Navy revolver.

4. Here is a photograph with a story. Both sergeant and private are wearing well-worn uniforms and are standing before a painted canvas backdrop. Beards would indicate that they have been in the field for some time. Both are equipped with a Model 1860 Colt revolver and Model 1860 light cavalry saber. Such photographs were almost always the work of an "army" photographer who specialized in such style.

5. An atypical Union cavalryman. His post 1863 issue arms indicate that this tintype was taken late in the war. His weapons are the Burnside .54 carbine, .44 Remington Model 1863 revolver and a Model 1860 Light Cavalry saber.

6. This Union Army corporal removed his Model 1863 .44 Remington from its holster and thrust it into his belt opposite his fine silver-hilted Bowie in order to present a more menacing appearance to the camera's eye.

7. When this young recruit sat for the camera, he wore a slight smirk. Why? Maybe because he had embellished his uniform with a pair of officer's straps. On the back of this photo is scratched a simple, but beautiful poem, possibly for his sweetheart at home.

8. During the war, Confederate militia-men often wore regulation uniforms. This one, however, continued to wear his pre-war organizational costume. He is armed with a Bowie-style knife and a Wesson & Leavitt revolver.

9. This dour individual is wearing a Colt Model 1849 revolver and an odd, non-regulation hat. However, similar headgear shows up repeatedly in pho-tos of Michigan enlisted men.

10. This young man is garbed in the battle shirt and blousy tie associated with Terry's Texas Rangers. His kepi is captured Federal issue; his pistol a small Springfield Arms.

paper cartridges

THE PROGENITOR OF THE MODERN CARTRIDGE, THE PAPER
CARTRIDGE WAS IN USE LONG BEFORE BRASS BECAME
THE POWDER CONTAINER. HERE IS A GUIDE FOR THESE SCARCE
AND UNUSUAL HISTORIC ITEMS.

by Charles R. Suydam

About 1540—perhaps 50 years after the first muskets (as distinguished from hand cannon) came into common use, it became evident that a faster and more convenient means of reloading would add to the efficiency of the musketeer—or add to the horror of war, depending on one's point of view.

One of the first methods used is admirably shown in the many reproductions of the illustrations from Jacob de Gheyn's book on the management of arms (Amsterdam, 1608). This was a belt, fitted across the left shoulder and under the right arm, attached to which were a number of small wooden flasks, each of which held one charge of powder. At the bottom was a pouch containing balls, and hung nearby a small flask of priming powder. Thus a measured charge, a ball and priming were readily available.

Shortly after—or perhaps at the same time—a paper packet holding both powder and ball was devised.

The powder was frequently of sufficient quantity that a small amount might be used for priming, thus eliminating the need for a priming flask. This packet was called a "cartouche" in French, signifying the *roll* of paper involved. The word became Anglicized as "cartridge"—pronounced "katt'ige" by old timers in the U.S. For about 300 years (circa 1575-1865) the cartridge remained this simple roll of strong paper containing powder and ball, and tied, glued, folded, or twisted at the ends. A small number—usually 10 to 20—were carried in a leather box at the waist of the soldier. An additional supply was available at the company area.

With the coming of breechloading arms and fulminating ignition in the second quarter of the 19th Century, two new types of non-metallic cartridge were developed: one of them was made of treated paper or other highly combustible material which, hopefully, would be consumed on ignition, to leave the breech ready

for insertion of another round. The second type, still of paper, added an ignition device—cap, tube, or pellet of fulminating material—in an attempt to devise a self-contained unit which did not require an external source of ignition.

The cartridges shown herewith cover a period extending roughly from 1780 to 1870, and are for muskets, rifles, carbines, and a few single-shot pistols. The special cartridge devised for percussion handguns, of 1850 to 1865, are not included. The earliest shown differ only in minor detail from those of the 16th Century. All specimens are believed to be original, with most from the United States, and with the period of the American Civil War predominant. The most interesting of the European specimens are those early attempts at a self-contained cartridge: these range from the French Demondion of 1831 through those used in the Franco-Prussian War of 1870-71. A few "near-paper" cartridges for capping carbines of the American Civil War era are also shown. Finally, a few bullets, cartridge packets, and other miscellany are added to complete this picture of the paper cartridge era. Notably absent are those self-contained cartridges with metallic head, rim, center, and pin fire, which constituted the loads for sporting shotguns and some rifles from about 1830; these are considered a version of the

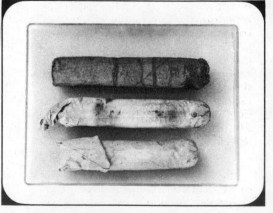

1. The first cartridge? A wooden "pulverflaschen aus Holz" (powder flask of wood) from the period of the 30 Year's War (c. 1620). Shown with it, a piece of "match" from a matchlock musket of the same period and a round ball of small caliber (for that period).

2. American cartridges from the period prior to the War of 1812 are very limited in number. These three follow the pattern of French musket cartridges used circa 1780-1810.

3. Few paper cartridges have as interesting a history as does this .69 caliber musket cartridge M1808. It is made of newspaper, and includes a testimonial for an eyewash dated "Norwich, Nov. 17, 1809." The cartridge was found with several others in a cartridge box circa War of 1812.

4. Many paper cartridges were made in the field by troops, or by citizens groups supplying a local company, or by an individual for his personal use. The five cartridges shown, generally following the military pattern, are among those whose origin it is impossible to determine.

5. Hall breechloader cartridges for the carbine of musket caliber and those for the pistol, both being .69 caliber are virtually indistinguishable: both used a .64 caliber ball, 75 to 86 grains of powder, and a red and white striped string. (From the left) The first two pictured meet the specifications for either type. (Right) Shown are two .58 caliber blanks for rifle, pistol or carbine. (Bottom) A .54 caliber pistol cartridge is shown as issued for the M1816-M1842 which took a .525 inch ball, 32 to the pound and about 50 grains of powder (M1842 pistol was loaded with 35 grains). The earlier cartridge is shown.

6. A standard European musket caliber for many years was the 18mm (.69 caliber). Shown are four typical specimens: the two on the left are of Mexican origin; those on the right, made of stouter paper, are of Swiss make.

7. The U.S. Rifle Caliber .54 M1841, known as the "Mississippi Rifle" was a favorite of both North and South. A fine rifle, but .58 caliber was standardized by the North. The first two rounds from left to right resemble some taken from a known Confederate packet but their provenance is uncertain.

primed metallic cartridge, not of the early paper cartridge.

It has been the purpose of this article to show the general development of the paper cartridge from its inception until its demise after the American Civil War. From the round ball through the various experiments in muzzle loading cylindro-conoidal bullets and the early self-igniting and capping breechloaders, the cartridge slowly developed to the centerfire cartridges of the late 19th and 20th Centuries. But history repeats, and the latest cartridges are again caseless and unprimed.

BIBLIOGRAPHY

The following works will be found of interest in the study of paper cartridges. They do not exhaust all possible sources, but in combination will be found to be of a wide range of content and period.

Logan, Herschel C. CARTRIDGES. Standard Publications, Inc. 1948.

Lewis, Col. B. R. SMALL ARMS AND AMMUNITION IN THE UNITED STATES SERVICE, Smithsonian Institute, 1956.

Greener, W. W. THE GUN AND ITS DEVELOPMENT, 1st & 9th Ed. Birmingham, 1881-1910.

Schmidt, R. DIE HANDFEUERWAFFEN. Basel, 1875-78.

Tackels, C. J. ETUDE SUR LES ARMES A FEU PORTATIVES. Paris, 1866.

Bosson, Clement. HISTOIRE ET DESCRIPTION DE L'ARME A FEU EN SUISSE (in) ARMES ANCIENNES, No. 9, Geneva, 1957.

paper cartridges

1. *These three "oldtimers" in calibers .58 and .64 appear to have been made by troops in the field: the method is quite satisfactory, but would not pass rigorous inspection in a cartridge factory. These rounds probably can be dated as belonging to the Civil War era.*

2. *Buckshot cartridges were used at least as early as 1780, when a .75 caliber Brown Bess charge had 9 buck and 154 grains of powder (10-12 grains for priming). Buck and ball loads (usually one .64 caliber ball and three buck) were listed in U.S. inventories as early as 1808. (Left to right) Buck and ball for Musket M1840; Musketoon M1847; another Musket M1840 and Buckshot for Musket M1861.*

3. *In the U.S. Army, prior to 1842, round balls were the standard projectile used in ammunition. In 1842 a caliber .685 conical ball, the Minie, was issued for the altered M1842 Rifled Musket and the M1842 Musketoon. (Left to right) A round ball musketoon load caliber .69 circa 1840; a M1855 elongated ball round for the 1842 Rifled Musket, and an unidentified .64 caliber elongated round, probably for the 1842.*

4. *Among the more successful bullets used during the Civil War era was the Williams patent "clean-out" bullet. This round had a dished zinc washer attached to the base of the bullet; upon firing the disc was flattened and forced into the rifling grooves, effectively scraping fouling from the bore. Early loadings are identified by salmon or blue outer wrappers. Later on they were made with no special color coded wrappings.*

5. *The longest elongated ball cartridge for the M1842 Rifled Musket and Musketoon used a 640 grain bullet, caliber .685 with a wood plug in the base. Later on the M1855 load was adopted using a 725 grain hollow base bullet. By 1865 a 695 grain hollow base bullet was made standard. (Left to right) An 1859 Frankford Arsenal .69 caliber musketoon cartridge; a M1855 model with the 725 grain ball, and the 695 grain bulleted cartridge, along with bullets for each model.*

6. *Firearms of the Confederacy are rare and highly desirable to the collector: far more uncommon are the cartridges issued for them. (Left to right) A caliber .69 buck and ball load from New Orleans Arsenal, and the unusual caliber .69 ball load from Selma Arsenal.*

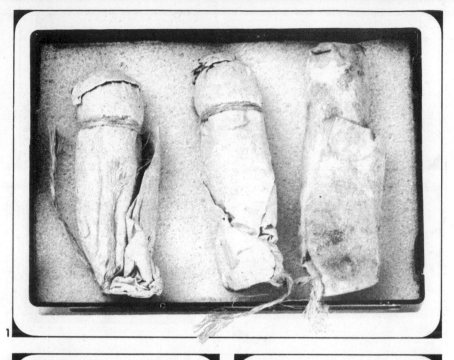

1

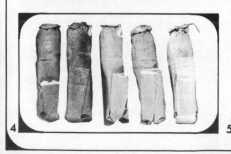

2

3

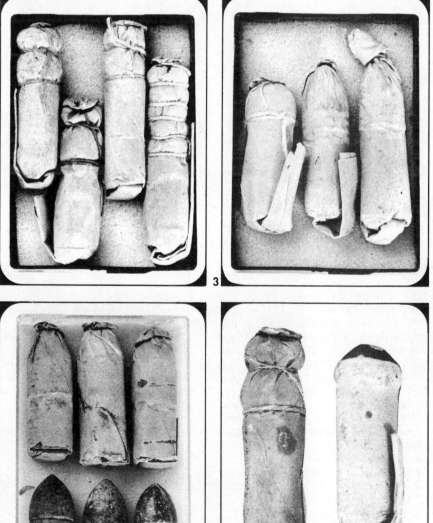

4

5

6

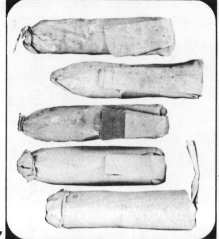

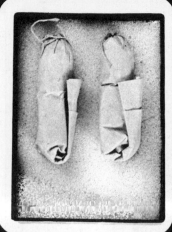

7. Shown here are five examples of the cartridge for the Rifled Musket and Rifle, caliber .58 (Top to Bottom) The first specimen is similar to those made at the Macon Arsenal, CSA, as is the second cartridge; but once removed from a packet, accurate dating is practically impossible. The third round has an unexplained gray inner wrapper. The fourth and fifth are unknowns.

8. One of the rivals of the Gatling in the Civil War was the Union Machine Gun, which used steel "cartridges" loaded via hopper into a revolving drum and fired through a single barrel. The cartridges were charged with special .58 pistol-carbine loads, taking a 582 grain Minie ball or a 525 grain Williams patent bullet. A standard "top hat" musket cap was placed on a nipple in the hollow base of the steel "chamber" to provide ignition.

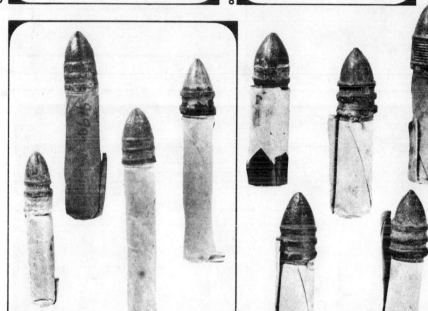

9. Robert Chadwick is known to have been a maker of cartridges for Colt's revolvers and other arms. The first two cartridges shown (left to right) have been identified as "Chadwick's patent", but no such patent is shown in Stockbridge's "Digest of Patents"—it may be that he designed cartridge-making machinery. The third and fourth rounds are linen cartridges for the Sharps' caliber .52 and Starr's caliber .54 rifles and carbines.

10. The slant-breech Sharps was one of the first reasonably successful American breechloading rifles, paper cartridges for them are quite rare. (Left to right) A .36 caliber, with paper pasted ball and three .44 caliber rounds, all with tied paper.

11. Although the Sharps linen cartridge is still available to collectors, the paper cartridges of military caliber are quite rare. Shown is a commercial (post-Civil War?) specimen with blue tissue paper base; two carbine rounds, probably military c. 1861; a rifle round, possibly pre-Civil War.

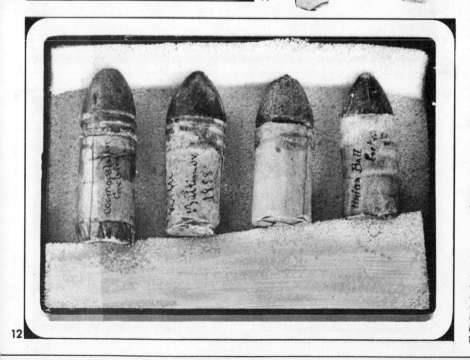

12. Among the rarest of cartridges used in the American Civil War are the combustible proprietary cartridges made up for use in the various breechloading capping carbines used in small numbers by the North. (Left to right) The Cosmopolitan (Union) carbine, the Merrill rifle, the Merrill carbine and a linen cartridge for the Cosmopolitan.

paper cartridges

1. The date of the Hingham, Massachusetts, Arsenal has been debated: it may have operated in the early 19th Century, or during the Civil War period —the former seems most likely. In any event, these distinctive .69 caliber rounds with their partially exposed ball are attributed to Hingham Arsenal.

2. The British Enfield musket Pattern 1851 utilized a .675 inch elongated, lubricated ball. This was the cartridge that was reported to have been one of the causes of the Sepoy Rebellion in India on May 10, 1857. Rumor had it that the lubricant was a mixture of beef tallow and lard (the Moslems consider the pig unclean; the Hindus revere the cow as a sacred animal; biting the bullet was the recommended instruction to open the cartridge). Variations are shown.

3. British smooth bore pistols used a round ball throughout their existence —as did those of other nations. (Left to right) The specimens shown are .75 caliber musket; .62 caliber carbine; the third round is not British but Austrian made for use in the 17.2mm Armee pistol, Model corrige 1777/05. The last cartridge is a British blank.

4. The story of Sir Joseph Whitworth and his famed hexagonal-bored rifle of 1854 is well known. This collection includes (from the top) a .45 caliber Whitworth hexagonal cartridge; a M1862 .45-70-530 military cartridge and three specimens of the M1853 .577 caliber cartridges. Bullets are a hexagonal with greased wad in loading tube, two "bare" bullets and one paper patched bullet.

5. Among the combustible cartridges used in the early capping breech-loaders were the thread-reinforced "skin" cartridges by Eley of London. Shown is a wrapped cartridge for the .577 Prince carbine (bolt action, experimental, 1855), an outer wrapper, a (damaged) cartridge, and a cartridge part way out of wrapper.

6. Another combustible cartridge was developed for the Terry, Greene and similar capping breechloading carbines. Following one British practice, the hollow base balls were of smooth exterior; a greased felt wad sealed the rear end of the chamber; after firing, this wad was pushed forward ahead of the succeeding round to help clean the bore.

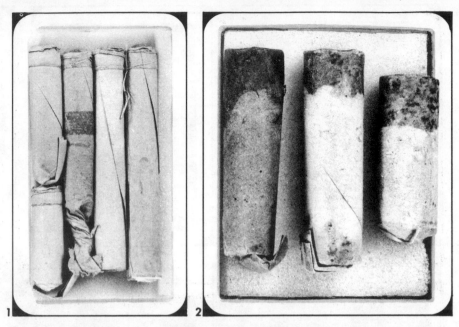

1

2

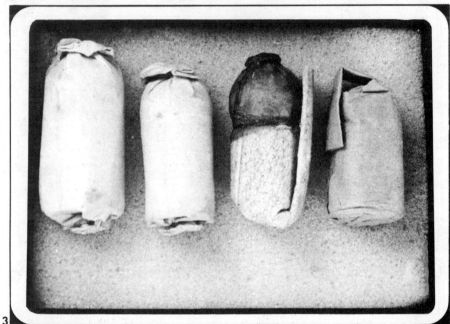

3

4

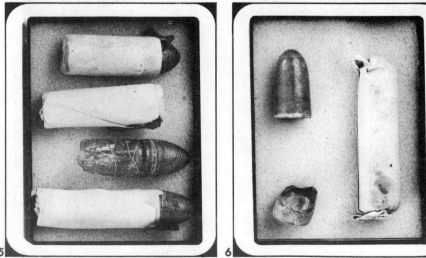

5

6

7. Among the unusual paper cartridges to be found are: (left to right) an unknown .75 caliber Minie pattern musket; a caliber .70 Austrian pattern circa 1861 (possibly attributed to Civil War contract muskets), and a caliber .75 French pattern of 1784.

8. Two other European rarities: a Model 1857 French infantry cartridge and a round for the Augustin (Austrian?) carbine with linen-wrapped ball and paper powder chamber.

9. Shown here are five cartridges for the Chassepot rifle Model of 1866 in 11mm caliber. (Left to right) An early all paper, one-piece case; two-piece case of paper; two-piece paper and linen, all ball cartridges. The fourth cartridge may be the first armor-piercing cartridge for small arms. At the top is a paper and linen blank.

10. All combustible cartridges for long arms devised during the Civil War are very scarce, from left to right: Johnson and Dow (skin) for the .574 British Enfield; same for the U.S. caliber .58 rifle; Bartholow's patent (powder mixed with shellac, attached to bullet with silk netting) in .58 caliber and a .56 caliber paper from Colt's cartridge works for their rifles.

11. The Prussian counterpart of the Chassepot was its "secret weapon" of 1846, the famed Dreyse needle gun. (Top to bottom) at top is a cartridge from an old European collection marked "No. 1 Prussien Zundnadel-gewehr 1841". Five or six models were made from 14 to 16mm, several are shown. Top right is the rare 10.5mm Schilling needle gun cartridge made for the Grand Duchy of Hesse-Darmstadt and an empty Dreyse case ready for loading.

12. The Requa volley gun—multiple barrels in a horizontal row, fired by one ignition—used an outside-primed metallic cartridge which could be reloaded. Available for loading or reloading was a Hotchkiss patent (seamless skin) cartridge; the specimen shown has lost much of its original "skin", but retains original bullet and compressed powder charge.

paper cartridges

1. This miscellany shows from left to right: (left upper) what is thought to be an unknown sabot-held ball of Dreyse type; (left, lower) a Dreyse ball and sabot; an original Dreyse military cartridge and two later Dreyse cartridges. The cartridge second from right is labeled "60-65-625 For Pruss. Needle Gun Pat'd 1836 B. V. Mod. 65" and could have been made for Bannerman's.

2. Not to be outdone, the Italians transformed their 17.6mm muzzle loaders to a needle gun pattern in 1865. This was the first of many arms developed by Lt. Col. of Artillery Salvatore Carcano between that year and 1896. This gun was of a turnbolt type.

3. Unlike the bolt actions, the 1867 Swedish Hagstrom was a complicated arm with a dropping block action like the Peabody. A locking lever on the side of the action served to actuate it and the cocking piece was similar to the Dreyse shotguns. The round is similar to the French Chassepot.

4. The end of the paper cartridge came in two ways: in Europe, via the self-igniting paper cartridges such as the Chassepot and the Dreyse, which were replaced by the capped metallic cartridges—the French Gras and the German Mauser. In the United States, the intermediate steps were rubber (as used by the Smith carbine), metal foil and paper, and unprimed metallic cartridges. Four variations of the metal foil and paper cartridges for the Smith are shown.

5. Continuing the paper-foil cartridges (left to right) are: the odd and rare Jackson patent, made of thin iron and paper; the rest are for the Gallagher carbine and are similar to the rounds for the Smith carbine.

6. Shown here (left to right) are: .52 and .54 caliber brass Gallagher cartridges; a tinned case .54 brass Gallagher, and two variations of the rubber case for the Smith carbine. The rubber case was quite impractical and it has been reported that a case of leather was made, but remains unconfirmed. These rounds shown are examples of the final developments in unprimed cartridges.

1

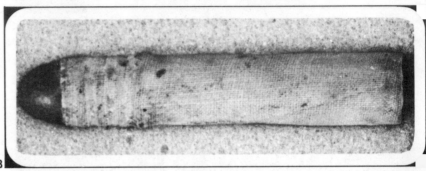

2

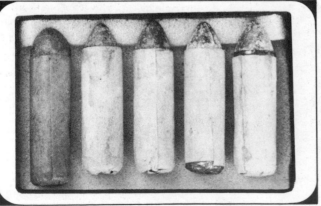

3

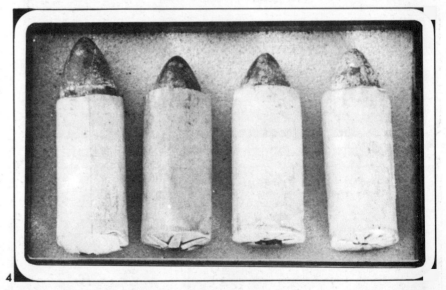

4

5

6

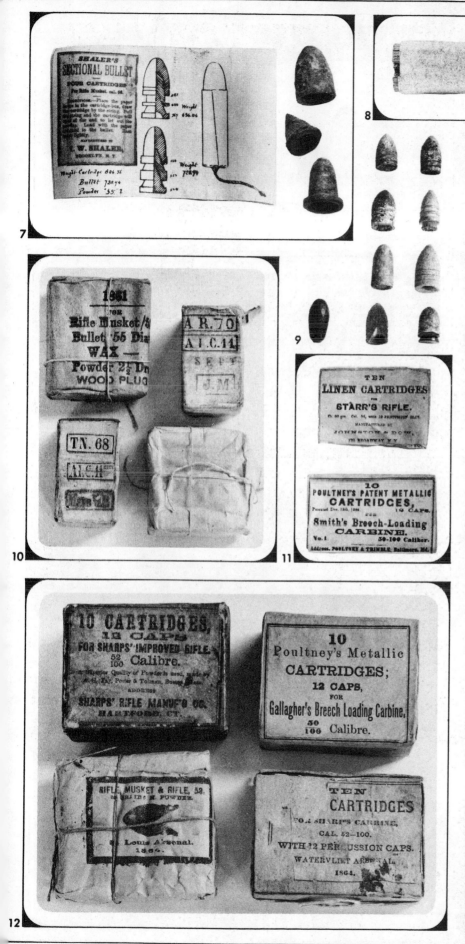

7. One of the secret weapons of the Civil War was Shaler's sectional bullet for the rifle musket, caliber .58. The label reads: Shaler's SECTIONAL BULLET four cartridges for rifle musket, cal. .58. Directions: Place the paper box in the cartridges box, draw the cartridge by the string. Pull the string and the cartridge will open at the end to let out the powder. Load with paper attached to the bullet. Ram home lightly. Manufactured by I. W. Shaler, Brooklyn, N.Y." Additional notes indicate two patterns of bullet, one with total weight of 636.06 grains; the other, 720.94 grains.

8. In the ninth edition of W. W. Greener's famed "The Gun and Its Development" a cross-section of the Demondion breech-loading rifle of 1831 is shown. Briefly, it is similar to a trap door Springfield, except that the breech closes at the very end of the barrel and is locked in place by a lever similar to the Westley Richards "monkey tail" design. The round is inserted with the priming tube in the six o'clock position and by pulling the trigger the hammer strikes against this tube, igniting the cartridge. This 16mm cartridge may be the first self-igniting cartridge.

9. Bullets of the period of the paper cartridge. (Top row, left to right) .56 Colt rifle, paper cartridge, solid base; .56 Colt rifle, skin cartridge, hollow base; .69 caliber ball, 625 grain, for rifled Musketoon M1855. (Middle row) Bullet for Sharps paper cartridge, caliber .54 for .52 caliber rifle; .577 Prichett bullet, clay plug, for British Enfield rifle; this specimen taken from salvaged Confederate blockade runner; ball, caliber .69 for M1842 altered, 730 grains. (Bottom row) Unknown for some type of Dreyse cartridge; sectioned caliber .58 Minie showing hollow base; Williams patent clean-out bullet.

10. Packets of paper cartridges. (Top row, left) British issue, made for the Pattern 1853 Rifle Musket; (right) a pack of French Chassepot cartridges, 1870. (Bottom, left) Chassepot cartridges, 1868; (right) a packet of U.S. issue caliber .58 rifle cartridges, c.1861.

11. Packets of cartridges for capping breechloaders. (Top) Johnston and Dow linen cartridges for Starr's rifle, c. 1863-1864. (Bottom) Brass foil and paper for Smith's carbine.

12. Packets of cartridges for capping breechloaders (Top row, left) Sharps linen by Sharps Rifle Mfg. Co. c. 1863-1864; (right) brass and paper for the Gallagher carbine, c. 1864. (Bottom left) "Rifle, Musket & Rifle" caliber .58 by St. Louis Arsenal, 1864; (right) Sharps linen by Watervliet.

PREPARATION FOR WAR · 1861

Shell and Solid Shell

Filling & Finishing Projectiles

The Union Shell

Pouring in the Lead

The manufacture of artillery ammunition. (engraving from Harpers)

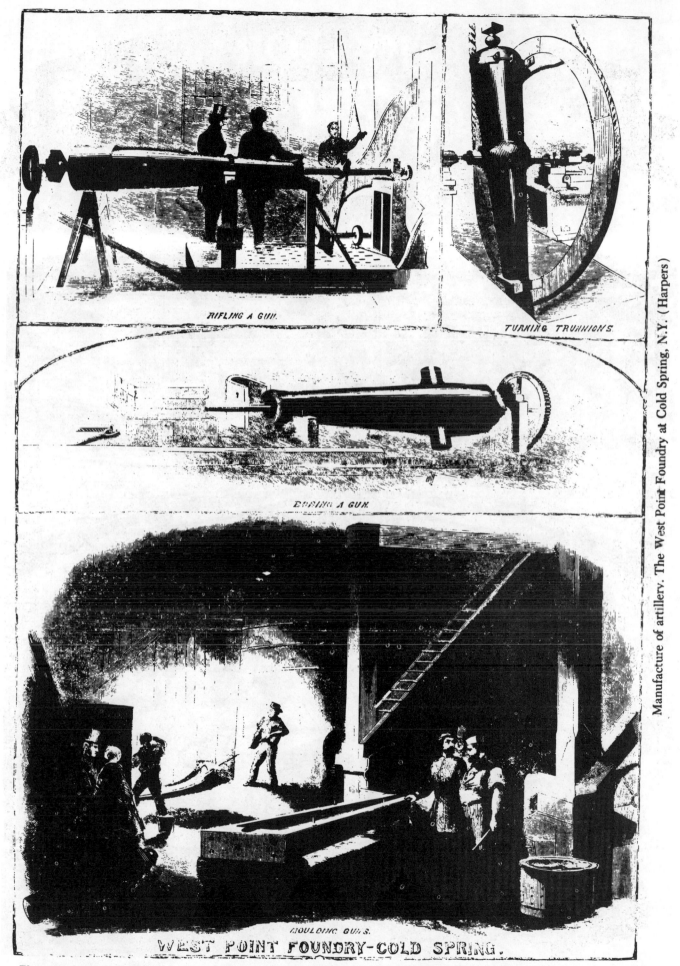

RIFLING A GUN.

TURNING TRUNNIONS.

BORING A GUN.

MOULDING GUNS.

WEST POINT FOUNDRY-COLD SPRING.

Manufacture of artillery. The West Point Foundry at Cold Spring, N.Y. (Harpers)

The manufacture of artillery at West Point Foundry in Cold Springs, N.Y. (engraving from Harpers)

The manufacture of ammunition. Filling cartridges at the arsenal in Watertown, Mass. (engraving from Harpers)

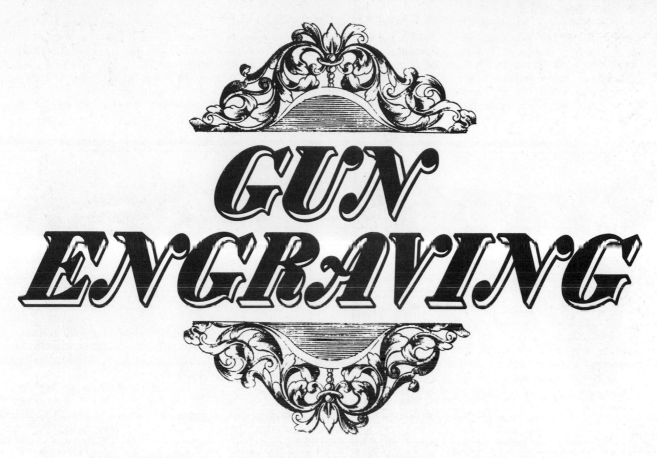

GUN ENGRAVING

THE HISTORY OF 400 YEARS OF EUROPEAN CRAFTSMANSHIP

by R.L. Wilson

The history of gun engraving in Europe covers over 400 years, encompassing the work of literally thousands of craftsmen and a myriad of styles and techniques. Such factors as nationalism, religious persecution, trends in art and design, the brilliance of individual gunmakers and engravers, and the whims and tastes of noblemen and rich merchants are all major ingredients in this broad field of concentration.

At first the Germans, then the Italians, then the French, and then the English were the dominant national schools in arms decoration. Today the Belgians, Germans, and Austrians are in command. In numbers of engravers they exceed the total of those in all other European countries by at least threefold.

The present article concentrates on the major schools, with a collection of illustrations drawn from major museum and private holdings of European arms. Many of the photographs wer made by the team of Bruce Pendleton and Merrill Lindsay, and have generously been made available by them for use here. Most of these arms are masterpieces worthy of exhibit in any major museum of art. Several are in the finest American collection of European arms, the Metropolitan Museum of Art, New York City.

The collector whose specialty is the so-called "high art" European firearm has many distinguished predecessors of like interest. Among the pioneer collectors in this field were the Emperor Charles V, King Henry VIII, the French King Louis XIII, and such millionaires as William Randolph Hearst and Clarence H. Mackay. Whereas in American antique arms, most of the best pieces now belong to private collectors, the vast majority of the finest in European high art firearms are in museum collections, mainly in Europe. This makes the study of the field easier for the enthusiast, but often frustrating (and costly) if he intends to build a comprehensive collection. Unfortunately, the field is not even conveniently studied through published works of reference.

As in American firearms, the vast majority of collector's books deal with details of construction, histories of makers, marks, and so forth. Only a few works cater to the connoisseur whose love is decoration. The key book, and the only comprehensive source, is John F. Hayward's classic "The Art of the Gunmaker." This two-volume study is complete through circa 1820, encompassing both European and American arms decoration. Other important books are Torsten

GUN ENGRAVING

Lenk's "The Flintlock," Howard L. Blackmore's "Royal Sporting Guns at Windsor," Merrill Lindsay's "100 Great Guns," Leonid Tarassuk's "Antique European and American Firearms at the Hermitage Museum," and Stephen V. Grancsay's two works on master French Gunsmith's designs.

The reader should also consult the 1972 issue of the "Guns & Ammo Annual," to contrast "The History of Gun Engraving in America" with the present article.

Before presenting this history of gun engraving in Europe, it should be pointed out that the article concen-

trates on the major schools of decoration. Thus it has not been possible to pursue the work of the Scandinavians, Swiss, Spanish, and Dutch; or to cover that of the English and the Belgians in the 16th and 17th Centuries. Russia receives a brief mention only.

Matchlock firearms with embellishments are rare, since the matchlock ignition system saw its primary service on military weapons. Fancy wheellock arms are common in comparison to the matchlock, one reason for which is the fact that the latter mechanism was considered beneath the dignity of the rich and titled. However, such tech-

niques as etching, engraving, chiselling, damascening, and applied ornaments are all known to have been used on those deluxe matchlocks that were made.

The matchlock musket pictured is attributed to Dutch gunmakers, and dates from the late 16th Century. The stock inlays of pearl and brass are the main decoration, with only light engraving (somewhat coarse at that) on the barrel and lock. Some of the mother of pearl inlays are themselves engraved.

The Dutch, Italians, and Germans were the major producers of the limited supply of elaborate matchlock

firearms. Italian gunmakers are credited with the earliest known fancy matchlocks, and these date circa 1530 to 1540.

From the collection of the late Joe Kindig Jr., piece No. 1 is believed to have once been in the "Cabinet of Arms" of the French monarch King Louis XIII. The King's Cabinet was composed primarily of richly decorated weapons, among them several matchlocks.

Except for military use, the matchlock followed the route of dinosaurs by the early 17th Century, and deluxe specimens nearly always predate circa 1625.

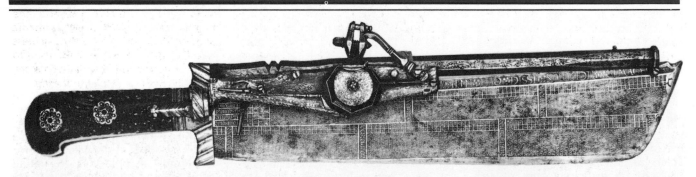

In 1546, a master etcher combined his skills with those of a knifemaker and a gunmaker to produce this unusual combination hunting knife, perpetual ecclesiastical calendar, and wheellock pistol. Now in the collection of the Metropolitan Museum of Art, the piece is an outstanding example of etched decoration. The lock, wheel, barrel and blade are profusely etched in minute detail.

Decoration on early European arms was a carryover from the embellishments lavished on contemporary armor. Of the various techniques employed on the metal, etching was the most prevalent in the 16th century,

followed by damascening and engraving, repoussé relief chiselling, and punched and applied ornaments.

The 1546 date proves the lock on this weapon, of German manufacture, to be an early specimen of the wheellock system. At present, the earliest known wheellock arms are Italian made and date from the first quarter of the 16th Century. In this period armor was still flourishing, and etching was the most common form of artistic decoration in use on the deluxe suits.

The Germans are considered to have been the major producers of

wheellock firearms, followed by the Italians. But the use of etching was commonly shared by European makers of wheellock guns, including on the type known as the Tschinke.

Early wheellocks, which were costly and considered in the province of the rich and the titled, were normally quite elaborate. Barrels on these arms are an important indicator in determining a date of manufacture; early wheellock arms (as represented in this article) featured profusely decorated barrels. Some barrels were even made in the form of an architectural column, the muzzle terminating in a relief-chiselled capital.

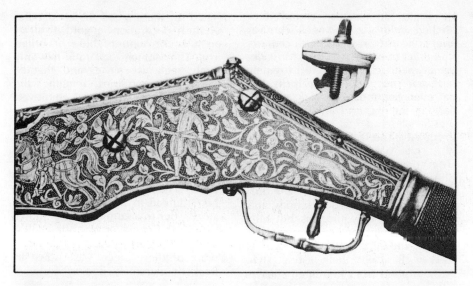

Augsburg was the city of manufacture for this very elaborate metal-stocked wheellock double-barrel pistol. It dates from circa 1560, and is now in the Musee de la Porte de Hal, Brussels. Metal stocks or metal-overlaid wooden stocks were not uncommon on wheellock pistols, particularly those of Germanic origin. The use of metal, mainly for structural advantages, provided the etcher (as seen here), the relief chiseller, and the engraver more space for their decorations.

The etcher of this pistol used a vine and leaf scroll pattern on the stock, with the central theme a mounted huntsman, followed by a footman bugling for game. Arabesques and portrait heads, also etched, appear on the bulbous butt. The barrel is profusely etched in a ribbon and scroll design. With the substitution of a military or non-hunting motif, the etched style of this pistol can be observed on various armors of noblemen from the 16th century.

Charles V, Holy Roman Emperor, had several outstanding decorated firearms in his collection, most of them made specifically at his behest. Some specimens are known with his motto "plus ultra," the double headed Imperial eagle, the columns of Hercules with the Imperial crown, and the collar of the Golden Fleece, all incorporated within a profusely etched regal decor. He was a pioneer connoisseur of fine firearms, and his reign covered the years 1519 to 1596.

The middle and late 16th Century was a period of extremely elaborate weapons. The Germans were then in a position of leadership, both in making guns and in decorating them, as this pistol clearly demonstrates.

Peter Pech of Munich made this double-barrel wheellock pistol of circa 1553, from the collection of the late Joe Kindig Jr. Pech had the distinction of working for the Spanish King Phillip II, and for the Emperor Charles V.

The piece illustrated is not one of his fanciest, but is shown here due to its use of pierced ornamentation, and of etching and a primitive sort of relief chiselling. The wheel covers appear to have been etched, while the barrel is partially relief chiselled. The wheel at the left is encircled at its bottom half with a pierced and lightly engraved external spring. Not all of the 16th Century wheellock arms were coated with fancy frills.

The major producers of elaborate weapons in the wheellock period were the Germanic cities of Munich, Augsburg, Nuremberg, and Dresden, and the Italian city of Brescia. Each featured an individual style but it is important to note that there are maverick specimens which sometimes challenge the most knowledgeable experts. This is mainly due to emigrating gunmakers and gun decorators, and to others who supplied major gun parts (locks and barrels) for export, sometimes these already bearing decorations.

Germanic styles have been and still are a major force in gunmaking. In the 16th and 17th Centuries this influence was especially prevalent. The popular sport of hunting and the wealth of the princes in the Germanic principalities gave the arms business in these districts great impetus. On decorated weapons by these makers, the hunt was a frequent theme.

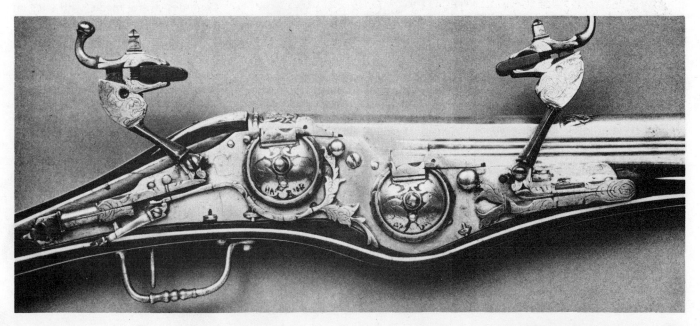

Casper Spät (active circa 1630 to circa 1665) is credited with the exquisite high-relief chiselling on this masterpiece of gunmaking now in the Metropolitan Museum of Art. On the lock are blued mythological figures contrasted against a gilt background of sea and sky. The barrel was chiselled in a ribbed, scroll and strapwork moti , again with a gilt background. The talents of an engraver were needed on many of the intricate ivory and bone stock inlays. Elias becker was the stockmaker; his theme was of mannerist (an art style of circa 1520—1590) beasts and musicians, engulfed in scroll and decorative borders.

The Spät-Becker gun represents the most involved and elaborate firearms decorations of all time. Custom order guns of this period (circa 1590 to circa 1665) are even known to have been made with silver and gold overlaid stocks, mounted in diamonds and other precious stones.

In the 16th century, engraved or etched lockplates of wheellock rifles were uncommon. In the 17th century, the exact opposite was true. Most deluxe wheellock rifles were extremely elaborate not only on the locks, but all over. Some of this work, particularly by the masters Daniel and Emanuel Sadeler and Spät was exceptional in quality. The Dukes of Bavaria were the chief patrons of these artisans. The combined period of activity for the Sadelers and Spät was from circa 1594 through circa 1665. Their output was from Munich workshops, and included not only firearms but hilts for edged weapons, mountings for purses, and all-metal boxes known as caskets. Basically, their distinct style was inspired from imprinted sheaves of engraved ornaments dating circa 1550 to circa 1575, primarily by the artist Etienne Delaune, a Frenchman. The extremely elaborate masterworks by the Sadelers and Spät were quite popular with the wealthy and titled. That these workmen had large shops with assistants is evident from the number of examples of their work extant.

A major decorative detail characteristic of this celebrated Munich group is the contrast of relief-chiselled steel against a background in gold. Their contemporaries generally relied on the applied or inlaid relief or flush decoration in gold or silver on a background of blue or bright iron. The Munich technique has only rarely seen use since, and that of their contemporaries remains the major deluxe method employed through modern times.

Stock decorations of ivory, bone, and exotic woods were prevalent on luxury German-made arms of the 16th and most of the 17th Centuries. French, English, and Italian gunmakers indulged in similarly embellished stocks, but to a comparatively limited extent. The engraver was often called upon to add his skills on the stockwork of these pieces—as shown by Becker's extremely fine example.

Coats of arms on the cheekpieces of hunting rifles was a frequently employed device. Classical mythology, hunting, and military themes were popular and are most often observed with scroll, strapwork, and floral encirclements and borders. In quality and design such stock decorations are regarded by connoisseurs as among the finest of Germanic decorative arts of the period. As with the contemporary workmen in the decoration of metals on firearms, the stockmakers seldom signed their pieces and only a few have been identified by name.

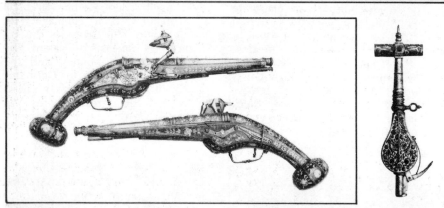

A French master gunmaker of circa 1560-1570 made this fine pair of deluxe wheellock pistols, now in the Metropolitan Museum of Art. The Lockplates are engraved and gilded, and the barrels are relief-chiselled iron with relief-cut figures in silver. The wheels have pierced covers and the stocks are inlaid with finely engraved staghorn and brass wire. Note the relief-chiselled iron details on the lock, including the cock. The combination spanner/powder flask was decorated to match. Its relief-chiselled floral and vine design matches that bordering the center section of each barrel.

Wheellock firearms were known early to French gunmakers and were preferred by the French nobility. As with guns by Germanic and Italian makers, and the other major European manufacturers, French matchlocks were seldom made in deluxe style, the fancy treatment being mainly lavished on wheellocks and successor lock types.

In studying the earliest known French wheellocks a group of combination arms are key examples. One of these, from the mid-16th Century, is a mace and pistol, decorated superbly with gilt bronze and silver, with a relief-chiselled shaft. The quality of the relief chiselling and chasing has been referred to by expert John F. Hayward as executed "in a manner that could not be bettered on the finest French silver of the time." Unfortunately, surviving examples of decorated French firearms of the 17th Century are far less frequently seen than their Germanic contemporaries.

A few French wheellock holster pistols of the late 16th and early 17th Centuries were made with elegant stocks of iron, decorated in gold and silver relief designs. The inlay was the same basic technique as employed by gun engravers of today, with undercutting of the iron and hammering of the soft metal into the resultant crevices. The French gun decoration of the 16th and early 17th Centuries was usually done in low or high relief.

The pistols illustrated here offer an exciting combination of engraving, piercing, silver inlay, relief chiselling, and chasing. They represent some of the most exceptional French work of the 16th Century, and for that reason are hardly typical of that country's deluxe manufacture. But they are important examples partly because they illustrate so many important techniques of the craft called for in the decoration of firearms during the 16th and 17th Centuries.

On the lockplate of this wheel-lock fowling piece is the signature of the gunmaker: *Jean Henequin a Metz, 1621.* On the buttplate are the arms of King Louis XIII of France. The stock is inlaid with engraved silver and the lock and barrel are relief chiselled and engraved. The importance of the Henequin gun is that it shows the influence of the French gunmakers of the 17th Century on their contemporaries, particularly in Alsace, Lorraine, and the southern part of the Netherlands. Metz is in the province of Lorraine, bordering both France and Germany. All the features of this piece are French in style, but internally the lock was made in the German fashion.

The cock is of quite unusual design, relief chiselled as a human figure terminating in grotesque animal motifs. The cock spring is finely chased, as is the dragon on the right side of the wheel. Decoration of the wheel and the lockplate is a very shallow engraving with animal, human figure, and scroll and floral designs. The quality of the lock and

wheel engravings does not compare with that which appeared in the important French gun engravers' pattern books published circa 1650-1660 by Marcou and Thuraine and Le Hollandois.

In the 17th Century, the French gunmakers took over the position of eminence which had previously been dominated by the Germans and, to a lesser extent, the Italians. Paris was the center of the French mastery, and the encouragement of the royal gun collector, Louis XIII (1610-1642) was influential in the emerging French dominance.

Special privileges were granted to gunmakers by the French monarchy; of particular significance beginning in 1608 was the allocation of rooms on the ground floor of the Louvre to exceptional craftsmen and artists with royal patronage. Among these individuals was generally a gunmaker. The first of the craft was Marin le Bourgeois, and among his successors were Francois Duclos and Bertrand Piraube.

Francois Duclos of the Louvre Galleries made this exquisite combination matchlock-wheel-lock gun in 1636. King Louis XIII added the piece to his personal arms collection and it bore inventory No. 151. The stock is of ebony, mounted with silver wire and engraved silver inlays, and with a gilt bronze figure

of Atlanta beneath the shooter's chin. The weapon is now in the Musee de l'Armee, Paris.

One of history's most distinguished arms collectors was Louis XIII. His collection was rich in the most elaborately decorated weapons, though he keenly appreciated mechanical details as well. His Highness was known

to have enjoyed taking apart, cleaning, and reassembling his guns. Known as the *Cabinet d'Armes,* Louis' collection of over 330 weapons was first inventoried in the year 1673.

Although Paris and the Louvre Galleries formed the hub of French gunmaking in the 17th Century, there were several master craftsmen in such provinces as Brittany, Normandy, Alsace, Lorraine, Burgundy, Dauphine Picardy, and Champagne. Much of the talent in these areas had come from Paris, usually to escape religious persecution of those who practiced the Huguenot faith.

Early 17th Century French wheellocks, of which the above gun is an exceptional example, are quite varied in their ornamentation. Metal inlays were part of the stock decoration of many guns, as on the Duclos piece illustrated. Note the delicately engraved gargoyle, floral and animal motifs, and the gracefully-inlaid silver wire forms. The engraving could have been from the hand of a specialist in decorating soft metals, or from a gun engraver normally working in steel. Such stock inlays as engraved staghorn and mother of pearl had been largely dropped by French gun craftsmen early in the 17th Century. Stocks after about 1610 emphasized the use of silver or brass wire inlays contrasting against plain wood. The gilt bronze Atlanta is quite unusual; its manufacture called on the skills of casters and chasers in bronze.

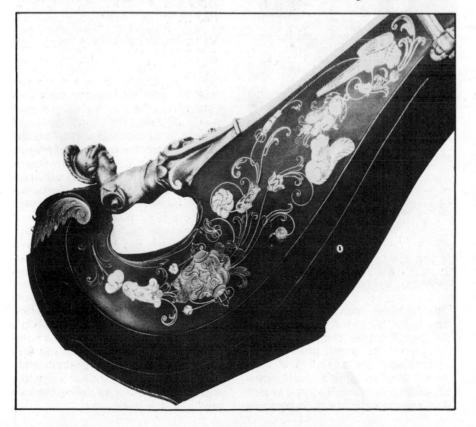

GUN ENGRAVING

The intricately pierced, chiselled, and engraved decoration on this superb pair of wheellock pistols immediately identifies the work as Italian, and more specifically, Brescian. Dated approximately 1650, the pistols are marked *Lazarino Cominazzo* on the barrels, and the mark of *Giovanni Antonio Gavacciolo* inside the locks.

The distinctive North Italian style of decoration as represented here appeared in a wide degree of quantity and quality—the most and the best coming from Brescia and its environs. Brescia's leadership was secure, with one of its minor rivals the city of Naples, which in itself offered a distinctive style. Brescia was already a major gunmaking district by the last quarter of the 16th Century. The use of pierced steel tracery work on the stocks was in fashion there by the 1580s; and at this early period they were already producing high art firearms. The style peaked from circa 1630 through circa 1700.

In the second half of the 17th Century, relief chiselling, often in the round, developed in the extreme. These frequently overdone decorations represent a decline in the Brescian style. The pistols illustrated (Metropolitan Museum of Art col-

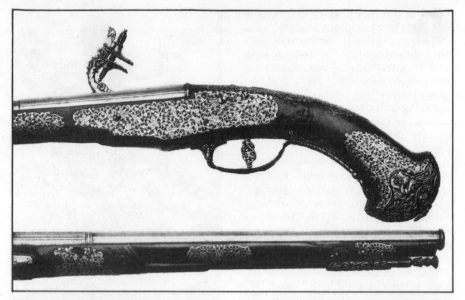

lection) are among the finest specimens of the best period of Brescian artistry. Fortunately for posterity, Brescian gunmakers permitted some decorated arms to carry the signature of the engraver; a practice unusual in European arms decoration to this day.

The Italian preference for pierced and engraved iron stock inlays (silver or gilt bronze also sometimes employed) has its most direct contrast to the German preference for bone. Both often required the engraver's skill to decorate the inlays. To the

connoisseur of European arms, a fine Brescian pistol ranks among the most desirable examples of Europe's mastery of the decorated weapon. One detail of artistic importance is that stockmakers carefully cut out the wood precisely to accept each tracery inlay. Buyers of fine guns circa the 1580s to circa 1700 recognized the great Brescian mastery and eagerly purchased specimens for their armories. The mechanisms used on these arms were wheellock, and later snaphaunce and flintlock.

The French introduced the flintlock early in the 1600s, and had dropped the wheellock almost entirely after the mid-17th Century. The early flintlock arms made in France were relatively plain, but in the 1630s and 1640s decorations of high relief chiselling came into evidence. By the 1650s this elaborate decor had reached a norm on deluxe guns of French manufacture.

Pictured is a three-barrel pistol of circa 1670, with silver wire stock inlays and engraved and relief-chiselled lock and hammer. The attribution is French and the gun is in the Tower of London Armouries.

An important factor which influenced the widespread preference for the French style in gunmaking and decoration was the pattern book of gun designs, one of the most important being that by Francois Marcou (1657). Such books were largely collections of work which had already been used on guns.

Another such book, that of Thomas Picquot (circa 1638) pictures pommels in a sculptured mode which became fashionable on French pistols in the period circa 1625 to 1650. These were made in varied materials and generally depicted animal motifs.

Otherwise the stocks of the period were quite plain, but elegant, while the locks, barrels, and mounts featured gold damascening of a very delicate quality.

Still another pattern book contributing to the prevalence of French style and decor in the 17th Century

was that depicting work by master gunsmiths Thuraine and Le Hollandais, (circa 1660; see No. 12). Themes were in the main animals, birds, grotesques, and the hunt. At a later date, classical history and mythological devices joined these themes in popularity. Lockplates of the period were flat and thus suited for engraving.

In the mid-17th Century the flat surfaces gave way to rounded ones, due to changes in the fashion as developed in Paris. Again pattern books of decorations served as a vehicle in spreading the new approach to gun decor—relief chisellings generally replacing the flat work of the engraver. Rather quickly, relief chiselling became the style throughout the gunmaking centers of Europe; previously that approach had been largely confined to specific areas.

The specimen illustrated, having the curved lock, shows both styles: The flat engraved design of a cupid and floral scrolls and borders, and the relief-chiselled combination of scrolls, leafs, grotesques, and a portrait bust. Sideplates of this period took on rich and often graceful forms, and many beautiful examples appear in the Marcou and Thuraine and Le Hollandais books.

This specimen plate is from the ornamental pattern book engraved by C. Jacquinet from gun designs used by the master French gunsmiths Thuraine and Le Hollandois. The initial date of publication was circa 1660. Stephen V. Grancsay authored a facsimile edition of these prints published in 1950 under the title: "Master Gunsmiths' Designs."

The Grancsay book later appeared in a greatly expanded form, entitled: "Master French Gunsmiths' Designs (1970)." Both volumes are important to the collector and are interesting and valuable aids to the modern gun engraver. The original pattern books occupied key roles in the dissemination of ideas to arms engravers in France and in several other gunmaking centers of Europe. The rare plate pictured here is in the Grancsay Library; it should be compared to illustrations No. 11, 12, 16, and 18.

One of the greatest of all French gunmakers was Bertrand Piraube, who was appointed to the galleries at the Louvre in 1670. Piraube made this magnificent fowling piece in 1658 for presentation by King Louis XIV to the first Duke of Richmond, an English nobleman. The barrel is chased solid silver. Motifs on the relief-chiselled steel lock are Jupiter with an eagle, dolphins, fame, and Mars in a chariot drawn by lions. On the stock are silver wire and engraved plaque inlays. The weapon is part of the Tower of London Armouries collection. Guns by Piraube are important in the study of European arms decoration because his shop was a style setter during nearly all of its period of production, and the Piraube workshop not only signed but usually dated its output.

The French gunmakers, of whom Piraube for over 50 years was foremost, set the fashion in European arms design and decoration from circa 1670 to circa 1770. Important vehicles in dissemination of the French style were pattern books from Paris by Claude Simonin and Nicholas Guerard. The first book of Simonin appeared in 1691 and the irst of Guerard appeared in the first quarter of the 18th Century. On the whole, 17th Century ornamentation featured delicate engravings, while the 18th Century style featured elaborately relief-chiselled iron, and chased mountings of iron, bronze, silver (sometimes), and gold (rare).

The French dominance spread to the gunmaking capitols of Europe,

and rich noblemen purchased their creations with enthusiasm. But in most countries one also notes in this period a secondary approach to gunmaking and decoration, one which held fast to older styles and traditions. This was confined largely to rural artisans. English 18th Century gunmakers remained independent of the French style, and would in the period of the American and French Revolutions begin to themselves influence continental fashions.

The earlier engraved style of ornament is referred to as baroque; while

the later more elaborate decor is categorized as rococo. As with nearly all styles in the history of gun engraving, they are closely allied and influenced by prevailing tastes and designs in contemporay art and architecture. The Louvre Galleries for example, brought together masters from all areas of decorative arts, as well as painters and architects. An authority in any of the non-gun art fields can generally examine a deluxe firearm and give a reasonably accurate date of manufacture based solely on decoration.

zoni. Interestingly, the work of Acqua Fresca and Lorenzoni shows the influence of French pattern books of arms decoration.

The gun pictured is of the so-called Lorenzoni magazine breechloading system, but made by the Bolognese and Roman gunmaker Giacomo Berselli. Dating circa 1690, the engraving and silver mounts represent decadence of decoration by Italian gunmakers. The uninspired combination of engraved scrolls (at left) and the relief-cut and punched matte decor at center and right are no comparison to the quality of relief chiselling as proliferated by the Italian masters in the second half of the 17th Century. Nor can the decor in the Berselli gun compare with the richness and elegance of contemporary French gunmakers.

Italy's decline continued into the 19th Century; with the center of gunmaking lost by Brescia circa 1750 to 1800 to such cities as Naples, Rome, and Florence and their environs. Even gun control laws contributed to Brescia's problems. The Neapolitan luxury arms of circa 1750 to circa 1820 were strongly influenced first by Spanish and later (in the Napoleonic and early percussion periods) by French styles. Though eclectic, some of this work was of a high quality.

Gunmakers in Northern Italy, spearheaded by the craftsmen of Brescia, were in a position of leadership in Europe in the mid-17th Century. Their status continued through into the 1690s, but came to be gradually overshadowed by the French. In the period circa 1650—circa 1690 the Italian mastery of relief chiselling had gone from the flat pierced work as seen in No. 10 to high relief, featuring figures, grotesques, and animals. Though their technical skill continued into the first half of the 18th Century, the Italian relief chisellers were gradually declining as major makers of elaborate guns. By continuing in the 17th Century style of relief work, and even resorting to brass rather than iron on occasion, the Italians offered no real competition to their more fashionable and artistic French contemporaries.. The Italian decline was thus attributable to what might be termed their artistic conservatism. Among the greatest of the Italian firearms artisans in the period circa 1650—circa 1700 were Matteo Acqua Fresca, Carlo Bottarelli, and Michele Loren-

---

After the mid-17th Century, the German cities of Nuremberg and Augsburg had lost their pre-eminence as gunmakers in the Germanic school. Succeeding them in the second half of the 17th and first half of the 18th Centuries were such cities as Dresden, Düsseldorf, Köln, Mainz, and a leader from the previous period, Munich. Generally speaking, wheellocks were being replaced by flintlocks in Germany during the second half of the 17th Century and French fashions in gun design and decoration were gaining in popularity. Interestingly, rifled longarms in Germanic countries continued to employ the wheellock well up through the mid-18th Century, but these too came under the French influence, at least in their decoration. Mountings of relief-chiselled steel, and cast and chased silver and brass were often used.

The French influence in Germany was significant. When a nobleman wished the finest in handguns or a smoothbore fowler, he would look to the Parisian gunmakers, or (after circa 1685) he could also look to French gunmakers who had come to German cities. Some Germanic gun-

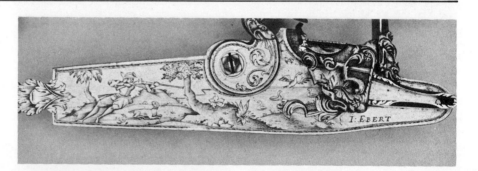

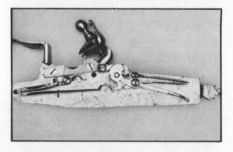

makers of the period were highly skilled at capturing the French style. Throughout Western Europe and Particularly in Germany, gunmakers often signed their pieces in French in addition to a general cribbing of the French style. One of the finest of the Germans in the production of the relief-chiselled flintlock firearms

was Armand Bongarde of Düsseldorf whom experts have compared favorably with the best contemporary French masters.

The very delicate engraving on this lock signed *I. Ebert* (Sonderhausen, Germany) dates circa 1725 to 1740, but is in the French fashion of the latter years of the 17th Century. Although the lock's contour and construction is Germanic, the engraving and relief chiselling show the strong influence of the French. Note the hunting scene, one of the most popular motifs found on German arms of the period. Hunting was the great passion of the German ruling families. To show the attention to detail and quality of decoration, the back of the lock is also illustrated.

These lavishly over-decorated but superbly executed pistols by the Parisian gunmaker La Roche (1734) are representative of the French fashion in deluxe guns prevalent from the 1730s through the 1770s. The stocks are inlaid with gold wire, and the blued-steel barrels are richly inlaid with gold and silver. The barrel breeches, the locks, the butt-caps, and the remaining mountings were heavily relief chiselled. As suggested also by the fleur-de-lis emblem embroidered on the velvet sheaths, the pistols have a royal provenance. They are now in the Musee de l'Armee, Paris.

In the periods of the rococo and the baroque, over-decoration was the mode. On the La Roche pistols (rococo) hardly any area remains void of excessive embellishments. Qualified craftsmen in the baroque and rococo spread from France to escape renewed religious persecution beginning in 1685. By 1700 these Huguenot gunmakers were to be found in most Protestant countries of Europe. Thus religious intolerance played a significant role in the dissemination of French gun decoration and craftsmanship in Europe.

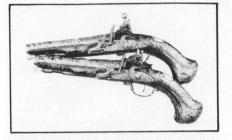

Except for the relatively practical and plain stocks, deluxe guns of the 18th Century were much more elaborate than those of the 17th. Relief-chiselled decorations, previously confined primarily to a select few of Europe's foremost gunmakers, now were widespread throughout Europe. Not only were arms specialists executing this work, but skilled die cutters were also called into play. To accentuate the relief-chiselled motifs, a gold matte background was usually applied.

La Roche was one of several contemporaries and successors to the master Piraube who were turning out over-decorated but superbly-executed fancy firearms in the great period of 1670-1770. In 1743, La Roche was honored by receiving an appointment as a gunmaker with the privilege of a workshop in the Louvre.

Among the distinctive features of rococo arms as represented by the La Roche pistols are: Gilded barrels with a bright blue background finish, maker's name and address gold damascened on the barrel top, and the proliferation of designs without the interference of a central sighting rib on the barrel. Relief chiselled or cast and chased decorations of the mounts had largely replaced engravings in the flat. Themes of flowers, trophies, and laurels proliferated.

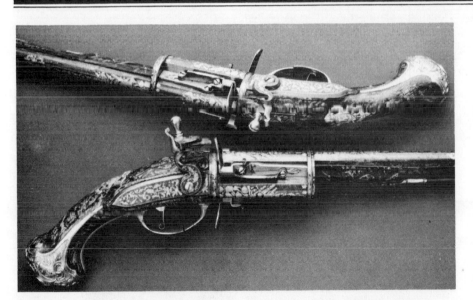

Now in the magnificent arms collection of the Tojhusmuseet, Copenhagen, these flintlock revolvers of King Christian IV were made in Austria, circa 1740. Their cast, chased, and gilded-bronze mountings are representative of the style in use by Austrian gunmakers in the period of the first half of the 18th Century. The engraved (as opposed to relief chiselled) and gilt locks, cylinders, and barrels are also representative of Austrian gunmaking style of the period. In overall design, however, even the Austrians showed the influence of French masters in their pistols and fowlers. Austrian-made rifled guns for target or hunting use also prove the French dominance, primarily in decoration.

The gunmakers of Austria had the good fortune of being ruled by emperors who were keen huntsmen and shooters. One of the world's finest arms collections is that formed by the Hapsburgs, now exhibited in Vienna's Kunsthistorisches Museum. Their patronage gave significant orders to Viennese gunmakers and served as a magnet in drawing talented craftsmen to that city. Some of the finest decorated Austrian guns were made by the Parisian La Marre, who emigrated to Vienna from Paris, circa 1680—1685. In decorative skills, he was a maestro in any technique —chiselling, inlay, and engraving. The names of several other Austrian master gunmakers of the period are known, and some of their works also show the influence of the French.

The gunmaking city of Ferlach, Austria, was active in filling large orders for firearms as early as the 1630s. Most of their production in the 18th Century was of military weapons, but they also made special order arms of high quality. As a rather remote town, their high grade arms usually show a distinct individual style in decoration—a fact which is still true in modern times.

Another gunmaking center worth noting for the quality of their decorated arms is Carlsbad, in what is now Czechoslovakia. As a major spa of 18th Century Europe, the city attracted the high society of the day from throughout the Continent. To cater to these wealthy notables, a community of manufacturers evolved, including some outstanding gunmakers. Specimens of Carlsbad firearms artistry are found in the major ancestral arms collections of Europe, and these arms are individual in style, though related to the work of gunmakers in Vienna and in Prague. A major feature of Carlsbad decoration was their great color—gilt and blued barrels, mounts of gilt bronze or silver, and rich woods of various shades, including yellow.

The schools of gun decoration, within and without the French influence, are so many and varied in all periods of European gunmaking, that just to master French firearms embellishments requires both an expertise in the technical history of firearms and in the history of European decorative arts. The true expert must be a gun authority *and* an art historian and connoisseur.

GUN ENGRAVING

The Empress Elizabeth of Russia was the proud owner of an exquisite garniture which included this sporting gun plus a pair of pistols, a set of stirrups, and a powder flask—all decorated *en suite*. Inlaid silver wire and plaques were lavished on the stocks, and the mountings are of chiselled and parcel-gilt iron. The set was made in the French style by Russian gunmakers in Tula, in 1752, and is now in the collection of The Armouries, H.M. Tower of London.

Russian arms of the 17th Century are not well known to students of gun decoration. As a generalization it may be said that the embellishments known on Russian 17th Century arms are oriental in the stocks and exhibit a coarse execution of European chiselled decor on locks and barrels.

In the 18th Century matters were changed significantly. The key to an improved output was the establishment of the Imperial armsmaking facility at Tula, primarily for manufacture of military weapons. Fortunately, the Imperial Court encouraged the production of deluxe sporting weapons, including swords. Tula's period of best quality was under the patronage of the Empress Elizabeth, who reigned from 1741-62. The major influences shown in these arms was French, and the chief craftsmen were emigrants from Denmark, Sweden, and Germany. They were assisted by Russian craftsmen who were specially trained.

The result was a specific school of arms decoration, with elaborate ornamentation, featuring relief chiselling which when closely studied usually does not live up to the finer quality of work which the Tula school was imitating. The Empress Elizabeth's fowling piece is one of the more successful eminations from the Tula workshops.

That city is still the gunmaking capitol of Russia, but their workmanship today, at least in engraving and inlay, is undistinguished. Gold damascened double-barrel shotguns examined by the author in Leningrad in 1967 were a far cry from the production of quality firearms made in Tula for the Russian Imperial Court over 200 years before.

Far more early Scottish firearms have survived the ravages of time than have English ones, due in the main to the frequent use of brass, iron and sometimes silver for the stocks. Gunmakers were active in Scotland as early as the 1580s. Ornamentation of Scots arms of the period was usually in the form of scroll, scale, cable and strapwork engraving, and on later guns included the added embellishment of silver inlay. A few remarkable pieces are known with inlays or overlays of precious stones or enameling.

The pistol illustrated is dated 1615, and is one of a pair of quite early Scottish manufacture. The engraved decorations of the pioneer Scottish guns were continental in style, as on the present specimen. The mounts are silver and brass, the barrel is blued with gold and silver bands, and the fishtail butt is silver. Barrels of some early Scottish pistols were quite a bit more elaborate than shown here, with profuse engraving similar to that on the lock. A few pistols had silver inlaid and engraved panels on the upper part of the barrels.

On these Murdoch flintlocks made in the mid-18th Century, in Dounne, Scotland, the stocks are of silver, engraved in scroll and leaf designs. The fluted and faceted barrels, of iron, are also scroll engraved, as are the locks. Note the pierced design of the belt hook mount. Some barrels after circa 1740 have relief inlaid silver bands between which were engraved decorations.

A major detail of Scottish gunmaking, of the 17th and 18th Centuries, was its independence from foreign tastes and styles. All-metal stocks were the norm for Scots pistols as late as the early 19th Century. Early iron stocks had been blued, to give an attractive contrast to the silver inlays. Beginning about the middle of the 18th Century, a flat circular disk was in popular use on the back of the hammer at its top. This added embellishment was usually pierced in either a star or floral motif.

Engraved patterns prevailing in the mid-18th and early 19th Centuries were similar to that appearing on the Murdoch pistols. Floral, scroll, and thistle motifs were popular, and silver inlays are often observed on Scottish arms of this period. A few extremely fancy Scots all-metal pistols were made late in the 18th Century. Among surviving specimens is a pair believed to have been made for King George III. The stocks, of gilded copper, bear engraved rococo scrollwork and are inset with enameled gold plaques. Similar plaques appear on the barrels, each a miniature portrait. Scrollwork on a gold background is chiselled on the locks, while the barrels are gold inlaid and blued. The belt hooks are finished in the same fashion.

The final configuration of Scottish all-metal pistols (many of which were made outside of Scotland, in Birmingham and London) was percussion with German silver, iron, or brass stocks, and engravings of what Hayward terms a "debased classical type."

Scottish pistols form a distinctive chapter in the involved history of European arms decoration. They are related to a group of extremely interesting longarms of which scarce few have survived. Known specimens, dating from the 17th Century, feature silver decorations on the wooden stocks, and mountings engraved in simple floral and foliate designs quite distinctly Scottish in style. By the second half of the 18th Century the major Scots gunmakers were producing, in quantity, sporting arms mostly English in appearance.

Beginning in the mid-18th Century, English gunmakers were emerging as the chief rivals of the French. However, in arms decoration the latter continued in a position of leadership until the middle of the 19th Century.

The government arms factory at St. Etienne turned out large quantities of quality firearms in the second half of the 18th Century. Some of these featured rich decorations of relief chisellings after the fashion of such masters as the La Roches (father and son), but hardly in their league. The rococo styles were dominant on deluxe French guns until the Revolution, in 1789.

Major changes in French gun decoration began to appear in the few years following the Revolution. These drastic developments affected both form and ornament and were the creation of the renowned Nicholas Noel Boutet (1761-1833). The dominant position of Boutet dates from his appointment in 1792 as the artistic director of the government workshops at Versailles. In the year following he was given the authority to assemble gunmaking equipment and to hire master gunmakers from Liége, Belgium. The major production of the Manufacture de Versailles was military firearms, but fancy weapons were made in a specially set up workshop. From 1794 through 1818, Boutet himself concentrated on the high-quality guns and it is from these that he earned his immortal fame as a gun designer and manufacturer. After the final collapse of Napoleon (1815) and the expiration of Boutet's government concession (1818), the master lived and worked in Paris, dying a debtor in 1833. His great period was from 1800 to 1815.

Boutet's reign as a premier maker of quality arms represents a unique era in the production of luxurious weaponry. To quote John F. Hayward's "The Art Of The Gunmaker": "The demand for luxury arms of all kinds was never greater than during the period of the Directoire, Consulate and Empire in France."

Presentation and custom grade arms were made in such a profusion that a system was devised to classify the various available grades. Among the decorative details which gave Boutets their vaunted reputation were gilt and matte blue finishes on the barrels, with imaginative tooled patterns formed by the gilding. Mountings were richly cast in silver or (on extra deluxe guns) in gold, or were in finely engraved bright steel. One form of pistol buttcap was of a mask or the head of Medusa. Stock inlays were usually finely engraved and inlaid sheet gold or silver. Chased silver or gold castings and gold or silver wire inlays were also lavished on some of the deluxe grade arms. Engraving, relief chiselling, and relief-cut gold inlays were often applied to locks in varying degrees of luxuriousness. Boutet's use of ornament left no source or range of design of the French Empire period untapped. The imaginative and exquisite embellishments which evolved from the complete and total approach of Boutet combined to earn for him and his Versailles workshop a reputation and stature in gunmaking unparalleled in his day. Many modern collectors rank Boutet as the premier maker of deluxe firarms of all time. It is fitting that he described himself as an artist, and is the only gunmaker on record to have done so.

Examples of Boutet artistry, all in the Metropolitan Museum of Art, are as follows:

Trigger guard detail of a double-barrel flintlock fowler attributed in ownership to Marshal Ney (1804). The mountings are cast and chased silver. Note the superbly carved stocks and the minute trigger guard detail.

A garniture with blued and gilt barrels and gold mounted stocks and silver mounts (circa 1810 to 1815). The stockwork is utterly magnificent. These arms, cased, sold for $103,000 at a Christie's auction in 1970.

Details of one of the most deluxe arms in existence; a double-barrel fowling piece made circa 1815 for Napoleon. Mountings are in gold, and an exchange set of matching percussion barrels and locks were made at a later date by another French gunmaker.

A cased muff pistol, of bright steel, with gold-mounted grip. The engraved decoration is quite delicate on both the pistol parts and the gold stock inlays.

Among the talented rivals of Boutet was Le Page, who as *Arquebusier de l' Empereur* held a position of stature in Paris which compared favorably to Boutet's situation at Versailles. LePage made longarms for the Emperor, while Boutet concentrated on his pistols. LePage handled each commission on an individual design basis, while Boutet's output was mainly in his set grades of predetermined designs. LePage was a close rival to Boutet, although the latter is decidedly pre-eminent in both historical and artistic significance.

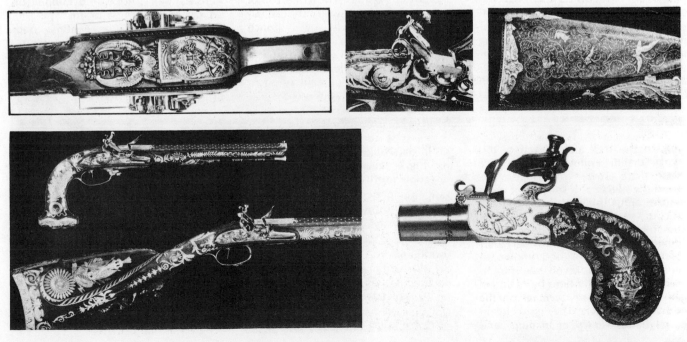

GUN ENGRAVING

The student and collector whose enthusiasm lies in decorated British firearms has recently been blessed with an excellent and detailed publication on the subject. Written by Clay P. Bedford and Stephen V. Grancsay, the book is entitled "Early Firearms of Great Britain and Ireland." Combining the expertise of Messrs. Grancsay and Bedford with that of such authorities as John F. Hayward, Claude Blair, W. Keith Neal, Geoffrey Jenkinson, Howard Blackmore, Peter Dale and L. C. Jackson, the book is without parallel in its field. Most of the firearms are decorated, although the majority of these are rather reserved, subject to period of manufacture. The Bedford-Grancsay book illustrates and identifies every item in detail, and covers the complete field of English, Scottish, and Irish firearms through the mid-19th Century. By studying the pictures alone, one absorbs a detailed knowledge of the evolution of decoration on the British firearm.

On this rare Joseph Manton smoothbore double gun with gravity safeties and water drain breech (circa 1814) one can observe the quite reserved, tasteful, and conservative engraving common to English and Irish firearms of the period circa 1780 to circa 1840. Simple scrolls, borders, and trophy themes were the norm. Paramount was the form and function of the gun; decoration, on the whole, was secondary. Such economy of embellishment provides a welcome relief from the excesses (no matter how exquisite) typical of the previous 250 years of deluxe gunmaking. Decorated mountings were generally limited to silver escutcheons and butt-caps (sometimes with coats of arms or masks, respectively) and engraved steel or silver trigger guards and ramrod pipes. Owing to their many innovations, English guns were taking the lead from the French in the manufacture of superior functional firearms. In the process, decoration on English non-military firearms was at

a minimum by the late 1790s.

However, some splendid deluxe arms were made by the English in the second half of the 18th Century. A fashion known as Chinoiserie (based on a rococo style popular with goldsmiths and cabinet makers) saw use on some deluxe English arms of the period circa 1750-circa 1770. These decorations were engraved on silver mountings or inlaid on wooden stocks.

Gunmakers who were gaining in stature during the period of the late 18th and early 19th Centuries rank as some of the greatest in British firearms history. Among them were Joseph and John Manton, Henry Nock, Durs Egg, H. W. Mortimer and Ezekiel Baker. These men were largely responsible for the developments which gradually shrunk gun engraving on English arms down to a minimum. In the period of circa 1780 to circa 1830, they enjoyed the patronage of George, Prince of Wales, who ordered quantities of deluxe firearms and was an enthusiastic collector of antique firearms as well. Though always superbly made, even Prince (later King) George's custom guns were on the whole conservatively decorated. All of them at least featured a royal crest of gold or silver on the grip or buttstock.

Duelling pistols were in vogue beginning circa 1780, and these were quite austere in decor, as were officers' pistols, and fine quality pocket pistols. These comprised the three popular types of English hand weapons that were made in large quantities into the 19th Century. All were masterfully designed and manufactured, but their technical perfection far overshadowed any engraved or applied decorations.

On pocket pistols of post-1800, only a silver buttcap in the form of a small lion head survived the quite conservative decorative approach to British non-military arms. Joseph Egg was an exception to this, with his jewel-like pocket pistols with engraved silver or (rare) gold mountings and the gold-inlaid maker's name on the finely blued barrels.

Interestingly, however, some elaborate arms were still made in the period circa 1775 to circa 1800 for the export trade by R. Wilson of London. Rundell, Bridge, and Rundell of London carried on with this type arm atfer the turn of the century. And the influence of ornaments by Boutet has even been noted on a superb pair of silver-mounted pistols by John Prosser, used in a presentation to a British Colonel in 1802.

On the lock and breech of this Forsyth volley gun of circa 1820 (Tower of London Armouries collection) a somewhat more deluxe embellishment was selected as compared to the Manton double. The animal head finial to the hammer came to be a standard on many percussion arms, and is best known to Americans on Colt revolvers—a treatment made popular here by emigrant gun engravers from Germany in the mid-19th Century. The gold inlaid barrel bands (singly or in pairs) and

scroll engravings of similar style on the trigger guard, and the guard's pineapple profile forward finial were basic components in English arms decoration from circa 1780 into the 1840s. The style illustrated here was used on such well-known guns as the London-made Collier revolvers and on the early products of the renowned firm of J. Purdey & Sons, and in variant forms on London-made Colt revolvers and on those of many of Colt's British competition.

The importance of Liége as a gunmaking center, and the fact that today it employs the greatest number of gun engravers concentrated anywhere in the world (over 150) calls or some comment and background on that city's role in the history of arms engraving. By the mid-18th Century, Liége gunmakers were producing military arms in quantities of approximately 100,000 guns per year. Records show that upwards of 6000 persons were active in this thriving trade by the end of the century. Although military arms comprised the lion's share of this output, certain Liége manufacturers were capable of and turned out a noteworthy number of finely executed and decorated non-military firearms. Again, and quite understandable from a geographic standpoint, the French influence was quite strong. Surviving weapons from the early 18th Century prove that Parisian fashion and French gunmakers pattern books were well known to Liége gunmakers and designers. A characteristic of their products at this time was the frequent use of cast and chased gilt bronze mounts, rather than the chiselled iron as still popular in France. However, the very finest Liége arms of the period did use relief-chiselled iron mountings, and chiselled designs on the locks and barrels. As the 18th Century progressed, the deluxe products of Liége arms manufacturers gained an increasing patronage from noblemen in Europe's northern and central countries and principalities. But to the connoisseur, the Liége firearms of the 18th Century lack the refinement and overall harmony of products by their French contemporaries.

As early as the mid-18th Century some members of the Liége trade were already using spurious markings such as London or Paris, and sometimes these even included fake proof marks. On such arms an attempt was made to capture the style of guns made in those cities, and their success is proven by the difficulty even among some authorities in identifying a Liége gun (spuriously Paris-marked) from the genuine French product.

Toward the end of the 18th Century, Liége concentrated even more than previously on military production, while their first quality deluxe output declined. In the latter area they concentrated on pocket pistols, often with two or more barrels. For decoration, rococo scrolls were cut on most, wtih relief chiselling reserved for the better grade. Again, spurious markings were used with frequency, usually *London*.

The production of pocket pistols continued well into the 19th Century, accompanied by an increasing concentration on all grades of sporting arms. Copies of the products of almost any successful foreign gunmaker were undertaken. On the whole, however, the engraving of these remained in a Belgian style. Most often scrollwork was used, with vine and floral finials. Gold and silver inlays, both flush and in relief, were also employed, though relatively limited in quantity and often in quality.

The crudely executed and uninspired scrolls and floral motifs on this Liége pocket pistol of the mid-19th Century has contributed to the general connotation of poor quality that is associated with Belgian firearms by collectors specializing in the 19th Century. The London marking was a device put on by the maker to help his product sell.

On a trip to Belgium in January, 1972, the author had the pleasure of studying a hand-drawn and colored sample book prepared in the period circa 1840 to 1860 to illustrate the prolific output of the Francotte firm in various grades of pocket arms for export sales. Some guns were of a quality equal to their finest foreign competition, and the balance were of average or low quality, allowing the client a wide choice. Besides engravings in Belgian floral and/or scroll styles, and the London markings, some pieces were pictured with engraving copying specific London patterns. The point of this anecdote is to emphasize the fact that beginning in the mid-19th Century—arms decoration, and particularly engraving—often is in the style of— one country, but appears on guns made in another. These circumstances were influenced by the proliferation of mass-produced, machine-made arms, and the increased emigrations which included gunsmiths, stockmakers, and engravers. It was not usually due to any one nation being a fashion-setter, as was true, e.g., with the French in their great periods of influence.

GUN ENGRAVING

Most German and Austrian gunmakers from the mid-18th into the first quarter of the 19th Century experienced difficulty. They were no competition for the French and English, and their trade was severely hampered by the excessive length of time that they had remained married to the wheellock system. In Germany and Austria the wheellock finally ceased to be fashionable by about 1750. They turned too late to concentrating on the flintlock, and it was not until the percussion period that they began anew to hold their own.

In any event, the decorative style of Germanic arms of this period became very much alike, losing the individuality previously displayed. Of all the German-Austrian gunmakers, only the Kuchenreuter family of Regensburg was renowned throughout Europe in the late 18th Century. For most of the rich nobility, acquiring a fine gun meant turning from the Fatherland to French or English makers. For guns of a lesser quality than Paris or London, the gun fancier could count on Liége.

A few distinguished makers of high quality arms were active in Germany and Austria in the mid-and late 18th Century. Among them, the Stockmars of Suhl, who turned out some exceptionally well-ornamented (relief chiselled) pieces for their royal patrons, the Electors of Saxony. The Stockmars were primarily engravers and are believed to have acquired unfinished locks and barrels from Suhl

gunmakers. Their privileged station as Court gunmakers not only brought select commissions, but kept them exposed to stylish arms of French and English manufacture, also acquired by their patrons. Many Stockmar guns were never meant to be fired, and were looked upon solely as masterworks of craftsmanship.

The Kuchenreuters were a family of gunmakers who remained active through several generations from the 17th to the 20th Century. In this long history, their best period was circa 1750 to circa 1820. In decoration these guns at first followed the German style of relief-chiselled locks and barrels and gilded brass mountings. However, the Kuchenreuters soon leaned towards practical, good-shooting designs, and avoided the over-decorated rococo type decorations. This practical approach must have been a key to the family's commercial success.

The Kuchenreuters were among several German makers who were influenced in varying degrees by the style of Nicholas Noel Boutet, in the Napoleonic period. But in quality their products never compared favorably to the originals by the Artiste himself.

Pictured here is a double-barrel German fowler of the mid-19th Century. Its decoration represents an over-embellished style popular with German and Austrian gunmakers prevailing during most of the 19th and early 20th Centuries. French manufacturers also fell for this excessive approach in the period circa 1835—circa 1880, but their creations were much more artistic and digestable. Unfortunately, vestigal influences of such decorative abominations as this fowler are still seen today in the many highly stylized German and Austrian sporting arms which include custom engraving and stockwork.

The last published pattern book exerting any major influence on European gun engravers was that released circa 1856 by Charles Claesen, Liége. The book was produced for guns specifically, as had been such predecessors as the works of Jacquinet (Thuraine and Le Hollandois) and Claude Simonin. Claesen called upon the design skills of several prominent artists of the day; the results were quite elaborate and bespeak a specific style representing the Victorian period's own interpretation of opulence and splendor.

The profusely engraved, relief-chiselled, and cast pistol illustrated is an artist's design from the Claesen book. Note the rather quaint title of "Pistolet Gothique." The Gothic influence from European art of the 12th through the 16th Centuries was quite prevalent in the mid-19th Century. "Ivanhoe" and other novels by Sir Walter Scott had been instrumental in bringing about a revival of this style.

Claesen's pattern book is known to have seen limited use in America, by emigrant German and Austrian craftsmen. Engraver R. J. Kornbrath had a Claesen in his large archive of source materials.

The employment of embellishments such as those published by Claesen was mainly on deluxe guns of French, Belgian, German, and Austrian production of the period

of the mid-to-late 19th Century. However, among the archives of the Greener arms company of Birmingham (liquidated in the 1960s) were pages from Claesen. The book was known to the English craftsmen, but not often used by them. Vestiges of the style published in the book, particularly in game scenes and scrolls, continue in popularity with the Germans and Austrians up to the present.

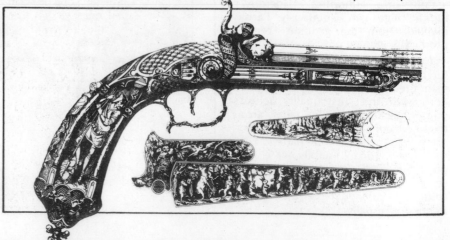

In this cast and relief-chiselled percussion pistol made of iron and stocked in ebony, the French gunmaker (either Gauvain or Antoine Vechte) employed designs in the Gothic manner a la Claesen. A touch of humor on the breech is an apelike figure covering his ears in anticipation of the noise of discharge.

The elaborate buttplate terminates in a gold crest. In quality of execution and detail such weapons were masterpieces of the gunmaker's art. However, they do lack the elegance and refinement of such magnificent firearms as those illustrated in the Jacquinet pattern book of the 17th Century (No. 11A).

Gold inlays were sometimes in use on guns of this type, but their overwhelming effect was based mainly on the rampant profusion of high relief Gothic details. The influence of artists in supplying designs for this type weapon is clear in the excellent blend of the overall form of the gun with the details of relief designs on both metal and wood. At the turn of the century another popular style would exert its influence on deluxe guns, but to a comparatively limited extent —this was *art nouveau*. Students of American gun decoration are familiar with *art nouveau* from the Tiffany-gripped Smith & Wesson revolvers prepared for the Chicago World's Fair of 1893.

After the period of the 1820s, mass production of firearms quickly developed in Europe and in America. For the first time, the American gun industry began to give their European contemporaries competition in the international gun market. In the study of gun engraving, this ascent of the Americans is important because they drew like a magnet many superb craftsmen from the Old World. The Germans almost exclusively provided the United States with engravers. All the prominent names of master gun engravers of middle and late 19th Century America are Germanic—L. D. Nimschke, Gustave Young (Jung), the Ulrichs, and Cuno Helfricht being most prominent. Understandably, the style they used here was based on their native habits. These artisans adapted their Old World patterns and scrolls to fit the new shapes of such U.S.

makes as Winchester and Colt.

Pattern books published circa 1840 in Vienna were discovered in the papers of L. D. Nimschke. Details from these books (by G. Ernst) have been found not only on guns by Nimschke, but in the work of Gustave Young and certain of the Ulrichs. Both Nimschke and Young are known to have brought with them ink impressions pulled from their own work done while in Germany. These too, served as sources of design for their production in America.

The Colt revolver pictured (circa 1870) is attributed to Young. The scroll and punched matte background are a major Germanic style, and the scroll is very close to designs found in the Ernst pattern books. One can state without hesitation that the major stylistic influence on American engraving from the 1840s through today has been Germanic.

The work of R. J. Kornbrath, who emigrated from Ferlach, Austria, to America early in the 20th Century, continued the influence of Germanic styles on American tastes in gun engraving. On the shotgun and revolver shown here, one sees a clear presentation of 20th Century Germanic engraving. These scroll, floral, leaf and animal designs also represent manifestations of the German-Austrian style which were widely accepted in the U.S. and were the major influence on many American-born engravers of the 20th Century.

The gun engravers of Germany and Austria developed engravings of this type during the 19th Century. Influencing this evolution was the Gothic taste which flowered in the second quarter of the Century, and an ever-increasing demand for finely-made and profusely decorated rifles and shotguns for hunting. The opening of such well-endowed game lands as the American West, Africa, and India all contributed to this dramatic increase in popularity of hunting and in guns of the chase.

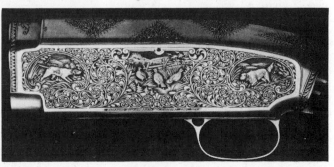

GUN ENGRAVING

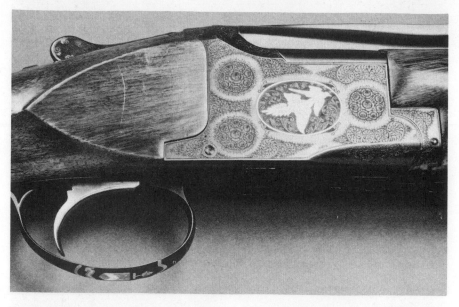

A protegé of Kornbrath who also emigrated to America from Ferlach was Joseph Fugger, who for many years has been Master Engraver at Abercrombie & Fitch (Griffin & Howe), New York. Fugger's style, as seen on his Browning over-and-under 12 gauge from the Russell Aitken Collection, has minute English type scrolls and floral rosettes, along with Germanic scrolls within the gold-inlaid bird motif. Top craftsmen like Fugger, although they prefer specific styles, can work in virtually any mode the customer may desire. On the whole, however, 20th Century European gun engraving is either the Germanic type by the German speaking craftsmen, English by the English, and Belgian, English, and German by the Liége engravers. Spanish engravers work usually in English or German patterns, and the Italians work similarly, but also rely on patterns having their origin in Italian Renaissance decorations.

It is interesting to note that some of today's Liége engravers are emigrant Italians, some of the engravers in the London gun trade are also Italian, and a few English manufacturers call on Liége craftsmen for some of their decorative needs. The exchange of engraving patterns and styles within European gunmaking has been greatly enhanced in the 20th Century by the swiftness of modern communications and the ease of travel.

Modern art has yet to effect today's gun engraver. Picasso and Jackson Pollack et al have had no influence whatsoever on the decoration of 20th Century firearms, European or otherwise. Gun engravers are traditionalists, as are the vast majority of their clients. Thus every engraved or inlaid decoration on a 20th Century gun has its roots in previous styles, and most always the results are of the types as shown in illustrations.

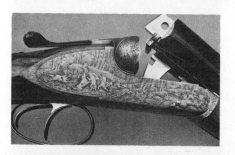

On this pre-WW2 Francotte double-barrel shotgun from the Musee d'Armes, Liége, the engraver cut a scene full of life and masterful detail. Francotte, one of Liége's oldest gunmakers, has patronized engravers since the firm's beginnings in the Napoleonic period. One of the great Liége master engravers of all time was Lemaire, which in French means "The Master." He is credited with having executed the quite artistic scene on this gun. The best Liége engravers combine technical skill with an innate artistry in design and composition. One of these artist-engravers, Denise Thirion, emigrated to America in 1971, and is now employed full time by the firm A. A. White Engravers, Inc.

In the 20th Century, accompanying the evolution of Fabrique Nationale and their association with John M. Browning and the Browning Arms Company, Liége has become the world center of the gun engraving trade. Not only does this city boast the largest number of gun engravers in the world (over 150, most of them working for FN and Browning), but its School of Mechanical Arts offers a three-year course for student craftsmen. Taught by former FN engraver Professor Rene Delcour, the program combines the art of engraving, along with the other gunmaking crafts (stockwork, filing, etc.), plus liberal arts training equal to an American junior college. Delcour's students are the future engravers at FN and Browning, and the apprentice program previously operated by FN was discontinued in favor of the School of Mechanical Arts.

After three years, a graduate (there are about a half dozen per year) is qualified to do scrollwork, lettering, and general engraving on steel. Any of these craftsmen would then qualify to work for most American and European gun manufacturers.

Delcour himself has traveled extensively in Europe and America, meeting engravers and studying the work of modern craftsmen and their predecessors as represented in dealer, collector, and museum holdings of decorated firearms. His influence in the world of gun engraving is significant. The lock plates pictured here are samples of his own mastery of the difficult art of steel engraving.

Russell J. Smith, Master Engraver for Smith & Wesson, devoted over 100 hours to the design and execution of this quite ambitious and effective sample plate. The eagle at center is gold inlaid in high relief, and the balance of the plate is cut in steel in eight basic decorative styles. In the scrolls of the two upper sections the strong influence of Germanic design is evident. The leaf motifs of the left and right borders are also of German inspiration. At center of the lower right corner the delicate scroll motif is quite French in feeling.

Russ Smith's imaginative and finely executed plate is a sample not only of his own artistry in metalwork, but of the European influences which affect the creations of any American gun engraver.

One of Europe's finest engravers is K. C. Hunt, of England. He specializes in engraving and gold inlay for J. Purdey & Sons and Holland & Holland, which means that every commission must be a modern masterpiece. Hunt has done a greater proportion of such high grade guns than any other active craftsman in the English speaking world. Though only in his 30s, on Purdeys alone he has decorated in a rich variety of deluxe weapons for many crowned heads of Europe, for Russian Premiers and American Presidents, for the richest families of Europe and America, and for a raft of Texas oil kings and cattle barons.

These illustrations of his work are photographs from so-called "gunmaker's pulls," i.e., paper impressions taken in ink or candle black directly from the engraved gun. The artistic perfection of a Ken Hunt, however, does not represent European gun engraving of today—any more than Alvin White's abilities represent contemporary American work, or Boutet was representative of the overall accomplishments of gun engravers of his day. There have been and always will be a limited number of supreme masters of the craft.

However, the standard of gun engraving in Europe, particularly in England, Germany, Austria, Italy, and Belgium continues to be relatively high. The quality of execution cannot be compared to the work of a Piraube, Boutet, or Casper Spät. But the modern practitioners are akin to the thousands of engravers, relief chisellers, and chasers whose skills preceded them over a period of four centuries. The major inspirations of the modern school are both practical and personal: (a) income, and, (b), the myriad of creations executed on firearms by their predecessors and contemporaries as available mainly through museums and books and periodicals for collectors and sportsmen.

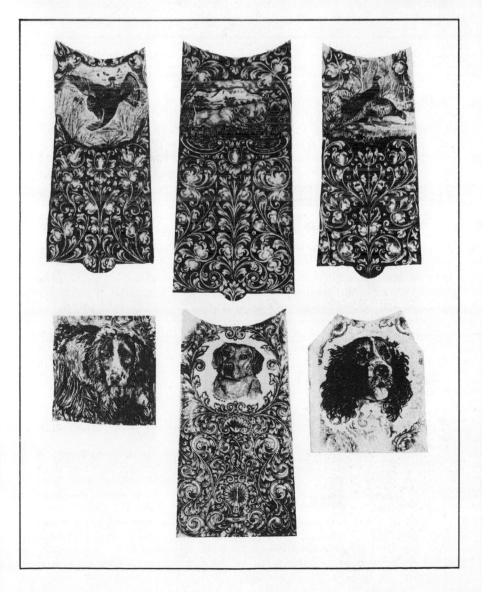

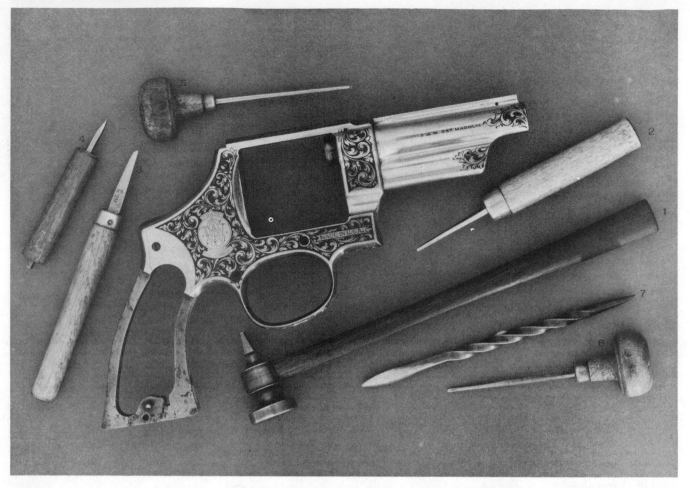

Of all the craftsmen in gunmaking, the engraver was helped the least by the great advancements of the machine age. The tools you see here belong to contemporary craftsman Lynton McKenzie, and are basically the same as those used by engravers and relief chiselers of firearms for the last 400 years. With the small hammer (made in varying weights and sizes), the chisels (No. 2 & 3) are struck, to cut the scrolls and most details of game scenes, borders, etc. Chisel No. 2 is one form of cutter, while No. 3 is a liner, for shading. The punch (No. 4) is employed in giving a matte finish to the background, which is usually cut away first to give relief to the scrolls. No. 5 is a hand-held liner and No. 6 is a hand-held chisel. Hand-held chisels are generally used only in cutting motifs of the most critical detail. The burnisher-awl (No. 7) is useful in taking ink impressions on paper of an engraved design (the paper is rubbed into the outlines after the ink or candle smoke has been applied to the engraved surface). Its primary use, however, is in burnishing metals (left end) and in laying out design by scratching lines on the metal surface or through a film of chalk (right end). Gold and silver are usually inlaid by cutting the metal with the complete profile of the item being inlaid (e.g., a duck or deer), then undercutting with an awl or chisel a profusion of prongs aimed in varying directions, and then pounding the silver or gold (in wire or plate form) into position. The engraving of the gold or silver is done after the metal is secured.

GLOSSARY

CHASING: Touch-up work on repousse or cast metal pieces. Chasing cleans up the item and puts on the final touches. Cutters, files, and punches are used.

CHISELLING: Sculpting iron, gold, or silver in low or high relief. To do well, this form of arms decoration calls for great skill and patience. Sometimes, such metals as copper or bronze are used.

DAMASCENING: Properly the word identifies the producing of the watered pattern in gun barrels ("Damascus barrels"), particularly on shotguns. However, it is often used by writers as a name for gold or silver inlay and overlay. As used in the present article it refers to the early form of overlay where a rough ground was cut on the iron and the gold and silver (in wire form) adhered when lightly hammered on.

ENGRAVING: Cutting designs on metal, ivory, mother of pearl or other hard materials using a hand-held chisel, or a hammer and chisel (one in each hand). The word is often confused with . . .

ETCHING: Cutting a design on metal or other hand materials (e.g., glass) by the action of an acid. Generally done on metal by coating the surface with a varnish or wax, then removing this resistant substance with a pointed instrument. Exposure is then made to acid, which eats the metal and leaves the design.

GILDING: Overlaying with gold by using heat and an amalgam of gold and mercury. Replaced in the 19th Century by the electrical process known as plating. **Parcel gilt** means partially gilded; masking off of parts not to be gilded was done with a varnish.

INLAYING: Setting gold, silver, or copper wire or sheet into undercut grooves on iron or steel. After the soft metal is inlaid, it is engraved and/or relief chiselled. If done correctly, such inlays will not fall out or fragment in any way. Solders are not used to adhere the soft metal to the iron or steel.

REPOUSSE: Relief decoration made by hammering or beating of the metal from the underside, using fine hammers and punches. The word is often used in modern times to include all relief work, even that done from the upper side. Usually accompanied by chasing or chiselling to bring out detail. Repousse was usually confined to items such as the fine sideplate pictured.

Master Engraver Lynton S. M. McKenzie has been with the New Orleans Arms Company since 1969, and prior to that worked for several years in England. Among his clients were Holland & Holland, and his skills in arms decoration encompass not only engraving and gold inlay, but virtually all the techniques known in the 400-year history of firearms embellishment.

He is shown at a specially-constructed vise which turns to every required angle, with a Purdey frame receiving some fine line cuts from hammer and chisel. On the work bench are odds and ends of engraver's tools. Note the positioning of the vise at the corner of the bench, this allowing for body movement. As an aid in cutting with greater speed, he works in a standing position, rather than seated as is the common practice among jewelry engravers, die cutters, and many of the American contingent of gun engravers. The standing approach is common to most European gun engravers, although master crafsmen may choose to sit when cutting finely detailed scenes with the hand graver.

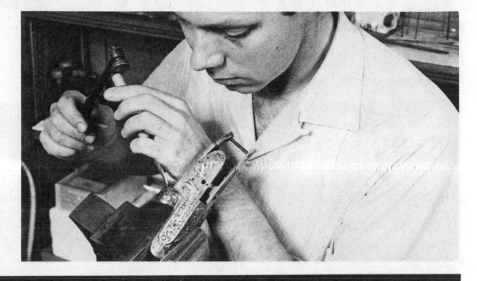

Entitled "Progress," this cartoon by Ken Hunt shows his comical invention for the engraver of the future—or for adoption by their shop boss or manager of the present. The bars on the window and the ball and chain on Hunt's ankle contribute to a concentrated, uninterrupted day's work.

Interestingly, the only machine thus far developed which could replace the centuries' old hammer and chisel is the American invention known as the Gravermeister. Engravers in the U.S. have increasingly taken to this ingenious product, which in effect is an automatic hammer and chisel. Most old time craftsmen do not seem readily adaptable to the Gravermeister, but for many of the newer crop, and for the beginner, it is highly recommended. Sales are now being made to some of Europe's gunmakers, and several of the U.S. arms manufacturers have already acquired the machine. This is quite a break from the 400-year hammer-chisel tradition, but the Gravermeister definitely is a valuable addition to the craft, and—after four centuries—isn't it about time!

Miniature Firearms

ALTHOUGH THEY SOLVE THE SPACE PROBLEM
HANDILY, THEIR VALUE IS DEFINITELY OUT OF
PROPORTION TO THEIR DIMINUTIVE SIZE

by Samuel Weill, Jr.

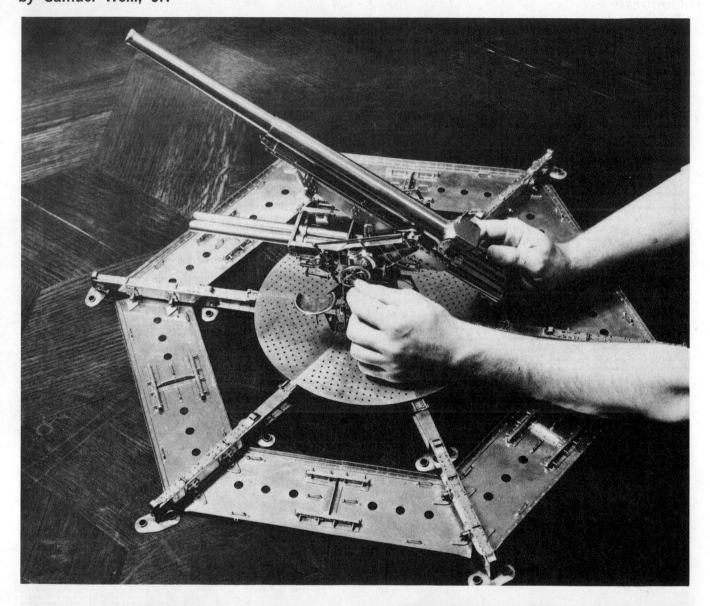

Miniature firearms have been with us, probably since the approximate time when gunpowder was first used, and a few examples may be found in various museum collections all over the world. Other miniature arms existed even before the beginning of the gunpowder era, as tiny swords, daggers and crossbows give evidence that unknown craftsmen of those ancient times duplicated these full-sized weapons in miniature, for reasons at which we can only guess.

Over a period of years, however, miniature firearms have been made for many reasons as toys for the children of royalty, exercises in skill on the part of the craftsmen, jewelry, salesmen's samples, and simply as commercial ventures.

Tom P. Weston, of Mexico City, is a good example of the latter. His output includes, among others, many scale models (all fully functional) of the following: Colt Walkers, Navies, Patersons, Pocket Revolvers, No. 3 Derringers, Remington Navies, Remington Falling Block Carbines, Hopkins and Allen "Parrot Heads", and Winchester '66 Saddle Ring Carbines. These range in size from models of less than two inches in overall length, to half scale models, and are of exquisite workmanship, most being true to the originals in every detail, including engraving.

During the 19th Century in Europe, many fine muff pistols and tiny revolvers, both rimfire and pinfire, were turned out as items of fine

1. Overall and detail views of the author's magnificent stainless steel model of the Japanese Model 1925 105mm AA gun. It was made at Nagoya arsenal in 1928, and is fully operable, right down to the fuse setting box. The 16½-inch barrel is chambered and rifled for the 11mm Murata round, and shows evidence of having been fired.

2. Brass model in .22 rimfire of the famous Model 1893 Police Gatling gun. No toy, the six steel barrels fire from the Accles drum feed.

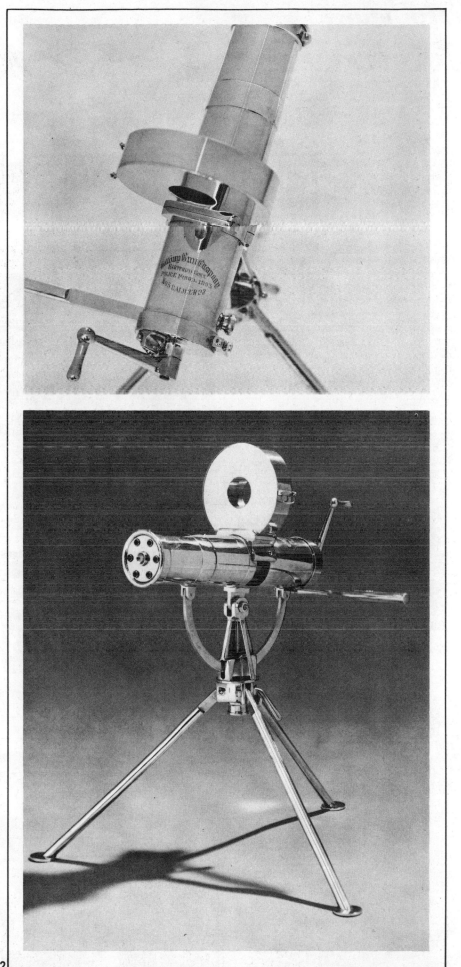

Miniatures

jewelry. Some of these were worn by men on their watch chains and were actually used to find their watches, as the bores were cut so that they fitted the winding mechanisms in the same manner as did the more familiar keys. Women also wore similar pieces as earrings and as bracelet charms, but many of these small guns were sold as cased sets with all accessories, and were almost too fine to wear in this fashion. This is all the more fortunate, as some beautiful examples exist in various collections today, unfired and in mint condition.

There is a fascination about these miniscule firearms which strikes almost everyone seeing them for the first time, not only because of their beauty (some being made of solid gold, fitted with ivory or mother of pearl grips and extravagantly engraved) but because of the intricacy of their mechanical parts. An operating wheelock for instance, may have up to 50 separate pieces making up

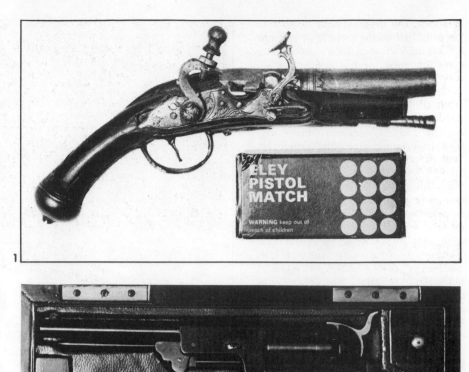

1

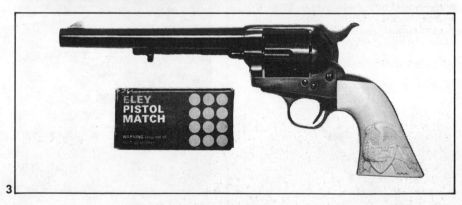

2

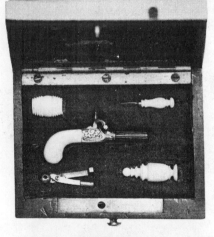

3

4

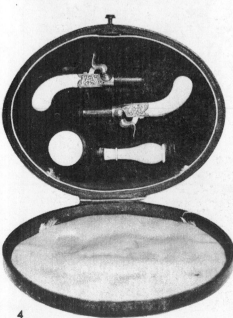

5

the lock, the total size of which may be only half as big around as a dime.

Gunsmiths and their apprentices have also turned out individual examples of these small guns and some, such as Joseph Childs and D. Egg, both of London, in the early 1800s, made fine miniatures which bear

1. *A miquelet firing a .38 caliber ball. Buffalo horn furniture. It was no doubt made in the 1600s, when this type of lock was in use.*

2. *Colt Walker, made by Weston. Length of pistol is six inches. It bears serial: A Co. No. 44.*

3. *Colt SAA, overall length, 7¾ inches, caliber .22 Short. No marks, but was probably made by Mr. Aguilar, a former Weston workman. Serial #3.*

4. *Miniature muff pistols, probably French. Superb workmanship. Pair are unusual in that they have side hammers.*

5. *Model 1928 Thompson made by Edmond de la Garrigue, pantograph work by Kest Hofstra. Serial #S-001. Detail is superb, right down to lettering.*

6. *Weston-made Colt Navy in case with stock. Originally from Berger collection.*

7. *Weston Winchester 1866, 20 inches overall, serial #5, caliber .22 Short.*

8. *Small Mauser, made in commemoration of Guatemala's October, 1944 revolution. Plaque in stock: "20 de Octobre de 1944 Recuerdo a la Juventud Revolucionaria".*

9. *Nonfunctional Stoner .223, complete with scale cartridge in magazine. Purportedly 12 were made for presentation purposes. No serial.*

10. *Purse pistol, 5mm pinfire.*

11. *Pair of "Colt" blank pistols.*

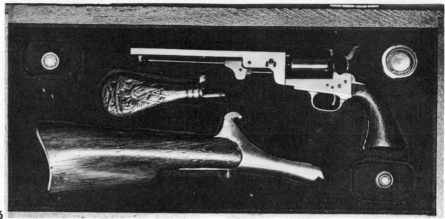

6

7

0

9

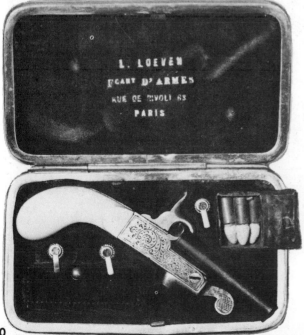

10

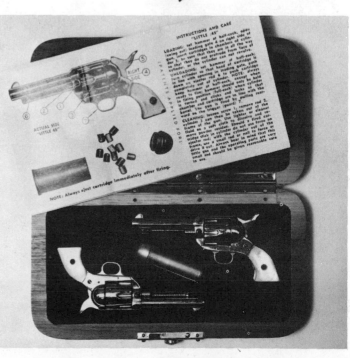

11

Miniatures

London and Birmingham proof marks.

Many of the great collections are presently in museums such as the Metropolitan in New York, the Victoria and Albert in London, and the Hermitage in Leningrad, but there are also many collectors who own, in their miniatures, what amounts to a small fortune. The constantly rising prices and extremely short supply of these fascinating little works of art puts their value on a par with rare stamps and coins, and collector interest in them seems to be at an all time high.

Not all period miniature firearms are antiques, even though the majority of the more highly ornamented pieces seem to have been made during or before the 1800s. While Weston has, for the most part, discontinued his manufacturing operations, Karl J. Furr and Paul Kuhni of Orem, Utah are still turning out a very fine functional scale reproductions of various models of the Gatling Gun. These

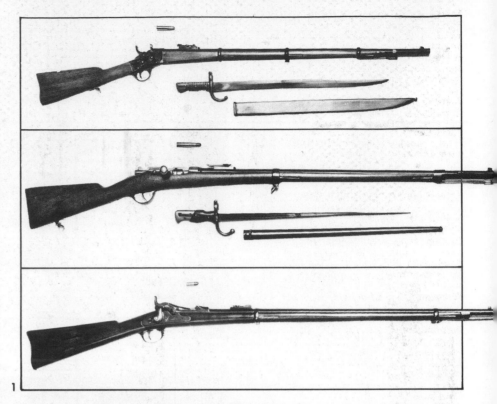

1

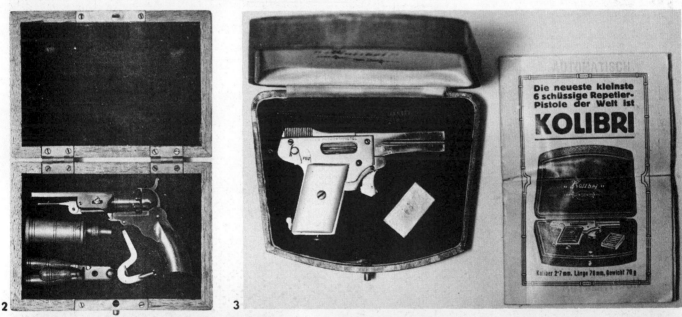

2

3

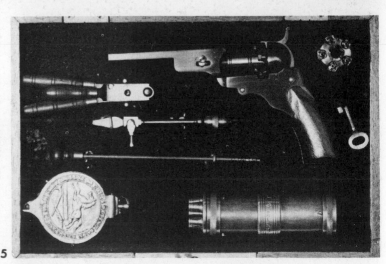

4

5

1. Remington, Gras and Model 1873 Springfield miniatures. Remington and 1873 in .22 Short, Gras has one handmade round of about .20 caliber. Made by Weston, duplicating a set commemorating election of Diaz by Mexican Arsenal.

2. Weston-made Colt Paterson. Length overall 3⅛ inches.

3. German-made Kolibri, caliber 2.7mm. A tiny, functional piece from the early 1900s. Nickel plated.

4. Weston Sharps derringer, 2mm.

5. Weston Colt Paterson, cased.

6. Probably English made, this small flintlock has a barrel length of only ¾-inch. Fairly recent manufacture.

7. Above, a "Binn's Patent" pistol. No information has been found on such a specification. Bottom pair are percussion, 2-5/16 inches in length.

8. Remington 1866 Navy pistols by Weston, serials #2, #3, .22 Short. Length of pistols, 6½ inches.

9. Model 1926 Lilliput, caliber 4.25mm. Shown is its original cardboard box. This particular specimen is in unfired condition. These tiny pistols, like the Kolibri were actually intended to be fired and used as weapons.

6

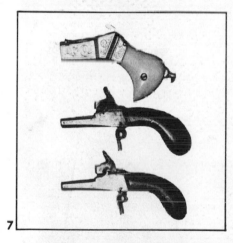

7

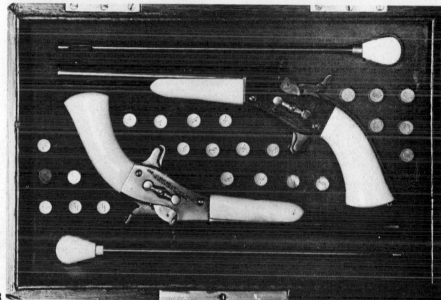

8

9

Miniatures

1

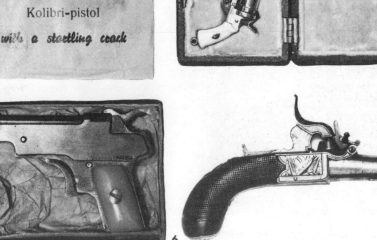

2

beauties, made mostly of brass, sell for about $1500.00 and up. Herschel Kopp, now living in Rochester, New York, has turned out a few fine miniatures, one example of which, a Frank Wesson over and under knife pistol, is presently in the author's collection. Kenneth Sonntag of San Antonio, Texas, has made more than 80 technically perfect miniatures during the past 38 years, but strictly as a hobby, and does not sell them. Other craftsmen in other countries still painstakingly turn out fine scaled down arms, and one completely functional wheelock only 2¼ inches long, which the author currently owns, was made by a professor in England, who reportedly took three years to complete it.

Unfortunately, for the dedicated collector, many of the older items have gone through so many hands that their age and origins are clouded. Many of their makers' names are unknown, and the histories that could make these little firearms so much more interesting are lost for all time. These sad facts notwithstanding, it should be easy to understand the feelings of pride and quiet elation that come from owning a veritable arsenal that fits easily into a shoebox!

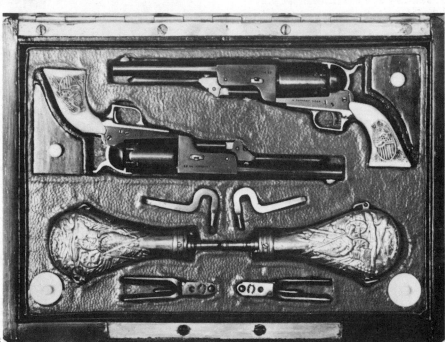

3

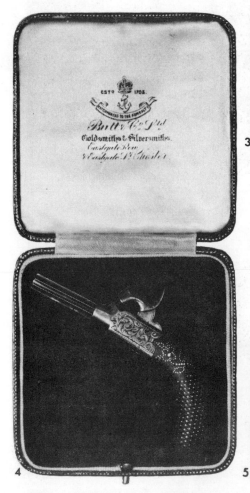

4

free of arms-certificate

Kolibri-pistol

with a startling crack

5

6

1. At top, a Brown Bess miniature, below it a French military flintlock. On the butt is engraved "Grenadiers", on barrel "Garde du Directoire" dating the piece from the early 1800s.

2. Winchester '66 by Weston, 19 inches overall. Gold plated, elaborate engraving, ivory stock and forend.

3. Cased pair of Walkers by Weston, serials #88 and #89. Carved ivory grips showing American Eagle. Four in. long.

4. Cap and ball by Durs Egg, London. Silver pin inlay in grip; 3½ inches overall length.

5. A rather old Kolibri miniature blank cartridge pistol. Tip-up action.

6. Above, a six-shot double action pinfire revolver fitted to a moulded hard rubber case. Below, a .23 caliber muff pistol by Smith of London.

7. Two caliber 2mm Belmex blank pistols made by Weston for tourist trade.

8. Pair of Colt No. 3 derringers by Weston to 2/3 scale, firing the .22 Short. Formerly in the Harry C. Knode collection in Dallas, Texas.

9. Completely operable wheellock made within past 10 years by a professor in England. Stock is gold, remainder steel. Author considers this to be the most meticulously made piece in his entire collection.

10. Frankenau purse pistol, 5mm.

11. Charm blank pistol grouping.

7

8

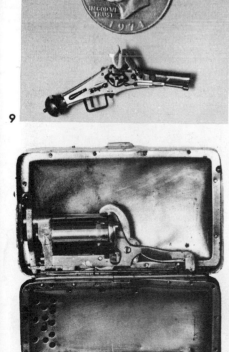

9

10

11

Proof Marks

One of the most positive methods of determining the origin of a foreign firearm is by its proof marks. England and most all European countries require, by law, that all arms manufactured or imported must have these markings affixed to them before they can be sold. Proofing consists of subjecting both barrel and breech mechanism to dynamic pressure higher than is to be expected from normal service cartridges. What this amounts to is discharging a cartridge through the arm which, on the average, is overloaded 20 percent above standardized ballistics.

The above procedures are carried out at either government, or government licensed "proof houses" in the presence of inspectors. This applies to commercial arms in most cases, since military arms are proved at arsenals.

Following is a listing of various British and European commercial proof markings. It is interesting to note that U.S. made arms will occasionally appear with these marks on them, usually the British examples. These are weapons imported to another country, proved there, and which have subsequently returned home. The United States has no proof laws, but for many years, all our major manufacturers have proved their products voluntarily. Familiar to all shooters is the interlocked "WP" (Winchester) and "REP" (Remington) on those markers' sporting arms.

BRITISH PROOF MARKS Under 1954 Rules of Proof

(chart 1 showing marks A through K)

BRITISH PROOF MARKS Under 1925 Rules of Proof

(chart 2 showing marks A through F, together with the words NITRO PROOF)

AUSTRIAN PROOF MARKS

(chart 3 showing marks A through G)

BELGIAN PROOF MARKS

(chart 4 showing marks A through J)

1. Britain, 1954 Rules of Proof: (A) Provisional proof, London. (B) Provisional proof, Birmingham. (C) Definitive proof, nitro powder, London. (D) Definitive proof, nitro, on barrel, London. (E) Definitive proof, nitro, on both barrel and action, Birmingham. (F) London, black powder only. (G) Birmingham, black powder only. (H) Special definitive proof, London. (I) Special definitive proof, Birmingham. (J) Reproof, London, (K) Reproof, Birmingham.

2. Britain, 1925 Rules of Proof: (A) Proof, London. (B) View, London. (C) Nitro, London. (D) Proof, Birmingham. (E) View, Birmingham. (F) Nitro, Birmingham.

3. Austria: (A) Provisional proof, Vienna. (B) Provisional proof, Ferlach. (C) Definitive black powder proof, Vienna. (D) Definitive black powder proof, Ferlach. (E) Nitro proof, Vienna. (F) Nitro proof, Ferlach. (G) Voluntary reinforced proof.

4. Belgium, Liege Proof House: (A) Provisional. (B) Provisional, double proof. (C) Provisional, triple proof. (D) Former definitive. (E) Definitive. (F) View. (G) Rifled arms. (H) Nitro. (I) Nitro, superior proof. (J) Definitive proof foreign arms. Note: Military rifles in which nitro powder is used, must bear the marks (E), (G), and (H) on the barrel and (F) and (H) on the action or principle parts thereof. On arms not of Belgian manufacture the mark (J) is used in lieu of mark (E). Revolvers must bear the marks (E) upon the cylinder, and, when rifled, (G) on the barrel. Automatic pistols must have (E) and (H) on the barrel and (H) on frame.

FRENCH PROOF MARKS The Paris Proof House

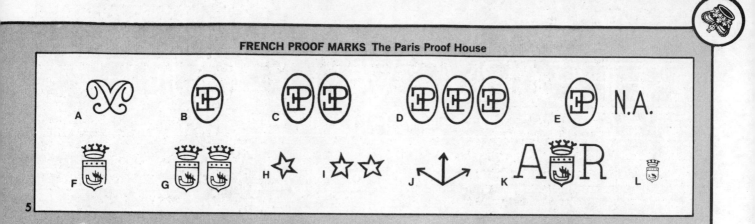

FRENCH PROOF MARKS The St. Etienne Proof House

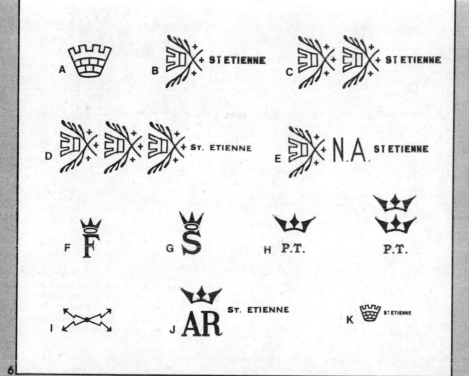

5. France, Paris Proof House: (A) Provisional, initial stage. (B) Assembled tubes, ordinary. (C) Double proof. (D) Triple proof. (E) Tubes proved separately, not assembled. (F) Definitive proof, black powder. (G) Black powder, superior proof. (H) Ordinary proof, smokeless. (I) superior proof, smokeless. (J) Additional supplementary mark. (K) Rifled arms. (L) Short barreled arms.

6. France, St. Etienne Proof House: (A) Initial stage, provisional. (B) Assembled tubes, ordinary proof. (C) Double proof. (D) Triple proof. (E) Tubes proved separately, not assembled. (F) Black powder (seldom used). (G) Superior black powder proof. (H) Rifled arms. (I) Smokeless, ordinary. (J) Smokeless, superior. (K) Supplementary mark. (L) Short-barreled arms.

7. Germany, post-war (in some cases applicable to pre-war marks) (A) Berlin. (B) Kiel (Eckernforde) (C) Hanover. (D) Munich. (E) Ulm (in Baden-Wurttemberg)). (F) Cologne. (G) Provisional, black powder. (H) Definitive, black powder. (I) Nitro proof. (J) Flobert (.22 rimfire) rifles. (K) Voluntary proof for hand held firearms. (L) Repair mark.

8. Italy, from the proof house at Gardone Val Trompia near Brescia. (A) Provisional. (B) Definitive. (C) Definitive, proofed in finshed condition or ready for sale.

GERMAN FEDERAL REPUBLIC PROOF MARKS

ITALIAN PROOF MARKS

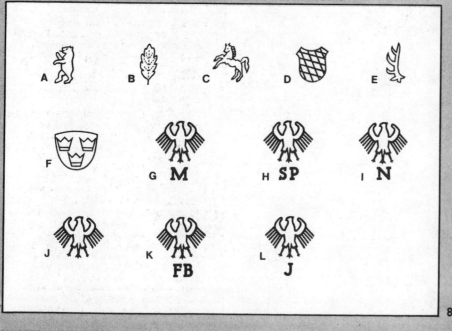

FIREARMS VALUE GUIDE

by Charles W. Fritz, *The Gun Report*

COLT PISTOLS AND REVOLVERS

COLT—Pocket model Paterson	2400-3700
COLT—BELT model Paterson	2850-4200
COLT—"Texas Model" Paterson 9" barrel	3000-5000
COLT—Walker model 1847	4700-14000
COLT—Dragoon 1st model	850-2000
COLT—Dragoon 2nd model	850-2000
COLT—Dragoon 3rd model	850-1800
COLT—Shoulder, stock for 3rd model Dragoon	500- 700
COLT—1848 Baby Dragoon	450- 900
COLT—1848 Wells Fargo type	325- 625
COLT—1849 Pocket .31 cal.	90- 270
COLT—1849 Pocket Model w/Thuer conversion	1200-2000
COLT—1851 Navy .36 cal.	85- 350
COLT—1851 Navy square back trigger guard, .36 cal.	600-1150
COLT—1851 Navy, marked COLT LONDON, .36 cal.	225- 400
COLT 1851 Navy conversion with bbl. cut out	95- 275
COLT—1851 Navy converted to .38 cal.	145- 325
COLT—1851 Navy conversion w/o bbl. cut out	175- 325
COLT—1851 U.S.N. markings	375- 600
COLT—1851 Navy Thuer conversion	1700-2500
COLT—1851 Navy cut for shoulder stock	250- 550
COLT BREVETTE—1851 Navy	225- 495
COLT—Pocket of Navy cal. often called Model 1853	175- 550
COLT—1855 Root or sidehammer	125- 450
COLT—1860 Army .44 cal.	85- 350
COLT—1860 .44 cal. (with fluted cylinder)	350- 600
COLT—1860 Army converted to .44 CF	100- 250
COLT—1860 Army converted to .44 CF (Thuer conversion)	1800-2850
COLT—Shoulder stock for 1860 Army	350- 500
COLT—Canteen shoulder stock for 1860 Army	500-
COLT—1861 Navy round barrel .36 cal.	200- 375
COLT—1862 Police or Belt model	125- 285
COLT—1862 converted to .38 CF	110- 225
1862 POLICE—Conversion round cyl.	85- 225
1862 POLICE—½ Fluted cyl. Engraved, ivory	325- 700
COLT FRONTIER—Army marked U.S. .45 cal.	110- 350
COLT FRONTIER—High Nos. smokeless powder	100- 225
COLT FRONTIER—Factory C engraving .45 cal.	275- 575
COLT FRONTIER—Flat Top .22 cal.	950-1350
COLT FRONTIER—Flat Top .32-20 cal.	250- 435
COLT FRONTIER—Flat Top .38 cal. Big Handle, marked 15 PALL MALL London	325- 500
COLT FRONTIER—(Storekeepers model w/o eject.)	150- 350
COLT BISLEY—Flat Top 7" barrel, .38 cal. spec.	250- 400
COLT BISLEY—4¾" barrel .38-40 cal.	85- 150
COLT Double action Frontier or Army, .45 cal.	65- 100
COLT—Old line open top .32 cal.	45- 75
COLT—Open Top with ejector housing, .22 cal.	250- 475
COLT DERINGER—No. 1, .41 cal.	150- 235
COLT DERINGER—No. 2, .41 cal.	90- 150
COLT DERINGER—No. 3, .41 cal.	50- 140
COLT—House pistol, .44 cal.	100- 210
COLT—House pistol, cloverleaf, .41 cal.	100- 225
COLT—Model 1872 type 1860 .44 cal.	175- 290
COLT—New Line .22 cal.	50- 90
COLT—New Line .32 cal.	45- 70
COLT—New Line police .38 cal. known as police-thug	175- 350
COLT—New double action (lightning)	45- 100
COLT—New Service target .45 cal.	65- 125
COLT—U.S. Marine model 1905 .38 cal.	45- 85
COLT—Officers model target 7½" barrel, .38 cal.	75- 135
COLT—P. P. target .22 cal.	50- 90
COLT—Model 1900 Automatic .38 cal.	95- 150
COLT—Model 1902 Automatic Navy, .38 cal.	95- 150
COLT—1903 model pocket automatic, .38 cal.	70- 125
COLT—Model 1905 Automatic .45 cal.	125- 285
COLT—Model 1911 Automatic .45 cal. Com.	85- 150
COLT—National Match Automatic .45 cal.	125- 200
COLT—Ace Automatic .22 cal.	175- 325

COLT—Automatic .25 cal.	55- 100
COLT—Automatic .32 cal.	50- 85
COLT—Automatic .380 cal.	35- 60
COLT—Army Revolver model 1917 .45 cal.	35- 75
COLT—Shooting Master	125- 185

PERCUSSION PISTOLS AND REVOLVERS

ROGERS & SPENCER—Revolver	125- 325
JOSLYN—Revolver	175- 425
SHARPS—Single Shot, percussion pistol	475- 600
PERRY—Single Shot, .56 cal. percussion pistol	300- 450
BUTTERFIELD—Army Revolver	600- 750
STARR—Single Action, Army	90- 200
STARR—Double action, Army	95- 250
UNION ARMS CO.—Navy .36 cal.	95- 135
UNION ARMS CO. POCKET—.31 cal.	60- 95
STARR—Double action Navy .36 cal.	85- 200
SAVAGE NORTH—.36 cal.	125- 250
SAVAGE NORTH—Figure Eight Iron Frame	550- 900
WHITNEY—Navy .36 cal.	85- 100
WHITNEY BEALS—Ring trigger	125- 200
MASS. ARMS—Wesson and Leavitts pat. .40 cal.	300- 375
MASS. ARMS—.28 cal. (Maynard Primer)	- 120
MASS. ARMS—.31 cal. (Maynard Primer)	- 150
COOPER—Navy .36 cal.	90- 150
METROPOLITAN ARMS CO.—Navy Revolver .36 cal.	265- 425
METROPOLITAN ARMS CO.—Pocket Navy Revolver .36 cal.	85- 160
METROPOLITAN ARMS CO.—Revolver .31 cal.	60- 85
ALLEN & WHEELLOCK—Army revolver .44 cal.	125- 285
ALLEN & WHEELLOCK—Navy revolver .36 cal.	125- 250
ALSOP—Navy revolver .36 cal.	325- 600
AMES—Navy marked U.S.R. box lock	90- 185
AMES—Navy marked U.S.N. box lock	90- 360
PETTINGILL'S PAT.—.44 cal.	165- 350
PETTINGILL'S NAVY—.36 cal.	115- 165
FREEMANS PAT.—.44 cal.	165- 350
MANHATTAN—Navy .36 cal.	60- 150
H. ASHTON—Pistol	70- 125
PALMETTO—Armory Model 1842	200- 350
I. N. JOHNSON—Model 1842	75- 160
DERRINGER—Model 1843 marked U.S.R. box lock	125- 195
DERRINGER—Dated 1847 marked U.S.N. box lock	105- 265
DERRINGER—Phila. 3½" barrel	125- 300
ELGIN—Cutlass Pistol (C. B. Allen)	1400-2200
DERRINGER—Phila. 3½" barrel	90- 225
DERRINGER—Phila. made with 2 sales agents names	175- 350
WALCH—10 shot pocket .31 cal.	125- 225
DIMICK—Derringer	150- 350
NEUPPERHAN F. A. Co.—5 shot .31 cal.	90- 200
BRUFF—Derringer	135- 225
WESSON & LEAVITT Army	400- 875
HOPKINS & ALLEN—5 shot .31 cal.	50- 75
SHARPS—Breechloading Pistol cal. .38	325- 700
SPRINGFIELD—Pistol-Carbine model 1855	200- 325
With original shoulder stock	350- 600
SPRINGFIELD Arms Co., (Warners Pat.)	- 100
WALCH—10 shot pocket .31 cal.	125- 225
STOCKINGS—S.S. perc.	45- 65
TYRON—Derringer	95- 105

REMINGTON HAND GUNS

REMINGTON—Army old model .44 cal.	85- 225
REMINGTON—Navy old model .36 cal.	90- 200
REMINGTON—Army new model .44 cal.	85- 325
REMINGTON—Navy new model .36 cal.	85- 235
REMINGTON—Belt model .36 cal.	85- 175
REMINGTON—Belt model double action .36 cal.	150- 285
REMINGTON—Police new model .36 cal.	90- 165
REMINGTON—New model police conversion	65- 125
REMINGTON—New model pocket	60- 90
REMINGTON—New model pocket conversion	60- 90
REMINGTON—New model conversion .44 cal. CF	60- 150

REMINGTON—Beals Navy .36 cal.	110-	190
REMINGTON—Beals Army .44 cal.	125-	200
REMINGTON—Revolving rifle .44 cal.	175-	425
REMINGTON—.31 cal. No. 3 Beals, outside pawl	150-	550
REMINGTON—Rider all brass .170 cal.	425-	550
REMINGTON—Rider pat. Navy fluted cyl., .36 cal.	175-	285
REMINGTON—Rider pocket .31 cal.	65-	125
REMINGTON—Rider pocket conversion	45-	80
REMINGTON—1875 model Frontier	165-	350
REMINGTON—1890 model Frontier	195-	500
REMINGTON—Navy 1st model 1865 .50 cal.	225-	350

MISCELLANEOUS CARTRIDGE PISTOLS AND REVOLVERS

CONNECTICUT ARMS—Hammond Bull Dog, .44 cal.	85-	150
MERWIN & HULVERT—Model 1876 Army .44 cal.	85-	125
MERWIN & HULBERT—Pocket Army .44 cal.	85-	125
PLANT CUP PRIMER—Army .44 cal.	85-	125
SOUTHERN—Derringer .41 cal.	75-	125
CHICAGO FIRE ARMS—Palm Pistol	85-	150
MARLIN—Standard revolver .32 cal.	15-	95
SHATTUCK—Palm Pistol 4 shot .22 cal.	90-	135
SHATTUCK—Palm Pistol 4 shot .25 cal.	90-	135
SHATTUCK—Palm Pistol 4 shot .32 cal.	90-	135
OSGOOD—Duplex cal. .22 & .32 R.F.	85-	150
MARSTON—3 bbl. Knife Pistol .22	135-	250
MARSTON—3 bbl. pistol .32 R.F. cal.	65-	135
WRIGHT ARMS CO.—"Little All Right"	150-	240
DERRINGER—(Philadelphia) 5 shot .32 R.F.	60-	90
NATIONAL NO. 1—Derringer .41 cal.	90-	175
NATIONAL NO. 2—Derringer .41 cal.	65-	125
H R—Knife revolver 5 shot .32 cal.	85-	150
REID DERRINGER—Knuckle duster .32 cal.	75-	110
FRANK WESSON—O. U. .22 cal.	85-	125
WARNER—.30 cal.	23-	40
SHARPS PEPPER BOX—No. 1 4 shot .22 cal.	65-	140
SHARPS & HANKINS—Pepper box .32 cal.	65-	140
SHARPS—4 barrel .32 cal.	65-	125
WILLIAMSON—Derringer	85-	175
STEVENS—Offhand target 8" barrel .22 cal.	28-	65
E. ALLEN—Derringer .41 cal.	65-	125
ALLEN—Cartridge Derringer .41 cal. iron frame	65-	125
STARR—4 shot Button Trigger .32 cal.	125-	200
DERRINGER—(Philadelphia) Revolver .22 cal.	50-	90
BACON ARMS CO.—Revolver .32 cal.	25-	45
BACON—Navy .38 cal.	70-	125
HOPKINS-ALLEN ARMY—XL-8 .44 cal.	55-	95
PRESCOTT—Revolver iron frame Army	50-	95
POND—Army .44 cal.	50-	95
BALLARD—Derringer .41 cal.	55-	85
FOREHAND & WADSWORTH—Derringer .41 cal.	55-	85
FOREHAND & WADSWORTH—Army .44 cal.	60-	125
FOREHAND & WADSWORTH—Improved model or Frontier 44 cal.	100-	135
WHITNEYVILLE—Armory revolver .32 cal.	15-	25
MOORE—Revolver 7 shot R.F. .32 cal.	38-	70
MOORE—All metal Derringer .41 cal.	85-	150
MARLIN—.32 cal. Derringer "Never Miss"	60-	95
J. C. TERRY—.32 cal. Derringer	75-	110
BALLARD—.41 cal. Derringer	65-	85
X. L. DERRINGER—.41 R.F.	60-	125
STARR SINGLE SHOT—.41 R.F.	75-	150

U.S. MUSKETS

1795 FL orig.	265-	450
1795 orig. C.P.	200-	325
1803 FL. Harpers Ferry orig.	400-	600
1803 FL. Harpers Ferry reconv.	275-	375
1814 Harpers Ferry orig.	350-	425
1814 FL. Harpers Ferry reconv.	300-	375
1819 FL. Harpers Ferry orig.	225-	400
1806 FL. orig.	210-	350
1808 FL. reconverted	125-	200
1812 FL. orig.	275-	425
1814 FL. Johnson orig.	250-	400
1814 FL. Johnson reconv.	100-	225
1814 FL. Derringer orig.	225-	400
1814 FL. Derringer reconv.	100-	225
1817 FL. Derringer orig.	235-	400
1809 FL. (Contract arm) orig.	175-	300
1809 FL. (Contract arm) reconv.	95-	150
U.S. FL. marked "Mill Creek Pa" 1845	175-	275
REMINGTON—Jenks pat. 52	90-	150
KENTUCKY—Percussion marked Bedford County	260-	500
KENTUCKY—F/L rifle, marked H. G. Lan	450-	800
KENTUCKY—F/F marked W. Barnhart, silver trim	500-	900
KENTUCKY—F/L unmarked	500-	900

KENTUCKY—F/L unmarked (New England Type)	-	300
J. MOLL F/L	650-	1000
SHARPS—.45/70 Old Reliable model target sights	125-	275
U.S. RIFLE—Model 1841 (The Mississippi Rifle)	150-	325
U.S. MUSKET—Model 1842 (percussion)	95-	150
U.S. RIFLE—Carbine Model 1855—Springfield .58 cal.	200-	425
LINDSAY—Two hammer musket	200-	425
U.S. COLT—Musket 1861	100-	250
U.S. COLT—Musket 1861	125-	450
COLT PATERSON Carbine	850-	1650
U.S.—Musket model 1843 Percussion Hall Pat. Made by S. North	150-	300
U.S. Model 1861-63 made by Savage R.F.A. Co.	100-	250
SPRINGFIELD—Model 1863 percussion	125-	250
SPRINGFIELD—1865 Rifle (Allin conversion) .58 cal.	125-	385
SPRINGFIELD—1866 Rifle .57/70 cal.	100-	160
SPRINGFIELD—1866 Cadet (2 bands) .50/70 cal.	85-	150
SPRINGFIELD—1868 Rifle .50/70 cal.	85-	150
SPRINGFIELD—1868 Cadet .50/70 cal.	85-	150
SPRINGFIELD—1869 Rifle .50/70 cal.	85-	150
SPRINGFIELD—1869 Cadet .50/70 cal.	85-	510
U.S. 1870 RIFLE—.50/70 cal.	85-	150
U.S. 1870 CARBINE—.50/70 cal.	85-	150
SPRINGFIELD—Model 1873 .45/70 cal.	100-	175
SPRINGFIELD—Carbine model 1873	150-	250
SPRINGFIELD—Officers model rifle .45/70 cal.	360-	600
U.S. SPENCER—Breechloading rptg. carbine	100-	175
U.S.—Joslyn carbine	90-	175
U.S.—Poultney & Trimble carbine	85-	160
U.S. Star carbine .50 cal.	90-	175
U.S.—F. M. Merrill carbine	90-	175
U.S. SHARPS .45/70 rifle	135-	225
U.S. Sharps carbine	100-	225
WARNER—Carbine .56/60 cal.	65-	100
U.S.—Burnside carbine 4th model	125-	200
U.S. Rifle Remington Arms Co. model 1863	125-	325
REMINGTON—Model 1858 (Maynard) .58 cal.	100-	150
REMINGTON—Model 1857 Maynard primer	125-	175
REMINGTON—Split Breech Carbine	135-	185
REMINGTON—Carbine Rolling Block .50/70 cal.	65-	135
REMINGTON—Keene Carbine .44/40 cal.	150-	300
REMINGTON—Hepburn Target .40/82 cal.	100-	175
REMINGTON—Jenks Navy	125-	245
MAYNARD CARBINE—.50 cal.	100-	150
EVANS—Repeating carbine	95-	165
GREEN CARBINE—British proofs .53 cal.	100-	145
JOSLYN Carbine made A. H. Walters & Co.	125-	245

SMITH & WESSON HAND GUNS

VOLCANIC ARMS—3¾" barrel .31 cal.	275-	600
VOLCANIC ARMS—6" barrel .41 cal.	350-	800
VOLCANIC PISTOL—Carbine 16½" bbl.	900-	1650
S&W—Model No. 1 first issue .22 cal.	135-	375
S&W—Model No. 1, second issue	50-	125
S&W—Model No. 1 third issue	50-	100
S&W—Model No. 1½	25-	65
S&W—Model No. 2 Army .32 cal.	35-	85
S&W—Model No. 3 American .44 cal.	85-	250
S&W—Model No. 3 Russian markings	85-	250
S&W—Model 3 SA Russian target cal. .38 & .44	85-	135
S&W—Model 3 Russian .44 cal.	60-	85
S&W—Schofield Pat. 1st issue .45 cal.	75-	200
S&W—Schofield Pat. 2nd issue, .45 cal.	75-	200
S&W—Model 2 .38 cal. Often called Little Russian	30-	50
S&W—Model 320 repeating rifle	350-	450
S&W—Model 320 repeating rifle with stock	500-	825
S&W—Regulation Police .38 cal.	35-	60
S&W—Ladysmith 1st model	100-	225
S&W—Ladysmith 2nd model	100-	200
S&W—Ladysmith 3rd model	90-	175
S&W—Ladysmith 3rd model with 6" barrel	75-	225
S&W—Ladysmith 3rd model with 6" bbl. w/target sights	150-	325
S&W—New Departure 1st model .38 cal.	40-	75
S&W—New Departure 2nd model .38 cal.	40-	60
S&W—New Century triple lock .44 cal.	55-	90
S&W—New Century target .44 cal.	90-	135
S&W—New Century triple lock .44 cal.	85-	150
S&W—Perfected model .38 cal.	60-	90
S&W—Straight Line Target with metal case, .22 cal.	125-	250
S&W—Hand ejector 1st model	40-	85
S&W—Hand ejector target .32/20 cal.	35-	60
S&W—Safety first issue .32 cal.	20-	40
S&W—Model 1917 .45 cal.	25-	65
S&W—22-32 target .22 cal.	35-	55

ANTIQUE ARMS & CARTRIDGE DEALERS

ANTIQUE ARMS DEALERS

Robert Abels
157 E. 64th St.
New York, N.Y. 10021

Ed Agramonte
41 Riverdale Ave.
Yonkers, N.Y. 10701

F. Bannerman Sons, Inc.
Box 26
Blue Point, L.I., N.Y. 11715

Fulmers Antique Firearms
Detroit Lakes
Minn. 56501

William Boggs
1783 E. Main
Columbus, Oh. 43205

Brass Rail
1136 N. La Brea
Los Angeles, Ca. 90038

Brick House Shop
Roma Pl.
New Platz, N.Y. 12561

Dixie Gun Works
Hwy. 51 South
Union City, Tenn. 38261

Donnin's Arms Museum
12953 Biscayne Blvd.
No. Miami, Fla. 33161

Farris Muzzle Guns
1610 Gallia St.
Portsmouth, Oh. 45662

Gold Rush Guns
P.O. Box 33
Afton, Va. 22920

A.A. Fidd
Diamond Pt. Rd.
Diamond Point, N.Y. 11338

Norman Flayderman & Co.
Squash Hollow
New Milford, Conn. 06776

Herb Glass
Bullville, N.Y. 10915

Holbrook Arms Museum
12953 Biscayne Blvd. N.
Miami, Fla. 33161

Gold Rush Guns
1567 California St.
San Francisco, Ca. 94109

Goodman's for Guns
1101 Olive St.
St. Louis, Mo. 63101

Griffin's Guns & Antiques
R.R. 4
Peterboro, Ont., Canada

Groote Guns
337 Fisher
Walpole, Mass. 02081

The Gun Corral
10302 S. Prairie Ave.
Inglewood, Ca. 90302

The Gun Shop
6489 Pearl Rd.
Cleveland, Oh. 44130

Heritage Firearms Co.
1 Danbury Rd., Rt. 7
Wilton, Conn. 06897

Ed Howe
2 Main
Cooper's Mills, Me. 04341

Inglewood Gun Shop
609 E. Manchester
Inglewood, Ca. 90301

Jackson Arms
6209 Hillcrest Ave.
Dallas, Tex. 75205

Jerry's Gun Shop
9220 Ogden Ave.
Brookfield, Ill. 60513

Lever Arms Service
716 Dunsmuir
Vancouver 1, B.C., Canada

William M. Locke
3607 Ault Park Rd.
Cincinnati, Oh. 45208

J. E. McKercher
Stumpfield Rd.
Hopkinton, N.H. 03301

Maverick Trading Post
3454 N. Halstead St.
Chicago, Ill. 60613

Charles W. Moore
R.D. 2
Schenevus, N.Y. 12155

John J. Malloy
Briar Ridge Rd.
Danbury, Conn. 06810

Museum of Historical Arms
1038 Alton Rd.
Miami Beach, Fla. 33139

National Gun Traders, Inc.
Box 776
Miami, Fla. 33135

New Orleans Arms Co., Inc.
240 Charles St.
New Orleans, La. 70130

Old West Gun Room
10855 San Pablo Ave.
El Cerrito, Ca. 94530

Pioneer Guns
5228 Montgomery
Norwood, Oh. 45212

Pony Express Western Gallery
17460 Ventura Blvd.
Encino, Ca. 91316

Glode M. Requa
Box 35
Monsey, N.Y. 10952

Ridge Guncraft Inc.
234 N. Tulane Ave.
Oak Ridge, Tenn. 37830

Martin B. Retting, Inc.
11029 Washington Blvd.
Culver City, Ca. 90230

San Francisco Gun Exchange
74 Fourth
San Francisco, Ca. 94103

Santa Ana Gunroom
1638 E. 1st St.
Santa Ana, Ca. 92702

Service Armament Co.
689 Bergen Blvd.
Ridgefield, N.J. 07657

M. C. Weist
234 N. Tulane Ave.
Oak Ridge, Tenn. 37830

Ward & Van Valkenburg
402-30th Ave.
No. Fargo, N. Dak. 58102

Yeck Antique Firearms
579 Tecumseh
Dundee, Mich. 48131

COLLECTOR'S CARTRIDGES

A. Donald Amesbury
4065 Montecito Ave.
Tucson, Ariz. 85711

J. A. Belton
52 Saure Rd.
Ste. Philomene, Que., Canada

Conjay Arms Company Ltd.
168 Church Road
Willesden
London N.W. 10
England

Elwood Epps
80 King St.
Clinton, Ont., Canada

The Gun Shop
1060 N. Henderson
Galesburg, Ill. 61401

House of Cartridges
12 Cascade
Barandon, Man., Canada

Ed Howe
2 Main St.
Cooper's Mills, Me. 04341

Jackson Arms
6209 Hillcrest Ave.
Dallas, Tex. 75205

Keokuk
616 Kingsley Dr.
Loves Park, Ill. 61111

McDaneld & Wheeler
Box 23
Osborne, Kans. 67473

Miller Bros.
Rapid City, Mich. 49676

Oregon Ammo Service
Box 19341
Portland, Ore. 97219

Powder Keg
R.R. 1
Coal Valley, Ill. 61240